Elements of Deterrence

Elements of Deterrence

Strategy, Technology, and Complexity in Global Politics

ERIK GARTZKE
and
JON R. LINDSAY

OXFORD
UNIVERSITY PRESS

Oxford University Press is a department of the University of Oxford.
It furthers the University's objective of excellence in research, scholarship,
and education by publishing worldwide. Oxford is a registered trade mark of
Oxford University Press in the UK and in certain other countries.

Published in the United States of America by Oxford University Press
198 Madison Avenue, New York, NY 10016, United States of America.

© Oxford University Press 2024

All rights reserved. No part of this publication may be reproduced, stored in a retrieval system,
or transmitted, in any form or by any means, without the prior permission in writing of Oxford
University Press, or as expressly permitted by law, by license or under terms agreed with the
appropriate reprographics rights organization. Inquiries concerning reproduction outside the scope
of the above should be sent to the Rights Department, Oxford University Press, at the address above.

You must not circulate this work in any other form and you must impose this same condition on any acquirer

Library of Congress Cataloging-in-Publication Data

Names: Gartzke, Erik, author. | Lindsay, Jon R., author.
Title: Elements of deterrence : strategy, technology, and complexity in
global politics / Erik Gartzke and Jon R. Lindsay.
Description: New York, NY : Oxford University Press, [2024] |
Includes bibliographical references and index.
Identifiers: LCCN 2023057081 (print) | LCCN 2023057082 (ebook) |
ISBN 9780197754443 (hbk.) | ISBN 9780197754450 (pbk.) |
ISBN 9780197754474 (epub)
Subjects: LCSH: Deterrence (Strategy) | Military art and
science—Technological innovations. | Asymmetric warfare.
Classification: LCC U162.6 .G378 2024 (print) | LCC U162.6 (ebook) |
DDC 355.02—dc23/eng/20231229
LC record available at https://lccn.loc.gov/2023057081
LC ebook record available at https://lccn.loc.gov/2023057082

Book Summary

Deterrence theory emerged early in the Cold War, as theorists and practitioners grappled with the new threat environment posed by nuclear weapons. Today, strategists and operators are confronting a novel set of technological challenges such as cyberattacks, drones, space weapons, and subversion, all in the context of a highly interdependent global economy. While policy makers aspire to integrate deterrence into a broader "whole of government" approach, deterrence is not a panacea for complexity. *Elements of Deterrence* presents detailed arguments and empirical evidence demonstrating that the practice of deterrence involves complex trade-offs between multiple political goals pursued via increasingly specialized military and non-military instruments. The result is a generalization of the standard deterrence framework and a more dynamic synthesis of venerable themes in deterrence theory.

Contents

Foreword	ix
Preface	xiii
Biographies	xix
List of Figures and Tables	xxi
1. Introduction: Revisiting Deterrence Theory	1

I. THE MEANS AND ENDS OF DETERRENCE

2. What Is Deterrence?	17
3. Deterrence Is Not (Just) One Thing	40
4. Politics by (Many) Other Means	73

II. THEORETICAL PROBLEMS IN THE CYBER DOMAIN

5. Cyberspace Is Unsuitable for the Strategy of War	109
6. Cyberspace Is Ideal for the Strategy of Deception	133
7. Cyber Deception versus Nuclear Deterrence	165

III. EMPIRICAL EVIDENCE IN MULTIPLE DOMAINS

8. Land: Presence and Credibility *with Koji Kagotani*	195
9. Sea: Maneuver and Uncertainty	224
10. Air: Automation and Cost *with James Walsh*	252
11. Space: Intelligence and Stability *with Bryan Early*	282

IV. STRATEGIC IMPLICATIONS OF COMPLEXITY

12. Trade: Asymmetry and Multipolarity *with Oliver Westerwinter*	303

viii CONTENTS

13. Cyber: Complements and Substitutes 319
    with Nadiya Kostyuk

14. Gray Zone: Ambiguity and Escalation 340
    with J. Andrés Gannon and Peter Schram

15. Conclusion: Summary and Implications 373

Bibliography 409
Index 445

Foreword
by Michael Nacht

Deterrence, defined as the threat of discouraging an action or event by instilling doubt or fear of the consequences, has been a centerpiece of US national security policy since the use of two atomic bombs ended World War II.

The prominent political scientist George Quester informed us more than a half century ago, in his *Deterrence before Hiroshima*, that deterrence was actually an element of US policy before the initial employment of nuclear weapons in 1945. Quester pointed out that the evolution of US airpower during the Second World War, including attacks against population centers as well as industrial and military targets, were key building blocks in the formulation of US deterrence policy.

While the United States began to grapple with the meaning of nuclear weapon use as the Cold War came to dominate US security concerns in the late 1940s and early 1950s, the RAND corporation (established in 1948 as an independent defense think tank separate from the Douglas Aircraft company of Santa Monica, California) initiated a study of where US nuclear forces should be deployed. The leader of the study effort, Albert Wohlstetter, spearheaded the formulation of "secure second-strike" capabilities as the key feature required by US forces to ensure that the US could respond with devastating effect in the event of an initial attack. The RAND study argued that such a capability was the most credible deterrent against an initial attack by the Soviet Union.

In the ensuing six decades, the United States engaged in a vigorous debate both in government and among scholars and analysts about how to modify its deterrence policies in the face of major changes in weapons technologies. Terms including "flexible response," "damage limitation," "counterforce targeting," "extended deterrence," "limited nuclear options," and "look, shoot, look," were adopted at one point or another to describe US nuclear targeting policy. From the 1960s through the 1980s a large number of publications evaluated all aspects of these approaches.

Yet, in my view, this publication, *Elements of Deterrence*, by colleagues and co-authors Erik Gartzke and Jon Lindsay, is the most comprehensive, well-documented analysis of the subject, combining a wealth of understanding of military technologies, strategic doctrine, organizational analysis of the key US agencies as well as considerations of Russian, Chinese, and other adversarial perspectives.

The twenty-first century brought with it important developments in cyber and space technologies. These led to a further review of US nuclear deterrence policy. In the spring of 2010, while serving as Assistant Secretary of Defense for Global Strategic Affairs, I was asked by the Undersecretary of Defense for Policy to lead a new study on "cross-domain deterrence." The details of this study remain classified, but aspects have been discussed in selected publications, such as a July 2010 report by James Lewis with the Center for Strategic and International Studies. Lewis pointed out that deterrence in space or cyberspace cannot be "domain limited" and will require threats in other domains, such as saying that an attack on our satellites could lead to an attack on terrestrial targets. The study identified several challenges including:

1. Declaratory policy—what should be US declaratory policy in the event of a cyberattack against US assets or an attack on US satellites?
2. Deterrence policy—what set of deployments in US space or cyber capabilities could strengthen deterrence against US adversaries contemplating cyber or space attacks against the US?
3. What explicit US government agencies should have formal authority and responsibilities over the use of space and cyber assets?
4. What congressional oversight should be put in place to monitor the deployment and possible use of US space and cyber assets?
5. International consultations—what should be US policy about the sharing of information and coordination with our allies, including the Five Eyes (the UK, Canada, Australia, New Zealand, and the US), NATO members, Japan, South Korea, the Philippines, India, and others?
6. Responses—what should be the explicit range of retaliatory options available to the US in the event of space or cyber attacks on US assets?
7. How can government-private sector cooperation be strengthened most effectively to maintain the US technological advantage in space and cyber technologies?

These were issues posed more than a decade ago by the Department of Defense cross-domain deterrence study. Since then, much progress has been made, and this book addresses many of these issues, among others.

The reader will find herein a rich and highly documented discussion of many topics. The book presents a careful discussion of deterrence theory including an explanation of the means and ends of deterrence and a powerful set of arguments that deterrence is not just one thing. The discussion of the cyber domain is innovative, including the controversial argument that cyberspace is unsuitable for the strategy of war but ideal for the strategy of deception. The authors provide very detailed case discussions of empirical evidence in multiple domains including land (presence and capability), sea (maneuver and uncertainty), air (automation and cost), and space (intelligence and stability). The last major section of the book considers strategic implications of complexity including trade (asymmetry and multipolarity), cyber (complements and substitutes), and the gray zone (ambiguity and escalation).

In the past decade the US government has moved beyond the concept of cross-domain deterrence to adopt the construct of "integrated deterrence," in an attempt to combine all aspects of deterrence across all domains. The authors conclude with a skeptical perspective of this approach.

In sum, this volume is "one-stop shopping" for all important aspects of deterrence, both in theory and in technological and doctrinal practice. The volume should be the standard reference on this subject for many years to come.

Preface

On the cover of this book on deterrence is a NASA file image of the Moon transiting across the Earth, taken by the Deep Space Climate Observatory (DSCOVR) satellite. The photograph may look incongruous for a study of international relations. It may even appear slightly menacing, with the Moon vaguely resembling the "Death Star," the giant space station that obliterated planets in *Star Wars*.

The perspective of this image from space invites us to think differently about objects and relationships that we think we already know, something we are asking readers to consider in rehashing a topic that seems to be thoroughly examined and understood. The Moon is a familiar celestial body for Earthlings, but technology enables us to see it anew. Deterrence theory, similarly, is a familiar body of literature, but technology is (again) pressing us to envision, and apply, it differently. New military capabilities in outer space and cyberspace prompt us to revisit the conceptual foundations of deterrence theory, a topic and task that may seem to many to be in turn unnecessary and immutable. Just as DSCOVR illuminates the dark side of the Moon, we find that deterrence also has had a dark side—features that have always been lurking in the shadow of nuclear weapons. This book offers a new, more general theoretical framing of deterrence theory. We also offer considerable systematic empirical evidence to substantiate our revised conception of deterrence.

For more than a millennium, the Aristotelian model of astronomy offered a tidy, concentric depiction of the solar system. Copernicus and others during the Enlightenment identified discrepancies between classical conceptions of the cosmos and the world as it actually operated. Galileo put a nail in the coffin when he tipped a telescope up to the heavens and observed impact craters on the Moon, and other moons around Jupiter. Celestial bodies could not be orbiting neatly around the Earth if they were running around, and sometimes into, one another. More to the point, the whole thing was much more chaotic and differentiated than the classical model implied.

Something similar is afoot in the "physics" of deterrence. Deterrence theory developed in the aftermath of World War II in response to the need for different approaches to security that could ensure survival in the face of nuclear annihilation. Deterrence theory itself turned much that was intuitive about national security on its head and required considerable rethinking of strategy. But the classical deterrence model itself has always been too neat. In practice, we see lots of interplay and variation between actors, interests, instruments, and circumstances. Others have noted for some time that the consensus Cold War framing of deterrence seemed to be struggling to adapt itself to evolving aspects of modern security, if indeed it ever applied at all. Why? Was it human psychology? Conditions of scope or scale? Or was there something fundamentally limiting about the classical model? Relaxing the tidy traditional perspective and seeing deterrence differently helps to advance and generalize deterrence as a concept, one that does justice to the growing complexity of strategy in practice.

This book is the product of a decade-long research agenda sponsored by the US Department of Defense Minerva Initiative. It would not have been possible without the hard work of many collaborators, colleagues, and friends. We are especially grateful to Michael Nacht for the initial inspiration to explore the deterrence challenges posed by cyperspace and outer space. We are also grateful to the scholars and practitioners who contributed to our 2019 edited volume with Oxford University Press, *Cross-Domain Deterrence: Strategy in an Era of Complexity*. They explored the frontiers of a problem that gets more complex every year, and their insights continue to resonate today. We did not elaborate on our own views in that volume in any detail, partly because our goal was to canvas the state of the art and partly because our views were still evolving. Since then, we have published a series of peer-reviewed articles on deterrence—together, separately, and with colleagues. Each of these articles has presented a portion of our reasoning, along with a range of empirical findings. Yet the respective strands have never been developed coherently and brought together in one place. This book accomplishes that and more.

In the coming pages, we present a distinctive argument about the strategic implications of specialized military means or "domains." This study integrates new material with several articles that have passed through the rigors and idiosyncrasies of peer review. We are grateful to the anonymous reviewers who provided constructive feedback on these articles, as well as to the two anonymous reviewers of the revised book manuscript, who shared with us their detailed, thoughtful suggestions. We are especially grateful to our co-authors for their permission to include their work in this new format; they are credited on the byline of chapters as appropriate. While we have tried to preserve the spirit of the original articles as much as possible, our revisions are substantial enough to warrant new titles that highlight their place in the overall argument. While some of these originally appeared several years ago, we believe that the claims they posed, and the evidence they provided, continue to stand up well, even in fields like cybersecurity that are clearly subject to rapid technological change. The consistency of these arguments over an admittedly brief period of time may stem from the enduring relevance of a few basic political logics.

Our focus throughout the manuscript is on the underappreciated incentives, and constraints, posed by the strategic specialization embodied by the technical details of any given operational capability. Here we present overarching themes by revising, reshuffling, and reissuing the original articles alongside new material not yet published elsewhere. This has required extensive revision to bring each chapter up to date with subsequent literature, standardize terminology, minimize redundant discussions, impose a consistent voice, and highlight connections across chapters. The new versions of this material appear here in a logical order that advances the argument of the book, which is not necessarily the order in which the respective articles were published (as listed below). We have also minimized the presentation of technical material, summarizing empirical findings in Chapters 8 through 14 as appropriate, in order to allow the general reader to focus on the main thrust of our arguments. Readers interested in delving into the technical details of formal models, empirical datasets, and statistical analysis, or who are curious about the historical context of each argument, are encouraged to consult the original articles and the online appendices:

- Erik Gartzke. "The Myth of Cyberwar: Bringing War in Cyberspace Back Down to Earth." *International Security* 38, no. 2 (2013): 41–73.
- Erik Gartzke and Jon R. Lindsay. "Weaving Tangled Webs: Offense, Defense, and Deception in Cyberspace." *Security Studies* 24, no. 2 (2015): 316–48.
- Jon R. Lindsay. "Tipping the Scales: The Attribution Problem and the Feasibility of Deterrence against Cyber Attack." *Journal of Cybersecurity* 1, no. 1 (2015): 53–67.
- Erik Gartzke and Oliver Westerwinter. "The Complex Structure of Commercial Peace: Contrasting Trade Interdependence, Asymmetry, and Multipolarity." *Journal of Peace Research* 53, no. 3 (2016): 325–43.

- Erik Gartzke and Jon R. Lindsay. "Thermonuclear Cyberwar." *Journal of Cybersecurity* 3, no. 1 (2017): 37–48.
- Erik Gartzke and Koji Kagotani. "Being There: US Troop Deployments, Force Posture and Alliance Reliability." International Studies Association annual meeting. Baltimore, 2017.
- Erik Gartzke and Jon R. Lindsay. "The Influence of Seapower on Politics: Domain- and Platform-Specific Attributes of Material Capabilities." *Security Studies* 29, no. 4 (2020): 601–36.
- Erik Gartzke "Blood and Robots: How Remotely Piloted Vehicles and Related Technologies Affect the Politics of Violence." *Journal of Strategic Studies* 44, no. 7 (2021): 983–1013.
- Bryan R. Early and Erik Gartzke. "Spying from Space: Reconnaissance Satellites and Interstate Disputes." *Journal of Conflict Resolution* 65, no. 9 (2021): 1551–75.
- Erik Gartzke and James Igoe Walsh. "The Drawbacks of Drones: The Effects of UAVs on Militant Violence in Pakistan." *Journal of Peace Research* 59, no. 4 (2022): 463–77.
- Jon R. Lindsay and Erik Gartzke. "Politics by Many Other Means: The Comparative Strategic Advantages of Operational Domains." *Journal of Strategic Studies* 45, no. 5 (2022): 743–76.
- Nadiya Kostyuk and Erik Gartzke, "Fighting in Cyberspace: Internet Access and the Substitutability of Cyber and Military Operations." *Journal of Conflict Resolution* (forthcoming).
- J. Andres Gannon, Erik Gartzke, Jon R. Lindsay, and Peter Schramm. "After Deterrence: Explaining Conflict Short of War." *Journal of Conflict Resolution* (forthcoming).

In sum, this book is not just a greatest hits album, but an extensive remix that re-imagines the originals. Of course, there is some madness in this method. We run the risk of creating the intellectual equivalent of Frankenstein's monster, an ungainly beast reanimated from the severed limbs of putrid scholarship. This is a risk we are willing to run, however, to present a holistic framing of our previous work. We leave it to the reader to decide whether our monster, like Shelly's, teaches us something novel about the impact of technology on the human condition.

This research was supported by US Department of Defense Minerva Initiative Grants N00014-14-1-0071, N00014-15-1-2792, FA9550-21-1-0143, and N00014-19-1-2491. Chapter 8 was supported by JSPS KAKENHI

PREFACE xvii

Grant Numbers 16KT0158 and 17KK0076. Chapter 13 was supported by The William and Flora Hewlett Foundation award #s 2018-7277, 2020-1961, 2021-2955. Early drafts of this work (including articles) benefited greatly from comments from Susan Aaronson, Victor Asal, Ben Bahney, David Blagden, Erica Borghard-Lonergan, Aaron Brantly, Ben Buchanan, Shannon Carcelli, Tai Ming Cheung, Peter Cowhey, Michael C. Desch, Rex Douglass, Peter Dombrowski, Bryan Early, Tanisha Fazal, Allan Friedman, J. Andres Gannon, Eugene Gholz, Florian Grunert, Stephan Haggard, John Horgan, Jenna Jordan, Jeffrey Kwong, Kirill Levchenko, Austin Long, John Mueller, William J. Perry, James Piazza, Heather Roff, Joshua Rovner, Scott Sagan, Jacqueline Schneider, Phillip Schrodt, Ryan Shandler, Frank Stech, John J. Szmer, Henrik Urdal, and Brandon Valeriano along with countless conference participants, journal editors, and anonymous reviewers. For research assistance we thank Oliver Davies, Rex Douglass, Lauren Gilbert, and Thomas L. Scherer. Special thanks goes out to the students and researchers at the Center for Peace and Security Studies (cPASS) at UCSD who were an integral part of this project over the course of many years, and especially to Jason Lopez for his steady administrative hand at cPASS. Vorathip Plengpanit performed yeoman's work in compiling the book manuscript, with assistance from J. Andres Gannon and Jasmine Moheb. We are especially grateful to David McBride for supporting this project and to the production staff at Oxford University Press.

Erik wishes to thank Tara, Allana, McGivney, and Farrell for their forbearance, tact, and frequent encouragement. Beside my chair in the living room is a small plaque, given to me by my daughter McGivney, that reads "please be quiet, I am pretending to work." Many hours of pretense, and some of rumination later, this book is the result.

Jon is grateful for the Elements of Family—Heather, Lily, and Eleanor. While deterrence may be a relationship between many means and ends, the meaning of family is an end in itself.

Biographies

Authors

- Erik Gartzke is a Professor in the Department of Political Science and the Director of the Center for Peace and Security Studies (cPASS) at the University of California, San Diego. His research on the causes of war and peace, alliances, the nexus between economic interdependence and conflict, nuclear weapons, deterrence, cyberconflict, technology, international organizations, geopolitics, and climate change has been published in numerous academic journals and edited volumes. He holds a PhD in political science from the University of Iowa, and he has served in both the US Navy and US Army Reserve.
- Jon R. Lindsay is an Associate Professor at the School of Cybersecurity and Privacy and the Sam Nunn School of International Affairs at the Georgia Institute of Technology. He is the author of *Information Technology and Military Power* (2020) and editor of two Oxford volumes on, respectively, cross-domain deterrence and Chinese cybersecurity. His latest book manuscript is *Age of Deception: Cybersecurity and Secret Statecraft*. He holds a PhD in political science from the Massachusetts Institute of Technology, and he has served in the US Navy.

Contributors

- Bryan R. Early is a Professor in the Department of Political Science and Associate Dean for Research at the Rockefeller College of Public Affairs Policy at the State University of New York at Albany.
- J. Andrés Gannon is an Assistant Professor in the Department of Political Science at Vanderbilt University and a Faculty Affiliate at the Data Science Institute.
- Koji Kagotani is an Assistant Professor in the Faculty of Policy Studies at Chuo University in Tokyo, Japan.

- Nadiya Kostyuk is an Assistant Professor at the School of Public Policy and the School of Cybersecurity and Privacy at the Georgia Institute of Technology.
- Michael Nacht is the Schneider Chair Emeritus Professor at the Goldman School of Public Policy at the University of California, Berkeley, and a former Assistant Secretary of Defense for Global Strategic Affairs.
- Peter Schram is an Assistant Professor in the Department of Political Science at Vanderbilt University.
- James Igoe Walsh is a Professor in the Department of Political Science, the School of Data Science, and the Public Policy Program at the University of North Carolina at Charlotte.
- Oliver Westerwinter has been affiliated with the Department of Political Science at University St. Gallen, Switzerland, and the Robert Schuman Centre for Advanced Studies at the European University Institute.

List of Figures and Tables

List of Figures

3.1	Basic components of the bargaining model of war	48
3.2	Manipulating parameters in the bargaining model of war	53
8.1	Overseas presence improves strategic stability	219
8.2	Offshore balancing erodes strategic stability	220
9.1	Effects of naval capability on dispute location	241
9.2	Effects of naval tonnage on diplomatic recognition	242
9.3	Effect of aircraft carriers on diplomatic recognition	243
9.4	Effect of coastline length on diplomatic recognition	244
9.5	Effects of naval capability on dispute propensity	245
9.6	Effects of specific naval platforms on dispute propensity	246
9.7	Effects of submarines on dispute propensity	247
10.1	Weekly terrorist attacks (gray) and civilians killed by drones (black)	269
10.2	Weekly terrorist attacks (gray) and leaders killed by drones (black)	270
10.3	Weekly terrorist attacks (gray) and militants killed by drones (black)	270
10.4	Percentage change in militant attacks for a one standard deviation increase in militants killed in the previous week	271
11.1	Reconnaissance satellites correlate inversely with conflict	294
12.1	The effects of asymmetric and multilateral trade on conflict	308
12.2	Trade interdependence increases non-miltiary conflict	314
12.3	Asymmetric dependency increases militarized conflict	314
12.4	Multilateral trade reduces conflict for more dependent states	315
12.5	Multilateral trade slightly reduces conflict for less dependent states	315
13.1	Attacker's internet access and its likelihood of experiencing conflict	336
13.2	Target's internet access and its likelihood of experiencing conflict	336
14.1	Challengers select gray-zone conflict without risking war	349
14.2	Challengers risk war in gray-zone conflict	350
14.3	Determining the optimal level of gray-zone conflict	353
14.4	Intensity of Russian intervention across time	359

xxii LIST OF FIGURES AND TABLES

14.5	Geographic representation of Russian intervention	359
14.6	Escalation dynamics in gray-zone conflict	367
15.1	Stability of strategies with different preferences over cost and demand	383
15.2	Proposed strategies to deter China reflect different preferences	392

List of Tables

1.1	Strategies to pursue distinct goals implied by the bargaining model	7
4.1	Comparative strategic advantages of military domains	86
8.1	Implications of force posture on strategic stability	217
14.1	Deterrence gradient in major Russian gray-zone conflicts	361
15.1	The multiple elements of deterrence	382
15.2	Implications of different means for strategic stability	389

1

Introduction

Revisiting Deterrence Theory

What more can possibly be said about deterrence? Few topics have attracted more detailed, extensive, and consistent attention in the field of international relations (IR). It is hardly an exaggeration to say that deterrence theorizing gave rise to the subfield of international security. During the Cold War, deterrence became a mainstay of the national security policies of numerous nations, and remains so today. Yet, while it is generally believed that deterrence is exceptionally well understood, there are some underappreciated challenges and contradictions that persist at the heart of deterrence theory. These challenges are becoming ever more difficult to ignore.

The basic idea of deterrence is deceptively simple. An actor threatens prospective costs or risks to discourage another actor or actors from crossing some threshold. Few would question the core concepts and features of classical deterrence theory, even as they might reject it as a solution to many or even most policy problems. Indeed, the effort here will initially strike some as confusing and others as redundant. Why bother revisiting deterrence theory when it is so well understood?

It turns out that deterrence may actually not be that well understood. The "classical deterrence model" as outlined above was always underspecified. It proved convenient during the Cold War because avoiding nuclear Armageddon was an obvious priority, but nuclear war was a special case. Deterrence began, and has generally been treated analytically, as a cohesive binary choice of action or inaction: to deter or not to deter. Deterrence either succeeds, likewise, or it fails catastrophically. In practice, however, deterrence policies can be implemented in a range of degrees, and in different areas. Nuclear powers may be deterred from attacking each other directly, but they might be encouraged to engage in conflict indirectly, or in peripheral areas. As such, deterrence is less like an on-off switch and more like a rheostat. Indeed, figuring out when to engage this security rheostat, and how much resistance to apply in a given context, entails non-trivial problems.

Elements of Deterrence: Strategy, Technology, and Complexity in Global Politics. Erik Gartzke and Jon R. Lindsay, Oxford University Press. © Oxford University Press 2024. DOI: 10.1093/oso/9780197754443.003.0001

2 ELEMENTS OF DETERRENCE

Nations and their leaders usually care about many different things, not just whether they or an ally are attacked. Countries, governments, and factions within societies also vary in their willingness to face risks and make sacrifices for some or all of their goals. This is one reason that perception and cognitive processes have featured prominently in studies, and critiques, of deterrence. Actors often differ in their goals or values in different circumstances, such as lowering the risk of war, gaining influence over the status quo, improving combat effectiveness in the event of a contest, reducing the costs of national security, or investing in other social priorities.

Deterrence by whatever means, for whatever purpose, has always had several moving parts. At the very least, practicing deterrence requires balancing different objectives, each of which is in tension with other goals. As Dr. Strangelove states in the eponymous classic, "Deterrence is the art of producing, in the mind of the enemy, the fear to attack!" Yet fear of what exactly? The risks of war? The failure to achieve cherished national objectives? The costs involved in generating credible deterrence threats? The hazards of having to fight after abandoning the element of surprise? Or the ignominy of defeat? At the same time, how exactly shall the enemy attack? And how shall we make them afraid of attacking?

The classical model says almost nothing about how actors should go about actually doing deterrence. This was perhaps reasonable during the Cold War, when the primary means were assumed to be nuclear, and the overriding goal was understood to be avoiding mutual annihilation. But new technologies often enable political groups and individuals to seek out new ways to cooperate and compete, and sometimes fight. How do actors threaten or use force when a wider portfolio of military and non-military tools is available? How does the emergence of historically novel domains complicate, and also shed light on, the venerable logic of deterrence?

From Cyberspace to Integrated Deterrence

One way to begin looking for answers to these questions is to examine the strategic implications of cyberspace, which is one the most pervasive and eclectic of the many emerging technologies affecting modern politics. Digital networks connect all kinds of military capabilities on land, on and under the sea, in the atmosphere, and in outer space. Nearly anything that drives, sails, flies, or orbits uses or is affected by cyberspace in one way or another, while every component of cyberspace is located in the other domains. In other words, the cyber domain is inherently cross-domain.[1] The possibility of cyber warfare, furthermore, raises some hard questions about deterrence. How and why does the interconnectedness of electronic networks enable or constrain cyberconflict? How can countries deter ambiguous, undetectable, or unattributable attacks? How can governments make credible threats with capabilities they cannot reveal? Should cyberstrategy simply abandon the concept of deterrence altogether? How, then, should countries integrate their cyberunits with their armies, navies, air forces, and space forces to achieve deterrence objectives?

The answers to the questions raised by cyberspace need not be specific to it. But just as the cyber domain connects all other domains, the problems of cyber deterrence are relevant for other types of deterrence. Our interest in the general problem of deterrence across domains grew out of an early interest in the strategic problems of the cyber domain. But this has culminated in much more than a theory of cyber deterrence. We find that the strategic problems of cybersecurity reveal general tensions in deterrence theory that have always been present, but which have not been fully appreciated. Similarly, we begin this book with a survey of theoretical problems in cyberspace. A deeper appreciation of specific trade-offs in cyberspace sets the stage for an empirical investigation of general problems posed by the availability of multiple domains of specialized military capabilities. This book thus explores the complex relationships between the multiple ends and means of deterrence strategy.

There is a revival of deterrence strategy in academic and policy circles today, as well as something of a crisis of confidence in these same communities. National security practitioners obsess over the intricate details of force structure, posture, and employment. These issues are not mere technical details but rather politically consequential choices. Security scholars are increasingly noticing that means matter. At the same time, the latest

---

[1] The "cyber domain" is a sociotechnical construct. We use the notion of "domain" as a shorthand for describing classes of technologies or military platforms with similar operational characteristics in terms of mass, speed, stealth, etc. States will often field specialized military units or services for different domains. For convenience, we will generally follow the modern Western practice of distinguishing five operational domains because this provides a useful first cut at technological specialization, which is what we are really interested in. Sometimes it will even make sense for us to distinguish the nuclear and conventional "domains," even as each relies on platforms in many other environments, real and virtual. We are ultimately more interested in questions of the comparative strategic advantages of different classes of technologies than in determining what is "really" a domain or not in any ontological sense. See Chapter 4 for further discussion.

4 ELEMENTS OF DETERRENCE

technological challenges and buzzwords that animate policy discourse on deterrence are often just reflections of classic political trade-offs.

The concept of "integrated deterrence" in the 2022 National Defense Strategy of the United States, for example, is a recent manifestation of a longstanding aspiration to combine all instruments of national power into a coherent security strategy. The NDS defines "integrated deterrence" as "working seamlessly across war-fighting domains, theaters, the spectrum of conflict, all instruments of US national power, and our network of Alliances and partnerships."[2] This degree of ambition may be novel, but the underlying impulse is not. When our research for this book began a decade ago, the same basic problem was known as "cross-domain deterrence."[3] Related concepts have evolved in the interim, including "full-spectrum deterrence," "comprehensive deterrence," and the Chinese notion of "integrated strategic deterrence."[4] It would not be wrong to describe integration at this scale simply as "grand strategy," which is always hard and may not even be possible.[5]

The technological challenges of strategic integration pose a few particular difficulties, which are the focus of this book. While the jargon used to describe the problems of integrating deterrence changes with Pentagon fashions, the underlying issues and challenges are enduring. The basic strategic problems that we uncovered in our research on "cross-domain deterrence" have not gone away. If anything, they are getting worse. Advances in artificial intelligence, autonomous weapons, quantum computing, hypersonic weapons, commercial spacecraft, and the "internet of things" tend to amplify interdependence across actors and their activities. The complexity of military strategy is increasingly embedded within the complexity of economic globalization. The NDS concept of "integrated deterrence" thus aims to integrate not only war-fighting domains but also political and economic policy in the United States, and with its coalition partners, across the entire spectrum of conflict. A fundamental question here is whether integration at this scale is possible, or even desirable.

The Elements of Deterrence

Deterrence as a strategy is not simply a matter of integrating multiple military and non-military tools, but of figuring out *what objectives* an actor

---

[2] Department of Defense 2022, p. 1.   [3] Lindsay and Gartzke 2019.
[4] Chase and Chan 2016.   [5] Betts 2000.

INTRODUCTION 5

seeks to pursue in the first place. Some force structures and postures are useful for "winning" particular kinds of wars. Others are more effective for "warning" adversaries of likely consequences or demonstrating resolve. Still others may accomplish these goals at a lower overall cost or achieve them alongside greater political stability. Many new technologies, moreover, are useful for "watching" for opportunities to collect secrets or manipulate perceptions. Any attempt to integrate all operational domains, therefore, will require national leaders to make difficult choices about what they really want and where they are willing to compromise. Orthodox deterrence theory has little to say about the trade-offs actors face in actually doing deterrence and how different actors are likely to weigh alternatives within the practical rubric of deterrence.

The emergence of new technological tools, let alone entirely novel operational domains, may provide new strategic options. Some technologies may even make some goals more salient than they were before. For example, cyberspace makes intelligence and covert action strategies more feasible than ever before, using information and subterfuge to pursue national goals at reduced political or material cost. Yet, any expansion of options will tend to complicate the practice of deterrence. Credible commitment, after all, often involves limiting options. New technologies may offer policy makers additional ways to mitigate risk, exert influence, minimize costs, and enhance power. But different actors in different contexts, with different national priorities and values, may find each of these objectives more or less compelling.

This book is about the enduring challenges of balancing multiple national security objectives and choosing from a growing portfolio of specialized military domains. We argue that deterrence is not a simple, monolithic strategy but rather a bundle of different goals and practices. If we conceive of deterrence as a collection of various "ingredients," then competent practitioners are forced to make tough decisions about how to combine these ingredients in order to produce different "recipes," according to their respective national "tastes" for cost, performance, risk, and reward. These systematic trade-offs help to explain patterns of conflict and restraint that seem otherwise surprising. Because the multiple political ends of deterrence are often in tension, the recipes used to pursue them may not be compatible or consistent.

Our argument unfolds in two parts. First, we highlight different goals implicit in the deterrence rubric. Second, we explore the implications of technological specialization for deterrence. These various strategic goals and military means are the "elements of deterrence" in the book's title.

6 ELEMENTS OF DETERRENCE

The Different Ends of Deterrence

Throughout this book, we explore tensions that have been lurking all along in what we refer to as the "classical" or "orthodox" model of deterrence. As we discuss further in Chapter 2, the classical model was elaborated in response to the emergence of a very specialized form of military power—nuclear weapons brandished for the overriding goal of political survival. Even here we already confront fundamental tensions between the goals of avoiding war and ensuring the status quo. If avoiding nuclear war were the only objective, then accommodation and disarmament might serve most adequately as strategies. In addition to stability, however, most governments also want to sustain or improve the status quo. This tension gives rise to the characteristic paradox of nuclear deterrence: threatening nuclear suicide in order to avoid it.

But other means and ends highlight additional trade-offs. We view nuclear deterrence as just a special case of a much older and more general practice, which we label "the deterrence rubric." States have been known to make different threats for different reasons. Most of the discourse on deterrence tends to conflate four distinct objectives: the avoidance of war or escalation (strategic stability), retaining or imposing a given state of the world (political influence), minimization of political and material costs (policy efficiency), and the preservation or enhancement of war-fighting effectiveness (military power). All of these goals are desirable, but perhaps not equally so. States will often differ in how they prioritize across and among these objectives. At the same time, each objective is seldom equally attainable.

These four objectives are nothing new. They follow naturally from basic parameters of the bargaining model of war, which informs a lot of modern scholarship on conflict.[6] Preferences over these parameters give rise to four basic strategies, which are the ingredients of deterrence in practice. Table 1.1 summarizes these relationships. We thus rebuild deterrence theory on the foundation of the bargaining model of war by highlighting the unappreciated trade-offs that are implicit in it. Chapter 3 presents the detailed argument, though we summarize it here.

Bargaining models typically feature two actors who compete over some contested good such as territory, prerogatives, resources, etc. The actors

---

[6] Blainey 1988; Fearon 1995; Powell 1999; Wagner 2000; Reiter 2003; Glaser 2010; Slantchev 2011; Fearon 2018.

Table 1.1 Strategies to pursue distinct goals implied by the bargaining model

Bargaining model parameter	Political preference	General strategy
Demand	Political influence	Coercion (warning)
Power	Military effectiveness	Defense (winning)
Cost	Policy efficiency	Deception (watching)
Uncertainty	Strategic stability	Accommodation (working)

have the outside option of going to war, the outcome of which will be determined by their relative military power. Yet war is costly in blood and treasure, destroying some of the benefits over which the actors compete. Thus, avoiding war creates a "surplus" that ensures both actors are better off negotiating, rather than fighting, provided that they can arrive at a mutually acceptable deal. The inability to arrive at such a bargain, then, explains why states or other actors fight; whatever prevents states from agreeing on terms that approximate the bargains that end contests is an explanation for conflict.

Even strong, capable actors would be better off conceding something whenever there is a non-zero cost associated with war. However, each side in a dispute would also like to get the best deal possible without fighting. Thus, actors faced with a contest have incentives to misrepresent their true strength, resolve, or willingness to compromise. Candor may mean losing out in the resulting bargain (a private, internalizeable loss), but bluffing can result in war (a costly social burden). The bargaining model thus implies that *uncertainty* about power, resolve, or other variables such as valuation for the stakes is an important cause of war, if not *the* cause of war.

The bargaining perspective offers a variety of useful insights about the dynamics of war and peace given the demands being made, the relative power of the actors, the costs of war, and uncertainty about these factors. However, there is nothing about this framework that presupposes that an actor should care more about one of these parameters than another. Actors could conceivably improve their expected payoffs or risks of war by pressing or moderating demands, enhancing or restraining power, raising or lowering costs, or reducing or augmenting uncertainty. To use technical language, preferences over these parameters are exogenous to the model. Actors may desire many different things, for a variety of reasons, ranging from personality and psychology, organizational culture and bureaucratic politics, electoral and factional perspectives, coalition and alliance dynamics,

8 ELEMENTS OF DETERRENCE

national ideology and religion, etc. Unit-level characteristics, while tremendously important for explaining behaviors and choices in any given case, are not hard-wired into the strategic model.

Given variable preferences over the basic parameters of the bargaining model, actors may pursue different strategies. The strategy of *coercion* puts a priority on protecting or improving the status quo through the credible communication of threats and assurances. This encompasses many traditional intuitions about coercive diplomacy and classical deterrence by punishment. The strategy of *defense* puts a priority on using military power to forcibly preserve or alter the distribution of power or benefits. This encompasses brute force, combat operations, territorial conquest, and physical denial. Under some conditions, defense also contributes to so-called deterrence by denial. The distinction between coercion and defense is relatively well understood in deterrence theory, but the bargaining model implies at least two other strategies. We use the term *deception* to describe intelligence, covert action, and secret diplomacy initiatives that lower the costs of security policy. Indeed, an efficient way to get what you want is to trick opponents into acting voluntarily, but unwittingly, against their own interests. A major problem with deception, as we shall see, is that secrecy is at odds with the credible communication of deterrent threats. This brings us to the last strategy, *accommodation*, which aims to improve strategic stability by reducing provocations, improving information, and making compromises. This category includes disarmament, diplomatic engagement, and economic exchange.

Informally we might describe these four options as *warning* of costly consequences, *winning* a war, *watching* for discreet opportunities to gain advantage, or *working* together for common ends. We focus here on basic trade-offs across these four "pure" strategies, even as they are typically combined in various ways in practice. Sometimes the combinations create synergies, as when military power optimized for defense yields deterrence by denial. Sometimes, however, combinations interfere with one another, as when ambiguous subversion undermines credible communication.

All four strategies are inherent in the simple bargaining model. And yet, different strategies that shape different parameters will give rise to different conflict dynamics. To the degree that some version of the bargaining model of war is actually lurking within deterrence theory, these trade-offs have been hiding in plain sight.

The Multiple Means of Deterrence

We do not provide an explicit theory of preference formation in this book. Our theory simply assumes that these preferences, whatever their source, encourage different force structures or postures. Our aim is to highlight the unappreciated complexity that is an inherent feature of the bargaining approach to war before even considering the complexity of preference formation, let alone deviation from rationalist norms. The scope of this book, therefore, is limited to clarifying and testing the relationship between specialized military forces and the dynamics of deterrence within the bargaining model framework. The domestic or institutional political processes that give rise to decisions to make specialized investments are outside of the scope of this study. Ours is not a theory of the causes of preferences, but rather of their effects.

The second step of our argument, therefore, focuses on technological specialization, guided by different political preferences, whatever their cause. Many strategic conundrums seem to be caused by new technologies themselves, for instance the complexity of computer network security or the autonomy of artificial intelligence. These seemingly technical problems often reflect underlying political contradictions in the ways that specialized means are used to pursue different ends.

As noted above, it has become fashionable to describe new classes of technologies, and the strategic challenges they create, in terms of "domains." The key theoretical concept that underlies the confusing notion of a "domain,"—one that we wish to stress here—is functional specialization. Specialization has been extensively analyzed in economic theory but not in security studies, where military power has generally been treated as an undifferentiated good. In economics, as Adam Smith argued centuries ago, specialization in the means of production tends to enhance efficiency, the number and quality of outputs associated with a given basket of inputs. The implications of specialization in the means of *destruction*, by contrast, are less straightforward, in part because efficiency is only one of several possible objectives. For example, states may decide *either* to accentuate battlefield impact (i.e., destructiveness) *or* economic cost. Indeed, in many circumstances, they may be forced to choose between these and peacetime political influence or strategic stability.

10 ELEMENTS OF DETERRENCE

The growing number and variety of military and non-military means available to nations (and increasingly non-state actors) tend to be more or less specialized and effective in producing different political ends. Some military instruments, for example ground forces and nuclear weapons, have specific advantages for the classical deterrence goals of improving credibility and preventing war. Others, especially stealthy and maneuverable air and maritime forces, sacrifice in terms of reduced credibility to achieve enhancements in war-fighting. Emerging technologies in space and cyberspace are particularly well suited to intelligence collection and deception, which differ in subtle ways from traditional strategies of deterrence and defense.

Non-military tools like cultural soft power or economic inducements, in turn, may be better suited for stabilizing strategies that eschew conflict altogether (i.e., accommodation or disarmament). In this book we focus disproportionately on military specializations for coercion, defense, and deception, which are complex enough. But to round out the discussion we do briefly consider the role of economic interdependence, which plays an increasingly important role in great power politics. China, most obviously, is both America's largest trading partner and its foremost military competitor. If integrated deterrence within the Department of Defense is already complex, then integrating grand strategy across the entire US government takes things to a whole new level of complexity and difficulty. In the conclusion, we show how debates about how to deter China are actually debates about which of the several objectives in the deterrence rubric the United States should prioritize.

If developing strategy is the process of unearthing relationships between means and ends, then successful deterrence involves linking some of the growing number and variety of means available in the twenty-first century with one's preferred ends. The particular forms that deterrence takes, and the outcomes it produces, depend on the specific ways in which actors with diverse motives use whatever combination of instruments are available to them. One reason that deterrence is so challenging in the *cyber* era, therefore, is that deterrence in *any* era draws from a repertoire of variegated processes or means to pursue discrete and often incompatible political ends. Put simply, deterrence is not just one thing, at least not any more.

Plan of the Book

As discussed in the acknowledgments section, this book combines new content and contextualization with thoroughly revised, updated, and remixed

INTRODUCTION 11

material from academic articles published elsewhere. In several chapters we are joined by coauthors who have generously allowed us to leverage their talents in this synthesis. While portions of our argument have appeared before, this material has never been presented holistically until now. The result, we believe, is an integrated framework that only becomes obvious to readers (and to some extent, ourselves) in the present format. We support our general argument about the effects of military specialization on the dynamics of deterrence with considerable empirical evidence.[7]

The book is organized in four parts. Part I presents the book's conceptual framework (Chapters 2–4). Part II details theoretical arguments about the strategic nature of the cyber domain (Chapters 5–7). Part III offers empirical evidence about strategic specialization in other domains (Chapters 8–11). Part IV turns to interactions and complications across domains (Chapters 12–14 and the conclusion). Each part begins with a brief summary of the portion of the overall argument of the book that is presented in that section.

In Part I, we begin by reviewing the literature on deterrence theory, highlighting implicit assumptions about means and ends in classic concepts such as escalation and deterrence by denial (Chapter 2). We then reframe the problem of deterrence within the modern bargaining model of war, highlighting four distinct strategic goals implied by the model (Chapter 3). We continue by arguing that different military operational domains have comparative advantages for these goals (Chapter 4).[8]

We next turn to cyberspace to explore the strategic implications of technological specialization. Part II explains why cyber operations are poor instruments of deterrence and only marginally useful for defense in combination with other military domains (Chapter 5).[9] However, cyberspace is excellent for deception; for the same reasons, cyberthreats can be defeated through counter-deception (Chapter 6).[10] Combining a deception-specialized domain like cyberspace with other military domains can introduce varied virtuous or vexing trade-offs. For example, offensive cyber operations could potentially be used to disrupt nuclear command and control, which would provide a war-fighting advantage in the event that nuclear deterrence fails; but this option makes it more likely that deterrence will fail in the first place, since stable nuclear deterrence depends on a high degree of transparency about capabilities (Chapter 7). We return to

---

[7] In this book we summarize technical findings for the general reader. Readers are encouraged to consult the original academic articles, footnoted with each respective chapter below, for full technical details. The most relevant articles for each chapter are cited below as appropriate and in the main text.
[8] Lindsay and Gartzke 2022.   [9] Gartzke 2013.   [10] Gartzke and Lindsay 2015.

12 ELEMENTS OF DETERRENCE

cyberspace in Part IV to consider additional complexities that arise at the intersection between conflict and economic interdependence.

Part III turns to additional strategic trade-offs highlighted by the four physical domains—land, sea, air, space. Forward deployed land forces are comparatively well suited for improving the credibility of extended deterrence, even as other forces may be more useful for fighting wars in a maritime environment (Chapter 8 with Koji Kagotani).[11] While naval forces can "show the flag" anywhere with a coastline, maritime maneuverability also increases the likelihood of deterrence failure, since challengers are free to question the commitment of forces that can be easily withdrawn (Chapter 9).[12] Automated air forces (drones) offer particular battlefield advantages, but they are also ambiguous signals of resolve, which may contribute to the protraction or redirection of conflict in undesirable ways (Chapter 10 with James Walsh).[13] Satellite reconnaissance tends to reinforce strategic stability be decreasing the attractiveness of surprise attack (Chapter 11 with Bryan Early).[14]

In Part IV, finally, we address the challenges of deterrence in an globalized world. The role of economic interdependence is every bit as complicated as deterrence, sometimes encouraging restraint and in other circumstances encouraging conflict, depending on underlying network conditions (Chapter 12 with Oliver Westerwinter).[15] The same economic trends that discourage traditional war, moreover, encourage intelligence contests in cyberspace (Chapter 13 with Nadiya Kostyuk).[16] Gray-zone conflict has different escalation dynamics depending on whether it is motivated by risk minimization or cost minimization (in Chapter 14 with J. Andres Gannon and Peter Schramm).[17] Different prioritizations of ends imply different prioritizations of means. We see this especially in the debate over US grand strategy toward China; while sponsors advocate different combinations of military and diplomatic instruments, each is actually an expression of different strategic priorities (Conclusion).

Getting deterrence right may ultimately be less about distilling an abstract ideal recipe of military threats and assurances and more about societies figuring out what they really value. What one achieves in practicing deterrence depends on how one pursues it, for what purposes, and with what tools. More

---

[11] Gartzke and Kagotani 2017.   [12] Gartzke and Lindsay 2020.
[13] Gartzke and Walsh 2022; Gartzke 2021.   [14] Early and Gartzke 2021.
[15] Gartzke and Westerwinter 2016.   [16] Kostyuk and Gartzke 2023.
[17] Gannon et al. 2023.

generally, most coercive strategies mobilize a range of different features, objectives, and values that differ and are often in tension. Successful (or unsuccessful) deterrence is not just a single coherent outcome, but rather an ongoing interaction among different tools and, importantly, different strategic objectives. As a result, actors will usually not be able to have all of the things they want, equally and simultaneously. While strategists cannot escape complexity, they can help decision makers appreciate the consequences—both good and bad—that stem from complexity, and to make more informed choices.

PART I

THE MEANS AND ENDS OF DETERRENCE

This book is about the enduring strategic problems of integrating new technologies and different operational domains—land, sea, air, space, cyberspace—into long-held and practiced strategies, such as deterrence. Concepts of "integrated deterrence" and "cross-domain deterrence" gesture at these longstanding problems, and new buzzwords are sure to appear in the future, but the underlying problems are not going to disappear any time soon. Whatever we call it, the desire to harmonize as many of the means of national power as possible to achieve deterrence objectives is an enduring ambition of strategists, and not only in the United States.

We argue, however, that it may not be possible to realize a truly integrated deterrence strategy. Different means support different ends. Any attempt to combine different domains into a single strategy will require states to make hard political choices about what they want, and where they are willing to compromise. These problems have always been relevant in practice, but they have not received as much emphasis in the classic deterrence literature. The overriding preoccupation with nuclear weapons in traditional deterrence theory focused on the vital problem of global survival, an admirable objective indeed. Yet, the growing diversity of military technologies draws our attention to facets of deterrence strategy that, while always present, have yet to be explicitly incorporated into a general theory of deterrence.

This section lays out the basic theoretical framework for this new general theory of deterrence. Chapter 2 surveys the conceptual landscape of deterrence theory and provides a glossary of deterrence concepts. Chapter 3 teases out different strategic objectives that tend to be conflated in the discourse on deterrence, namely improving political influence, enhancing military power, lowering peacetime costs, and strengthening strategic stability. These are all desirable, but they cannot be achieved at the same time, to the same extent. Chapter 4 analyzes how military specialization at the operational level supports different political goals at the strategic level.

2

What Is Deterrence?

Deterrence as traditionally understood is a good deal, if you can get it. By proscribing behavior and threatening consequences, actors gain influence over their rivals without being forced to bear the horrendous burdens of war. But this is also the fatal flaw of deterrence logic. Actors who have no interest in going to war in the first place will be tempted to posture in order to gain the benefits of deterrence. Bluffers will seek to obtain concessions on the cheap. Targets will suspect, in turn, that threats are nothing but cheap talk, and so they will not be deterred.[1]

Threatening and bluffing are ancient practices. Non-human species produce threatening displays when provoked, while less dangerous creatures mimic these displays. Leaders and soldiers throughout history have brandished and blustered, and they have considered the consequences of attacking stronger foes, or of making commitments they could not defend. If targets were not convinced, or they decided to call a bluff, then it might be necessary to fight. For much of history, deterrence strategies were lumped in with every other kind of military strategy. The same forces that states used to fight and win wars were also used to produce warnings about the possibility of war. Subtle distinctions between winning and warning were largely ignored and strategic concepts remained pragmatic, rather than analytic.

The need for an explicit theoretical treatment of deterrence only became ineluctable when humanity invented nuclear weapons. The possibility of nuclear annihilation encouraged careful theorizing about the difference between coercion and war-fighting. A single nuclear weapon can decimate a city. An exchange of weapons can render large swaths of territory uninhabitable. The advent of long-range nuclear bombers and intercontinental ballistic missiles, furthermore, made it possible for nuclear nations to inflict comprehensive devastation within hours, or even minutes. The inability to effectively defend against nuclear attack, in turn, encouraged careful reflection about strategies designed to avoid extermination. At the same

[1] Fearon 1995.

Elements of Deterrence: Strategy, Technology, and Complexity in Global Politics. Erik Gartzke and Jon R. Lindsay, Oxford University Press. © Oxford University Press 2024. DOI: 10.1093/oso/9780197754443.003.0002

18 ELEMENTS OF DETERRENCE

time, adversaries were keen to find ways to advance the national interest in the face of unusable weapons and impossible forms of war. Deterrence theory was the result.

The classic dilemma about influence on the cheap became more acute than ever. States sought the benefits of nuclear deterrence without the costs of nuclear war. Their rivals had to wonder whether they were bluffing. All sides asked, what benefit could be worth the risk of mutual suicide? Politicians, soldiers, and civilian strategists all began to take an intense interest in the "ultimate weapon," in hopes that such destructive implements would never have to be used. Nuclear weapons dramatized the difference between "winning" a war and "warning" about one. This distinction is fundamental and remains essential today. Yet, it is reasonable to wonder whether other forms of military specialization may highlight other dimensions of deterrence.

The nuclear age catalyzed an intensively creative period of thinking about deterrence which largely culminated by the end of the 1960s.[2] Thomas Schelling famously declared that nothing new in deterrence theory had been written since 1966, coincidentally the publication date of his second book, *Arms and Influence*.[3] Nevertheless, an enormous amount of work has been done since this period to refine, test, extend, and challenge deterrence theory. Scholars have examined many varieties of deterrence—extended, immediate, general, denial, punishment, etc.—and have applied them to a range of different contexts—nuclear and conventional warfare, cyber and space operations, terrorism and insurgency, economic statecraft, law enforcement, and even parenting. This book is part of a modern resurgence of interest in deterrence theory inspired by all this new complexity, as well as by the growing sense that the world may not always and for ever more remain peaceful, i.e., that history has not reached an end.[4] But first it will be helpful to revisit some essential intellectual roots.

This chapter proceeds in five parts. First, we review the classical literature on deterrence theory. Our review is of necessity proscribed and selective; we focus on portions of the huge literature on deterrence that we consider most characteristic or deem most salient to our efforts here. Second, we provide a glossary of key distinctions in classical theory that continue to be

[2] Freedman 1986; Trachtenberg 1991a.
[3] Schelling 1966, confirmed in a personal conversation with the authors.
[4] Fukuyama 1989.

relevant, even as implicit assumptions about military specialization have not (yet) been fully appreciated. Third, we discuss modern challenges and the reemergence of deterrence theorizing. Fourth, we detail the manifestations of these challenges in US deterrence policy, with special focus on the recent notion of "integrated deterrence." We conclude with a call for revisiting first principles in (re)theorizing deterrence in the twenty-first century.

Classical Deterrence Theory

Politics, of course, did not end with the nuclear revolution. Superpower competition unfolded in the shadow of nuclear holocaust. Elaborations of deterrence theory attempted to explain how states could continue to compete and even "win" in an era when the consequences of great power war were prohibitive. Paradoxically, weapons too destructive to be inflicted could be mobilized to prevent war, or even to further political interests through "brinkmanship," the mere risk of their use. A vast literature evolved to analyze deterrence as a problem of high-stakes nuclear bargaining.[5] This enterprise implicitly assumed that nuclear weapons would, indeed must, be used to deter nuclear war. Theorists focused on the challenge of credibility in the shadow of annihilation, while empiricists debated the applicability and scope of deterrence theory.[6] Even departures from orthodox theory were generally conceived in the context of, and as adjuncts to, the overarching nuclear contest between superpowers.

Deterrence in practice frequently diverged from theory. US policy makers pursued counterproliferation and damage-limiting counterforce policies in the face of reasoned advice about the stability of "Mutual assured destruction" (MAD).[7] MAD theorists tended to see such policies as irrational, even dangerous, products of parochial or misguided domestic interests. As the new historiography of the Cold War reveals, US policy makers did not share, and routinely ignored or even opposed, the academic consensus regarding MAD, often for sound strategic reasons.[8] Military commanders and arms control negotiators obsessed about the details of

---

[5] Classic treatments include Brodie et al. 1946; H. Kahn 1960; G. Snyder 1961; George and Smoke 1974; Schelling 1966; Jervis 1989; Powell 1990. Book-length reviews of the foundational literature include Kaplan 1986; Freedman 2004.

[6] Huth 1999; Quackenbush and Zagare 2016; Carcelli and Gartzke 2017.

[7] Waltz 1981; Jervis 1984; Glaser 1990.

[8] Gavin 2012; Long and B. Green 2014; Gavin 2019; B. Green 2020.

20 ELEMENTS OF DETERRENCE

force structures and postures on land, at sea, in the air, and in orbit, while the superpowers jockeyed for advantage in low-intensity, non-nuclear conflicts around the globe.

Deterrence theorists have elaborated many specialized extensions to deterrence theory, including analyses of the credibility of nuclear guarantees to allies,[9] incentives for conventional war in the shadow of nuclear deterrence,[10] deterrence in conventional war,[11] the role of the offense-defense balance,[12] risks of inadvertent escalation from conventional to nuclear war,[13] the conduct of limited nuclear war,[14] the dynamics of arms racing and arms control,[15] and the safety and reliability of nuclear command and control systems.[16] As Lawrence Freedman notes in a book-length review of the literature, "We have seen how complicated a theoretical tangle developed around deterrence even during the cold war, a period of unusual clarity and continuity in international affairs."[17] All of this complexity suggests that there has always been more going on than what was captured in classical conceptions of deterrence.

Classical Complications

In this section we provide a short glossary of several important distinctions that emerged during the golden age of deterrence theorizing. They remain relevant today, and will appear throughout the book. These important nuances reveal complications in deterrence theory that raise questions about the simple appeal of influence on the cheap. They also belie tacit assumptions about the means of deterrence that have not been fully appreciated. Here we simply sketch these problems, unpacking them further at various points in the book.[18]

---

[9] G. Snyder 1984; Stein 1987; Huth and Russett 1988
[10] G. Snyder 1965; Jervis 1989; Powell 2015.   [11] Mearsheimer 1985.
[12] Jervis 1978; Glaser and Kaufmann 1998; Lieber 2000.
[13] Posen 1991. Recent elaborations in the US-China context include A. Goldstein 2013; Talmadge 2017; Acton 2018.
[14] Kissinger 1957a; Larsen and Kartchner 2014.
[15] Wohlstetter et al. 1974; Trachtenberg 1991b.   [16] Blair 1985; Sagan 1995.
[17] Freedman 2004, p. 117. Some critics describe such complexity as evidence of a degenerative research program, e.g., Vasquez 1997. We prefer to see this as an opportunity for starting afresh with the bargaining model of war, as we argue in Chapter 3.
[18] Useful primers include Art and Greenhill 2018; T. Biddle 2020.

Peace

Deterrence theory focuses on avoiding war in contexts where warfare is a possibility. This is often referred to as *negative peace*. *Positive peace*, by contrast, refers to the presence of ideas and institutions that eschew or otherwise obviate the need for violence.[19] Deterrence is fundamentally about threatening war to avoid it. The absence of the possibility of war, either because of the lack of motives or because there exist other mechanisms— such as institutions—that supplant warfare, also eliminates the utility of deterrence. Disarmament may or may not be a good idea for humanity, but some arms must be retained for deterrence to be a meaningful strategy. One could argue that positive peace provides the most effective form of security by making war unthinkable. The counterargument is that actors need a military insurance policy in case humanitarian norms fail.[20] Put another way, deterrence strategy relies on the existence of warlike means. If war is politics by other means, positive peace eschews those other means altogether. Yet, this also means that a basic differentiation of means underlies the entire practice of coercive diplomacy. Deterrence theory has always been a theory of specialized means.

Coercion

The concept of coercion encompasses *deterrence* and *compellence*. Deterrence is to compellence as defense is to offense. Deterrence says: "come no closer or I will shoot." Compellence says: "come closer (and give me your money) or I will shoot." This distinction is blurry in practice. Just as defenders will counterattack and attackers will protect themselves by adopting a (temporary) defensive posture, deterrence and compellence can be combined or merged, so that the two are difficult to differentiate empirically. Moreover, actors often disagree about the status quo; one actor's deterrence becomes another actor's compellence. As this indicates, the distinction between deterrence and compellence hinges on the reversion point (the status quo), which itself is routinely contested, artfully composed, and socially

---

[19] Galtung 1996.

[20] Schelling 2009 argues that Global Zero—the movement to eliminate nuclear weapons popularized by prominent political figures in 2008—would lead to significant risk and instability.

constructed. A routine practice is for opposing sides to point to different boundaries, conditions, claims, agreements or points in history as the status quo, thus ensuring that one side's deterrence is another's compellence and vice versa. For example, China and its neighbors dispute the status of large portions of the East and South China Seas based on different interpretations of ownership at different points in history. In this book we generally discount the distinction between deterrence and compellence. We use "coercion" as an umbrella term, meaning either deterrence, compellence, or both. Deterrence and compellence are each forms of political communication about or through threats, i.e., *coercive diplomacy*. Coercion and its derivatives are in turn distinguished from war-fighting or defense (i.e., brute force). Coercion succeeds through the promise of harm, while war-fighting involves the actual imposition of violence.

Assurance

Deterrence depends on both *threats and assurances*. Coercive diplomacy is the art of making credible promises of at least two different sorts. A threat is a promise to inflict harm if a condition is not met. An assurance is a promise not to inflict harm if a condition is met. A target has no reason to comply with a threat if there is no benefit for doing so. Threats and assurances, moreover, can be sequenced in different ways. The classic threat of punishment only materializes if the target does not comply. In cases of ransomware, kidnapping, or limited war, however, the punishment is applied *until* the target complies. In either instance, assurances provide some promise of relief from punishment. This raises a question about whether the same means that make threats credible are also useful for making credible assurances.

Allies

Deterrence can be *direct* or *extended*. Direct (or homeland) deterrence refers to efforts to discourage attacks on one's own sovereign territory, population, or assets. Extended deterrence, by contrast, is used to protect another sovereign nation's territory, population, or assets from attacks by a third party. Direct deterrence is generally thought to be more credible, as actors may be more willing to fight for themselves than for a friend. Choices about force structure and posture are particularly important for extended deterrence, especially if the patron state (defender) has to project power over long distances to protect its client (protégé). The defender also has to provide assurances to the protégé that it will make good on its promise of protection, as well as to the target (challenger) that it will exercise restraint. Three-body problems, while solvable in some circumstances, are naturally more difficult than two-body problems.

Crises

Deterrence can be *immediate* or *general*. Immediate deterrence refers to situations where a specific challenger initiates a militarized crisis and the defender makes threats to persuade the challenger to back down. General deterrence, by contrast, discourages any challengers from initiating crises to begin with. Immediate deterrence tends to be more focused, but also more difficult, because challengers who initiate crises tend to be more committed to subsequent action, either because they are more resolved (or capable) or because they are more invested in a particular course of action (e.g., reputation). An underappreciated feature of immediate deterrence is that challengers make specific choices about what and how to mount their challenge. In other words, specific challenges usually involve specific means.

War-fighting

Deterrence is *distinct from defense*. Both deterrence and defense attempt to protect the status quo. But deterrence relies on credible threats to discourage attacks, while defense relies on military power to defeat them. Military war-fighting operations are described with actions like attack and defend, conquer and resist, strike and shield, destroy and protect, etc. These actions use force in the *present* to change or preserve the distribution of benefits. Coercive diplomacy by contrast communicates demands and threats of *future* punishment, denial, or conquest. This distinction is foundational for deterrence theory.[21] In this book we show that the availability of diverse modes of defense also has implications for how deterrence operates.

---

[21] Schelling 1966, pp. 2–6 famously describes this in terms of coercion vs. brute force.

Denial

Deterrence of any sort may threaten *punishment* or *denial*. Most classical formulations of deterrence emphasize that punishment must be sufficiently costly to outweigh the benefits of aggression (e.g., through nuclear retaliation against enemy cities, etc.). Deterrence by denial, by contrast, is the threat of preventing successful aggression in the first place, or successfully defending against it (e.g., effective strikes against enemy nuclear forces). Deterrence by punishment merely requires some ability to impose a cost. The threat of armed popular resistance, for example, could deter an invader through the promise of an exorbitantly expensive occupation, even if the insurgency itself is unlikely to succeed militarily. Deterrence by denial, in contrast, necessitates a degree of military war-fighting capacity sufficient to convince an aggressor that it cannot win a war.[22] The distinction between punishment and denial also applies to compellence. Compellence by denial is the threat to take something by force if it is not conceded voluntarily, while compellence by punishment is the threat to impose a cost on an opponent until the opponent makes the required concessions, even if the coercer cannot obtain what it wants directly, by force.

Counterforce

While there are obvious parallels, the distinction between *countervalue* and *counterforce* targeting does not map perfectly onto the distinction between punishment and denial. While countervalue targets (i.e., cities and economic targets) are generally associated with punishment strategies, counterforce targeting may serve both denial and damage limitation strategies.[23] Damage limitation, as the name implies, is about limiting the enemy's ability to inflict damage by any means possible. Damage limitation capabilities do

---

[22] The 2022 US National Security Strategy distinguishes between "deterrence by denial" meaning the capacity to defeat enemy forces, and "deterrence by resilience" meaning the capacity to absorb enemy attacks (Department of Defense 2022, p. 8). From an orthodox perspective, these are both aspects of deterrence by denial, since they deny an adversary the benefits of aggression, enabling the United States to fight through attacks. Yet, resilience can also be seen as part of a counter-punishment strategy that denies the enemy the ability to impose costs. The NSS describes deterrence by punishment with the ungainly phrase, "deterrence by direct and collective cost imposition."

[23] To the extent that the enemy intrinsically values its military forces, they can be targeted for punishment as well. Economic targets might also degrade enemy military capability. The distinction between countervalue and counterforce is ultimately more about intention.

not have to be communicated to the enemy in advance; indeed, they may be more effective if kept secret (e.g., subtle electronic warfare attacks on enemy command and control). Deterrence by denial, by contrast, requires the credible communication of the willingness and ability to resist attack. In the conventional realm, likewise, an attack that rolls through a hidden minefield may be defeated but not deterred, since the minefield has not been advertised. As with counterforce strategies in the nuclear realm, minefields can either be advertised (making them an attempt at deterrence by denial) or not advertised (implying that they are designed to defeat an enemy, rather than deter them). The simple act of advertising rather than concealing changes the strategy and its effects.

Arsenals

Deterrence can be described as *minimal* or *maximal* depending on the range of scenarios it covers. The classic minimal deterrent is a small, secure, second-strike force used for direct deterrence by punishment. Few weapons are needed to cover one very important objective: the deterrence of nuclear attack on the homeland. The arsenal is able to ride out any first strike (because weapons are dispersed in hardened silos or deployed on submarines at sea) so they do not need to be kept on a hair-trigger alert. A maximal deterrent requires a much larger and more differentiated force structure, and a more aggressive alert posture, to respond to a wider range of contingencies for extended deterrence, deterrence by denial, and damage limitation. Note that the nuclear arsenal is sometimes described simply as "the deterrent," which nicely captures the conflation of deterrence theory with nuclear weapons in practice. Clearly, once we begin debating minimal versus maximal deterrents, we are taking into account multiple objectives and a portfolio of military options.

Abstraction

Deterrence can work at the *strategic* or *operational* level. Strategic deterrence is about preventing the onset or escalation *of war*. Operational deterrence is about preventing the use of certain weapons or operations to gain an advantage *in war*. This distinction flips deterrence by denial on its head.

26 ELEMENTS OF DETERRENCE

Instead of using military capabilities to bolster (strategic) deterrence, here deterrence is used to protect or enable the use of military capabilities. The classic example is using covering fire to discourage the enemy from firing on maneuvering troops. Likewise, airpower can deter armor from concentrating in the open. Operational deterrence is more preoccupied with the comparative advantages of different capabilities. This might help to explain why orthodox theory tends to ignore it. More generally, deterrence theory is abstract enough to apply to any level of analysis. Deterrence can describe interactions of soldiers warning their enemies to avoid a minefield, litigants offering to settle out of court, or nations contemplating nuclear retaliation. But this also means that actors at any of these levels of analysis, or at different times, may opt to rely on strategies other than deterrence. War-fighting at the strategic level can, and frequently does, involve a lot of deterrence at the operational level, and vice versa.

Escalation

Deterrence policies can target either the *onset* or *escalation* of war. The severity of war may vary from a special operations raid to global thermonuclear catastrophe. Deterrence, therefore, might be used not only to discourage actors from starting a war but also from expanding the war to different regions, actors, weapons, or levels of severity. Classical deterrence theory focuses on the former for good reasons: the outbreak of nuclear war is inherently a disastrous failure of deterrence. But nuclear war planners must also worry about how to keep a war limited, for instance, to the use of tactical weapons in a particular geographical area. Clearly, the means used to fight or threaten a wider war become extremely salient here.

Expansion

Escalation can be described as *vertical* or *horizontal*. Vertical escalation describes moving to a higher level of severity or lethality. Horizontal escalation describes expanding the war to different areas or using different types of forces at the same level of severity. This can also be described in terms of widening or expanding the conflict. Classical treatments of escalation focus on the vertical dimension, often described as "climbing the escalation ladder." In practice, horizontal escalation may be more common. When actors have more means available, military or non-military, or more domains for political competition, then they have more opportunity for horizontal escalation, and perhaps for vertical escalation as well. Air operations can range from unmanned surveillance to nuclear bombardment. Cyber operations might produce irritating webpage defacements or catastrophic failures of critical control systems. Rather than a one-dimensional ladder, we gain additional dimensions in a multi-dimensional matrix of escalation.[24]

Stability

The concept of *strategic stability* is complicated for all these same reasons. Intuitively, strategic stability is synonymous with deterrence success. But as we have seen, deterrence is complicated. Success in one area may imply failure in another (or vice versa). We can distinguish between the willingness to engage in arms races, the frequency or likelihood of militarized crises, the potential for crises to end in war, the likelihood of escalation into different domains or regions, and so on. It is possible for political rivals to experience a great deal of arms racing and intelligence contests and yet endure few dangerous crises or wars, implying that some forms of strategic instability reinforce other forms of stability. In many ways this describes the Cold War. Arms racing should be unimportant if MAD works as theorized (since a few nuclear weapons are almost as dangerous as many, especially when using countervalue strategies), but it was clearly an important feature of the Cold War. Again, this highlights the importance of force structure in the practical dynamics of deterrence.

Instability

The *failure or success* of deterrence is ultimately relative to the scope of the policy. An important implication of all the distinctions above is that

---

[24] This is also a helpful way to think about arms racing. It is intuitive to think about an arms race as a tit-for-tat interaction where each side buys more of the same thing to try to outbid each other. In practice, arms racing has a pronounced horizontal dimension as actors seek out countermeasures and offsets by innovating new kinds of capabilities, rather than by just producing greater quantities of the same. Thus, the modern combined-arms team is not simply a bigger army but a more diversified system containing a range of specialists.

28 ELEMENTS OF DETERRENCE

deterrence success or failure is not absolute. The most famous manifestation of this insight is the so-called *stability-instability paradox*. This is the idea that successful nuclear deterrence may encourage conventional or peripheral aggression in areas where nuclear threats are much less credible.[25] Put another way, nuclear deterrence may fail to prevent the onset of a limited war even as it deters escalation to the highest levels of mutual annihilation. The classic form of the stability-instability paradox is inherently a cross-domain phenomenon, because it contrasts the different deterrence dynamics of nuclear weapons and conventional or special forces. As there are now more ways to threaten undesirable consequences at the high end, and engage in political competition at the low end, we should expect the stability-instability paradox to reappear in many new manifestations. We could even flip the argument on its head and describe an *instability-stability paradox*, whereby the availability of new domains of competition without war (cyberspace) makes the resort to traditional war less attractive.

Complexity

The further we move away from the simple goal of deterring the onset of war by any means, and the more we layer on other goals and values, the more concerned we become with the details of force structure, posture, and employment. Thus, deterrence may fail to prevent the onset of war, but succeed in deterring its vertical escalation, yet fail to deter its horizontal escalation. For example, the United States was not deterred from entering the war in Vietnam, and eventually escalating its bombing campaign there, but it was deterred from using nuclear weapons. It was not deterred from starting adjunct secret wars in Cambodia and Laos, which were intended both to weaken Vietcong operating bases (war-fighting) and to warn Hanoi about potential escalation (coercion). While US strategic bombing campaigns ultimately failed to persuade Hanoi to end the war (strategic deterrence), US tactical airpower was successful in shaping North Vietnamese Army decisions on the battlefield (operational deterrence).[26] In short, deterrence has always been complicated in practice, and these complications have always involved a diversity of ends and means.

[25] G. Snyder 1965; Powell 2015.   [26] Haun and Jackson 2016.

The Renaissance of Deterrence

Deterrence theory was born in the nuclear age, and its inherent tensions were already present then. Nuclear weapons have not been used in anger since the closing days of World War II, in 1945. Yet, according to deterrence theorists and military professionals at US Strategic Command, they are used every day to keep the peace. Deterrence seems to offer a humane alternative to war, even as the threat to extinguish civilization seems immoral in the extreme. Many credit nuclear deterrence with the absence of major war and a "long peace" among the major powers since 1945, even as nuclear weapons have made mass extinction more likely. Given that nuclear arsenals are often described simply as "the deterrent," deterrence could amount to whatever it is that we do with nuclear weapons. Yet nuclear weapons can also be used for war-fighting or damage limitation when deterrence fails. Deterrence appears, variously, as a Western conceit, a potent magic, and an article of quasi-religious faith. Stretched to fit many different situations, it is no wonder that the concept often disappoints, even as hope for resurrection springs eternal.

Deterrence thinking has experienced something of a renaissance in recent years.[27] The military modernization and economic growth of China, in particular, reinvigorated interest in superpower deterrence. Russia, meanwhile, clings to a superpower-sized arsenal in an attempt to preserve influence in a period of relative decline. Yet compared to the Cold War, deterrence now operates in a different geographic and political context of greater technological complexity and economic interdependence.

In the nuclear realm, new technologies for reconnaissance, communications, and precision strike have made nuclear counterforce and damage limitation postures even more feasible than they were in the past.[28] The emergence of new nuclear states like India, Pakistan, and North Korea have created multipolar dynamics that call into question the implications of classical dyadic theory, even as multilateral extended deterrence has always been central to American policy.[29] Longstanding concerns about

---

[27] Several recent volumes explore new challenges to and extensions of deterrence theory: Paul, Morgan, and Wirtz 2009; Shultz, Drell, and Goodby 2011; Greenhill and Krause 2018; Lindsay and Gartzke 2019.

[28] Lieber and Press 2017; Kroenig 2018.

[29] Crawford 2003; P. Morgan 2003; Zagare and Kilgour 2000; Sartori 2013.

30 ELEMENTS OF DETERRENCE

proliferation and nuclear latency are newly urgent given regional rivalries in the Arabian Gulf and on the Korean Peninsula, among others.[30]

Challenges have also emerged beyond the nuclear realm.[31] Coercing terrorists, for example, is problematic to the degree that irregular operatives are tough to find and possess fewer assets or ties that one can hold in jeopardy. Actors who are willing to commit suicide for their cause may be difficult to deter.[32]

Deterrence appears to be understood and practiced in different ways by different societies. One may persuasively assert, for example, that deterrence can have Chinese or Israeli characteristics.[33] America's geopolitical competitors have also grappled with the increasing complexity of deterrence. Their aspirations for strategic synergy should not be mistaken for a workable solution that has somehow eluded Western strategists. The Russian concept of "strategic deterrence" prioritizes the integration of non-nuclear, informational, and nuclear means, to counteract the threat of Western "hybrid warfare."[34] Likewise, the Chinese concept of "integrated strategic deterrence" stresses an imperative to coordinate nuclear, conventional, space, and cyber capabilities.[35] Middle and smaller powers may adopt very different deterrence postures.[36] Since the practice of deterrence hinges critically on common understandings and expectations about red lines and consequences, specialized cultural or subjective understandings of deterrence pose an obstacle to deterrence success, even more so when complex emerging technologies are added into the mix.[37] Viewed in a certain way, the widely accepted claim of cultural variation is really just another way of saying that our conceptualization of deterrence is overly parochial. A truly universal concept should not need to be reformulated for every application, in every setting, with each different adversary, at different points in history.

New technological domains have also inspired new commentary on deterrence. Domain-specific critiques of deterrence assume implicitly that military-technical specialization is strategically consequential. Highly

---

[30] M. Bell 2016; Volpe 2017; Narang 2017.

[31] Lupovici 2010; Knopf 2010.

[32] Trager and Zagorcheva 2006; Talmadge 2007; Wilner 2015. The very factors that motivate terrorists are presumably subject to cost or risk. Defense of possible targets and offensive operations designed to hunt down terrorists succeed in part by discouraging future terrorism. Someone who is pessimistic about the prospects that political violence will prove successful is presumably less likely to become a terrorist. Terrorists themselves rely on coercive diplomacy, see Kydd and Walter 2006.

[33] Twomey 2011; Adamsky 2017.   [34] Ven Bruusgaard 2016; Adamsky 2018.

[35] Chase, Engstrom, et al. 2015; Fravel 2018.   [36] Yoshihara and Holmes 2012; Narang 2014.

[37] Jervis, Lebow, and Stein 1985; Adler 2009; Morrow 2019.

technological domains like space and cyberspace are rife with uncertainty about weapons effects and threat attribution that appear to compromise deterrence.[38] Is it possible to retaliate against aggression without a return address? Does non-lethal or reversible aggression even merit retaliation? Some strategists reject deterrence altogether as an inappropriate strategy for countering disinformation, subversion, and espionage in the cyber domain, looking instead to alternatives described in terms of "persistent engagement" and "defending forward."[39] Many technological trends combine to produce apparent deterrence failures in so-called gray-zone conflicts, in which nuclear-capable states like Russia, China, and the United States employ unconventional means below the threshold of full-scale military retaliation,[40] a new spin on the old stability-instability paradox.

The Dream of Integrated Deterrence

Deterrence remains a fixture in US national security discourse. Novel formulations of deterrence concepts typically highlight the challenges of technological and political complexity with the addition of a new adjective. Deterrence thus becomes "complex," "tailored," "cross-domain," "multidomain," "full-spectrum," "comprehensive," and, most recently, "integrated." These variations may seem to offer new solutions, but they really just describe the same underlying problem of strategic complexity.

Classical deterrence theory arose in the bipolar context of the Cold War, but deterrence in practice has always involved a more complex set of interactions among multiple states or coalition actors. This gives rise to concerns about "complex deterrence."[41] In the new millennium, the George W. Bush administration sought "tailored deterrence" to deal with regional problems of counterterrorism and counterproliferation in situations deemed too nuanced for a general deterrence policy.[42]

The Barack Obama administration worried further about "cross-domain deterrence" in reaction to emerging challenges in space and cyberspace, which were dramatized by the 2007 test of a Chinese anti-satellite weapon

---

[38] Libicki 2009; F. Morgan 2010; Manzo 2011; Nye 2017; J. Schneider 2019a; Bahney, Pearl, and Markey 2019; Lonergan and Lonergan 2023.

[39] Harknett and Fischerkeller 2017; Schneider, Goldman, and Warner 2020; Fischerkeller, Goldman, and Harknett 2022.

[40] Gannon et al. 2023; Lanoszka 2016; M. Green et al. 2017.

[41] Paul, Morgan, and Wirtz 2009.   [42] Bunn 2007.

32 ELEMENTS OF DETERRENCE

and a barrage of Russian cyberattacks in Estonia that same year. US defense strategists concluded that "cross-domain deterrence dynamics will constitute a core analytic issue for the US defense, diplomatic, and intelligence community, particularly as shifts in the actual or perceived balance of power in sea, air, space, and cyberspace become more opaque."[43] Sometimes the term "cross-domain" is used specifically to describe the use of means of one type to deter another type (e.g., using economic sanctions to discourage cyberattacks), while the term "multidomain" refers more generally to combinations of multiple types of operational forces in any kind of strategy. The special operations community also floated the notion of "comprehensive deterrence" to counter low-intensity threats in this more complex strategic environment.[44]

The Donald Trump administration attempted to turn cross-domain deterrence from a vulnerability into a strength. As the 2018 Nuclear Posture Review (NPR) observed, "There now exists an unprecedented range and mix of threats, including major conventional, chemical, biological, nuclear, space, and cyberthreats, and violent non-state actors. These developments have produced increased uncertainty and risk."[45] The Trump NPR explicitly raised the possibility of nuclear retaliation for catastrophic cyberattacks, highlighting the comparative advantage of nuclear weapons: "US nuclear capabilities make essential contributions to the deterrence of nuclear and non-nuclear aggression. . . . Non-nuclear forces also play essential deterrence roles, but do not provide comparable deterrence effects."[46]

Not to be outdone, the Joseph Biden administration set forth an ambitious concept of "Integrated Deterrence" in the 2022 National Defense Strategy (NDS).[47] The ostensible goal is to coordinate US and Coalition strategy and operations in all domains and across the entire spectrum of conflict. This concept thus "integrates" three previous notions of deterrence: (1) the idea of "cross-domain deterrence" involving multiple military and non-military instruments; (2) "complex deterrence" involving relationships among multiple actors and coaltions; (3) and "comprehensive deterrence"

---

[43] Brimley 2010. See also Brimley 2010; Lewis 2010; Denmark and Mulvenon 2010; Manzo 2011; Creedon 2012; Nacht, Schuster, and Uribe 2019.

[44] Wasser et al. 2018.   [45] *NPR* 2018, p. v.

[46] *NPR* 2018, p. vi. The 2022 NPR clarifies that "the fundamental role of nuclear weapons is to deter nuclear attack on the United States, our Allies, and partners," and yet it still asserts that "our nuclear posture is intended to complicate an adversary's entire decision making calculus, including whether to . . . conduct strategic attacks using non-nuclear capabilities," Office of the Secretary of Defense 2022, p. 8. We return to this problematic combination in Chapter 7.

[47] Department of Defense 2022.

spanning the "full spectrum" of threats from the "gray zone" to global thermonuclear war.

The phrase "integrated deterrence" first appeared in a speech by US Secretary of Defense Lloyd Austin III on April 30, 2021.[48] The occasion was a change of command ceremony at US Indo-Pacific Command, which underscored the real motivation for the speech: the growing military threat posed by the Chinese People's Liberation Army (PLA). Indeed, the Pentagon increasingly describes China as "the pacing threat" for US defense strategy. The PLA has been modernizing in all domains in recent decades, with special emphasis on space, cyber, and missile capabilities to counter the ability of the US military to project power in East Asia. To counter this threat, Austin spoke of revitalizing deterrence by creating synergies across domains, organizations, and operations. Austin's speech is worth quoting here in some detail because it clearly lays out several themes that reoccur regularly in US deterrence discourse, and which are sure to reappear under future administrations:

> Deterrence still rests on the same logic. But it now spans multiple realms, all of which must be mastered to ensure our security in the 21st century. And deterrence now demands far more coordination, innovation, and cooperation from us all. Under this integrated deterrence, the US military isn't meant to stand apart, but to buttress US diplomacy and advance a foreign policy that employs all of our instruments of national power....
>
> We can't predict the future. So what we need is the right mix of technology, operational concepts, and capabilities—all woven together and networked in a way that is so credible, flexible, and formidable that it will give any adversary pause. We need to create advantages for us and dilemmas for them. That kind of truly integrated deterrence means using some of our current capabilities differently. It means developing new operational concepts for things we already have. And it means investing in quantum computing and other cutting-edge capabilities for the future, in all domains....
>
> But this isn't just about technology. It's about thinking differently— for all of us. That means that our view of deterrence has to rise above the old stovepipes that can build up in any organization.... Integrated deterrence means all of us giving our all. It means that working together

---

[48] Austin 2021.

34 ELEMENTS OF DETERRENCE

is an imperative, not an option. It means that capabilities must be shared across lines as a matter of course, not as an exception to the rule. And it means that coordination across commands and services needs to be a reflex, and not an afterthought.

Austin may be right that "we can't predict the future" in detail, but US policy makers still have agency in how and where they will use American military power. The US military may be unprepared to invade and occupy a major European country, but perhaps the United States has no interest in doing so. Only a subset of all possible scenarios are worth deterring or fighting. Moreover, whatever force structure or posture the United States adopts will be an invitation for adversaries to counter or offset. States get to influence the future by how they build and develop their forces, but this usually means influencing *how* competitors respond, rather than discouraging competition altogether. Wise strategies may thus try to channelize adversary behavior, much as castle builders of yore constructed visible weaknesses to lure enemies into a killing zone.

A key assumption in Austin's narrative is that all forms of power can and should be harnessed to improve deterrence. One way to understand this is as a straightforward application of operational concepts like combined arms warfare and joint military operations. In a combined arms team, infantry provide flexibility and reconnaissance, tanks provide mobile fires and protection, artillery and aircraft deliver massed fires, and helicopters provide battlefield mobility. In "joint" or "multidomain" operations, navies project power on land, air forces shape the battlefield, and everyone relies on satellite communications and intelligence. These kinds of war-fighting synergies are essential for victory at the operational level. Achieving these synergies necessarily involves extensive training, refined doctrine, and high-quality troops, so not every state is willing or able to achieve them.[49]

It is natural to assume that what works at the operational level will also work at the strategic level. The principles of "joint operations" are simply applied to "whole of government" integration. The concept is simple enough, but implementation is wickedly complex. Achieving joint command and control has involved a long, difficult institutional saga for the US military.[50] Integrated deterrence is an even harder organizational problem, with a scope encompassing not only all of the Department of Defense but also

---

[49] S. Biddle 2004; Talmadge 2015.   [50] Allard 1996.

non-military policy and coalition partners. Thus Austin stresses the imperative to "rise above the old stovepipes." Faced with formidable institutional challenges of implementation, it is easy to ignore the basic strategic assumptions of integrated deterrence. It is an open question, however, whether the same combination of domains that produces war-fighting synergies at the operational level can also succeed in achieving similar efficiency gains at the strategic level.

The 2022 NDS assumes that strategic synergies are indeed achievable: "Integrated deterrence is enabled by combat-credible forces prepared to fight and win, as needed, and backstopped by a safe, secure, and effective nuclear deterrent."[51] There is much going on here. The same forces that are capable of winning in combat are also supposed to improve the credibility of warning in deterrence. Conventional war-fighting capabilities will be bolstered by, and not undermine, nuclear deterrence. It is not self-evident, however, that combat-capable forces are also "combat-credible," or that *winning* is sufficient for *warning*.

Things get even more complicated as we layer on cyber and intelligence capabilities for *watching*, let alone the normal *working* of the global economy in peacetime. Credibility is in the mind of the adversary, but secret sources and methods are not supposed to be communicated at all. As we discuss extensively in Chapters 5, 9, and 10, there are features of military forces that are useful for winning wars, like stealth, mobility, and automation, respectively, that are not necessarily useful for deterring them. It is especially puzzling to imagine how concepts like US Cyber Command's "persistent engagement" that were proposed explicitly as an alternative to deterrence are now to be impressed into service for "integrated deterrence."[52]

Effective deterrence depends on transparency. An actor cannot deter with capabilities or intentions that remain opaque to a potential attacker. A key feature of nuclear weapons is their continued viability in the face of revelation. When there is no effective defense against nuclear attack, states can freely share information about their nuclear capabilities with other nations. This in turn leads nuclear weapons to be unusually effective in achieving deterrence. The ability to brandish nuclear capabilities without paying a substantial price in terms of diminished effectiveness (even over relatively long periods of time) is one of the most important and under-appreciated attributes of nuclear security. By contrast, one cannot minimize the risk of

---

[51] Department of Defense 2022, p. 1.   [52] Billingsley 2023.

war with capabilities or intentions that are concealed from an adversary. One can lower the cost of implementing or maintaining deterrence through secrecy and can also heighten operational effectiveness in the event of active conflict. Yet secret capabilities are ineffective as leverage in maintaining the status quo. An adversary will demand more than one is willing to give, in part because the adversary does not realize the true balance of power. This is problematic insofar as many exquisite military capabilities are highly classified, or too complicated to perfectly understand.

The NDS further argues that the US military "strengthens deterrence" through "campaigning—the conduct and sequencing of logically-linked military activities to achieve strategy-aligned objectives over time. Campaigning initiatives change the environment to the benefit of the United States and our Allies and partners, while limiting, frustrating, and disrupting competitor activities that seriously impinge on our interests, especially those carried out in the gray zone" (i.e., low-intensity conflict between peace and conventional war, to include most special operations and cyber campaigns).[53] But there is a lurking contradiction here. If the United States finds itself conducting military campaigns, then at some level deterrence has failed. While a gray-zone challenger may be deterred from starting a large war, the very existence of the challenge implies that it is undeterred from lesser provocations.

Military force can be used to either alter the balance of power (i.e., "limiting, frustrating, and disrupting competitor activities") or to influence decisions about additional uses of force. Shaping and signaling are not mutually exclusive, but neither are they the same. The fact that the NDS includes both "integrated deterrence" and "campaigning" in the same strategy suggests that deterrence is more complicated than widely assumed. To achieve deterrence, the strategy says, it is important to include capabilities to mitigate deterrence failure. These capabilities are not merely brandished, as classical nuclear deterrence theory might assume, but actively used to shape the battlefield and frustrate adversary operations. Not to put too fine a point on it, the NDS says in effect that deterrence cannot achieve all security objectives of the United States, and thus US forces must do things other than deterrence to achieve them. How will these same forces be integrated into deterrence?

This tension comes to a head in the NDS discussion of "How we will deter."[54] To achieve "deterrence by denial" the Department of Defense "will develop new capabilities, including in long-range strike, undersea,

---

[53] Department of Defense 2022, p. 12.　　[54] Department of Defense 2022, pp. 8–9.

hypersonic, and autonomous systems, and improve information sharing and the integration of non-kinetic tools." These are precisely the kind of tools that rely on sensitive sources and methods and are difficult to factor into any net assessment of the military balance of power. This begs the question of the "role of information in deterrence," where the NDS proposes: "To strengthen deterrence while managing escalation risks, the Department will enhance its ability to operate in the information domain—for example, by working to ensure that messages are conveyed effectively." Put differently, the capabilities needed for pure military denial may not be useful for deterrence by denial. Even worse, the ability to fight the war the United States hopes to deter may make it more likely that such a war actually occurs. We are doomed to fight the wars for which we are unprepared, but blessed with the opportunity to avoid the wars for which we prepare.

The concept of "integrated deterrence" is not the first attempt to grapple with the challenge of deterrence across domains. It is also not the first to assume that all good things go together, and it will not be the last. Future administrations will undoubtedly come up with a new buzzword. But buzzwords in defense policy often overlook enduring contradictions rather than reconcile them, let alone offer feasible solutions. Seen in this light, "integrated deterrence" may well refer to the difficulty, or even the impossibility, of integrating deterrence. Concepts such as "integrated deterrence" and "campaigning" through "multidomain operations" promise to improve both diplomatic influence and military performance. What government would not like to achieve both of these goals? The problem is that this is an extremely difficult balance to achieve in practice; who would not like to have their "peace" of deterrence "cake," and eat it too? Indeed, it may not even be possible in principle.

The Need to Revisit Deterrence

An enormous body of literature on deterrence emerged in the twentieth century to meet the need for new understandings in the era of nuclear weapons. Deterrence scholarship continues to burgeon in the twenty-first. Deterrence strategy has long been a mainstay of national security doctrines, and it has been extensively studied by scholars of international relations, criminal justice, economics, and other fields. Indeed, it might seem as there is little new that can be said on the topic. For perhaps the same reasons, the

38 ELEMENTS OF DETERRENCE

concept of deterrence has been stretched to fit so many situations that one might question the implicit assumption that deterrence is even a coherent phenomenon. Strategists have extended deterrence far beyond its initial formulation in an attempt to cover capabilities and issues that were not contemplated by the original theory or in its applications in national policy or strategic doctrine.

Indeed, the discourse of deterrence abounds with paradox and contradiction. We are as likely to hear that deterrence remains vibrant today as that it is failing or cannot function properly in this new era. We are told that deterrence must impose costs and deny benefits, but also that it reduces costs and provides benefits. Some call for clear red lines, while others try to keep the other side guessing. Some advocate for deterrence as a hard-headed alternative to norms against violence, even as deterrence depends on norms of appropriate behavior and proportionate response. Some see deterrence failure in the outbreak of any aggression whatsoever, while others may herald a success, provided that an adversary's aggression is subdued to some extent. Deterrence may be described both as a way to avoid a war and as a way to prepare to fight one. Deterrence is both the opposite of force, and the continuous use of force. Deterrence somehow allows us to have peace but exploit our power also.

Nations or other actors are bound to differ in their preferences for these different goals, even if they are faced with similar trade-offs. Indeed, the sources of national preferences, and thus the valuation of the stakes of a crisis or conflict, are largely external to the basic logic of deterrence. As the eminent theorist Robert Powell concludes at the end of a seminal article on nuclear deterrence:[55]

> Deterrence theory takes these stakes for granted by holding the fundamental conflict of interest underlying a crisis fixed. Yet conclusions about significant changes in the likelihood of major war are claimed to follow from this theory. Accordingly, the causes of these changes are not to be found in variations in the underlying conflict of interest. . . .
>
> Thus, nuclear deterrence theory implicitly assumes that a better explanation of the likelihood of major war is to be found by examining the actions of states rather that by examining the situations in which states act. A reductive approach to explaining the outcome of a crisis is assumed to

---

[55] Powell 1985, p. 96.

provide a better explanation than a more systemic approach that focuses on how states stand in relation to each other as described by the underlying conflict of interest. This may be so. But regardless of the usefulness of this assumption in accounting for the presence or absence of major war, this is an assumption of a theory of international politics. It is not an assumption of the theories of strategic nuclear deterrence. . . .

To claim that such conclusions [about strategic stability] follow from the theory of strategic nuclear deterrence is to claim too much for these theories.

We take Powell's charge seriously. Deterrence theory provides no account of why states want what they want, even as the dynamics of deterrence turns on strong assumptions about state preferences. Our argument thus begins by relaxing orthodox assumptions about what deterrence is for and what it can achieve. We let state preferences vary so that we can explore the strategic consequences of this variation. Our theory assumes that different goals like stability, credibility, efficiency, and effectiveness give rise to different force structures and force postures, with important consequences for the dynamics of deterrence.

There may be some value in stepping back from this conceptual tar pit and returning to first principles. This is what we pursue next, in Chapter 3.

3

Deterrence Is Not (Just) One Thing

Policy makers look to deterrence as an attractive solution for difficult foreign policy problems. They hope deterrence will preserve the peace, advance a nation's interests, liberate resources to invest elsewhere, and preserve military options in case deterrence fails. Practiced successfully, deterrence is supposed to persuade rivals to do what the government wants of them, without a fight, at an expedient cost, while helping our side win any wars that do in fact occur. It would be nice indeed if strategy could achieve all of these goals. In practice, this can seldom be the case.

Deterrence strategy combines various objectives that are in tension with one another. Successfully resisting revision may raise the costs of vigilance and readiness and increase the risks of deterrence failure. Successfully lowering costs may compromise the credibility of deterrence and undermine the goal of war avoidance, unless one also accepts some revision of the status quo. A declaratory policy, force structure, and force posture optimized to win wars is not necessarily ideal for ensuring that war does not occur. Strategic actors must balance the disparate goals of peace and stability, retaining the status quo, lowering the costs involved in implementing and maintaining a deterrence posture, and preserving latent combat power.

The various objectives of deterrence may be best served by specialized policies, strategies, and military or non-military capabilities. But doing well in some areas usually entails doing less well in others. The increasing complexity and specialization of military power, moreover, tends to exacerbate these tensions and trade-offs. At the operational level of war, by analogy, some forces that operate particularly well in a given domain or environment may be ill-suited to functioning elsewhere. Navies are of limited utility far inland, for instance, while armies cannot secure sea lanes of communication. Land forces move slower than air forces, which struggle to locate concealed ground forces. So too at the level of strategy, some platforms, force structures, or policy instruments are especially adept at providing political leverage, promoting stability, cutting costs, or winning a fight, should one occur, but they may not perform each of these functions equally well, or simultaneously.

Elements of Deterrence: Strategy, Technology, and Complexity in Global Politics. Erik Gartzke and Jon R. Lindsay, Oxford University Press. © Oxford University Press 2024. DOI: 10.1093/oso/9780197754443.003.0003

The theme of this book is that deterrence is a complex relationship between many means and multiple ends. We present an overview of this theory in two chapters. This chapter tackles the many ends of deterrence. The next chapter will delve into its many means. This chapter proceeds in three parts. First, we return to first principles and delineate the basic features of the bargaining model of war. The bargaining model suggests four different objectives for deterrence strategy, even as it is silent about which of these actors should prefer. Second, we discuss the general tensions across these objectives. These tensions have always been inherent in deterrence, but are rarely considered together. Third, we emphasize that the source of complexity is ultimately rooted in domestic preferences over the various objectives of deterrence.

Disaggregating the Politics of War

Clausewitz famously claimed that war is "a true political instrument, a continuation of political intercourse, carried on with other means."[1] But if war is politics by other means, then politics itself is a choice between at least two different types of means. Normal politics is full of nominally peaceful pursuits such as governing, speaking, negotiating, trading, allying, colluding, or bribing. Compared to these things, war is extremely costly in blood and treasure and fraught with risk. Or as Clausewitz puts it, war is a "peculiar" means that combines passion, chance, and reason in a "paradoxical trinity."[2] Given all the danger and misery that war entails, leaders are wise to choose it if and only if they hope to achieve something that peaceful means cannot.

The Bargaining Model of War

Politics is about authoritative allocation: who gets what, when, and how.[3] In modern IR theory, this idea is encapsulated in the bargaining model of war.[4] The bargaining model is a workhorse in the field and has been applied to

---

[1] Clausewitz 1976, p. 87.
[2] Clausewitz 1976, pp. 87, 89. See also Beyerchen 1992; Waldman 2016.   [3] Lasswell 1936.
[4] Overviews include Blainey 1988; Fearon 1995; Powell 2002; Reiter 2003.

everything from nuclear deterrence and terrorism to electoral politics and institutional design.

Politics is profoundly concerned with the distribution of goods (resources, territory, etc.) or prerogatives (rights, reputations, etc.). Political actors bargain over these distributions, sweet-talking and cajoling, offering carrots and sticks, and potentially threatening or using military force in the process. War can be likened to the outside option in a negotiation (i.e., the expected utility of terminating the diplomatic conversation). In a job negotiation, to take a more everyday example, the outside option is taking another job or remaining unemployed rather than accept employment on unfavorable terms. Actors with better outside options (more job offers) generally have more leverage to get a better deal. Actors with more military power, likewise, generally have additional leverage to negotiate a more favorable deal. If coercive diplomacy fails to achieve a bargain, a sovereign state can always go to war to forcibly redistribute, or defend the distribution of, disputed resources.

Because war is profligate (people suffer and resources are destroyed), states and other actors ought to be able to arrive at a division of resources that leaves each side better off without fighting. However, the same actors have incentives to misrepresent their power and interests to lobby for a better deal in peacetime or in a crisis.[5] In a job negotiation, actors may lie about their outside offers, but employers can verify their claims with other companies. Validating the outside option in anarchic politics is more difficult because it is hard to verify an actor's willingness or ability to fight. Diplomats may bluster about redlines, and adversaries may question their resolve. It is hard to know what a government is willing to do until guns start blazing.

Bargaining models assume that actors are broadly rational. This may sound problematic, or even implausible, but it is actually quite simple. "Rationality" here means only that actors want things and that they act according to their (own) understandings of how to get what they want, adjusting for costs and risks. The technical language used is that actors have preferences that they seek to realize. There is no requirement that decision makers be of sound mind in setting preferences. Indeed, a leader who is mentally ill in medical terms can be "rational" in this sense of acting according to what she or he believes is true. This assumption is important because it is difficult to make, and test, claims about cause and

[5] Fearon 1995.

effect involving human behavior if we do *not* imagine a connection between preferences and behavior. Most of the causal claims we make every day follow this pattern. If a driver cuts you off in traffic, you may call them "crazy," but no doubt you imagine they have their reasons for driving the way they do, even if you don't like that they are driving so aggressively.

Classical deterrence theory largely adopts this same rationality assumption.[6] A massive literature in cognitive psychology disputes various aspects of rationality.[7] Most often the challenge from psychological perspectives is regarding the ability of actors to connect what they want with how they behave. Again, if leaders, or the states they represent, are not guided by preferences, then we cannot do much to explain their usage of deterrence theory or explain how deterrence works, positively or normatively. If you don't accept that people, leaders or govenments can think their way through problems and make decisions designed to achieve their goals, even imperfectly, then this book probably does not have much to offer you.

Even locally rational decision making can lead to apparently irrational outcomes in the emergent dynamics of complex systems.[8] The technological and cultural complexity of modern deterrence across different technological and political domains may well make these problems more salient. Nevertheless, it is still desirable to articulate a baseline of reasoned choices before considering the important conditioning effects of decision heuristics and institutional pathologies.[9] This baseline can serve as a reference or point of comparison. It could also act as an "ideal type" or goal, one that is imperfectly realized in the "real world," precisely because of growing complexity and other factors that we emphasize. Still, it can often be useful to decompose a process in a simpler setting, to see how it works in basic terms before confronting all the variables that actually impinge on our behaviors in a more complex world.

Rational theory can advise decision makers about how to operate given their (exogenous) preferences. But it has less to say about how to choose among different preferences. Before looking beyond rationality to explain the complexity of deterrence in practice, it is important to ask how much of the complexity attributed to psychology and sociology may actually be a function of tensions within rational theory itself.

---

[6] Schelling 1960.
[7] Jervis 1976; Jervis, Lebow, and Stein 1985; Goldgeier and Tetlock 2001; Stein 2017.
[8] Jervis 1998.   [9] Glaser 2010.

44 ELEMENTS OF DETERRENCE

As we aim to show, there are basic tensions built into the rationalist foundations of deterrence theory, even before one considers the nuances of institutions or psychology. Stripped to its essentials, the bargaining model emphasizes a few simple concepts:

- The division of a disputed resource;
- The relative military power of the competitors;
- The costs of fighting, preparing for, or threatening war;
- Uncertainty about any of these factors.

The last of these is particularly important with respect to the likelihood of war (i.e., deterrence failure). Uncertainty from any source—ignorance, bluffing, secret plans, secret weapons, inherent complexity, stochastic error, Clausewitzian friction—can lead to incompatible expectations about what a war is likely to achieve (war outcomes), which in turn can trigger bargaining failure and a military conflict.

Uncertainty and War

There is a growing consensus that uncertainty is a fundamental cause of war.[10] Fearon's foundational formulation of the bargaining model highlights two main causes of war: asymmetric information and commitment problems.[11] The former describes incentives to misrepresent capabilities or resolve—exaggerating martial strength or willingness to fight, hiding vulnerability or lack of conviction, feigning commitment or weakness, etc.— to get a better deal in peacetime, which in turn leads to miscalculations about acceptable bargains. The latter describes incentives for one side to renege on a deal in the future—due to secular shifts in military strength, emerging alliance structures, seasonal fluctuations in battlefield advantage, etc.—which makes an opponent reticent to accept a deal. Therefore, it seems that costly conflict is possible even when there is complete information

---

[10] Blainey 1988; Gartzke 1999; Meirowitz and Sartori 2008; Slantchev and Tarar 2011; Ramsay 2017; Kaplow and Gartzke 2021.

[11] Fearon 1995. Fearon mentions, but discounts, a third war-causing problem of indivisible goods, which he points out can generally be addressed through side payments and issue linkages.

about the balance of power, especially when there are large, rapid changes in relative power.[12]

There is an important nuance here. The commitment problem logic assumes that actors have perfect information about the balance of power *today*, but they actually have imperfect understanding about how interests might change *tomorrow*. To see this, assume that there is a preventative war to resolve a commitment problem. This war, like all wars, will destroy some of the surplus that the actors could have divided between themselves. Assume, furthermore, that this preventative war ends, as wars generally end, when both sides eventually prefer to negotiate a settlement over further fighting. Now, if both sides had completely perfect information about the costs of this preventative war, then they would have both preferred a settlement prior to starting it. The same reasoning applies to any future preventative war that might emerge to solve the commitment problems of *those* future settlements. Through backward induction from the final settlement, therefore, actors who are perfectly informed about all shifts in relative power and the costs of fighting all wars will be able arrive at an ex ante deal that both sides prefer to ever fighting in the first place.

Assuming this degree of prescience is fantastically unrealistic, not to mention deeply incompatible with the chaotic nature of war.[13] But this only highlights the scarcity of information in power politics. Relaxing assumptions of rational unitary action introduces still other sources of uncertainty. In a world where the present or future are uncertain, and/or people make mistakes, some actors will be willing to gamble on fighting. From this perspective, uncertainty is not just a cause of war, but *the* cause of war. In any case, the uncertainty explanation for war causation is sufficient to frame the discussion of deterrence that we anticipate here.

Anything that creates uncertainty about the present or future balance of power or resolve, and of the true costs and consequences of war, will tend to make war more likely (i.e., possible). To take a recent example, Putin's invasion of Ukraine in February 2022 seemed to be inspired in part by the Russian leader's optimism about the ability of Russian forces to conduct a quick, successful attack. While clearly wrong in retrospect, Putin's view was shared by many international experts. Few imagined that Russia's invasion

---

[12] Powell 2004b.   [13] Beyerchen 1992.

46 ELEMENTS OF DETERRENCE

would iteratively bog down into a costly, relatively static attritional contest. Indeed, Ukrainian leaders, for their part, seemed either to be skeptical that Russia would invade—they thought Putin was bluffing—or they were more optimistic about the ability of Ukrainian forces to resist a Russian onslaught, given private information about Ukraine's military capabilities.

Conversely, anything that improves the common understanding of respective capabilities, motives, and costs will tend to make (negative) peace more likely. Put simply, information improves stability. Actors can cultivate a better mutual understanding of war through processes of costly signaling and credible commitment.[14] These options are often described with metaphors like "tying hands," "burning bridges," "sinking costs," "burning money," and "threats that leave something to chance." Visible preparations for war, for example, as well as the process of fighting a limited war, help to reveal how much actors are willing and able to pay for what they want.

Military mobilization is a particularly potent signal because it both ties hands, by making fighting more attractive by increasing available military power, and sinks costs, because maintaining a high level of readiness is not cheap.[15] Even so, actors are tempted to wonder whether mobilizations are bluffs. Many NATO allies questioned whether the Russian mobilization in late 2021 was serious. The US government took the extraordinary step of releasing intelligence in an attempt to convince allies that Russian preparations were genuine. The release of intelligence was intended mainly to promote alliance cohesion and counter-mobilization. Russian coercive diplomacy failed, and war ensued, because Russia badly misjudged the willingness and ability of Ukraine and its Western patrons to resist aggression.[16]

This implies that there are costs associated with deterring wars as well as fighting them. Deterrence is an informational process insofar as informing an adversary about unwanted consequences is tantamount to making the actual playing out of warfare unnecessary. But signals must often be made costly to become more credible. Some actors may opt for aggression on the cheap, therefore, wherever the costs of exploitation or conflict seem low and the price of effective deterrence or coercion seems high.

From this perspective, limited forms of conflict or instability can be interpreted as bargaining in the shadow of a larger war. Fighting a small war can marginally alter the distribution of resources and clarify the costs

---

[14] Schelling 1966; Jervis 1970; Fearon 1997; Gartzke, Carcelli, et al. 2017.
[15] Slantchev 2011. [16] We return to these dynamics in Chapter 14.

DETERRENCE IS NOT (JUST) ONE THING   47

and interests at stake in a potentially bigger war (i.e., more intense or longer duration of fighting).[17] Modest aims or high risks will tend to encourage military restraint. Clausewitz thus observes that the "degree of force that must be used against the enemy depends on the scale of political demands on either side. These demands, so far as they are known, would show what efforts each must make; but they seldom are fully known—which may be one reason why both sides do not exert themselves to the same degree."[18]

Implicit Strategic Objectives

The basic parameters of the bargaining model of war are demands, power, costs, and uncertainty. Given these parameters, the model allows us to make inferences about where actors will prefer negotiation over fighting. But the model tells us nothing about how actors might go about setting or changing these parameters in the first place. This process is exogenous to the model. Actor preferences might arise from personalities and cognitive biases, factional or coalition dynamics, electoral politics and domestic disputes, organizational culture and bureaucratic politics, alliances and alignments, ideology and religion, international norms, geographical constraints, or any number of reasons. The list of factors that can shape strategic goals can go on and on, which is part of why it can be so difficult to formulate or assess national strategy. But even holding these inputs to the model constant, there are certain complexities in the model itself that must be appreciated.

We will return to the problem of preferences below. For now, we simply highlight the fact that actors can, for whatever reason, prioritize different objectives:

- *Political Influence* prioritizes gaining or maintaining a state's *demands* in disputes over territory, resources, policies, or prerogatives.
- *Military Effectiveness* prioritizes maximizing military *power* in war to forcibly alter or protect the distribution of resources, territory, or prerogatives.
- *Policy Efficiency* prioritizes minimizing the *costs* of the bargaining process, which include the costs of signaling, fighting, and contesting the "gray zone" between peace and war. Economizing on costs enables

---

[17] Wagner 2000; Slantchev 2011.   [18] Clausewitz 1976, p. 585.

actors to invest in domestic policy goals other than security (i.e., butter over guns).

- *Strategic Stability* prioritizes minimizing the risks of war, accidents, or escalation, which implicitly requires reducing mutual *uncertainty* about the balance of power and resolve. Stability, in turn, enables actors to focus on peaceful pursuits that maximize prosperity such as economic trade.

We can illustrate these different goals in Figure 3.1, which builds on the canonical model of bargaining between state A and state B.[19] The two states negotiate to divide some good like territory. Payoffs are zero-sum, meaning that A's profit is B's loss (and vice versa). The x-axis represents A's demand for a share of the disputed good. The y-axis represents A's military power to win a potential war over the dispute.[20] Each state pays some cost to fight

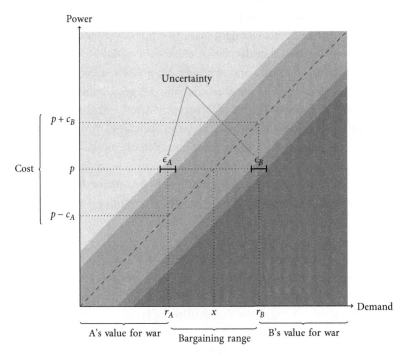

Fig. 3.1 Basic components of the bargaining model of war

---

[19] Fearon 1995.
[20] The division of the good—the payoff for A—is represented on the x-axis by $x \mapsto [0, 1]$. State A wants to shift x as far right as possible, while state B wants to shift x to the left (i.e., A's

a war, indicated respectively by $c_A > 0$ and $c_B > 0$, also on the y-axis. There is some uncertainty about the true values of p, c_A, and c_B, which is illustrated by the error bands ϵ_A and ϵ_B in Figure 3.1. In this example, for the sake of illustration, the costs of war are fixed for all values of p and x and equivalent for both actors, which creates the diagonal band shown. This is a simplification (e.g., the state "hosting" a war will often see more of its territory devastated); we will discuss the effects of manipulating costs and uncertainty later. We will also discuss how these costs can be consumed in bargaining tactics and conflict short of war in an attempt to improve credibility or revise the status quo.

This simple model already depicts fundamental relationships between getting more in a dispute (influence), winning a war (power), economizing on the costs of politics by other means (efficiency), and avoiding war and ensuring peace (stability). Strategic stability is represented by shading (darker indicates more instability). Intuitively, if A asks for less, then (negative) peace is more likely, but if A demands too much, then B will go to war. But if A asks for *too* little, then A might regret its weak demand and B will worry that A will not honor its deal. As we shall see, the lightest shade of gray is not necessarily stable. The interesting dynamics take place in between, where there is a range of deals that both sides would prefer over open warfare, yet there is uncertainty about the precise contours of the bargaining range.

Each state is willing to fight past some reservation point. These reservation points—the point at which actors are indifferent to war or peace—are determined by their respective estimates of power and cost: $r_A = p - c_A$ and $r_B = p + c_B$. A's expected value for war is r_A, which is the chance of winning discounted by the cost of fighting, and B's expected value for war is $1 - r_B$ or $1 - p - c_B$. State A prefers the outside option of war if $x < r_A$, while state B prefers war if $x > r_B$. Between these two values is a range of outcomes $r_A < x < r_B$ that both states prefer to war. The interval $r_A < x < r_B$ is always positive because fighting involves positive costs. The size of the bargaining range is defined by the sum of costs $c_A + c_B$, while relative power

---

payoff is x and B's payoff is $1 - x$). By convention, power is typically represented as a probability $p \mapsto [0, 1]$, which can be interpreted as the chance of winning $x = 1$ with probability p or a sure bet of receiving just $x = p$. The diagonal dashed line from the origin plots the risk-neutral indifference curve of costless conflict, capturing the idea that more power can elicit larger demands (A risk-averse or risk-accepting indifference curve would be bowed, and the degree of risk aversion is another source of uncertainty that we do not represent here.). But conflict is costly and uncertain. Coding p is notoriously difficult (see Beckley 2018) and has spawned a large literature about the so-called offense-defense balance, which we discuss in Chapter 6. Measurement uncertainty itself is an important factor in the bargaining model.

50 ELEMENTS OF DETERRENCE

only affects its location. Thus, the diagonal band in Figure 3.1 depicts the shifting location of the bargaining range as A's power increases relative to B. This implies that even relatively powerful states have reasons to compromise.

To simplify Figure 3.1, both states' war costs are held constant. The bargaining range thus has a fixed dimension at every level of p. In reality, the relationship between power and costs is ambiguous. Powerful states may win wars easily at low cost, or they may fight costly wars that they may not even win. An expensive military might not translate into greater relative power if the other side invests in a big military, too. Power is interactive; one side can spend more in an effort to improve relative power, but this will just drive up costs if the other side does the same (e.g., arms racing). In Figure 3.2 we will relax these assumptions, but first we want to clarify the implications of the basic model for strategic stability.

State B is resolved to fight at r_B, and so any demand $x > r_B$ is the least stable from the perspective of state A—the darker gray shaded region. Conversely, state A is resolved to fight at r_A, and if state B understands this, then state B has no reason to insist on $x < r_A$. If instead state A is willing to concede even more than it could get through fighting by demanding only $x < r_A$, then state B is likely very pleased. B has no reason to start a war when it receives more from A's offer than from fighting—the lightest gray shaded region. However, A has a commitment problem whenever $x < r_A$, since A can expect to get r_A by going to war.[21] Thus, while A can reduce the risk of *B starting a war* by choosing $x < r_A$, B must worry about *A starting a war* whenever $x < r_A$. If military-technical factors create first-mover advantages for preemption, moreover, then B may be tempted to initiate the war on favorable terms to minimize its losses in the war that A has incentives to start. Given A's incentives for war, the lightest gray shaded region is not really a zone of peace at all! If A wants to reassure B that it will not initiate a war, A must visibly change its incentives (e.g., through disarmament), in effect spending down some of the surplus that could be captured through fighting and thereby expanding the bargaining range in B's favor.

Figure 3.1 depicts the bargaining range between r_A and r_B as a gray zone with fuzzy borders. Within this range, each state still wants to get as much as possible. In this "zone of potential agreement," we can expect to see all sorts of negotiating tactics, signaling behavior, and even non-military conflict as

---

[21] This is a variant of the security dilemma, the idea that one state's efforts to improve security make other states insecure.

DETERRENCE IS NOT (JUST) ONE THING 51

the actors try to forge a better deal without going to war. War is always possible, but it is less likely so long as both actors can agree on the boundaries of $r_A < x < r_B$, and provided they can accurately predict the outcome of a possible future conflict. This is obviously an heroic assumption. Indeed, uncertainty is the main cause of war in this model.

The error terms ϵ_A and ϵ_B reflect uncertainty about where exactly r_A and r_B lie, whether for intrinsic reasons (costs are unknowable ex ante) or strategic reasons (actors are deceptive). Therefore, Figure 3.1 depicts bands of uncertainty around the cutoff points in different shades of gray. Negotiators often seek to bluster and bluff in pursuit of a better deal without having to fight. They may also misrepresent their abilities (exaggerating strength or feigning weakness) for various reasons. Moreover, war and politics are inherently complex and unpredictable processes. Governments and peoples themselves may even be unsure about what they want or how much or little they are willing to fight for. Some nations discover new resolve once the fight is on, while others decide that the game is not worth the candle. Given all the uncertainty about p, c_A, and c_B, it will usually be quite difficult for A and B to share a clear understanding about where r_A and r_B really lie. War is in the error terms ϵ_A and ϵ_B.[22]

What can states do to reduce this dangerous uncertainty? One solution is to make honest threats and assurances, backed up with costly signals of commitment. A credible commitment to act on a clearly communicated threat entails a reduction of uncertainty. Assuming an agreement $r_A < x < r_B$, state A can spend up to the entire surplus $x - r_A$ to get it and still be strictly better off than fighting a war, which gives state A just r_A. An influence-maximizing state A, therefore, might elect to spend up to $c_B + c_A$ to persuade B to accept r_B. Even if state A is only interested in some lesser degree of influence, it will still be necessary to take steps to make sure that state B correctly understands the red line at r_A. As before, state A may burn up some of the surplus to maximize its influence over the status quo.[23]

---

[22] Gartzke 1999. There may even be some ambiguity about the precise status quo x, or A's demand to change it. In reality, states may have very different understandings of the status quo, or of each other's demands for protecting or revising it. The simple version of the model does not include this complexity, for the sake of explanatory simplicity, but this is yet another source of destabilizing uncertainty.

[23] This is known as a "sinking costs" signal. "Tying hands" by contrast works by building in triggers, effectively reducing A's option to back down below some $x > r_A$. We discuss tripwires in Chapter 8. On the variety of signals see Fearon 1997; Gartzke, Carcelli, et al. 2017.

52 ELEMENTS OF DETERRENCE

Alternatively, states may opt to lie, cheat, and steal. They may engage in subversion in an attempt to manipulate foreign elites and polities, in effect changing foreign preferences. They can invest in intelligence infrastructure to penetrate their rivals' secrets. And they can engage in elaborate subterfuge or other forms of bluff and bluster. All of these activities may enable them to capture more of the surplus without spending on signaling. State A can spend up to the entire surplus $x - r_A$ on a covert conflict and still be strictly better off than fighting an open war, which has an expected value of just r_A. Leaders can even exaggerate their strength or minimize their costs to demand something *outside* of the bargaining range, in effect gambling on the other side's uncertainty about what it really wants or is willing to pay.

The basic bargaining model offers no advice about which strategy states should prefer to improve bargaining outcomes. Depending on which aspect of the bargaining model state A prioritizes, it can attempt to improve its fortune in several ways:

- If A prioritizes political *influence*, then it should produce costly signals that persuade B to accept a deal within the bargaining range, which is valued at $r_B - r_A = c_B + c_A$. This in effect reduces the uncertainty ϵ_A and ϵ_B about the bounds of the peaceful bargaining range by drawing a brighter line between peace and war.
- If A prioritizes military *effectiveness*, then it should invest in improving p. This shifts the entire bargaining range to the right. Improving power also enables other objectives, since assessments of p figure into all decisions. Improving p and shifting the bargaining range potentially provides more influence over the stakes, depending on how costs and information evolve as well.
- If A prioritizes policy *efficiency*, then it should take steps to reduce c_A. This shifts the lower bound of r_A to the right. Lower costs make military action more attractive for marginal revisions of x. Efficiency measures may even make conflict more attractive than costly signaling, especially for means that rely on stealth, maneuver, and deception, as discussed further in Chapters 4 and 6.
- If A prioritizes strategic *stability*, then it should moderate its demands and concede more of x to B while simultaneously reducing uncertainty and offering assurances to B. This shifts A to the safest edge of the gray zone, and may even shift the boundary further left as a costly signal of assurance. Because mutual agreement about p, c_A and c_B is notoriously

hard to predict, moreover, a highly risk-averse, stability-maximizing state might even be willing to accept some $x < r_A$ to limit the chance of miscalculation.[24]

Figure 3.2 provides an example of how the bargaining range shifts with different assumptions about the values of the parameters. In this example, state A spends to increase its relative power (prioritizing effectiveness). But, given some circumstances internal to state A and the particular dispute, this also increases the costs of war (de-prioritizing efficiency) and exacerbates uncertainty (de-prioritizing stability) whenever A makes larger demands (prioritizing influence). Some contingent structure of the situation in this example (i.e., geography, technology, domestic politics) results in the costs c_A and uncertainty ϵ_A about its reservation point r_A scaling faster than

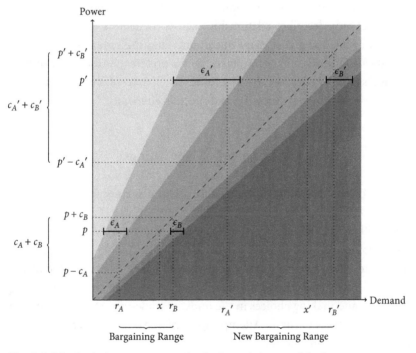

Fig. 3.2 Manipulating parameters in the bargaining model of war

---

[24] Extremely moderate demands $x \ll r_A$ require that A solve its own commitment problem, assuring B that A will not start a war. This might be done by openly spending some of the prospective gains of war on unambiguously defensive arrangements, peaceful policy initiatives, or other costly and thus credible signal of assurance.

54 ELEMENTS OF DETERRENCE

c_B and ϵ_B, resulting in greater overall uncertainty $\epsilon_A' + \epsilon_B'$ when state A demands x'. This could happen for many reasons. Perhaps the constituents of state A are more likely to punish their leaders for war, or perhaps state B has developed some very efficient automated weapons that are particularly effective at exploiting state A's vulnerabilities. The point is that costs and uncertainties may be variable for any number of unit-level and dyadic factors. As a result, the new bargaining range becomes much larger, which creates more opportunity for gray-zone conflict, and there is more overall uncertainty about its bounds, which create more risk of war. Complexity in this case emerges (a) through the interaction of the four basic parameters and (b) situational constraints including domestic preferences that inform them.

In sum, states have different options for manipulating bargaining outcomes. Which they choose will reflect different political preferences about the four basic factors of the bargaining model, within the constraints of the social, technological, and geographical context of the dispute. The bargaining model only describes relationships across the factors of relative power, demands, bargaining costs, and uncertainty and the outcomes of strategic stability and the division of the stakes. Actor preferences about any of these are necessarily exogenous to the model. In Chapter 4 we will link these preferences to different strategies and specialized means.[25]

Deterrence Is Many Things

So what do we talk about when we talk about deterrence? With apologies to Raymond Carver, we talk about many things. Strategists hope that deterrence will enable them to keep (or take) what they want, at a bargain price, while avoiding a fight, all while retaining the ability to win a contest, should one occur. These are all attractive goals, certainly, but they are different, and they are in tension with one another. Politics, and strategy, is about setting priorities, and making choices in the midst of trade-offs. Deterrence cannot smooth over these tensions. Attempts to force it to do so weaken the concept and muddle national policy.

Classical deterrence theory has little to say about how actors come to have the interests and resolve that guides their political behavior. Given the traditional focus on existential survival in nuclear security competition this

---

[25] See also Table 1.1 linking bargaining parameters, preferences, and strategies.

is perhaps understandable. States facing extinction or the liquidation of their regimes should be highly resolved to avoid paying the ultimate price. Yet there are many additional benefits beyond survival, ranging from an extra margin of security to the acquisition of wealth and enhancement of prestige. How much should governments be willing to pay to obtain these arguably secondary goals? Geographic endowments, economic development, institutional character, national culture, ideology, and leader personality can all influence political preferences. The ultimate origin of what states want is beyond the scope of any theory of deterrence, even one that is already relaxing the rigid classical structure. Yet preferences matter greatly in determining which objectives matter most for deterrence. Different types of actors, with different goals, will be more or less willing or able to allocate resources to protect the status quo as they understand it. To paraphrase Alexander Wendt, deterrence is what states make of it.[26]

The disparate goals of deterrence create trade-offs that are mutually constraining. For example, an actor might value influence over the status quo more than peace at any price, but also care more about strategic stability than about controlling costs. This implies that the same actor must also value maximizing influence over minimizing costs (i.e., they are willing to pay for a credible posture to defend the status quo). Let us further assume that this actor is not completely insensitive to cost and is willing to compromise on military power to a degree to save some resources. It then follows that they must also value status quo influence over enhancing military power and, furthermore, reductions in the risk of war over improvements in the ability to win a war. These logical entailments are consistent with an actor whose guiding preferences are to ask for little, but defend this minimum resolutely.

This example corresponds roughly to actors' preferences as assumed by the classical MAD model. No doubt, they are a reasonable approximation of what states want when the stakes involve the annihilation of populations and/or national survival. States can credibly threaten to use nuclear weapons to defend core interests such as territorial integrity or the maintenance of the regime, thus accepting some risk of costly nuclear war. Other nations will prefer to reduce this risk. However, different actors/nations likely vary to a greater degree in their valuation for alternatives in less extreme situations.

---

[26] Wendt 1992. Constructivism is sometimes framed as a challenge to rationalism, representing historically contingent intersubjective ideas as an alternative to hard-headed calculations about power, but it turns out that some of the complexity that constructivists highlight as an alternative to rational models is actually implied by those same models.

56 ELEMENTS OF DETERRENCE

Indeed, the same actors could express different preference orderings given different strategic and technological circumstances. Varying a country's value for the various objectives of deterrence will tend to prompt different decisions about what, how, and where to deter.

Goals tend to diversify as the cost of war subsides. The prospect of nuclear Armageddon limits preference heterogeneity. Almost everyone has the same goal when war involves annihilation. States don't fight when fighting is more costly than any conceivable benefit. Indeed, they look for proxies like brinkmanship under such circumstances. States have to move into the domain of risk (rather than war) before salient differences in preferences emerge about how much risk is too much.[27] As the expected costs of war decline, some will be more willing to fight. Others at least find fighting more acceptable than making too many concessions. Still others will be unwilling to fight, or will only contemplate war when an adversary is particularly intransigent and will issue a deterrent threat only if the costs are low.

Inherent Tensions in Deterrence

We are not introducing anything new to deterrence. On the contrary, we are utilizing the well-understood bargaining model to unearth what has been within deterrence, hidden and unrecognized, all along. This constitutes familiar terrain for international relations. Yet it leads to unfamiliar implications. Implicit in the bargaining model is considerable complexity for deterrence. Given the four basic objectives in the bargaining model (but exogenous to it), there are six logical trade-offs across them:

1. *Influence versus stability*: improving the status quo versus the risk of war;
2. *Stability versus effectiveness*: satisfaction with the status quo versus the ability to achieve a better position;
3. *Efficiency versus stability*: the costs of producing signals versus the willingness of the opponent to believe them;

---

[27] The same point can be made about benefits. Everyone likes free ice cream or beer, but few would pay a million dollars for a cone or a pint. In between these extremes, preferences matter.

DETERRENCE IS NOT (JUST) ONE THING 57

4. *Efficiency versus influence*: the ability to efficiently expand deterrence coverage to more areas versus the ability to deter effectively in any given area;
5. *Efficiency versus effectiveness*: the costs of exquisite technologies versus the ability to use them successfully in war;
6. *Effectiveness versus influence*: the ability to win on the battlefield versus the risk of making it necessary to do so.

These are all intimately related. As an explanatory convenience, we will group these into three short discussions on protecting and improving the status quo, the scope and effectiveness of deterrence, and the relationship between winning and warning. Most of these issues have been examined in previous studies of deterrence. But they have not been considered together, which means the systematic aspect of these interrelated constraints has not been apparent. More importantly, the inevitability of trade-offs across deterrence objectives has not been tied to policy alternatives. The implication of this new (old) perspective is that deterrence is an amalgam of choices, with contrasting consequences, rather than one unified strategy. The ambiguities in any deterrence policy can never be resolved completely and consistently.

Protecting and Improving the Status Quo

The problem of credibility in deterrence encompasses entwined trade-offs between (1) influence over the status quo versus the risk of war and (2) satisfaction with the status quo versus the power to demand—or take—a little bit more. The former is a question of resolve: how much is an actor willing to risk to persuade the target of its willingness to defend its interests? The latter is a question of interests or preferences: how credibly can an actor convince a potential adversary that it is only interested in protecting the status quo rather than revising it? This is one reason why the extent and/or legitimacy of coercion (i.e., is it deterrence or compellence?) so often resides in the subjective eye of the beholder.

Another way to understand this problem is in terms of where to draw a given line delineating who controls what prerogatives or territory in global affairs. More risk averse actors are willing to give ground to avoid a war, which at the extreme is indistinguishable from appeasement. Actors that value a given set of stakes (territory, control over politics or policies) more

58 ELEMENTS OF DETERRENCE

highly prefer to revise the status quo in their favor, which at the extreme is indistinguishable from aggression and conquest.

Few politicians would publicly advocate maintaining only "good things" in hand and doing nothing about "bad things." Deterrence policy thus faces a dual problem in establishing red lines, first in persuading an opponent not to cross them and second in reassuring opponents and others that the actor will not cross them itself.

Ambiguous declaratory policies have a similar dual aspect, at once tempting adversaries to consider opportunism ("salami tactics" and faits acomplis) while also preserving the option to press an opponent, if convenient. Ambiguity can enhance influence for low-value actors by, in effect, discounting the expected costs of carrying out a threat (e.g., while it is not credible to threaten nuclear suicide, it may be credible to risk accidental nuclear war).[28] Conversely, ambiguity can also undermine influence by making an actor appear less resolved and thus vulnerable to predation or, conversely, more aggressive and untrustworthy.

Numerous examples exist of finessing the status quo. George Kennan's classic advocacy of containment in confronting Soviet expansionism in the aftermath of World War II acknowledged the practical necessity of a Soviet sphere of influence—a geographical region surrounding the borders of the U.S.S.R. where the United States would accept Soviet dominance—rather than insisting on tightly constraining Soviet influence within its pre-World War II borders. Defining a status quo is itself a political process, where individual or national "truths" respond to interest and practicality as much or more than historical precedent or international law.

China's current approach to its littoral waters is another case in point. While contesting China's definition of its territory, the United States has not made clear what actions it will take to prevent China from expanding its control in the region. Nor has the United States formally declared what definition of Chinese territory it would accept, other than China's formal borders under international law. Even here, Taiwan is a major point of ambiguity, both belonging to Beijing and not. The 1979 treaty between the United States and China makes clear that there is one China, though it fails to specify which China it is. The treaty further restricts the PRC from using force to compel reunification, though it allows that coercion is not incompatible with China's interpretation of international law. In the

---

[28] Schelling 2008.

South China Sea, the United States and other nations have disputed China's construction of artificial islands and military outposts, while taking few steps to actually prevent China from changing facts on the ground (or in the sea). Thus the problem of "gray-zone conflict" where an adversary attempts to operate below the threshold that would clearly trigger major conflict, while still wielding a degree of influence or protection.

The converse is also true. When formal alliance commitments alone prove inadequate to limit aggression, tools like declaratory policy or a forward force posture can ensure additional security or influence, but only by heightening the risk of military confrontations, both accidental or intentional. NATO's forward force posture in Europe in the Cold War protected the inter-German frontier from Warsaw Pact incursions. It also limited the military effectiveness of allied forces, particularly armored units that require room to maneuver and strategic depth to counter the anticipated armored onslaught from the Warsaw Pact. Nevertheless, a forward posture assured NATO allies of US resolve and made the nuclear trigger more credible. This is the flip-side of the stability-instability paradox: NATO conventional vulnerability reinforced the credibility and leverage provided by the nuclear umbrella.[29]

Deterrence is constrained in scope by where commitments are made, to whom, and under what conditions. By extension, polities and places that are not explicitly delineated as protected by the defender can be seen as lacking sufficient value to justify the defender accepting the risk of war for their protection. Failing to make explicit the scope of one's commitments can thus also lead to war. Secretary of State Dean Acheson neglected to specify whether the United States would protect South Korea among other states in Asia. Goaded by the Soviets, North Korea attacked, believing that the United States would not intervene.

The ways in which alliance coverage is extended impinges similarly on a basic deterrence trade-off between war risk and influence over the status quo. Any defender confronted by a deterrence crisis must choose between insisting that nothing be conceded to the challenger, at some significant risk of war, and giving the challenger some of what it wants, but also maintaining peace. In the Taiwan Strait Crises of the mid-1990s, American aircraft carriers were deployed to signal US protection of Taiwan in the face of Beijing's growing concern that the island was drifting toward formal

---

[29] Lanoszka 2018.

60 ELEMENTS OF DETERRENCE

independence. While the deployment was regarded as a immediate extended deterrence success, there are reasons to challenge this interpretation.

Most of the conditions we think about when we consider deterrence conceptually were not met in the Taiwan Strait Crisis. For example, it is extremely doubtful that China would have invaded Taiwan in 1996, even if it were assured that the United States would not intervene. China simply lacked the ability to conduct a major amphibious assault at the time. China could, and did, engage in other coercive actions, but conquest was not in the cards. Thus the US naval presence may have helped sooth Taiwan's sense of vulnerability and limit the extent of PRC aggression, but it was not pivotal to Taiwan's territorial integrity, at least not at that time.

Similarly, the literal status quo in the Taiwan Strait Crisis was *not* retained. China initiated the firing of ballistic missiles over the island, a practice that continues to this day. This was a change in the status quo, one that frightened Taiwanese citizens and frustrated the United States. But US officials chose to concede this revision, rather than seek to deter missile overflights, or compel their cessation, once they began. This does not mean that deterrence failed, of course, only that its terms were finessed and outcomes incomplete, as political policies are inevitably.

The nuclear arms control debate is largely animated by the trade-off between influence and stability (or credibility and risk). Nuclear forces in a deployed and alerted posture may be good for signaling a commitment to retaliate promptly if attacked. Yet the accompanying reduction in decision time and increase in command and control complexity raises the possibility that policy makers and operators might misinterpret signals and early warning indicators amidst the fog of a crisis.[30] Even without misperception, one nuclear power may race to preempt a possible attack in an effort to limit damage or even disarm the aggressor (first-mover advantage).[31]

Nuclear arsenals are complex systems with hard-to-understand, tightly coupled decision and operational linkages. The integration of decision making and command and control introduces the risk of "normal accidents" with catastrophic consequences.[32] The risks of misperception and accident can be lessened by de-alerting, decoupling, or redeploying forces, but this can potentially embolden an aggressor. Either the arsenal becomes vulnerable to a preemptive strike, or the attacker is increasingly tempted to render a fait accompli, in the expectation that it will be futile to retaliate afterwards.[33]

---

[30] Blair 1985.   [31] Schelling 1966.
[32] Perrow 1999; Sagan 1995.   [33] Altman 2017.

An arsenal optimized for safety may suggest to an aggressor that the country is more interested in avoiding a war than backing up its commitments.

Moreover, the actual structure and functioning of nuclear command and control organizations are designed to morph, to change the trade-offs between different facets/objectives of deterrence in response to evolving conditions.[34] Going on "heightened alert" increases the credibility of a response even as it exacerbates the risk of unwanted action. This is done in a context where the cost of deterring is greatly increased, but where the likelihood that an enemy can exploit learning about the organization, to utilize during war, is also diminished, because of increased risks and a compressed time line. The very ethos of heightened alert is that it is temporary, meaning both that it is not sustained and that it involves a set of behaviors and priorities that differ from day-to-day deterrence. In the absence of crisis, the deterring state accepts a set of trade-offs that differ, involving less willingness to endure cost, less willingness to risk accidental escalation and war, but also a greater acceptance that time gradually, inevitably favors the challenger (i.e., the enemy is given more opportunities to engage with one's own systems and explore weaknesses and vulnerabilities). Both routine operations and heightened alert are supposed to generate deterrence, but clearly each is doing so differently, and to differential effect.

The complementary trade-off between influence and power is most acute when nuclear arsenals are designed not just for credible punishment (i.e., secure second strike), but rather for counterforce and damage limitation (nuclear war-fighting). Damage limitation necessarily requires preempting enemy forces before they strike, which further decreases warning times. Yet insofar as damage limitation and counterforce postures require larger and more varied arsenals (to fight through attacks in a variety of circumstances), countries that have them may be tempted to further leverage their arsenal for coercive diplomacy.[35] This too raises the risk of war, as targets may be inclined to disbelieve compellent threats.[36]

The Scope and Effectiveness of Deterrence

One important reason why policy makers find deterrence attractive is because it promises protection without necessarily having to pay the costs of

---

[34] Wirtz and Larsen 2022.   [35] Kroenig 2018.   [36] Sechser and Fuhrmann 2017.

war. For this same reason, an opponent might well suspect that declaratory statements are just cheap talk. Expensive actions provide credible signals that inform others about what is important to a nation.[37] Deterrence on the cheap, by contrast, invites more challenges (general deterrence failures), which themselves may lead to riskier crisis diplomacy and costly military responses (immediate deterrence failure).

The problem of efficiency encompasses the trade-offs between (3) the costs of producing signals and the willingness of the opponent to believe them and (4) the ability to expand deterrence coverage to more areas and the ability to deter effectively in any given area. More simply, how much posturing and expense is enough to protect a given nation's interests? After all, money not spent on weapons is money available for tax cuts, economic development, and other policy agendas.

While keeping deterrence cheap makes the strategy more attractive in the familiar "guns versus butter" trade-off, there are also "guns versus guns" trade-offs in terms of what to buy and what to protect. Some forces are more mobile or maneuverable than others, for instance, such as cavalry, helicopters, or ships, although not all of them can be deployed to the same places. Mobility has important implications for strategy, so we will spend some time on it here to illustrate this type of "guns versus guns" trade-off. Other features (stealth, automation, etc.) offer other implications.

Mobile forces can relocate to more places, increasing the potential scope of a nation's influence. While individual platforms (aircraft or ships) might be expensive on a per unit basis, they can be employed to cover more places or commitments without incurring the additional costs of building a new army to protect each new ally. In short, mobility reduces the ratio of overall expenditures to commitments.

At the same time, however, mobility creates ambiguity about where and how long forces will remain. Mobile forces can be deployed to protect an ally in the event of a crisis, but crises are themselves the product of expectations about the local balance of power. A challenger that does not believe the defender will intervene is more likely to attack. Thinning out the line (or overstretching forces) suggests a lack of resolve, inadvertent or otherwise. The discretion implied by mobility itself produces increased risk of deterrence failure and the potential for military confrontation.

---

[37] Fearon 1997; Gartzke, Carcelli, et al. 2017.

DETERRENCE IS NOT (JUST) ONE THING   63

Prior to historical changes in military technology that rendered positional warfare obsolete, nations and other groups used forts and castles to defend strategic territory. This increased the defender's advantages by making it more difficult to attack a given location. Robust fortifications also acted as an effective deterrent. The location of a fort was obvious, so potential attackers knew its potential. In an era before effective cannons, this knowledge could not be used to reduce the defensive potential of the fort. The fort also could not move and would attack no one by itself, so building the fort created mutual knowledge about the intentions of the defender.

Any potential attacker had to consider whether the added cost or risk of laying siege to a fortified position was worthwhile. Alternately, one could take a fort by deception, but this made it difficult to obtain concessions from a foreign power diplomatically, without the use of force. "Give me some of your territory or I will surprise you in some as yet unstated way" is hardly a persuasive negotiating position.

In contrast, a defender *could* use the deterrent effect of a purely defensive capability such as a fort or castle for diplomatic gain. Rather than just passively accepting that a given strong point made an attack at that location less likely, the defender could shift the deployment of troops to other locations. Building new forts was slow and expensive, but infantry and cavalry could move quickly and cheaply. This reality allowed a defender to become more assertive in negotiating, demanding concessions wherever it might choose to deploy. "Give me some of your territory or I will take it with the troops I freed up due to my new fort" is perhaps more persuasive.

Some of the reduction in the risk of attack generated by the original fort could thus be redistributed to new locations. Alternately, a defender could create a stronger mobile reserve to cover more places and reinforce weaknesses in a defensive system. This reserve could even return to the original fort to reinforce or relieve the garrison in a crisis. Mobile forces expand the scope of deterrence offered by the original fort, without the considerable expense of actually building more forts.

At the same time, however, the mobile reserve is not *quite* as effective at discouraging aggression in any particular place. A potential attacker does not know how stiff will be the resistance it will face on an open plain, as opposed to at the fort or castle. Mobility imparts contingency and discretion. The reserve might not show up to relieve a siege in time. It could be busy elsewhere, have too far to travel, or be otherwise employed by the crown. Mobile force commanders might even decide not to fight. This in turn

64 ELEMENTS OF DETERRENCE

increases uncertainty on the part of attackers about the local balance of power. The deterrent effect achieved by fortifying a given location has been converted into an increased chance of the defender prevailing in battle when and where it desires. But it has also left the attacker less certain about where this event will occur, inviting errors that undermine the deterrence goal of war avoidance in favor of doing better in a fight (on average), if one occurs.

The efficiency gained through mobility also activates the aforementioned trade-off between influence and power, whereby deterrence is mobilized not just to protect but to revise the status quo. Much as the shield protects the sword, a fort that cannot attack anyone facilitates an attack by liberating defenders to fight elsewhere. Thus, a purely defensive structure can deter, facilitate aggression, or something in between.

This may just be yet another incarnation of deterrence. The fear of retaliation (punishment) from a defender's mobile capabilities could be used to discourage attack, just as nuclear ballistic missiles dissuaded Soviet attacks on forward deployed NATO ground forces along the Central Front in Europe. Still, policy makers who would not risk Armageddon with their mobile reserve might be tempted to move the status quo in a more favorable direction. The defensive advantages of fixed fortifications could thus be converted into a mobile attack, which not only advantages a defender and lowers costs, but also blurs the distinction between deterrence, defense, and aggression. Indeed, nuclear weapons themselves have created conditions where states are able to free up a greater portion of their conventional forces for foreign adventures, confident that the homeland will remain safe from major attack.

It is ultimately a policy choice, not an intrinsic technological characteristic, that determines how the deterrent effect of a fort is to be utilized. The fort option could be exercised completely for local stability and peace, limiting the risk of attack in a given place or over a given set of circumstances. It could also be leveraged by mobile forces, diluting the effect on stability in any given place but providing additional protection or influence everywhere. It could even lead to a thinning out of forces, as a cost-saving measure. At the extreme, an empty fort might be worse than useless.[38]

---

[38] Fort Ticonderoga in upstate New York was so well situated, planned and constructed that it was never taken by siege or frontal assault. Its reputation deterred any such effort. Instead, confidence in its impregnability led defenders to thin out its garrison to a point where it was vulnerable to subterfuge and *coup de main*. Ticonderoga thus both deterred formal attack and invited adversaries to capture it through surprise, a mode of aggression that is inherently more destabilizing.

Policy choices about posturing, positioning, and provisioning defensive forces thus shape the quality of deterrence. A defender with unlimited resources might erect impregnable defenses at every point on its borders to deter any attack. But making one's own territory impregnable encourages a defender to look farther afield, to other territories and issues that might prove more vexing and problematic. Conversely, it might lead the defender to shift priorities elsewhere, to lowering the burden of defense, and thus making its defenses more porous. France's famous Maginot line was an immovable object. This in turn led recurring French administrations to underfund French divisions and the French military to adopt a passive doctrine inconsistent with modern mobile warfare. Conversely, it led German commanders to look for a way around the Maginot defenses, which of course they found. In this respect, the Maginot Line was an operational deterrent but not a strategic deterrent.

In reality defenders must make choices about what forces to buy, where to employ them, and which operating budgets to allocate. A defender might choose to protect more places from attack, however imperfectly. Alternately, the defender could choose to only protect critical assets, ensuring that the probability of attack in these areas is minimized, but at the cost of a greater risk of aggression elsewhere. This dilemma poses a classic quantity-quality trade-off. It is also a choice about prioritizing peace versus influence (protecting some things well or many things moderately).

If the defender seeks to protect more territory from attack, it must accept that its defenses at any given point will be less effective and thus deterrence is less likely to result in an absence of aggression. A defender intent on avoiding attack could withdraw to a defensible perimeter, a portion of territory or issues that are unlikely to be challenged because they are so well defended. If instead the defender wishes to continue to protect much or all of its territory, it most accept a higher risk of a challenge, either by distributing its forces widely or, again, creating a mobile force, capable of intervening anywhere, but of course not everywhere.

National leaders intent on pursing deterrence at the international level face similar trade-offs. Promising protection to more allies ensures that the protection available to any given ally is reduced. Promising protection under all circumstances invites skepticism (and probing) to see just where, or on which issues, a defender will actually act. Protecting fewer allies more intensively is more likely to discourage aggression—provided that the ally

66 ELEMENTS OF DETERRENCE

does not convert the shift in the local balance of power into influence—but it also abandons the security interests of other states.

Similarly, telegraphing military intent, which is necessary in order to reduce uncertainty and minimize the risk of war, can weaken one's defense. Just as defenders can "shape" but not prevent aggression, so too deterrence choices shape the tenor and content of international politics and strategy, but do not do away with it altogether.

Nations will still seek to pursue their interests, conditioned by others' deterrence choices. In most cases, adversaries will not cease to act altogether. Rather, deterrence will affect the kinds of actions they take, and where and when they take them. Thinking about deterrence in this more dynamic manner—an approach that is more consistent with the conduct of warfare itself, and with the conduct of policy in international affairs—is destined to be more accurate and useful.

Winning and Warning

Deterrence, and coercion generally, works through the building, brandishing, fielding, and even limited use of military force. Schelling distinguishes coercion from brute force as the holding of punishment in reserve.[39] Coercion involves a surplus "power to hurt" that is not actualized. Threats succeed when the threatened punishment does not have to be applied, or when some ongoing punishment can be relieved.

Military forces can thus be utilized in two distinct ways in international politics. Most obviously they can be used to fight wars, which directly shapes the balance of power and benefits the victor through conquest or defense. Brute force is costly in blood and treasure, but it can also quickly and effectively change facts on the ground. Military forces can also be used to convey information about the balance of power, interests, or resolve. Signaling is usually less costly than war but also less effective. As discussed previously, there are commonly understood incentives to bluff.

It is often assumed that force is fungible across these two functions, but this may be exaggerated, or even mistaken. Some weapons, particularly nuclear weapons, are better suited for deterrence than war-fighting. Conversely, other weapons are ill-suited for credible signaling. The problems

[39] Schelling 1966.

with mobile forces have already been discussed. The next chapter will highlight other operational features and challenges.

Military forces that improve the ability to fight and win a war may not be equally useful for preventing a war in the first place. Worse, some latent war-fighting capabilities can even cause deterrence to fail. The problem of effectiveness thus encompasses the trade-offs (5) between the exquisite technological capabilities of modern military forces and the ability to use them successfully in war and (6) between the ability to win on the battlefield and the risk of making it necessary to do so. The way in which military forces deter influences the quality of deterrence achieved.

Military power has historically relied on an ability to field more troops on the battlefield. Winning in war was costly in material terms. The advent of maneuver and combined arms warfare, however, put a greater premium on force employment over material preponderance and technological sophistication.[40] Operational art enabled smart forces to do more with less. More recent innovations in information technology and doctrine further enhance intelligence, coordination, and maneuver.

A theme common to the Soviet "reconnaissance-strike complex," American "network-centric warfare," or Chinese "informatized warfare" is that fewer, lighter, faster, smarter, networked forces can produce more precise, targeted, coordinated, lethal, decisive effects (i.e., both efficiency *and* effectiveness). Cost-sensitive actors, especially casualty averse democracies, appear especially attracted to technology that substitutes for manpower.[41] Unfortunately, there are hidden costs in the employment of networked technologies on the battlefield, especially in land warfare and counterinsurgency.[42] Systems malfunction, people suffer from information overload, enemies do not behave as engineers had expected, and the fog of war sadly persists.

Failure to appreciate the true costs involved in conflict may lead policy makers to recklessly opt for war. The 2003 invasion of Iraq has become the poster child for ill-placed faith in technology. Light, fast, networked coalition forces were able to decisively defeat the ponderous Iraqi army, but they were unable to occupy and subdue a nation determined to resist.[43] Moreover, forces that only impose costs but do not absorb them provide little information to opponents about national resolve. Long-range, precise,

---

[40] S. Biddle 2004; Grauer 2016.　　[41] Gartzke 2001a; Caverley 2014.
[42] S. Biddle 1998; Harknett 2000; McMaster 2015; Lindsay 2020.　　[43] Shimko 2010.

68 ELEMENTS OF DETERRENCE

automated forces (i.e., drones) may seem like an attractive alternative to boots on the ground, but they also encourage opponents to drag out contests for longer periods of time in an attempt to test and undermine the resolve of more capable adversaries.[44] More efficient military power, or misperceptions of digitally enabled efficiency, can cause deterrence to fail. The result is war and/or escalation.

A declaratory policy, force structure, and force posture that is optimized to fight wars is not necessarily ideal for ensuring they do not occur. Components of combat power that benefit from remaining opaque to an adversary must be concealed to maximize war-fighting effectiveness, limiting or eliminating their utility in discouraging aggression. Japanese diplomats in 1941 were in negotiations with the United States to resolve differences that had led US officials to ban sales of scrap iron and petroleum to Japan. Disclosure of Japanese war plans targeting Pearl Harbor might have caused a stir in the US diplomatic corps, but it would almost certainly have deeply degraded Japan's combat power, since much of the military effectiveness that Japan was relying on to win depended on the critical element of surprise.

States that practice deterrence but also desire to "keep their powder dry" for possible military contests must either accept that war is more likely, that they will have to make concessions to possible aggressors that are not in fact necessary in terms of the actual military balance, or that they will have to spend more to mobilize and orient their forces toward the potential challenger.

Furthermore, a state with important battlefield advantages that cannot be revealed without degrading military effectiveness may decide that deterrence is not sufficiently promising as a tool of foreign policy. In general, plans or weapons that require secrecy to remain effective militarily cannot be revealed in advance, since revealing these capabilities allows a target to adopt countermeasures. Publicizing the strength of defenses may encourage an attacker to fight elsewhere or to refrain from aggression altogether. However, revealing information about defensive capabilities also enables the adversary to improve its own military effectiveness, should it decide to attack. The defender may benefit from pulling its forces back from the front line to ensure a more dynamic, mobile defense. Yet doing so invites minor or incremental incursions from the adversary. Sticking close to the frontier will help ensure that the enemy does not set foot in friendly territory, unless a

---

[44] As discussed extensively in Chapter 8.

DETERRENCE IS NOT (JUST) ONE THING 69

major attack breaks through dramatically due to the brittle, static character of the defender's posture.

This trade-off between "winning" and "warning" can also be described as the "military commitment problem" because an actor cannot credibly commit to a threat that will be sufficiently degraded by the very act of communicating it.[45] Analogously, the "cyber commitment problem" is a major issue for cyber operations that rely on sensitive intelligence and special access programs.[46] In the intelligence realm this trade-off is known as the "intelligence gain-loss" dilemma: is it better to protect secret sources and methods or act on the information they produce and risk their disclosure? Secret information and capabilities can allow modern networked forces to exploit and surprise an adversary across the entire breadth and depth of the battlefield. Yet this creates a double liability, first because low-cost forces provide little information about resolve, and second because secrecy precludes credible signaling.

The Problem of Preferences

Politics is, and always has been, centrally about preferences. Voters in democracies, and citizens generally, do not always see eye-to-eye about the guns-or-butter trade-off, for instance. Even if all populations want to be protected from harm, some are more willing to pay a steep price for protection than others, either directly or in terms of opportunity costs for other policies. Some political actors want more defense, while others want lower taxes or additional social programs. Interest groups, political parties, and foreign lobbies differ about whether and where a nation should devote its attention, recognition or resources. There are vast literatures exploring these dynamics. The role of preferences is so ubiquitous that definitions of politics are framed around "the authoritative allocation of values" or something similar.

Classical conceptions of international security emphasize the objective and monolithic nature of state preferences. States seek to exercise influence or protect themselves or others from harm. These alternatives are sometimes described in terms of power-seeking versus security-seeking. States may be compelled by circumstances and the anarchy of international affairs to seek

---

[45] Gartzke 2001b.   [46] As discussed further in Chapters 3 and 5.

70 ELEMENTS OF DETERRENCE

dominance, or at least survival. The fact that there are at least two camps of realists—defensive[47] and offensive[48]—should itself imply some subjectivity, since international behavior presumably depends *simultaneously* on whether actors believe in and/or adopt an offensive or defensive world view *and* on what they believe others believe and will do.

Economic theory, on which Kenneth Waltz based his famous theory of structural realism,[49] is at once more flexible and less ambitious. Preferences in economic theory are largely treated as exogenous. Rather than claiming to know what they are and how they originate, economists generally accept that they must either assume them or measure them empirically in some way. The main contribution of economic theory, then, is to predict (explain) what an actor will do, subject to information about what actors want. There are thus limits to what economic theory aspires to tell us about human behavior in the absence of empirical data about human preferences.

Any theory of deterrence, or indeed any theory of international relations generally, is an explanation for how states or other actors are likely to behave, given a set of preferences over outcomes and information about the resources available to actors to pursue these interests. Theories of international politics that explicitly seek to incorporate the preferences of actors have been present for some time.[50] Rational deterrence has also been expressed in terms of the preferences of actors.[51] However, little attention has been paid to the trade-offs between different objectives in the deterrence rubric and to how different actors may differ in their evaluation of these trade-offs. Similarly, while uncertainty about the willingness of states to fight if necessary has been tied to preferences, studies of resolve and credibility have yet to analyze how respective objectives interrelate. We have explored these interactions here.

If we accept that states or other actors may opt to pursue either security or influence, or some mix of the two (as well as other objectives), then any theory of deterrence will need additional empirical input to make sense of behavior, or to make recommendations about intelligent courses of action. In any given context, we have to know whether states are seeking influence, efficiency, power, stability, or some combination of these, or something else entirely. While this requires more work, and more data, considering the trade-offs inherent in different objectives can still prove efficient in terms of parsimony, provided the approach covers either pure alternatives and

---

[47] Jervis 1976; Glaser 2010.　　[48] Mearsheimer 2001; Lieber 2005.
[49] Waltz 1979a.　　[50] E.g., Mesquita 1985; Glaser 2010.　　[51] Zagare 1990.

accounts for additional implications (mixed cases). This additional empirical content may not be as problematic as it sounds, particularly for policy practitioners.

While successful deterrence involves retaining the status quo without resorting to the use of force, within this rubric are several trade-offs between, for instance, how much one is willing to risk war, how closely to the status quo one expects to remain, or indeed, how much of what exists is deemed part of the "status quo" that must be retained for deterrence success, and whether the status quo is to be defended forcibly. Even if the defender finds a balance that is most likely to achieve its preferred mix of stability and influence, it does not follow that deterrence will be realized.

Adopting deterrence as a policy also implies some willingness to sacrifice wartime military performance for other policy objectives that compete with military goals and budgets. To the degree that surprise is a component of military effectiveness, furthermore, it is costly in performance terms to deter, since deterrence requires revealing military secrets to impact an adversary's calculations of cost or risk.

Finally, for deterrence to be preferable to defense (or outright preventative war), it must be sustainable at a cost that is attractive to practitioners. Indeed, moderating the cost of providing protection and securing influence is critical to make deterrence a useful option to policy makers. Understanding the trade-offs across the different objectives of deterrence can provide the basis for more nuanced thinking about how deterrence works theoretically and how it is best put into practice.

One thing that politicians pay attention to better than most academics or pundits is what actors want. Elected officials are especially keen observers of popular values, what costs or trade-offs citizens will tolerate, and what they will not. While it may be difficult for researchers or even military officials to isolate national values in every instance, this does not mean that a theory of deterrence that incorporates foreign or domestic preferences is problematic for policy practitioners. To the contrary, such a theory promises to inform policy in precisely the ways that political officials are uniquely, or at least distinctively, equipped to understand and implement. Evaluating this empirical claim is beyond the scope of this study.

A key rationale for civilian control of the military is to bring public preferences to the table. The military generally knows how best to conduct battle (or to a slightly lesser extent, deterrence) but not to what end. War itself is as often a contest in cost tolerance as it is a test of relative power. Indeed, as the very notion of a test of wills implies, any theory of international politics that exiles values and intentions is going to prove problematic, either as a guide to policy or as a predictor of behavior.

If deterrence has become more complex, or requires more extensive efforts at integration, the source of that complexity is ultimately to be found at home, not simply in the technological array of threats out in the world. The root problem with integrated deterrence is not (just) that large institutions are hard to coordinate, but that prioritizing the objectives of deterrence is a political judgment call. Even worse, domestic political rivals are likely to seize on debates about preferences and judgment to score political points. But governments that cannot figure out what they want, and where they are willing to compromise, are unlikely to succeed in foreign policy.

4

Politics by (Many) Other Means

Deterrence theory was the product of a very specific kind of military innovation. With the advent of nuclear weapons, and platforms to deliver them, a few states gained the ability to inflict catastrophic devastation on others. Deterrence strategies thus became necessary as exclusive reliance on military defense became exceedingly risky, if not impossible. Ironically, the specialized nature of nuclear forces also masked the general importance of military specialization in deterrence strategy. As the initial focus of deterrence theory was on using nuclear weapons to deter nuclear war, theorists generally did not consider alternative forms of military or non-military power in much detail.

The prompt delivery of ghastly destruction gives nuclear weapons a distinctive political quality compared to conventional forces in *any* domain. Part of what makes nuclear weapons so distinctive, furthermore, is that they can be delivered rapidly through the air and space domains, or withheld through reliable control in the cyber domain.[1] Insofar as an intercontinental ballistic missile trajectory through outer space can deliver devastation to any point on Earth with low probability of interception, the nuclear age and the space age are one and the same. Yet, the specific insight that military means matter in shaping political ends has yet to be incorporated into deterrence theory.[2]

While nuclear deterrence may secure civilizations from direct attack, massive retaliation has little salience in more modest disputes, such as "gray-zone" subversion or cyberconflict, let alone fixing respective tariff levels in trade negotiations. Furthermore, states have a larger portfolio of choices available to pursue such interests. Indeed, the military, technological, and economic means by which states influence or subdue others have

---

[1] We take an expansive view of the cyber domain encompassing not only digital networks but also the shared sociotechnical infrastructure for communication and computation in any era.

[2] If means matter, then vulnerabilities in nuclear force structure and posture matter greatly too. Secure nuclear deterrence is not a simple given, but an ongoing achievement. If the actual nuclear balance is not stalemated but rather delicate, as B. Green 2020 argues, arms racing and counterforce may not be as irrational as orthodox deterrence theorists believe.

Elements of Deterrence: Strategy, Technology, and Complexity in Global Politics. Erik Gartzke and Jon R. Lindsay, Oxford University Press. © Oxford University Press 2024. DOI: 10.1093/oso/9780197754443.003.0004

74 ELEMENTS OF DETERRENCE

become more diverse throughout the industrial and information revolutions. Innovation in all the domains of modern warfare—land, sea, air, space, cyberspace—has led to a greater range and variety of military capabilities.

To bring Clausewitz into the twenty-first century, war is politics by *many* other means. And so, for that matter, are military operations *other than war*. Adding an explicit discussion of choice among multiple means, therefore, not only makes sense for contemporary national security challenges, but can also make better sense of classical nuclear deterrence, which involved a very specific choice of means.

Specialization provides a surplus; more can be produced (or saved) with the same number of actors by allowing actors to specialize. To a greater extent than ever before, any action that a political actor can take can be countered by a response that is likely to be relatively effective, provided the right response is chosen. Just as there are specialized responses to the actions of every element on a modern combined arms battlefield (armor, infantry, artillery, aviation, etc.), certain actions or capabilities in a portfolio of political options will be particularly adept at achieving one or another of the various objectives of deterrence, or any other national security strategy. Different domains in turn can be mixed and matched in complementary or less constructive ways. For instance, combining nuclear weapons with forward troop deployments can enhance the credibility of extended deterrence policies. Air and naval power offer important force multipliers when deterrence fails. Space and cyberspace enhance the scope and efficiency of military operations by improving intelligence and communications, and they offer some alternatives to using military force.

The different ends nations choose to emphasize in crafting deterrence policies leads states to emphasize, implicitly or explicitly, different types of military instruments. Most national leaders would like their coercive threats to be believed, their military forces to be victorious, and their security policies to be affordable. Some might even like to avoid war altogether. These goals are all desirable, but they generally cannot be achieved simultaneously, or to the same extent. Military specialization imposes opportunity costs in terms of what a nation does well and where it must compromise its capabilities. Choices about what to buy, and where and how to field the nation's military might, then pose certain constraints on political strategy.

Force structure and posture, therefore—not just the raw size of armed forces—are politically consequential. Political calculations concerning national defense must consider not only the classic trade-off between "guns

POLITICS BY (MANY) OTHER MEANS   75

and butter" but must also account for complements and trade-offs between "guns and guns."

While the previous chapter discussed the diverse ends of deterrence, this chapter turns to its many means. Here we focus on the political utility of different military building blocks, setting aside for now the complex problems of crossing or combining them. We proceed in three parts. First, we highlight the role of military specialization in classic strategic thought. Different domains have varying suitability for the pursuit of different deterrence objectives, as discussed in the previous chapter. Second, we discuss nuances and exceptions that arise within and across the five primary domains, with special consideration of nuclear missiles in the air and space domains. Finally, we return to the problem of combinations and trade-offs across domains.

The Strategic Role of Military Specialization

There are many kinds of war and many ways to wage it. Clausewitz notes that "wars can have all degrees of importance and intensity, ranging from a war of extermination down to a simple armed observation."[3] Attack and defense, further, "are two distinct forms of action,"[4] best served by different combat arms: "the essence of defense is to stand fast, as it were, rooted to the ground; whereas movement is the essence of attack. Cavalry is totally incapable of the former, but preeminent in the latter, so it is suited only to attack. Infantry is best at standing fast, but it does not lack some capacity to move."[5] Artillery, by contrast, "is the most destructive of the arms. Where it is absent, the total power of the army is significantly weakened. On the other hand, it is the least mobile and so makes an army less flexible."[6]

One might add that warships can combine the destructiveness of artillery with movement across entire oceans. Clausewitz says little about war at sea, but Corbett picks up his line of argument to highlight the different strategic objectives of different services: "The object of naval warfare is the control of communications, and not, as in land warfare, the conquest of territory. The difference is fundamental."[7] If war is the continuation of politics by other

---

[3] Clausewitz 1976, p. 81.   [4] Ibid., p. 84.   [5] Clausewitz 1976, p. 285.
[6] Ibid., p. 287.   [7] Corbett 1911, p. 45.

76 ELEMENTS OF DETERRENCE

means, then the diversity of means in modern warfare suggests a diversity of political effects, for a diversity of political objectives.

In the centuries since Clausewitz wrote, there has been a dramatic increase in the variety of military options available to policy makers and commanders. Cavalry and artillery have become mechanized, and infantry units have become more versatile and specialized. Evolved versions of traditional formations are joined by new specialists in aviation, air defense, intelligence, special operations, and civil affairs. Naval operations, furthermore, are now conducted on, over, and under the waves at a truly global scale. Entire new services have emerged, from the rise of air forces in the twentieth century to the creation of space forces in the twenty-first. It has become fashionable to describe all of these different operating environments as "domains." When the United States officially established US Cyber Command (CYBERCOM) in 2010, for instance, the Deputy Secretary of Defense declared that "cyberspace is a man-made domain . . . just as critical to military operations as land, sea, air, and space."[8] NATO followed suit in 2016 as the "Allies recognised cyberspace as a domain of operations— just like air, land and sea."[9] Military writers increasingly to refer to strategy and operations as "multidomain."[10] Combined-arms warfare on regional battlefields has thus evolved into multidomain operations in a global battlespace. As in Clausewitz's day, military commanders still attempt to sequence and combine diverse capabilities to achieve "a more complete use of them all."[11]

The venerable tradition of geopolitics is founded on the assumption that land and sea powers have different strategic constraints and opportunities.[12] It would be surprising if new arenas of conflict, such as space and cyberspace, did not also have distinct strategic features. The choice to use or mix different types of forces, within or across domains, is not simply an operational military consideration. On the contrary, choices about which military means to apply matter for political ends.

Clausewitz states that war "is nothing but a duel on a larger scale," but there are many ways to duel. Rivals who choose pistols must be deadly serious because at least one of them may not survive. Duelists who choose rapiers, by contrast, might simply agree to settle their quarrel at the first

---

[8] Lynn 2010. [9] North Atlantic Treaty Organization 2018.
[10] US Army 2018. [11] Clausewitz 1976, p. 285.
[12] Classic works include Mahan 1890; Mackinder 1904; Spykman 1938. Modern extensions include Art 1998; Ross 1999; Posen 2003; Levy and Thompson 2010.

shedding of blood. A skillful duelist might persuade his opponent to drop the dispute altogether, or conversely could cause an adversary to select means that narrow the odds. A dab hand with a foil presumably prefers swords to pistols, while a less practiced fencer may select pistols despite the increased risk of mortality. A duelist prioritizing safety over honor, alternatively, can spy out flaws in a rival's swordsmanship, sabotage his pistol, or pay bandits to murder him en route to the dueling green. War is politics, to be sure, but different threats or modes of fighting reflect and imply different political objectives.

The integration of diverse capabilities is and always has been vital in military practice. Students of strategy have developed a rich set of insights about warfare by land, sea, and air.[13] Even so, the comparative political utility of different military instruments has not received much systematic attention.[14] Our emphasis here is on the strategic utility of different types of military forces, which have specific operational characteristics in the physical environments in which they are employed.

Different Strategic Objectives

Clausewitz defines strategy as "the use of the engagement for the purpose of the war."[15] More generally strategy has been considered as a "theory" of how military means advance political ends.[16] There are a great many different possible strategies. Here we focus on broad categories of strategy that prioritize the different objectives of deterrence discussed in the previous chapter. We then link these objectives to different types of military force. The choice of *how* to threaten or utilize military violence is then as much a political act as the decision of *whether* to resort to coercion or force.

To summarize the discussion about the various ends of deterrence in Chapter 3, political actors tend to have multiple national interests and priorities. They may choose to prioritize military effectiveness, political influence, resource efficiency, or strategic stability. These four values correspond to

---

[13] Extended reviews include Heuser 2010; Freedman 2013.

[14] There are exceptions, of course, notably Wylie 1989. See also the special issue introduced by Sechser, Narang, and Talmadge 2019.

[15] Ibid., p. 177.

[16] Inter alia, Posen 1984; Betts 2000. War colleges often differentiate "ways" and "means" to distinguish policies and instruments, but here we will consider the concept of "means" as generally as possible to encompass force structure, posture, and employment.

78 ELEMENTS OF DETERRENCE

basic parameters of the rational bargaining paradigm (i.e., power, demands, costs, uncertainty). The canonical bargaining model of war, however, is silent about which of these should be preferred over others. Actor preferences are exogenous to the model, meaning they are often found at the "unit level" rather than in the pure logic of strategic interaction at the "system level." The sources of strategic preferences might include factors such as leader personalities, cognitive psychology, national ideologies, bureaucratic culture, and domestic politics. These factors are beyond the scope of our study. We simply assume that preferences exist and that they may vary from state to state or situation to situation. Our focus is on the trade-offs that exist across these objectives, and how these tensions manifest in choices about force structure and posture.

The four basic factors of the bargaining model and actor preferences about which factor(s) to prioritize, in turn, give rise to four different fundamental strategies:

- *Defense* uses effective military force to change or maintain the distribution of territory, resources, political prerogatives or other benefits.
- *Coercion* communicates threats and assurances to protect or improve the status quo; this captures the intuitions around classical deterrence.
- *Deception* exploits the willing but unwitting assistance of others to gain benefits at reduced cost.
- *Accommodation* seeks a mutually beneficial agreement to improve information and promote stability, avoiding forms of costly political friction, such as war.

These general categories have been described with many other labels, such as war-fighting, coercive diplomacy, secret statecraft, and institutional engagement (or less charitably, appeasement). More colorfully, they might be described as *winning* a war, *warning* of consequences, *watching* for opportunity, and *working* together.[17] Whatever the label, the key point is that governments prioritize different objectives, for whatever reasons, and thus they may use different strategies to achieve them.

---

[17] We are grateful to Ryder McKeown for suggesting "watching" as the distinctive contribution of intelligence strategies. See also Table 1.1 in Chapter 15 linking bargaining parameters, preferences, and strategies.

POLITICS BY (MANY) OTHER MEANS   79

Note that the category we have labeled "coercion" is closest to the classical conception of "deterrence" in terms of credibly threatening punishment to prevent revision of the status quo. But deterrence in practice, as we have seen, can also make use of defensive capabilities ("deterrence by denial"),[18] while military capabilities in turn may leverage deception strategies (including maneuver and information operations) to operate more efficiently, and some military capabilities might even be deliberately withdrawn to accommodate and reassure an adversary for the sake of strategic stability. While "coercion" carries the unpleasant colloquial connotation of extortion, we follow Schelling in using it as a general term covering the art of using the "power to hurt" to communicate information about interests and consequences.[19] The point we seek to make is that deterrence in practice is a blend of objectives of influence, effectiveness, efficiency, and stability that create both opportunities and trade-offs.

If a state's overriding priority is to avoid conflict altogether (stability), then its leaders are likely to rely on strategies of accommodation. They will look for ways to minimize the use of military instruments altogether (i.e., de-escalation, compromise, appeasement, arms control institutions, demobilization, disarmament, and collective governance). These may be wise policies in many circumstances, but they amount to reliance on "regular" politics rather than politics "by other means." Our emphasis in this chapter is on specialization in *military* means, so we will not have much to say about accommodation here. In Chapters 12 and 13 we will return to the relationship between mutually beneficial economic interdependence (which is a form of accommodation in this general sense) and conflict (of various types).

The other three goals are best served, respectively, by strategies that use military operations to enforce favorable distributional outcomes, prioritize credible communication to achieve influence without war, or rely on intelligence or subversion to seek to capture political benefits without having to absorb all of the costs of fighting or credible signaling. The strategies of defense and influence correspond to Thomas Schelling's classic distinction between brute force and coercion, i.e., "the difference between defense and deterrence, between brute force and intimidation, between conquest and blackmail, between action and threats... Brute force succeeds where it is used, whereas the power to hurt is most successful when held in

---

[18] G. Snyder 1961; Mearsheimer 1985.   [19] Schelling 1966.

80 ELEMENTS OF DETERRENCE

reserve."[20] Indeed, the notion of "coercion" applied here captures much of classical sense of the concept of "deterrence." The strategy of deception is different from both defense and influence: "watching" is neither "winning" nor "warning."[21]

Defense strategies, accordingly, attempt to use military capabilities to directly impose or protect preferred policy outcomes. Actors who care most about maximizing their power to ensure that they get what they want, and who are less sensitive to the costs of getting it, should be strongly attracted to war-fighting strategies. Actors who prioritize pure strategies of defense will be more preoccupied with military effectiveness (accomplishing the mission) than resource efficiency (doing more with less). Money is no object when survival is on the line. "Defense" should be understood broadly here to encompass war-fighting, denial, disruption, and conquest.

By contrast with pure defense strategies, strategies of coercion threaten to use force in the future under some specified circumstances. "Coercion" should be understood broadly here to encompass coercive diplomacy, classical deterrence, and reassurance. This category includes deterrent threats to protect the status quo and compellent threats to change it. Whereas military forces used for defense act to change the balance of power or shift the distribution of benefits, forces used for "pure" deterrence communicate information about power or resolve. Coercive diplomacy is attractive because it promises benefits without having to pay the costs of fighting for them, but this also tends to encourage coercers to bluff, and thus leads prospective targets to suspect bluffing. Without some sort of costly signal of ability and resolve, targets are liable to disregard or misperceive threats as cheap talk.

Some actors, however, may prize cost-savings over *either* power or credibility. This might be because actors have few resources available or other important non-military spending priorities (i.e., butter over guns). Even well-resourced actors will often prefer to moderate their costs, especially when the stakes are diminutive. Conversely, when a weaker actor seeks to prevail over a more capable one, avoiding direct military confrontation may be tempting, even essential. Trickery and stratagem become more attractive in resource-constrained circumstances because they promise greater reward

---

[20] Schelling 1966, p. 3.

[21] Deception is also subtly different from "working" insofar as it subverts cooperation for competitive gain, as discussed in greater detail in Lindsay 2017 and Chapter 6.

POLITICS BY (MANY) OTHER MEANS   81

at less risk.[22] Intelligence, for example, uses deceptive tradecraft to enable a weaker defender to employ scarce resources more efficiently to offset a stronger opponent's intentions and capabilities rather than attempt to defend everywhere.[23]

We use the concept of "deception" broadly here to refer to espionage, disguise, subversion, disinformation, active measures, covert action, sabotage, counterintelligence, clandestine diplomacy, and any form of secret statecraft. Deception is not just a tactic but rather a distinct strategy for gaining political benefits without the cost and risk of direct confrontation.[24] What these diverse shadowy activities all have in common is that they work by tricking another actor into harming itself or foregoing opportunities. Thus disinformation and seduction persuade their victims to behave differently than they should, because they've been persuaded of a falsehood, while camouflage and concealment persuade them not to act as they would, if they knew the truth. Simulation shows something that is absent, while dissimulation hides something that is there.[25] The essence of deception is that the victim voluntarily, but unwittingly, provides benefits to the deceiver through its own action or inaction.

Defense, coercion, and deception are logically distinct. Deception tries to hide the truth, while coercion signals to improve information. Coercion or deterrence promises to act tomorrow, while defense uses force, and deception uses something other than force, today. Defense physically overpowers an enemy, while deception gains the willing assistance of the victim. Coercion explicitly communicates, defense openly fights, and deception slyly manipulates.

These pure strategies are often combined in practice. Deterrence by denial relies on the credible threat of effective military defense to improve influence over the status quo. Maneuver warfare may rely on deception in the form of feints, camouflage, and ambush to improve the efficiency of military power relative to costly attrition strategies. Coercive diplomacy might combine credible deterrence threats (sticks) with accommodations and side payments (carrots) to achieve a more stable agreement. Institutions may work more efficiently when they have surveillance mechanisms to monitor compliance with agreements. Yet these same combinations often require actors to make

---

[22] Ettinger and Jehiel 2010; Zhuang, Bier, and Alagoz 2010.   [23] D. Kahn 2001.
[24] See Chapter 6 for extensive discussion of the unique strategy of deception.
[25] Whaley 1982.

82 ELEMENTS OF DETERRENCE

trade-offs, precisely because different strategies emphasize different political goals. Secret weapons may boost military effectiveness but cannot be used to augment the war avoidance, stability, or cost-reduction aspects of deterrence. Secret weapons may also boost the efficiency of military operations, so long as they remain secret. Revelation and compromise, however, can undermine military effectiveness. The ideology of "network-centric warfare" (i.e., the information technology "revolution in military affairs") is premised on the idea that intelligence, surveillance, and reconnaissance (ISR) and precision munitions provide an efficiency advantage by "substituting information for mass," while criticism of the same ideology emphasizes the need for mass, protection, reserves, and overwhelming firepower to compensate for the "fog of war."[26] Deception and deterrence are an especially unstable combination insofar as bluffing and misrepresentation are at odds with credible signaling.

Different Operational Features

Military forces have long been used to advance the three competitive strategies that we will focus on for the remainder of this chapter: defense, coercion, and deception. Armies have conquered, princes have threatened, and spies have conspired for millennia. Yet the advent of different technologies at different points in history alters and focuses their respective relevance. During the Cold War, most obviously, nuclear weapons encouraged hard thinking about deterrence strategy, precisely because nuclear war-fighting seemed impractical in the extreme. Deterrence was practiced long before nuclear weapons encouraged careful theorizing about it. Today, cyber espionage and covert influence are drawing more attention to classic strategies of deception. While espionage and subversion are ancient practices, the scale and manner in which they are practiced in cyberconflict encourages new theorizing.[27]

The main thrust of our argument is that specialized technological and institutional capabilities have comparative advantage for different strategies:

- *Defense* and most forms of war-fighting are enhanced by speed, range, mobility, maneuver, networking, adaptation, flexibility, lethality,

---

[26] Van Riper 1997; S. Biddle 1998; McMaster 2003.   [27] Lindsay 2021; Carnegie 2021.

protection, sustainment, preponderance, integration, combined arms warfare, protection, etc.

- *Coercion* and most kinds of deterrence are enhanced by unambiguous declaratory policies, explicit red lines, costly signals, durable commitments, clear assurances, transparent capabilities, advertised defenses, fixed fortifications, transparent consequences, painful punishments, secure and resilient forces, etc.
- *Deception* and other types of covert action are enabled by secrecy, stealth, precision, deniability, ambiguity, espionage, intelligence, confidence games, subversion, disinformation, sabotage, proxy and paramilitary operations, etc.
- *Accommodation* is facilitated by transparency, de-escalation, de-alerting, demobilization, arms control, disarmament, commerce, soft power, common institutions, cosmopolitan norms, international law, collective governance, etc.

These lists are intended to reflect relevant features supporting each strategy. They are neither exhaustive nor mutually exclusive. Indeed, strategies can and often are used together. Deception can enable defense, and defense can provide political influence. But there are also trade-offs. The clarity and transparency of deterrence, for instance, is in tension with the secrecy and ambiguity of deception.

We can take this one step further by linking these enabling features to the character of different operational domains. We use the term "domain" here in a loose sense to describe categories of specialized military technologies that have interestingly different operational characteristics, often as a result of the environment in which military technologies operate. The physical environments of land, sea, air, and space are each interestingly different from one another because platforms optimized for them face specific geospatial constraints on power-projection, movement, and coordination.

Technology can diminish geographical constraints, as when railroads increased the scope and scale of terrestrial mobilization. But the effects of geography cannot be eliminated altogether. Even in cyberspace, borders matter.[28] The opening of a new domain can allow actors to transcend constraints in other domains (e.g., aircraft overfly coastlines and mountain ranges, and electronic communications move at the speed of light).

---

[28] Goldsmith and Wu 2006.

84 ELEMENTS OF DETERRENCE

The virtual realm of cyberspace is interestingly different from the physical domains because it relies on human-built constructs to protect and exploit the command and control of things that drive, sail, fly, or orbit in other domains.[29]

While geography and technology do not directly determine politics, they do facilitate or constrain political behaviors. Actors make purposeful choices about how to deploy, employ, and counter material capabilities.[30] However, technology and geography both enable and constrain the options available to politico-military actors, broadening or restricting the outcomes that are possible in any given case. While technology and geography do not determine, they do shape and channel.[31]

As a simple heuristic, a state's decision to divide different classes of capability into different services or major functional commands is a prima facie indicator of coherent functional specialization. Indeed, the description of a certain set of capabilities as a "war-fighting domain" has proved useful for consolidating bureaucratic control over military resources, most notably in the cyber community's quest for recognition and resources in the early 2000s. Consideration of a distinct "missile domain" appears in other national contexts (e.g., China's PLA Rocket Force). The different organizational cultures of military services often reflect particular historical experiences in specific operating environments.[32] Military cultures may provide additional resources for, or obstacles to, the formulation of national security strategy above and beyond the operational characteristics of domains. We focus here less on military culture per se and more on strategically relevant functional specialization.

The notion of a "domain" is ultimately an analytical convenience and a social construction. Armies get wet, navies fly, and computers are everywhere. One might further subdivide the "big five" domains to consider, for instance, an undersea domain, or variation across different service branches,

---

[29] Territorial metaphors about "cyberspace" are extremely problematic, as discussed by Branch 2021. We do not consider the cyber "domain" to be a separate geography or "virtual terrain" but rather the sociotechnical information infrastructure that enables command and control in any physical environment whatsoever. Note that our usage is more expansive than the Joint Chiefs of Staff 2018 definition of cyberspace as "A global domain within the information environment consisting of the interdependent networks of information technology infrastructures and resident data, including the Internet, telecommunications networks, computer systems, and embedded processors and controllers." We take a broader view of the human and technological infrastructure of communication and computation, of which digital networks form an important subset, but a subset nonetheless.

[30] Bijker et al. 1987; Smith and Marx 1994; Herrera 2006.

[31] Mumford 2010; Winner 1977; McNeill 1982; Dafoe 2015.   [32] Builder 1989; Long 2016.

weapon platforms, or labor specialties. Thus we see attempts to distinguish the "electromagnetic domain" and the "cognitive domain" from the "cyber domain" by communities that wish to differentiate nuances of electronic warfare and psychological operations, respectively, from computer security. One could also embrace non-military domains such as economic statecraft or coercive engineered migration that are sometimes used in lieu of, or in response to, military force.[33] We leave this "rectification of terms" to others. We are most interested in the empirical question of how operational differences matter politically, not in some dogmatic ontological inquiry into what is "really" a domain. From this perspective, it would be reasonable to distinguish the "nuclear domain" from conventional warfare, even as nuclear weapons are deployed on land and at sea, delivered through air and space, and controlled via cyber networks, because nuclear weapons are qualitatively different from other types of military technology.[34] All delineations of domains are wrong, but some can be useful.

To keep the analysis tractable, this chapter (and the book as a whole) focuses on six different categories of military capability: land, sea, air, nuclear (missile), space, and cyber. There is already enough diversity across these "domains" to enable us to make the first-order point that different means have different political utility.[35]

Analysis of Comparative Advantages

We next explain how the geographic and technological features of different operational domains create different advantages for the strategies of defense, deterrence, and deception. We omit accommodation here as we are focusing on military means. We will paint in broad brushstrokes, drawing on stylized insights from scholarship on each domain. We do so at the risk of eliding important distinctions and debates in specialized literatures, but to do them

---

[33] Drezner 2018; Greenhill 2019.

[34] It is in the nature of complex systems that they combine separate, unlike elements. Weapons systems that operate across domains create definitional problems, but they also symbolize the discussion here about trade-offs and the need to combine unlike attributes to achieve various ends.

[35] This differentiation by domains is of course arbitrary and fails to address a multitude of other variables. Our theoretical approach is completely compatible with a more detailed typology of military capabilities, technologies, and human capital. For example, one could consider different military platforms and occupational specialties, applying our framework to this more detailed inventory of means. However, this would also be extremely cumbersome descriptively. We prefer the admittedly imperfect setup of domains as a simpler foil within which to present our arguments.

86 ELEMENTS OF DETERRENCE

Table 4.1 Comparative strategic advantages of military domains

Strategy	Nuclear	Land	Sea	Air	Space	Cyber
Coercion	+	+	?	?	?	−
Defense	−	+	+	+	?	−
Deception	−	?	?	?	+	+

all justice is impossible without spilling over into multiple volumes. We hope to make up for the lack of technical nuance by providing synthetic insight into the political implications of specialized capabilities.[36]

Table 4.1 summarizes the comparative political advantages and disadvantages of military domains (indicated by plus and minus, respectively). In many cases, the advantages are indeterminate for various reasons (indicated by a question mark). They might be indeterminate because there is a diversity of specialized platforms and units within a domain. Also, the relevant effects might be created by combining capabilities across domains. This is especially true of space, which is the most "cross-domain" domain of all. We proceed to unpack some of these nuances in the following sections.

We have ordered technological domains in Table 4.1 to highlight an overall *functional* pattern of specialization. Nuclear weapons are most specialized for coercion. Land forces are generalists. Sea and air forces are specialized for war-fighting, relying on the space domain as an important force multiplier. Space and cyber forces are information specialists, which makes them particularly useful for deception.

Holding aside nuclear weapons for the moment, Table 4.1 also suggests an interesting *historical* pattern. In the broad sweep of history, most of military history is concentrated in the land domain (for obvious reasons). Before the articulation of deterrence theory, land forces were used for both deterrence and defense without anyone making clear distinctions between these functions. States still use their armies for both coercion and war-fighting. Smaller, mobile units can also employ deception as well (i.e., ambush, raiding, infiltration), even as large armies are harder to hide. The venerable land domain is the *most versatile* because it is also the *least specialized* domain. Ground forces are jacks of all trades, doing everything OK. But by extension other domains are more specialized, doing certain things even better.

---

[36] This chapter trades efficiency for effectiveness, but we hope to preserve some credibility!

Historical innovation in the other domains adds specialized war-fighting capability. Greater maneuverability and lethality enables military forces to increase the scope and scale of power projection. Armies supported by sea lines of communication and air power are much more capable armies. And these new domains become contested theaters of war in their own regard. But war-fighting specialization comes at the price of reduced credibility for influence, as we shall see. Deception also becomes more feasible with technological improvements in mobility, stealth, and networking. Innovation in the technologies of information—space and cyber—is especially useful for intelligence and subversion. Cyberspace, from this perspective, is peculiarly specialized for deception, just as nuclear weapons are specialized for coercion.[37]

Returning to nuclear weapons, they emerged historically between the air and space domains. Nuclear weapons, delivered by bombers through the air or missiles transiting through space, represent a sharp break in the historical pattern of *decreasing deterrence* and *increasing deception*. Nuclear weapons, in effect, returned the pendulum back toward deterrence, after the sacrifice of credibility in the air and space domains. The extreme, and obvious, destructiveness of nuclear weapons, when combined with prompt global delivery platforms, recovers some of the strategic deterrence utility of the traditional land domain that was sacrificed in the quest for greater military effectiveness and efficiency in the highly technological domains.

The nuclear exception illustrates the importance of context and combination. Specialization for mass destruction of nuclear weapons (which enhances the credibility of punishment strategies) offsets the mobility and stealth of delivery platforms moving through air and space (which undermines credibility). In cyberspace, conversely, specialization for information (which enhances the efficiency of both economic and military coordination) can augment the employment of forces in other domains, either through providing better intelligence or manipulating enemy communications.

We expand on these comparative advantages and highlight several instructive exceptions below, delving into specific examples and detailed argumentation in the chapters which follow. For convenience we consider these technologies in rough historical order. Note that this is not the order displayed in Table 4.1, which highlights a functional rather than historical

---

[37] We present our detailed argument about cyberspace and deception in Chapter 6.

88   ELEMENTS OF DETERRENCE

pattern. We will thus discuss nuclear weapons after the air domain, i.e., the emergence of nuclear ballistic missiles flying through space.

Land

Land is the oldest warfare domain, and also the least specialized. Strategic specialization in this context must not be mistaken for geographical differentiation. The land domain is highly complex and differentiated. Sea, air, and space, by contrast, are more homogeneous domains. The forces that operate in these environments tend to be more specialized for specific missions. Land forces, by contrast, tend to possess considerable organic capabilities to deal with geographical and cultural complexity.

States have long used armies to invade, occupy, or defend territory. Armies have also always been useful for making credible threats.[38] While small units can hide and harass, large ground deployments are hard to disguise. This turns out to be good for signaling, because a target knows that a dangerous capability is present. The logistic entourage of an army moves slowly, so the target knows that a capability will remain present. Mobilized forces are expensive to maintain in the field, so a target knows that the threat is serious. By paying the financial and political costs to deploy and sustain troops in harm's way, political leaders can more credibly communicate their willingness to conquer or defend an interest. Even ground forces that cannot defeat an attack on their own still signal a defender's interest in a particular place or issue. Further, they can also act as a tripwire, committing a defender to deploy additional forces in a crisis or war. So much the better for deterrence (or compellence) if ground forces are large and strong enough to also mount a successful defense (or invasion).

During the Cold War, as today, the United States extended nuclear guarantees to some of its allies. Concerns about the credibility of the nuclear umbrella were pithily summed up by the question of whether the United States would trade Washington for Paris or Bonn. American officials addressed the problem with a cross-domain solution. US troops were deployed to Europe to commit the United States to a larger, and most

---

[38] Slantchev 2011; Hunzeker and Lanoszka 2015; Gartzke and Kagotani 2017; Frederick et al. 2020. We document the stabilizing effect of land forces in Chapter 8.

likely nuclear, war if the Soviet Union attacked Central Europe. Tripwire forces in the Cold War, as in the Baltic region today, may not have been able to defeat an enemy attack, but their failure to do so would have helped to generate the will required to respond with even more force. Schelling describes their mission with characteristic flair: "Bluntly, they can die. They can die heroically, dramatically, and in a manner that guarantees that the action cannot stop there."[39]

Indeed, NATO adopted a concentrated forward deployment in Western Germany that was politically efficacious, even though a defense in depth would probably have better suited mobile warfare, and thus defensive fighting power. Innovations in technology and doctrine eventually helped to relieve the painful trade-off policy makers faced between defense and deterrence. The adoption of AirLand Battle doctrine by the US military (and Follow-On Forces Attack by NATO) substituted the possibility of forward air interdiction in Eastern Europe for the politically less attractive option of defense in depth in Western Europe. Once again, this was a cross-domain solution, leveraging the war-fighting potency of air forces to complement the deterrent credibility of ground forces. The improvement in NATO's conventional power during the late Cold War greatly enhanced deterrence by denial (the threat of successful defense) and thereby relieved NATO of exclusive reliance in the early Cold War on nuclear deterrence (the threat of costly punishment).

John Mearsheimer points out that attrition, as contrasted with maneuver warfare, is the foundation of coercive strategy with conventional land forces.[40] Attrition relies on mass—large numbers of troops and heavy firepower—to absorb and inflict damage, which raises the costs of conflict (coercive punishment) and wears down the enemy's ability to keep fighting (war-fighting denial). While a willingness to engage in attrition can be useful for deterrence, it is also a liability for war-fighting effectiveness. Attrition also wears down friendly forces and political will.

Maneuver strategies, by contrast, attempt to flank or penetrate enemy formations to throw them into disarray. Throughout history, commanders

---

[39] Schelling 1966, p. 47.
[40] Mearsheimer 1985. See also Nolan 2017. We are grateful to a reviewer for pointing out that we are talking about the American distinction between attrition and maneuver here rather than the Prussian distinction between attrition and annihilation, which do not necessarily overlap.

90　ELEMENTS OF DETERRENCE

have struggled to restore maneuver to attritional battlefields.[41] Maneuver warfare can potentially force a battlefield decision, shorten a conflict, and conserve friendly forces. Modern ground forces rely on combinations of different capabilities within the land domain itself to survive the lethality of the modern battlefield, and to restore mobility.[42]

In combined-arms warfare, the strengths of each branch—infantry, armor, artillery, aviation, etc.—cover the weaknesses of the others, creating synergies that enhance the fighting power of the overall force. Joint doctrines like AirLand Battle leverage forces from other domains to shift the emphasis from mass to maneuver in war-fighting.[43] The result is inherently complex in structure and operation.

Yet even at its best, maneuver warfare remains constrained by terrain features, weather, material infrastructure, and local politics. Schemes of maneuver often fail to go according to plan because, as Clausewitz stressed, vehicles break down, troops panic and make mistakes, intelligence proves unreliable, or the enemy behaves surprisingly.[44] When speed and maneuvers falter, armies must fall back on mass to take the hits and keep on fighting.[45] Napoleon may have been a genius of maneuver warfare, but even he is reputed to have believed that God favors bigger battalions.

Special forces are an exception that proves the rule. Commando units rely on stealth and speed to achieve advantage.[46] More often than not, however, they do so by leveraging air, naval, space, and communications platforms from other domains that have comparative advantages other than mass. Special operators who find themselves outgunned in land encounters usually fare badly.[47] Moreover, some forms of irregular warfare recapitulate the classic ground force emphasis on mass; for instance, counterinsurgency doctrine calls for troops to "surge" in order to "clear, hold, and build."[48] In general, the land domain incentivizes ground forces to rely more on mass than maneuver. Mass, in turn, facilitates costly signaling that disproportionately—relative to other domains—enables greater credibility in coercive strategies.

---

[41] Weigley 1973; Roland 1994; Nolan 2017.　　[42] S. Biddle 2004.

[43] AirLand Battle was a US Army doctrine in the late Cold War. Its NATO counterpart was known as Follow-On Forces Attack. Both emphasized agile maneuver and proactive targeting of enemy forces deep in the rear via battlefield surveillance networks and precision munitions.

[44] Clausewitz 1976, pp. 113–21.　　[45] S. Biddle 2007.　　[46] McRaven 1995.

[47] See, for example, Naylor 2005.　　[48] Ucko 2009.

Sea

Navies, by contrast, enable maneuver on a grand scale. Vessels can move heavy cargo around the world at relatively low cost. Naval fleets can project supporting fires, land expeditionary troops, and deliver logistical supplies to any region with a coastline. The ocean becomes a highway for nations that can afford the enormous cost of capital-intensive maritime capabilities, and a barrier for those that cannot.

Naval mastery enabled Great Britain in its heyday to minimize its standing army, yet still shape Continental, and eventually global, politics.[49] The mobility and flexibility of sea power provides strategic advantages for projecting forces, imposing blockades, resupplying troops, and keeping sea lanes open for trade. Navies can support armies to enable a sort of combined-arms warfare on a grand scale. Corbett notes that the Royal Navy served as an invaluable auxiliary for Wellington's campaigns against Napoleon on the continent, by supplying British expeditionary forces and interdicting French sea lines of communication.[50] Importantly, however, the defeat of the French navy at Trafalgar failed to translate directly into British victory in the war, which lasted another decade. Command of the sea was more important for maritime Britain than continental France. Again, nations vary in their goals and in the military implements and domains where these goals are best realized.

The operational features of navies are politically consequential. As Francis Bacon observed, "he that commands the sea is at great liberty, and may take as much and as little of the war as he will. Whereas those that be strongest by land are many times nevertheless in great straits."[51] The vastness of the sea enables navies to withdraw from danger and opt into engagements when conditions favor them, or their goals. Land armies are more likely to find themselves caught in desperate situations.

Yet the discretion that enhances defense is not good for deterrence: navies can renege on commitments by simply sailing away, while more cumbersome ground forces remain committed to fight (or surrender). Navies provide a state with expanded options for power projection relative to ground forces, but the availability of options also undermines the credibility of promises. The same mobility that creates war-fighting options also enables

---

[49] Kennedy 2017.   [50] Corbett 1911.   [51] Bacon 1909.

92 ELEMENTS OF DETERRENCE

commanders to protect these advantages by avoiding risky encounters. Athenians sacrificed their city, after all, but not the fleet.

Fleet battle is rare, even historically, because the loss of capital ships, and the resulting compromise of supply lines and power projection, threaten catastrophic consequences for a maritime nation. Churchill thus characterized Admiral John Jellicoe, commander of the Royal Navy's Grand Fleet during the Battle of Jutland, as "the only man on either side who could lose the war in an afternoon."[52] As in the Napoleonic Wars, maritime defeat would have been a disaster for Britain. Instead, even though Jutland turned out to be operationally indecisive, it marked the end of Germany's effort to contest the high seas, a strategic victory for the Allies not unlike that resulting from Nelson's decisive action at Trafalgar. Once again, Britain had re-asserted its command of the sea, if in a much less dramatic fashion. Yet, control of the seas did not translate into prompt Allied victory on the land, any more than it had for Nelson. The naval standstill gave Britain a free hand in sustaining its blockade and embargo of German commerce, while also underscoring that the main theater of war was on the Continent. Britain's primary adversaries were deterred from mounting any further significant maritime challenge, but they were still free to redirect their energies into the ongoing contest on land.

Naval deterrence, therefore, must be understood in a cross-domain context. The "stopping power of water" is a natural barrier to invasion.[53] One need look no further than the current tensions between Taiwan and mainland China to see that this is so. If not for the Taiwan Strait, this dispute would have ended long ago, in China's favor. For similar reasons, naval powers might credibly signal defensive intentions and thereby discourage the formation of balancing coalitions against them.[54] While naval forces operating in peripheral theaters can reasonably claim that a state is pursuing limited aims, states that cross an enemy border with land forces find it harder to commit not to march on the enemy capital.[55] Contrast Russia's (admittedly unsuccessful) invasion of Ukraine and China's ineffective posturing against Taiwan.

Naval missions to "show the flag" through port visits and "freedom of navigation operations" can demonstrate the ability to move firepower into an area, which can enhance coercion and assurance to allies. Moreover, navies

---

[52] H. White 2016.   [53] Mearsheimer 2001.
[54] Levy and Thompson 2010.   [55] Corbett 1911.

must assume some risk by sailing into a potential adversary's engagement envelope, which demonstrates some degree of resolve, or a willingness to run risks in a brinkmanship crisis. The credibility of "presence" missions is weakened, however, by the degree to which mobile platforms like naval vessels can simply sail away at another moment. Alternatively, navies may be too far away to arrive in time and in sufficient mass to be of much help. Mobility and vulnerability are twin liabilities for coercion.[56]

The sea-based leg of the nuclear triad offers another rule-proving exception. Much as special forces rely on other domains to exploit maneuver rather than leaning on mass to achieve their mission, ballistic missile submarines (SSBNs) rely on the air and space domains to impose horrific punishment. SSBNs can disappear for months at a time to evade counterforce targeting, which improves the survivability of forces available for nuclear retaliation. Military uncertainty about the location of mortal threats improves political certainty that they will be available when called upon, in much the same way as the infeasibility of missile defense enhances the credibility of deterrent threats. Thus, nuclear states tend to converge on SSBN forces once they are able to master the significant challenges involved in maritime deployments.[57]

Submarines can also use their advantages in maneuver and stealth for intelligence collection, but this may have a negative effect on the transparency required for stable deterrence. Information gleaned from covert intelligence collection must generally be kept secret, so that one side does not know what the other side knows. Indeed, one objective of clandestine operations is to convey no information at all. Yet this very tension creates questions for allies about whether extended deterrence through SSBNs is as credible as nuclear capabilities based on the client's own soil.[58]

As a general rule, the mobility and stealth of navies weakens the credibility of influence strategies relative to armies, even as the ability to transport expeditionary forces and project firepower in substantial quantities affords some additional bargaining leverage. The formidable costs involved in building—and risking—a navy can also provide a marginal advantage in making credible threats relative to other capabilities that are even more maneuverable and vulnerable, such as air forces.

---

[56] This argument is developed further with supporting empirical data in Chapter 9.
[57] Gartzke, Kaplow, and Mehta 2014.   [58] Mehta 2019.

Air

The comparative advantage of modern air power is the rapid delivery of firepower and other effects over great distances. Aircraft can project precision fires to targets far inland that naval fires simply cannot reach. Aircraft can also serve as reconnaissance platforms to target fires from, or into, other domains. This enhances the efficiency of combined arms warfare (or variants like joint force maneuver or multidomain operations), reducing reliance on mass. By limiting the number of personnel in harm's way, moreover, modern air power can increase military power while decreasing political risk, which is especially attractive for governments that are sensitive to casualties.

Yet while air power exceeds naval power in speed, maneuverability, and global reach, aircraft are far more fragile than ships. Warships with modern close-in weapon systems and damage control systems can continue fighting under missile attack, but gravity dooms a damaged aircraft. Air superiority is thus a critical precondition for effective use of the air domain to project power into the land and sea domains. Air forces are also needed to oppose enemy air forces that threaten them.[59]

To an even greater extent than naval forces, air forces rely on stealth and speed to compensate for their disadvantages in mass and protection. The political trade-off between power and credibility is thus even greater. While the rise of air power is closely associated with the articulation of coercive punishment strategies, the historical record casts doubt on the political efficacy of strategic bombing.[60] One problem is that the same efficiencies of air power that enhance military effectiveness at the operational level also undermine the credibility of influence at the political level.

An important nuance here is that air power *can* generate effective deterrence at the *operational* level. This works by using the mobility and firepower of air power to deny the ability of ground forces to concentrate mass, provided that there is some degree of air superiority to reduce the risk to friendly forces.[61] Aircraft can also draw away enemy fighters that might attempt to do the same to friendly ground forces. The military features of air power make it a highly desirable instrument for fighting and winning

---

[59] Surface-to-air missiles can be considered disposable unmanned aircraft tailored for the aerial denial mission. SAMs are a cross-domain response to the threat posed by the air domain to the land domain.

[60] Pape 1996; T. Biddle 2002; Haun 2015; Post 2019.

[61] Haun and Jackson 2016; Haun 2019.

a war. Yet these same features make air power alone somewhat less useful for credibly signaling political interests and consequences. The fact that it is relatively easy, and not particularly costly, to fight from the skies makes use of air power less convincing as a demonstration of resolve. Consider, for example, the air campaign preceding the coalition land invasion of Kuwait in the First Gulf War; had the former been credible the latter would not have been necessary.

Recent US drone campaigns highlight some of the advantages of air forces for war-fighting, at least in permissive airspace, together with their disadvantages for strategic coercion. The remote location of aircrew protects them from lethal exposure to enemy fires. The range and endurance advantages of drones have improved intelligence coverage in politically sensitive areas that are off limits to US troops, which has improved the precision and accountability of aerial targeting.[62] Empirical studies of drone campaigns find a significant effect in suppressing insurgent violence in areas around drone strikes, while arguments about blowback from civilian casualties appear to be exaggerated.[63] Yet as effective as drones may be for denial, drone strikes provide little information to targets on the receiving end about the resolve of the nation that relies on drones. The chronic attrition of limited war has the useful political function of separating weaker but more resolved actors from stronger but less resolved types. If, however, the stronger actor only imposes rather than pays costs, then the weaker actor receives no information about the political resolve of the stronger actor. The targets of drone strikes thus have incentives to target more vulnerable civilian populations in an effort to test the resolve of the stronger power.[64]

Nuclear Weapons

Nuclear weapons, typically delivered through air and space, create a major exception to our generalization about the coercive limits of air power. Certainty about the extreme costs of nuclear punishment compensates somewhat for the uncertainties associated with stealthy, long-range, maneuverable platforms. Nuclear weapons are uniquely devastating and, when

---

[62] McNeal 2014; Lyall 2017.   [63] Walsh 2013; Johnston and Sarbahi 2016; Shah 2018.

[64] See Chapter 10 for more detailed discussion. For an alternative view that overweights the power to impose costs and underweights the willingness to absorb them, cf. Zegart 2018.

delivered by volleys of long-range missiles, extremely difficult to intercept. In theory, a state with a secure second-strike capability—an arsenal that can survive a preemptive first strike—can openly advertise to others that it has the ability to carry out punishing nuclear attacks.[65]

The political certainty of retaliation, interestingly, depends on tactical uncertainty about the location of delivery platforms and the inability to intercept a critical portion of an enemy's nuclear arsenal. It is difficult to target mobile or hidden platforms and to intercept warheads speeding in from outer space. A single missed warhead, moreover, can incinerate an entire city. The typical importance of aggregate military power is somewhat muted in the nuclear domain as a result. Above a certain threshold, the marginal damage inflicted by additional mass destruction adds little to the horrendous damage already inflicted. The orthodox theory of the nuclear revolution—stability through mutual assured destruction (MAD)—holds that small arsenals and conservative force postures are sufficient for effective deterrence.[66]

The central problem in nuclear deterrence theory is credibility. Executing a nuclear threat entails significant risks of enemy retaliation, collateral consequences from friendly nuclear strikes, and the potential opprobrium of transgressing the "nuclear taboo."[67] An actor must be perceived to have an extremely high value for the stakes in a contest before it can credibly make such a threat. Deterrent threats to protect vital interests, such as regime survival, are regarded as more credible than compellent threats to advance revisionist goals, which are more likely to be seen as bluffs.[68] Loss-aversion heuristics tend to reinforce the asymmetry of stakes.[69]

One implication is that actors who rely mainly on nuclear deterrence will tend to compromise on disputes over less-than-vital interests. Nuclear threats may credibly deter major war, but it is not credible to threaten Armageddon in response to minor acts in peripheral theaters, which gives rise to the so-called stability-instability paradox.[70] The Kennedy administration's pursuit of "flexible response" as an alternative to Eisenhower's "massive retaliation" reflected, in part, a desire to fashion additional tools for coercion

---

[65] See Chapter 2 for a review of this literature.

[66] Inter alia, Jervis 1989; Glaser 1990; Glaser and Fetter 2016.

[67] The precedent of nuclear non-use appears to have a weak but non-zero effect on public preferences, which may not reflect policy makers preferences: Press, Sagan, and Valentino 2013.

[68] Sechser and Fuhrmann 2017; Kroenig 2018.   [69] Jervis, Lebow, and Stein 1985.

[70] G. Snyder 1965.

and influence below the threshold of nuclear credibility.[71] Nuclear weapons discourage attacks on vital interests, even as credibility suffers, and even encourages challenges, in less-than-vital arenas.

Nuclear deterrence in practice has involved a dizzying variety of capabilities for nuclear war-fighting (i.e., defense and deception are often mixed with deterrence). MAD skeptics point out that modern reconnaissance and precision strike capabilities make nuclear war-fighting more feasible than generally appreciated.[72] Counterforce strategies tend to require larger and more varied arsenals, with more aggressive postures, to deal with a wider range of scenarios. The ability to track and target enemy nuclear forces would enable a state to limit the damage an enemy could inflict in a nuclear war, even as the same ability creates temptations for nations possessing these capabilities to engage in a preemptive counterattack.

Yet even the most vocal advocates of counterforce still consider nuclear war-fighting to be a last-resort option to be exercised only in the event that deterrence fails. Because even a small nuclear war entails considerable risk for all sides, nuclear weapons are ill-suited as an instrument of conquest.[73] Despite all the debate about counterforce and strategic stability, a rough consensus endures that the primary utility of nuclear weapons is for deterring major war and ensuring state survival.

Space

Many of the reconnaissance functions first performed by aircraft can now be performed more effectively by satellites. Yet there are important differences between the air and space domains. Outer space is more difficult to access. Despite being physically vast, maneuver in space is highly constrained by orbital physics, extremely high orbital velocities, and hazardous environmental conditions including radiation and debris. Debris created by asteroids, derelict satellites, rocket bodies, or kinetic strikes might create orbiting

---

[71] "flexible response" was never actually implemented as an operational nuclear doctrine during the Kennedy or Johnson administrations according to Gavin 2012.

[72] Inter alia, Lieber and Press 2006; Long and B. Green 2014; Lieber and Press 2017; Kroenig 2018.

[73] An interesting dilemma has been exposed by Russian threats involving low-yield nuclear weapons, designed to isolate and protect their actions in Ukraine. Low-yield nuclear capabilities "split the difference" between conventional conflict and large-scale nuclear war, while also foreshadowing a general nuclear exchange. Bringing the threshold of nuclear use down advantages the less capable but more resolved actor by introducing brinkmanship dynamics.

98 ELEMENTS OF DETERRENCE

hazards that imperil any satellite in the same orbit, including those operated by the attacker.[74]

Unfortunately, spacecraft have limited fuel stores for defensive maneuver, and remote control from ground stations might not be timely in tactical situations. The replacement of damaged or derelict satellites is expensive and time-consuming, particularly for highly specialized platforms like US Space-Based Infrared System (SBIRS) satellites. All of these factors put a premium on centralized command and control. Russia and China already have dedicated military space agencies, and the United States has consolidated operational capabilities into a new Space Force.[75] Given the steep barriers to entry for viable programs, most space powers are major powers.[76]

As with the sea, space is strategically salient because of what it means for operations on Earth, not because of what happens in space per se.[77] Space is primarily, but not exclusively, an informational domain that enables intelligence collection, communications, and precision navigation on Earth. Low-Earth, mid-Earth, geostationary, and elliptical orbits each offer unique vantage points for locating and interconnecting assets in the land, sea, and air domains. A parabolic path through space is also the quickest way to move between two widely separated points on Earth. Combining these features, satellite-based targeting and early warning capabilities enable ballistic missile operations that transit through space. The space age and the missile age are one and the same; space is a big reason why nuclear deterrence is practiced at planetary scale.[78]

The informational and kinetic applications of space have an important but underappreciated strategic similarity in this respect: it is difficult to defend against them. Warheads reenter the atmosphere at many times the speed of sound, which makes missile defense a difficult technical challenge. Decoy warheads and volley fire add to the difficulties. Reconnaissance satellites, meanwhile, provide continuous or near-continuous coverage of the entire globe across the full electromagnetic spectrum. While it is possible

---

[74] A single weapon test by China in 2007 and an accidental satellite collision in 2009 increased the amount of trackable space debris by 40 percent; see N. Johnson 2010.

[75] Bahney and Pearl 2019.

[76] Moltz 2014. There is a growing commercial space industry, but leading firms are largely from countries with robust government space programs. The commercial firm SpaceX provided thousands of Starlink satellite internet terminals to Ukraine during the war with Russia, but this was in the context of significant US government support for the war and little Russian counterspace effort.

[77] The metaphor of space as a global littoral area is developed by Bowen 2020.

[78] Deudney 1983.

to conceal activity and shield signals, it is difficult to concentrate large land formations or to move big metal platforms at sea while remaining undetected from space.[79] Satellite vehicles may be easy to track from Earth against the blackness of space, but their intelligence payloads remain closely guarded secrets. This, in turn, creates many opportunities for non-intrusive intelligence, early warning, and arms control verification. Put simply, the space domain is fundamentally cross-domain.

The strategic stability of space is a complicated matter, in large part because of changing relationships, and greater dependencies, across domains. Stability appears to be eroding since the end of the Cold War due to improvements in ASAT technology and the increased reliance on space for conventional operations.[80] ASAT technology was immature in the Cold War, and the superpowers were deterred from using it given the close coupling between early warning satellites and nuclear forces.[81] As space assets become more entangled with conventional operations in other domains, the deterrence dynamics of space are harder to predict.

The informational advantages of space, together with the difficulty of defending against missiles and reconnaissance from space, helped to make deterrence a feasible grand strategy during the Cold War. Indeed, states with reconnaissance satellites have been less likely to be targeted with military aggression.[82] Today, however, there are growing incentives to preempt in space during a conventional military crisis. Ironically, this may improve the credibility of Russian and Chinese deterrence against the United States given the heavy reliance of the latter on space for power projection. Increasing dependence on space by new space powers for all kinds of peacetime and wartime missions could also result in some degree of mutual vulnerability and restraint similar to that experienced during the Cold War.[83] At the same time, war in space might injure only spacecraft rather than people, creating credibility problems similar to those discussed above regarding drone campaigns.

---

[79] This is especially true of the operational (theater) level of war, but tactical detection of individual platforms from space became feasible in the Cold War. See Friedman 2000.

[80] Bahney, Pearl, and Markey 2019.

[81] An excellent primer on ASAT operations, still relevant despite considerable technological change and thus reflecting the important physical constraints on the space domain, is Carter 1986. On Cold War stability see Stares 1985; Moltz 2008.

[82] See further discussion in Chapter 11.   [83] Gompert and Saunders 2011.

Cyberspace

Space and cyberspace are both informational domains. Indeed, portions of cyberspace are literally in outer space. For example, the Global Positioning System (GPS) supports the synchronization of global financial transactions and enables mobile phone users to find themselves on digital maps. Space also relies on cyberspace insofar as satellite operations depend on electronic data links to ground stations, computer hardware, and software control systems. Global information infrastructure is physically located in all four environmental domains, improving intelligence, communications, and control. Much like space, cyberspace is a cross-domain domain.

Yet there are also significant operational differences between these domains. Outer space is mostly empty and constrained by unforgiving physical laws. Cyberspace, by contrast, is a flexible, human-built, institutionally governed, sociotechnical infrastructure.[84] There are few spacefaring nations, but billions of people interact online. Low barriers to entry enable many weaker states and non-state actors to cause problems in cyberspace, but space infrastructure is a major investment. ASAT threats are almost exclusively military in nature, but civilian technology in the global economy is the source of most cyber vulnerability. Satellites collect intelligence from above a target, but cyber operations get inside the target's networks.

Cyberspace is essentially the information infrastructure of economic globalization. The irony is that while trade interdependence tends to discourage militarized conflict, it also encourages intelligence contests.[85] Any domain (or capability in a domain) that is useful for information and communication functions will be particularly relevant for intelligence and deception. Because cyberspace is built out of information and communication technology, the possibilities for deception are limitless. The economic viability of cyberspace depends on the willingness of millions of users to entrust valuable data to remote servers. Increased trust and lowered transaction costs, in turn, make it possible for malicious actors to abuse trust at scale and at low nominal cost.[86] Pervasive digital networks offer unprecedented opportunities for secrecy, deception, obfuscation, manipulation, and subversion.

---

[84] DeNardis 2014; Choucri and Clark 2018.
[85] We provide evidence on both sides of this proposition in Chapters 12 and 13.
[86] Bodmer et al. 2012; Bejtlich 2013.

Cyber operations exploit technical vulnerabilities and manipulate human gullibility for intelligence collection (surveillance and espionage), network disruption (sabotage and covert action), or indirect influence (subversion and disinformation). Organizations that depend on digital networks for their operations must be especially concerned about electronic attack, cyber exploitation, and other forms of disruption and disinformation, let alone self-inflicted friction within complex systems.[87] Defense is difficult in cyberspace because offense has many opportunities for deception, but network defenders can employ deception as well to monitor and entrap attackers. Cybersecurity is perhaps most usefully understood as an intelligence-counterintelligence contest, conducted with new means at a historically unprecedented scale.[88]

Deception, by its very nature, undermines credibility. Secrecy and tactical flexibility tend to make cyber coercion difficult.[89] Interestingly, these same features may make cyber tools useful for signaling a willingness to back down from a militarized crisis.[90] Using ambiguous attacks with reversible effects enables an actor to save face by "doing something" without provoking further escalation. Cyber operations are potentially useful for de-escalation for the same reason that they are not useful for signaling resolve: there is lots of room at the bottom in cyberspace.

Ransomware (e.g., the WannaCry attacks of 2017) offers another rule-proving exception.[91] This method employs a surprise attack to embargo a user's data and then demand payment to unlock it (or to avoid releasing embarrassing documents). The threat only works if the ransom is less than the target's replacement cost. More generally, a cyberthreat that is specific enough to be believable is also specific enough to enable a target to patch or reconfigure its networks. For the same reason, offensive cyber operations are often careful to avoid losing access to target networks. Too aggressive exploitation can prompt a target to disconnect from common networks, generally terminating exploitation, and it may invite retaliation in other domains.

Incentives for restraint in cyberspace create a new twist on the Cold War stability-instability paradox. The risks of cross-domain retaliation, the

---

[87] Benbow 2004; J. Schneider 2019b; Lindsay 2020.

[88] Rid 2013; Rovner 2019a; Lindsay 2021; Chesney and Smeets 2023.

[89] Libicki 2009; Stevens 2012; Lupovici 2014; Lindsay 2015; Borghard and Lonergan 2017; J. Schneider 2019a; Lonergan and Lonergan 2023.

[90] Lonergan and Lonergan 2022.   [91] Jun 2021.

102 ELEMENTS OF DETERRENCE

benefits of continued intelligence exploitation, and reliance on interdependence for future exchange, all tend to discourage major aggression, while at the same time encouraging minor harms.[92] The cyber domain becomes useful for marginal revisions of the balance of power, rather than dramatic coercion, costly punishment, or large-scale attack.

Strategic Complexity in Multiple Domains

It is mistake to treat military power as an undifferentiated good. The details of implementation are relegated to military professionals or considered mere technicalities of policy. Policy makers and commanders, by contrast, have long appreciated, if only intuitively, that the ways in which political actors decide to generate and employ force are politically salient. Choices about force structure and force posture have consequences for grand strategy and, given their pecuniary expense, alternative domestic priorities. An increasingly differentiated portfolio of military capabilities makes these considerations more difficult, and arguably more important.

Any cross-domain or multidomain operation or strategy is inherently complex. Our basic argument is that the complexities are as much political as military. Military capabilities that offer advantages in mass—large numbers of troops or enormous destruction—enhance the credibility of influence strategies (including coercion). For the same reason, however, they are liabilities for efficiency since they require the actor to absorb considerable cost or risk of punishment. Capabilities that offer advantages in speed and maneuver, by contrast, such as air and naval fleets that can deliver long-range precision fires, enhance the effectiveness of defense (war-fighting) strategies. The same mobility that enhances war-fighting has the potential to improve the coverage of coercion (i.e., efficiency), but this benefit comes at the price of reduced credibility (making it easier to abandon commitments). Domains that offer advantages for information—intelligence and communication infrastructure in space and cyberspace—enhance the efficiency of strategies that seek political-military benefits at vastly reduced cost and risk.

---

[92] Lindsay 2017; Lindsay and Gartzke 2018; Valeriano, Jensen, and Maness 2018; Schram 2021. We provide further argument and evidence on the ways in which successful deterrence can encourage "gray-zone conflict" in Chapter 14.

Yet secrecy and deception are usually incompatible with credible communication and strategic signaling.

Our analysis is admittedly extremely coarse, but we believe that it captures important underlying features that differentiate broad categories of military capabilities. Each of the general operational domains has a distinctly recognizable political flavor. We have also attempted to highlight important variation and subtlety within each domain, which in turn offer more nuanced strategic choices. Different platforms and types of units in each domain can, in certain circumstances, offer countervailing (or amplifying) advantages with respect to the general trend in the domain. Furthermore, it is only for the sake of analytical clarity that we explore domains and strategies separately. Even so, we have already encountered interdependence and synergy across domains, as well as trade-offs and interference. Indeed, many of the most useful capabilities in practice involve combinations of branches and domains. We expect that much of the nuance observed in real circumstances will often be the product of combinations of comparative advantages in mass, maneuver, and information at a more fine-grained level.

Our aim in this chapter has been to articulate the political characteristics of the operational building blocks of military strategy. Much work remains to be done analyzing whether and how political actors combine and sequence these building blocks. The logic of complementarity across domains is intuitive and underwrites classic doctrines of combined-arms warfare as well as contemporary emphasis on joint, combined, and multidomain operations. Close air support (tactical airpower) and airborne operations each leverage the air domain to enhance the range or combat power of land forces. Similarly, aircraft carriers leverage the air domain to improve the power projection of warships.

Military specialization in pursuit of efficiency and effectiveness tends to put an imperative on integration. The integration of complementary weapon systems and domains is especially attractive in a war-fighting context where power maximization is a primary consideration: all forces can be concentrated in a unified effort. Efficiency—cost minimization—is also desirable insofar as every military must operate within a budget of blood and treasure, especially for democratic states seeking to minimize exposure to casualties. Information-leveraging via space and cyberspace is attractive as a "force-multiplier," i.e., a way to do more with less. These informational domains can enhance the efficiency and scope of maneuver in all domains by providing ISR and reliable command and control. At the same time,

104 ELEMENTS OF DETERRENCE

nuclear weapons underscore the enduring relevance of "mass" underwriting the credibility of deterrence. Indeed, nuclear mass destruction puts an upper bound on the dynamics of any cross-domain strategy. Politics continues in the shadow of nuclear threats because actors still look for other ways to improve or undermine political-military advantages and strategic credibility.

Historical doctrines such as "AirLand Battle" in the late Cold War and "AirSea Battle" in recent US-China strategy seek power-improving synergies; their critics have also highlighted liabilities, such as crisis instability and inadvertent escalation.[93] Cross-domain combinations can sometimes interfere with, rather than enhance, strategic objectives. Increasing reliance on the sea and air domains comes at the price of reduced credibility for coercion, precisely because mobile forces might choose to move away from their commitments. Strategies of offshore balancing that aim to deter a would-be challenger may end up sacrificing the credibility of the very deterrence that they aim to create while attempting to minimize cost and risk. Capabilities create vulnerabilities.[94]

The informational capabilities in space and cyberspace that integrate military and economic power at an unprecedented scale, improving efficiency, are also vulnerable to remote exploitation and disruption, imperiling effectiveness. Space and cyberspace can, in different circumstances, amplify or interfere with advantages of other domains for war-fighting or coercion. Space-based ISR makes surprise attack less likely to succeed, which is stabilizing. Cyber exploitation of enemy nuclear command and control, by contrast, could be profoundly destabilizing.[95] The pursuit of synergies and avoidance of interferences is by necessity an ongoing and dynamic process. Because this balancing act is politically consequential, moreover, it cannot be relegated to technical functionaries.

The weapons that a nation chooses to deploy, or even with which to equip itself, can reveal to observers what it is interested in achieving and what it wants to emphasize to other world actors. What weapons nations purchase, and where they put them, determines how their efforts to shape expectations and behavior turn out. Deterrence in practice, then, is the process of fitting force structure, posture, and declaratory policy to national preferences. Yet, with a larger portfolio of tools potentially available to every

---

[93] Posen 1991; A. Goldstein 2013; Talmadge 2017; Acton 2018.
[94] J. Schneider 2019b.   [95] Discussed further in Chapter 7.

side of a strategic interaction, choosing the right option at the right time is increasingly challenging. This leads us to expect greater variability in the outcomes of military engagements. Best responses to a given actor's actions require skill, sometimes even luck, in the application of the right tools to a given crisis or action. Picking from the multidomain menu will inevitably lead to policies that are ideal for some situations but counterproductive in others.

Clausewitzian insights about war remain relevant, indeed vital, in the modern world. War remains a "paradoxical trinity" of popular passions, unpredictable events, and raison d'état. Yet this chaotic interaction now moves through even more complicated geometries of defense, deterrence, deception, and accommodation in the highly interdependent context of economic and technological globalization. While Clausewitz discussed the comparative tactical advantages of different combat arms at the beginning of the nineteenth century, today entirely new military domains offer novel comparative strategic advantages and conundrums. The proliferation of domains and complex interactions across them are both increasing the practical difficulty of strategy and creating new demand for theoretical concepts to guide it. Our attempt to disaggregate ends and means is not the final word, to be sure. But even this modest effort to improve the conceptualization of the coercive strengths and weaknesses of different technologies may prove useful in theory and in practice.

PART II

THEORETICAL PROBLEMS IN THE CYBER DOMAIN

This section develops a deeper understanding of the deterrence trade-offs associated with specialized technology by exploring the strategic dynamics of cyberspace, the domain that connects all other domains, setting the stage for our later exploration of other trade-offs in other domains. Chapter 5 expands on the rational bargaining model of war that we introduced in Chapter 3 and argues that "cyberwar" is a poor substitute for traditional means of coercion. The same secrecy and inexpensiveness that make offensive cyber operations attractive, at first blush, also undermine their utility for compellence or deterrence.

But this does not means that cyberconflict is not useful. On the contrary, cyberspace increases the salience of the undertheorized problem of deception. Chapter 6 argues that the logic of deception differs fundamentally from deterrence and defense, even as all three strategies can be combined in practice. As a fundamentally informational domain, cyberspace is especially well suited for strategies of deception, which can benefit both offense (espionage and subversion) and defense (counterintelligence). The central role of deception in cyberconflict necessitates a reconsideration of the notion of the offense-defense balance in cyberspace, which is not as lopsided as widely believed.

A basic strategic challenge in cyberspace is the tension between deterrence and deception. Chapter 7 explores an extreme manifestation of this tension in the combination of two very different types of military technology. Nuclear weapons and cyber operations have converse informational characteristics. The former can be brandished for influence, while the latter must be hidden for effectiveness. Actors who hold cyber operations in reserve in case deterrence fails, therefore, may make deterrence failure more likely. This is just one way in which integrated deterrence can produce risk as well as synergy.

5

Cyberspace Is Unsuitable
for the Strategy of War

In the early years of the twenty-first century, a blitz of media, punditry, and official pronouncements raised the specter of "cyberwar." Future conflicts that "could devastate a modern nation" would take place "at the speed of light" as hacker "attacks rapidly go global" to knock out critical systems "without first defeating a country's traditional defenses."[1] As Secretary of Defense Leon Panetta famously warned in 2012, "The collective result of these kind's of attacks could be a cyber Pearl Harbor; an attack that would cause physical destruction and the loss of life. In fact, it would paralyze and shock the nation and create a new, profound sense of vulnerability."[2] A decade later, former Director of the National Security Agency Keith Alexander drew an analogy to another historical tragedy: "Cybersecurity remains the exposed underbelly of democracies around the world. Ukraine is already facing the cyber equivalent of a howitzer. We will all be faced with a 9/11-scale threat in cyberspace: the question is simply when."[3]

To be sure, fears of disruptive attacks in and through cyberspace are not mere speculation. A barrage of distributed denial of service (DDoS) conducted by Russian "patriotic hackers" against Estonia in 2007 and Georgia in 2008 underscored the possibility that cyberwar might substitute for or complement traditional military aggression.[4] The discovery in mid-2010 of the Stuxnet worm targeting Iranian nuclear centrifuges, allegedly a joint US-Israeli operation, provided an existence proof that cyber operations could indeed create physical disruption.[5] Not surprisingly, Panetta did not mention Stuxnet, but he did call attention to the fact that "a very sophisticated virus called Shamoon infected computers in the Saudi Arabian State Oil Company Aramco.... This routine replaced crucial system files with an image of a burning US flag.... More than 30,000 computers that

[1] Clarke and Knake 2010, p. 31.   [2] Panetta 2012.   [3] Alexander 2022.
[4] See Chapter 13 for further discussion of these cases.   [5] Lindsay 2013; Slayton 2017.

Elements of Deterrence: Strategy, Technology, and Complexity in Global Politics. Erik Gartzke and Jon R. Lindsay, Oxford University Press. © Oxford University Press 2024. DOI: 10.1093/oso/9780197754443.003.0005

it infected were rendered useless and had to be replaced.... These attacks mark a significant escalation of the cyber threat and they have renewed concerns about still more destructive scenarios that could unfold."[6] Iran also retaliated with DDoS attacks on the US financial sector,[7] while Israel and Iran continued to exchange cyberattacks throughout the next decade.[8] Russian cyber campaigns have also inflicted varying degrees of damage. These include a pair of brief electrical outages inflicted on Ukraine in 2015 and 2016, the NotPetya worm that wiped computers in Western Europe in 2017, temporary disruption of the Korean Olympics in 2018, and persistent engagement in Ukrainian networks following Russia's invasion in 2022.[9] This is to say nothing of the persistent cyber espionage and disinformation campaigns that, for more than three decades and counting, have been exploiting government and commercial networks and civil society actors around the world. It would seem that the era of cyberwar has already arrived.

War, however, is fundamentally a political process. States, groups, and individuals threaten or inflict violence to deter or compel, generating influence through the prospect of damage or loss. Military force can also be exercised to maintain or alter the balance of power and resist or impose disputed outcomes. We argue that the internet is generally an inferior substitute to terrestrial force in performing the functions of coercion or conquest. According to Hannah Arendt, "The chief reason warfare is still with us is... that no substitute for this final arbiter in international affairs has yet appeared on the political scene."[10] Cyber "war" is not likely to serve as the final arbiter of competition in an anarchical world and so should not be considered in isolation from more traditional forms of political violence.

The capacity for internet coercion is further limited by some of the same factors that make cyberwar appear at first so alarming. Secrecy, unpredictability, and anonymity are often cited as worrisome features of war on the internet, but these same features imply that it is difficult to make threats in cyberspace that victims will believe. Given the inherent difficulty of credibly threatening cyberattacks without also compromising operational effectiveness, it may be tempting for actors to inflict damage rather than engage in coercive threats. This means that of the two major political functions of military force—altering the material balance of power or influencing the decisions of other actors (i.e., "winning" versus "warning")—cyber

---

[6] Panetta 2012.   [7] Office of Public Affairs 2016.   [8] Work and Harknett 2020.
[9] Greenberg 2019; Greenberg 2022.   [10] Arendt 1970.

CYBERSPACE IS UNSUITABLE FOR THE STRATEGY OF WAR   111

operations are more attractive for the former and negligible for the latter. Here, too, however, key limitations exist regarding what can be achieved over the internet. It is one thing for an opponent to interrupt a country's infrastructure, communications, or military coordination and planning. It is another to ensure that the damage inflicted translates into a lasting shift in the balance of national power or resolve.

In this chapter we argue that cyberattacks are unlikely to prove particularly potent in grand strategic terms unless they can impose substantial, durable harm on an adversary. In many, perhaps most, circumstances, this will occur only if cyber warfare is accompanied by conventional military force or other actions designed to capitalize on any temporary incapacity achieved via the internet. Those initiating cyberattacks must therefore decide whether they are prepared to exploit the windows of opportunity generated by network-enabled attacks through other modes of combat. If they are not willing and able to do so, then in grand strategic terms, there are few compelling reasons to inflict large-scale digital destruction. This chapter explains why the *technical possibility* of catastrophic damage via the internet should not be conflated with the *political probability* of an actor actually doing so.

The Debate about Cyberwar

The basic argument in this chapter was first published as an academic article over a decade ago.[11] At the time, the IR literature on cybersecurity was still in its infancy. It has been growing steadily ever since.[12] The IR cyber scholarship has evolved from a negative critique of the notion of "cyberwar" to a more positive assessment of empirical patterns of cyberconflict. It perhaps more accurate to liken competition in cyberspace to an "intelligence contest" rather than military combat.[13]

In the debate over cyberwar, one side highlights the potential for significant escalation and disruption.[14] The majority of IR scholars, however, tend to take a more skeptical view. Critics have focused alternately on theoretical problems with cyber coercion,[15] the lack of empirical evidence

---

[11] Gartzke 2013.   [12] For a review see Gorwa and Smeets 2019.

[13] Chesney and Smeets 2023.

[14] Kello 2013; Junio 2013; Nye 2017; Buchanan 2017; Healey and Jervis 2020.

[15] Rid 2012; Stevens 2012; Lupovici 2014; Lindsay 2015; Borghard and Lonergan 2017; Maschmeyer 2021a; Branch 2021; Lonergan and Lonergan 2022.

112 ELEMENTS OF DETERRENCE

for large-scale catastrophe or escalation,[16] the social and technical challenges of conducting offensive cyber operations,[17] and the institutional incentives for threat inflation.[18]

The IR debate has since moved beyond these useful correctives to assess the actual patterns of interaction between digital spies and counterspies.[19] From this perspective, cyber operations have far more in common with classic forms of espionage, subversion, covert action, disinformation, counterintelligence than military defense or conquest. The difference is more a matter of degree than kind. State intelligence agencies can now conduct intelligence at greater scale against a wider range of targets, while commercial threat intelligence firms also conduct sophisticated offensive and defensive network operations, for better and worse.[20] Even those who reject the intelligence framing of cybersecurity—arguing instead for novel strategic concepts like "persistent engagement"[21]—still agree that the vast majority of cyberconflict occurs beneath the threshold of armed conflict.

This does not imply that cyber operations do not inflict harm; on the contrary, cyberspace expands the repertoire for censorship, surveillance, counterintelligence, state repression, family violence, and other human rights abuses.[22] These human security threats are notable insofar as they tend to occur *within* collective institutions, rather than *between* political actors in anarchy. This suggests that cyberconflict is governed by a different political logic than that which governs traditional coercion and warfare.[23]

This chapter circles back to the beginning of the IR debate to clarify our negative critique of the concept of "cyberwar." A decade of burgeoning scholarship on cyberconflict has only reinforced our belief that cyberwar is not a useful concept. IR scholars now have more nuanced insight into the limitations of cyber coercion and can draw on more evidence about the muted severity of cyberconflict. But the basic fact remains: cyberspace

---

[16] Valeriano and Maness 2014; Lindsay 2014; Valeriano, Jensen, and Maness 2018; Kreps and Schneider 2019; Kostyuk and Zhukov 2019; Kaminska 2021.

[17] Rid and McBurney 2012; Lindsay 2013; Slayton 2017; Smeets 2022.

[18] Dunn Cavelty 2008; Hansen and Nissenbaum 2009; Lawson 2013; Dunn Cavelty 2013; Stevens 2016; Gomez and Whyte 2021.

[19] Rid 2013; Gartzke and Lindsay 2015; Rovner 2019a; Gioe, Goodman, and Stevens 2020; Rid 2020; Lindsay 2021.

[20] Work 2020; Egloff 2021; Deibert 2022.

[21] Warner 2019; Harknett and Smeets 2022; Fischerkeller, Goldman, and Harknett 2022. For contrasting views in the intelligence contest debate see Chesney and Smeets 2023.

[22] King, Pan, and Roberts 2013; Deibert 2018; Egloff and Shires 2021; Slupska and Tanczer 2021; Shandler, Gross, and Canetti 2023.

[23] Lindsay 2017.

is ill-suited to perform the classic functions of war. The next chapter will go beyond this negative view and provide a more positive account of why cyberspace is very well suited to perform intelligence and counterintelligence functions. But before we explain why cyberspace is so useful for strategies of deception, we want to first explain why cyberspace is less useful for strategies of coercion and deterrence.

In the classic cyberwar narrative, the potency and scope of the cyberthreat is unprecedented. According to a former member of the Russian Duma, "In the very near future, many conflicts will not take place on the open field of battle, but rather in spaces on the internet, fought with the aid of information soldiers.... [A] small force of hackers is stronger than the multi-thousand force of the current armed forces."[24] Apparently this future is still not so near, as Russia did not trust its war in Ukraine to its hackers alone. Indeed, cyberwar was largely missing in action in the opening phase of the war in Ukraine.[25]

William Lynn III, writing as the US Deputy Secretary of Defense during the first administration of President Barack Obama to announce the creation of US Cyber Command in 2010, argued that cyber warfare was a substantial, imminent threat.[26] Cyberthreat actors, in this view, are virtually unlimited by financial or physical constraints, and their attacks on commercial industry will seriously damage consumer trust in the internet. The US military has become increasingly dependent on new technology to dominate modern battlefields, paradoxically rendering itself more vulnerable and prone to ever-increasing incidences of potentially crippling cyberattacks.[27] Such threats require the United States to treat cyberspace as an operational domain like land, sea, air, and space where it can practice deterrence and defense.

The focus of the cyberwar narrative is typically on the potential for harm, rather than on the motives and operational logic of perpetrators. Yet if ambiguity and anonymity are a challenge for the ostensible targets of cyberattacks, they are also awkward problems for initiators. Most terrorists spend as much time marketing their exploits as they do fighting, bombing, assassinating, and so on. Where anonymity protects an aggressor from retribution, it also dilutes credit for the deed. Vandals often "tag" their handiwork—creating an identity where none need exist—precisely because real anonymity means not receiving credit for one's handiwork. Internet

---

[24] Cited by Korns and Kastenberg 2008.   [25] Kostyuk and Gartzke 2022b.
[26] Lynn 2010.   [27] J. Schneider 2019b.

114   ELEMENTS OF DETERRENCE

vandals also brand their exploits, presumably because they wish to receive credit for their exploits, even at some risk to their anonymity. Cyberattacks from unidentified sources, furthermore, not only do not give the target a way to retaliate, but they also fail to provide the target with the means to acquiesce. As with the use of identifying symbols in war, it is in an attacker's interest to "brand" its actions to most effectively elicit concessions from a target.

Espionage, covert operations, and certain kinds of political theft or murder function most effectively when the perpetrators are unknown, or indeed when the operations themselves remain undisclosed. Strategic or tactical advantage can also stem from anonymity and surprise in terrestrial military missions, though nations and groups often sacrifice surprise and advertise their role in contests to extract concessions or tacit or formal admission of defeat. How does one surrender to no one in particular? The advantage of anonymity will persist for peripheral forms of warfare on the internet, just as it has played a role in terrestrial competition and conflict. Most forms of political conflict, however, encourage disclosing an initiator's identity. Coercion requires attribution. Ransomware and kidnapping are exceptions that prove the rule: an anonymous demand for payment in exchange for the return of precious data or family members still requires some signal of credibility or reputation on the part of the ransoming actor.[28]

In an influential article from the early IR debate about cyberwar, Thomas Rid argues that cyberwar is not really war because it fails to conform to Clausewitzian definitions of conflict.[29] One of Rid's chief points is that cyber operations are not sufficiently violent or lethal to be considered war. As such, "cyberwar" is a misnomer. Yet, the focus on violence alone tells us little about whether or not cyberconflict might supplant military violence as the ultimate arbiter of international politics. Cyberwar does not necessarily need to be war to make war obsolete. Instead, it must fulfill the existing functions of terrestrial warfare if it is to rival the utility of existing forms of conflict. As we shall see, however, the internet is extremely unlikely to substitute for, or serve as an alternative to, conventional warfare.

Technical Possibility vs. Political Probability

It is far from clear that the internet is transformational in military terms, let alone revolutionary. Lacking information about whether developments are

[28] Jun 2021.   [29] Rid 2012. This argument is expanded in Rid 2013.

radical or merely incremental, it may make sense to adopt a few guidelines that will help to determine whether there is cause for panic. Imagining what others could do to injure each of us can quickly descend into paranoia.

Even in the safest of societies, individuals, groups, and entire communities are subject to an enormous variety of potential hazards. Few of these possibilities are ever exercised, or experienced, with any regularity. The physical world hosts a multitude of venues for extremely unlikely accident or disease. A small number of people prefer to remain indoors rather than risk being struck by lightning or struck down by botulism. Still, individuals with these concerns may merit more attention from psychiatric professionals than from military planners. Being vulnerable will be novel to no one living in our modern, highly integrated world. Indeed, the capacity to hurt is so ubiquitous in densely populated portions of the globe that blood would coat the streets if it were not true that relatively little relationship exists between the capacity to attack and the actual prospect that one will be invaded, assaulted, or otherwise harmed.[30]

Just about anything is possible. Someone may have put poison in your corn flakes at breakfast. Terrorists may have singled you out for vengeance, or you might just become one of the unlucky few who are in the wrong place at the wrong time when a train derails. When a commuter steps outside to start her car or to catch the bus, it is impossible to be certain that no truck will jump the curb and that every asteroid will remain in its usual orbit. And yet, despite endless potential for injury or death, few of us have chosen to harden our living rooms against cruise missile attack or immersed ourselves in real-time plots from NASA charting the trajectories of space detritus. In dealing with known unknowns, we became comfortable with not being protected. California homeowners typically do not carry earthquake insurance, for example, even though "the big one" is almost certainly an eventuality.

We run risks against technically possible but unlikely threats, in part, because security is expensive. Being indemnified against unlikely events may literally not be worth the effort. One could buy that bulletproof vest listed on Ebay, but then how often would it prove fashionable at the office or in the classroom? Unlike possibilities, the probabilities of esoteric catastrophe are by their nature minute. Unlikely events are unlikely, and so most of us go

---

[30] Contemporary fascination with vampires (in popular culture) and zombies (among academics) illustrates the basic point. Aggression becomes endemic if harm has an intrinsic payoff (e.g., human beings are food). Vampires and zombies threaten not just individuals but the whole of civil society, because interdependence and specialization require that vulnerability not equal insecurity.

116   ELEMENTS OF DETERRENCE

about our business, paying little attention to the potential menace from the skies or, for that matter, from one another.

Governments face similar realities. Many threats are conceivable, but relatively few actually materialize. A holistic approach to security involves assessing risks, and then allocating finite resources to address tractable threats, making the largest improvements in protection or, conversely, the greatest increases in influence. The distinction between security and influence is often missed or misrepresented in policy debates. For example, although discussions often center on protecting the American people (security), much of US defense spending actually purchases discretion abroad (influence). Every dollar spent on national defense must be taken from objectives such as improving education, building or repairing infrastructure, or paying down the debt. Only extremely affluent (or extremely paranoid) populations will be willing pay the price of pursuing protection from the most exotic hazards. More to the point, protection is inevitably incomplete, and comes with its own consequences, including other forms of insecurity. The risk of attack is never zero, given that a potent defense or deterrent endangers the security of others.[31]

If violence is ecological, why do human beings not live in consummate fear? Most of us are safe because the multitudes capable of causing us harm have little interest in doing so. Humanity is protected by an invisible shell of indifference or inefficaciousness. The stranger coming toward you on a busy city street could swing out his arm, catching you under the chin. He could be carrying an Uzi, which in a fit of rage will leave you and other passersby on the pavement in a pool of intermingling fluids. Yet, you are probably not going to die a violent death in the next minute, or at any other time. The potential for violence is both ubiquitous and seldom realized because striking out, though often possible, does little to benefit the violator. The use of force is costly, risky, and mostly unproductive. When we learn of violence, our natural inclination is to ask "why?" Like a police detective, we seek a motive. Violence requires a cause. When on occasion we cannot identify the logic behind a perpetrator's choice of a target, the experience is remarkable, and puzzling.

The mere capacity to harm is simply not a very good predictor of aggression. Causing harm is usually inconvenient, unnecessary, or pointless for

---

[31] On the security dilemma, see Jervis 1978.

potential perpetrators. For most actors, most of the time, and for most instruments of potential harm, attacking other actors serves no purpose.

The internet, of course, makes it possible to interact with people just about anywhere on the globe. The supply of targets for cyber acts of aggression is huge relative to the supply of perpetrators of physical violence. Viewed in this way, it is remarkable that cyberspace has yet to become exclusively the domain of fraud, identity theft, and other acts of predation. Yet, if the internet makes it easy to reach out and touch others, it in no way makes those contacts profound. Predation continues unabated on the World Wide Web, but if it is easy to reach us, contact is all the more superficial. There are crimes on the internet, to be sure, but it is unclear whether these have increased the overall crime rate. Organizations and certainly countries have personnel and property that can be targeted with cyberattacks. But the question we must is not just *what* could happen, but *why* individuals, groups, or nations might attack.

Nations and organizations can be attacked through the internet, just as they have long been attacked in physical space. The ease with which such attacks can be perpetrated is a much-discussed phenomenon. Physical space has always been an important barrier to conflict.[32] Even today, the single best predictor of interstate conflict is contiguity.[33] Lowering the cost to transmit an attack, however, only increases its appeal if the attack is also capable of achieving the actor's desired ends. Beyond numbers and anonymity, the main factor protecting individuals is even more potent for institutions. How force will produce the desired change is often unclear. Cyberattacks can be appealing as political acts only to the degree that they affect the decisions that organizations and sovereigns make.

Cyberwar vs. the Logic of War

We will make the working assumption that understanding how cyberwar can (and cannot) influence politics must be embedded within a more general understanding how *any* form of military violence acts on politics. States and non-state actors make war to further their interests when incompatibilities exist between those interests, and when alternative methods of conflict resolution are deemed ineffective or inefficient. Although many conflicts

---

[32] Boulding 1978; Buhaug and Gleditsch 2006.   [33] Hensel 2000; Senese 2005.

118   ELEMENTS OF DETERRENCE

are conceivable, most potential wars do not occur because the participants recognize that threats or uses of force are futile. Only some acts of violence are likely to achieve the objectives for which political actors strive. If the futility of violence discourages the bulk of terrestrial conflict, it is an even larger concern in cyberwar.

The modern theory of war, which is grounded in rational bargaining models as discussed in Chapter 2, provides two basic mechanisms for the expression of political interests through physical violence. First, force can be used to conquer, directly imposing one's will by capturing and controlling inhabitants or resources contained in a given physical space. Second, force can be used to punish or compel, indirectly affecting the state of the world by harming an enemy to make it do something that the enemy would not do otherwise, or alternately discouraging change by raising the price of aggression. Just about everyone from parents to police and prime ministers seems to grasp the intuition behind creating consequences to modify behavior. Put simply, force can be used for "winning" or "warning." The operational ability to conquer or compel can, in turn, be used to achieve these objectives through actual force (offense or defense), overt threats (deterrence or compellence), or the shadow of war (e.g., diplomacy).[34]

During the Cold War, the two superpowers could easily have annihilated each other, along with much of the rest of the world. Yet, vast nuclear arsenals remained dormant and the prospect of mutual harm even led to the peculiar stability of mutual assured destruction. Again, the mere capacity to hurt tells us relatively little about the actual advent of violence, even though the potential in the Cold War was extraordinary and mutual assured destruction, by its nature, meant that devastation could not be prevented. Indeed, it was this mutual vulnerability that many credit with the Cold War remaining cold.

The threat or exercise of physical conquest can be effective provided the perpetrator finds it worthwhile to engage in the costliest form of politics. Here, again, the simple ability to act aggressively is not itself sufficient to predict aggression. The United States could probably conquer Canada if it chose to, and yet Canada remains free and independent. Most states, groups, and individuals persist in peace because they can conceive of no benefit from force, even if violence, and victory, are feasible.

The mere ability to cause harm over the internet does not suffice to predict that cyberwar will substitute for terrestrial conflict, or even that it will be

---

[34] Blainey 1973; Fearon 1995.

CYBERSPACE IS UNSUITABLE FOR THE STRATEGY OF WAR 119

an important independent domain for the future of warfare. Force, or the threat of force, is useful as punishment to the degree that the harm imposed is substantial and durable. Damage that can be quickly or easily undone will not do much to deter or compel, but it will alert an enemy to vulnerabilities in its defenses, and certainly also antagonizes an opponent, increasing the risk of counterattack, and general hostility.

Beyond questions of means and motive, two basic features make cyber warfare different from other types of conflict: (1) temporary effects and (2) secret means. We will consider these in turn.

Temporary Effects

The assumption among many cyber pessimists that the potential for creating harm is sufficient to make cyberspace a suitable substitute for, or indeed alternative to, terrestrial conflict is incorrect. Shutting down power grids, closing airports, or derailing communication could be tremendously costly, but much damage of this type can fixed quickly and at comparatively modest investment of tangible resources. Regardless, damage of this type is sunk. Losses experienced over a given time interval cannot be recovered whatever one's reactions and so should not have much direct impact on subsequent policy behavior.

Harm inflicted over the internet or any other medium will matter politically when it alters the subsequent balance of power, or when it indicates enemy capabilities that must be taken into account in future plans. Because cyberwar does not involve bombing cities or devastating armored columns, most damage inflicted will have a short-term impact on its targets.[35]

Temporary damage can be useful if compromising or incapacitating networks give an enemy valuable tactical, or even strategic, advantages. An opponent that cannot shoot, move, resupply, or communicate will be easier to defeat. To accomplish politically meaningful objectives, cyberattacks must contribute to other aspects of a more conventional war effort. And to affect the long-term balance of power, for instance, cyberwar must be joined to other, more traditional, forms of war. Nonetheless, the advantaged party

---

[35] In the 1970s, the so-called neutron bomb promised high casualties with minimal damage to physical structures. It might be tempting to think of cyberweapons as anti-neutron bombs, because they damage infrastructure, leaving people largely unharmed. Yet, this is also a key limitation of cyberwar, as damage is temporary and far from complete.

120   ELEMENTS OF DETERRENCE

must still act through some medium of combat to seize the initiative. Notions that cyberattacks will themselves prove pivotal in future war are reminiscent of World War I artillery barrages that cleared enemy trenches but still required the infantry and other arms to achieve a breakout.

Whether an actor can benefit from cyberwar depends almost entirely on whether the actor is able to combine a cyberattack with some other method—typically kinetic warfare—that can convert temporary advantages achieved over the internet into a lasting effect. In the parlance of war, cyber-attacks produce a "soft kill" that is valuable only when attackers prosecute follow-on attacks with traditional military force or permanently weaken an enemy in some other way.[36]

The notion of a devastating surprise attack is a particularly baroque aspect of cyberwar paranoia, and is certainly frightening to the degree that such scenarios are accurate. Yet, the idea of a surprise internet attack is misleading and relies on a fundamental misconception of the role of internet-based aggression. Modern warfare seldom allows any one element of combat to prove pivotal. Instead, it is the ability to combine elements into a complex whole that increasingly distinguishes the adept utilization of force.[37]

The archetype of modern, combined arms warfare is the blitzkrieg, where the lethality and decisiveness of conventional military violence is enhanced by actions designed to disrupt the enemy's military and civilian infrastruc-ture. An important element of blitzkrieg was the use of terror weapons, such as the Ju 87 "Stuka" dive bomber, to sow panic, causing enemy populations to flood roads and railways, thereby crippling transportation grids needed by the defense. Yet, fear is temporary and in the absence of substance, subsides. The Stukas were effective only as long as Germany held other military advantages over its enemies. Similarly, unless Stuka attacks were accompa-nied by a ground attack or an invasion, their role as terror weapons was largely redundant. Stukas contributed little to Germany's effort to subdue Great Britain, for example. Stuka units experienced heavy casualties when engaged against a sophisticated air defense and were eventually removed from service in the Battle of Britain. The hubris of Luftwaffe Commander in Chief Herman Göring in promising victory while exploiting just one

---

[36] Non-lethal weapons have similar functionality. Immobilizing an enemy with sticky foam works until it does not; non-lethal weapons are effective only if they are followed up by other actions, such as physical restraint or redeployment of forces away from the immediate area.

[37] S. Biddle 2004.

domain (the air) was precisely that he exaggerated the effectiveness of a new technology in isolation from other elements of an integrated offense.

There is no reason to believe that cyberwar will be any more useful as an isolated instrument of coercive foreign policy. An attack that causes temporary harm will inevitably be followed by countermeasures and heightened vigilance, as happened, for example, in Estonia in the aftermath of the 2007 attacks. For cyber aggression to have lasting effects, a virtual attack must be combined with physical intervention. Knocking out communications or power infrastructure could cause tremendous disruption, but the ability to quickly recover from such attacks implies that the consequences for the balance of national power would be negligible. The need to follow virtual force with physical force to achieve lasting political consequences suggests that the application of cyber warfare independent of conventional forms of warfare will be of tertiary importance in strategic and grand strategic terms. If one cannot foresee circumstances where the terrestrial use of force is plausible independent of cyberwar, then cyberwar is also unlikely to constitute a fundamental threat.

Secret Capabilities

The second problematic element of the logic of cyberwar has to do with influence. Rather than attacking directly, an actor might attempt to use the potential to inflict harm (i.e., cyber deterrence or compellence). The ability to shut down the US energy grid, say, might be used to compel US officials to refrain from aggressive policies or actions, or to persuade the United States to make diplomatic concessions. Yet, the problem with the standard deterrence or compellence logic in the context of potential cyberattacks, is that revealing a given set of cyber capabilities tends to degrade their usefulness. Deterrence and compellence are therefore marginal as "pure" actions in cyberspace. Indeed, concerns that nations will not be able to deter cyber aggression amount to recognition that neither will cyberthreats prove very effective as threats or inducements.

Imagine for a moment that a foreign power has hacked into the communications systems of the United States or another major Western power. Imagine further that this foreign power can disable cellular phone systems or military radio networks more or less at will. The foreign power could threaten its target with this capability, but obviously the leadership of the

122 ELEMENTS OF DETERRENCE

target state must be skeptical of such a threat, because the foreign power could easily be bluffing. The foreign power could make vague threats to protect the details of its secret capability, but this will be indistinguishable from vague threats to exaggerate a nonexistent capability. The target needs some convincing proof of its vulnerability to exploitation if it is going to change its behavior to avoid it, but such evidence would, in turn, jeopardize the potency or effectiveness of the cyberattack. Communicating a specific threat will indeed change target behavior, but in precisely the wrong ways, resulting in the loss of the threat.

Contrast this with the revelation in the 1990s that the United States had developed radar-evading "stealth" aircraft. Knowledge by foreign powers that a confrontation with the United States would necessarily involve the risk of attack by stealthy fighters and bombers in no significant way lessened the military effectiveness of these weapons systems, given that countermeasures to stealth technology have been slow to develop. Stealth technology thus serves as an excellent deterrent/compellent, because it can be used to coerce an opponent without sacrificing much of its military value. It is only feasible to reveal sensitive capabilities for signaling purposes if the signaler can substitute redundant capability or the adversary has limited ability to counter it.[38]

In contrast, Japan kept even its own diplomats in the dark about its plans to attack US bases in the Philippines and Hawaii because it could not share information about its intentions with US officials without fatally weakening the effectiveness of such a plan.[39] Whether force is threatened or carried out depends on whether threats can be made without degrading the instruments of military advantage. Revelation of the ability to harm can prove sufficiently compelling to cause a target to make concessions or to alter the target's behavior. Conversely, if threatening an enemy makes an eventual attack less effective, then the temptation may be to strike rather than threaten. Deterrent/compellent threats work best when they are tied to capabilities that are not much affected by enemy knowledge of the capabilities, whereas the opposite is true for capabilities that are compromised by the revelation of forces, technologies, or attack plans.

Cyber operations are generally not robust to revelation. Upon learning enough detail for the threat to be credible, the target will take steps to mitigate, patch, or other wise close its vulnerabilities or adopt some other

---

[38] B. Green and Long 2020.   [39] Slantchev 2010; Gartzke 2006.

countermeasures. This is clearly a problem for "zero day" vulnerabilities, which are known to the attacker but not the vendor or target and are thus particularly vulnerable. In practice, most cyber operations rely on known exploits and social engineering techniques, in the same way that most human intelligence operations rely on known tradecraft such as brush passes and dead drops. But even when the tradecraft in general is known, the target does not know that some combination of techniques is being mobilized against it in any specific situation. If it does, then it can use known counters against known techniques. The perishable nature of capabilities in cyber warfare mean that advantages generally yield time-bound deterrent or compellent threats,[40] and thus create little in the way of leverage for states that have, or plan to invest in, cyber warfare assets.

We refer to this general problem as the *cyber commitment problem*. Thomas Schelling famously describes coercion as the art of publicly committing oneself to punish the target if it does not comply with demands (and to refrain from punishment when it does comply).[41] Any failure to publicly commit will be a problem for credible coercion. Actors who want to "keep their options open" are not making a commitment, as anyone hoping for a marriage proposal knows well. Secret capabilities, moreover, much like secret liaisons, enable unscrupulous actors to escape their commitments. Cyber warfare provides an actor with useful capabilities for secretly shaping the balance of power or stealing information, but not for publicly committing to act in predictable ways in specific circumstances. The whole point of cyberwar is to be unpredictable. We will return to further implications of the cyber commitment problem in Chapter 7.

Many of the most potent offensive cyber advantages are thus "use and lose" capabilities. Revealing the capacity to harm via the internet typically also means tipping the enemy off to vulnerabilities that can be remedied or compensated for, while inflicting harm seldom has a durable effect on the balance of power. "Use and lose" capabilities cannot compel or deter, because convincing evidence of the capacity to inflict harm is itself useful information in nullifying the threat. If instead cyberwar is waged rather than threatened, then the temporary nature of cyber harm dictates that an enemy follow internet attacks with more kinetic action. Otherwise, the use of cyber force is punitive, even provocative. As such, cyberwar remains adjunct to

---

[40] Smeets 2017.   [41] Schelling 1966.

124   ELEMENTS OF DETERRENCE

terrestrial force unless some way is found for cyberattacks to permanently alter the balance of power.

The Myth of Cyber Pearl Harbor

Popular analogies to a cyber Pearl Harbor may be apt, but almost certainly not for the reasons contemplated by politicians like Secretary Panetta or futurists like Winn Schwartau. The situation in 1941 serves as a basis for comparison and a point of departure in examining cyberwar.[42] To understand why a cyber Pearl Harbor is not as threatening as it sounds, it helps to review what the air raids on December 7, 1941, were meant to accomplish and what they achieved.

The air strikes against US military installations in Hawaii and in the Philippines were an important tactical and even strategic victory for Japan. Yet, as is now widely understood, they were a prodigious failure in grand strategic terms, setting up a nearly inexorable path to Japanese defeat and surrender. Officials on both sides recognized this almost immediately. The 1970 film *Tora! Tora! Tora!* thus dramatized Admiral Isoroku Yamamoto offering stark commentary: "I fear all we have done is to awaken a sleeping giant and fill him with a terrible resolve." No event in the twentieth century has done more to realign US public opinion than the Japanese surprise attack on Pearl Harbor, which mobilized the nation psychologically for entry into World War II.

The Japanese decision to strike at the United States was a calculated gamble, balancing the imperatives of seasonal weather patterns and the impending decline in power projection capabilities for the resource-starved empire with the realization that much was being staked on a complex plan linking the conquest of oil fields in Southeast Asia with a temporary shift in the regional balance of power in the Pacific.[43] With almost no indigenous sources of iron, rubber, and especially oil, Japan was dependent on foreign-held reserves to feed its factories and allow it to sustain its occupation of Manchuria and war in China. The US embargo led Japanese officials to consider stark alternatives. Either Japan must relent and withdraw its forces from East Asia, or it would have to capture oil-rich regions in the south. This, in turn, put Japan in direct conflict with the United States.

---

[42] Lawson and Middleton 2019.   [43] Morton 2000.

The Japanese plan was to blunt US naval and military capabilities temporarily, long enough to prepare a defense in depth in the Western Pacific and present the United States with a fait accompli, one that would compel the Americans to submit to a compromise, a negotiated settlement that would end the war. The Japanese plan was a closely guarded secret. Japan kept even its own diplomats in the dark about its plans to attack US bases in the Philippines and Hawaii because it could not share information about its intentions with US officials without fatally weakening the effectiveness of such a plan.[44] Whether force is threatened or carried out depends on whether threats can be made without degrading the instruments of military advantage. If threatening an enemy makes an eventual attack less effective, then the temptation may be to strike rather than threaten.

The prospect of an impending and significant relative decline in power and optimism about the potential benefits of a military victory giving Japan a temporary advantage in the region were critical elements of Japan's decision to go to war. Importantly, Japan underestimated the psychological impact that the Pearl Harbor raid would have in mobilizing US public opinion. Japanese commanders also overestimated the damage they could inflict on US forces. The surprise assault famously failed to catch the US aircraft carriers in port. It was this inability to impair US naval airpower that seemed to vex Yamamoto the most.[45] Even allowing for Japanese optimism and error, however, Tokyo was reluctant to act against the United States prior to the end of 1940, when events in Europe laid bare Dutch holdings in Asia and dramatically weakened the ability of British forces in the region to resist.

Tactical or strategic surprise is useful as a temporary force multiplier; an attack such as that on US and European forces in December 1941 could shift the balance of power in Japan's favor for a time, but the real value of a surprise attack is what it allows an assailant to accomplish subsequently. An attacker can exploit the effect of surprise to prepare a more effective defense or, alternately, to prosecute additional offensive action against the target or others. By itself, a surprise attack has limited utility, precisely because surprise fades in time.

---

[44] On the strategic incentives to feign weakness see Slantchev 2010.

[45] Evidence of this is reflected in subsequent efforts by the Imperial Japanese Navy to realize the original strategic objective to destroy US aircraft carriers. Midway, in particular, was an elaborate trap, masterminded by Yamamoto, to locate and destroy the remaining US carrier force in the Pacific. See Prange 1983; Fuchida 1986; Parshall and Tully 2007; Symonds 2011.

126 ELEMENTS OF DETERRENCE

Japanese war planners anticipated the temporal nature of advantages gleaned from the Pearl Harbor attack. It was hoped that Japan would be able to secure critical resources in the south, fortify its gains in depth, and wait out the American onslaught. As Louis Morton writes, "Japan planned to fight a war of limited objectives and, having gained what it wanted, expected to negotiate for a favorable settlement."[46] At no time did Japan seriously consider unlimited war with the United States. Indeed, Japanese planners recognized the impossibility of directly defeating the United States. Admiral Yamamoto's other famous quotation, which was meant as an ironic reference to total war with the United States, claims, "To make victory certain, we would have to march into Washington and dictate the terms of peace in the White House."[47] Japanese forces later landed in the Aleutian Islands as a feint to distract attention from Midway, and Japanese submarines shelled a few isolated coastal communities, but there were never any serious plans to carry the war to the continental United States.

Now suppose that Japanese officials recognized from the outset that they would not be able to target the US carriers or other US military assets with permanent destruction. Instead, imagine (not very plausibly) that Japanese dive bombers and torpedo planes were fitted with special "delay bombs" that, unlike delay fuses, would simply disable a ship for hours, days, or possibly weeks, rather than permanently, or at least for months or years. Faced with this altered reality, Japanese officials and military planners would have been forced to contemplate a very different war, one that they would almost certainly have preferred *not* to initiate. In effect, Japan would have had to choose to precipitate total war, as surprise attacks themselves would not do much to diminish or delay a military response from the United States. The only value one could anticipate from a surprise attack, then, would be if it facilitated a follow-up invasion of the United States mainland, which Japan had no interest or ability to carry out. Yet this is the basic conceit of cyberwar. Because cyberattacks involve temporary "soft kills" of a target's military capabilities and civilian infrastructure, the point of the attack is largely nullified if an attacker cannot reasonably be expected to accompany internet aggression with terrestrial strikes designed to make permanent short-term damage to a target's security capabilities. In short, the attacker must have strong motives to initiate the major war that cyberwar merely enables.

---

[46] Morton 2000.
[47] The private letter from Yamamoto to Ryoichi Sasakawa is quoted in Prange 1981.

No foreign military force is capable of subduing the United States, now or in the foreseeable future, with or without the assistance of a phenomenally successful coordinated cyberattack.[48] If cyberwar is unlikely to allow a foreign power to permanently overtake US or allied capabilities, and if temporary damage is useful only when practiced in conjunction with more conventional military operations, then an opponent must plan and evaluate its use of cyberwar in relation to its complementarity to terrestrial combat, not as a fully independent method of force. If instead a cyberattack is carried out in which conventional force is either ineffective or not contemplated, then an attack of this kind fails to serve a meaningful strategic purpose, degrading neither the target's longer-term capabilities nor its resolve.

There will not be a cyber Pearl Harbor, except possibly when and if a foreign power has decided it can stand toe-to-toe with conventional US military power. This, admittedly, may be cold comfort when contemplating future conflict scenarios with China.

Cyberwar and the Balance of Power

The connection between internet aggression and traditional forms of military force imply an unfashionable prediction: cyberwar should be particularly appealing to *capable states confronting weaker opponents*. The popular assumption that cyberwar is an asymmetric weapon of the weak may be precisely backwards. Cyberwar is a weapon of strong actors who both have the requisite ability to plan sensitive technical operations and a military insurance policy to deter retaliation if the operation is compromised. Rather than threatening to overturn the existing world order, cyberwar may perpetuate or even increase current military inequality.

If cyberwar functions not as an independent domain, but as part of broader, coordinated military action, then the conventional military balance is the best indicator of where the most important threats exist in cyberspace. Thus, unless someone believes that economically and militarily advanced nations are in danger of physical attack from a foreign power, the threat of cyberattack cannot be treated as particularly serious in political terms. Most experts view an attack that subdues US military capabilities and subjects the US mainland to a foreign power as remote, even fanciful. To the degree that

---

[48] Some creative novels attempt to envision such a scenario, e.g., Ackerman and Stavridis 2021. This is fiction for a reason.

128 ELEMENTS OF DETERRENCE

powerful states are immune to conventional attack, cyberattacks are at most a nuisance and not a fundamental threat.

Cyberwar is not a revolution in military affairs in strategic (military) terms, nor is cyberwar likely to prove revolutionary in political terms, by threatening or transforming existing global or regional power structures. In this sense, cyberwar appears to provide a marginal reinforcement of the advantages of states that already possess significant conventional military advantages. The need to prosecute cyberattacks with more kinetic forms of force, and the perishability of cyber capabilities in the face of revelation, mean that nations with capable militaries are best equipped to exploit the type of damage that cyberwar inflicts, even as they are better able to credibly threaten cyberattacks and to "reveal and replace" a given capability to target an enemy's cyber vulnerabilities. This new mode of warfare, oft represented rhetorically as a serious threat to technologically advanced states, may pose greater grand-strategic challenges to the technologically backward or weak (which has troubling implications in the context of authoritarian repression of civil society).

This is not to say that the sophisticated computer-dependent nations of the West are immune to attack. The United States and other advanced countries are certainly vulnerable to internet aggression. We would all like to live in a world where no one could harm us even if someone fervently wished to do so. To the degree that this is not possible, a useful second best is for others to possess disincentives to inflict injury or death, even if they still can. An inability to exploit temporary opportunities created by cyberwar is a disincentive to conduct concerted internet attacks. In contrast, powerful nations continue to possess both the ability and interest in intervening in the developing world, even if they do so only episodically.

An open question exists in any crisis about how far competitors are willing to escalate, but an ability to counter cyberattack with other, more kinetic forms of military violence serves alternately to deter or to facilitate the use of cyber capabilities, giving those nations with terrestrial military power yet another option that, even if available to their opponents, may prove extraordinarily dangerous to practice. As we see today with US drone attacks and Special Operations raids on foreign sovereign territory, the power to do much more ensures that an opponent maintains a level of discretion in its response to provocation. Few can doubt the reaction of the United States, for example, if Pakistan attempted to mount a commando raid in suburban Baltimore, say, to assassinate a local resident. Nations that can physically

CYBERSPACE IS UNSUITABLE FOR THE STRATEGY OF WAR   129

punish others for transgressions in any domain, electronic or otherwise, are better able to operate in all domains. Once one distinguishes between simple vulnerability and actual threats, terrestrial capabilities become pivotal in determining who exercises cyberwar.

Even if cyberattacks are available to weaker actors, their effectiveness will be stymied where these actors lack the ability to prosecute advantages generated by cyberwar, and where weakness in more traditional modes of diplomatic, economic, or military competition ensure that these actors are exposed to countermeasures. The resort to cyberwar by terrorists, for instance, would not imply that cyberterrorism is an important threat to national security, any more than the appeal of the lottery to the poor or financially desperate implies that the odds of winning are somehow inversely tied to income. Cyberterrorism may be relatively ineffective, not unlike terrorism generally. Terrorism is a marginal business, not because airports and diplomats are too well protected or because guns or bombs are hard to come by, but because most people, even if very unhappy, do not believe that bombings, hijackings, or assassinations will effect positive change. Incapable of achieving their objectives directly, terrorists seek to mobilize fear and to cause overreaction, mechanisms that mobilize the targets of terror to assist in accomplishing terrorist objectives.

Terrorism is a form of compellence via punishment.[49] Lacking the ability to impose their will on others, terrorists rely on the prospect of harm to influence the behavior of a government or its population. Indeed, because their ability to harm is limited, the terrorist relies on psychology (fear and uncertainty) to multiply the impact of relatively finite capabilities on opposing populations or states. How will internet attacks be able to instill the quality of fear needed to magnify the terrorist's actions? No one will be happy when the power goes out or when one's bank account is locked down, but attacks of this type evoke feelings of anger, frustration, even resignation, but not terror. Terrorism relies on generating a particularly visceral emotion—putting the "terror" in terrorism. The old journalistic adage that "if it bleeds, it leads" implies the need for graphic trauma and lurid imagery. While there is some experimental evidence that destructive or lethal cyberattacks produce immediate psychological effects on par with kinetic attacks,[50] cyberwar may not be the best instrument for fomenting terror. The very attributes that make cyberwar appealing in abstract—the

---

[49] Kydd and Walter 2006.   [50] Shandler, Gross, and Canetti 2023.

130   ELEMENTS OF DETERRENCE

sanitary nature of interaction, the lack of exposure to direct harm, and strikes from remote locations—all conspire to make cyberterrorism less terrifying. White collar terrorists are probably not going to prove any more effective, and perhaps less, at shaping hearts and minds than the traditional model.

This is even more the case with long-duration, low-intensity conflicts that are a key component of both non-Western attempts at resistance and Western efforts to protect the status quo international order. From the perspective of the insurgent, asymmetric warfare has never been about attacking to diminish an opponent's strengths, but is instead focused on max-imizing one's own strengths by targeting enemy weaknesses.[51] Insurgency seeks out kinetic close physical combat where sophisticated technology is least effective. Damaging the technology may draw an enemy into direct contact, but it might also cause that enemy to withdraw and reschedule operations. Mobility, to the extent it is possible, is prized on every battlefield for this very reason. Internet attacks in the midst of close contact make little sense as it is here that the comparative advantage of cyberwar (distance and asymmetry) is least potent. The ability of internet-dependent armies to perform in superior ways on existing dimensions means that this is generally a process of leveling, not revolution.

Advanced industrialized countries, despite their dependence on high technology, will find that they can better exercise cyberwar as a political tool. Attacks against prosperous Western powers, if well publicized and the source of considerable anxiety, will turn out to be less consequential. While other technological or social changes may well transform contemporary hierarchies, cyberwar will most likely function more to perpetuate than to undermine existing inequalities of influence.

Bringing War on the Internet Back Down to Earth

In war, ideally, tactics must serve strategy and strategy must serve grand strategy. The tendency among pundits of cyberwar has been to focus on tac-tics and possibly strategy, showing that harm is possible without explaining how the harm generated is likely to shape the product of political differences. In the absence of a convincing logic of consequences, the internet becomes an adjunct domain to more traditional forms of warfare. Cyber warfare

---

[51] Mao 1961.

CYBERSPACE IS UNSUITABLE FOR THE STRATEGY OF WAR   131

is an evolving dimension of military operations and a source of concern, but in grand strategic terms, it remains a minor feature. A failure to focus on grand strategy is an all-too-familiar by-product of the war on terror, where the objectives have been to harm and not be harmed, rather than to effect meaningful changes to the disposition of world affairs. A grand strategic rationale becomes even more important in an era of great power competition.

Nations or groups that strike through the internet in minor ways may be ubiquitous. Those that threaten critical national security goals, however, will be rare if for no other reason than that "cyberwar" is not really war in any politically meaningful sense. By far the most compelling scenario for the transformation of political conflict through the internet, and the one that makes new headlines daily, involves the use of the internet for espionage, to include covert influence and disinformation campaigns. Spies can now work from home collecting information without leaving the territory of the sponsoring state, making it difficult to deter or capture cyber spies. At the same time, the detection of cyber spies may be easier than conventional espionage, given computer forensics and the trail left when remotely accessing digital files. We will turn to the dynamics of deception in the next chapter.

One implication of more extensive espionage, furthermore, may be that nations may find it increasingly difficult to convince themselves that their secrets are safe, even if they are. Secrets are not sacrosanct when every network is exposed to infiltration, making it more difficult to carry out the conspiracies so often associated with coercive politics. War will still occur, as Russia's 2022 invasion of Ukraine and Hamas's 2023 assault on Israel makes apparent, but surprise in war will be increasingly difficult to achieve, in turn reducing at least part of the motivation behind the use of coercive military force. With fewer surprises, identifying bargains that competitors prefer to the costly exercise of war should become easier. We will explore this argument in detail in Chapter 10, on the pacifying effect of satellite reconnaissance.

Indeed, it would be absurd to infer that there is no role for the internet in twenty-first-century conflict. The internet will be affected by conflict, just as is the case with every other domain in which individuals, groups, and societies interact. Indeed, the real message for soldiers and politicians is that cyberwar involves a broadening of the dimensions of warfare to include more extensive intelligence contests as well, rather than a narrowing of future conflict due to some digial weapon of mass disruption. In most cases,

132 ELEMENTS OF DETERRENCE

the internet is not a viable, free-standing venue for the pursuit of national interests. It would be surprising if a country intent on attacking another nation failed to carry out preparatory or simultaneous attacks of target's defense capabilities via the internet. It would be even more surprising if an aggressor successfully substituted cyberwar for conventional, tangible forms of conflict by only using the internet.

The threat of cyberwar cannot deter or compel particularly effectively, except possibly within a short window prior to remediation, and only with the consequence that an attacker will have forfeited the potential to exploit a given set of vulnerabilities in the future. While the threat of cyberattack will be unlikely to deter anything, it is possible that other forms of threats may deter some forms of cyber warfare, so long as those other threats do not suffer the same liabilities of transient effects and secret capabilities. In Chapter 13 on gray-zone warfare, we will present a model that shows how credible deterrence may discourage war at one level but encourage low-level cyberattacks and other forms of hassling.[52]

We expect that cyber warfare will most often occur as an adjunct to conventional warfare, or as a stop-gap and largely symbolic effort to express dissatisfaction with a foreign opponent. It is best to discuss cyberwar in these contexts, not as an independent, or even alternative form of conflict, but as an extension of the logic already expressed in combined arms battle. In most cases, cyber operations cannot achieve the objectives that have historically prompted nations to commit to tangible military violence. Thus "cyberwar" is only warfare within the context of traditional forms of military threats or combined arms operations. By itself, cyberwar can achieve neither conquest nor, in most cases, coercion. Russian military planners obviously understood this in preparing to invade Georgia and Ukraine, not just with an army of hackers, but with tanks. Indeed, the tanks appear to have done far more for Georgian and Ukrainian insecurity than anything accomplished by information soldiers. In this regard, the next Pearl Harbor is much more likely to occur in Hawaii than in cyberspace.

[52] See also Schram 2021.

6

Cyberspace Is Ideal for the Strategy of Deception

The previous chapter argued that large-scale disruptive cyberattack ("cyber-war") is a poor tool of coercion. Secret sources and methods cannot be revealed in advance for signaling. More ambiguous threats to use secret exploits and vulnerabilities are indistinguishable from bluffing, and thus more likely to be disregarded. We describe this as the "cyber commitment problem" because a coercer cannot publicly commit to follow through on a threat based on private information; revelations of capabilities that are specific enough to be credible are also specific enough to patch or counter. Commitment involves *limiting* options, after all, but cyber tools are attractive precisely because they offer *more* options. This suggests that cyber operations may be more useful for shaping the balance of power than signaling for about capabilities and interests.[1]

Another problem is that many cyber options rely on perishable vulnerabilities and create reversible or temporary effects.[2] If coercion depends on "the power to hurt," then cyberattacks that do not hurt very much, or for very long, do not provide much coercive leverage. Even worse, the targets of ambiguous cyberattacks might interpret the attacker's choice as an aversion to war, especially if more damaging capabilities are left on the shelf. Interestingly, however, this same feature may be useful at the low end, insofar as "doing something" that doesn't really hurt much can enable an actor to telegraph its interest in avoiding escalation or save face while backing down from a crisis.[3]

By contrast, even temporary cyber effects may be potentially useful in a war-fighting scenario, assuming they can by coordinated with other miltiary operations. Much as electronic warfare can suppress enemy radars during an airstrike, cyberattacks might create windows of opportunity for employing smaller conventional units with more precision or less risk.[4] The hope here is that cyber provides an *efficiency* advantages that also improves military

---

[1] Buchanan 2020; Lonergan and Lonergan 2023.   [2] Smeets 2017.
[3] Carson 2016; Lonergan and Lonergan 2022.   [4] E.g., Fulghum 2007.

Elements of Deterrence: Strategy, Technology, and Complexity in Global Politics. Erik Gartzke and Jon R. Lindsay, Oxford University Press. © Oxford University Press 2024. DOI: 10.1093/oso/9780197754443.003.0006

effectiveness, assuming that everything goes as planned. If the cyber operation fizzles or is compromised in the process, however, then military forces dependent on them could find themselves dangerously exposed. This cyber warfare scenario thus depends on both successful surprise attack and skillful integration with traditional military forces–no mean feat. As such, cyber warfare appears to be more useful as a complement for "winning" rather than a substitute for "warning." Military cyber complements will appear more attractive, furthermore, as military forces become more dependent on networks to do anything at all,[5] assuming that actors have calculated that there is something worth fighting about in the first place.

To use the terms from Chapter 4, the cyber domain is ill-suited for strategies of coercion, and only marginally useful for strategies of *defense* when combined with other military domains. Cyber operations thus provide little political influence, and they can only augment the use of military power with careful coordination in the right context.[6] These negative arguments clarify what cyber operations can *not* accomplish. But what *can* they do?

In this chapter we move beyond negative correctives by describing positive ways in which strategic actors pursue and protect their interests in cyberspace. We argue that cyber operations exemplify the distinct strategy of *deception*. Deception differs in interesting ways from defense and coercion. Rather than prioritizing power (defense or "winning"), influence (coercion or "warning"), or stability (disarmament or "working" together), the motivating goal of pure deception ("watching" for opportunity) is *efficiency*. Efficiency means doing more with less. Strategies of intelligence, subversion, disinformation, covert action, and other forms secret statecraft enable leaders to pursue their interests at reduced cost and risk relative to openly threatening or fighting. The strategy of deception is ancient, of course, but it has become newly relevant in the information age.

Claims about the revolutionary potential of cyberspace are misleading in many ways, but they do highlight the appeal of lowering the costs of aggression. If offense is relatively easier than defense in cyberspace, then

---

[5] J. Schneider 2019b.

[6] We use the word "influence" in Schelling's sense to describe efforts to shape behavior by manipulating incentives, typically through costly signaling. Confusingly, the word "influence" has also been used to describe forms of online deception, which is the opposite of costly signaling. Insofar as disinformation, marketing, information operations (IO), and psychological warfare rely on misdirection or lying, we would describe them as forms of deception, motivated by a desire to reduce costs as described below, rather than influence. Marketing is most influential when it promotes a product that customers actually want to buy again and again, rather than attempting to trick them into buying something they do not want to buy. For a critique of IO along these lines see C. Jackson 2016.

weaker ("asymmetric") actors can afford potent capabilities and employ them with less risk. One reason why this conventional wisdom is misleading, however, is that deception can be used not only to attack networks but also to protect them. Any attacker who relies on secrecy to reduce the risks of exposure and the costs of conflict must also worry about being detected or manipulated by network defenders. A spy must play defense if a counterspy plays offense. Offense and defense are so interwoven in cyberspace that it is hard to interpret the claim that offense dominates defense. Alternatively, if we understand cyberconflict as a contest in deception, rather than a new form of warfare, then the actors' relative willingness and ability to engage in deception in any given situation becomes more relevant. The offense-defense balance, therefore, is not determined by the systemic nature of cyberspace, but rather the contingent circumstances of deception and counterdeception for any given pair (dyad) of actors.

The information revolution has dramatically increased the potential for deception. The telegraph, introduced well over a century ago, enabled instantaneous communication at distance, but it also invited interlopers to tap the wire. Pioneers of military and diplomatic telecommunications quickly realized that there was no way to prevent an enemy from listening in or from jamming or incapacitating their circuits. By the traditional standards of defense, which focused on preventing access by intruders, telegraphy and telephony were a disaster. Fortunately, the inherent vulnerability of electrical communication to eavesdropping or attack was not in itself an insurmountable problem and could even be used to advantage by the target. If one could not prevent the adversary from intercepting or disrupting communications, one could still manipulate what was learned and thus what conclusions opponents were likely to draw from available information. Disguise, disinformation, and other counterintelligence practices came into their own as security strategies in the telecommunications era, albeit in shadowy agencies with limited or supporting roles within a broader military and diplomatic apparatus. With the further innovation of pervasive digital networks, however, deception became more democratized. Commercial companies and non-state hacker groups have become intelligence targets and collectors as well.

This chapter proceeds in four parts. We begin with a critique of the conventional wisdom about offense dominance in cyberspace, highlighting the absence of empirical activity to substantiate this belief. We also review recent scholarship on political secrecy that encourages a reconeptualization of cyberconflict as intelligence rather than war. Second, we explore the

136 ELEMENTS OF DETERRENCE

fundamental potential for deception inherent in information technology. Third, we explain how deception can also improve network protection, as computer security engineers have already recognized. Fourth and finally, we bring our argument full circle by pointing out that the salience of cyber deception actually calls into question categorical assumptions about offense dominance, along with other implications for the conceptualization and practice of strategic affairs.

The Hacker Will Always Get Through?

Actors seeking to maintain the status quo against revisionist aggression are generally believed to possess three well-known options: disarmament, deterrence, and defense.[7] Cyberspace seems like a disaster for all of them. Because hackers exploit the same open channels used for legitimate commerce and communication, then offensive techniques cannot simply be prevented or proscribed. Cyber disarmament treaties, moreover, are less than credible because the same actors that are threatened by cyberattacks in one moment will benefit from exploitation and espionage in the next.[8] If hackers can evade detection and disregard threats of retaliation, then deterrence loses its credibility.[9] Deterrence requires a return address.[10] If hacking tools are cheap and easy to use, while security engineering and incident response are hard to coordinate, then attackers have the advantage.[11] Cyber defense must succeed everywhere and every time, but attackers need only succeed once to compromise a system.[12]

These problems are often summarized with the claim that cyberspace is intrinsically offense-dominant. In an article written to announce the creation of US Cyber Command, for example, the Deputy Secretary of Defense asserts that "the offense has the upper hand." Unplugging (disarmament) is not an option because "Information technology enables almost everything the US

---

[7] Disarmament is a variant of the general strategy of accommodation, which prioritizes stability and prosperity over power and influence, as discussed in Chapter 3. The word "disarmament" is perhaps more intuitive in this context as we consider the futility of banning cyber "weapons," which are not weapons at all.

[8] Goldsmith 2011.

[9] Libicki 2009; National Research Council 2010; Solomon 2011; J. Schneider 2019a.

[10] This is misleading. Indiscriminate retaliation is always possible, but rarely popular or cost-effective.

[11] D. Peterson 2013; Saltzman 2013.

[12] This cyber shibboleth is also misleading. Attackers need to succeed continuously if they want to maintain persistent access in sensitive systems, while a single mistake might compromise the entire operation.

CYBERSPACE IS IDEAL FOR THE STRATEGY OF DECEPTION   137

military does." Traditional deterrence models of assured retaliation falter because "it is difficult and time consuming to identify an attack's perpetrator. Whereas a missile comes with a return address, a computer virus generally does not." Defense, finally, cannot be assured because "programmers will find vulnerabilities and overcome security measures put in place to prevent intrusions. Thus a fortress mentality will not work. The United States cannot retreat behind a Maginot Line of firewalls or it will risk being overrun." Therefore, he concludes, "Deterrence will necessarily be based more on denying any benefit to attackers than on imposing costs through retaliation. The challenge is to make the defenses effective enough to deny an adversary the benefit of an attack despite the strength of offensive tools in cyberspace."[13] In other words, all strategies are problematic in cyberspace, but defensive denial seems like the least bad option.

Categorical offense dominance would seem to have revolutionary consequences. Societal dependence on digital networks and cheap hacking tools enable nation-states and non-state hacking groups to reach across borders, without warning, to access vital data and critical infrastructure. Once inside an organization's network, hackers can pilfer valuable secrets or disable control systems. Because they are anonymous or operating remotely from a protected jurisdiction, they are immune from punishment. These implications are often assumed to be determined by the nature of digital technology. Lucas Kello, for instance, highlights the "unpredictability and undetectability" of attacks on machines that are "inherently manipulable by pernicious code" together with the "fragmentation of defense" across private sector firms and "supply chain risks" of "off-the-shelf and offshore manufacturers" which combine to "underscore the immense disadvantages of defense against cyberattack."[14]

According to a prominent IR literature known as "offense-defense theory," high levels of offense dominance should be tied to a heightened risk of war.[15] If geographic, technological, or organizational conditions make conquest feasible at low cost or risk in comparison with the effort of defending the same objectives, then aggressors should be more tempted to launch an attack, the security dilemma and negative spirals should be more intense, and greater uncertainty and secrecy should lead to more miscalculation and war.[16] The futility of disarmament, defense, and deterrence in cyberspace should make cyberwar the sum of all fears.

[13] Lynn 2010.   [14] Kello 2013.
[15] Quester 1977; Jervis 1978; Glaser and Kaufmann 1998; Van Evera 1999; Adams 2003.
[16] Glaser 2010.

The Empirical Anomaly

That cyberwar remains unusual is puzzling in light of the widely held belief that offense is easier than defense in cyberspace. The most alarming scenarios of a "digital Pearl Harbor" or "cyber 9/11" have yet to materialize, despite decades of warning.[17] Actual patterns of cyberconflict are more restrained and regionalized than disruptive and global.[18] Computer espionage and cybercrime thrive, to be sure, yet skeptics describe US losses as "a rounding error" in a fifteen trillion dollar economy.[19] The absence of evidence in the study of cyberwar is a source both of relief and concern. In the previous chapter, we highlighted a general lack of motive for catastrophic cyber-physical damage, but there are additional complementary explanations for the absence of evidence of cyberwar. In addition to a lack of will to employ cyberwar at the strategic level, there may also be unappreciated difficulties in employing cyberwar at the operational level.

Scholars have challenged the assumption that cyberspace is offense-dominant.[20] Serious cyberattacks against complicated infrastructure require not only technical exploit tools but also intelligence preparation, test and evaluation infrastructure, planning capacity, technical expertise, and administrative support.[21] One possibility, therefore, is that offensive advantage is relative rather than absolute. Perhaps there is a lot of low-cost hacktivism, website defacement, cybercrime, and low-grade espionage because offense is easy against targets that are not strategically significant. But perhaps defense dominates for more harmful or complicated forms of attack.[22] If the costs of offense cyber operations vary relative to the complexity and risk of the target, then it would be a categorical error to mistake the frequency of irritating activity in cyberspace for a more general tendency toward offense dominance across the entire cyber domain.

Alternately, offense-defense theory itself might be incoherent or in need of repair, as some of its critics have argued.[23] Offense and defense may vary across levels of analysis. An armored counterattack can support the defense

---

[17] Lawson 2013; Dunn Cavelty 2013; Lawson and Middleton 2019.

[18] Valeriano and Maness 2014; Lindsay 2014; Valeriano, Jensen, and Maness 2018; Kostyuk and Zhukov 2019; Kaminska 2021.

[19] The quote is from Lewis 2013.   [20] Lieber 2014; Slayton 2017; Garfinkel and Dafoe 2019.

[21] Denning 2009; Lindsay 2013; Slayton 2017; Smeets 2022.

[22] Lindsay 2015; Lindsay and Gartzke 2018.

[23] Lynn-Jones 1995; Davis et al. 1998; Glaser and Kaufmann 1998; Lieber 2000; Gortzak, Haftel, and Sweeney 2005.

even as defensive entrenchment can support an advance. Technologies may be difficult to categorize as functionally offensive or defensive. Military effectiveness, after all, relies on a number of factors other than technology including geography, labor, culture, bureaucracy, doctrine, and even diplomacy. These factors might not be the same in every engagement; it would be surprising if they were. Blitzkrieg was more than just a collection of tanks, radios, and aircraft, but also a doctrine of combined arms warfare. It only worked, moreover, when the enemy failed to defend in depth. This implies that the offense-defense balance is not a systemic feature of technology, but rather a dyadic feature of the balance of material and non-material capabilities.[24]

Evaluating the general validity of offense-defense theory is beyond the scope of this chapter. Instead, we simply call into question the more contained consensus that offense has the advantage in cyberspace. Many of the assertions delineated above about disarming, deterring, and defending in cyberspace can be or have been criticized or modified. Still, our recitation represents a consensus in the cybersecurity discourse, and so confusion remains where we began. If all three strategies are ineffective against a determined attacker, then why is it that cyberspace has not already erupted into unremitting warfare? Something additional is needed to account for the apparent robustness and stability of the internet. The troika of protective strategies assumes that no alternative exists that could either prove more effective or that would combine with deterrence and defense to form a more comprehensive, and potent, strategy set.

The Rise of Secret Statecraft

In fact, there is a fourth option, one that has been overlooked conceptually, if not operationally. Indeed, the internet's potential for deception is a common yet unarticulated assumption in arguments about offense dominance. The ubiquity of information technology provides attackers with opportunities to hide anywhere and abuse any data, potentially, so deception undermines disarmament. Anonymous hackers have many ways to disguise their identity, avoid detection, and mislead investigators, so deceptive attackers flout the credibility or effectiveness of deterrent threats. Infrastructural complexity

---

[24] S. Biddle 2001.

140 ELEMENTS OF DETERRENCE

enables attackers to exploit hidden vulnerabilities and gullible users, so deception facilitates the penetration of network defenses. Deception not only enables cyberattack, it is necessary: attackers who fail to be deceptive will find that the vulnerabilities on which they depend will readily be patched and access vectors will be closed.[25]

IR scholars long treated deception as a minor adjunct to the more central concerns of war, peace, and deterrence.[26] This does not mean that deception was absent. On the contrary, a major preoccupation of classic deterrence theory, as we have seen in Chapters 2 and 3, is distinguishing bluffing and cheap talk from credible threats.[27] The modern bargaining model of war, furthermore, implies that political actors have incentives to misrepresent their capabilities or interests.[28] In this sense, deception has long been central to strategic theory, but it has tended to be treated as a degenerate mode of bargaining. The unique strategic dynamics of deception were largely ignored in analytical studies, much as deterrence received little intellectual attention prior to the nuclear age.

But times have changed. In recent years there has been a burgeoning of IR scholarship on political secrecy,[29] intelligence,[30] and covert action.[31] It is perhaps no coincidence that the field of IR is experiencing a renaissance in deception theory at the same time as governments have become more concerned about digital espionage, disinformation campaigns, and cybersecurity. The advent and growth of the internet has increased interest in deception theory, just as deterrence theory came into its own in the nuclear era.

IR scholarship on cybersecurity, accordingly, has moved on from its initial critique of "cyberwar," as discussed in Chapter 5. Instead, scholars have increasingly turned to intelligence history for inspiration and precedents.[32] Scholars are now more likely to describe cyberconflict as an "intelligence contest" rather than a new form of warfare.[33] This framing remains

---

[25] This inverts reasoning by Van Evera 1998 that offense dominance makes secrecy more likely, which in turn raises the potential for war (his "Explanation H"). In cyberspace, secrecy comes first as enhanced potential for deception is required to change the offense-defense balance. However, as we argue, secrecy need not make conflict more likely if it also improves protection or makes attackers paranoid.

[26] Andrew 2004.　　[27] Schelling 1966; Jervis 1970.　　[28] Fearon 1995; Slantchev 2010.

[29] Yarhi-Milo 2013; Carnegie 2021.

[30] Zegart 2000; Mahnken 2002; Rovner 2011; Yarhi-Milo 2014; Matovski 2020.

[31] Downes and Lilley 2010; Carson and Yarhi-Milo 2017; O'Rourke 2018a; Poznansky 2020.

[32] Rid 2020; Egloff 2021; Maschmeyer 2021.

[33] Rid 2013; Gartzke and Lindsay 2015; Rovner 2019a; Lindsay 2021.

contested, however.[34] The most prominent alternative to date is the notion of "persistent engagement," which features prominently in the emerging doctrinal worldview of US Cyber Command.[35] This view holds that cyberspace creates a new structural condition of "constant contact" that enables, or requires, ongoing competition for advantage beneath the threshold of armed conflict. Rather than attempt to deter cyberattacks or defend the network perimeter, US Cyber Command should instead "defend forward" to disrupt and impose costs on cyber adversaries closer to home.

But this may be a distinction without a difference. Proponents describe "persistent engagement" as an explicit alternative to deterrence and warfare, and they acknowledge that secrecy is a key feature of the cyber domain. We suspect that "persistent engagement" simply reflects a rediscovery of the distinct strategy of deception at an historical moment when the classic practices of intelligence have become more salient, and more complex.[36] Intelligence and deception have always depended on common systems of trust and knowledge, as we discuss below, but the increasing complexity and pervasiveness of collective information systems creates more opportunities to practice them, by government and non-government actors alike. This is less a matter of "constant contact" (a military metaphor) than "common protocol" (an institutional metaphor) used in bad faith. It is hardly surprising that a "network-centric" force like the US military would become interested in the increased intelligence opportunities (and counterintelligence liabilities) posed by more sophisticated information systems. There are legitimate doctrinal and institutional questions about whether the activities of a military unit like Cyber Command should be properly described as "operations" or "intelligence" within the context of legal authorities specified in Title 10 or 50 of the US Code, to say nothing of the parochial organizational cultures of military units and intelligence agencies.[37] But from our perspective as international relations scholars rather than defense policy makers, this is more of a question of institutional implementation than of strategic logic, which is our focus here. Deception by any other name is still deception, even if practiced at unprecedented scale.

---

[34] Warner 2019; Harknett and Smeets 2022; Fischerkeller, Goldman, and Harknett 2022; Chesney and Smeets 2023.

[35] Schneider, Goldman, and Warner 2020.

[36] In much the same way, "integrated deterrence" is a rediscovery of the fact that deterrence has always had many moving parts.

[37] Boeke and Broeders 2018; S. White 2019.

142   ELEMENTS OF DETERRENCE

Cyber operations further exemplify interactions between the strategy of deception and other strategies. The same factors that are believed to weaken disarmament, deterrence, and defense also make it possible to lay traps for an adversary online. In cyberspace, deception is the most promising form of defense, just as counterintelligence provides the best security against espionage. This perspective leads us to question the widely accepted conventional wisdom that cyberspace is offense-dominant. Relative advantages for offense and defense are not determined by categorical features or attributes of digital networks. The offense-defense balance in any given cyberconflict, rather, is the result of relative organizational capacity for employing deception, integrating it with broader strategic initiatives, and identifying and redirecting deception. Cyberattackers rely on deception for almost any offensive advantage, but they do not have a monopoly on duplicity and stealth. The strategy of deception is not without risk for an attacker who cannot abide compromise. Because successful deception is highly sensitive to context, the offense-defense balance is highly contextual, too.

The Technology of Deception

We argue that conflict in cyberspace exemplifies the strategy of deception, which is logically distinct from the competitive strategies of deterrence (coercion) and defense (warfare), as well as from the more cooperative strategy of accommodation (disarmament). The distinct strategy of deception has always been a part of politics, but it has become more salient because of increasing digital connectivity. As humanity develops better systems of information to coordinate economic and social relationships, those same systems offer new ways and means for abusing trust and manipulating information. Building on decades of innovation in information technology, nearly every industrial and governmental sector has experienced tremendous productivity gains.[38] But if cyberspace is attractive because it enables innovation, then aggression is just one more creative application of the same productive assets.[39] As discussed further in Chapter 13, economic globalization is the wellspring of cyberconflict. Digital networks connect sovereign governments, bureaucratic agencies, individual citizens, private

---

[38] Beniger 1986; Yates 1989; Cortada 2008; Brynjolfsson and Saunders 2010; Starrs 2013.
[39] Zittrain 2006.

companies, international organizations, and almost everything else, because political-economic actors believe there is some value in mutual connection. In much the same way as large-scale capacities for violence gave rise to large-scale patterns of deterrence, therefore, large-scale networks of globalized prosperity give rise to large-scale patterns of deception. Another way to put this is that strategies of deception are parasitic on strategies of accommodation.

Deception of any kind manipulates information, so it should not be surprising that technology designed to processes information also serves to facilitate deception. As information technology has grown more sophisticated, from the dawn of writing to the internet, the opportunities for fraudulence and trickery have also grown more sophisticated. Gullible people and vulnerable machines are now linked together at an unprecedented scale. The risk of deception cannot be engineered away, moreover, because user trust and software abstraction are required in order for computer applications to be useful at all. Signals designed to certify the authenticity of communications simply become additional tools for deception.[40] Hackers send phishing e-mails to employees impersonating coworkers or give away infected thumb drives at trade shows in order to gain a foothold on protected networks.[41] Stuxnet combined a number of ruses, including antivirus detection and evasion, self-hiding propagation controls, and an innovative "man in the middle" attack that created bogus feedback for human operators in order to mask the alarms caused by malfunctioning centrifuges. Similarly, the National Security Agency has employed various tools to "muddle the signals of the cell phones and laptop computers that insurgents used to coordinate their strikes" and "to deceive the enemy with false information, in some cases leading fighters into an ambush prepared by US troops."[42] The internet's capacity for deception is what facilitates its malicious use: no deception, no cyberattacks.

Deception in Theory
Deception is a strategy designed to improve one's prospects in competition. It can deny a benefit to an opponent, as when camouflage, concealment,

---

[40] Edelman 2011 find that websites certified as safe from malware by a well-known commercial authority end up being twice as likely to be untrustworthy as uncertified sites.

[41] For a review of social engineering tradecraft for exploiting reason and emotion online, see RSA 2011.

[42] These incidents refer to activity during the 2007 surge in Iraq, according to Nakashima 2012.

144   ELEMENTS OF DETERRENCE

and decoys obstruct target discrimination. It can impose a positive cost, as when a sabotage or ambush create casualties or a scam defrauds money. It may do both simultaneously, for example, by distracting the adversary from attacking vulnerable assets while covering a surprise attack in return. Many deceptive ploys, especially in espionage tradecraft, seek to create the illusion of cooperation so that the vicitm does not even realize that it is being targeted until it is too late. Even if the target suspects a stratagem, it can still suffer costs in terms of the time and resources expended on operational security.

The two basic tactics of deception are dissimulation and simulation, or hiding what is there and showing what is not, respectively.[43] Sometimes the word "deception" is used only for active simulations that create bogus information to trick an opponent into taking the bait. We use the concept more broadly to cover also passive dissimulations, such as concealment and camouflage, that hide information opponents would want to know (and might act on if they were aware). Deception masks or adds information in order to influence indirectly the beliefs that affect an opponent's voluntary decisions to act.[44] This indirection is both a strength and a weakness for deception because the target acts willingly, but the desired action is not assured. Seduction promises influence with little overt conflict, but the deceiver has to be talented, careful, and lucky to translate a manipulative approach into a decision by the target to be manipulated in the desired way.

Not surprisingly, much of the literature on deception focuses on the psychological aspects of credibility. The deceiver acts to manipulate beliefs to produce false inferences.[45] Because deception provides competitive advantages, there are also advantages in being able to detect deceit. Primates have evolved sophisticated lie detection heuristics as well as hard-to-fake gestures like the facial expressions of love and shame.[46] A deceiver therefore must also work within the constraints of counter-deception efforts as well.[47] Intelligence scholar Richards J. Heuer, Jr., points out that "deception seldom fails when it exploits a target's preconceptions. The target's tendency to assimilate discrepant information to existing mental sets generally negates the risks to deception posed by security leaks and uncontrolled channels of

---

[43] Whaley 1982; J. Bell 2003.

[44] Here, "information" is used in the colloquial sense of suppressing or providing material signals. From an information theoretic standpoint, both dissimulation and simulation remove information, the former by suppressing signals and the latter by injecting noise. The net effect is that the target's decisions are governed by chance (or bias) rather than transmitted constraint. In either case, the deceiver creates degrees of freedom in the world that the target believes are constrained.

[45] Ettinger and Jehiel 2010.   [46] Seabright 2010.   [47] Johnson et al. 2001.

information."[48] Indeed, street conmen succeed in parting the gullible from their money even when hindsight reveals plenty of obvious clues—the wrong part of town, hurried actions, pressure tactics, conspiratorial bystanders, stereotypical frauds, etc. Deceiving entire organizations is perhaps more difficult because there are more individuals who might smell a rat, but deception can still work by exploiting organizational routines, corporate culture, and groupthink.

Evolution has equipped the human mind with sophisticated lie detection capacities that work by subconscious correlation of many different behavioral signals. Trust among primates is never absolute, of course, and suspicion may persist across interactions. But human face-to-face interaction is guided by subtle, high-context counter-deception heuristics.

By contrast, computers are blind to subtleties that they have not been explicitly programmed to recognize (or trained in the case of machine learning). Deterministic algorithms either accept forged credentials completely or reject them completely, oblivious to social cues or shades of agreement. Cyber deception, once accepted, is often total. Security engineers attempt to implement detailed error-checking routines or multifactor authentication schemes in an effort to increase context and error-correction channels. But these are still just deterministic routines that encode simplified assumptions about the world. Software works by simplifying the world into models that can be readily computed and compactly encoded for transmission. For example, the original internet protocols were designed to treat all machines the same and to accept connection requests from anyone on the network. That same openness later facilitated DDoS attacks that flood servers with more connection requests than they can handle.

Abstraction is the essence of software development. The magic trick of computer programming, so to speak, is to coordinate the internal state of a machine—its data and computational processes—with the external state of the world. Good programmers anticipate all of the ways in which this coordination might fail, and they write rules to handle those cases. If software is well engineered, then we don't notice all this complexity. Our digital map remains coordinated with the real roads. But when the software abstraction does not fit with the state of the real world, we experience glitches, bugs,

---

[48] Heuer 1981. By the same token, schemes that seek to alter or implant, rather than reinforce, existing beliefs are much less likely to prove successful. Heuer provides a helpful summary table of cognitive biases and their implications for deception (ibid., pp. 315–16).

or other errors. The software developer has failed to foresee some run-time use case. Now the map does not match the territory. Bugs cause machines to behave in unexpected ways, violating the intentions and expectations of developers and users. Bugs become vulnerabilities, then, when mismatches between programmer intentions and computational implementations create exploitable opportunities for an adversary.[49]

In this sense, malware engineering is a form of deception that exploits intentionally. The software designer and the user make inappropriate assumptions about what the machine can do and is doing. Thus they enable their own exploitation. Malware may cause legitimate code to run in unexpected circumstances, for instance by escalating privileges to the administrator level to install a rootkit. Or it may cause an application to fail to execute in expected circumstances, as when antivirus software fails to detect and block a new malware signature. As in any form of deception, the intentions of the target are the ultimate vulnerability. The only difference here is that human intentions are intermediated by deterministic machines. Good intentions today lead to malicious exploitation tomorrow. Even "noisy" forms of cyberattack, like distributed denial of service (DDoS) attacks, can be understood as deception in this sense because the attacker takes advantage of existing functionality for a new purpose. The server that accepts connections by default and stops working when there are too many requests is still following the logic of deception, insofar as the server engineer has voluntarily but unwittingly enabled the attack. This approach differs fundamentally from brute force.

Once software engineers understand the mismatch between encoded simplifications and dangerous variation in the world, they strive to correct the discrepancies through debugging and patching, but these merely change rather than eliminate the simplification. It is simply not feasible to review every line of code and configuration setting, most of which are compiled or set prior to runtime by a multitude of vendors, developers, and network operators. For example, the Heartbleed bug discovered in April 2014 in the OpenSSL protocol was caused by a failure to check the length of a string in a ping request, an alarming flaw that was hiding for years in plain sight in openly available code developed and reviewed by security engineers. The less technically savvy majority utilize their e-mail and smart phones even less critically.

---

[49] This possibility is analyzed as a "weird machine" by Bratus et al. 2011; Dullien 2020.

When machines mediate human interactions with one another, they strip out much of the context that we primates rely on to establish gradations of trust. Low-context interaction is thought to account for some cyber bullying, offensive e-mails, and other bad internet behavior.[50] The lack of context also makes it harder to detect "social engineering" scams to persuade users to part with passwords or provide access to machines. Deception is well suited to the cyber domain, a global network of gullible minds and deterministic machines. Widespread faith in the internet facilitates productive economic and administrative exchange, but by the same token, it is easy for a deceiver to exploit this trust. Even the savviest users must assume that their software and hardware will perform as expected.[51] The upshot is that the targets for the classic techniques of dissimulation or simulation now include not only the cognitive constructs of human beings but also the deterministic rules that software developers have programmed.

Deception in Practice
Deception is obviously not a new strategy. Ancient strategists like Sun Tzu and Kautilya wrote extensively about the role of subterfuge and espionage in politics.[52] Virgil's *Aeneid* offers an example of deception so famous that it has become a byword for modern malware. Greek warriors intent on subduing Troy, but unable to scale its strong walls, instead resorted to the ruse of a hollow wooden tribute stuffed with Hellenic commandos. Rather than persuading Trojans to draw massive equine contraptions through unassailable city gates, cyber deception capitalizes on the fact that targets are already credulously immersed in a digitized infrastructure.

The Second World War featured several famous plots in this spirit. The Allies concocted a bogus First US Army Group for Nazi eyes and ears, complete with phony radio traffic and inflatable tanks, all "commanded" by the flamboyant General George S. Patton. The ruse deceived Hitler and other German officials about the true location of the Allied invasion, leading to controversy and indecision in the Nazi high command and lessening resistance at the critical moment, on the beaches in Normandy. Allied diversions included other imaginative schemes like Operation Mincemeat, which planted false war plans on the corpse of a British soldier, and the Double

---

[50] Levmore and Nussbaum 2011.   [51] K. Thompson 1984.
[52] Warner 2006; Shoham and Liebig 2016.

148   ELEMENTS OF DETERRENCE

Cross System, which fed disinformation through compromised Abwehr agent networks in Britain and Europe.[53]

Tactical surprise, stealthy movement, and feints are commonplace, even essential, in modern joint and combined arms warfare, distracting the defender long enough for the main blow to be dealt from another axis (and potentially undermining peace negotiations). Tactical surprise consists of keeping an enemy guessing about how and where a state already at war will employ its military means; strategic surprise involves creating uncertainty about whether and why a state might decide to employ them.[54] Most of this activity, however, plays a distinctly secondary role in war and cannot be divorced from the material ability to inflict damage or to recover from deception gone awry. Deception is thus generally treated as a useful adjunct to the larger thrust of military operations.[55]

The picture changes dramatically when shifting from military to intelligence operations. Indeed, most of the WWII-era British schemes mentioned above involved military intelligence operations targeting (pathologically credulous) Abwehr collection efforts. Deception is essential for secret intelligence, not just an optional adjunct. Secret agents use disguises and hidden signals to avoid detection by an enemy that can easily overpower the spy's meager self-defenses. If the covert sources or methods used to create a surreptitious information channel are compromised, then the target of collection can rapidly change its behavior or otherwise move secrets out of the spy's material reach. Alternatively, the target may elect to add another layer of deception by spying on the spy. The compromised agent can then be used as a conduit for disinformation.[56] The spy or her handlers, in turn, may suspect deception even when there is none and thus cast doubt on information the spy obtains. Paranoid suspicion alone degrades the effectiveness of intelligence collection. Disinformation operations can likewise be used against normal information channels for psychological "warfare." The intelligence-counterintelligence contest is a funhouse of mirrors with endless possibilities for case officers and novelists alike.[57]

One legendary CIA counterintelligence operation during the Cold War targeted Soviet industrial espionage against the West. Through a "massive,

[53] Howard 1994.   [54] Leventoglu and Slantchev 2007.
[55] Some countries emphasize it more than others. The concept of *maskirovka* figures prominently in Russian writings on cyberstrategy, as discussed by Adamsky 2019.
[56] Sun Tzu thus distinguishes between "converted spies" (doubled enemy agents) and "doomed spies" (enemy agents subject to disinformation).
[57] Herman 1996.

CYBERSPACE IS IDEAL FOR THE STRATEGY OF DECEPTION   149

well-organized campaign" known as "Line X," the Soviets recovered "thousands of pieces of Western equipment and many tens of thousands of unclassified, classified, and proprietary documents" that benefited "virtually every Soviet military research project."[58] Once alerted to the danger by a defector, the CIA arranged for altered versions of Western technology and scientific disinformation to make their way into Line X. According to one participant, "The program had great success, and it was never detected."[59] Thomas Reed reports that faulty control software installed on a Trans-Siberian oil pipeline caused "the most monumental non-nuclear explosion and fire ever seen from space."[60] This episode is frequently cited in the cybersecurity literature to illustrate the dangerous potential of attacks on material supply chains. What authors usually fail to emphasize, however, is that the Line X sabotage is also an example of successful defensive deception. Although Soviet agents were able to use offensive deception to penetrate Western industry, their actions also made them vulnerable to defensive deception conducted by CIA counterintelligence. Students of cyberstrategy would do well to bear in mind that the Line X caper teaches lessons about both supply-chain insecurity and the disruptive potential of counterintelligence.

Intelligence agents must take elaborate precautions to avoid compromise. Going to a café is easy, to take an everyday example, but meeting a source at a café who intends to betray her country, while surrounded by cameras and incognito policemen in the same café, is far riskier. Any logistical friction can be the undoing deception, especially if someone is assiduously searching for clues. Intelligence collectors have been able to significantly reduce personal risk through arms-length technical collection since the dawn of the telegraph.[61] Targets of intelligence collection attempted to protect their communications from eavesdroppers by shielding cables, guarding exchanges, encoding transmissions, and criminalizing unauthorized wiretaps, yet signal collectors in remote locations were hard to catch, and the benefits of spying were too great. Something additional was needed, not to prevent or inhibit an opponent from interdicting correspondence,

---

[58] Agency 1985.   [59] Weiss 1996.

[60] T. Reed 2004. Some dispute this account for want of corroborating evidence; see, for example, Rid 2012.

[61] In Alexandre Dumas' novel *The Count of Monte Cristo*, the protagonist wipes out an enemy's fortune by sending false information over the semaphore network. The Chappe semaphore preceded electric telegraphy by five decades.

150 ELEMENTS OF DETERRENCE

but to make the effort futile. The resulting intelligence-counterintelligence contest gave rise to the modern profession of high-tech espionage.[62]

In an intensively technological world there are more things to know, more ways to know them, and more ways to manipulate knowledge. The computer network exploitation we experience today is only the most recent manifestation of a long evolution of technological espionage.[63] The attacker can also be fooled, however, and the defender can also deceive. Offensive advantage in cyberspace depends critically on the potential for deception, but defenders also gain advantages from deception, provided opportunities are identified and exploited effectively. This ability to deceive, and to coordinate deception with complex strategies and operations, is analytically distinct from a systemic offense (or defense) dominance rooted in technology.

Deceiving the Deceivers

Most of the literature on deception focuses on feints and ruses exercised by an aggressor to distract a victim.[64] Yet these techniques can also be implemented by defenders to foil an attack. Modern soldiers wear camouflage whether they are taking or holding territory. Insurgents likewise dress like civilians both to avoid targeting by security forces and to infiltrate them. As a protective strategy, deception differs from disarmament, deterrence, and defense in how it achieves protection. Whereas those three strategies seek to prevent, discourage, or block the attack, deception relies on the attacker getting through, at least to a degree. Both simulation and dissimulation rely on the dupe deciding to take the bait and walk voluntarily into the trap. Deception then uses an attacker's own capabilities and energy against him, by first inviting, and then redirecting, the attacker's self-interested action. Deception may even benefit the deceiver. In a meaningful sense, the deceived attacker can also be blamed for the punishment it receives.

Cyberattacks can be foiled, not just by blocking intrusions, but by converting the penetration into something that confuses or harms the attacker. If it is easy for a covert attacker to gain access to an organization's data, it is

---

[62] Headrick 1991; Hugill 1999; Nickles 2003; Gioe, Goodman, and Stevens 2020.

[63] Technology augmented age-old human intelligence (HUMINT) with new disciplines, like communication signals (SIGINT), photographic imagery (IMINT), underwater acoustics (ACINT), and assorted measures and signatures (MASINT).

[64] Whaley 1982; Ferris 1989; Godson and Wirtz 2000; Grazioli and Jarvenpaa 2003.

also easy for a network protector to feed the attacker data that are useless, misleading, or harmful. The cyberattacker can become confused, even if the defender does not do anything deliberately, simply because of the inherent complexity and uncertainty involved in accessing and understanding remote computer network targets. The attacker cannot take for granted that all is as it seems. Indeed, in the practical world inhabited by security engineers, this reality has already begun to take hold. In this section, we clarify the utility of the protective strategy of deception and explore the strategy's applications to computer security.

Deception as a Distinct Strategy

Disarmament (accommodation), deterrence (coercion), defense (denial), and deception have always been available and appear intermingled throughout history, but shifting material conditions have necessitated rebalancing among strategies. If the information age makes defense and coercion alone seem ineffective for protection in cyberspace, as many experts believe, then it may be appropriate to reevaluate deception as a distinct strategic option. The heightened potential for deception in ubiquitous dual use technology, whether used by the offense or the defense, also bodes poorly for disarmament if risks cannot be reliably measured or proscribed. The implications for denial and deterrence are less straightforward because the defender can use deception to bolster each of these strategies.

Deception is logically different from denial even though they are often combined. Pure defense is the act of physically confronting attackers so that they cannot cause harm to the assets that are being defended. Deception, by contrast, conceals assets and pitfalls from the enemy. Castle walls protect a lord and his vassals by obstructing or canalizing invaders and by providing fighting platforms from which to repel an attack. Peasants seeking shelter in the castle can bury their wealth to prevent plunder by either side. Those that stay and fight are practicing defense; those that flee after secreting assets engage in deception.

Tactical forms of deception have become essential on the modern battlefield. Armies once wore gaudy uniforms and employed tight, visible formations to improve coordination and esprit, thus optimizing their concentrated efforts for defense (or the attack). As the range, precision, and lethality of fires improved, however, armies began to emphasize deception—in the form of dispersion, concealment, and mobility, along with a starkly different doctrine and training regimen—in order to keep the enemy guessing about

152   ELEMENTS OF DETERRENCE

their location. Navies likewise abandoned the line of battle in favor of dispersed formations and faster or stealthier vessels such as destroyers and submarines. Tactical deception so increased combat effectiveness that today we think of camouflage and dispersion as intrinsic to military organization and operations.[65] Yet deceptive measures are not themselves a defense, since stealth and concealment alone do nothing to prevent an attacker from dominating the battlefield. Moreover, an active defense inevitably compromises deception as, for example, muzzle flashes reveal the defender's location. Deception may be more or less effective when combined with the offense or defense, but deception as a strategy should not be confused with either of these actions.

In a similar fashion, coercion differs logically from defense, even though the threat of a credible defense can serve to deter. Deterrence has always been a factor in world politics. Since antiquity, elites used the prospect of military mobilization to dissuade or compel their opponents. Yet because deterrence often failed, the ability to defend was critical in its own right. Nuclear weapons changed this calculus by making defense seem futile. Ballistic missiles capable of leveling cities could not be prevented or intercepted, thus promising unacceptable devastation. Policy makers were forced to consider strategies of pure deterrence in a world in which the prospect of annihilation made conquest meaningless but where threats of nuclear retaliation could still be useful tools of brinksmanship.[66] As Bernard Brodie famously observed, the object of strategy shifted from winning wars to avoiding them altogether.[67] Deterrence was bolstered by the inability to defend, and by the mutual prospect of unacceptable harm, even as deterrence skeptics sought counterforce options that would allow them to fight and win a nuclear war.

As nuclear weapons isolated, highlighted, and made the strategy of deterrence pivotal, so too cyberspace makes deception more salient as a regulating option in an increasingly wired and integrated world. Nuclear capabilities augmented the ability to deter, even as they prevented effective defense. Similarly, cyberspace heightens the effectiveness of deception but with ambiguous implications for the other, more traditional, strategies. Deception is

---

[65] Deception does not always improve defense; it can also limit it. Artillery can be better concealed if shells are smaller and gun tubes shorter, but this takes away some of the lethality of firepower. The general effect of deception as implemented in the "modern system" should be to improve overall military effectiveness; S. Biddle 2004.

[66] Jervis 1989.   [67] Brodie et al. 1946.

The Limits of Offensive Deception

As useful and necessary as deception is for cyberattack, faith in the internet is not misplaced for most users most of the time. On the contrary, critical financial, logistic, and public utility functions have moved online *because*, not in spite of, growing confidence in the reliability of network technology. In markets with highly asymmetric information, bad products should crowd out the good ones, yet the internet has thus far not devolved into a pure "market for lemons."[68] Cyberattackers do not run rampant like raiders on the steppe. Indeed, actors who rely on fraud have incentives to show restraint if they want to protect their enabling capabilities and preserve the option to keep using them.[69]

An oft-quoted passage from Sun Tzu reads, "All warfare is based on deception. Hence, when able to attack, we must seem unable; when using our forces, we must seem inactive; when we are near, we must make the enemy believe we are far away; when far away, we must make him believe we are near."[70] In reality, Sun Tzu's advice is easier given than followed. Carl von Clausewitz notes that surprise is both useful and difficult to achieve.[71] A potent military force takes time and effort to assemble. Large-scale preparations are difficult to conceal.[72] Smaller or simpler formations are easier to disguise, but they typically lack firepower or sufficient reserves, making them less potent on the battlefield. All forces require planning, manning, sustainment, and communications, but these activities are subject to mishaps and misperceptions. Clausewitz described these problems as collectively subject to "friction" and the "fog of war." One tactical mistake or clue left behind could unravel an entire deception operation. Conspiracies have a way of being compromised, especially as the number of conspirators grows, and troops who are not in on the deceptive ruse might become just as confused as the enemy. Even if deception planning goes well, the target of deception may simply misunderstand the stratagem.

---

[68] Akerlof 1970.   [69] Lindsay 2017.   [70] Sun-tzu 2002.   [71] Clausewitz 1976.
[72] Because it is costly, mobilization can serve as a credible signal of resolve. See Slantchev 2005.

154 ELEMENTS OF DETERRENCE

Large-scale military deception is logistically difficult to manage and depends on significant organizational integration, cooperative enemies, and luck. These conditions are rare. Surprise attacks of any significance—the Japanese raid on Pearl Harbor, the North Vietnamese Tet Offensive, Egypt's initiation of the Yom Kippur War, or al Qaeda's 9/11 attacks—are unusual events brought about as much by political conditions as by intelligence failures.[73] These attacks bought only temporary advantages for their perpetrators and more often than not invited fearsome retribution that eliminated the benefits of the original attack. These episodes, like the elaborate British deception conspiracies mentioned previously, are the exceptions that prove the rule that serious deception is difficult and rare. Countless schemes have no doubt been abandoned at the planning stage for want of adequate resources, command support, or feasibility, while other deception operations failed because they were impractical or poorly executed.[74] Commanders instead tend to emphasize attack and defense via mass and firepower. Tactical surprise and inventive maneuvers supporting larger military and naval efforts are prevalent, even essential, in modern warfare. These work best, however, in the service of hard military power, itself facilitated by deceptive cover, concealment, and maneuver, able to capitalize on the temporary windows surprise may create, and to absorb setbacks produced by failed deception.

The success of cyber operations, which cannot fall back on brute force or military mass, depends on the success of deception. Martin Libicki points out that "there is no forced entry in cyberspace," meaning that all intrusions depend on a user or engineer leaving a logical door open.[75] The most valuable targets tend to involve complex organizations, heterogeneous infrastructure, vast repositories of data, and critical tacit knowledge not exposed to digital recovery. Failure to control adequately for this complexity could result in mission failure when the malware "payload" does not perform as intended or nothing of value is exfiltrated from a target network.

The complexity of the target makes it more likely the attacker will leave forensic clues behind. The seriousness of the attack makes it more likely the victim will mount a major investigation. As the Defense Science Board

---

[73] Betts 1982.

[74] There is a critical bias in the historiography of deception; successful ruses receive considerably more attention. For examples of schemes that were planned but not implemented, see Twigge and Scott 2001; Scott and Dylan 2010.

[75] Libicki 2007.

CYBERSPACE IS IDEAL FOR THE STRATEGY OF DECEPTION   155

points out, competent network defenders "can also be expected to employ highly-trained system and network administrators, and this operational staff will be equipped with continuously improving network defensive tools and techniques (the same tools we advocate to improve our defenses). Should an adversary discover an implant, it is usually relatively simple to remove or disable. For this reason, offensive cyber will always be a fragile capability."[76]

Offensive deception thus reduces but does not eliminate the effectiveness of defense and deterrence. An attacker with a strong requirement for anonymity has strong incentives to show restraint.[77] Many cybersecurity measures seek to exploit the attacker's sensitivity to compromise by seeking to enhance authentication, intrusion detection, and forensic attribution. Since the attacker must spend time reconnoitering a network to understand defensive threats and target opportunities (building up its situational awareness in a low-context environment), the defender also has more time to detect and observe the attacker. Unfortunately, standard security strategies by themselves can only be pursued so far. More complex defensive measures simply provide more potential for deception. Deterrence in any case will not be effective against highly resolved attackers. Fortunately, there is another, more indirect, strategy to counter offensive deception.

Using Deception to Complement Defense and Deterrence

Ubiquitous dependence on the internet makes distinguishing malignant from benign activity difficult. Disarmament schemes are foiled even before participants can defect from them. For the same reason, however, it is difficult for the attacker to detect whether it has entered a virtual minefield or tripped silent alarms. A threat actor may be welcomed, indeed encouraged, to penetrate a network. Unable to distinguish between data that are useful and data that are harmful, adversaries can be lulled into a false sense of security, even impunity. As cyber spies vacuum up terabytes of data from a target's networks, what is to keep them from contracting a virus? As they open exfiltrated files, how can they be sure they have not installed malware that will subvert their own systems? If these traps degrade the adversary's

---

[76] Defense Science Board 2013.
[77] Nuclear terrorism is another threat that is supposedly premised by attribution problems. For a discussion of why political context helps the defender solve even technically difficult attribution, see Lieber and Press 2013.

156 ELEMENTS OF DETERRENCE

ability to keep on operating at the same level of efficiency or effectiveness, then deception will provide a defensive benefit.

Likewise, if the fear of deception dissuades an attacker from attacking a target, or attacking at the same level, then deception will provide a deterrent benefit as well. A non-zero risk of identification means that the attacker cannot discount retaliation completely. Anonymity in cyberspace is by no means guaranteed. The defender's deceptive minefield can include broadcasting beacons that ensnare an attacker and follow it home, as well as silent intrusion detection systems to provide attribution clues. More effective counterintelligence may make for a more convincing attribution case, and thus a more legitimate targeted punishment. Moreover, the adversary that would like to use deception to evade deterrence has no way to deter deception against itself. An adversary that wanted to complain about defensive deception would also have first to reveal its identity.

Even against an attacker that manages to remain anonymous, deception can still restore the threat of punishment. A duped intruder may punish itself by carrying a Trojan horse back with its plunder or getting lost amidst mountains of disinformation and decoys. The first time this happens, it is pure defense. But if the intruder pauses the next time, it is deterrence. Alternately, hackers may start to imagine that everything is a trap. They may worry whether their actions have tripped a silent alarm that will bring their activities to the attention of incident responders. They may worry that they are interacting with a persona or a machine that is actually controlled by a counterintelligence agent. Paranoia about the possibility of deception could make intruders more reticent to enter certain networks, worried that they might thereby lose capabilities to compromise or worse.

Deception-as-defense and deception-as-deterrence both tend to impose costs on the intruder, the first more directly by disrupting capability and the second by encouraging more careful and circumspect behavior. As the adversary's operators navigate a network, they must be alert to find exploitation opportunities while not getting entrapped. As the adversary's intelligence analysts work their way through enormous haystacks of exfiltrated data, they must be alert to find useful needles while not getting poked. Defensive deception—real or feared—will tend to exacerbate the intrinsic potential for attacker confusion. Deception adds to the ambitious attacker's already significant intelligence burden by: creating more use cases that attack

CYBERSPACE IS IDEAL FOR THE STRATEGY OF DECEPTION 157

code is required to handle; covering up heterogeneity so that all targets look similar; and hiding factors that can lead to failure against particular targets.

There is no escaping trade-offs, however. Defenses invested disproportionately in only the most valuable target can inadvertently signal attackers as to the value of a target, paradoxically encouraging more attacks. It may prove rational to spread defenses around.[78] But this, of course, implies additional cost, meaning that the effectiveness imperative of defense will eat into the efficiency advantages of deception. Generating paranoia for the attacker, similarly, may encourage it to improve the sophistication of its tradecraft and counter-counterintelligence posture, meaning that the influence imperative of deterrence will eat into the effectiveness of defense.

A challenge of deception planning is to ensure that legitimate users do not become collateral damage of defensive deception operations. Although this risk can never be eliminated completely in an intelligence-counterintelligence contest, it might be addressed by luring attackers into situations that authorized users would avoid. There remain serious legal and policy considerations associated with defensive deception or active defense. In particular, the democratization of deception raises the problematic issue of cyber vigilantism, especially if private sector actors can use deception to counterattack ("hack back") threats. Some forms of defensive deception, for example that involve infecting an attacker's computer with a Trojan horse virus, might expose civilian defenders to liability under domestic laws like the US Computer Fraud and Abuse Act. Uncontrolled deception could evolve from defensive deception to predation, somewhat akin to the experience of the great powers with naval privateers, a practice that was eventually curtailed.[79] Defensive deception also further exacerbates the civil liberties concerns raised by revelations of pervasive internet surveillance by the US government.[80] We do not mean to play down these practical challenges. Nevertheless, it is clear strategically that deception is now, and will continue to become, an attractive option for public and private actors in cyberspace. Cyber conflict brings to the fore an ancient category of strategy

---

[78] Powell 2007.

[79] Egloff 2021.

[80] The Edward Snowden leaks contain references to defensive deception capabilities developed by the NSA including bogus packet injection, redirects to phony servers, and other man in the middle techniques to defend against cyberattacks on military networks. See Weaver 2014.

158   ELEMENTS OF DETERRENCE

that has been long practiced but until recently under-theorized. Strategic theory can no longer afford to ignore it.

Engineering Deception

Defensive deception is not just a theoretical possibility but an increasingly potent feature of network defense.[81] One of the first cybersecurity uses was by Clifford Stoll in 1986 after he detected attempts to break into the Lawrence Berkeley Laboratory network. Stoll created bogus systems and documents to assess the intruder's methods and targets. His bait included fake classified information to which digital alarms were attached. The hacker was eventually apprehended and found to be a West German citizen selling secrets to the KGB.[82] The use of "honeypots" has become a basic tool of computer network defense. Lance Spitzner describes a honeypot as "an information system resource whose value lies in unauthorized or illicit use of that resource.... If the enemy does not interact or use the honeypot, then it has little value." The honeypot works as a simulacrum of actual systems and files, databases, logs, etc. It is not only a decoy, but also an intrusion detection system: "By definition, your honeypot should not see any activity. Anything or anyone interacting with the honeypot is an anomaly." Spitzner also describes more complex "honeynet" systems of many honeypots or individual "honeytoken" files that an adversary might be encouraged to steal. The key is to design "a honeypot realistic enough for the attacker to interact with" that will vary depending on whether the intruder is a casual outsider or possibly a more knowledgeable insider.[83] Because one can expect intruders to start anticipating honeypots, engineers have even begun to experiment with "fake honeypots" in which legitimate machines try to look like an obvious honeypot in order to scare attackers away. The further possibility of "fake fake honeypots" begins to mirror the double agent games that are a fixture of spy novels.[84]

There are countless technical examples. A project sponsored by the Defense Advanced Research Projects Agency features a system of decoy documents and misbehavior sensors designed to protect distributed virtualized (cloud) data systems. Unauthorized access triggers a disinformation attack

---

[81] Yuill, Denning, and Feer 2006; Heckman and Stech 2015.   [82] Stoll 1989.
[83] Spitzner 2003.   [84] Rowe, Custy, and Duong 2007.

CYBERSPACE IS IDEAL FOR THE STRATEGY OF DECEPTION   159

yielding bogus data nearly indistinguishable from live customer data. The authors argue that the system is useful for detection, confusion, and potential deterrence of adversaries.[85] Another project protects banking systems with dummy password-ID pairs. The only way for the attacker to distinguish between real and fake accounts is to try to extract money; the large number of decoys makes detection likely, allowing network monitors to observe the intruder's cash-out strategy.[86] Particular classes of hacker tools are also vulnerable to tailored counter-deception, such as a technique to flood key-logging malware with false data.[87] Other concepts include memory fragmentation and distribution schemes that make it difficult for an attacker to assemble a complete picture of the data with which the attacker is interacting. Machine learning techniques offer many opportunities for defensive deception ranging from generating realistic lures or traffic and actively interacting with attackers to providing false patches or data resources.[88] Moreover, deceptive ruses need not work perfectly to be effective; they can be combined for "deception in depth." One validation concept employed "deception as a service" to redirect network attacks and provide realistic responses through an active honeypot network, thereby reducing the volume of attacks mitigated through more traditional network defenses.[89]

Importantly, network defense and deception are not just conducted by mindless algorithms. Law enforcement agents and computer security experts are tactically active in the cyber defense ecosystem. Whereas an undercover agent like Joseph Pistone, alias Donnie Brasco, faces great personal risk in infiltrating a criminal gang, internet crime police can safely lurk in chat rooms and exploit the low context of internet interactions to avoid criminal detection. If an online undercover agent is compromised, he just shuts down the compromised persona and returns with a new one, with body parts and family members intact. Law enforcement stings, counterintelligence activities, and corporate network operators can all monitor and subvert attacker infrastructure.

Through a process of convergent evolution (responding to the opportunities for deception in the cyber domain), academic researchers also use deception (although perhaps not by that name) as a methodology to

---

[85] Thompson et al. 2011. In the same vein another project floods a an adversary with decoys and beacons: Wick 2012.

[86] Herley and Florêncio 2008.

[87] Ortolani and Crispo 2012. Another technique uses decoy traffic through the Tor anonymizer to detect attempts at endpoint eavesdropping and HTTP session hijacking; see Chakravarty et al. 2011.

[88] Mohan et al. 2022.   [89] Couillard 2023.

160 ELEMENTS OF DETERRENCE

study cyberthreat actors. Botnet control servers have been infiltrated by researchers who then use the criminals' own infrastructure to map the extent of compromise, their command and control methods, and their reaction to takedown.[90] In an example of intelligence-counterintelligence competition, a team of computer scientists posed as gray market customers, or sometimes as cybercriminals themselves, in order to study the economic structure of online illicit markets; miscreant targets responded by blocking the researchers' web crawlers, emitting bogus spam to confuse them, requiring voice contact from purchasers, etc., and the researchers responded in turn with technical and human adaptations to overcome the criminals' countermeasures.[91] These classic counterintelligence techniques, updated for the digital age, have enabled researchers to identify major portions of the global spam and counterfeit pharmaceutical underground, particularly the financial infrastructure, aiding law enforcement and official regulators with information leading to significant regulatory interventions and criminal prosecutions. Sometimes digital forensics also include elements of human intelligence. In one bizarre example, a former Israeli intelligence officer working as an undercover private investigator attempted to lure a researcher from Citizen Lab, a digital human rights watchdog at the University of Toronto, into a meeting in order to pressure Citizen Lab into recanting public statements about NSO Group spyware, which had been implicated in human rights abuses; however, the Citizen Lab researcher turned the tables and exposed the operation to the media, a completely privatized example of a counter-counterintelligence sting.[92]

The everyday practice of cybersecurity thus has much in common with the classic give-and-take of intelligence-counterintelligence contests. Adaptations and counteradaptations occur on an ongoing basis in the shadows of the generally productive internet. In global networked information systems, however, the players now include engineers rather than just intelligence operatives, and the private and non-governmental sectors rather than just government officials. Attackers of any stripe rely on deception to gain economic or political advantages, but they are also subject to deceptive exploitation by the very targets they attack.

---

[90] Cho et al. 2010; Fuller et al. 2021.   [91] Levchenko et al. 2011.   [92] Satter 2019.

The Balance of Deception

It is widely assumed that offense is easier that defense in cyberspace, but this should really be understood as a claim about the ways in which information technology lowers the costs of deception. If deception becomes easier, furthermore, then both sides must learn to expect it. The spy-versus-spy arms race can go on indefinitely. Even if deception does not impose direct costs, paranoid counterintelligence efforts and operations security measures impose indirect burdens. Mutually assured deception, to coin a phrase, is a boon for network protection. The result is to dull the power of a cyber offensive, even leading to unexpected stability as adversaries can no longer trust plundered data or be sure that an attack will perform as expected.

The net effect on the overall offense-defense balance remains unclear. Data on deception are, unsurprisingly, difficult to collect or obtain. Perhaps cyberspace is still marginally offense-dominant in some sense even if defenders use deception. We believe this is not the case. We believe instead that the cyber offense-defense balance is contingent on the complexity and severity of the attack and the resolve of the opponents and the institutional context of their interaction. A high potential for deception, evenly distributed among the players, would yield offensive advantages against low-risk, low-reward targets while conferring defensive advantages for high-risk, high-reward targets. This helps to account for the observed distribution of cyberconflict to date, with many relatively minor criminal and espionage attacks but few larger attacks that matter militarily or diplomatically (i.e., a lot of a little but little of a lot).

Deception allows an attacker to intrude with low risk of detection or punishment, but only as long as it attacks objectives of relatively low value to the defender. The more effort that is required per attack, the less likely a target will be attacked.[93] For untargeted scalable attacks, failure against some or even most of the targets does not matter. As attacks become more ambitious, offensive costs increase in terms of planning, confusion, and risk.[94] Even without deliberate defensive deception, attackers must contend

---

[93] The majority of cyberspace nuisances indiscriminately attack homogenous resources, such as identical copies of software programs and standardized bank accounts, because the effort invested in an attack does not scale with the number of targets. It does not matter if untargeted scalable attacks fail against some or even most of the targets. Herley 2013. Nigerian spammers thus concoct ludicrous stories to filter out all but the most gullible victims, because sending bulk spam is cheap but responding to replies is much more costly; see Herley 2012.

[94] Lindsay 2015.

162   ELEMENTS OF DETERRENCE

with sociotechnical complexity that risks failure and compromise. Most attackers will attempt to fly below the radar in order not to waste their resources, blow their cover, or invite retaliation.

Offensive advantages become more tentative as risk exposure becomes more severe. High-reward targets—those systems and infrastructures on which an attack produces big financial, informational, or destructive outcomes—are more likely to be protected with defensive deception, including both intentional disinformation measures and the de facto complexity of internetworked targets (which makes attacker self-deception more likely). These deceptive means are more likely to confuse, compromise, or injure the attacker due to the greater attention and higher deceptive posture of the defender and the innate complexity of the target. It is critical to understand that in such situations, deception is not acting alone. Instead, deception is reinforcing the effectiveness of the defense of high-reward targets and the deterrence of actors who might attack those targets. Where deception enhances defense, the ability to attack high-reward targets is less easy than is widely believed. Where deception enhances deterrence, those few with the ability to attack (nation-state spy agencies and high-end financial criminals) are likely to be dissuaded by fear of the consequences.

The existence of high-reward targets in cyberspace is a large part of what makes the cyberthreat narrative compelling. Critical infrastructure and command and control systems are increasingly interconnected and, in principle, they are vulnerable to attack. The prevalence of attacks against low-reward targets by well-disguised attackers makes these high-reward targets appear to be all the more vulnerable. Yet appearances are misleading. The reality is that, although the technical possibility of attacks against high-reward targets can never be ruled out, the probability of a successful attack against a high-reward target is quite low. High-reward targets pose greater risks and costs to those who attack them. If the attacker cannot be sure that its anonymity is secure, or the attacker has doubts that its malware will execute as intended (and without unwanted collateral damage or fratricide), or that its resources will not be wasted, then the benefits of attacking a target must be sharply discounted.

The asymmetric actors featured in cybersecurity discourse—rogue states, lone hackers, criminals, and terrorists—will tend to focus on the low-risk, low-reward bonanza, avoiding "deception-dominant" high-risk, high-reward operations. Advanced industrial states will also partake in low-risk, low-reward espionage and harassment in cyberspace. Capable countries will, however, employ risky computer network attacks against lucrative targets only when they are willing and able to follow them up or backstop them with conventional military power. Because intelligence is costly and its exploitation is complicated, wealthier and larger states tend to have more sophisticated, robust intelligence capacities. Only capable actors, such as major powers, are likely to be able to master the complex tango of deception and counter-deception necessary to execute high-intensity operations. Powerful actors thus have an operational advantage in cyberspace. Even then, the frequency of complex and risky action should still be relatively low. Stuxnet is an outlier for a reason.

If offense dominance does not apply to the most important targets— since they are protected by complexity and deception—then over-arming and sowing fear are wasteful and destabilizing. Such efforts might even interfere with economically productive aspects of the internet. There is also the potential for tragedy if officials hastily resort to aggression in the mistaken belief that relations are fundamentally unstable. A more pernicious form of deception is the attempt to represent cyberspace as categorically offense-dominant when there may in fact be relatively affordable defenses. Doomsday scenarios such as a "cyber Pearl Harbor" are useful in the pursuit of bureaucratic resources and autonomy. Deception-prone environments increase the risk of threat inflation.

To sum up, deception is essential for offensive cyber operations. Kinetic operations can simply break down a door and force their way into a room. But in cyberspace, targets must be persuaded to open the door, or leave it open, or be distracted from closing it. The utility of deception for cyber defense as well as offense, furthermore, necessitates reconsideration of the superficially intuitive but overly deterministic claim that cyberspace is offense-dominant. The offense-defense balance is probably not as unbalanced as usually believed. It is in fact conditioned on attack severity, organizational competence, and actor resolve in any given dyad of actors.

Strategic interaction in a deception-prone world is typically something other than war. Deception is an exploitative act that takes advantage of a competitor's preconceptions, encoded in human minds or technological designs. Deception matters most, politically, in increasing the options available for competitive and aggressive interactions other than war or for providing adjunct support to military operations. In this respect, computer network operations should mainly be understood as expanding the scope

164 ELEMENTS OF DETERRENCE

of intelligence and covert operations, not as a new substitute for war. As intelligence in general has become more critical for security operations and diplomacy, cyberspace is an important channel for information and influence. Intelligence has always been important in peace and war, yet now it involves a growing number of people both in and out of government, as well as ever expanding budgets. The democratization of deception can account for both the historical continuity of cyber operations with traditional espionage and stratagem and their novelty in terms of ubiquity and complexity.

This ongoing, chronic low-intensity conflict behavior can manifest in isolation in peacetime, as part of a combined-arms military operation in wartime, or, increasingly, in the ambiguous "gray zone" between war and peace.[95] At the same time, competition and conflict at the threshold of war can be complex and risky, reflecting both brinkmanship dynamics and the asymmetry and interdependence of parties tied together by mutual risk. This is clearly the case in the subsurface maritime domain as well: collisions between submarines led to negotiation of the Incidents at Sea Agreement to avoid inadvertent escalation between the United States and Soviet Union. Alternatively, cyber and other special or intelligence operations could provide a safety valve to help de-escalate crises and promote caution among adversaries who either fear being duped or discount the expected gains of aggression. The very secrecy of operations in space, cyberspace, or undersea is, however, what complicates strategic signaling immensely. Cyber warfare is not a sui generis phenomenon, but rather a member of a class of phenomena—intelligence and covert operations—that has received little attention from IR scholars until relatively recently.[96] Placing cyber operations in context with other forms of strategic and tactical deception can help to move the discussion beyond the debate over whether or not the cyber revolution is a disruptive military innovation and begin to explore how cyber means actually work in conjunction with other strategic instruments for multiple objectives. Put simply, cybersecurity is a major historical evolution in intelligence affairs.

---

[95] Chapter 14 delves into these issues in detail.
[96] Carnegie 2021; Chesney and Smeets 2023.

7

Cyber Deception versus Nuclear Deterrence

Throughout this book we have stressed the importance of strategic specialization. Sometimes specialized capabilities can be combined to realize synergies, as in combined arms warfare. This usually works best when the combinations are all directed toward the same goal, such as battlefield victory. In the previous chapter, we discussed ways in which deception can be used to augment defense and deterrence within the cyber domain: honeypots and silent alarms can impede intruders while paranoia about counterintelligence can encourage restraint.

However, specialization can also create dangerous interference, especially if different technological means are optimized for different political ends. In Chapter 5 we argued that "cyberwar" is *not* useful for coercion, and in Chapter 6 we argued that cyberspace *very* useful for deception. In this chapter we examine the interaction of military technologies with very different strategic characteristics: cyber operations and nuclear weapons. We argue that the use of cyber deception to improve counterforce defense can undermine nuclear deterrence. Strategic instability here arises not from cyberspace itself but through the interaction of cyberspace with military forces and characteristics in other domains.

In the classic 1983 movie *WarGames*, a teenager in a hoodie hacks into the North American Air Defense Command (NORAD), which almost triggers World War III. After a screening of the film, President Ronald Reagan reportedly asked his staff, "Could something like this really happen?" The Chairman of the Joint Chiefs of Staff replied, "Mr. President, the problem is much worse than you think." The National Security Agency (NSA) had been hacking Russian and Chinese communications for years, but the burgeoning personal computer revolution was creating serious vulnerabilities for the United States as well. Reagan directed a series of reviews that culminated in a classified national security decision directive (NSDD-145) entitled "National Policy on Telecommunications and Automated Information

Elements of Deterrence: Strategy, Technology, and Complexity in Global Politics. Erik Gartzke and Jon R. Lindsay, Oxford University Press. © Oxford University Press 2024. DOI: 10.1093/oso/9780197754443.003.0007

166 ELEMENTS OF DETERRENCE

Systems Security." More alarmist studies, and potential remedies, emerged in the following decades as technicians and policy makers came to appreciate the evolving threat.[1]

In this telling, fictional concerns about the security of nuclear weapons encouraged broader US government policy about cybersecurity. We can also turn this concern around to ask: what are the implications of decades of improvement in U.S. cyber operations capability for nuclear strategic stability? Most analyses of inadvertent escalation from cyber or conventional conflict to nuclear war focus on "use it or lose it" pressures and fog of war created by attacks that become visible to the target.[2] In a US-China conflict scenario, for example, conventional military strikes in conjunction with cyberattacks that blind sensors and confuse decision making could generate incentives for both sides to rush to preempt or escalate.[3] These are plausible concerns, but the revelation of information about a newly unfavorable balance of power might also cause hesitation and lead to compromise. We argue that a more insidious threat to crisis stability arises from clandestine attacks that remain undetected by the target.[4]

Theorists and practitioners have long stressed the unprecedented destructiveness of nuclear weapons in explaining how nuclear deterrence works. But it is equally important that capabilities and intentions are clearly communicated. Knowledge of nuclear capabilities is necessary to achieve a deterrent effect.[5] Strategic stability requires a degree of transparency about capabilities and consequences. Cyber operations, by contrast, rely on undisclosed vulnerabilities, social engineering, and creative adaptation to generate indirect effects via information systems. As discussed in Chapter 6, cyberspace is very attractive for espionage, subversion, and other forms of deception, so long as activities or agencies are kept hidden. The essential problem here is that transparency and deception do not mix.

An attacker who hacks an adversary's nuclear command and control apparatus, or the weapons themselves, will gain an advantage in war-fighting that the attacker cannot reveal, while the adversary will continue to believe it wields a deterrent that may no longer exist. The dangers of escalation

---

[1] Kaplan 2016; Schulte 2008; Warner 2012.   [2] Posen 1991; Cimbala 2011.

[3] A. Goldstein 2013; Gompert and Libicki 2014; Talmadge 2017; Acton 2018.

[4] Lindsay 2022 describes twenty-one different ways in which cyber operations might lead to nuclear escalation, most of which require assumptions of subrational decision making. This chapter focuses on only one of these mechanisms, but it is the most dangerous because even rational actors have incentives to escalate.

[5] Powell 1990.

are greatest in brinksmanship situations where actors are willing to use secret offensive cyber operations—which cannot be revealed in advance—to limit the damage of a nuclear exchange. The same strategic logic that leads us to view cyber warfare as a limited political instrument in *most* situations, as discussed in Chapter 5, also leads us to view it as incredibly destabilizing in *rare* situations. While cyberwar is not itself a weapon of mass destruction, the use of offensive cyber operations targeting actual weapons of mass destruction will tend to undermine crisis stability.

There are both theoretical and empirical reasons for taking seriously the effects of offensive cyber operations on nuclear deterrence. We will highlight some historical evidence that nuclear command and control systems may be vulnerable to attack and that the United States has targeted them in the past. More recent war-gaming experiments provide additional evidence that supports the argument developed in this chapter.[6] Below we lay out this argument in detail, and we explain why we expect the dangers to vary with the relative nuclear force structures and cyber capabilities of the actors in a crisis interaction. This makes asymmetric dyads like the United States and North Korea particularly worrisome, as the stronger cyber-capable superpower will be tempted to preempt the smaller rogue state. We close with a few implications for policy.

Nuclear Command, Control, and Communications

Nuclear command, control, and communications (NC3) is the nervous system of the nuclear enterprise.[7] NC3 encompasses intelligence and early warning sensors located in orbit and on Earth, fixed and mobile command and control centers through which national leadership can order a launch, operational nuclear forces including strategic bombers, land-based intercontinental missiles (ICBMs), submarine-launched ballistic missiles (SLBMs), and the communication and transportation networks that tie the whole apparatus together. NC3 should ideally ensure that nuclear forces will "always" be available if authorized by the National Command Authority (to enhance deterrence) and "never" used without authorization

---

[6] Schneider, Schechter, and Shaffer 2023.

[7] Carter, Steinbruner, and Zracket 1987; Office of the Deputy Assistant Secretary of Defense for Nuclear Matters 2015; Wirtz and Larsen 2022.

168   ELEMENTS OF DETERRENCE

(to enhance safety and reassurance). Friendly errors or enemy interference in NC3 can undermine the strict "always-never" criterion.[8] As the 2022 US Nuclear Posture Review (NPR) states, "Our NC3 system must provide command and control of US nuclear forces at all times and under all circumstances, including during a following a nuclear or non-nuclear attack by any adversary."[9]

NC3 Vulnerability

NC3 has long been recognized as the weakest link in the US nuclear enterprise. According to a declassified official history, a Strategic Air Command (SAC) task group in 1979 "reported that tactical warning and communications systems...were 'fragile' and susceptible to electronic countermeasures, electromagnetic pulse, and sabotage, which could deny necessary warning and assessment to the National Command Authorities."[10] Two years later the Principal Deputy Under Secretary of Defense for Research and Engineering released a broad-based, multiservice report that doubled down on SAC's findings: "the United States could not assure survivability, endurability, or connectivity of the national command authority function" due to "major command, control, and communications deficiencies: in tactical warning and attack assessment where existing systems were vulnerable to disruption and destruction from electromagnetic pulse, other high-altitude nuclear effects, electronic warfare, sabotage, or physical attack; in decision making where there was inability to assure national command authority survival and connection with the nuclear forces, especially under surprise conditions; and in communications systems, which were susceptible to the same threats above and which could not guarantee availability of even minimum-essential capability during a protracted war."[11]

The nuclear weapons safety literature likewise provides a number of troubling examples of NC3 glitches that illustrate some of the vulnerabilities attackers could, in principle, exploit.[12] The SAC history noted that NORAD has received numerous false launch indications from faulty computer components, loose circuits, and even a nuclear war training tape

---

[8] Bracken 1985; Blair 1985.   [9] Office of the Secretary of Defense 2022, p. 22.
[10] US Joint Chiefs of Staff 1982.   [11] U.S. Joint Chiefs of Staff 1982.
[12] Gregory 1990; Sagan 1995; Schlosser 2014.

loaded by mistake into a live system that produced erroneous Soviet launch indications.[13] In a 1991 briefing to the STRATCOM commander, a Defense Intelligence Agency targeteer confessed, "Sir, I apologize, but we have found a problem with this target. There is a mistake in the computer code.... Sir, the error has been there for at least the life of this eighteen-month planning cycle. The nature of the error is such that the target would not have been struck."[14] It would be a very challenging clandestine operation to intentionally plant undetected errors like this in an American strategic system, but the presence of bugs like this does reveal that such a hack is possible.

Following many near-misses and self-audits during and after the Cold War, American NC3 improved with the addition of new safeguards and redundancies. General Robert Kehler, the Commander of US Strategic Command (STRATCOM) in 2013, stated in testimony before the Senate Armed Services Committee that "the nuclear deterrent force was designed to operate through the most extreme circumstances we could possibly imagine."[15] Yet vulnerabilities remain. In 2010 the US Air Force lost contact with fifty Minuteman III ICBMs for an hour because of a faulty hardware circuit at a launch control center.[16] If the accident had occurred during a crisis, or the component had been sabotaged, the USAF would have been unable to launch and unable to detect and cancel unauthorized launch attempts. Bruce Blair, a former Minuteman missileer, points out that during a control center blackout the antennas at unmanned silos and the cables between them provide potential surreptitious access vectors.[17]

The unclassified summary of a 2015 audit of US NC3 stated that "known capability gaps or deficiencies remain."[18] Perhaps more worrisome are the unknown deficiencies. A 2013 Defense Science Board report on military cyber vulnerabilities found that while the "nuclear deterrent is regularly evaluated for reliability and readiness..., most of the systems have not been assessed (end-to-end) against a [sophisticated state] "cyber attack" to understand possible weak spots. A 2007 Air Force study addressed portions of this issue for the ICBM leg of the US triad but was still not a complete assessment against a high-tier threat."[19]

If NC3 vulnerabilities are unknown, it is also unknown whether an advanced cyber actor would be able to exploit them. General Kehler stated

---

[13] US Joint Chiefs of Staff 1982. [14] Butler 2016.
[15] Levin, Kehler, and Alexander 2013, p. 18. [16] Ambinder 2010.
[17] Blair 2010. [18] Government Accountability Organization 2015.
[19] Defense Science Board 2013.

170   ELEMENTS OF DETERRENCE

in 2013 that "we are very concerned with the potential of a cyber-related attack on our nuclear command and control and on the weapons systems themselves." As he notes laconically, "We don't know what we don't know."[20] Kehler further emphasized that "there's a continuing need to make sure that we are protected against electromagnetic pulse and any kind of electromagnetic interference."[21]

Even if NC3 of nuclear forces narrowly conceived are a hard target, cyberattacks on other critical infrastructure in preparation to or during a nuclear crisis could complicate or confuse government decision making. General Keith Alexander, Director of the NSA in the same Senate hearing with General Kehler, testified that "our infrastructure that we ride on, the power and the communications grid, are one of the things that is a source of concern...we can go to backup generators and we can have independent routes, but...our ability to communicate would be significantly reduced and it would complicate our governance....I think what General Kehler has would be intact...[but] the cascading effect...in that kind of environment...concerns us."[22]

Many NC3 components are antiquated and hard to upgrade, which is a mixed blessing. Kehler points out, "Much of the nuclear command and control system today is the legacy system that we've had. In some ways that helps us in terms of the cyber threat. In some cases it's point to point, hard-wired, which makes it very difficult for an external cyber threat to emerge."[23] The Government Accountability Office noted in 2016 that the "Department of Defense uses 8-inch floppy disks in a legacy system that coordinates the operational functions of the nation's nuclear forces."[24] While this may limit some forms of remote access, it is also indicative of reliance on an earlier generation of software when security engineering standards were less mature. Admiral Cecil Haney, Kehler's successor at STRATCOM, highlighted some of the challenges of NC3 modernization in 2015: "Assured and reliable NC3 is fundamental to the credibility of our nuclear deterrent. The aging NC3 systems continue to meet their intended purpose, but risk to mission success is increasing as key elements of the system age. The unpredictable challenges posed by today's complex security environment make it increasingly important to optimize our NC3 architecture while

---

[20] Levin, Kehler, and Alexander 2013, p. 10.
[21] Levin, Kehler, and Alexander 2013, p. 18.
[22] Levin, Kehler, and Alexander 2013, p. 18.
[23] Office of the Secretary of Defense 2022, p. 10.
[24] Powner 2016.

leveraging new technologies so that NC3 systems operate together as a core set of survivable and endurable capabilities that underpin a broader, national command and control system."[25]

Upgrades to the digital Strategic Automated Command and Control System initiated in 2017 have corrected some problems. General Charles Richard, the Commander of STRATCOM in 2022, described "an enterprise-wide approach to harden the current architecture until complete fielding of the NC3 Next Generation. As an example, the Air Force is leading the effort to modernize the NC3 data pathways for the Strategic Automated Command and Control System (SACCS), replacing legacy telephony to sustainable and secure modern technology with upgraded at-risk cryptographic devices."[26] The 2022 NPR states that "these technologies and platforms—including those enabling NC3—must be inherently cyber-security, joined by resilient, redundant and hardened networks, and monitored by an agile defensive cyber force operating under a clear, unified C2 construct."[27]

Yet, as with any increase in the complexity of digital control systems, adding additional layers of control also has the potential to introduce new access vectors and vulnerabilities.[28] The NPR's attempt to provide reassurance simply highlights the complexity of the NC3 attack surface: "We will employ an optimized mix of resilience approaches to protect the next-generation NC3 architecture from threats posed by competitor capabilities. This includes, but is not limited to, enhanced protection from cyber, space-based, and electromagnetic pulse threats; enhanced integrated tactical warning and attack assessment; improved command post and communication links; advanced decision support technology; and integrated planning and operations."[29]

In no small irony, the internet itself owes its intellectual origin, in part, to the threat to NC3 from large-scale physical attack. A 1962 RAND report by Paul Baran had considered "the problem of building digital communication networks using links with less than perfect reliability" to enable "stations surviving a physical attack and remaining in electrical connection...to operate together as a coherent entity after attack."[30] Baran advocated as a solution decentralized packet switching protocols, not unlike those realized in the ARPANET program. The emergence of the internet was the result of

---

[25] Haney 2015. [26] Richard 2022, p. 10.
[27] Office of the Secretary of Defense 2022, p. 9. [28] Futter 2016.
[29] Office of the Secretary of Defense 2022, p. 21. [30] Baran 1962.

172   ELEMENTS OF DETERRENCE

many other factors that had nothing to do with managing nuclear operations, notably the meritocratic ideals of 1960s counterculture that contributed to the neglect of security in the internet's founding architecture.[31] Fears of NC3 vulnerability helped to create the internet, which then helped to create the present-day cybersecurity epidemic, which has come full circle to create new fears about NC3 vulnerability.

NC3 vulnerability, finally, is not unique to the United States. The NC3 of other nuclear powers may even be easier to compromise. It is unclear whether other members of the nuclear club have are willing or able to invest in the same degree of modernization as the United States. Especially concerning is the NC3 capacity of new entrants to the nuclear club like North Korea.

Targeting NC3

So far we have only discussed potential vulnerabilities in NC3. Now we turn to efforts to target those vulnerabilities. During the Cold War, the United States developed an extensive set of capabilities and war-plans for nuclear counterforce and damage limitation.[32] "Counterforce" describes efforts to target enemy forces rather than "countervalue" population centers. Counterforce capabilities, if known to the enemy in advance, could conceivably enhance deterrence by denial. "Damage limitation" describes the use of counterforce capabilities are used to literally limit the damage enemy nuclear forces can inflict on the United States and its interests. Because this is a purely defensive effort, rather than a form of defensive signaling, there is no requirement to reveal these capabilities to the enemy. Indeed, secrecy might be essential for their success. In addition to a variety of nuclear, anti-submarine warfare, and air options, US counterforce plans also included NC3 attacks.

A rare example of these activities and capabilities is a Special Access Program named Canopy Wing. East German intelligence obtained the highly classified plans from a turncoat in the US Army in Berlin, and the details began to emerge publicly after the Cold War. An East German intelligence officer, Markus Wolf, writes in his memoir that Canopy Wing "listed the types of electronic warfare that would be used to neutralize the Soviet Union

---

[31] Clark 1992.   [32] Long and B. Green 2014; B. Green 2020.

and Warsaw Pact's command centers in case of all-out war. It detailed the precise method of depriving the Soviet High Command of its high-frequency communications used to give orders to its armed forces."[33]

It is easy to see why NC3 is such an attractive target in the unlikely event of a nuclear war. If, for whatever reason, deterrence fails and the enemy decides to push the proverbial nuclear button, one would obviously prefer to disable or destroy missiles before they launch than to rely on possibly futile efforts to shoot them down, or to accept the loss of millions of lives. American plans to disable Soviet NC3 with electronic warfare, furthermore, would have been intended to complement plans for decapitating strikes against Soviet nuclear forces. Temporary disabling of information networks in isolation would have failed to achieve any important strategic objective. A blinded adversary would eventually see again and would scramble to reconstitute its ability to launch its weapons, expecting that preemption was inevitable in any case. Reconstitution, moreover, would invalidate much of the intelligence and some of the tradecraft on which the blinding attack relied. Capabilities fielded through Canopy Wing were presumably intended to facilitate a preemptive military strike on Soviet NC3 to disable the ability to retaliate and limit the damage of any retaliatory force that survived, given credible indications that war was imminent. Canopy Wing allegedly included:[34]

- "Measures for short-circuiting . . . communications and weapons systems using, among other things, microscopic carbon-fiber particles and chemical weapons."
- "Electronic blocking of communications immediately prior to an attack, thereby rendering a counterattack impossible."
- "Deployment of various weapons systems for instantaneous destruction of command centers, including pin-point targeting with precision-guided weapons to destroy 'hardened bunkers.'"
- "Use of deception measures, including the use of computer-simulated voices to override and substitute false commands from ground-control stations to aircraft and from regional command centers to the Soviet submarine fleet."
- "Us[e of] the technical installations of 'Radio Free Europe/Radio Liberty' and 'Voice of America,' as well as the radio communications

---

[33] Wolf and McElvoy 1997.   [34] Fischer 2014.

174   ELEMENTS OF DETERRENCE

installations of the US Armed Forces for creating interference and other electronic effects."

Wolf also ran a spy in the US Air Force who disclosed that "the Americans had managed to penetrate the [Soviet air base at Eberswalde]'s ground-air communications and were working on a method of blocking orders before they reached the Russian pilots and substituting their own from West Berlin. Had this succeeded, the MiG pilots would have received commands from their American enemy. It sounded like science fiction, but, our experts concluded, it was in no way impossible that they could have pulled off such a trick, given the enormous spending and technical power of US military air research."[35]

One East German source claimed that Canopy Wing had a $14.5 billion budget for research and operational costs and a staff of 1,570 people, while another claimed that it would take over four years and $65 million to develop "a prototype of a sophisticated electronic system for paralyzing Soviet radio traffic in the high-frequency range."[36] Canopy Wing was not cheap, but even so, it was only a research and prototyping program. Operationalization of its capabilities and integration into NATO war plans would have been even more expensive. This is suggestive of the level of effort required to craft effective offensive cyber operations against NC3.

Preparation for surprise attack comes to naught when a sensitive program is compromised. Canopy Wing was caught in what we have described as the cyber commitment problem, the inability to disclose a war-fighting capability for the sake of deterrence without losing it in the process. According to *New York Times* reporting on the counterintelligence investigation of the East German spy in the Army, Warrant Officer James Hall, "officials said that one program rendered useless cost hundreds of millions of dollars and was designed to exploit a Soviet communications vulnerability uncovered in the late 1970's."[37] This program was probably Canopy Wing. Wolf writes, "Once we passed [Hall's documents about Canopy Wing] on to the Soviets, they were able to install scrambling devices and other countermeasures."[38] It is tempting to speculate that the Soviet deployment of a new NC3 system known as Signal-A to replace Signal-M (which was most likely the one targeted by Canopy Wing) was motivated in part by Hall's betrayal.[39]

[35] Wolf and McElvoy 1997.   [36] Fischer 2014.
[37] Engelberg and Wines 1989.   [38] Wolf and McElvoy 1997.   [39] Fischer 2014.

Canopy Wing underscores the potential and limitations of NC3 subversion. Modern cyber methods can potentially perform many of the missions Canopy Wing addressed with electronic warfare and other means, but with even greater stealth and precision. Cyber operations might, in principle, compromise any part of the NC3 system (early warning, command centers, data transport, operational forces, etc.) by blinding sensors, injecting bogus commands or suppressing legitimate ones, monitoring or corrupting data transmissions, or interfering with the reliable launch and guidance of missiles. In practice, the operational feasibility of cyberattack against NC3 or any other target depends on the software and hardware configuration and organizational processes of the target, the intelligence and planning capacity of the attacker, and the ability and willingness to take advantage of the effects created by cyberattack.[40] Cyber compromise of NC3 is technically plausible though operationally difficult, a point to which we return in a later section.

To understand which threats are not only technically possible but also probable under some circumstance, we further need a political logic of cost and benefit.[41] In particular, how is it possible for a crisis to escalate to levels of destruction more costly than any conceivable political reward? Canopy Wing highlights some of the strategic dangers of NC3 exploitation. Warsaw Pact observers appear to have been deeply concerned that the program reflected an American willingness to undertake a surprise decapitation attack: it "sent ice-cold shivers down our spines."[42] The Soviets thus designed a system called Perimeter that, not unlike the Doomsday Device in *Dr. Strangelove*, was designed to detect a nuclear attack and retaliate automatically, even if cut off from Soviet high command, through an elaborate system of sensors, underground computers, and command missiles to transmit launch codes.[43] Both Canopy Wing and Perimeter show that the United States and the Soviet Union took nuclear war-fighting seriously and were willing to develop secret advantages for such an event. By the same token, they were not able to reveal such capabilities to improve deterrence to avoid having to fight a nuclear war in the first place.

The modern threat environment includes a few new wrinkles. Russia retains a large nuclear arsenal that is similarly sized to that of the United States, but with a very different force structure and posture, featuring a larger proportion of so-called non-strategic nuclear weapons.[44] China has

---

[40] Owens, Dam, and Lin 2009; Herrick and Herr 2016.   [41] Gartzke 2013.
[42] Fischer 2014.   [43] D. Hoffman 2009.   [44] Adamsky 2018.

176   ELEMENTS OF DETERRENCE

recently embarked on an ambitious modernization and expansion program to improve the diversity and survivability of its nuclear forces, which makes it "the overall pacing challenge for US defense planning and a growing factor in evaluating our [US] nuclear deterrent."[45] In addition to this "two peer" deterrence problem, North Korea has acquired a small but dangerous arsenal and increasingly capable missiles, and Iran is just a decision away from a breakout effort (as of this writing).

This is an extremely complex deterrence environment. There are natural incentives for the US military to seek out hedges to deal with so many simultaneous threats without having to greatly expand the US arsenal, which may be politically unpopular. Counter-NC3 options would be one way to improve the efficiency of counterforce coverage. Indeed, it would be surprising to learn that the United States has failed to upgrade its Cold War NC3 attack plans to include offensive cyber operations against a wider variety of potential targets.

The United States has already demonstrated both the ability and willingness to infiltrate sensitive foreign nuclear infrastructure through operations such as Olympic Games (Stuxnet), albeit targeting Iran's nuclear fuel cycle rather than NC3.[46] There is also speculation that the United States fielded, and potentially used, a suite of cyber and electronic warfare options allegedly part of program code-named "Nimble Fire" designed to interfere with North Korean missile tests "left of launch."[47] North Korea suffered numerous unsuccessful tests, including some catastrophic failures, although it is impossible to rule out accidents. In principle, now that North Korea has a functional deterrent, the same methods could be used to disrupt an actual wartime launch. Preemptive cyberattacks could complement kinetic counterforce missile strikes to neutralize a North Korean missile before it departed its launch pad. This would be an attractive military alternative to relying exclusively on antimissile systems like Terminal High Altitude Air Defense (THAAD), the Aegis Ballistic Missile Defense System deployed on warships and Aegis Ashore batteries, and the Ground-based Midcourse Defense system. The electronic attack and offensive cyber operations tested as part of the Nimble Fire program are updated digital analogues of Cold War programs like Canopy Wing.

---

[45] Office of the Secretary of Defense 2022, p. 4.
[46] Slayton 2017.   [47] Sanger and Broad 2017.

How Cyber Deception Undermines Nuclear Deterrence

Unfortunately, as we shall argue, when one side depends on covert counterforce capabilities to preempt the other side's nuclear deterrent, then deterrence failure becomes even more likely. Offensive cyber operations planned and employed "left of launch" are just such a capability. Moreover, strategic instability is greatest in confrontations between asymmetric nuclear powers, where only the stronger side has effective covert cyber counterforce capabilities. This is, more or less, the situation with the United States and North Korea.

In the language of game theory, the ability to win the war-fighting subgame of the deterrence game makes playing the subgame more likely. Our theoretical argument proceeds as follows. We first describe the importance of transparency in nuclear deterrence and the importance of secrecy in cyber operations. Then we analyze the ways in which the combination of these two domains can affect crisis decision making. We highlight relative nuclear force structure and cyber capacity factors that could potentially condition the instability of this combination.

Nuclear Deterrence and Credible Communication

Nuclear weapons have some salient political properties. They are singularly and obviously destructive. They kill in more, and more ghastly, ways than conventional munitions through electromagnetic radiation, blast, firestorms, radioactive fallout, and health effects that linger for years. Bombers, ICBMs and SLBMs can project warheads globally without significantly mitigating their lethality, steeply attenuating the conventional loss-of-strength gradient.[48] Defense against nuclear attack is very difficult, even with modern ballistic missile defenses, given the speed of incoming warheads and use of decoys; multiple warheads and missile volleys further reduce the probability of perfect interception. If one cannot preemptively destroy all of an enemy's missiles, then there is a non-trivial chance of getting hit by some of them. When one missed missile can incinerate millions of people, the notion of winning a nuclear war starts to seem meaningless for many politicians.

---

[48] Boulding 1962.

178   ELEMENTS OF DETERRENCE

As defense seemed increasingly impractical, early Cold War strategists championed the threat of assured retaliation as the chief mechanism for avoiding war.[49] The Cold War was an intense learning experience for both practitioners and students of international security, rewriting well-worn realities more than once.[50] A key conundrum was the practice of brinkmanship. Adversaries who could not compete by winning a nuclear war could still compete by manipulating the risk of nuclear annihilation, gambling that an opponent would have the good judgment to back down at some point short of the nuclear brink. Brinkmanship crises—conceptualized as games of Chicken where one cannot heighten tensions without increasing the hazard of the mutually undesired outcome—require that decision makers behave irrationally, or possibly that they act randomly, which is difficult to conceptualize in practical terms.[51] The chief concern in historical episodes of chicken, such as the Berlin Crisis and Cuban Missile Crisis, was not whether a certain level of harm was possible, but whether an adversary was resolved enough, possibly, to risk nuclear suicide. The logical inconsistency of the need for illogic to win led almost from the beginning of the nuclear era to elaborate deductive contortions.[52]

Both mutual assured destruction (MAD) and successful brinksmanship depend on a less appreciated, but no less fundamental, feature of nuclear weapons: political transparency. Most elements of military power are weakened by disclosure.[53] Military plans are considerably less effective if shared with an enemy. Conventional weapons become less lethal as adversaries learn what different systems can and cannot do, where they are located, how they are operated, and how to devise countermeasures and array defenses to blunt or disarm an attack. In contrast, relatively little reduction in destruction follows from enemy knowledge of nuclear capabilities. For most of the nuclear era, no effective defense existed against a nuclear attack. Even today, with evolving ABM systems, one ICBM still might get through and annihilate the capital city. Nuclear forces are more robust to revelation than other weapons, enabling nuclear nations better to advertise the harm they can inflict.

The need for transparency to achieve an effective deterrent is driven home by a critical plot twist in the satirical Cold War film *Dr. Strangelove*: "the whole point of a Doomsday Machine is lost, if you keep it a secret! Why didn't

---

[49] Brodie et al. 1946; Wohlstetter 1959; H. Kahn 1960; G. Snyder 1961.
[50] Trachtenberg 1991a; Gavin 2012; Gartzke and Kroenig 2016.   [51] Powell 1988
[52] Schelling 1960; Zagare 1996; Schelling 1966.   [53] Slantchev 2010.

you tell the world, eh?" During the real Cold War, fortunately, Soviet leaders paraded their nuclear weapons through Red Square for the benefit of foreign military attaches and the international press corps. Satellites photographed missile, bomber, and submarine bases. While other aspects of military affairs on both sides of the Iron Curtain remained closely guarded secrets, the United States and the Soviet Union permitted observers to evaluate their nuclear capabilities. This is especially remarkable given the secrecy that pervaded Soviet society. The relative transparency of nuclear arsenals, at least after the late 1960s, ensured that the superpowers could calculate risks and consequences within a first-order approximation, which led to a reduction in severe conflict and instability even as political competition in other arenas was fierce.[54]

Despite other deficits, nuclear weapons have long been considered to be stabilizing with respect to rational incentives for war (the risk of nuclear accidents is another matter).[55] If each side has a secure second strike— or even a minimal deterrent with some non-zero chance of launching a few missiles—then each side can expect to gain little and lose much by fighting a nuclear war. Whereas the costs of conventional war can be more mysterious because each side might decide to hold something back and meter out its punishment due to some internal constraint or a theory of graduated escalation, even a modest initial nuclear exchange is recognized to be extremely costly. As long as both sides understand this and understand (or believe) that the adversary understands this as well, then the relationship is stable. Countries approach other nuclear-armed powers with considerable deference, especially over issues of fundamental national or international importance. At the same time, nuclear weapons appear to be of limited value in prosecuting aggressive action, especially over issues of secondary or tertiary importance, or in response to aggression from others at lower levels of dispute intensity. Nuclear weapons are best used for signaling a willingness to run serious risks to protect or extort some issue that is considered of vital national interest.

As mentioned previously, both superpowers in the Cold War considered the war-fighting advantages of nuclear weapons, quite apart from any deterrent effect, and the United States and Russia still do (to some extent and in different ways, with the US focusing on the credibility of extended deterrence and Russia focusing on coercive uses of so-called non-strategic weapons).

---

[54] Powell 2015.   [55] Sagan and Waltz 2012.

180 ELEMENTS OF DETERRENCE

High-altitude bursts for air defense, electromagnetic pulses for frying electronics, underwater detonations for anti-submarine warfare, hardened target penetration, area denial, and so on, have some battlefield utility. Transparency per se is less important than weapon effects, when considering only war-fighting uses, and can even be deleterious for tactics that depend on stealth and mobility. Even a single tactical nuke, however, would inevitably be a political event. Survivability of the second-strike deterrent can also mitigate against transparency, as in the case of the Soviet Perimeter system, as mobility, concealment, and deception can make it harder for an observer to track and count respective forces from space. Counterforce strategies, platform diversity and mobility, ballistic missile defense systems, and force employment doctrine can all make it more difficult for one or both sides in a crisis to know whether an attack is likely to succeed or fail. The resulting uncertainty affects not only estimates of relative capabilities but also the degree of confidence in retaliation. At the same time, there is reason to believe that platform diversity lowers the risk of nuclear or conventional contests, because increasing the number of types of delivery platforms heightens second-strike survivability without increasing the lethality of an initial strike.[56] While transparency is not itself a requirement for nuclear use, stable deterrence benefits to the degree to which retaliation can be anticipated, as well as the likelihood that the consequences of a first strike are more costly than any benefit.

The Cyber Commitment Problem

Offensive cyber operations, by contrast, are neither robust to revelation nor as obviously destructive as nuclear weapons. Combat performance often hinges on well-kept secrets, feints, and diversions. Many military plans and capabilities degrade when revealed. The need to conceal details of the true balance of power in order to preserve battlefield effectiveness gives rise to the so-called military commitment problem.[57] This refers to situations where the military benefits of surprise (winning) trump the diplomatic benefits of coercion (warning).

To sum up our discussion in Chapter 5, cyber operations are extremely constrained by the military commitment problem. Revelation of a

[56] Gartzke, Kaplow, and Mehta 2014.   [57] Gartzke 2001b; Powell 2006.

cyberthreat in advance that is specific enough to convince a target of the validity of the threat also provides enough information potentially to neutralize it. Stuxnet took years and hundreds of millions of dollars to develop, but it was patched within weeks of its discovery. The Snowden leaks negated a whole swath of tradecraft that the NSA took years to develop. States may use other forms of covert action, such as publicly disavowed lethal aid or aerial bombing (e.g., Nixon's Cambodia campaign), to discreetly signal their interests, but such cases can only work to the extent that revelation of operational details fails to disarm rebels or prevent airstrikes.[58]

In Chapter 6 we argued that cyber tradecraft relies on stealth, stratagem, and deception. This is especially true of highly technical cyber operations that rely on exquisite vulnerabilities and other sensitive sources and methods. This is not necessarily true of all cyber operations (most of which rely on known vulnerabilities but exploit the gullibility or negligence of human users), but it is almost certainly true of those targeting enemy NC3. Operations tailored to compromise complex remote targets require extensive intelligence, planning and preparation, and testing to be effective. Actions that alert a target of an exploit allow the target to patch, reconfigure, or adopt countermeasures that invalidate the plan. Therefore, hacking NC3 must be conducted in extreme secrecy as a condition of the efficacy of the attack.

In short, the cyber domain on its own is better suited for "watching" for opportunities to gain an advantage in covert competitions for information, and perhaps for supporting military efforts at "winning" through preemption in other domains, than "warning" adversaries in coercive diplomacy. As such, cyber and nuclear weapons fall on extreme opposite sides of a spectrum of strategies.

Dangerous Complements

Nuclear weapons have been used in anger twice—against the Japanese cities Hiroshima and Nagasaki—but cyberspace is abused daily. Considered separately, the nuclear domain is stable and the cyber domain is unstable. In combination, the results are ambiguous.

In one direction, nuclear deterrence provides an extreme bound on the intensity of destruction that a cyberattacker will be willing to inflict on a

---

[58] Carson and Yarhi-Milo 2017.

182   ELEMENTS OF DETERRENCE

nuclear-armed adversary. Nuclear weapons, and military power generally, create an upper bound on cyber aggression to the degree that retaliation is anticipated and feared. US declaratory policy suggests that unacceptable cyberattacks may prompt a military response; while nuclear weapons are not explicitly threatened, neither are they withheld.[59] Nuclear threats have no credibility at the low end, however, where the bulk of cyberattacks occur. This produces a cross-domain version of the stability-instability paradox, where deterrence works at the high end but is not credible, and thus encourages provocation, at low intensities.[60]

In the other direction, however, the unstable cyber domain can undermine the stability of nuclear deterrence. Most analysts who argue that the cyber-nuclear combination is a recipe for danger focus on the fog of crisis decision making.[61] Stephen Cimbala points out that today's relatively smaller nuclear arsenals may perversely magnify the attractiveness of NC3 exploitation in a crisis: "Ironically, the downsizing of US and post-Soviet Russian strategic nuclear arsenals since the end of the Cold War, while a positive development from the perspectives of nuclear arms control and nonproliferation, makes the concurrence of cyber and nuclear attack capabilities more alarming."[62] Cimbala focuses mainly on the risks of misperception and miscalculation that emerge when a cyberattack muddies the transparent communication required for opponents to understand one another's interests, red lines, and willingness to use force, and to ensure reliable control over subordinate commanders. Thus a nuclear actor "faced with a sudden burst of holes in its vital warning and response systems might, for example, press the preemption button instead of waiting to ride out the attack and then retaliate."[63]

The outcome of fog of decision scenarios such as these depend on how humans react to risk and uncertainty, which in turn depends on bounded rationality and organizational frameworks that might confuse rational decision making.[64] These factors exacerbate a hard problem. Yet within a rationalist framework, cyberattacks that have already created their effects need not trigger an escalatory spiral. While being handed a fait accompli may trigger an aggressive reaction, it is also plausible that the target's awareness that its NC3 has been compromised in some way would help to convey

---

[59] Office of the Secretary of Defense 2022.
[60] Colby 2013; Lindsay 2015; Lindsay and Gartzke 2018.
[61] Fritz 2009; Cimbala 2012; Futter 2015.   [62] Cimbala 2014.
[63] Cimbala 2012.   [64] Jervis, Lebow, and Stein 1985; Goldgeier and Tetlock 2001; Stein 2017.

new information that the balance of power is not as favorable as previously thought. This in turn could encourage the target to accommodate, rather than escalate. While defects in rational decision making are a serious concern in any cyber-nuclear scenario, the situation becomes even more hazardous when there are rational incentives to escalate. Although "known unknowns" can create confusion, to paraphrase Donald Rumsfeld, the "unknown unknowns" are perhaps more dangerous.

A successful clandestine penetration of NC3 can defeat the informational symmetry that stabilizes nuclear relationships. Nuclear weapons are useful for deterrence because they impose a degree of consensus about the distribution of power; each side knows the other can inflict prohibitive levels of damage, even if they may disagree about the precise extent of this damage. Cyber operations are attractive precisely because they can secretly revise the distribution of power. NC3 neutralization may be an expensive and rarified capability in the reach of only a few states with mature signals intelligence agencies, but it is much cheaper than nuclear attack. Yet the very usefulness of cyber operations for nuclear war-fighting ensure that deterrence failure during brinksmanship crises are more likely.

Nuclear states may initiate crises of risk and resolve to see who will back down first, which is not always clear in advance. Chicken appears viable, ironically, because each player understands that a nuclear war would be a disaster for all, and thus all can agree that someone can be expected swerve. Nuclear deterrence should ultimately make dealing with an adversary diplomatically more attractive than fighting, provided that fighting is costly—as would seem evident for the prospect of nuclear war—and assuming that bargains are available to states willing to accept compromise rather than annihilation. If, however, one side knows, but the other does not, that the attacker has disabled the target's ability to perceive an impending military attack, or to react to one when it is underway, then they will not have a shared understanding of the probable outcome of war, even in broad terms.

Consider a brinksmanship crisis between two nuclear states where only one has realized a successful penetration of the rival's NC3. The cyberattacker knows that it has a military advantage, but it cannot reveal the advantage to the target, lest the advantage be terminated. The target does not know that it is at a disadvantage, and it cannot be told by the attacker for the same reason. The attacker perceives an imbalance of power while the target perceives a balance. A dangerous competition in risk taking ensues. The first side knows that it does not need to back down. The second side feels confident that it

184 ELEMENTS OF DETERRENCE

can stand fast and raise the stakes far beyond what it would be willing to if it understood the true balance of power. Each side is willing to escalate to create more risk for the other side, making it more likely that one or the other will conclude that deterrence has failed and move into war-fighting mode to attempt to limit the damage the other can inflict.

The targeted nature and uncertain effects of offensive cyber operations put additional pressure on decision makers. An intrusion will probably disable only part of the enemy's NC3 architecture, not all of it (which is not only phenomenally difficult to achieve but also more likely to be noticed by the target). Thus the target may retain control over some nuclear forces, or conventional forces. The target may be tempted to use some of them piecemeal to signal a willingness to escalate further, even though it cannot actually escalate because of the cyber operation. The cyberattacker knows that it has escalation dominance, but when even a minor demonstration by the target can cause great damage, it is tempting to preempt this move or others like it. This situation would be especially unstable if only second strike but not primary strike NC3 was incapacitated. Uncertainty in the efficacy of the clandestine penetration would discount the attacker's confidence in its escalation dominance, with a range of possible outcomes. Enough uncertainty would discount the cyberattack to nothing, which would have a stabilizing effect by returning the crisis to the pure nuclear domain. A little bit of uncertainty about cyber effectiveness could heighten risk acceptance while also raising the incentives to preempt as an insurance measure.

Adding allies into the mix introduces additional instability. An ally emboldened by its nuclear umbrella might run provocative risks that it would be much more reluctant to embrace if it was aware that the umbrella was actually full of holes. Conversely, if the clandestine advantage is held by the state extending the umbrella, allies could become unnerved by the willingness of their defender to run what appear to be outsize risks, oblivious of the reasons for the defender's confidence, creating discord in the alliance and incentives for self-protective action, leading to greater uncertainty about alliance solidarity.

The direction of influence between the cyber and nuclear realms depends to large degree on which domain is the main arena of action. Planning and conducting cyber operations will be bounded by the ability of aggressors to convince themselves that attacks will remain secret, and by the confidence of nuclear nations in their invulnerability. Fears of cross-domain escalation will tend to keep instability in cyberspace bounded. However, if a crisis has risen to the point where nuclear threats are being seriously considered or made, then NC3 exploitation will be destabilizing. Brinksmanship crises seem to have receded in frequency since the Cuban Missile Crisis but the war in Ukraine since 2022 can be interpreted as a slow-motion nuclear brinksmanship contest. President Vladimir Putin of Russia has insinuated more than once in recent years that his government is willing to use tactical nuclear weapons if necessary to support his policies.

Dyadic Variation in Instability

Not all crises are the same. Indeed, their very idiosyncrasies create the uncertainties that make bargaining failure more likely.[65] So far our analysis would be at home in the Cold War, with the additional introduction of the technological novelty of cyber operations. Yet not every state has the same cyber capabilities or vulnerabilities. Variation in cyber power relations across dyads should be expected to affect the strategic stability of nuclear states.

The so-called second nuclear age differs from superpower rivalry in important ways.[66] There are fewer absolute numbers of warheads in the world, down from a peak of over seventy thousand in the 1980s to about fifteen thousand today (less than five thousand deployed), but they are distributed very unevenly.[67] The United States and Russia have comparably sized arsenals, each with a fully diversified triad of delivery platforms. China, India, Pakistan, Britain, France, and Israel have modest arsenals in the range of several dozen to a couple hundred weapons, but they have very different doctrines, conventional force complements, domestic political institutions, and alliance relationships. Yet, China has embarked on a modernization and expansion program to improve survivability against a perceived American counterforce threat. The recent nuclear powers lack the hard-won experience and shared norms of the Cold War to guide them through crises, and even the United States and Russia have much to relearn.

Cyber warfare capacity also varies considerably across contemporary nuclear nations. The United States, Russia, Israel, and Britain are in the top tier, able to run sophisticated, persistent, clandestine penetrations. China is a uniquely active cyber power with ambitious cyber warfare doctrine, but its operational focus is on economic espionage and political censorship,

---

[65] Gartzke 1999.   [66] Yoshihara and Holmes 2012.
[67] Kristensen and Norris 2016.

186 ELEMENTS OF DETERRENCE

resulting in more porous defenses for military purposes.[68] France, India, and Pakistan also have active cyber warfare programs, while North Korea is the least developed cyber nation, dependent on China for its expertise.

The risk of crisis instability is not the same for all dyads. It is harder to compromise the NC3 of strong states because of the redundancy and active defenses in their arsenal. Likewise, strong states are better able to compromise the NC3 of any states but especially of weaker states, because of strong states' greater organizational capacity and expertise in cyber operations. Stable deterrence or MAD is most likely to hold in mutually strong dyads (e.g., the United States and the Soviet Union in the Cold War or Russia today to a lesser extent). Deterrence is slightly less likely in other equally matched dyads (India-Pakistan) where defensive vulnerabilities create temptations but offensive capabilities may not be sufficient to exploit them. Most states can be expected to refrain from targeting American NC3 given a US reputation for cyber power (a general deterrence benefit enhanced by Stuxnet and Snowden).

The situation is less stable if the United States is the attacker. The most dangerous dyad is a stronger and a weaker state (United States and North Korea or Israel and Iran). Dyads involving strong and middle powers are also dangerous (United States and China). The stronger side is tempted to disrupt NC3 as a war-fighting hedge in case deterrence breaks down, while the weaker but still formidable side has a reasonable chance at detection. The marginally weaker may also be tempted to subvert NC3, particularly for reconnaissance; the stronger side is more likely to detect and correct the intrusion but will be alarmed by the ambiguity in distinguishing intelligence collection from attack planning.[69] In a brinksmanship crisis between them, windows for coercion may be available yet fleeting, with real risks of spiral and war.

Policy Implications

Skeptics are right to challenge the hype about "cyberwar." The term is confusing, and hacking rarely amounts to anything approaching a weapon

---

[68] Lindsay 2014. Improving Chinese capacity for cyber warfare is suggested by Microsoft Threat Intelligence 2023.

[69] Buchanan 2017.

of mass destruction. Cyberspace is most usefully exploited on the lower end of the conflict spectrum for intelligence and subversion, which will tend to be more useful for peacetime intelligence contests or as a wartime complement to rather than a substitute for military power. Yet the logic of complementarity has at least one exception regarding conflict severity, and it is a big one.

Offensive cyber operations targeting NC3 raise the risk of nuclear war. They do so because cyber operations and nuclear weapons are extreme complements regarding their informational properties. Cyber operations rely on deception. Nuclear deterrence relies on clear communication. In a brinksmanship crisis, the former undermines the latter. Nuclear crises were rare events in Cold War history, thankfully. Today, the proliferation and modernization of nuclear weapons may raise the risk slightly. Subversion of NC3 raises the danger of nuclear war slightly more. Cyberwar is not war per se, but in rare circumstances it may make escalation to thermonuclear war more likely.

NC3 is a particularly attractive counterforce target because disruption can render the enemy's arsenal less effective without having to destroy individual platforms. US nuclear strategy in practice has long relied on counterforce capabilities such as Canopy Wing.[70] Deterrence theorists expect this to undermine the credibility of the adversary's deterrent and create pressures to move first in a conflict.[71] If for some reason deterrence fails, however, countervalue strikes on civilian population centers would be militarily useless and morally odious. Counterforce strikes, by contrast, aim at preemptive disarmament or damage limitation by attacking the enemy's nuclear enterprise.

Counterforce capabilities are designed for "winning" a nuclear war once over the brink, but their strategic purpose may still include "warning" if they can somehow be made robust to revelation. During the Cold War, the United States found ways to inform the Soviet Union of its counterforce ability to sink SSBNs, hit mobile ICBMs, and show off some electronic warfare capabilities without giving away precise details.[72] This improved mutual recognition of US advantages and thus clearer assessment of the consequences of conflict, but the military commitment problem was real nonetheless. The commitment problem is even more pronounced for offensive cyber operations targeting NC3. As one side builds more sophisticated

---

[70] Long 2008; Long and B. Green 2014; B. Green 2020.   [71] Jervis 1984; Van Evera 1999.
[72] B. Green and Long 2019.

188 ELEMENTS OF DETERRENCE

NC3 to improve the credibility of its nuclear "warning," the other side engages in cyber operations to improve its capacity for nuclear "winning." The ability to prevail in the damage limitation conest, should deterrence fail, makes it more likely that deterrence will fail in the first place.

The prohibitive cost of nuclear war and the relative transparency of the nuclear balance has contributed to seven decades of nuclear peace. If this is to continue, it will be necessary to find ways to restore and maintain transparency. If knowledge of a shift in relative power is concealed, then the deterrent effect of nuclear capabilities is undermined. This will tend to occur in periods where concern over nuclear attack is heightened, such as in the midst of a militarized crises. Yet there is no reason to believe that states will wait for a crisis before seeking to establish advantageous positions in cyberspace. Indeed, given the intricate intelligence and planning required, offensive cyber preparations must precede overt aggression by months or even years. It is this erosion of the bulwark of deterrence that is most troubling.

Anything that can be done to protect NC3 against cyber intrusion will make the most dangerous possibility of successful but undetected compromises less likely. The Defense Science Board in 2013 recommended "immediate action to assess and assure national leadership that the current US nuclear deterrent is also survivable against the full-spectrum cyber...threat."[73] Significant progress was made in the following decade modernizing NC3, but more work remains to be done.

Defense in depth for NC3 will generally include redundant communications pathways, error correction channels, isolation of the most critical systems, component heterogeneity rather than a vulnerable software monoculture, and network security monitoring with active defenses (i.e., a counterintelligence mindset). Older technologies, ironically, may provide some protection by foiling access of modern cybertechniques (Russia reportedly still uses punch-cards for parts of its NC3);[74] yet vulnerabilities from an earlier era inadequate safeguards are also a problem. For defense in depth to translate into deterrence by denial requires the additional step of somehow advertising NC3 redundancy and resilience even in a cyber-degraded environment. General Richard thus goes on to offer reassurance in the survivability of US NC3 in a hostile cyber environment: "The relative isolation and the

---

[73] Defense Science Board 2013.
[74] S. Peterson 2004.

redundancies of the systems comprising the Nuclear Command and Control System (NCCS), combined with ongoing cybersecurity enhancements, ensure our ability to respond under adverse cyber conditions."[75]

This is fine and well for the security of US NC3 from foreign intrusion. The destabilizing scenario contemplated in this chapter, however, concerns the security of adversaries' NC3 against, for instance, American intrusion. We argued that instability is greatest when one side has a potent cyber exploit of the enemy's NC3 that it cannot reveal due to the cyber commitment problem. Our argument here is theoretical, but war-gaming experiments have produced supporting evidence for this mechanism: nuclear initiation was found to be more likely among players that had a secret cyber exploit against enemy NC3 than among players who became aware of their own NC3 vulnerabilities.[76] Hardening one's own NC3 against cyberattacks while simultaneously exploiting the NC3 of the other side can lead to precisely this scenario.

What else can be done? Arms control agreements to ban cyberattacks on NC3 might seem attractive, but the cyber commitment problem also undermines institutional monitoring and enforcement. Even where the US would benefit from such an agreement by keeping this asymmetric capability out of the hands of other states, it would still have strong incentives to prepare its own damage limitation options should deterrence fail. Nevertheless, diplomatic initiatives to discuss the dangers of cyber-nuclear interactions with potential opponents should be pursued. Even if cyber-nuclear dangers cannot be eliminated, states should be encouraged to review their NC3 and ensure strict lines of control over any offensive cyber operations at that level.

Classified studies of the details of NC3, not just the technical infrastructure but also their human organizations, together with wargames of the scenarios above, may help nuclear war planners to think carefully about subverting NC3. Unfortunately the same reconnaissance operations used to better understand the opponent's NC3 could potentially be misinterpreted as attempts to compromise it.[77] More insidiously, private knowledge can become a source of instability insofar as knowing something about an adversary that improves one's prospects in war increases the incentive to act through force or to exploit windows of opportunity in a crisis that could inadvertently escalate.

---

[75] Richard 2022, p. 18.   [76] Schneider, Schechter, and Shaffer 2023.   [77] Buchanan 2017.

190   ELEMENTS OF DETERRENCE

Finally, every effort should be made to ensure that senior leaders—the President and the Secretary of Defense in the United States, the Central Military Commission in China, etc.—understand the implications of and think carefully about authorizing any cyber operations against any country's NC3 for any reason. Even intrusions focused only on intelligence collection should be reviewed and approved at the highest level. Education is easier said than done given the esoteric technical details involved. But ignorance at the senior level of the implications of compromised NC3 is a major risk factor in a crisis contributing to false optimism or other bad decisions. New technologies of information are, ironically, undermining clear communication.

Cyber disruption of NC3 is fundamentally a cross-domain deterrence problem. Linking domains could also be part of the solution. As noted above, nuclear deterrence will intrinsically work to bound the severity of instability in the cyber domain by threatening, implicitly or explicitly, the prospect of military, economic, law-enforcement, or diplomatic consequences. The 2018 NPR explicitly included a modified declaratory policy that appears to consider a nuclear response to a catastrophic cyberattack: "The United States would only consider the employment of nuclear weapons in extreme circumstances to defend the vital interests of the United States, its allies, and partners. Extreme circumstances could include significant non-nuclear strategic attacks. Significant non-nuclear strategic attacks include, but are not limited to, attacks on the U.S., allied, or partner civilian population or infrastructure, and attacks on U.S. or allied nuclear forces, their command and control, or warning and attack assessment capabilities."[78]

The problem is that this is a more ambiguous, and potentially more provocative, declaratory policy. How big would a cyberattack have to be to justify a nuclear response? Would a nuclear response ever be justified in response to even a massive cyberattack? Doubts in these areas led to a more tightly scoped declaratory statement in the 2022 NPR: "As long as nuclear weapons exist, the fundamental role of nuclear weapons is to deter nuclear attack on the United States, our Allies, and partners." And yet the same document asserts, "our nuclear posture is intended to complicate an adversary's entire decision making calculus, including whether to ... conduct strategic attacks using non-nuclear capabilities."[79] Any conceivable threshold for a nuclear response to a cyberattack is doubtlessly very high, as it should be,

[78] Office of the Secretary of Defense 2018, p. 21.
[79] Office of the Secretary of Defense 2022, p. 8.

but it seems that it is not off the table. The vast majority of cyberattacks we can contemplate will fall well below this rarefied threshold, of course. Perhaps it is possible to set a lower threshold for a non-nuclear response via other military domains, but that will raise similar quandaries about proportionality and credibility. We can expect cyberattacks to flourish well below any credible threshold of conventional deterrence, and rapidly tail off as it is approached.[80]

But cross-domain deterrence may help in nuclear crises in other ways, by providing policy makers with options other than nuclear weapons, and perhaps options when NC3 is compromised. A diversity of options provides a variation on Schelling's classic "threat that leaves something to chance" by leaving brinksmanship to an expanded portfolio of options. In some dyads, particularly with highly asymmetric nuclear arsenals and technical capabilities, cross-domain deterrence may provide options for conventional war and coercion short of initiating nuclear war. This does not necessarily improve deterrence and in many ways is predicated on the failure of general deterrence (i.e., the outbreak of a crisis), but the broadening of options may lessen the consequences of that failure.[81] To return to the *WarGames* scenario with which we began, it is helpful to have options available other than "global thermonuclear war" when a machine asks, "Do you want to play a game?"

---

[80] Lindsay 2015.   [81] Lieber and Press 2023.

PART III

EMPIRICAL EVIDENCE IN MULTIPLE DOMAINS

Specialized military capabilities can be more or less useful for different political strategies. The previous section focused on the theoretically distinct features of cyberspace, which is both a highly technological domain and extremely specialized. We argued that cyberspace is especially useful for strategies of deception, but for the same reasons, it is problematic for deterrence.

In this section we explore other painful trade-offs showcased in other domains. Military specializations become useful for goals other than strategic stability, to include influence over the status quo, the power to win wars, and economizing on the costs of national security policy. But it is not usually possible to pursue all of these desirable goals at once. The following chapters provide empirical evidence on the deterrence implications of military specialization. Chapter 8 discusses the relationship between the forward deployment of ground forces and the credibility of extended deterrence. Chapter 9 assesses the implications of naval mobility, which enhances power projection at the price of lower credibility for deterrence commitments. Chapter 10 shows how the decoupling of killing and dying, exemplified in the use of aerial drones, can have inadvertently tragic consequences for civilian populations. Chapter 11 demonstrates a relationship between improved satellite reconnaissance and strategic stability.

Measuring deterrence in any given case is challenging because success often means that nothing happens. Qualitative case studies might look for evidence about how policy makers consider explicit and implicit threats when formulating policy options. Another strategy is to look for quantitative patterns of conflict across a large set of cases. Hypotheses can be tested by looking for statistically significant correlations between these conditions and

194 ELEMENTS OF DETERRENCE

the onset of conflict (controlling for other conditions associated with war and peace). This provides evidence about general trends, even as individual cases may vary for idiosyncratic reasons.[1]

Most of the empirical studies in this book measure deterrence failure in terms of the incidence of militarized interstate disputes (MIDs).[2] MIDs code the use of military force in international politics, ranging from coercive displays to major wars. While the historiography of any given data point may be contested, and some historical incidents may be missing altogether, this is only a problem if there are reasons to believe there are systematic biases or auto-correlated errors in the data. For better or worse, reliance on MIDs is standard practice in quantitative peace research. Here we assume that if we see a MID, then at least one actor decided that mobilizing or employing military power was more attractive than the alternatives; that is, the actor was not deterred. If we observe systematic patterns in the distribution of MIDs in circumstances predicted by a theory of deterrence, therefore, then it is reasonable to conclude that deterrence is *not* credible under those circumstances.

[1] Gartzke 1999.   [2] Maoz et al. 2019.

8

Land

Presence and Credibility

with Koji Kagotani

The United States is a capitalist democracy that wields a disproportionate share of the world's military power (i.e., it is a "liberal hegemon"). In an earlier era, the British played a similar role. Like the United Kingdom in its heyday, the United States today relies on its navy to keep the oceans open for commerce and project power in defense of its global interests. But this also requires the United States to prioritize its interests overseas. Navies can go anywhere, but they cannot be everywhere at the same time. The very strengths of naval power—stealth, mobility, and the ability to concentrate fires at a time and place of a commander's choosing—ensure that navies are also more mercurial than comparable land forces.

Sending expeditionary land armies wherever a nation has interests is expensive, and thus often unpopular. Alliances offer a much cheaper alternative. Alliances are also particularly attractive for a country like the United States that desires to influence foreign affairs but has little direct need for more territory (outside of a few niche interests like space ground stations and other intelligence collection platforms). The distant sea power can partner with a local land power, again provided that their objectives are similar or compatible. The United States and Great Britain have thus relied on alliances as a key component of their respective grand strategies. The United States has numerous formal alliances including the multilateral NATO treaty in Europe and the "hub and spokes" system of bilateral alliances with Japan, South Korea, the Philippines, Australia, and New Zealand. But allying also introduces an additional set of dilemmas involving choices about force structure and posture.

To protect and reassure US allies overseas, should Washington rely on inherently mobile naval and air forces, or should it forward deploy ground troops for an extended territorial stay? Maintaining multiple garrisons at

Elements of Deterrence: Strategy, Technology, and Complexity in Global Politics. Erik Gartzke and Jon R. Lindsay, Oxford University Press. © Oxford University Press 2024. DOI: 10.1093/oso/9780197754443.003.0008

196 ELEMENTS OF DETERRENCE

levels sufficient for every contingency is prohibitively expensive. Further, if the United States deploys land forces to one region, they will not be immediately available in another. Mobile naval and air forces provide more flexibility for covering commitments over the vast expanses of the Pacific. They can also redeploy quickly to other regions as circumstances require. However, force structure and posture decisions affect more than (just) military tactics. Where a country deposits what kinds of military power ultimately signals different things about the nation's priorities and values: committing to protect a few things that matter most, or attempting to influence more areas with somewhat reduced credibility.

In this chapter we begin our empirical exploration of the specific differences between land and sea power by focusing on the signaling benefits of fixed forward (ground) force deployments. Then in Chapter 9, we will show that the strategic flexibility of naval mobility comes at the price of strategic stability.

The Obama administration's announcement in November 2011 of its intent to "pivot" a sizable portion of US military power to Asia generated considerable anxiety among America's European allies. NATO is one of the most durable and highly institutionalized security agreements in world history. Nevertheless, there were fears that the pivot signaled waning US interest in European affairs.[1,2] President Vladimir Putin of Russia may also have interpreted the pivot this way, since Russia's aggression toward its European neighbors increased in intensity (and frequency) in subsequent years.

At the same time, there is an active debate in academic and policy circles about where in Asia US forces ought to go.[3] At least part of the basis for controversy lies in a lack of information; it is simply not clear what deployments accomplish and where they might prove unnecessary or even counterproductive. "Presence" involves the physical deployment of ships or other forces or platforms abroad, to some distant place. There is a perception among policy makers and military experts that presence

---

[1] Kim and Simon 2021b.

[2] Kim and Simon discuss yet another force structure/posture balancing act (Kim and Simon 2021a). While repositioning forces may raise doubts about reliability, the recipients of increased protection should presumably also perceive benefits in the defender's change of priorities.

[3] Layne 1997; Layne 2002; Layne 2012; Brooks, Ikenberry, and Wohlforth 2013; Montgomery 2014a; Lanoszka 2022. The Obama pivot turned out to be more aspirational than actual, as crises in the Middle East and Europe continued to capture American attention and military resources. Instead of a pivot, US policy was a "pirouette." But it is very likely that the attempt to realign US force posture toward Asia will persist in coming decades, especially given the rising power and influence of China. For background, see Manyin et al. 2012; R. Ross 2012.

makes a difference, shaping foreign perceptions of US power, for instance. This could be consequential, even in the context of an existing alliance. Yet, systematic theory and evidence substantiating (or challenging) this intuition is lacking. A forward posture could (further) warn adversaries and reassure allies, reinforcing the conflict-inhibiting effect of the basic alliance treaty.[4] Presence could also facilitate more rapid and decisive intervention in a crisis or conflict.

Foreign deployments also have clear downsides. They are expensive and unpopular, both at home and abroad. Deployments could prove provocative, destabilizing rather than stabilizing international affairs. Finally, durable deployments on allied territory are redundant if alliances themselves are adequate to deter or reassure.

Alliance networks represent both opportunities and liabilities in deciding whether and where to deploy troops abroad. Allies may offer a welcoming destination for one's soldiers, ships, and aircraft. An ally's geographical location can also provide access to distant places or a platform for intelligence collection, an attractive feature for basing and projecting power.[5] Yet, defenders seldom send forces sufficient to actually protect a partner. Direct defense is cost prohibitive, particularly when confronted with the need to secure a network of allies. Relying on less tangible commitments—such as alliance treaties or even informal alignments—is cheap by contrast and scales well with a large number of partners.

A military presence may thus be unnecessary if the alliance treaty does a sufficient job of creating commitment or signaling resolve.[6] Previous research suggests that the critical contribution of deployments may be in how they telegraph the defender's existing (but possibly unrecognized) willingness to intervene to protect an ally,[7] rather than through attempts to enhance the defender's (possibly inadequate) level of commitment. Defenders that position substantial proportions of their military capabilities on a given ally's territory are more likely to maintain successful extended general deterrence. Conversely, for a defender capable of protecting a partner and projecting power, the nominal quantity of forces deployed, and their overall cost, may be less critical, since size by itself may not convey the intensity of

---

[4] The "Washington Declaration" between South Korea and the United States provides for port visits by US submarines, among other platforms. While symbolic—US nuclear submarines literally *cannot* perform their missions while in port—these visits may shape perceptions of the tightness of the alliance, enhancing deterrence, or influence, through greater presence.
[5] Morrow 1991. [6] Fearon 1997. [7] Gartzke and Kagotani 2016.

198 ELEMENTS OF DETERRENCE

the defender's preferences, or the priority assigned by the defender to a given security partner.

Every ally clearly cannot equally be the defender's favorite. Some protégés must be a lower priority, at least in relative terms. The defender's force posture decisions thus signal intent, not just in terms of which states will be protected, but also which allies might be protected first, or most vigorously, if this becomes necessary. The choice of force posture therefore determines winners and losers within and across alliance structures, something very nearly matching standard definitions of politics. Indeed, this logic serves to explain why assurance—the quality of convincing allies that they are the ones on the top of the pecking order—has both been a central feature of alliance politics and why it has not received more scholarly attention previously. There is in fact a downside to a defender for reassuring an ally, provided that the alliance treaty is already discouraging challenges from abroad. If instead, the alliance treaty is only *part* of the mechanism by which defenders deter—if deployments "top off" or supplement alliance treaties in the manner described here—then allies can quite reasonably be expected to compete with one another for these additional security benefits. *Where* a defender deploys its forces abroad can then reflect, and indeed effect, which allies appear to be at the top of a hierarchy of protection. Seen in this light, the US pivot to Asia may very well have contributed to Europe's anxiety, and to Russia's recent emboldenment.

Perhaps being near an ally is almost as effective as, and more flexible than, land-based deployments? The strategy of "offshore balancing" is intended to enable a defender to intervene quickly and decisively if needed and may be comparable, even preferable, to a fixed physical presence in military terms.[8] Offshore balancing refers to a strategy of limited, and often indirect, intervention, inspired in part by British grand strategy vis-à-vis Europe in the seventeenth and eighteenth centuries.[9] While not explicitly articulated in this fashion, the approach relies on mobile forces, able to position combat power at the place and time of the balancer's choosing. But no country can keep more than a modicum of troops at sea indefinitely. Soldiers designed to be airlifted into battle (such as the US rapid reaction forces) actually spend the bulk of their time in garrison somewhere. As a practical matter, offshoring requires the establishment of regional bases and logistics hubs,

---

[8] Layne 1997; Layne 2002; Mearsheimer and Walt 2016; Posen 2014.
[9] Mearsheimer 2001.

from which power can be projected when needed. The bulk of personnel (support, training, logistics, administration, etc.) are located at these remote locations, or even in the continental US (CONUS). Thus, while mobile formations (naval and air forces) are clearly a defining characteristic of offshore balancing, these forces exist in some physical place, generally on land.

The ability to act is of course not the same thing as the imperative to do so; force postures that retain greater discretion for a defender also allow the defender to demur. For the same reasons that a military presence onshore signals the defender's priorities, the decision *not* to deploy to a given country is more likely to elicit uncertainty as to a defender's exact or ultimate willingness to intervene or protect an ally. Offshoring thus increases the risk of error or misperception. Uncertainty about a defender's intentions *must* in turn undermine the peace-promoting objective of deterrence, given the role that uncertainty plays in triggering the onset of military contests. Force postures deploying proportionately large capabilities near, but not on, an ally's soil may thus yield a surprising counter-intuitive effect; they can exacerbate, rather than diminish, deterrence failures, increasing, rather than decreasing, instability.

This tendency is magnified when one considers the dual role of power in either increasing deterrence or compellence. As a third party to possible conflict, the state extending deterrence (the defender) must balance protection with a protégé's incentive to treat military advantage as influence. In effect, the defender faces the equivalent of type I and type II errors in inferential statistics (or false positives and false negatives). The defender cannot increase protection without also increasing incentives for the protégé to insist on more advantageous bargains from the challenger.[10] Offshoring capabilities can limit a partner's ability to chain-gang, but only by increasing the ecological hazard of buck-passing. Deployments near, but not on, an ally's territory, while increasing local capabilities and influence, also exacerbate the risk of general deterrence failure by allowing the protégé and challenger to diverge in their perceptions of the true balance of power.

Forward force postures are costly, as are alliances themselves.[11] All things considered, defenders should presumably prefer to protect the homeland, lower costs, and recycle defense revenues through local tax payers. A forward posture also has its benefits, including better and more immediate access to distant locations.[12] However, neither of these incentives necessarily accounts

---

[10] Christensen and Snyder 1990.   [11] Alley and Fuhrmann 2021.   [12] Morrow 1991.

200 ELEMENTS OF DETERRENCE

for particular decisions about forward presence, which presumably hinge more on the deterrence logic outlined above.

Here, we detail the effects of US foreign deployments on extended general deterrence success. After reviewing the relevant literature, we provide a theory of extended deterrence in which defenders balance finite capabilities with the complementary hazards of entrapment and abandonment. We then estimate these effects on data on troop deployments in the post-World War II US alliance network.[13] We examine the effects of US force posture (how much of US capabilities are deployed abroad) and presence (what proportion of US forces are deployed to different allies), considering whether and how deployments influence extended deterrence. We further estimate the effect of US military capabilities located "offshore," weighting the "spill-in" effect of deployments by geographical distance from the protégé.[14]

Our findings strongly support our claims; a proportionally large onshore presence helps US allies enhance deterrence success, while offshore deployments do the opposite, increasing deterrence failure. As a final step in the chapter, we discuss some of the implications of these findings for international politics and national policy.

Alliances, Extended Deterrence, and Deployments

There are a number of allied processes that deal with, or impact on, security cooperation among states. What do scholars and practitioners believe they know about these processes? A review of the literature in this setting will necessarily be brief, given the number and diversity of relevant works. We have organized discussion into three sections, dealing with: alliances, deterrence, and military deployments.

Alliance Theory

IR scholars offer a number of reasons for alliance formation.[15] Structural realists, in particular, emphasize the role of alliances in "bandwagoning" or

---

[13] Kane 2006; Allen, Flynn, and Machain 2022.

[14] US military personnel are assigned to quarters on a base, port, camp or airbase. Even naval personnel onboard ships are home ported somewhere. In a crisis or war, the forces that are *not* already deployed to the protégé would be transported by air (sometimes by sea) from their permanent duty stations. The countries where troops are stationed are the locations we use later in the chapter to measure proximity and offshore balancing.

[15] Lanoszka 2022.

"balancing," aggregating power either with or against the hegemon, respectively.[16] In this conceptualization, the proximate goal of alliances is to accumulate power. However, there are other things alliances can do or achieve, even as it is far from clear empirically that the majority of alliances meaningfully add to aggregate power.

The bulk of alliances pair weak states with strong states or weak states together.[17] Since weak states offer very little to augment the capability of other nations, some other factor must be at work in promoting the majority of alliance ties. Indeed, most potential alliances never occur; only about 1% of pairings of states involve an alliance. In other words, states are leaving a substantial amount of capabilities un-tasked and un-recruited. Following and building on insights from Altfeld, Morrow argues that alliances act as a contract for supplying complementary, rather than symmetrical "alliance goods," increasing security for some (weaker states), while providing others (powerful states) with greater autonomy in the form of access to facilities and remote locations.[18] However, argument in turn provides no direct logic for standing military deployments, since the protection afforded by presence is incidental, although access can of course prove quite useful.[19]

Fearon offers a different, compatible justification for alliance formation.[20] Alliances can act as a "signal," either advertising a defender's resolve (credibility), or augmenting the defender's determination to intervene, should a protégé become the target of aggression (commitment). Fearon's framework offers two mechanisms through which alliances shape perceptions and/or behavior. An alliance can "tie hands," linking the future reputation of a defender to current promises through a formal agreement (the public alliance treaty).[21] Tying hands commitments are "cheap talk" signals since a state's reputation is only affected if the defender fails to honor its treaty obligations. Fearon argues that tying hands is more attractive, especially to reliable defenders, because of the contingent nature of this cost.

Fearon's second alliance mechanism does not actually require an alliance, though some agreement may prove practical. A defender can "sink costs," spending money or other resources that cannot later be recouped in a manner that demonstrates an existing, unobservable, alignment with the

---

[16] Waltz 1979; Henry 2020. Henry sees allies as balancing abandonment and entrapment risks, which are more complex in alliance networks than in bilateral treaties. Intriguingly, he focuses on Taiwan, which is highly unusual in political terms (a small, developed, "non-state" state, claimed by a major power). For various assessments of structural realism, see Vasquez 1997; Schweller 2004.

[17] Morrow 1991. Kim (2016) offers a book-length treatment with a similar market framework evaluating complementary incentives states may have to ally.

[18] Altfeld 1984.   [19] Morrow's 1991.

[20] Fearon 1997.   [21] Fearon 1997; Morrow 2000.

202 ELEMENTS OF DETERRENCE

protégé's interests. Sinking costs is expensive, precisely because it involves up front, wholly non-contingent expenditures in time, money and, possibly, military power. A defender that is willing to shell out resources on behalf of another state clearly has an interest in the other state's welfare. Indeed, the potency of such a signal is enhanced by a budget constraint. "Large" is in the eye of the beholder, but a disproportionately sized effort or expenditure imposes clear opportunity costs. One cannot simultaneously put most of one's eggs in one bucket and also deposit them elsewhere.

One of the most important developments in the study of alliances in the past two decades has been major improvements in data.[22] Somewhat less has been achieved in terms of demonstrating or refining existing theoretical perspectives, such as Fearon's typology. Some work has begun to examine how alliances and military power interact.[23] The tying hands reasoning offered by suggests that the decision of defenders to adopt a forward force posture is somewhat peculiar.[24] To the degree that alliances credibly commit a defender to intervene in the case of a crisis or conflict, ongoing deployments are unnecessary. Brian Blankenship and Erik Lin-Greenberg explore elite attitudes about deployments, finding that they are indeed perceived to be of relatively little value.[25] Criticisms of the utility of deployments are fairly widespread in the contemporary literature on international security. We discuss these more extensively in the "Deployments" section below.

Perceptions may differ from reality. What people (even experts) believe about a process, and how it actually works, may not align. Reconciling empirical reality with logical constructs may best be accomplished through a fuller understanding of how deployments affect actual behavior, rather than (simply) through subjective assessments. Sunk costs may prove much more informative than tying hands given budget constraints and by demonstrating where costs actually accrue. To explore this further, however, we need to look more closely at the related process of deterrence.

---

[22] Leeds 2003; Leeds, Mattes, and Vogel 2009.
[23] Allen, Flynn, Machain, and Stravers 2020; Nieman et al. 2021.
[24] Fearon 1997.   [25] Blankenship and Lin-Greenberg 2022.

Logics of Extended Deterrence

Deterrence involves efforts by a possible target of attack to raise the costs or risks of aggression.[26] Extended deterrence occurs when the deterring state is a third party to a potential conflict.[27] The study of extended deterrence is also appealing for inferential reasons; it is easier to observe deterrence success affecting third parties.[28]

Deterrence is a psychological process.[29] Convincing an adversary to refrain from acting aggressively based on what might come to pass requires someone to paint a convincing mental image of what the future likely entails. Mistakes are bound to happen. However, examples of errors are not evidence of systemic bias.[30] Getting something wrong is not prima facie proof that the actor was not trying to get things right, or that coming up with an (approximately) correct answer is impossible. The presence of "noise" in a process is thoroughly compatible with attempts at optimization, however imperfect they may be. Nor is it clear how misperception plays out in the context of extended deterrence, where actors must presumably make cognitive errors while failing to notice similar errors in others. Psychological challenges to extended deterrence theory thus seem to demand a second explanation for why protégés ever accept mere assurances, rather than insisting on "boots on the ground."

Empirical studies of extended deterrence echo the call for localizing troops.[31] Indeed, systematic research has struggled to demonstrate a relationship between broader defender capabilities and extended deterrence success.[32] The empirical salience of the local balance paradoxically highlights the role of perception. Given that defenders typically deploy forces locally that are insufficient for defense, the deterrent effect of presence would appear to be heavily influenced by expectations of additional deployments in a crisis or wartime. A defender that positions relatively few capabilities abroad may be viewed as unlikely to intervene quickly or effectively. To the degree that the defender and/or the protégé believe that deterrence works, peacetime

---

[26] P. Morgan 1977.   [27] Freedman 2004.   [28] Huth 1988b.
[29] Jervis, Lebow, and Stein 1985.
[30] Huth and Russett 1990; Lebow and Stein 1989; Achen and Snidal 1989.
[31] Huth and Russett 1984; Huth 1988a.   [32] Huth and Russett 1984.

204 ELEMENTS OF DETERRENCE

deployments should not occur. In this sense, a forward force posture is actually evidence of a *dearth* of optimism about deterrence via alliance ties.

For not dissimilar reasons, many innovations in deterrence theory have focused on perceptions, rather than capabilities. A critical determinant of deterrence failure concerns foreign beliefs about deterrent claims.[33] Manipulating what actors believe about extended deterrence involves raising one's commitment or credibility. A willingness or ability to intervene may not be recognized. Actions designed to demonstrate, but not necessarily increase, the defender's willingness or ability to defend signal credibility. Sunk costs are behaviors that reduce uncertainty but which have mostly marginal effects on subsequent defender decision making (i.e., they foreshadow future behavior, rather than altering behavior through ex post incentives).[34] It is difficult to identify empirical contexts where the costs of deterrence in one period are isolated and do not carry over to payoffs in subsequent periods. For example, mobilization by a defender not only demonstrates resolve in the face of significant costs and inconvenience, but it also alters the short term balance of power, creating a commitment problem in which the defender may prefer a military decision.[35] However, some behaviors of this type exist. In particular, we focus on costs that are largely consumed in a given interval of time, such as salaries and benefits for military personnel.

Deployments: Determinants and Effects

The study of military deployments has been less systematic or logically grounded than the literatures on alliances and extended deterrence. Recently, however, questions of force posture and presence have received increasing attention from researchers. In general, the tone of assessments of the effects of deployments is cautionary, even skeptical. Rovner and Talmadge, for example, make the point that the forward US force posture in the Middle East does not appear to have been critical for stable access to energy supplies, a public good, at least for consuming nations.[36]

A "tripwire" is a relatively small deployment of forces to an ally or other security partner's territory. One purpose for such a deployment could

---

[33] Lebow and Stein 1989; Powell 1990; Kilgour and Zagare 1991; Zagare and Kilgour 1993.
[34] Fearon 1997.   [35] Slantchev 2005.   [36] Rovner and Talmadge 2014.

be to trigger a larger intervention in the event of a crisis or war.[37] Such deployments have much in common with the presence argument outlined here and discussed in greater detail in the next section. The mechanism behind tripwires is commitment (i.e., "tying hands"), but relatively modest, durable deployments could also generate credibility ("sinking costs"). Indeed, the two processes can operate independently, with each influencing deterrence or alliance reliability separately or together.

Skepticism about tripwires emerges from several quarters. Blankenship and Lin-Greenberg use a survey experiment of elite European respondents to compare the perceived impact of "high-resolve, low-capability signals" with the converse (low-resolve, high-capability), finding that the former are not any more effective at reassuring allies. The authors find that "tripwire forces in allied territory are not viewed as any more reassuring than high-capability, low-resolve signals such as forces stationed offshore."[38] Blankenship and Lin-Greenberg's findings thus appear to contradict the argument proposed here. However, perceptions and reality can differ, as is often noted in the study of deterrence. What subjects appear to think, and how they behave, may not always align. Similarly, the claim that tripwires do not reassure is not equivalent to demonstrating that they fail to deter, or indeed that they fail to trigger larger interventions, when appropriate.

Dan Reiter and Paul Poast argue directly that tripwires do not work as advertised, using informal deductive reasoning and citing examples of deterrence success, and failure. They argue, "Not only are small tripwire deployments unlikely to prevent an attacker from capturing its objective and establishing a strong defensive position, tripwire-force fatalities may be insufficient to provoke broader intervention. To deter, forward deployments must be sufficiently substantial to shift the local balance of power."[39] Again, if their arguments and evidence are correct, we are barking up the wrong tree. There are reasons to question the authors' conclusions, however, if not necessarily their interpretations of particular historical events. To begin with, we know from research on the causes of war that the last sentence of their explanation quoted here must be incorrect. Shifts in the balance of power do not alter the probability of war, except possibly at the boundaries (i.e., in extreme cases).[40]

What then can explain deterrence success? The answers, while complex and varied, are knowable and readily evaluated. Alexander Lanoszka and

---

[37] Schelling 1966.   [38] Blankenship and Lin-Greenberg 2022.
[39] Reiter and Poast 2021.   [40] Fearon 1995.

206 ELEMENTS OF DETERRENCE

Michael A. Hunzeker argue, for example, that NATO's attempts to reorient to the growing threat from Russia have been more successful than many critics feared, in part because of a series of nuanced, practical and iterative steps taken by the alliance network.[41] Others, such as James Goldgeier and Joshua Shifrinson, offer a more conditional and generally less sanguine interpretation of NATO's post-Cold War contributions to European stability.[42] Goldgeier and Shifrinson frame the debate among contributors to their edited volume as muted and subject to controversy. Scholars argue that NATO under-invested in or over-extended its security umbrella, or both.

Contests are avoided as a product of establishing consensus expectations about what the contests will achieve. Deterrence as war avoidance is thus an act of communication; instilling in the minds of an adversary "the fear to attack" as Dr. Strangelove so memorably observed.

While large deployments can commit or signal resolve, they are clearly expensive. The claim that large deployments do a better job signaling is not the same as saying that small deployments completely fail to inform. Smaller deployments should convey credibility, provided they "separate," or distinguish different "types" of defender from one another. This implies that there will be failures, as well as successes. Given probabilistic outcomes, net effects will be in terms of tendencies. Tendencies are difficult to unearth by means of cases. Just because one can find examples where something did not work does not mean that there are not also cases where it did. Indeed, the net effects of phenomena and processes are often obscured by a combination of probabilistic tendencies and our own penchant to act in ways that tend to cover over evidence of success.

Consider an analogous inferential problem. Hospitals have high death rates; a superficial assessment would encourage people to avoid them, especially if one is sick. But of course there are reasons that hospitals are associated with mortality. People go to hospitals when they are sick because they believe (correctly) that the hospital is likely to make them better. Evidence that hospitals exhibit worse health outcomes than other institutions reflects adverse selection (people in poor health go to hospitals *because* of the health benefits of hospitalization). The sick usually get better at hospitals, but not always, and because so many sick people concentrate there, hospitals (superficially) appear to be unhealthy, even dangerous.

---

[41] Lanoszka and Hunzeker 2023.   [42] Goldgeier and Shifrinson 2023.

This chicken-or-egg problem of inference also affects interpretations of deployments. Defenders place tripwires in bad neighborhoods, places where the risk of attack is relatively high. Indeed, Nieman et al. find that there is a positive feedback cycle involving non-invasion troop deployments; major powers are mutually drawn to the same states and regions.[43] This finding is clearly in tension with the view that tripwires are unsuccessful. It would be odd if states react to one another's deployments, but not to their own. Similarly, Allen et al. examine the effects of the presence of US forces on public opinion in host countries.[44] In contrast to abundant journalistic accounts and other scholarly, though subjective assessments, the authors show that engagement with deployed US military forces generally has positive effects. By and large, the populations of host nations perceive a US military presence as efficacious and worthwhile, even if the elites in some of these countries may not.

Thus, thinking and evidence about the role of military deployments on deterrence has yet to resolve a core conundrum. It may be tempting to conclude that military deployments are ineffective. However, the behavior of states in conducting, funding and hosting deployments suggests otherwise. Clearly, while there is skepticism about the value of stationing troops abroad, there is also continued reliance on precisely this behavior by both defenders and protégés. If current conclusions in the literature are to be believed, this is a waste of time, and taxpayers dollars, if not worse. We therefore move forward to provide additional reasoning, and assessment, with a strong dose of humility, mindful that there are reasons to be cautious in believing in the utility of deployments. The persistence of presence in the face of both skepticism and possible redundancy (alliances) suggests the need for another, more careful, look.

Presence, Offshore Balancing, and Force Posture

One of the more striking features of the Cold War was where NATO placed its military forces. Rather than deploying in depth as indicated by modern military tactics, a large portion of NATO conventional capabilities were forward deployed, right on the inter-German border. On the one hand, a forward defense posture was clearly in tension with NATO's wartime doctrine

---

[43] Nieman et al. 2021.   [44] Allen, Flynn, Machain, and Stravers 2020.

208   ELEMENTS OF DETERRENCE

of mobile warfare ("Follow-On Forces Attack" was the NATO manifestation of the US "AirLand Battle" doctrine). A forward defense posture reduced the ability of NATO forces to maneuver against an enemy advance and to redeploy in response to the rapidly evolving realities of an enemy armored attack.[45] On the other hand, forward defense made NATO's commitment to West Germany incontrovertible. It would be extremely difficult for Warsaw Pact forces to practice "salami tactics," for example, isolating Bonn militarily. Thus, NATO's forward defense doctrine maximized the deterrent effect of the alliance, even if this approach also weakened conventional defense.[46]

NATO's force posture illustrates trade-offs between deterrence and defense. Deploying in depth, especially if this meant moving forces to other countries, would have simultaneously strengthened NATO's ability to prevail in a conventional contest (if one occurred) and weakened the credibility of NATO's commitment to the FDR, undermining deterrence. Relaxing the forward force posture would have indicated that NATO was not indisputably a unified whole, that pressure on the FDR from the east might potentially yield diplomatic fruit. Thus, to some degree, NATO planners had to choose between credibility in deterrence and effectiveness in combat.

Different conceptions of extended deterrence imply very different things about the utility of a defender's force posture and the impact of military presence. Classical conceptions emphasize the complementarity of deterrence and defense, noting that a good defense improves the quality of deterrence and implying that large local deployments should be associated with peace.[47] However, this appears untenable in practical terms. Powerful defenders generate economies of scale in the provision of security by leveraging their capabilities, committing to defend more allies than is actually possible at any given time.[48]

Modern conceptions have taken an entirely different approach to extended deterrence, arguing that alliances and deployments are largely substitutes and that treaties are much cheaper than infantry brigades. States can form binding commitments that tie their hands, allowing defenders to deter aggression independent of force posture.[49] This of course implies

---

[45] Mearsheimer 1981 argues for forward defense, but his target appears to be advocates of mobile warfare, which was adopted as NATO doctrine. The question remains why, after adopting AirLand Battle, did NATO still choose to concentrate its forces near the border?

[46] The strategy also heightened the credibility of NATO's US-based nuclear deterrent by making it difficult for the Americans to disengage or for NATO to prevail in conventional terms. Every major war scenario between NATO and the Warsaw Pact was meant to end in a nuclear exchange.

[47] Huth 1988a; Huth 1988b.   [48] Gartzke and Markowitz 2015.   [49] Fearon 1997.

that deployments are unnecessary, or even that they are a signal of a *lack* of confidence in the actual alliance mechanism.

Existing conceptions of extended deterrence thus offer contrasting predictions about the role of troop deployments, neither of which appear obviously correct, given US force posture decisions and deployment patterns. Allies often host long-standing, but moderate, foreign military contingents. These deployments are redundant or inadequate, depending on one's preferred theory of extended deterrence. In contrast to alliance signaling, deployments are costly ex ante, and thus can prove more informative, especially in certain circumstances. Force posture decisions can also prove informative on an ongoing basis, since deployment patterns can vary from year to year. While the tripwire metaphor has garnered considerable attention, there is again an important conceptual and empirical distinction between the classical emphasis on tripwires as commitment mechanisms (a linkage that forces intervention) and an effort to generate credibility (a costly action that signals the intent to intervene).[50] The US deployment of force in Japan, for example, functions through credibility, rather than commitment.[51] It is the signal of the relative importance the defender places on the protégé that matters most for deterrence, not the forcing function of compelling the defender to intervene.

Japan serves as an especially useful case in clarifying the nature of these relationships. As the only country that is constitutionally precluded from acting through force even to assist its own allies, Japan is highly unlikely to entrap an ally or precipitate a conflict spiral. Thus, the dynamics of alliance behavior in the US-Japan case appear largely to be driven by uni-directional concerns over abandonment. At the same time, however, it remains unclear whether the use of presence primarily to enhance credibility, rather than to generate commitment, is a unique feature of the Japan-US alliance dyad, or whether it is generally the case that presence, and force posture more broadly, work best to deter when they signal defender credibility through (dis)proportionate deployments of expensive military personnel.

Alliance dynamics across multiple security relationships may or may not function in the same way as substitutes or complements to the basic dynamic of increased credibility through presence. While proportionately costly deployments may prove informative, other mechanisms may turn out to be equally, if not more effective, particularly when considering substitution

---

[50] Schelling 1966. [51] Gartzke and Kagotani 2016.

210 ELEMENTS OF DETERRENCE

or re-deployment from one ally to another. Deployments near a given US protégé (offshore balancing) simplify defense. Placing forces regionally, to be used wherever (and whenever) needed, may be a superior military option, and so it is tempting to assume that offshoring forces *also* signal credibility. However, much as defense in depth and full realization of AirLand Battle in Europe required a force posture that compromised deterrence, so too offshore balancing may achieve flexibility and responsiveness at the expense of credibility.

A defender with many allies cannot hope to be, or even be perceived to be, everywhere at once. Defenders and their partners may well imagine that proximity is a convex set, that being close is almost as good—possibly even superior to—"being there." This appears to be the expectation of Japan and the United States, for example, in the discussion over re-positioning of US Marine units from Okinawa to Guam. However, there are reasons to be pessimistic about the deterrent effect of a force posture that positions one's immediate protection offshore. Flexibility is fundamentally incompatible with the predictability needed for deterrence; relying too heavily on re-positioning in a crisis invites speculation about whether the defender will intervene. A defender that is able, indeed expected, to be in many places still cannot be in every place at once. In contrast, force postures that make discretion less meaningful encourage compatible beliefs about the likely evolution of a contest.[52] Spending resources in one place as opposed to another suggests a hierarchy of salience, one that is difficult to mistake or misinterpret. Offshore balancing is thus much like Schelling's forcing function in reverse. The absence of a formal deployment commitment "in country" invites doubts about whether other forms of commitment, such as the alliance itself, will prove sufficient to trigger intervention in a crisis.

Being offshore *may* mean that a defender will take its obligations seriously and rush to protect the protégé. An offshore presence certainly helps the defender to arrive more quickly, if it chooses to intervene, while at the same time allowing the defender to operate in more places, which is appealing from a policy perspective. However, this by no means guarantees intervention. Nor does spending operating funds elsewhere imply that a given ally is a priority. The balance of power or threat in a crisis depends on the mix of

---

[52] This is an increasing problem as new technologies emphasize mobility, range, and stealth critical components of military effectiveness. Features that allow countries to maintain a competitive edge in future military operations probably also make it harder to maintain a credible conventional deterrent. Offshoring and mobility lead to questions about intent.

forces that are available and that are committed by interested parties. In contrast, beliefs about the balance in the event of conflict—the critical dynamic for deterrence—depends on perceptions of the defender's willingness to intervene. Actions ex ante that clearly indicate the defender's intentions, such as positioning forces within a given ally's territory, reduce uncertainty about the local balance, thereby reducing incentives for a challenger to probe or provoke. Again, the critical issue is not whether the defender will intervene, but whether other actors disagree about the likelihood that this will happen. Thus, even with something like the pivot, which is designed to increase the defender's offshore forces, and may be interpreted by both friends and foes as altering the local balance, the risk is that adversaries see the world differently. The protégé may factor in the defender's offshore capabilities into its expectations of the balance, while the challenger interprets the lack of presence as a sign of equivocation, and an opportunity.

This dynamic is clearly reflected in terms of the standard alliance trade-off of abandonment and entrapment, what Christensen and Snyder refer to as "buck-passing" and "chain-ganging."[53] Politicians like options, but options are antithetical to commitment because they increase the likelihood that a defender will act with discretion, failing to intervene, or at least that the defender will dither or delay, creating the potential for a fait accompli. A gap in time and space between what the local balance might be and what it will become, if an attack occurs, creates a window in which a challenger can differ in its expectations about the likely outcome of aggressive action. Abandonment is a problem in alignments. Alliances institutionalize alignments, shoring up perceptions about intentions (credibility or sinking costs) or enhancing intentions (commitment or tying hands). States can also commit or signal credibility through a military presence, although this is complex and is arguably becoming more difficult with the mobility of modern military capabilities. Military deployments that act as tripwires could cause a defender to intervene.[54] On the other hand, a commitment to intervene may not be believed, so that credibility and signaling remain important dynamics, regardless of the commitment mechanism.

Alliances, as commitment devices, are conversely prone to exploitation (entrapment), since a protégé can take a tougher stance with adversaries, confident that it is protected by the defender. This phenomenon of chain-ganging thus poses a risk for the defender, but may not be observed in terms

---

[53] Christensen and Snyder 1990.   [54] Schelling 1966.

212 ELEMENTS OF DETERRENCE

of deterrence success or failure, since the deterrent effect of the defender's presence can be converted into influence by the protégé. A defender should be concerned about entrapment to the degree that the defender's objectives or interests differ from those of the protégé. At some point, preferences differ so much that the defender is unwilling to sustain an alignment. A middle step is for states to ally, but to leave the extent of the commitment in doubt. The defender can rein in chain-ganging by limiting its commitment ("untying hands"), but credibility may be affected if the defender abandons an ally.[55]

The dangers posed by public perceptions of abandonment may be acceptable, given the defender's perceived risk of entrapment. However, deployments "dial-in" the effect of alliance ties in at least two ways, increasing the precision of the defender's security policy. First, physical deployments are a costly signal of the value placed on an ally by the defender. Financing force postures is expensive; putting money in the ground at one location says something different from placing it elsewhere. Second, force postures evolve, allowing the defender to alter the details of security relationships on an ongoing basis in a manner that is more flexible than nominal alliance ties, and in a way that incentivizes the protégé to behave. A defender with excessive exposure and an ally prone to chain-ganging can dial down the size of a deployment or even change its force posture to limit risk. However, doing so also invites the challenger to update its beliefs about alliance reliability.

Offshoring military capabilities is both a mechanism for increasing flexibility for the defender and a signal that the defender's emphasis in managing risk is closer to abandonment than entrapment. Abandonment is a problem for the protégé and an opportunity for a challenger. Offshore balancing at the expense of some presence on the soil of an ally is an important delimitation, indicating that the defender is less (not more) likely to protect a given security partner. Challengers facing adversaries that are not directly protected by a defender must have greater doubts about what actions the defender will take. Indeed, cases of extended deterrence failure seem replete with examples where the defender either failed to deploy its forces onshore (e.g., Kuwait) or drew these forces down to the point where intervention became questionable (e.g., Korean War). The defender may or may not intervene, increasing the challenger's uncertainty about the balance of power or threat in the event of a crisis or a contest, weakening deterrence and

[55] Gibler 2008; Crescenzi et al. 2012; Mattes 2012.

fueling instability. Again, while the defender can reduce uncertainty either by firmly signaling through an onshore presence or by removing forces from the region, either option also comes with consequences that are magnified by the relationship of interests between the parties.

Hypotheses

A physical presence augments alliance credibility, which should increase deterrence success. Because forward deployments are elective and much of their costs must be borne and renewed regularly, they are less subject to entrapment than the alliance itself. More importantly, deploying forces onshore indicates a lower likelihood of abandonment, increasing the deterrent effect of the alliance. Such a presence is informative because it achieves two critical functions. First, at least part of deployment costs are sunk, unrecoverable, and vested in a given place and time. In particular, personnel costs and benefits—as rents on labor—cannot be re-used. Pay and support for US forces in Germany, say, cannot be recovered and utilized subsequently elsewhere. Nor is the fact that soldiers or airmen are paid in a given year particularly relevant in the future. Continued service requires new personnel expenditures, unlike other expenses on infrastructure or capital goods. The physical deployment of forces ("presence") thus localizes the effects of personnel spending to a given time and place, while future decisions are not dictated by past practice (i.e., forces can be redeployed or moved about).

A second component of presence that affects credibility, but which is often overlooked, is the need for an observable baseline. The magnitude of a cost is in the eye of the beholder. It is difficult to determine how "costly" a costly signal might be without having something to compare it to. Budgets are a useful way to parameterize the size of a cost in politics because spending on some item or issue always poses a loss in terms of what else *cannot* be purchased. Government budgets are by their nature a product and record of controversy. Every expenditure that is present exists only because it forced out some other candidate for funding that was deemed less important. The overall costs of maintaining a forward force posture, as well as the details of where money was spent, in what proportions, and forces deployed, is much more informative than spending in an absolute sense, where budget constraints or alternative candidates for funding are not directly addressed.

214 ELEMENTS OF DETERRENCE

If evidence of a commitment is increased (credibility) by proportionately expensive deployments targeted at particular US allies (presence), then the opposite should be true for deployments that avoid a given ally's territory (offshoring). Spending a large portion of the US defense budget on a force posture that places military personnel near but not on the soil of an ally limits entrapment but only by increasing the risk of abandonment. Challengers can reasonably doubt the willingness of the defender to intervene in wartime if the defender is unwilling to commit forces onshore in peacetime. More to the point, offshore deployments require some additional trigger to move forces from offshore to onshore, while deploying these forces onshore signals the likelihood of their involvement. A proportionately small forward presence in a given ally implies the possibility that the relationship is a lower priority to the defender and/or the protégé. This may cause a challenger to act aggressively or, more conservatively, to adopt a more assertive posture of its own in order to assess the local balance of power or threat through diplomatic challenges or probing attacks that allow the challenger to evaluate alliance tightness. These low-level conflicts, while not necessarily destined to trigger abandonment or war, are themselves destabilizing general deterrence failures.

The arguments here can be contrasted with more traditional interpretations of presence and offshore balancing. Schelling emphasizes the tripwire metaphor as a commitment (i.e., tying hands) and a deterrent.[56] A military contingent deployed abroad can engage a larger force, signaling to adversaries the intention of the defender to intervene more extensively in the event of an attack on the protégé. A challenger can be deterred by a tripwire to the degree that the tripwire acts to mobilize this intervention. To do so, however, the tripwire must be vulnerable to the challenger, valuable to the defender, and difficult to extract from harm. These attributes may be driven by many things, but a readily observable feature of presence that correlates with both value and mobility is size. The larger the deployment the more difficult it would be to displace it quickly out of harm's way. A deployment that is large *in absolute terms* is at once both more valuable and harder to re-deploy. However, as already noted, long-term deployments to US allies are typically small in proportion to the security needs of most protégés. Thus, the size of the force located in a given ally should accurately characterize the possible tripwire/tying hands rationale for US military

---

[56] Schelling 1966.

deployments (i.e., commitment), while measuring changes in the nominal size of deployments (in terms either of dollars or soldiers) should capture the impact of changes in the level of US commitment.

While the theoretical logic is clear, there are problems with commitment as an explanation on the empirical level. Since much of the impact of commitment is in *changing* the willingness of the defender to intervene, commitment is much less important *if a defender already intends to protect the protégé*. Commitment matters most where a defender lacks resolve and wants to increase the likelihood it will act. It will also be tempting for the defender or protégé to "draw off" some of the increase in defender resolve as leverage to backstop a more assertive foreign policy (this is implied directly by the logic of chain-ganging). If one's protector just doubled down, perhaps this is a good time to demand more from an opponent, or at least to compromise less. Commitment thus "stiffens" resolve, in effect changing reality, while credibility works more to advertise what one state perceives reality to be (when doubts about resolve exist but are unfounded). Credibility is closer to a "pure" informational mechanism that communicates reality without much altering the balance of power or threat. As such, credibility acts more directly on the war avoidance aspects of deterrence. Credibility (through mechanisms like sinking costs) is most valuable where resolve exists, but opponents do not recognize its presence, while commitment (achieved most often by tying hands) matters most where resolve is flagging.

Ongoing debates about offshore balancing reflect differing predictions, and at times preferences, concerning causes, costs, and consequences.[57] The size of deployments (absolute or relative), mobility versus presence, and force posture all do different things to different aspects of security. At its simplest, offshoring forces involves abandoning presence in favor of maintaining influence and minimizing cost, which in turn means that fluctuations in the balance of power should have much more effect on who gets what than whether states fight. An increase in absolute capabilities in a region allows a defender or its allies to resist a change in the status quo. A shift in the local balance of power or influence is then being exercised for (re)distribution, rather than primarily as a way to affect beliefs about the balance. This should thus have relatively little effect on deterrence success, as conventionally measured by the (in)frequency of challenges directed at

---

[57] Layne 1997; Mearsheimer 2001; Holmes and Yoshihara 2012; G. Jackson 2012; Brooks, Ikenberry, and Wohlforth 2013.

216 ELEMENTS OF DETERRENCE

a specific protégé. In contrast, shifts in the military balance that are not accompanied with a stiffening of policy positions could well act to reduce the likelihood of conflict. Unfortunately, leaders seldom continue to speak softly when carrying a bigger stick. Offshore balancing must tempt resistance or at least a reluctance to compromise among allies and thus should fail to generate credibility and, where it generates commitment, this should tend to be exercised as influence, rather than deterrence.

Geography provides a useful context in which to assess and recognize the differential effects of onshore and offshore deployments. Increased capabilities allow a defender to reinforce existing commitments or to seek to control or contest more land, air or policy space more tenuously. A more forward force posture must come at some cost in terms of additional defense burdens or reduced deterrence effectiveness. Retrenchment does the opposite, saving dollars or the risk of war but also proscribing influence. Force structures that emphasize mobility enhance power projection and leverage at the cost of some decline in credibility.[58] Observers can reasonably disagree about whether minimizing cost, maximizing influence or avoiding war are the most desirable objectives, but it is important to recognize that one cannot avoid the fact that each alternative is a consequence dictated in part by reactions to the other alternatives. Below we provide formal hypotheses drawn from the discussion above:

- Hypothesis 1: Presence—Credibility. Extended general deterrence *success* (i.e., an absence of challenges in the form of militarized aggression directed at the protégé) should be significantly predicted by the *proportion* of US spending on US military personnel deployed to a given US ally.
- Hypothesis 2: Offshore—Credibility. Extended general deterrence *failure* should be significantly predicted by the *proportion* of US spending on US military personnel deployed near, but not on, a US ally's territory.
- Hypothesis 3: Presence—Commitment. Extended general deterrence *success* should be significantly predicted by the *absolute size* of US military personnel or spending on US military personnel on a US ally's territory.
- Hypothesis 4: Offshore—Commitment. Extended general deterrence *success* should be significantly predicted by the *absolute size* of US military personnel or spending on US military personnel deployed

[58] Gartzke and Lindsay 2020.

LAND 217

Table 8.1 Implications of force posture on strategic stability

Hypotheses	(type/source and predicted effect)	Force Posture	
		Presence	Offshore
Signaling Method	**Credibility**	H1: Sunk Cost Personnel & Budget (+)	H2: Flexibility → Uncertainty (−)
	Commitment	H3: Schelling's "tripwire" (+)	H4: Offshore Balancing (+)[−]

near, but not on, a US ally's territory. (Note: This hypothesis is a foil for defensive realist expectations for offshore balancing. We expect that this will not significantly predict strategic stability but rather offshore deployments will marginally predict instability, hence the brackets in the H4 cell in Table 8.1.)

Together, these four hypotheses can be represented in the form of a 2-by-2 matrix described in Table 8.1. Columns represent a chosen force posture strategy, while rows constitute mechanisms for signaling. Presence should work differently than posturing offshore, just as commitment differs in its dynamics and consequences from credibility. Presence is predicted to function well in generating extended deterrence, though the micro-foundations are a subject of our analysis here. While the distinction between commitment or credibility may appear at first to be relatively minor, the conclusions one can draw are highly consequential. If presence works through credibility, for example, then proportional changes in emphasis are more important than absolute differences, suggesting that presence can continue to deter even in an era of relative military decline. A moderately weaker defender does not necessarily weaken deterrence, as long as the defender is sufficiently discriminating in emphasizing protection for its most critical allies.

Offshoring of capabilities, on the other hand, implies more variable deterrent effects for variable causal mechanisms. While commitments locally or regionally may compel intervention, they are unlikely to have strong observable effects, particularly since the increase in leverage available creates incentives for chain-ganging on the part of the protégé, defender or both, as we have already noted. In contrast, credibility is likely to plummet as defenders move offshore, since their actions speak louder than their written words (alliance treaties).

218 ELEMENTS OF DETERRENCE

Summary of Findings

We test the effects of the four hypotheses about presence and offshore balancing using the random-effects logit model.[59] The dependent variable takes on dichotomous values representing deterrence success or failure. General deterrence failure occurs when an adversary initiates a MID to challenge the status quo. The two key credibility independent variables are associated with the proportion of US troops stationed in a given ally (*presence*)[60] or in its neighborhood (*offshore balancing*).[61] We examine several component measures of credibility and commitment including total and relative US personnel and spending.

Alongside these key variables, alternative measures, and their components, we include other explanatory variables that could influence the deterrence outcomes of US allies. To address the structural effects of the dyadic relationship between a potential adversary and a US ally, we include the local balance of power, domestic political institutions, and economic interdependence. To consider domestic political factors for US foreign policy making, we also add the partisan identity of the US president and a dummy variable coded for the US presidential election year. We also introduce measures to control for time dependencies.

Our findings provide extremely robust support for our two main hypotheses (1 and 2) and strong disconfirming evidence for offshore balancing (hypothesis 4). Despite including numerous controls and components of our key measures, the presence credibility and offshore credibility variables are each statistically significant in the expected direction. Increasing presence in a way that enhances credibility, as a proportion of overall personnel spending for a specific ally, leads to deterrence success. Moving forces offshore, in a large proportionate manner to neighboring US allies, increases the risk of deterrence failure.

---

[59] Additional details on model specification, regression results, and robustness checks are discussed further in Gartzke and Kagotani 2017.

[60] Spending for military personnel is roughly proportional to the number of troops stationed overseas, although military personnel salaries vary by rank. We calculate US military personnel spending devoted to a given ally i and the distance-weighted sum of spending for all other American allies.

[61] As troops stationed with other US allies are farther away from a given alliance partner i, they are less able to intervene in a timely manner. Thus, we use the inverse of the distance between an ally i and the location of US overseas troops to capture the loss of salience (discount) for forces by proximity.

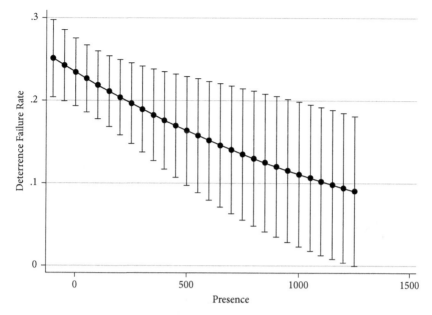

Fig. 8.1 Overseas presence improves strategic stability

Figures 8.1 and 8.2 show the predicted deterrence failure rate, while fixing other variables at their means. The connected line represents the mean predicted probabilities and vertical bars indicate the 95 percent confidence intervals. A one-unit change in *offshore balancing* has a greater impact on the probability of deterrence failure than an equivalent change in *presence*. For a one percentage increase in US forces engaged in offshore balancing, the US must devote over twelve percent of its forces to presence to remain equally effective at preventing militarized threats directed at its allies.

Presence commitments, or tripwires, fielded in an ally's territory, tend only marginally to enhance deterrence. Interestingly, this mirrors part of the findings from Blankenship and Lin-Greenberg,[62] though other aspects of their study are contradicted by the findings here. Further, offshoring such commitments to neighboring US allies has no impact on deterrence outcomes. Neither the size of budget nor the number of troops for a particular ally and its neighboring US allies significantly affect the likelihood of challenges. We also verified that a deterrence failure in the previous year

---

[62] Blankenship and Lin-Greenberg 2022.

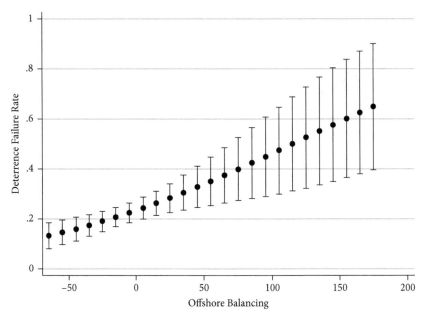

Fig. 8.2 Offshore balancing erodes strategic stability

has no correlation with Presence in the current year; thus, our findings are robust to concerns about reverse causation.

We offer three main implications derived from these results. First, annual changes in patterns of US presence update challengers' beliefs about US resolve, while annual levels of US troop deployments have no comparable effect. Second, the guns-versus-butter trade-off implied by comparisons with the federal budget is a salient baseline in signaling US resolve. Conversely, the domestic-versus-overseas security comparison plays little role in deterrence success. Third, stationing more troops in a specific ally (presence) leads to deterrence success by mitigating the risk of abandonment, while in contrast deployments to neighboring US allies or elsewhere (offshoring) yields an increased number of deterrence failures by introducing uncertainty about alliance priorities and by alleviating the risk of entrapment.

Some of the control variables also have some effect on deterrence. First, only a challenger's polity is associated with deterrence, not the regime type of the protégé. Challengers that are democracies are less likely to be deterred than are challengers that are non-democracies. The effect of the United States as the defender and a democracy is constant. Interesting dynamics may occur involving non-democratic defenders, but of course we cannot evaluate these here. The effect of regime type on challengers implies that diversionary incentives induce democratic leaders more often to resort in adventurous foreign policies.[63] Second, the party affiliation of the incumbent US president influences deterrence success. Democratic presidents are more likely to invite foreign challenges that lead to extended general deterrence failure. This result is consistent with the conventional belief that Democratic presidents tend to focus more on domestic issues and are less assertive regarding foreign policy concerns, or alternately that Democratic US presidents are perceived by challengers as more "dovish" than their Republican counterparts.

Conclusion

Issues of force posture and the effects of deployment strategies (presence versus offshore balancing) are exceedingly important yet poorly understood. This chapter provides systematic evidence of the effects of the positioning of military capabilities on deterrence outcomes. The next chapter will provide systematic evidence that disproportionate reliance on naval forces is associated with deterrence failure. Taken together, the implication is that the land domain, in effect, can compensate for the deterrence liabilities of the maritime domain.

Onshore presence—forces deployed on an ally's soil—are shown to matter, especially in proportional terms. When the United States demonstrates that an ally is a priority by stationing relatively large contingents of US troops in the country, deterrence tends to succeed. In contrast, de-emphasizing presence increases deterrence failures, even with the benefit of robust alliance treaties.

The same cannot be said for offshore balancing. A forward force posture that is pursued "on the cheap," without presence but instead relying on military capabilities positioned remotely—from which forces would need to be redeployed "onshore" in a crisis or conflict—appears often to be counterproductive in terms of its impact on local or regional stability and extended general deterrence. Forces positioned near but not on an ally's territory significantly increase the probability of deterrence failure. This phenomenon is most likely the result of the adverse signal that offshoring

---

[63] Leeds and Davis 1997.

222 ELEMENTS OF DETERRENCE

implies: The defender does not care enough to send its very best. Instead, it hopes to provide protection from afar, leveraging limited capabilities or interest for a more extensive set of commitments (more allies) or greater leverage in world affairs (more influence), rather than focusing on increased credibility, and stability, regarding its most important alliance relationships.

The effects of commitment are much less apparent. Absolute size does not matter for deterrence. A larger presence, both in human and financial terms, has no statistically significant effect on whether an ally is attacked. Similarly, the absolute size of an offshore commitment cannot be shown to be meaningful in a statistical sense, at least in terms of its effect on the likelihood of extended general deterrence failure. Offshoring capabilities does not help and often hurts stability. The motives for offshore balancing then depend much more heavily on other possible effects, such as extending finite or declining influence more broadly than is possible otherwise or minimizing the cost of a given alliance structure. In basketball, a team with a player off the court due to penalties typically shifts to a zone defense. It does not follow, however, that a mobile, dynamic defense, where coverage is always chasing the action, is better at avoiding crises in the first place. As we have noted, the benefits of influence on the cheap come with a high price tag in terms of instability and the risk of deterrence failure.

The absolute size of deployments is not a critical factor affecting deterrence. Instead, it is proportions that make a much more import contribution, both in pacifying (presence) and exacerbating (offshore) international affairs. Interestingly, this finding says a great deal about the durability of existing US alliance structures. One of the chief arguments for offshore balancing has to do with cost; presence is expensive and many students of international security have argued that a forward force posture is prohibitive and may perhaps even become "brittle" as a defender faces increasing demands on its capabilities in a period of relative decline. In contrast, our results indicate that the greatest damage in the short to medium term for the United States and its allies may come from emphasizing a force posture that increases US reliance on offshore balancing. Relative decline is not itself critical for maintaining deterrence success, at least not as long as a declining defender maintains significant military capacity. It is the *way* that the United States practices a forward force posture that matters. Put more precisely, a critical issue involves *where* US capabilities are forward deployed. A disproportionate emphasis on America's chief allies is telling. It ensures that potential challengers receive a clear message (signal) of US priorities.

This signal, as we have shown, is telling, and thus consequential. As long as presence is practiced with proportions in mind, deterrence may continue to function effectively, even in the event of significant US decline.[64]

The fate of nations is too important to be left to loose conjecture and plausible anecdote. The lack of rigor in the study of force posture has led to many misconceptions, only a few of which have been touched on here. Future research can make better sense of presence and other, related processes. Indeed, force posture has yet to be measured directly. Instead, we have inferred posture by the proximity of offshore forces to each ally in the US alliance network. As always, additional research can extend, clarify, and even qualify these findings. Still, the results here serve perhaps to inform, not unlike credible presence itself.

---

[64] US decline relative to China's rise is often assumed but is contested, both theoretically and empirically; cf. Brooks and Wohlforth 2016b; Beckley 2018. Our findings should be welcome news to both sides of this debate, insofar as interpretations are predicated on assumptions of relative power rather than discrepant preferences for US policy.

9

Sea

Maneuver and Uncertainty

One of many disagreements between the "restraint" and "engagement" camps in debates about US grand strategy is the efficacy of "offshore balancing" versus basing troops on foreign soil.[1] The previous chapter argued that the forward deployment of ground forces provides a credible signal of commitment to allies and adversaries alike. This implies that "being there" is often more useful for extended deterrence than flexible naval and air power, even as the latter may provide more potent military options.

Although proponents of offshore balancing strategies expect navies to bolster deterrence,[2] sea power may in fact undermine strategic stability. The irony is that naval means of "restraint" may end up making war more likely, as allies and adversaries alike come to question US deterrence commitments. Yet, this should not be surprising insofar as another motivation for offshore balancing is avoiding alliance entrapment, which implies escaping commitments.

Renewed Sino-US strategic antagonism invites a reassessment of arguments about the use of naval power, its characteristics, and its effectiveness as a political and economic tool. The special political salience of sea power has long been an accepted fact. Nations spend vast sums to equip specialized oceangoing vessels (i.e., warships) to influence international politics. Yet, faith in the utility of naval power is largely underpinned by logic and anecdote, and at times by institutional interest, not by systematic evaluation. Nor has there been a careful examination of the possible trade-offs imposed by exploiting the maritime domain. Such an examination is possible, given available data.[3]

---

[1] Posen 2014; Brooks and Wohlforth 2016a; Avey, Markowitz, and Reardon 2018.
[2] Gholz, Press, and Sapolsky 1997; Art 1998; Posen 2014; Mearsheimer and Walt 2016.
[3] For technical details on these data, our research design, and our statistical findings, see Gartzke and Lindsay 2020 and its online appendix.

Elements of Deterrence: Strategy, Technology, and Complexity in Global Politics. Erik Gartzke and Jon R. Lindsay, Oxford University Press. © Oxford University Press 2024. DOI: 10.1093/oso/9780197754443.003.0009

In this chapter we offer detailed argument and evidence about the distinct influence of sea power on international politics.[4] One of the defining characteristics of naval force is its special role in projecting power. Navies enable countries to influence politics in more places, more decisively, farther from home. But the advantages of navies for influence come with disadvantages for credibility. The heightened mobility and stealth of warships and submarines create ambiguity about where, and for how long, naval power will be concentrated. This creates uncertainty for political actors that undermines signals of commitment, which increases the risk of conflict.

The operational characteristics of naval force have two important strategic implications. First, naval nations are tempted to intervene in more places, especially where warships can create locally favorable concentrations of power. Second, it is not clear whether they will intervene in any given place, especially where there is heightened risk of losing those precious warships.

Consistent with this argument, we find that countries with disproportionately large navies tend to receive *more diplomatic recognition and project power further* from home (controlling for military spending and other factors). This in itself is unsurprising, but it is helpful to validate navalist expectations.[5] Yet, we also find that maritime nations also tend to be involved in *more militarized disputes*, which runs counter to conventional wisdom about the stabilizing influence of sea power.

We further assess the heterogeneous effects of specific naval platforms on influence and stability. Ship classes differ in their ability to improve military effectiveness or provide credible signals of intent. Submarines—the "silent service" is emblematic of stealthy reach—should be better at projecting power than exerting influence, also leading to increased uncertainty about the intensity or permanence of national interests. Aircraft carriers seem to be especially good at providing "presence"—Huntington Ingalls Industries advertises its capital product as "100,000 tons of diplomacy"—but may not necessarily enhance power projection more than other types of warships, which travel equivalent speeds and distances. We explore these and other implications of platform diversity to show how different means have strategic qualities that affect national security in varying ways.

---

[4] We follow Mahan 1890 in using the term "sea power" to describe the military utility of navies, as contrasted with the character of a maritime nation, which is sometimes referred to using the closed-form term "seapower." Cf. Lambert 2018.

[5] This is consistent with findings reported by Crisher 2017.

The Strategic Literature on Sea Power

International security scholars often rely on aggregate measures of military power, thus ignoring important differences across military domains.[6] But this was not always the case. Indeed, multidomain strategy is an ancient problem. Thycydides' account of the Pelopennesian War describes a conflict between domain specialists. Athens enjoyed comparative advantages at sea, while Sparta enjoyed comparative advantages on land. The Hellenic cross-domain rivalry has inspired comparisons to Britain and France in the Enlightenment era, and to the United States and the Soviet Union during the Cold War.

Joshua Rovner shows that Athens and Sparta each tried to use their domain-specific advantages to discourage war.[7] Cross-domain deterrence failed, however, because shifting alliances muddied perceptions of the cross-domain balance of power, leading each side to gamble on a quick and decisive war. Unfortunately, these same respective advantages led to a prolonged contest. Athens was hesitant to commit to a land war while Sparta was hesitant to go to sea. Both nations were deterred from engaging in decisive offensive operations in the opponent's favored domain. Rovner draws a cautionary lesson for today's rivaly between the United States and China: "China's hope of seizing the initiative and controlling the modern 'informationized' battlespace might prove to be a techno-fantasy. So, too, might the US desire to guarantee access by forcing China into a state of operational sclerosis after a rapid blinding attack. Like Sparta and Athens, both sides may be disappointed after the first volley but perfectly able to continue skirmishing. The United States can fall back to its blue water refuge, confident that its durable advantages in power projection and undersea warfare allow it to continue operations indefinitely. China enjoys a vast land refuge of its own, of course, and has built a large arsenal of ballistic missiles it can use to harass US allies and US bases in a protracted campaign."[8]

Thucydides credits Pericles with the argument that Athenian sea power could offset Spartan military prowess: "For our naval skill is of more use to us for service on land, than their military skill for service at sea." Pericles offers at least four reasons for this claim. First, Spartan land victories could not prevent Athens from imposing costs by sea: "A mere post might be

---

[6] On the problem of measuring power see Beckley 2018.
[7] Rovner 2019b.   [8] Rovner 2019b, p. 182.

able to do some harm to the country by incursions and by the facilities which it would afford for desertion, but can never prevent our sailing into their country and raising fortifications there, and making reprisals with our powerful fleet." Second, high barriers to maritime competence prevented Sparta from mounting a serious naval challenge: "The restraint of a strong force will prevent their moving, and through want of practice they will grow more clumsy, and consequently more timid." Third, commercial wealth and offshore holdings enabled Athens to prosecute a long war, whereas Sparta had to conclude wars quickly to protect its agriculture: "The desolation of the whole of Attica is not the same as that of even a fraction of Peloponnese; for they will not be able to supply the deficiency except by a battle, while we have plenty of land both on the islands and the continent." Fourth, sea control offered Athens an "impregnable position" safe from "battle with the numerical superiority of the Peloponnesians."[9]

In short, the flexible mobility, technical capability, commercial utility, and defensive potency of the Athenian fleet provided strategic advantages over Sparta. As Pericles summarizes, "The rule of the sea is indeed a great matter."[10] Classic navalists like Sir Walter Raleigh would agree: "Whoever commands the sea commands the trade; whosoever commands the trade of the world commands the riches of the world and consequently the world itself."[11] Triremes have long since been replaced by submarines and aircraft carriers, yet the same basic virtues of sea power extolled by Pericles have become even more pronounced.

The most famous modern naval strategist, Alfred Thayer Mahan, argues that the core purpose of a navy is to enable maritime commerce and economic growth.[12] The high seas, according to Mahan, are a "great commons" which no one owns, and so long as enemy warships cannot be excluded from it, friendly commerce can be interdicted, and dispersed warships can be defeated in detail. Mahan thus urges commanders to concentrate forces and seek decisive battle to achieve command of the sea, which enables the victor to blockade enemy ports, choke off enemy commerce and supply to land armies, and dictate terms ashore. Command of the sea thereby provides a highway for commerce and barrier to enemy action.

British naval strategist Julian Corbett argues, by contrast, that the vastness of the sea enables navies to advance national interests even if they cannot or

---

[9] Thucydides 1996, pp. 82–83.   [10] Thucydides 1996, p. 83.
[11] Quoted in Rubel 2012. See also Heuser 2017.   [12] Mahan 1890. See also Sumida 1997.

228 ELEMENTS OF DETERRENCE

choose not to defeat the enemy fleet in battle.[13] Naval assets can be inserted at specific places and times to raid merchant shipping (guerre de course), land expeditionary marines, escort merchant convoys around enemy concentrations, or assert local naval supremacy when an enemy fleet is occupied elsewhere. Sea power also enables a nation to fight limited wars far away from vital interests at home without risking a more general conflict. Corbett argues that sea power ultimately serves the objectives of terrestrial states: "Since men live upon the land and not upon the sea, great issues between nations at war have always been decided—except in the rarest cases—either by what your army can do against your enemy's territory and national life or else by the fear of what the fleet makes it possible for your army to do."[14]

Mahan and Corbett both inferred strategic verities from the age of sail, but they wrote in an era of major technological upheaval (steam propulsion, armor plating, big guns, submarines, aircraft, etc.). Other contemporaries speculated that these developments had revolutionized naval warfare.[15] In the mid-twentieth century, Bernard Brodie charted a middle path between the historical and matériel schools: "Naval strategy remains relatively unchanged over a long period of time and is only moderately altered by changes in weapons, [but] tactics change almost from day to day and tend to become constantly more complicated."[16] Brodie argued, along with Corbett, that "naval warfare differs from land warfare in the objectives aimed at, the implements used, and the characteristics of the domain on which it is used."[17] Yet Brodie also points out that specific platforms have contrasting effects on classic naval missions. Submarines undermine close blockade by surface vessels but facilitate commerce raiding even with enemy control of the surface. Aircraft extend the range of naval power projection but increase the vulnerability of warships to aircraft. Radio facilitates fleet concentration but undermines the secrecy of maneuver when the enemy intercepts transmissions.

An important consequence of technological improvements in speed, range, lethality, and stealth is the increasing importance of naval intelligence. As Norman Friedman argues, "Naval combat is usually about attacks on particular moving ships or groups of ships, and merely finding those targets is an important theme."[18] The targeting problem has been transformed, but definitely not eliminated, by improved reconnaissance and communication networks integrating distributed platforms on, over, and under the sea.[19]

---

[13] Corbett 1911.   [14] Ibid., 16.   [15] Heuser 2010.
[16] Brodie 1944.   [17] Ibid., 12.   [18] Friedman 2001.
[19] Ford and Rosenberg 2005; Friedman 2009.

Political scientists have also explored the political utility of sea power. Barry R. Posen builds on the Mahanian concept of "command of the sea" to explain the geopolitical significance of the network-centric revolution in military power, arguing that the United States enjoys "command of the commons"—the ability to project power globally at sea, in the air, and in space, and to prevent other states from doing the same.[20] Command of the commons enables American hegemony, but its influence is limited in littoral and terrestrial "contested zones" where resolved challengers can impose costs on the US military. Posen advocates for a grand strategy of "selective engagement" or simply "restraint," which would preserve command of the commons but avoid costly foreign commitments where US vital interests are not at stake, thereby reducing overseas interventions and alliance commitments favored by grand strategies of "primacy" or "liberal hegemony."[21] Several scholars argue that US command of the commons is eroding due to rising Chinese military power and growing technological threats in space and cyberspace,[22] although the relative potency of Chinese "anti-access/area-denial" (A2/AD) is disputed.[23]

Why has the United States managed thus far to avoid counterbalancing coalitions and remain hegemon? Jack Levy and William Thompson argue that balance of power theory is underspecified in that it fails to account for differences between continental and maritime hegemons.[24] Land-based powers inherently threaten the core interests of neighboring states via control of an adversary's territory and/or resources. Maritime powers, which benefit from and protect freedom of navigation, are less likely to challenge other states' core interests. Access to the liberal public goods provided by the maritime hegemon outweigh the costs of conceding control of the sea. The strategic nature of the maritime domain thus undergirds more general arguments about the stabilizing effects of liberal hegemony.[25] Scholars have also linked navalism with liberal politics (and conversely, disproportionate reliance on armies with autocracy).[26]

John J. Mearsheimer, by contrast, argues that limitations on maritime hegemons have less to do with bandwagoning liberal interests and more

---

[20] Posen 2003.   [21] Posen 2014.

[22] Denmark and Mulvenon 2010; Erickson 2014; Montgomery 2014.

[23] Biddle and Oelrich 2016; Beckley 2017; Erickson et al. 2017.

[24] Levy and Thompson 2010.   [25] Ikenberry 2001; Brooks and Wohlforth 2016a.

[26] Heginbotham 2002; Solingen 2007; Böhmelt, Pilster, and Tago 2017. Although mindful of the need to incorporate domestic (second image) dynamics in a full account of the influence of sea power on politics, our initial focus here is on systemic (third image) factors.

230 ELEMENTS OF DETERRENCE

with "the stopping power of water."[27] Naval wisdom, often (mis)attributed to Rear-Admiral Sir Horatio Nelson, holds that "a ship's a fool to fight a fort."[28] Amphibious invasions must solve difficult logistical challenges and penetrate littoral defenses before tangling with shore powers. Mearsheimer thus concludes, "Great powers separated by water are likely to fear each other less than great powers that can get at each other over land."[29] The United States, surrounded by vast oceans, is fortunate in this respect. East Asia's "geography of the peace" may also blunt incentives for military conquest.[30]

At the same time, oceans have facilitated conquest since antiquity.[31] Polynesian, Viking, Greek, Portuguese, Spanish, Dutch, and British mariners all created vast empires. To the extent that outright conquest is less prevalent today, this has much to do with global commerce as the common basis for both military power and limited motives for conquest.[32] Chapter 12 will return to the interaction of trade and conflict in more detail. Here we simply highlight the maritime underpinnings of economic interdependence.

The most efficient way to transport large volumes of goods or war material today is still by sea. Over 80 percent of global trade moves by sea, while seaborne tonnage has increased 3 percent annually on average since 1974.[33] Shipping delays associated with the global supply chain crisis in the wake of the COVID-19 pandemic, or the 2021 grounding of the *Ever Given* container ship in the Suez Canal, demonstrate how limitations on maritime trade can have a significant impact on global commerce. Maritime travel is also a hazardous and capital intensive endeavor, even in peacetime. Big ships are expensive investments that can be lost at once in a storm or an accident. In wartime, enemy patrols, blockades, and shore defenses make commerce and overseas expeditions even riskier.

As in ancient Greece, navies provide more options in more places, for commerce and war, but naval technology is a serious investment. Navies enable a maritime nation to access the world, while also keeping the world at bay. The loss of naval power, conversely, may lead to isolation or invasion. Thus the ocean is described as both highway and barrier. Disagreements over the origins of instability reflect classic tensions between characterizing oceans as barriers or highways and are a point of departure for our efforts here. The oceans are as important as ever for economic globalization, which

[27] Mearsheimer 2001.   [28] Ferreiro 2016.   [29] Mearsheimer 2001.
[30] R. Ross 1999.   [31] Sharman 2019.
[32] Rosecrance 1985; Gartzke 2007.   [33] United Nations 2017.

is often thought to be stabilizing, as well as global power projection, which may or may not be.

Political Trade-Offs in the Maritime Domain

Much of politics is captured by the paired dynamics of distribution and efficiency. If fighting directly over the distribution of benefits is costly, then competitors have incentives to forge bargains that avoid unnecessary military contests. But costly force is unnecessary only if competitors can agree on the likely distributional effects of fighting. In any given dispute, actors may be mistaken about relative resolve (the willingness to pay for a preferred outcome) or capabilities (the balance of power). If components of military power differ in their transparency or ease of interpretation, then these capabilities or platforms should differentially affect bargaining failure. It is not just the overall military balance, but the specific qualities of force structure and posture, that affect whether any given bargain is achieved efficiently or through costly conflict.

To appreciate the political attributes of sea power, imagine for a moment removing the massive cannon and turrets from a battleship and placing them instead in a concrete casemate somewhere on land.[34] The main guns will be devastating to anything within range. Fixed in place, there can be little doubt what consequences confront an adversary, should they wander into the field of fire. However, the fixed turret can only dominate territory at a given radius around it. Now imagine that we again mount these guns on a warship. Afloat, their devastating firepower can go anywhere there is sufficient water beneath the keel. Unopposed, the battleship can dominate the same area as the fixed guns, but it can do so in a nearly infinite number of locations, massively increasing the geography over which force can be applied. However, the same attributes that enable sea power to exert influence in more places also make it possible that one's forces will be moved or withheld. Perhaps the captain will be afraid to risk the ship and withdraw, or the admiral will call for his guns elsewhere. A specific platform cannot be at more than one location at any one time. The likelihood that military power will be exercised, influencing

---

[34] For example, a turret from the German battleship *Gneisenau* was installed ashore near Trondheim, Norway, in 1944; Zaloga 2011.

232 ELEMENTS OF DETERRENCE

the local balance of power, must decline in the number of places a capability can be deployed.

Although states may contest travel on or under the high seas, they do not conquer and control oceans in the same way as territory. Where armies can occupy ground, naval vessels can only pass through trackless ocean from one point to another. Whereas terrestrial lines of communication are canalized by roads and terrain, ships at sea have the freedom to vary routes to avoid detection, except where they must pass through terrestrial choke points like the Straits of Hormuz or Malacca. Oceanic mobility ensures that the influence acquired from force can be used in more places. Mobility also facilitates the massing of fires, which concentrates the impact of a nation's military might, even when that nation faces an adverse overall military balance.

Mobility thereby allows sovereigns greater discretion to decide where they will act to protect, punish, or plunder. Naval forces might intervene anywhere along a contested coastline, which imposes a sort of "virtual attrition" on landbound foes, who must pre-position many slow units to hedge against the sudden arrival of a few fast ships.[35] A weaker but capable "fleet in being" can tie up a stronger fleet—in effect deterring its use to project power elsewhere—without actually engaging in decisive battle.[36] Navies also enable maritime nations, such as Great Britain in its heyday, to punch above their weight in coalition strategies, for instance, by aiding local allies who will fight on land while shielding the maritime power from cost and risk.[37] Stealth further supports discretion and mobility by making it harder to respond to concentrated firepower with counter-concentrations. Victory at sea thus becomes a function of strategy and maneuver rather than brute strength.

Yet the capability, mobility, and stealth of naval assets come with two important political liabilities. First, the ability to project power in more places with less risk creates the temptation to intervene in more places. Navies can create locally favorable balances of power, for instance, by deploying a carrier strike group to threaten a distant dictator. The target, however, might be willing to absorb some punishment rather than make concessions.

---

[35] Friedman 2001.

[36] "Most men were in fear that the French would invade; but I was of another opinion . . . that whilst we had a fleet in being, they would not dare to make the attempt," Torrington to Queen Mary II, quoted in Brodie 1944.

[37] Kennedy 2017.

SEA 233

Coercion by stronger but less resolved actors often fails when they miscalculate against weaker but more resolved actors.[38]

Once fighting makes the unfavorable terms of the conflict more apparent, the naval power can more easily cut its losses. Second, naval power projection can be very risky indeed if countered by littoral defenses or an enemy fleet. Warships are expensive to maintain, limited in number, and vulnerable to sinking, making them attractive targets. Yet warships can usually sail away in unfavorable circumstances to preserve valuable capital assets for later actions that might be more successful or decisive. Competitors may thus reasonably wonder whether a naval power will be willing to risk its most valuable assets in any given dispute, especially if the stakes are limited. In the first case, the ability to project power creates risks of miscalculation about interests, even as there may be less uncertainty about the local balance of power (yet questions about how long it will be maintained). In the second case, the ability to relocate power undermines signals of commitment, precisely because the local balance is mutable.

The ability to easily relocate military power is in direct tension with the objectives of commitment. Reducing the stealth or mobility of naval platforms for the sake of credible signaling, moreover, would greatly reduce their military performance and increase their vulnerability.[39] Navies generally want their firepower to be highly mobile, to ensure its greatest potential impact. In short, even as the inherent flexibility of sea power increases a nation's influence, it also heightens uncertainty about where, when, and what action will take place. Uncertainty about intentions, in turn, raises the likelihood that opponents will miscalculate about resolve or underestimate the local balance of power. Different expectations about whether and how long an actor will stay or go (or never arrive) can generate asymmetric information about power and resolve, which heightens the risk of war, escalation, or protraction.

Note that we do not empirically test the effects of platform diversity in land warfare in this book, but a similar logic should apply. On land, cavalry, armor, or airborne units supply the attributes of mobility, observation, and shock that most naval platforms exhibit at sea. These mobile land elements

---

[38] Sechser 2010; Haun 2015.

[39] On the restrictive conditions for signaling with sensitive assets such as submarines or antisubmarine warfare capabilities, see B. Green and Long 2020.

234 ELEMENTS OF DETERRENCE

often prove decisive in battle, either by concentrating against enemy vulner-abilities, deterring the enemy from concentrating in strength, or by failing to engage or fleeing the battlefield, thus rendering one side weaker than expected. The cavalry in old Hollywood westerns was famous for showing up in the nick of time to chase off the bad guys. But the fact that the cavalry rode over the hill late in the action reveals a core problem. The wagon train was not adequately protected—it was attacked (and deterrence failed) because the bad guys decided that the cavalry would not arrive in time. The bad guys may have judged the opportunity wrong this time, but their bet was not in general unreasonable. Imagine instead a well-defended band of settlers, with soldiers already accompanying the column. Attacking such a target is inherently more difficult, and so deterrence is more likely to succeed. The trade-off posed by this example is that there may not be enough soldiers to go around. Putting them on horses and allowing them to roam means that they can cover more territory and more wagon trains, if imperfectly. Military history is replete with examples where hubris or simple miscalculation led to disaster and where soldiers and units that lacked the advantage of mobility became an impassible barrier to their enemy. Those who are most mobile turn and run, not because they are cowards, but because they can. The "bridge too far" of Operation Market Garden was not too far for the paratroopers who, once deployed, were largely committed in their positions (and fought with extraordinary valor). It was too far for the armored units that were slowly pounding their way to the rescue.

These dynamics are thus not unique to navies but they are particularly pronounced, given their global mobility, operational flexibility, and high platform costs. There are at least three major observable implications.

Power: Fighting Farther from Home

Firstly, the interests of powerful actors are less likely to be disputed where they are highly salient and/or close to home—these attributes are highly correlated. Tertiary interests in distant locales raise questions about whether the powerful care enough to make the necessary effort to have their way, given they will still shoulder non-negligible costs and risks in military action abroad, especially when territory or the issues involved are much more salient to local actors. This environment suggests a political geography in which power is projected farther by capable states and less so by the weak.

The military "loss of strength gradient"[40] thus tends to be correlated with a gradient of political interest. A "balance of place" occurs where distance, interests, and disparate capabilities cancel each other out.

Rather than creating peace and stability, a balance of this type could be associated with increased conflict.[41] As one moves from (core) locations in which one nation is predominant and challenges cannot be contemplated to (peripheral) places where power is disputed and capabilities—attenuated by distance—are comparable, one should see an increase in uncertainty about which actor would win a contest, should one occur. The empirical implication of this argument is conflict should be much more common at the geographical extremities of power, where the greatest uncertainty exists about whether conditions favor one side or the other, and whether capable actors are sufficiently about the stakes.

Sea power comes into special focus because the effects of navies on power projection are so distinctive. Controlling for overall capabilities, a given country's naval power should increase the geographical distance between its contests and its core. Put another way, countries with navies that are disproportionately large relative to national capabilities, or the defense effort of these countries, should tend to project power further than comparable countries without disproportionate navies, in turn ensuring disputes occur at greater distances from core centers of power. This implies a direct test of the classic notion of power projection, at least in the incarnation conceived here.

- *Hypothesis 1*. Countries with disproportionately large naval capabilities tend to fight farther from home.

Influence: Diplomatic Recognition

If power involves possessing greater discretion in where to fight and the ability to intervene in more places, then influence is the ability to shape foreign decision making. The capability to fight at greater distance from one's capital means there should be more places on the globe where a given nation is influential, even without exercising force. The naval term for this process

---

[40] Boulding 1962. [41] W. Reed 2003.

236 ELEMENTS OF DETERRENCE

is "presence."[42] Navies seek to continually remind other nations—friend and foe alike—that they can act with relatively little warning to protect or harm. This kind of influence should manifest in terms of increased political access and attention. If diplomacy often operates in the shadow of power, then the shadow cast by naval power covers more nations than other forms of military capabilities.

One indication of increased naval presence (influence) is, then, the number of countries that seek out and attend to a given country's concerns. Diplomatic recognition has proven to be a useful measure for assessing the presence of influence in previous research.[43] Diplomatic recognition, although increasingly common, is not universal. Countries that recognize one another are more likely to be able to influence one another through normal political discourse, negotiation, patronage or development, and intelligence activities run from diplomatic installations. At the same time, the possibility of military assistance or intervention must be critical in local officials deciding which nations merit their limited time and attention. Evidence of influence can be gleaned from looking at which nations send diplomatic representation to one another.

The influence of naval power on politics can be inferred by the degree to which maritime capabilities achieve a special impact on diplomatic recognition. Naval nations have disproportionate influence because of their ability to exercise presence. Unlike other forms of military influence, navies can "show the flag" without necessarily being based in a particular region. Navies also affect critical components of national prosperity through control and protection of commerce. Because diplomatic recognition is an imperfect measure of influence, it paradoxically constitutes an especially demanding test. Since the threshold for recognition is relatively low, many countries will have some level of representation in other nations' capitals, regardless of influence. There is thus considerable "noise" in our chosen measure. If diplomatic recognition proves to be affected by national emphasis on naval power despite this bias against significance, our findings may increase confidence in the theory.

---

[42] McNulty 1974. Related, though distinct, notions of social ordering through implied punishment or reward exist in social science. "Prestige" involves a social hierarchy where some actors defer to others due to obligation or underlying power relations. "Identity" organizes actors that self-identify in terms of subjective sameness, creating cleavages and a balance of power.

[43] Boehmer, Gartzke, and Nordstrom 2004. Diplomatic recognition is not necessarily the best measure of influence, but there are few available alternatives. Official visits, basing agreements, and participation in joint naval exercises may say more about the geographic and material endowments of a state than its diplomatic pliability. This area of scholarship could benefit from further attention.

Traditionally, carriers are seen as having a special role in encouraging other nations to adopt the policies and preferences of a naval power. Nations with aircraft carriers are recognized, and probably listened to, more often than other countries, and more often even than nations with comparable investments in sea power or with equivalent overall national capabilities. Aircraft carriers enhance the probability that other countries will recognize a nation, something generally consistent with "showing the flag," but which also reflects the special role of carriers as "floating diplomacy."

Access to the sea is also a critical delimitating factor for naval influence. Navies project power across bodies of water. Innovations in firepower have steadily increased the ability of naval platforms to direct fires inland. Yet a navy is still fundamentally a maritime asset. Kyrgyzstan, for example, should be less affected by naval power than Japan, Cyprus, Bahrain, or the United Kingdom. A country's exposure to naval power, furthermore, depends on the extent of its coastline. Nations with no frontage on the sea are least exposed to influence by naval capabilities. Conversely, countries with extremely long coastlines might be less vulnerable to influence than countries with moderate coastlines but considerable civilian coastal development. Blockades, a major tool of naval coercion, depend on the ability of one nation to bottle up an adversary, cutting off access to maneuver and to world markets. Long coastlines tend to diffuse the potential concentration that makes threats from the sea effective. The influence of sea power may thus be curvilinear, varying with the length of a country's coastline. To summarize:

- *Hypothesis 2a.* Countries with disproportionately large naval capabilities are more likely to be recognized diplomatically.
- *Hypothesis 2b.* Countries with aircraft carriers are more likely to be recognized diplomatically.
- *Hypothesis 2c.* The influence of a country's naval capabilities should be curvilinear and concave to the origin, initially increasing and then decreasing in impact with respect to the length of a target's coastline.

Uncertainty: More Militarized Disputes

Naval capabilities are flexible, dynamic, and possibly pivotal in more places, advantaging maritime powers by increasing their influence in world affairs. But, as emphasized previously, naval power also has a quixotic aspect, namely increased risk of uncertainty or miscalculation. Competitors that

238   ELEMENTS OF DETERRENCE

reasonably imagine that a naval adversary won't intervene, or will do so in a limited fashion, or will disengage shortly after intervening, will be tempted to talk and act more aggressively. Knowing naval forces could prove pivotal, but not knowing whether an adversary will act, may cause a leader to make mistakes. Conversely, a naval nation that can quickly deploy to a crisis area with less apparent risk to itself may miscalculate about target nation's resolve. The increased number of ways that navies can become relevant to localized conflicts, over and above land forces, greatly adds to the ways that opponents can misperceive or simply err in assessing the risk of facing a particular adversary.

The naval forces of either the initiator or target of a dispute will tend to increase uncertaintly. There is uncertainty about whether the initiator will actually use its threatened forces or keep them engaged if it does. There is uncertainty, likewise, about whether the target will meet a challenge with its precious fleet. Uncertainty associated with the willingness to commit naval assets to battle, initially or indefinitely, implies sea power is destabilizing for crisis bargaining. Naval power thus acts as a "wild card" in diplomatic terms, increasing uncertainty and thus heightening the propensity of nations with disproportionate naval capabilities to experience conflict.

Yet another way to think about this issue is in terms of leverage. A key trade-off of naval mobility is that although one can concentrate military power against a particular target or place, concentration can still only occur somewhere (not everywhere). It follows that naval power is leveraged, much like cash in modern banking systems, to more places than it can physically inhabit. The ability to target more potential opponents means that any given opponent is proportionately less likely to be an actual target at any particular time. At sea, no enemy is the focus of attention all the time. Instead, concentrating forces for victory means conflict tends to be episodic. Adversaries contemplating aggression against or involving naval nations may be tempted by the fact that they are less likely to be targeted even if, should they be targeted, the consequences may be more severe. Choice under increased risk is inherently more uncertain, producing the possibility of miscalculation and error.

We do not differentiate here between uncertainty about whether the naval power will disengage after intervention or whether the naval power will intervene at all. These may be associated with subtly different mechanisms. For instance, there may be little question about the balance of power when a stronger naval state intervenes against a weaker state that poses little threat at sea, yet the stronger state might still miscalculate about the weaker state's greater resolve. By contrast there may be more question about the local balance of power between peer competitors, which makes miscalculation about credibility more likely. The uncertainty in either case is a function of the naval power's freedom to move, either to abandon the contest or avoid it in the first place. Additional research and attention to these issues may prove useful.

Stealth is particularly potent in causing adversaries to underestimate intent. We discussed the general logic of the cyber commitment problem in Chapters 5 and 7. Secret sources and methods are useful for revising the balance of power (winning), but not for sending information about it (warning). Secrecy improves military power at the same time it increases efficiency, as it becomes possible to do more with less. Yet the efficiency gain of secrecy cannot be converted into a costly signal of commitment. Credibly signaling the existence of the stealthy asset makes it easier for the target to counter it.

Submarines should, therefore, play an especially prominent role in increasing the propensity for militarized conflict. By their nature, submarines are not ideal platforms for signaling or "showing the flag." The "silent service" optimizes the ability to attack through stealth and concealment. Deterrence requires a clear quid pro quo; enemy submarines would have to signal their presence and display their capabilities to deter. However, this is inconsistent with the wartime role of submarines and the culture of submariners. Given the extreme vulnerability of submarines to anti-submarine warfare countermeasures once detected and their advantages while submerged, submarine tactics emphasize stealth. Submarines are an important intelligence collection and special operations platform (watching), optimized for deception or surprise in battle (winning), as opposed to deterrence or compellence (warning).

States with disproportionately large submarine forces should thus be more likely to experience conflict. This does not mean submarines are more likely to be used in military disputes (which would be difficult to test because nations do not share location data on submarines), but simply that they cannot be used to signal interests. Nuclear ballistic missile submarines (SSBNs) provide an exception that proves the rule. SSBNs improve the credibility of nuclear deterrence by protecting weapons from preemption. Transparency about the existence of deployed and ready SSBNs, together with tactical uncertainty about their location, improves

240   ELEMENTS OF DETERRENCE

political certainty that retaliatory forces will remain available. At the same time, allies and adversaries may question whether a nuclear patron will be as willing to use SSBNs for extended deterrence as it would more vulnerable—committed—forces.[44]

- *Hypothesis 3a.* States with disproportionately large naval capabilities endure more militarized disputes.
- *Hypothesis 3b.* Countries with more attack submarines experience a greater number of militarized disputes.

More fine-grained hypotheses might be enumerated for other types of platforms, but for the sake of brevity we will move on to our empirical tests.

Summary of Empirical Findings

Here we summarize key findings demonstrating the destabilizing effects of naval power.[45] We conduct multivariate tests of three dependent variables—militarized disputes (MIDs), geographic distance of MIDs to capital cities, and diplomatic recognition—on a range of possible causal variables. We include a number of independent variables including naval order of battle, contiguity and distance, coastline length, land area, military alliances, major power status, and democratization. We also control for temporal effects. In most cases we use directed dyad years as the unit of analysis, which allow us to differentiate between factors affecting initiators and targets.

In support of hypothesis 1, Figure 9.1 details the substantive effects of naval tonnage. We find countries that spend disproportionately more on naval power are more likely to challenge, and to be challenged, farther from their own capitals than counties that spend proportionately less on naval power, regardless of overall military capacity. Initiators with proportionately larger navies experience disputes at greater distances from their capitals, while targets with capable navies are more likely to fight at longer standoff distances. Results are marginally influenced by whether distance is measured from the initiator or target's capital, but the general pattern is consistent across measures. The effect of naval tonnage in projecting power cannot

[44] Mehta 2019.   [45] For detailed analysis see Gartzke and Lindsay 2020.

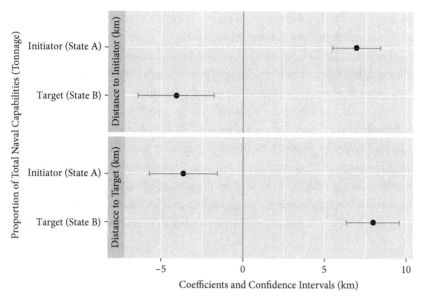

Fig. 9.1 Effects of naval capability on dispute location

be explained away by proximity (distance) or by either country's defense spending.

We also find that the basic effect of tonnage on distance remains for all classes of capital ships, although each platform type demonstrates distinctive effects on the distance at which disputes occur from a nation's capital.[46] Indeed, the effect of battleships is to reduce power projection, below that of equivalent naval tonnage by other platforms. For example, both Britain and Germany appeared to be reluctant to deploy their largest battle wagons close to enemy coastlines or formations in World War I. But aircraft carriers are different. The latter must engage enemy platforms at or near visual range, directly confronting an adversary and experiencing proportionate risk of damage or destruction. Aircraft carriers, in contrast, use their aircraft to conduct attacks while (hopefully) remaining obscured from an enemy, using distance and mobility to lower risk of attack. Accordingly, we find that more intensive use of aircraft carriers appears to (modestly) increase power projection.[47] Submarines also influence power projection differently. We find that a target's submarines do not reduce power projection by an initiator,

---

[46] Not shown here but see Gartzke and Lindsay 2020.
[47] It is, however, difficult to draw conclusions from these values, as there are few countries that have aircraft carriers, and a limited number of possible dyads generates large standard errors.

but they do affect the distance a dispute occurs from the target. This asymmetry may result from how submarines operate and are deployed. Major surface engagements often occur along the boundaries between national spheres of influence; however, submarines patrol sea-lanes, rather than contest boundaries, interdicting ships bound for enemy harbors. Although submarines project power, they do not necessarily do so in a linear manner, operating on laterals and denying access rather than along great circle distances.

In support of hypothesis 2a, Figure 9.2 reports the impact of proportional naval tonnage on diplomatic recognition. Even controlling for the effect of coastline on this decision, as well as the effects of other independent variables, naval tonnage is positively and significantly correlated with diplomatic recognition of the naval state by other states.[48] This does not reflect power

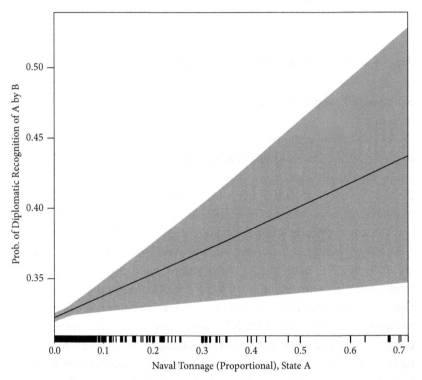

Fig. 9.2 Effects of naval tonnage on diplomatic recognition

[48] The effect is variable with increasing confidence intervals at high values are due to small sample size, but always positive.

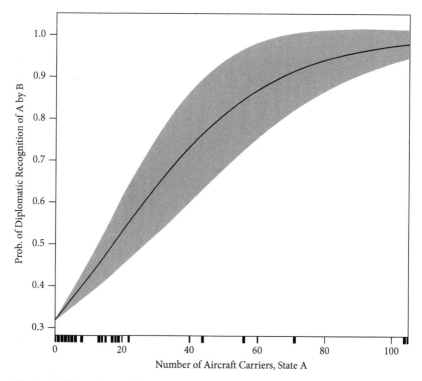

Fig. 9.3 Effect of aircraft carriers on diplomatic recognition

broadly, which is included separately in the model, but rather the special role of sea power in affording influence.

In support of hypothesis 2b, Figure 9.3 depicts the effect of a count of aircraft carriers on diplomatic recognition. The relationship between carriers and influence is positive and concave to the origin. This may help to explain both the historical appeal of aircraft carriers—even in peacetime—and the acquisition of flattops by aspiring great powers. This finding militates against claims that carriers are mere status symbols without strategic import.[49]

In support of hypothesis 2c, Figure 9.4 plots the curvilinear relationship between coastline and diplomatic recognition. The relationship produces a declining upward sloping curve, concave to the x-axis. Although the influence of naval power is minimal for landlocked nations, this influence increases rapidly but at a declining rate as national coastlines lengthen. The function flattens for the longest coastlines, suggesting long coastlines

---

[49] Gilady 2018.

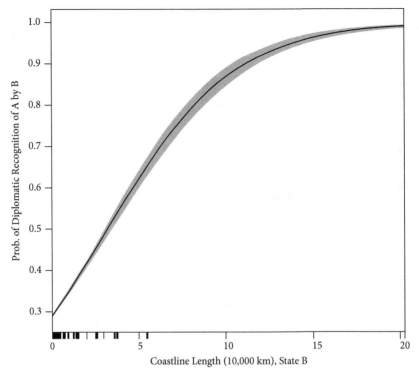

Fig. 9.4 Effect of coastline length on diplomatic recognition

form a natural defense against naval coercion, in effect diluting potential concentration. Nations with the longest coastlines are not disproportionately vulnerable because long coastlines provide additional opportunities to thwart blockades, disperse maritime assets, use redundant ports, etc.

In support of hypothesis 3a, Figure 9.5 illustrates the effects on dispute probability of both proportional and absolute sea power. By both measures, we find that rather than achieving deterrence, big navies (in relative terms) are disproportionately associated with MIDs. Measured in proportional tonnage, initiators are marginally more likely to experience deterrence failure, which might be interpreted as naval powers being more willing to make threats or their targets less willing to believe them. While navies can attempt to deter in more places, naval deterrence is also more likely to fail.

The increased dispute propensity of sea power cannot be written off as an endogeneity effect. Although a nation may decide to invest in sea power because it expects to fight more often, this does not explain why other actors might also be willing to fight them more often, too. We argue that a deficit

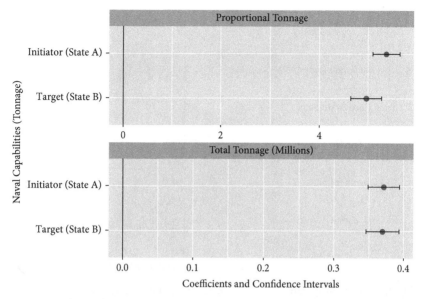

Fig. 9.5 Effects of naval capability on dispute propensity

of mutual information is further required to explain conflict. Even if a state expects to engage in gunboat diplomacy more often, and therefore invests in a bigger navy, this investment decision still sends ambiguous signals about that state's actual willingness to go to war. Targets have a hard time distinguishing whether the initiator is brandishing its navy as a bluff or as its most effective military option. We will explore a similar trade-off in more detail in Chapter 10 on drone warfare. All else being equal, and regardless of the intentions of the naval state, bigger navies tend to marginally increase uncertainty due to asset mobility, firepower, and stealth.

All types of platforms significantly impact conflict propensity. However, these effects are not uniform. Figure 9.6 depicts the marginal effects of different naval platforms on dispute propensity. Battleships (to a greater extent) and submarines (to a lesser extent) are each associated with a heightened risk of dispute behavior, beyond that attributable to naval tonnage or overall military power. In contrast, aircraft carriers have a slightly lower impact on conflict.

This does not mean that carriers pacify; quite the converse. Instead, it shows carriers impose less uncertainty than other platforms, ceteris paribus. How could this be? Consistent with hypothesis 2b, the carrier can achieve some influence without having to fire a shot or by conducting limited

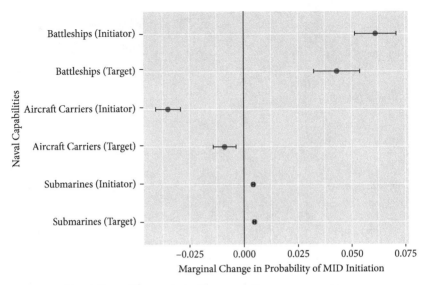

Fig. 9.6 Effects of specific naval platforms on dispute propensity

strikes. Carriers can menace a foreign shoreline at stand-off distances, in international waters. The relative visibility, mobility, and range of a carrier and its entourage make the strike group an attractive platform for coercive diplomacy.

Battleships and other surface combatants must go further into harm's way when approaching enemy formations or shorelines to influence affairs. This makes them riskier to employ. They are easy to move into a conflict area, and easy to remove as well, in ways that are visible to adversaries. Stealthy submarines, however, are generally unable to "show the flag." Indeed, submarines may be so stealthy that adversaries can do little better than assume, with some discount factor, that they could be present anywhere, thus diluting their effects on specific disputes. Figure 9.6 appears to provide only weak support for hypothesis 3b, which focuses specifically on subs.

Yet, not all submarines are alike. As with platform types, different types of submarines play different roles, leading to contrasting effects on dispute propensity. Key findings are detailed in Figure 9.7. Attack submarines are aggressive, intended to shape the tide of battle, should nations fight. Submarines are not especially useful for making credible claims about limited objectives with any certainty. Providing some support for hypothesis 3b, diesel attack submarines are rather poor at keeping the peace, precisely because their strengths in quietly delivering lethal firepower affect the

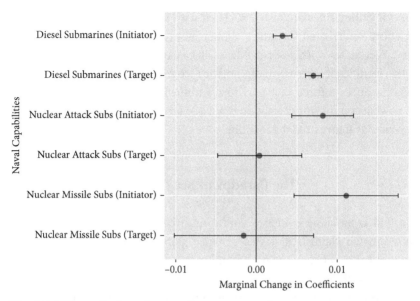

Fig. 9.7 Effects of submarines on dispute propensity

conduct of battle more than they warn and inform. SSBNs, conversely, may do more to warn. *Targets* with more SSBNs have a marginally lower dispute propensity as the existence of SSBNs is typically declared to enhance strategic deterrence, but there are large errors since their impact on war depends less on their location, which is kept secret to enhance tactical survivability. The effect of nuclear propulsion for *initiators* is positive for both attack and missile subs, but this not statistically significant and the sample size is small (and may be an artifact of US dispute propensity).

In sum, the general effects of sea power on politics—more influence but less stability—are reflected in different naval platforms. Aircraft carriers and submarines tend to increase the distance at which an actor fights from its own territory, should a contest occur. Battleships do the opposite. Indeed, battleships as a platform class do not appear to offer many advantages that cannot be gleaned from naval tonnage generally. Battleships make disputes more likely, without increasing diplomatic recognition or augmenting the projection of power. This may have contributed to their rapid demise once they proved vulnerable in fleet operations with the advent of more versatile aircraft carriers and submarines. Carriers and submarines have only marginal effects in shortening the distance to disputes, a finding that seems to confirm the traditional distinction between denial and sea control. Submarines are also associated with increased conflict propensity, an effect exacerbated for attack submarines (especially diesels) but absent for target states with SSBNs. Meanwhile, carrier inventory is associated with a significant increase in diplomatic recognition. A carrier-focused navy thus produces a force that maximizes influence and reduces conflict but, somewhat counter-intuitively, does not add significantly to power projection beyond naval investment generally.

The Paradox of Sea Power

We find compelling evidence confirming the widely assumed but rarely substantiated claim that navies enhance global power and presence. The amount (or proportion) of naval tonnage a nation possesses coincides with an increase in the range at which that nation projects power, even when accounting for other military expenditures. Sea power also produces influence that can be measured in terms of diplomatic recognition. Interestingly, countries with longer coastlines are more likely to submit to the influence of sea power, though this effect diminishes as coastlines become extremely long.

Yet, we also find that sea power destabilizes international affairs, which runs contrary to most navalists' expectations. Disproportionate naval tonnage (and platforms) is associated with an increase in dispute propensity, over and above the effect for defense spending generally. The paradox of sea power is that greater influence comes with greater instability.

Why would nations accept this additional risk? The answer surely lies in the additional political benefits of sea power. Navies win influence in more places, in peacetime and war. Warships can concentrate power offshore to threaten a troublesome rival, reassure an ally, or provide material assistance. At the same time, friend and foe alike may wonder if the possibility of concentration will be actualized, and for how long. The war-fighting strength of navies, ironically, raises questions about relative resolve and credible commitment. Even weaker targets without the ability to threaten the fleet directly may gamble that they can outlast naval punishment. They might also worry that a naval power will not keep to an agreement to suspend punishment, since it is so easy for them to return repeatedly with little risk to themselves. Stronger targets, conversely, may reasonably doubt whether a rival will be willing to risk its fleet in a dispute.

In short, great navies are a great temptation for policy makers: they are tempted to use them in more places and to withdraw in crises. Naval presence may become indistinguishable from diplomatic bluff, and naval maneuver invites political brinksmanship.

This is not simply an artifact of large naval nations like the United States. These results hold for even small naval powers in our dataset, even as small navies tend to have rather different missions in practice.[50] Yet the defining characteristic of any naval platform is its mobility, potentially across the entire ocean, which in turn creates uncertainty about where it will be at any given time, now or in the future. It is this feature which marginally improves influence yet undermines stability.

Yet, the policy implications are perhaps most important for large naval nations, since they are the ones investing in this peculiarly specialized form of power. The nominal purposes of America's historic investment in naval power has been to deter and stabilize relationships, signal US resolve, and increase US combat effectiveness. US maritime strategies routinely assume that all of these good things go together. The 2020 "Advantage at Sea" tri-service strategy aimed to "boldly modernize the future naval force to maintain credible deterrence and preserve our advantage at sea." The 2015 "Cooperative Strategy for 21st Century Seapower" stated, "Naval forces achieve all domain access as part of joint operations, improving relationships and deterrence in peacetime and enabling success against our enemies in wartime." Its 2007 predecessor stated similarly, "Maritime forces must contribute to winning wars decisively while enhancing our ability to prevent war." None of them acknowledge the inherent tensions between deterrence and defense, or any of the fundamental strategic trade-offs of naval power.

A heavy investment in the most mobile military capabilities will tend to weaken the goal of deterrence in any given place. The United States very well may have to invest in a larger and more capable navy to better defend its maritime allies in Asia. But it will also be tempted more often to use that power in other places as well, far from the Pacific, thus distorting US posture over time in response to new hotspots and tensions elsewhere. America's so-called pivot to Asia (during the decade of the 2010s) offers a case in point. The pivot became a pirouette as the United States flexed to respond to other priorities in the Central Asia and Europe. Mobile strike forces with an expeditionary punch enable US leadership to respond to unexpected crises

---

[50] McCabe, Sanders, and Speller 2021.

250   ELEMENTS OF DETERRENCE

in faraway places. Yet the exercise of military power in places other than planned attenuates force commitments in the Pacific. As America thins its lines in the effort to extend itself further, it will experience additional rounds of instability in Asia that it will unlikely be able to address efficiently.

One of the least studied and most troubling features of deterrence strategy, moreover, is what might be called "aspiration creep." Leaders often convert deterrence into compellence, using the power to discourage aggression against a given target to wrest greater influence elsewhere. A US naval vessel in Yokohama, nominally protecting Japan, may find itself tasked to head to the Indian Ocean, say, because it is stationed relatively closer than other members of the Third or Seventh Fleets. Increasing naval power could discourage aggression, but it could also tend instead to lead to additional commitments.

A simpler solution—*if* US policy makers decide that strategic stability is more desirable than other goals—is to put ground-based forces in places that are America's highest priorities. Security in the Pacific, for example, seems obviously to be a naval domain. But one of the best ways to prove US priorities is with shore-based land and air forces that signal, and indeed provide, a clear commitment to a particular security partner. The Navy clearly will still prove pivotal in any contest in the Pacific. But a fight is paradoxically much less likely the more the United States invests in forces that signal defensive intentions and credible deterrence, rather than maximizing US offensive options and influence. During the battle for Guadalcanal, the US Navy responded to a Japanese attack by retreating. The Marines on Guadalcanal stayed, because they had no other option. Especially on islands in the Pacific, land forces are inherently more likely to stay and fight, and thus are more effective at deterrence. Investment of specific assets in a given location might seem like a military disadvantage from the point of view of flexibility and survivability. Yet the reduced mobility and increased visibility of land forces provide key political virtues.

As discussed in Chapter 8, land-based forces demonstrate to allies and adversaries alike that a given location is a priority for the foreign patron that will be defended vigorously. Reduced mobility also means that land powers have to forego opportunities to rapidly redeploy to other locations, fostering assurance. Land-based forces (and to a lesser extent land-based maritime infrastructure) could be more useful than high seas forces for US deterrence policy. Their usefulness increases where and when their inability to move about easily ensures that they commit the United States only where they are posted. Forward deploying troops, as opposed to sailing naval vessels, improves the credibility of US extended deterrence by creating tripwires designed to mobilize a more robust US response if attacked.

The United States could also help allies like Japan and quasi-allies like Taiwan to develop their own shore-based defenses. Strategies of "active denial" or "defensive defense" essentially turn China's anti-access and area denial (A2/AD) techniques against it. Shore-based reconnaissance and strike forces would be less useful for attacking China directly. The same cannot be said of proactive offshore interventions by the US Navy. Shore-based denial also reduces the risks of inadvertent escalation that are inherent in attacking command and control targets on mainland China, a likely feature of any US campaign to roll back Chinese A2/AD. Of course, increasing the self-reliance of allies also reduces US influence over them. Maintaining US troops abroad is also expensive. Indeed, this policy is a credible signal precisely because it is costly. It also exposes the United States to a heightened risk of under-provision and entrapment by easy-riding allies. And all of these shore-based options will restrict America's flexibility to use forces elsewhere. But these are the trade-offs faced by the United States.

Ultimately, there can be no one right strategy for all goals. Different goals call for different force structures and postures. The prioritization of goals, moreover, cannot be deduced in a vacuum from the bargaining model of war. Unit level factors like domestic politics and ideology will often determine what matters. Trying to achieve power, efficiency, influence, and stability all at the same time is untenable for any navy and is, in effect, an abandonment of strategy. We will return to the implications of different goals for US China strategy in the conclusion.

10

Air

Automation and Cost

with James Walsh

The previous chapter argued that the range and maneuverability of warships are valuable features for power projection, but these same features become liabilities for credible signaling. Military units that can quickly deploy anywhere can more easily escape political commitments to fight in specific places. Given that warplanes are even faster and more agile than warships, it is plausible that air power might recapitulate, if not amplify, the deterrence liabilities of sea power.

Indeed, the punishment theory of strategic bombing has not fared well in history.[1] There is more evidence that air power is effective for denial strategies, especially at the operational level of war.[2] Recall that punishment strategies threaten to impose costs on an enemy by destroying things that it values, which may or may not include its military forces, while denial strategies threaten to disarm the enemy, preventing its military forces from conquering or defending. In this sense, air power deters when it discourages the enemy from massing ground forces, forcing the enemy to rely on more dispersed or disguised operations.[3] But as a strategic instrument, air power has been generally more useful for "winning" than "warning."

In this chapter we explore another strategic trade-off that is acute for air power. Modern warplanes can deliver tremendous firepower on short notice, and they can do this at greatly reduced risk to friendly forces. In other words, air forces make it possible to separate killing from dying. For most of military history, harming others meant exposing oneself to harm. But the emergence of long-range artillery began to put distance between the killers

---

[1] Pape 1996; T. Biddle 2002; Haun 2015; Post 2019.
[2] Pape 1996; Haun and Jackson 2016; Haun 2019.
[3] Chapter 14 on gray-zone conflict will explore these ambiguous deterrence dynamics.

Elements of Deterrence: Strategy, Technology, and Complexity in Global Politics. Erik Gartzke and Jon R. Lindsay, Oxford University Press. © Oxford University Press 2024. DOI: 10.1093/oso/9780197754443.003.0010

and the killed. Even so, artillerymen remained vulnerable to counter-battery fire. With the advent of airplanes, however, bombers could deliver violence over the horizon without putting substantial numbers of troops in harm's way. Aircrew were still vulnerable to air defenses, of course, but there were far fewer of them. Loss ratios became ever more lopsided, culminating in the 1999 air war for Kosovo in which NATO forces did not suffer a single fatality.

The rise of unmanned aerial vehicles (UAVs) or "drones" takes the separation between aircrew and their targets to an unprecedented extreme.[4] UAVs like the US MQ-1 Predator and MQ-9 Reaper are among the most recognizable examples of a class of systems that are conceivably making war safer, at least for one side. Operators who physically reside in Nevada, for instance, can strike targets in Afghanistan or Somalia with great precision. The ability to wage relatively effective precision bombing campaigns against enemy forces makes denial strategies feasible, even as effectiveness varies across campaigns and target sets. The United States has used drone technology extensively for targeting militant fighters. The depletion of militant ranks makes it difficult for targeted groups to recruit and retain members and supporters, threatening the organization's most fundamental resource.[5]

Military automation, together with reconnaissance systems and communication networks for intelligence and control, has evolved to a point where it is possible to contemplate conflicts in which human beings are no longer directly engaged in combat. While there will still be incentives to attack soldiers, cover and concealment are enhanced dramatically by the ability of military personnel to operate remotely, far from combat areas. The proliferation of drones, moreover, means that a growing number of actors will be able to inflict damage or death with little prospect that those causing harm will themselves be subject to death or injury. What are the strategic implications of the fraying link between imposing and incurring harm? Can warfare be "efficient" or even "costless" in this way and truly remain war? More to the point of this book, can low-cost military denial options support coercive diplomacy?

---

[4] Singer 2009; Callam 2010; Schmitt and Thurnher 2012; Crootof 2014; Franke 2014; Mayer 2015; Walsh 2015; Walsh and Schulzke 2015; Fuhrmann and Horowitz 2017.

[5] The partial automation of combat has been evolving for quite some time. For example, the Wehrmacht deployed the Goliath tracked land mine carrier in 1940. The device, which was remotely controlled and expendable, was intended to carry an explosive charge to targets like enemy tanks or armored defensive emplacements, such as bunkers, etc. The German V weapons, similarly, were the first modern precedents for guided ballistic and cruise missiles. Modern drones differ mainly in the degree of remote control they afford, along with the attractive feature of being reusable.

254 ELEMENTS OF DETERRENCE

The arguments in this book suggest not. Effective coercion is not simply about imposing costs, but also about demonstrating a willingness to pay them. The separation of killing from dying in the operational instrument of automated air power forces us to separate these two functions of coercive diplomacy. Theories of strategic bombing are essentially theories of killing: impose enough costs on the enemy population, or destroy the right critical nodes, and the enemy will capitulate. But theories of coercion furthermore stress the importance of dying, or at least demonstrating a willingness to die for a cause. This is one reason why guerrillas can win against more capable counterinsurgents: while the latter can kill more guerrillas in any given battle, the former can demonstrate their resolve to keep on fighting a long war.

The problem with costless conflict is that it fails to produce costly signals of resolve. A nation that does not need to imperil what it values most in fighting will have more difficulty demonstrating its values. Combatants will be tempted, therefore, to find ways to make costless conflict more costly. To the extent that machines dominate the battlefield, the decisiveness of contests will hinge on the willingness of actors to inflict and incur human harm. To the degree that automation removes humans from the battlefield, we should expect patterns of violence to shift as well.

The irony is that as machines become able to kill more efficiently without risking human operators, militaries may become less effective at ending wars quickly and decisively. Even more troubling, a world made safer for military personnel may become more dangerous for civilians. Effective automated airpower may provide a form of deterrence by denial that *discourages* direct reprisals on military forces, yet *encourages* more aggression against civilian targets. Successful deterrence in one area translates into deterrence failure in another. Lethal action through the air domain can have counterproductive effects in the land domain.

This chapter begins with a review of debates about the use of drones in US counterterrorism operations, one of the most extensive uses of military UAVs to date. Then we apply the themes of this book to explain why automated warfare has the potential to make asymmetric conflicts longer and increase civilian suffering. One reason is that drone strikes that kill rank-and-file militants encourage militant groups to increase terrorist attacks in urban areas, which both protects the loss of a valuable resource (militant fighters) and demonstrates the group's continued viability as a political force. We then present empirical evidence that militant deaths from drone strikes in Pakistan have led to more terrorism in urban areas and have reduced militant attacks on government and military targets. Finally, we take a step back to consider the use of UAVs in other types of conflict. Asymmetric war is just one model. Recent wars in Nagorno-Karabakh and Ukraine showcase a different model, with UAVs targeting enemy ground forces in high-intensity land warfare. The first of these ended after only a month, while the second drags on as of this writing. In all of these cases, relative resolve conditioned the ways in which automated airpower was used, and to what effect.

Debates about Drones

UAVs have been a prominent feature of the US military's long war against militant groups. The objective of drone strikes is to degrade targeted organizations by killing their active militants and leaders. The capacity of UAVs to closely monitor potential targets for long periods of time makes it possible to collect more accurate intelligence on militants hide-outs, vehicles, and movements. Drones are armed with precision-guided munitions, allowing their operators to act on intelligence and more reliably strike their targets. The absence of an on-board crew greatly reduces the cost of UAV operations and also ensures that the United States does not suffer military casualties if a drone malfunctions or is shot down. UAVs also require far fewer "boots on the ground" to sustain operations in combat areas, dramatically lowering exposure of US personnel to threats of all kinds and encouraging the use of force in environments where the risks of military casualties would otherwise outweigh the benefits of military intervention.[6] As President Barack Obama's counterterrorism advisor, John O. Brennan, explained "the purpose of these actions [using UAVs] is to mitigate threats to US persons' lives."[7]

US strategy is based on the expectation that targeting militants with drone strikes will degrade their capacity to engage in violence. But scholarly research suggests that such strikes could actually increase attacks by militant groups. Many observers argue that drone strikes serve to strengthen the hand of militant groups. A diverse set of critics—human rights organizations,[8] military experts,[9] and United States and Pakistani government officials[10]—claim in particular that drone strikes that kill civilians do more harm than

---

[6] Walsh and Schulzke 2018.   [7] Becker and Shane 2012.
[8] Cavallaro, Sonnenberg, and Knuckey 2012.
[9] Kilcullen and Exum 2009.   [10] Gerstein 2011; DeYoung 2013.

256 ELEMENTS OF DETERRENCE

good. Militants highlight civilian deaths from drone strikes to demonstrate US brutality, and justify their own use of violence. Civilian deaths provide powerful narratives used to recruit or sustain support from residents and sympathizers overseas. Pakistani militants have defended their own attacks as retaliation for US drone strikes. A man convicted of attempting to bomb Times Square in New York, who was trained by the Pakistan Taliban, planned the attack in response to drone strikes that were "killing Muslims."[11] Research also finds that drone strikes designed specifically to kill militant leaders contributes to a rise in terrorism. Leadership decapitation reduces the ability of militant organizations to control their subordinates, who may be tempted to attack softer, civilian targets, rather than engage in dangerous combat with military forces.[12] If this is the case, then the US reliance on drones could be fundamentally misguided, leading to "blowback."[13] While drone strikes against militant leaders might be intended to weaken these organizations, the result may actually be to increase violence and instability in the form of increased terrorist attacks.

Each of these lines of criticism invites some skepticism, however. Civilian deaths due to drone strikes, while disconcerting, may actually be less pronounced than for other forms of military violence.[14] We discuss evidence below that civilian casualties and leadership decapitation are not consistently related to any form of political violence. While one cannot doubt the outrage that drone strikes engender, it is not clear that targeted killings using manned aircraft or special operations personnel would be regarded as more benign by local populations. Similarly, the death of militant leaders need not result in heightened attacks against civilians. Leaderless militants could just as well refrain from taking any aggressive actions, or they might choose to consolidate with other militant groups.

Existing research identifies three channels through which drone strikes influence the use of terrorism, or other forms of violence, by militant groups. Most of this work, like the present study, examines empirical evidence from the drone campaign in Pakistan, where UAVs have been employed by the United States most frequently and have continued for the longest period of time.

---

[11] Elliott 2011.   [12] Abrahms and Potter 2015.
[13] C. Johnson 2001.   [14] Plaw and Fricker 2012.

A first perspective, which justifies US use of drones, holds that drone technology is uniquely well-suited to degrading or destroying militant organizations. Proponents argue that technological features of drones allow for more selective targeting of militants while minimizing civilian casualties.[15] The ability of UAVs to loiter for long periods, track movements by foot or vehicle, collect real-time information from sensors that can be integrated with other sources, and fire precision-guided missiles makes them especially effective at combatting insurgent movements, which requires identifying militants and distinguishing them from civilians. Historically this has proven difficult, particularly in the application of air power.[16] Militant groups typically do not possess extensive logistical infrastructures, in part to limit their vulnerability to the likely dominance of the skies by their enemy. For similar reasons, militants often resist becoming fixed to specific territory, and seldom choose to operate as massed units.

Drones do offer some improvements in the effectiveness of air power in countering militant groups and their preferred tactics. The sensors and increased loiter time of UAVs allow operators to better distinguish combatants from non-combatants, making drones particularly effective in undermining the militant organizations they target. Indiscriminate attacks can drive civilians into the arms of militants. Such violence reduces the benefits of siding with the authorities in a conflict, "[b]ecause it approximately equalizes the probability of victimization for participants and nonparticipants, indiscriminate violence increases participation in insurgencies by raising its payoff vis-à-vis nonparticipation."[17] Selective violence thus accentuates the "rebels' dilemma"—making participation in insurgency more risky or costly—while indiscriminate violence has the opposite effect.[18] A pair of careful and sophisticated empirical analyses, by Johnston and Sarbahi and by Mir, find that drone strikes are associated with short-run reductions in a range of measures of militant violence in the Federally Administered Tribal Areas (FATA) of Pakistan, where many militant groups are based.[19] This relationship also extends to areas immediately surrounding the FATA. Both studies conclude that the surveillance and targeting technology that underpin drone strikes are a key element of this relationship.

---

[15] Schwartz 2003; Brown 2007; Mir 2018; Mir and Moore 2019.   [16] Pape 1996.
[17] Kocher, Pepinsky, and Kalyvas 2011.   [18] Lichbach 1995; Goodwin 2001; Kalyvas 2006.
[19] A. Johnston 2017; Mir 2018.

258   ELEMENTS OF DETERRENCE

Consistent with claims that drones lead to more selective use of violence, Plaw and Fricker developed a dataset of the victims of drone strikes in Pakistan.[20] Their data collection effort divides victims into three categories: militants, civilians, and those whose status cannot be determined. Based on a careful review of media reports, they measure the ratio of militants killed in drone strikes to civilians that die in such attacks. Using only information from media sources in Pakistan, they estimate that over 26 militants are killed for each confirmed civilian death in a drone strike. This ratio falls slightly to 19 militants per civilian death if they also rely on international media sources. Plaw and Fricker then compare these ratios of militants and civilians killed by drone strikes with corresponding ratios for other types of armed conflict, including Pakistani military operations in the FATA and the Swat Valley, United States military operations in Pakistan that use other types of force besides drones, targeted killings in the West Bank and Gaza Strip carried out by Israel between 2000 and 2008, and all conflicts in the world in the year 2000. All of these other types of force yield a higher ratio of civilian deaths than even the lowest estimates for the proportion of civilian deaths per militant by drone strikes. It should be acknowledged that it remains difficult to generate accurate counts of civilian and military victims during armed conflicts. Still, these findings seem to indicate that the proportion of civilian victims from drone strikes is comparable or lower to that of other types of military violence. In addition, Plaw, Fricker, and Williams find that the ratio of civilian to military deaths in the drone campaign in Pakistan has dropped over time.[21] Over time, US drone operators have become more adept at distinguishing civilians from military targets.

A second perspective holds that civilian deaths from drone strikes provide militants with political gains that outweigh the harm inflicted on their organizations by successful targeted killings. In the context of drone strikes in Pakistan, the argument is that militant organizations can publicize civilian deaths in propaganda campaigns that mobilize supporters and alter public opinion. This propaganda emphasizes to the larger population—which may not feel vulnerable to targeted killings themselves—that civilian victims share their ethnic, religious, and national identities and thus merit support. Drone attacks, and the resulting propaganda, also make it easier for militants to justify their own use of violence in the face of a more powerful and threatening state security apparatus. For example, Al Qaeda Central and

---

[20] Plaw and Fricker 2012.   [21] Plaw, Fricker, and Williams 2011.

AIR 259

allied groups used drone strikes as part of propaganda campaigns intended to mobilize recruits and raise financial donations from overseas diasporas and other groups, portraying drones as unfair exploitation of technology by a powerful foe unwilling to risk the lives of its own soldiers and citizens.[22]

Drone strikes have aroused considerable controversy about civilian deaths in Pakistan. One survey conducted in the tribal areas of Pakistan finds that most respondents believe that the drones kill more non-combatants than militants. Respondents were asked if drones "accurately target militants" or "largely kill civilians." Only 16.2% of respondents believed that drones accurately kill militants alone, while 47.8% concluded that they kill civilians and an additional 33.1% believed drones killed both militants and civilians.[23] Consistent with this perspective, a number of studies of more conventional manned air strikes, which often victimize non-combatants, were associated with subsequent increases in militant violence in Vietnam and Iraq, and reduced popular support for the authorities during the conflict in Afghanistan after 2001.[24] This logic holds that drone strikes that kill civilians increase support for militant groups, enabling them to justify and to engage in additional violence.

A third perspective considers how the scale and position of militants killed by the authorities influence subsequent militant violence. Abrahms and Potter focus on how attacks on the leadership of militant groups, influence subsequent group behavior.[25] The authors challenge the contention that terrorist attacks are typically counter-productive for the groups that mount them because they reduce the likelihood of concessions by the government. Why, if this is the case, would militant organizations engage in such violence? Abrahms and Potter distinguish between the incentives of leaders and of rank-and-file members in militant organizations. Leaders have incentives to behave strategically, limiting attacks on civilian targets. Rank-and-file members, in contrast, have incentives to carry out such attacks, which place them at a lower risk of harm than they face in attacks on military targets. Targeted killings of militant commanders produce leadership "deficits" that empower the rank-and-file to act in accordance with their preferences. Abrahms and Potter test this theory using several sources, including data on drone strikes and terrorism in Pakistan. Their key independent variables

[22] Smith and Walsh 2013; Pape and Feldman 2010.   [23] Terror Free Tomorrow 2010.
[24] Condra and Shapiro 2010; Kocher, Pepinsky, and Kalyvas 2011; Lyall, Blair, and Imai 2013.
[25] Abrahms and Potter 2015.

are the occurrence of drone strikes and of drone strikes that kill militant leaders. The authors find that drone strikes are associated with an increase in terrorist attacks, regardless of whether the strike kills a militant leader. However, only strikes that actually kill leaders lead to reductions in attacks on military targets.

Existing research has thus identified three ways that drone strikes could influence terrorist attacks by militant groups: degradation, civilian casualties, and leadership decapitation. The first expects drone strikes to reduce militant violence, while the second and third claim that drone attacks increase such violence. We build on this work in two ways. First, we test these arguments directly with data that disaggregates drone strikes by the number of civilians, militant leaders, and rank and-file militants that they kill. Disaggregating in this way allows us to identify which, if any, of the existing theories are supported by the data. Second, we offer a new theory in which UAV strikes that kill rank-and-file militants lead militant groups to increase terrorist attacks in urban areas.

The Costs of Costless War

If war is truly costless, then there are no material incentives to refrain from fighting. With no financial, social, or human consequences, war ceases to function as an organic and binding method for the arbitration of disputes. Peace could ensue, but politics will still require some means to conquer or compel. The recourse to violence reflects dissatisfaction with either the method or outcome of other means for determining winners and losers. Costless war must therefore trigger a search for other methods of imposing costs, even as opponents seek security and new ways to harm in return. It is again this relationship between hurting and being hurt that characterizes conflict. If war imposes little or no cost on some practitioners but imparts harm to others, then it will be practiced freely, and frequently, by those that are asymmetrically free of its burdens.

Today, as in the past, powerful countries fight less powerful nations and non-state actors more often in part because they can act with relatively little harm to themselves. Yet, relatively little information is revealed by the capable party engaging in such an exercise, since fighting is cheaper or easier for the powerful actor. A decisive outcome favors the more capable power, so the weaker actor avoids decisive combat, and both sides end up pursuing attrition strategies. The comparative advantage of the weak is to go for a longer contest in which a stronger enemy may reveal itself to be less resolved.[26] But this also means that stronger opponents will be able to demonstrate resolve, where such resolve exists. Asymmetries of capabilities are typically matched with asymmetric stakes. Insurgents fight for their homeland while the capable adversary is projecting power far from home. Asymmetric wars tend to drag on because time is a proxy for resolve and because at least one actor prefers attrition to decisive engagements; one side cares but is limited in what it can do, while the other side is less resolved, but is better able to inflict considerable harm.

One of the potentially revolutionary features of automated warfare is the degree to which technology may free one or both sides from the need to mobilize political support before deploying military capabilities. As recent events should make clear, technological powers are increasingly able to initiate, or to broaden the scope or intensity of, conflicts often with relatively limited internal debate. Uses of force are thus likely to increase as automated systems reduce the risk of friendly casualties. At the same time that automating combat reduces the costs faced by the technological power, however, it also reduces the ability of the country substituting robots for people to demonstrate resolve. Pilotless vehicles tell us very little about an actor's willingness to face high costs or risks. Deploying automation rather than flesh-and-blood soldiers may even imply the opposite, since the side fighting remotely may or may not care enough to do anything but risk machines. As outlined above, capabilities strongly favoring one side tend to coincide with resolve favoring the less capable actor. The weak must compensate for a lack of capabilities with a greater willingness to risk or sacrifice wealth, territory, or personnel. Indeed, opponents tend to concede disputes when one side is clearly favored by both capabilities and resolve.

Deployment of increasingly sophisticated automated systems appears destined to dramatically weaken the ability of non-technological actors to prevail in direct combat with technological powers. This would seem at first to be a linear extension of previous effects of technology on the battlefield (fire, maneuver, command and control, ISR, etc.). However, it is not the increased effectiveness of these systems over human counterparts that is

---

[26] Mao 1961, Arreguin-Toft 2005.

262 ELEMENTS OF DETERRENCE

their most salient feature. The most distinctive political quality of UAVs is their ability to *limit exposure of friendly personnel*. Human combatants from the technological power already tend to be rare and so are harder to locate and interdict. The scarcity of human adversaries reflects supply and demand; technological actors suffer more from human losses and thus try to limit them, even as relatively low valuations for the stakes in a contest makes them more sensitive in general to war costs. As automation makes it possible to relocate human cognition away from the battlefield, valuable human targets will become scarcer still, breaking the bond between harming and the risk of being harmed.

A technological power that utilizes remote systems is communicating at least two messages about its preferences. First, it is emphasizing its sensitivity to casualties in its willingness to substitute machines for people on the battlefield. Second, one cannot rule out the possibility that the technological state's resolve is very thin, since it may have chosen to fight at least in part because automation lowered the expected costs of fighting. This also means, however, that the technological power could well be persuaded to quit the conflict after experiencing relatively modest harm. "Kill" the machines and the machines will be replaced. Kill citizens or the citizens of allies of the technological power, and the opponent might relent, much as the Somali warlord Muhamed Farrah Aidid convinced President Clinton to withdraw from Mogadishu by inflicting eighteen American casualties. With few human combatants, wars against technological powers are paradoxically won by inflicting human carnage.

If technology finally removes those responsible for imposing harm from direct combat, then opponents must look elsewhere to reimpose the relationship between harm inflicted and incurred. Less technological actors must therefore succumb, or seek out new ways to prevail, often by choosing some other setting in which to take their fight to the enemy. One-sided robot wars are therefore destined to shift targeting away from the battlefield and toward the leadership, logistics, allies, and ultimately the populations of the technological power. Put simply, asymmetric drone war should lead to more attacks against non-combatants through bombing, terrorism and related techniques.

Since the role of combatants and non-combatants is defined in ethical terms, use of force against civilians is viewed by many as immoral. Still, with no human enemy to confront in battle, the less technological actor must choose between attacking non-combatants or defeat.[27] Conversely, to the extent that actors fail to overcome inhibitions against targeting civilians, they will be forced to concede to technological powers. Since disputes occur in places and over issues where contention exists (the parties must generally disagree about who will win and by how much in order for a dispute to occur), consensus about the outcome of a contest should lead adversaries to forge bargains, not to fight. In other words, rather than primarily affecting the frequency of conflict, automation should relocate contests; peace will break out in some places, while force will be used in areas previously considered marginal.

In the extreme, with no human adversaries available in the battle space, the less technological opponent will have no reason to expose him- or herself to harm. Almost as soon as automated combat becomes a reality, the enemy will find other ways to fight, leaving the battlefield altogether in favor of unconventional methods of conflict. Just as insurgent forces have learned to avoid the fires of combined arms warfare, hiding in the terrain or among civilian populations or alternately closing with the enemy to avoid the worst effects of air power and artillery, so too the strategy of the weak in the age of automated warfare will involve immersing combatants in urban populations, to blunt enemy advantages and to increase the ability of insurgents to inflict harm.

To sum up: the ability to defeat an opponent in open combat with very little cost or risk to a nation will mean that less resolved adversaries will be defeated, concede, or reconcile themselves with available compromises. Victory against automated systems will be rare precisely because their low cost in human terms makes defeating them fatuous. The nature and value of machines designed for combat conditions suggests that, for many issues, material destruction will not suffice to dissuade or deter. Submission, avoidance, or terrorism will then be appealing asymmetric responses to military automation.

---

[27] Note that what appears on its face to be a neutral ethical position, prohibitions against the targeting of civilians, has the effect of favoring the capable and more technologically advanced over the more backward or weaker. Unless the allocation of technology reflects some moral "oughtness," we have a classic tension between "might" and "right." Indeed, what may appear to be natural or innate ethical values may well be the product of technological evolution and strategic action. Moral and immoral killing are strategic variables that can determine winners and losers.

Evidence from the US War on Terrorism

Our theory generates two testable hypotheses: drone strikes that kill militants lead to (1) more urban terrorism, and (2) fewer attacks on military targets. Drones and related technologies are attractive to Western leaders because they remove (expensive and politically sensitive) troops from the line of fire and do not require large (expensive and controversial) deployments in unstable regions abroad. These characteristics led to rapid expansion of the "drone war" in Pakistan and in other conflict zones. At the same time, extensive targeting of militants with UAVs encourages militant groups to adapt their own battlefield strategies. Militant groups are strategic actors that are bound to adapt their own behavior to new threats. We find empirical support for both hypotheses.

Militant organizations, like all organizations, need resources to survive and to achieve their objectives. The specific resource needs of militant groups vary depending on context and their strategy; a rebel group seeking to overthrow a government with a conventional military strategy needs heavy weapons and a robust logistical supply chain, while a group pursing a guerrilla strategy would find these military resources unsuitable, for example. All militant organizations, though, need to recruit and retain fighters. UAVs, supported by robust ISR, are particularly effective at targeting and killing rank-and-file militants. Drone strikes thus pose a direct threat to a militant organization's core need for human capital.

UAVs also disrupt the ability of militant organizations to maintain command and control of their fighters and supporters, whose motives often differ from those of an organization's leaders and commanders. These differences lead militant organizations to establish methods of communication and record-keeping that ensure that subordinates are acting in ways consistent with leaders' larger political and strategic objectives.[28] Drone strikes disrupt these methods of command and control. Their ability to surveil suspect locations for long periods requires targeted militant organizations to regularly relocate their fighters and to search for new hide-outs. Intercepts of electronic communications allow drone operators and the intelligence organizations that support them to track and locate likely militants. This, in turn, makes it more difficult to conceal the activities of militant organizations that

---

[28] Shapiro 2013.

are concerned with managing human capital, including recruiting, training, supplying, and deploying militant forces.[29]

Beyond the immediate tactical objective of killing active militants, drone strikes also seek to deter potential fighters and supporters from enlisting with, or aiding, a militant organization. By eliminating their current manpower and disrupting their methods of communication and concealment, drone strikes increase the need for militant organizations to recruit fighters and to maintain a network of non-combatant supporters who can provide it with donations, resources such as safe houses or vehicles, and intelligence about government and military operations. Potential fighters and supporters are less likely to join a militant organization if they fear that they will be identified and targeted by drone strikes themselves. Furthermore, they may conclude that drone strikes that kill militant fighters will weaken the organization, making it less likely to survive or achieve its political, ideological, or social objectives. Instead, potential supporters may shift their allegiance to other militant organizations, decide not to involve themselves in the conflict, or even provide intelligence about the identity and location of militant operatives to the authorities.

To remain viable, militant organizations targeted by drone strikes need to convince their current and potential supporters that they remain capable and effective after drone strikes deplete their ranks. Over the longer run, militant organizations can signal their resilience in the face of UAV attacks in a variety of ways, such as issuing propaganda, maintaining an armed presence in locations they control, and providing security and other services to citizens in these locations. But these actions will be difficult to sustain if drone strikes lead current and potential supporters to begin to abandon the organization. Militants thus have incentives to issue prompt signals of their viability in the wake of drone strikes. As specialists in the use of force, they are well positioned to respond to drone strikes by launching violent attacks soon after drone strikes occur. Conducting violence in response to drone strikes demonstrates to current and potential supporters that the organization retains the capacity to use force. It also implies that this capacity can be directed at their members or network of supporters who abandon the militants or betray them to the government.[30]

---

[29] Abrahms and Potter 2015.

[30] See Topalli, Wright, and Fornango 2002 for a discussion of this behavior in the context of criminal organizations. Lyall 2017 makes an argument similar to the one we advance here, although

266 ELEMENTS OF DETERRENCE

The loss of regular militant fighters to drone strikes thus threatens a targeted organization's ability to retain and attract soldiers and supporters. It further creates an incentive for the militant organization to respond with violent attacks of its own to demonstrate their continued resilience. Retaliatory attacks are best undertaken shortly after drone strikes occur; a prompt response will most effectively counter any perception that drone strikes have undermined the group's viability.

Hypotheses on Militant Violence

We next turn to the types of violence that militants will employ in response to drone strikes: either conventional and irregular attacks on government and military targets, or terrorism directed at civilian targets. Drone strikes make attacks on military targets less attractive. They degrade the militants' military capacity, making it more difficult for them to strike at well-defended targets. This makes terrorist attacks a more attractive option for militant groups, as they typically require fewer human and physical resources and can be planned and undertaken on shorter notice.

We expect, then, that drone strikes will lead militant organizations to increase their use of terrorism. We further argue that such attacks should tend to target locations beyond the normal base of militant operations in remote, rural regions of the country. Attacks in more distant urban areas transport violence away from militant bases. It is more difficult for drones to strike at militants in urban areas. Denser populations make it harder to track militants and increase the likelihood of civilian casualties, countering key advantages of UAVs as observation and fire platforms. Relocating at least part of militant operations to urban centers shields militant soldiers from being targeted by drones. This offsets the threat of drone strikes to current and potential fighters and supporters.

This shift in the location of militant violence also publicizes militant grievances, as domestic and international media will devote more coverage to attacks that kill civilians in locations where they have reporting

---

his work does not theorize about the form of violence that militants will use in response to government attacks, a point we take up below.

infrastructure in place.[31] Terrorist attacks pressure the government to stop or at least modify its support for drone operations. Urbanized Pakistani civilians may begin to perceive that they are bearing the burden for a contest between militants and the American superpower, a dispute in which they have little to gain and much to lose. This process reorients the focus of conflict away from regions where drones dominate to areas where drone warfare is less effective.

The impact of drone strikes in terms of militant casualties will then produce an increase in operations against civilians and others in areas where terrorist attacks were previously less common. The use of drone strikes destabilizes conflict geographically and shifts targeting of retaliation by militant groups towards civilians, since direct retaliation against UAVs is not practical. Our main hypothesis thus predicts that drone strikes should be associated with a rise in urban terrorism.

The increased tempo of militant operations in distant urban environments poses opportunity costs for militant groups. At the same time that their ranks are depleted by drone strikes, the organization must divert militants and resources away from other tasks to planning and carrying out terrorist attacks in cities. This reduces their capacity to engage in other types of violence, such as conventional or irregular attacks on military and police targets. Furthermore, one motive for shifting operations to urban areas is to shield current rank-and-file militants from drone strikes. Continuing to attack military targets in areas of the country where drone strikes occur compounds exposure of militant fighters to danger, from both the air and on the ground. These factors suggest that militant organizations facing UAV strikes will curtail attacks on government or military targets.[32]

A secondary hypothesis, therefore, is that militant "kills" from drone strikes should tend to influence the timing, type, and location of subsequent militant violence. Drone strikes could have short-term effects (days and weeks), as well as operating over the longer run. We focus on the short-run effects here. This is not to suggest that longer-term effects are less interesting

---

[31] While urban violence is more likely to be reported, the change in terrorism we identify occurs across time, within the same urban setting. Our findings are not (just) a result of geographic bias in reporting.

[32] Johnston and Sarbahi 2016 argue that drone technology is particularly well suited to disrupting militant organizations. We focus on how this disruption influences the willingness and ability of militant organizations to undertake terrorist attacks far from their base of operations. While Johnston and Sarbahi analyze the effects of drone strikes in rural areas controlled by militants, we show that militants shift their violence to other regions of the country.

268 ELEMENTS OF DETERRENCE

or powerful. Instead, our effort is motivated by the fact that the drone campaign in Pakistan has only been conducted with high intensity for a few years. Our hypotheses suggest that militant deaths should lead to an increase in attacks on civilian targets in more distant, populous areas. Militants need to counter the perception that drone strikes may have undermined the group's ability or willingness to fight. Engaging in violent attacks shortly after drone strikes demonstrates that this is not the case, communicating to current supporters and fighters that the organization can respond to threats to its survival quickly and decisively. At the same time, the need to sustain the organization discourages militants from attacking well-protected targets such as military and government facilities at a time of relative weakness, particularly when such operations are likely to be compromised by the very same drones attriting militant members.

- *Hypothesis 1.* Militant deaths caused by drone strikes, even more than the deaths of civilians or militant leaders, should lead to a short-term increase in terrorist attacks in major population centers.
- *Hypothesis 2.* Drone strikes should also be associated with a shift in militant tactics, emphasizing attacks on civilians in populous areas and deemphasizing attacks on military and government targets.

Summary of Findings

This section summarizes the results of several empirical tests of the relationships between civilian, militant, and militant leader deaths caused by drone strikes and militant violence in Pakistan.[33] Our main dependent variable is the count of urban terrorist attacks per week in Pakistan. To determine if drone strikes lead to a displacement of violence from combat against government forces to urban terrorism, we also use as a second dependent variable measuring weekly attacks directed at state institutions and conventional and irregular attacks on military, paramilitary, police, and intelligence targets. Our main independent variables describe US drone strikes in Pakistan, relying on Bureau of Investigative Journalism (BIJ) data

---

[33] Our analysis begins on January 1, 2006, about two years before the time period when the pace of US drone strikes accelerated, and ends on November 8, 2011, the last date for which the Political Violence in Pakistan Dataset records violence in Pakistan; Bueno de Mesquita et al. 2015. For more extensive analysis and discussion of data see Gartzke and Walsh 2022.

based on media reports as well as interviews with witnesses and victims to identify the occurrence, timing, location, and victims of each drone strike.[34] We also control for other developments (other counterterrorism operations, elections, etc.) that could influence the willingness or ability of militant groups to launch attacks in Pakistan.

Figures 10.1, 10.2, and 10.3 plot relationships between the number of urban terrorist attacks in Pakistan's twenty most populous districts plus the capital Islamabad (plotted in gray) and, respectively, the weekly counts of civilians, leaders, and militants killed in drone strikes (plotted in black). There is a plausible relationship between civilian killed and urban terrorism (Figure 10.1), offering apparent support for the conviction that civilian deaths due to drone strikes lead to increased terrorism. Leaders killed (Figure 10.2), in contrast, does not track closely with urban terrorism. For example, a spike in militant leaders killed in drone strikes in 2009–10 is not associated with an increase in urban terrorism. The pattern of militants killed (Figure 10.3), however, appears to closely coincide with that of urban terrorism.

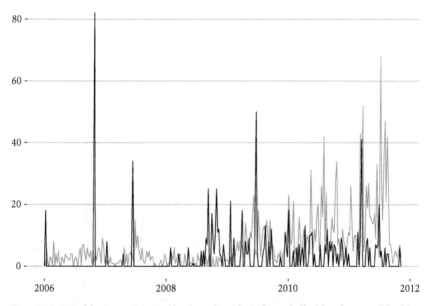

Fig. 10.1 Weekly terrorist attacks (gray) and civilians killed by drones (black)

---

[34] Bureau of Investigative Journalism 2017.

270   ELEMENTS OF DETERRENCE

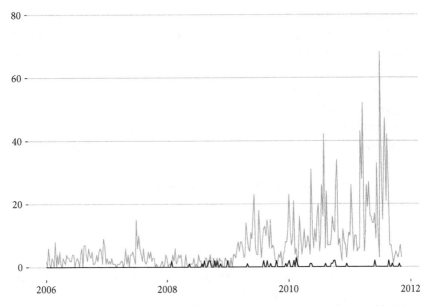

Fig. 10.2 Weekly terrorist attacks (gray) and leaders killed by drones (black)

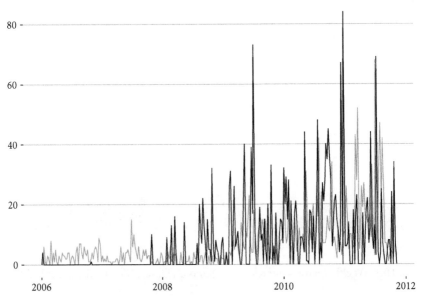

Fig. 10.3 Weekly terrorist attacks (gray) and militants killed by drones (black)

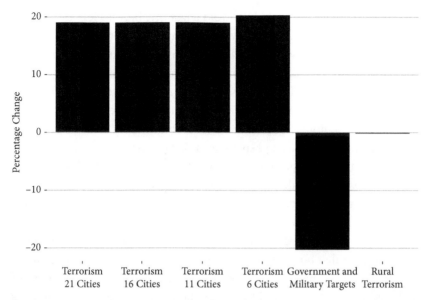

Fig. 10.4 Percentage change in militant attacks for a one standard deviation increase in militants killed in the previous week

For a more precise assessment, however, we turn to multivariate regression analysis. Figure 10.4 plots the percentage change in militant attacks against different target sets for a one standard deviation increase in the number of militants killed in drone strikes in the previous week.[35] We find a statistically significant relationship to a nearly 20 percent *increase* in urban terrorist attacks on civilian targets and 20 percent *decrease* in attacks on government and military targets. We find no effect on rural terrorism.

We also find that civilian deaths from drone strikes are *not* associated with urban terrorism or attacks on military and government targets. The apparent correlation in Figure 10.1 turns out not to be statistically significant (unlike the relationship in Figure 10.3, which is significant). This finding contradicts widespread claims that the deaths of civilians in drone strikes in Pakistan have provided militant groups with the means or motive to engage in greater violence. Recall that much of the research on repression finds that indiscriminate use of violence that harms civilians often backfires, and strengthens militant groups. The findings reported here suggest that drone

---

[35] To assess how variation in the inclusion of fewer or more populous districts influences the analysis, we report results using the number of terrorist attacks per week in the 5, 10, 15, and 20 most populous districts plus the capital Islamabad.

272 ELEMENTS OF DETERRENCE

strikes may be selective enough to avoid triggering blowback in the form of increased militant violence. However, our focus is only on the short term. It remains possible that civilian or militant leader deaths due to drones increase popular support for militant organizations over the longer term.

We also find that militant leader kills are *not* associated with urban terrorism. This is some evidence that a more limited drone campaign targeting militant leaders alone might have avoided contributing to the increase in civilian attacks that Pakistan experienced during our study period. Prior to mid-2008, this was the primary objective of drone strikes in the country. The United States launched drone strikes when it was able to identify the location of a named individual leader of a militant group. These "personality strikes" were few in number; two were launched in 2006, and four in 2007. These rules of engagement were altered in early 2008 to allow attacks against groups of armed men that bore the "signatures" of militants as long as no civilians were nearby. This change meant that strikes increasingly targeted groups of rank-and-file militants in addition to militant leaders. Our finding suggests that the introduction of signature strikes may have been counter-productive, triggering an increase in terrorist attacks.

In sum, only the deaths of rank-and-file militants are associated with subsequent increases in urban terrorism in Pakistan. Existing research on this topic has theorized that civilian and leader deaths lead to more terrorism. Our findings cast doubt on these explanations, at least for this important case and in the short run.

These results provide some good news for advocates of drone-based counterterrorism strategy. The evidence we summarize here is consistent with the argument that drone strikes do not generate enough civilian deaths to motivate militants to engage in more terrorism or attacks on government and military targets. The finding that targeting militant leaders is not associated with increased militant violence suggests as well that focusing on leadership decapitation is not producing significant blowback effects, at least not over the short term. It is possible that targeting leaders weakens militant groups in the longer run, a possibility debated in the literature on leadership decapitation,[36] although we are not able to assess this possibility with the data used here. We also find evidence that this choice to launch more urban terrorist attacks led to a decline in attacks on military and government targets, suggesting that militants responded to drone strikes by substituting

---

[36] Jordan 2009; Jordan 2014; P. Johnston 2012; Price 2012.

their efforts away from military targets and toward urban terrorism. This might be a worthwhile outcome for the United States if attacking militants in this manner reduces the ability of militants to undertake irregular attacks in Afghanistan or terrorism overseas.

From the perspective of Pakistani civilians, however, substitution puts them more directly in the cross-hairs of militant violence. The same trends that make one type of aggression unattractive may make other types more attractive. Indeed, these findings create considerable doubt about the effectiveness of the US strategy underlying its drone campaign in Pakistan. Drone strikes appear to contribute to more terrorist attacks on civilians and to generate negative and unforeseen externalities for the US relationship with Pakistan. Although drone strikes themselves may result in fewer civilian deaths compared to other forms of violence that the United States or Pakistan might employ, they lead indirectly to harm against a larger number of civilians, by creating incentives for militants to shift to terrorist attacks in urban centers of Pakistan. This relationship has received little attention in the United States, but attracted a great deal of comment in Pakistan, where the drone campaign was blamed for increasing instability and has fueled militant violence against civilians. This in turn likely made it more difficult to persuade Pakistani authorities to end their support for some militant groups and to pursue more effective counterinsurgency tactics against others. This could help to persuade current and potential supporters of the insurgency to offer assistance to the militant group, and lead the United States to conclude that the campaign of drone strikes, by undermining the Pakistani state's ability to protect its citizens and politicizing the debate over cooperation with the United States, was less effective than hoped.

Beyond the US War on Terror

Beyond the Pakistan theater, policy makers have to consider the nature of an insurgency when deciding whether to employ drone strikes. Drone technology is rapidly diffusing within the United States military and across other military and paramilitary organizations. UAVs are a key priority for research and development by all branches of the US military. Drones have also been used in other areas where terrorists operate against US interests, including Yemen and east Africa. The results presented here suggest the need for caution regarding the rapid expansion of the use of armed

274 ELEMENTS OF DETERRENCE

drones, or at least consideration of their as yet unanticipated liabilities. There are good reasons to believe that drones should work most effectively in Pakistan if they prove effective against militant organizations anywhere. Militant groups in Pakistan are concentrated in a small geographic area. The United States devoted enormous intelligence resources to understanding this area after 2001. It also receives important logistical and, on occasion, intelligence support from its local partner. These characteristics may not hold in other conflict zones, where the United States is unlikely to have as much intelligence and may lack a cooperative local government. If this is the case, then the rapid introduction of drones into other conflicts may again produce similar dynamics to those we report for Pakistan. Militants everywhere will suffer attrition from drone strikes against their leadership and personnel. The vulnerability of militants to drone strikes may also drive them to re-position personnel and operations to urban centers and other "soft" targets. Drone strikes that disrupt militant organizations may also prove destabilizing for civilian and governmental affairs in these regions.

Of course, the use of drones is not limited to the US war on terror, which has perhaps seen their most extensive use to date, nor to asymmetric war in general. In the Second Nagorno-Karabakh War of 2020, Azerbaijan made extensive use of drones and loitering munitions to target Armenian armor and fighting positions. The war ended in victory for Azerbaijan after only a month. If we assume for the sake of argument that drones did tip the scales for Azerbaijan,[37] this would be an example of a weaker party opting to capitulate before the demonstrated strength of the stronger party with drones. Armenia did not value the stakes enough to convert this into a wider or longer war, so the contest was decided by revelation of the balance of power, which drones apparently improved in favor of Azerbaijan.

If the prospective loser does not care too much about the stakes of a contest, then it might agree to make modest concessions without further coercion by its technologically superior adversary. Replacing humans with machines is intended in part to make war less costly. The value of military machines may also be more predictable. To the degree that losses can be anticipated, they should prompt different bargains rather than leading to war, as both parties are better off with these compromises. The very fact

---

[37] This point is contested, cf. Calcara et al. 2022. In this case the authors find, "when employed with other systems, such as manned aircraft, land-based artillery, electronic warfare systems, and ground based radars—as Azerbaijan did—[drones] proved to be a significant force multiplier. But without such infrastructural and operational support, drones remained vulnerable to air defense systems."

that a contest occurs implies disagreement over the value of some aspect of the dispute. If adversaries are mutually able to price each other's war materiel, then ambiguity over the value of the stakes in a contest, or the likelihood or value of human casualties, must motivate the contest. To the degree that fighting with robots reveals only limited information about these values, other modes of warfare may ensue. If the putative loser of techno-war refuses to accept defeat, then there is relatively little about the techno-contest itself that can force a resolution of the dispute. Defiance is a quality that is most meaningfully exhibited by the weak. As long as an enemy is willing to live with the consequences of persisting in a lop-sided contest, then there is nothing about what has happened on the battlefield that fundamentally alters political realities. Months of one-sided bombing in the First Gulf War by coalition air forces left Saddam Hussein with numerous wrecked palaces, but it did not compel him to withdraw from Kuwait. As long as coercion was the dominant strategy practiced by the US-led coalition, it was Saddam alone who determined the status of Iraq's nineteenth province.

The Russian invasion of Ukraine in 2022 (ongoing as of this writing), which has resulted in the most serious combat in Europe since World War II, illustrates a different possibility. Extensive use of drones by both sides has not by itself decided the contest, and to some extent is implicated in its protraction. The Ukrainian army has used drones and loitering munitions effectively to identify and target Russian armor and other battlefield targets.[38] Of course, the Ukrainian army has benefited from a wide range of other material and intelligence support from its Western patrons as well, to say nothing of lessons in effective combined arms warfare. Both sides appear to be using drones much as mechanized armies in the past have used snipers and forward observers to target artillery and air strikes. This includes opposing drone teams trying to target each other, in the case of tactical drones with a standoff range of only a few miles. Automation at this range still requires human intelligence and judgment on the battlefield, which exposes tactical drone operators to lethal harm. Indeed, this war has been anything but costless for both sides. In many ways the war in Ukraine appears more similar to earlier episodes of land warfare than any imagined future of costless robotic war. Assuming again for the sake of argument that

---

[38] Andrew E. Kramer, and Lynsey Addario. "Budget Drones Prove Their Value in a Billion-Dollar War." The New York Times, September 22, 2023. https://www.nytimes.com/2023/09/22/world/europe/ukraine-budget-drones-russia.html.

276 ELEMENTS OF DETERRENCE

Ukraine has gained a relative military advantage through its use of drones, this means that the local exchange ratio of military casualties may favor the more automated side.[39] The Russian response to the operational gains of the Ukrainian army, and the operational frustration of the Russian army, has been to unleash waves of missile and (Iranian-made) drone attacks against Ukraine's population, in addition to sporadic blockades of grain supplies. Not to put too fine a point on it, the military advantages of Ukrainian drones on the battlefield have encouraged Russia to target drones at Ukrainian civilians. This correlation is consistent with the argument in this chapter but more empirical work is needed to support stronger claims of causality in this case.

Military automation changes the distribution of war costs, making it easier to pursue force at a much lower risk in the form of battlefield casualties. However, automation does not imply improvements in the ability to resolve more intense disagreements, precisely because bigger issues require a willingness to impose higher costs on an enemy in order to prevail. Because the "losing" side in a robot contest will only concede when the issues in dispute are not particularly critical,[40] even nations wielding highly effective remotely piloted systems will have to consider targeting humans, precisely because humans are valuable, especially for societies pursuing military automation. Again, with no humans on the battlefield, looking elsewhere for targets becomes a practical necessity. War must involve the prospect or practice of human casualties to be highly costly and coercive, especially in the face of military automation, where military labor is scarce and protected.

Sadly, this is neither new nor speculative. The principle war-fighting strategy of the Allied powers in World War II was effectively to kill civilians in extremely large numbers. Both Britain and the United States entered World War II as technological powers, intent on bringing war to the enemy—and avoiding the heavy casualties of trench warfare—by exploiting a comparative advantage in capital-intensive, multi-engine bombers. First the British RAF and then the US Army Air Force learned that precision bombing was impractical under wartime conditions. Aircrews were hardly ever able to

---

[39] In addition to automation, Ukrainian operational advantages might be credited to better intelligence, better doctrine, better training, better morale, better strategy, or whatever. Whatever their source, these advantages are extremely circumstantial, as slow, grinding attrition has been the more common pattern in this war.

[40] Technically, the losing side should concede when it understands that an adversary is willing to impose sufficient costs to force the loser to concede eventually, whether or not the additional level/intensity of fighting actually occurs.

accurately bomb military targets. Much like the massed fires of World War I (and Korea), the Allies conducted massed bombing raids in which it was hoped that at least a few of the hundreds or thousands of bombs dropped would hit military installations. However, massed bombing in built-up areas was in practice targeting civilians. This led to a rapid evolution of applied ethics, as the Allies decided that bombing civilians was justified by Axis atrocities, enemy recalcitrance, and the need for victory. The irony of course is that a technological solution intended to limit casualties ensured that many more civilians were killed or injured. It was precisely the inability to coerce an opponent from a distance by destroying equipment that led principled governments to intentionally adopt less and less discriminate approaches to targeting.[41]

The purposive mass killing of enemy civilians in World War II is a highly distasteful aspect of the Allied war effort. It is important to emphasize, however, that it was conducted by leaders and militaries that had consciously prepared for a very different kind of war, one in which technology would allow the Allies to minimize all types of casualties. Leaders fielding automated armies in the future will face similar ethical and practical challenges. Those that imagine using precision to avoid killing civilians may well find that the ability to hit what one is aiming at does not necessarily make war any less bloody in the end. Attempts at "dialing in" harm have in the past backfired. Examples such as McNamara's incremental bombing strategy in Vietnam failed to compel and/or enabled the adversary to adjust to the threat. Precision makes war less costly to all but the intended target, but it does not mean that war can be costless. For the reasons outlined above, killing will remain an important component of war, especially when an enemy stubbornly resists defeat.

Ethical precepts require that civilians should not intentionally be targeted in war. Combatants and war planners are supposed to take the vulnerability of non-combatants into consideration in deciding how and whether to exercise force. These precepts have even led on occasion to leaders or combatants that hold their own populations hostage in an attempt to deter enemy aggression.

As the ability to sow destruction extended beyond visual range, dramatic increases in civilian casualties were not only possible, but threatened the venerable principle of protecting civilians from harm. The ability to destroy

---

[41] Sherry 1987; Schaffer 1988; Crane 1993.

278   ELEMENTS OF DETERRENCE

vastly outstripped the ability to only destroy intended targets. Efforts to kill combatants endangered civilian populations. Non-combatants became "collateral damage." Conveniently, human rights standards evolved that require combatants not to target civilians, but which do not preclude killing them as part of the process of attempting to kill enemy combatants.[42]

The Grim Future of Automated Airpower

The automation of war is just a small part of a much broader process involving the replacement of human labor in productive processes. Conflict is of course different from production, as politics differs from economics. However, all production involves inputs of factors that are needed in different combinations and qualities at different points in history. Changing the mix of factor inputs to war means changing the nature of warfare and potentially altering who wins and how.

The automation of war makes it possible in principle to avoid killing altogether. Shooting down remotely piloted vehicles or machine gunning a combat robot murders circuits rather than flesh and bone. To the extent that machines are substitutes for biological combatants and to the degree that fighting occurs in unpopulated places, future war could dramatically reduce human loss of life. The question remains, however, whether the mere destruction of technology will prove adequate to accomplish the objectives typically associated with military violence.

It is entirely possible, based on the political logic of war, that automation (combined with precision) will lead to a resurgence in targeting civilians, precisely because few human combatants will remain on the battlefield. Civilians will be targeted because they are available and because enemies typically wish to win. World War I is rightly remembered as a land contest. The great naval fleets that had been the focus of so much pre-war maneuvering and expense spent the war in port, too valuable to be risked in actual combat.[43] More to the point, use of these forces endangered too much *else*. Neither Britain nor Germany were willing to hazard the consequences of a decisive naval engagement. Perhaps automation will create similar forces that are too critical to the survival of the state to risk in open combat. Perhaps

[42] Dill 2014.   [43] Massie 2007; Halpern 2012; Kennedy 2014.

states might protect civilian populations by foregoing robotics and forcing a return to human combatants. Perhaps this grim situation might deter war all together, but that is perhaps too optimistic.

Still, contemplation of this scenario also requires considering other information. The British blockade eventually starved Germany into submission, even as combat in the trenches continued to draw blood on both sides. Had adversaries acknowledged this, they might have saved innumerable lives by settling their differences at sea. Yet, the outcome of a naval contest appeared all too predictable. The greatest human tragedy in the Great War was experienced where the outcome of the contest was most in doubt, on the Western front, leaving the greatest concentration of military capital dormant. Military automation advantages societies by lowering costs and increasing influence, but it does not necessarily address the origins of war, which lie in the imperative of imposing and enduring costs to reveal relative capability or resolve.

Rather than making war costless, automation may encourage wartime commanders to target enemy civilians, much as investments in long-range "precision" bombing led to mass civilian casualties in World War II. Conversely, robot armies also make it easier for leaders to contemplate much more frequent uses of force at lower intensity levels. Modest uses of UAVs, designed to erode power relations rather than suddenly alter them—"gray-zone conflicts"—may become more or less continuous practice among rivals, just as cruise missiles, drones, and cyberwar have stretched the definitional boundaries of war. The risk is that minor skirmishes will escalate, in extent if not in severity. In a process mirroring brinkmanship in the Cold War—but at much lower intensity levels—leaders may play chicken with the prospects of broader conflict, with one side usually, but not always, backing down.

Automation may also change where states and other actors fight. A low risk of casualties is already encouraging the use of UAVs in places that otherwise would have proven prohibitive or insufficiently central to the interests of Western powers. One of the things that appears to have ended European colonialism and limited interest in conquest in the latter half of the twentieth century was the high labor cost involved in military occupation.[44] Suppressing populations is labor intensive. Heavy bombers and submarines are pretty poor at crowd control. It became efficient to "out source" predation, relying on local dictators and demagogues to govern.

[44] Gartzke and Rohner 2011b.

280 ELEMENTS OF DETERRENCE

Military automation may thus revitalize occupation, particularly if there are other strategic or economic benefits to direct physical control of territory, such as plundering resources or denying assets to competitors in a complex, multipolar world. Cheap automated ground systems could patrol and conduct the other routine activities of occupation at a much lower cost than reliable human occupiers. Already, Israel has deployed remotely controlled combat systems for patrolling its borders. Automated combat systems may even allow states to "dial in" occupation from afar.

Yet, Israel's automated defenses around Gaza failed spectacularly to prevent a massive terrorist attack by Hamas on October 7, 2023. This is sadly consistent with our argument. Hamas, unable to face the Israel Defense Forces directly, planned a surprise massacre that killed over 1,200 Israeli civilians. The attack appears to have been cynically designed to provoke an Israeli counterattack that would kill many thousands more Palestinian civilians and thereby draw outside supporters to their cause. Note that Israel's "Iron Wall" was a successful deterrent in the same way that France's Maginot Line was successful: both encouraged the enemy to find a more creative axis of advance. Israeli defenses managed to deter Hamas for a very long period, but they also forced Hamas to adopt an unexpected strategy, a provocative and punitive assault, which in turn forced Israel to conduct a bloody invasion in urban territory, where conditions are slightly more favorable to Hamas. The Hamas plan also exemplifies our earlier argument about secret capabilities that can only be used rather than threatened. The military plan for using commercial drones, bulldozers, and gliders to breach Israeli border defenses had to be kept completely secret, including from elements of the Hamas political leadership and its regional allies. Hamas would only get one chance at this particular vulnerability, so it had to make it count by maximizing Israeli casualties directly, and thereby Palestinian casualties indirectly. Thus, automation is implicated in a double tragedy: Israeli automated defenses encouraged Hamas to search out new vulnerabilities and civilian targets, while Hamas gained an automated advantage that it could only use for slaughter rather than coercion. As of this writing, the combatants have not yet come to an agreement about the balance of power and resolve, a complex calculus of multipolar politics in a volatile region, and the only thing that is certain is that civilians are suffering grievously. Time will tell whether a successful surprise attack will translate into a grand strategic disaster for Hamas, as happened in the cases of Imperial Japan and Al Qaeda.

A final implication is that automation has the potential to change the balance between populations and power. Nations with better factories have long had an advantage in modern warfare. If force can be achieved through machines making machines, then the relationship between labor and victory will be largely severed. While highly speculative, this could create an impetus in tension with the shift in modern times toward popular rule. Democracy is at least partly the product of the growing difficulty of coercing mass populations in contrast to the low cost of governing by consent. Practical liberal government also reflects a certain congruence of interests between masses and elites. The holders of the means of production still need labor to assist them. Paying workers and giving them the vote are two sides of the same coin. Military automation at once lowers the cost of coercion, increases the distance between the interests of elites and ordinary citizens, and reduces the utility of cultivating loyalty among the population. If it is cheaper to compel the masses in a foreign land, then it is also cheaper to use machines to repress at home.

The recent rise, or perhaps recovery, of populism in the West implies that tensions between elites and masses are growing as machines drive a wedge between ever more skilled and unskilled productive labor. What has been missing is a way for elites to impose their will against popular opposition. Military automation may well provide this means. We are dismayed by the plausibility of this projection.

11

Space

Intelligence and Stability

with Bryan Early

The previous chapter explored the potentially destabilizing effects of automated air power. Drones send ambiguous signals about resolve because they separate killing from dying. This makes it difficult for targets to distinguish whether high-resolve attackers are using drones as the most effective way to maximize costs for the enemy, or whether low-resolve attackers are using drones to minimize their own costs in a conflict they would otherwise avoid. This ambiguity gives the enemy an incentive to widen the war or shift targeting patterns in order to test the resolve of the attacker. The tragedy is that reliance on drones to protect military personnel may lead to civilians suffering more violence.

But not all forms of automation are destabilizing. Some robotic systems may even contribute to strategic stability. All space satellites are *unmanned orbital vehicles*, so to speak. And as President Jimmy Carter stated in a speech at the Kennedy Space Center in 1978, "Photoreconnaissance satellites have become an important stabilizing factor in world affairs in the monitoring of arms control agreements. They make an immense contribution to the security of all nations."[1] In this chapter we offer argument and evidence that surveillance satellites can indeed foster peace by disproportionately benefiting defensive policies and discouraging aggression.[2]

What accounts for the difference between drones and satellites? The difference, in a word, is information. As we have argued throughout this book,

---

[1] Office of the Federal Register 1978, p. 1686.

[2] This chapter does not discuss satellite communications, anti-satellite weapons, counterspace defenses, or ballistic missiles transiting space, which can be expected to have different implications for strategic stability. Here we focus on the implications of reconnaissance, which remains one of the most significant functions of the space domain. On strategic implications of outer space generally, see Dolman 2001; Johnson-Freese 2007; Moltz 2014; Bowen 2020.

Elements of Deterrence: Strategy, Technology, and Complexity in Global Politics. Erik Gartzke and Jon R. Lindsay, Oxford University Press. © Oxford University Press 2024. DOI: 10.1093/oso/9780197754443.003.0011

uncertainty is an important cause of war.[3] The previous three chapters on land, sea, and air forces, respectively, focused on the credibility of signaling, which provides information about an actor's willingness to follow through on its commitments. We argued that forward deployed land forces provide more reliable information about resolve than mobile naval or automated air forces. But nations endeavor to not only signal information but also *collect* it. The space domain is especially well suited for collecting imagery and signals intelligence on terrestrial targets. While automated drones are poor sources of information about one's own *resolve*, reconnaissance satellites are excellent sources of information about other states' *capabilities*.

However, we must not jump to the conclusion that intelligence is stabilizing just because it provides more information. Many sources and methods of intelligence must be kept secret to remain useful. If only one side enjoys the benefit of secret information, then intelligence can worsen rather than improve information asymmetries. As we argued above in Chapter 7 on nuclear command and control, the secrecy of offensive cyber operations has the potential to undermine the transparency of nuclear deterrence. Because secret intelligence can be used for targeting as well as warning, moreover, the more informed actor may be tempted to act on its secret advantage.[4] Thus, Japanese advanced reconnaissance of Pearl Harbor, and Al Qaeda reconnaissance of commercial airliners, enabled them to pull off successful surprise attacks against the United States. The terrorist attack by Hamas on Israeli civilians in 2023 can be added to this list. Secret information that provides an offensive advantage can be destabilizing.

Satellites are an important source of intelligence. A state with eyes in the sky is better equipped to anticipate and to react to the actions of a foreign power. Thus, we should expect reconnaissance satellites to affect patterns of interstate conflict. However, knowledge of enemy activity is valuable to both sides in a crisis. Sun Tzu's famous admonition to know both ourselves and our enemy implies that intelligence is an integral component of both offense and defense. Intelligence can be used for targeting as well as warning. Satellite reconnaissance would seem at first glance to offer major distributional benefits to those that possess it, and to impose significant liabilities on those that do not. The desire of nations to acquire reconnaissance satellites, and the reluctance of most countries to share satellite technology with others, speaks

---

[3] Fearon 1995; Gartzke 1999; Ramsay 2017. Uncertainty can even be described as *the* cause of war insofar as commitment problems imply uncertainty about the future, otherwise backward induction would enable a mutually preferable settlement without war.

[4] Matovski 2020.

to zero-sum elements of spying from space. How then can this technology prove pacifying, as Carter argued?

An interesting feature of space reconnaissance is that it is a slightly more public form of espionage compared to other modes of spying. While the technical details of satellite payloads are secret, it is infeasible to hide heavy launches and orbiting satellites, which are easy to observe from Earth. Yet whereas sensitive cyber intrusions must remain secret to be viable, the obviousness of space reconnaissance does not obviate its usefulness, at least not to the same degree. "National technical means" in space remain effective *despite* being apparent to their targets. Space reconnaissance is especially effective for identifying activity that is infeasible to bury, disperse, or camouflage, such as preparations for a large-scale land invasion. This transparency is an important feature of satellite reconnaissance, in contrast to secret cyber exploitation or classic human espionage.

An observable implication is that there should be some reduction in conflict whenever once-secret activities become transparent due to technological change. Surprise attacks that are no longer surprising are less likely to materialize as attacks. There are some important exceptions that prove the rule, such as Russia's recent invasion of Ukraine in 2022 despite advance public warning from the United States. We will return to this notable case in the conclusion to this chapter. First, we explain why special attributes of reconnaissance satellites are likely to produce observable changes in conflict behavior. Then, we summarize statistical tests using data about space reconnaissance and conflict in the post-World War II period.[5] We find that countries that operate reconnaissance satellites are significantly less likely to be involved in substantial militarized disputes, either as initiators or targets. Finally, we discuss some key implications and exceptions.

Spying from Space

Ancient armies relied on human scouts to reconnoiter terrain and to report on the disposition of enemy forces. Julius Caesar, for instance, sent an advance force before invading Britain in 55 BCE. For their part, British tribal leaders also received warnings from merchants about the impending Roman attack.[6] For Sun Tzu, victories are best achieved by using knowledge of an

[5] For a full discussion of data and technical results see Early and Gartzke 2021.
[6] Richmond 1998, pp. 4–5.

adversary to prevail before fighting begins. Given the tendency for states to exercise power as influence in peacetime, military advantages often fail to play out in an intuitive manner in terms of battlefield success. Sun Tzu also highlights the importance of espionage: "Advance knowledge cannot be gained from ghosts and spirits, inferred from phenomena, or projected from the measures of Heaven, but must be gained from men for it is the knowledge of the enemy's true situation."[7]

The strategic value of information has long been recognized in world affairs. Knowledge of enemy capabilities is useful for at least two reasons. First, intelligence is a force multiplier that can shift the effective balance of power. Knowledge of enemy capabilities or dispositions can be used to achieve victory in war or to prevail in peacetime. Second, information about an enemy's capabilities or intentions can prevent war and ensure peace by making leaders more effective at identifying acceptable bargains that substitute for military contests. This duality means that study of the effects of espionage is often convoluted. Intelligence advantage can be used to win a war or to prevent a war from happening, but it cannot simultaneously accomplish or influence both objectives.

Traditional intelligence collection methods are extremely vulnerable to revelation. If I tell you I have a spy in your midst, then you will seek out my spy, doing away with a valuable intelligence asset. For the purposes of signaling, secret intelligence is a "use it and lose it" capability. We discussed this in Chapters 5 and 7 in terms of the "cyber commitment problem." This quality of traditional espionage means that it is more attractive to apply the fruits of espionage to winning intelligence contests, and improving performance in politics or war, than to avoiding war through deliberate signaling. To the degree that spying is a force multiplier, secrecy can cause leaders who are the unwitting victims of spying to overestimate their own nation's performance in military contests, and to underestimate the success of other leaders who have effective spies. The bargaining model of war leads us to expect more disputes when clandestine knowledge of enemy secrets (spying) cannot be revealed, and any source of uncertainty is a potential cause of war.[8]

A core problem historically has been that leaders are often much more concerned about "winning" than "warning." The fact that politics has two related but distinct uses for information implies an inherent tension in how intelligence can best be exploited. On the one hand, the prospects for victory

---

[7] Sawyer 1984, p. 231.   [8] Gartzke 1999.

286 ELEMENTS OF DETERRENCE

are typically improved through surprise. Hiding what one has gleaned from intelligence operations maximizes the military effect of espionage. On the other hand, concealing information about what one knows, much as with concealing capabilities, makes it more difficult for an enemy to accommodate an adversary's demands. Deterrence (and compellence) require the actor seeking to deter to share information about the military balance with the actor that is being deterred. Again, however, utilizing intelligence to seek to deter risks degrading the quality of future intelligence.

Trade-offs between winning versus warning with intelligence need not be uniform across time, or space. While the choice of whether to use information to prevent a war, or to win one, is a question of values, it must also reflect the conditions under which information is obtained. For much of history, humans were the main means of intelligence collection (HUMINT). This form of espionage is inherently delicate, and perilous. Exposure reduced a spy's utility and often cost their lives. This fragility of traditional espionage means targets typically cannot be told that they are compromised. Information gleaned through HUMINT thus tends to be used to win, not warn.

The nature of espionage took a dramatic turn in recent decades with the advent of space surveillance. Information collected by countries with aerial reconnaissance capabilities allows them to monitor areas and behaviors of concern, ensuring that they are much less likely to be surprised by enemy activity. "President Eisenhower, who championed photoreconnaissance," for example, "was briefed on the results of every U-2 and satellite mission. At a time when the surprise attack on Pearl Harbor still resonated, Eisenhower saw the technology as a means of preventing another such traumatic experience in the future."[9] An adversary contemplating harm will have difficulty avoiding detection. Almost as crucially, transparency operates at both ends; an enemy typically knows it is being watched. Strategic surprise—perhaps the most crucial and consequential of all advantages to any attacker—has become more elusive.

Compared to traditional forms of intelligence, satellite reconnaissance is more robust to revelation, difficult to subvert, and is less risky and more persistent. Reconnaissance carried out by aircraft is more dangerous, violates international law, and risks escalating hostilities. When a US U-2 spy plane was downed in the Soviet Union in 1960, it became a major international

[9] Brugioni 1996, p. 82.

incident that derailed détente between the two nations. Indeed, the United States ended overflights of Soviet territory, ensuring that US officials were "blind" concerning important features of the Cold War standoff. In yet another incident, the downing of a US U-2 surveillance aircraft by anti-aircraft fire over Cuba during the Cuban Missile Crisis in 1962 significantly escalated tensions during the crisis. Satellites provide much more consistent, broad, durable and predictable coverage than reconnaissance aircraft, making their effects a subject of government strategy and debate, and allowing researchers to observe their impact, a critical feature promoting transparency.[10]

Strategic Surprise and Military Aggression

Armed with superior information, military leaders can magnify the effectiveness of their forces. Sun Tzu observed the advantages of attacking "where [adversaries] are unprepared" and going "forth where they will not expect it".[11] According to Clausewitz, "One of the strongest weapons of offensive warfare is the surprise attack. The closer we come to it, the more fortunate we shall be."[12] Yet, Clausewitz doubts the feasibility of surprise attacks due to the risk of detection and the fog of war.[13] Even Sun Tzu is not sanguine about the challenges involved, emphasizing that only exceptional leaders will make the best use of spies and deception. Leaders must make substantial efforts to achieve strategic surprise. Even then, bad luck, or a vigilant adversary, can make surprise difficult to achieve.

Intelligence not only plays a central role in planning surprise attacks, it also determines which targets are most likely to be taken by surprise. As Colin Gray observes, "If war can be prepared and launched with scant detectable evidence, then strategic surprise should be achievable. If, in contrast, war can be prepared and launched only in a manner that must yield massive signatures for enemy intelligence-gatherers, then operational or tactical surprise must constitute the outer bounds of prudent ambition."[14] Leaders may consider closely the likelihood of detection in planning an attack. The availability of coherent intelligence to both an attacker *and*

---

[10] Greenwood 1972; Richelson 1990; Dobbs 2008, 17, 43, 241–43, respectively.
[11] Sawyer 1984, p. 168; Gray 1999.   [12] Gatzke 1999.
[13] Handel 2005, pp. 171–75.   [14] Gray 1999, p. 35.

288   ELEMENTS OF DETERRENCE

target help to determine whether surprise is viable, a feature facilitated by surveillance satellites.

Advance warning of a surprise attack is only half the battle, however. Leaders must also marshal an effective response. According to Richard Betts, "The principal cause of surprise is not the failure of intelligence but the unwillingness of political leaders to believe intelligence or to react to it with sufficient dispatch."[15] Betts concludes that surprise attacks seldom occur "out of the blue," but rather follow "prolonged political conflict."[16] Leaders should thus actively monitor potential threats. Yet, leaders could also misinterpret or cast doubt on information alerting them to an attack. To avoid being taken by surprise, leaders must not just possess accurate intelligence, but must also receive information in a clear and persuasive format.

Debate continues about whether surprise attacks occur primarily as the result of failures to warn, or due to failures to heed warnings.[17] While much depends on how leaders utilize intelligence, having access to accurate, timely information is a necessary prerequisite to an effective response.[18] Regardless, new technologies that enable rapid collection and dissemination and feature less ambiguous results should allow leaders to react more effectively to the warnings they receive. At the very least, a potential aggressor must consider the risk that spying from space makes this so.

Empirical Patterns of Conflict

The most salient issue in applying our argument is how advantages are utilized by participants (winning versus warning). As informational devices (insofar as spy satellites "show" rather than "do"), satellites operate primarily by changing what actors know or believe. Since satellite capabilities are observable (states know whether other states have reconnaissance satellites) and in important respects immutable (states cannot avoid being seen from space), the primary effects of satellite surveillance should be in reducing conflict rather than helping determine wartime outcomes. In the terms of Chapter 3, satellites enable a strategy of "watching" to improve "warning" rather than "winning."

---

[15] Betts 1982, p. 4.   [16] Betts 1982, p. 95.
[17] Handel 1977; Betts 1982; Levite 1987; Betts 2002; Bar-Joseph 2005; Jervis 2006.
[18] Betts 1982, p. 268.

States that possess reconnaissance satellites should be better able to detect an adversary preparing an attack. A potential aggressor that is denied the element of surprise should be less likely to win a conflict. The durable nature of intelligence from reconnaissance satellites allows governments to leverage intelligence to ensure advantages in bargaining. A target can inform a potential aggressor that it knows what the potential aggressor is doing without undermining its own ability to continue to monitor an adversary's actions. This in turn can dissuade the potential aggressor from choosing to attack. That potential aggressors are unlikely to gain advantage from a surprise attack against a target that possesses reconnaissance satellite capabilities should be generally recognizable to both parties. This can then discourage militarized aggression.

Our argument also predicts that potential aggressors with surveillance satellites should be less likely to need to act aggressively. A potential aggressor spying from space possesses advantages in the attack that are both valuable and durable. The revelation of military advantage is possible when a target cannot thwart future surveillance, nor necessarily undermine an attack in the short term. Information can be shared freely with the target, confident that intelligence will continue to be obtained. There are situations where intelligence would have to remain secret for an attack to be successful—such as targeting a mobile platform, or where countermeasures can be taken—but the general durability of satellite surveillance ensures that it can more often be used to warn, or compel, rather than harm, compared to more sensitive sources of intelligence.

An additional test for our argument concerns what happens when both states possess reconnaissance satellites. Classical arguments from offense-defense theory make it difficult to discern whether satellites should provide net offensive or defensive advantages.[19] Classical theory predicts that advantages conferred on targets and potential aggressors during military conflicts should tend to cancel one another out. In contrast, our argument predicts that mutual possession of reconnaissance satellites creates an information-rich environment that should mutually reduce the likelihood of conflict initiation.

Targets benefit from possessing reconnaissance satellites by being able to substantially reduce the likelihood that a potential aggressor can launch a successful surprise attack. Potential aggressors with reconnaissance satellites

---

[19] Quester 1977; Jervis 1978; Van Evera 1998; Van Evera 1999.

290 ELEMENTS OF DETERRENCE

can confirm that a target state is not itself considering a surprise attack. This reduces incentives to strike first, a dynamic that is closely associated with instability. Strategic stability—embodied in concepts like mutual assured destruction (MAD)—relies implicitly on the ability of states to observe aggression. Fear of surprise attack was rampant during the Cold War, but satellite surveillance of nuclear launch systems ensured that neither side could strike without fear of retaliation. In other settings, where a debilitating surprise attack could plausibly be achieved, instability has tended to be more prevalent, and conflict more likely.

The ability of both sides to verify conditions in an enemy's territory without the need to physically intervene also enables arms control and other de-escalatory activities, reflecting the role of common knowledge in bargaining. These and other aspects of transparency enhance opportunities to avoid military violence in resolving disputes and lead to two testable hypotheses:

- *Hypothesis 1.* States with reconnaissance satellites are less likely to initiate or be the targets of serious militarized disputes than states without reconnaissance satellites.
- *Hypothesis 2.* Dyads in which both states possess reconnaissance satellites are less likely to experience militarized disputes than other equivalent pairings of states.

Examples of Surveillance as Stabilizing Factor

Tensions between the United States and the Soviet Union intensified in the 1950s, as US concerns about growing Soviet capabilities and Soviet fears of US intentions had yet to be matched by an ability of either state to effectively monitor the other. Efforts by the United States to infiltrate spies were largely unsuccessful and heighted Soviet anxieties. Overflights of the Soviet Union were risky, provided incomplete information, and regularly led to international incidents. It was only with the deployment of surveillance satellites by both nations in the early 1960s that mutual tensions began to decline.

A formative example of the pacifying effect of satellite surveillance emerges from the Cuban Missile Crisis. US suspicions about Soviet activity on Cuba were initially triggered by spies on the ground. However, HUMINT could not provide details of what the Soviets were up to, and could not be disclosed without endangering America's human assets on the island. Nor were the claims of a spy likely to generate much credibility for the United States, or condemnation of the Soviets. Instead, the United States revealed photographic imagery of Soviet IRBM and MRBM missile emplacements in Cuba.[20] Rather than having to bomb these sites, as many US officials advocated, and which almost certainly would have triggered a devastating nuclear conflict with the Soviet Union, the United States was able to compel the Soviet Union to withdraw the missiles peacefully.

Contrast the evolution of US-Soviet détente under the sponsorship of watchful eyes in space with rising tensions between the Soviet Union and China. A series of clashes occurred on the Sino-Soviet border in the latter half of the 1960s, culminating in March 1969 with a large Chinese attack on Soviet-controlled Zhenbao Island. In response, Soviet commanders began preparations for a large retaliatory strike.[21] A Soviet military build-up of "overwhelmingly superior forces" went unobserved by the Chinese.[22] Meanwhile, American intelligence officials drew on satellite reconnaissance to monitor Soviet preparations in the summer of 1969 with growing concern.[23] But they did not share this information with the Chinese. Therefore, "... when the Soviets suddenly went on the offensive in Xinjiang and seemed to be preparing for a large-scale attack on China, Mao was surprised."[24] If the conflict had broken out into a full-scale war, the Chinese would not have been prepared.

Soon after the incident, China initiated a crash program to acquire its own satellite reconnaissance capabilities. Since China's acquisition of reconnaissance satellites in the 1970s, the Sino-Soviet/Russian strategic relationship has stabilized significantly. This is not solely attributable to satellite reconnaissance, of course, but it is a stabilizing factor that reinforces other trends. Having these capabilities earlier would have allowed China to signal its awareness of Soviet preparations and intention to counter a Soviet attack, in a manner comparable to U.S actions four years later during the Yom Kippur War.

---

[20] The photographs were taken by U-2 spy planes. America's first surveillance satellites were also deployed at this time. They provided President Kennedy with critical information on Soviet ICBMs, giving him confidence that the Soviet Union could be coerced with a modest risk of war.

[21] Kuisong 2000, pp. 32–34.   [22] Burr 2001, pp. 82, 86–87.

[23] Burr 2001, pp. 85–90.   [24] Kuisong 2000, p. 35.

292 ELEMENTS OF DETERRENCE

Apparent technical problems in the lead up to the 1973 war prevented the United States from sharing its satellite imagery with Israel.[25] Yet that same year, US satellites identified early signs of Soviet forces being mobilized for operations in the Middle East. Officials of the Nixon Administration heightened the readiness of US naval and nuclear force postures in ways designed to be apparent to Soviet leaders.[26] Given satellite surveillance, both sides were able to gauge the resolve of the other and to contain a crisis said to have brought the world closer to nuclear war than at any time since the Cuban Missile Crisis over a decade earlier.[27]

Like China before it, the military failings of 1973 encouraged Israel to pursue its own space launch capabilities.[28] Israel launched its first independent satellite in 1988 and, according to the criteria we employ, obtained effective reconnaissance satellite capabilities in 1995.[29] Israel's satellites allow it to anticipate and better confront a repeat of the surprise attack like the one that took place in 1973. Even if satellite capabilities cannot protect Israel from non-state actors, the capability has enhanced its ability to monitor state-based threats in the region.

While in no way definitive, these examples provide some confidence that our causal argument is plausible. Knowing what an adversary is doing equips a nation with major strategic advantages. Being able to show others that you know what they are doing promotes stability and peace.

Summary of Statistical Findings

We argue that the information provided by reconnaissance satellites can play a significant role in shaping leaders' decisions about the deliberate use of force. Satellite intelligence will have the greatest impact in shaping important decisions about the potential use of force and in protecting states from strategic threats. Our hypotheses focus on the role that space reconnaissance plays in whether leaders deliberately initiate serious militarized conflicts.

We test our theory quantitatively to determine how the possession of reconnaissance satellites by potential aggressors and targets affects the likelihood of a serious militarized interstate dispute (MID) within a given dyad.

---

[25] Zorn 2001, pp. 33–35.   [26] Israelyan 1997.   [27] Rabinovich 2012.
[28] Simpson, Acton, and Crowe 1989; Harvey, Smid, and Pirard 2010.
[29] The "Ofeq 3" was Israel's first satellite that had photo-reconnaissance capabilities. See Early 2014; Early and Fahrenkopf 2017.

We focus on major lethal MIDs rather than compellent threats because we are interested in the relationships between satellites and serious armed conflict. Satellites very well may enable more successful coercion through the same informational mechanisms, enabling powerful states with space-enabled militaries like the United States to extract more concessions. We also do not argue that satellites prevent lower levels of aggression; indeed they may even encourage more furtive forms of subversion, as discussed in the conclusion. But the marshaling of significant ground units or the movement or use of major naval platforms or air formations necessary to inflict a minimum of a hundred battlefield casualties is much more likely to be noted by the operators of surveillance satellites ex ante than are statements of leaders, attacks by small bands of skirmishers, or the flight of a solitary plane.[30]

Our sample dataset of satellite capabilties covers the period 1950–2010.[31] The US satellite program began in 1955 and Sputnik was launched in 1957. We started the analysis in 1950 to provide a baseline for what international conflict within the international system looked like before the introduction of satellite technology. On the other end of the sample, in the year 2000, 4-meter resolution satellite imagery from the US-owned IKONOS satellite became commercially available for the first time. The advent of commercial space surveillance means that even more modestly funded governments can afford access to information that previously was the purview of a relatively small group of nations, possibly obscuring the nominal association between possession of satellites and peace. While only 11 countries obtained national reconnaissance satellite capabilities from 1950 to 2000, 16 additional countries thus obtained those capabilities from 2001 to 2010.

Out of the 139 instances of salient MIDs from 1950 to 2010 in our sample, 14 occurred when the potential aggressor had reconnaissance satellites,

---

[30] Given that serious MIDs occur infrequently, we rely on rare events logit as our main method of estimation in these analyses. For more detail on data sources, model design, regression results, and robustness checks see Early and Gartzke 2021. In choosing an appropriate dependent variable, we thus seek to exclude accidental, unauthorized, and/or minor MIDs between states, focusing instead on MIDs that are most likely to be the result of a chief executive's deliberate decision making. Similarly, events leading up to more modest militarized events may not be observable from space or will not pass notice by satellite operators. We assessed whether using a lower fatality cut point for our dependent variable affects our findings. When we re-estimated our analysis using a dependent variable that reduced the MIDs fatality threshold to from 100 to 25+ casualties, the statistically significant correlations identified in our analysis were still present but were weakened. It thus appears that the effects of reconnaissance satellites on conflict behavior are credibly limited to reducing the incidence of only serious military aggression, not to reducing minor militarized disputes.

[31] Early and Fahrenkopf 2017.

nine occurred when the target had them, and only one occurred when both states possessed them. The only recorded case of two states possessing reconnaissance satellites getting involved in a salient MID pertained to the Sino-Vietnamese War in 1979, in which the People's Republic of China (aggressor) attacked Vietnam, which had the backing of the Soviet Union (target). Even in that case, the dispute did not involve direct attacks on either reconnaissance satellite possessors' forces or territory.[32] Consistent with our two hypotheses, then, salient militarized disputes almost never occur when both sides possess reconnaissance satellites and rarely when only one dyad member does.

Our statistical findings lend considerable support to our hypotheses. Figure 11.1 depicts the coefficients and confidence intervals of three variables describing possession of reconnaissance satellites. The negative and significant effects of having reconnaissance satellites are negative and

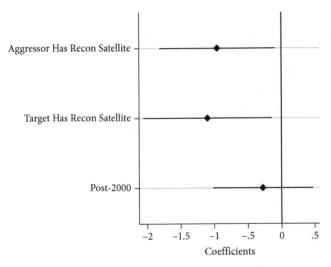

Fig. 11.1 Reconnaissance satellites correlate inversely with conflict

---

[32] The Soviet Union signed a defense accord with Vietnam in 1978. The Soviet Union had deployed a small naval force off the coast of Vietnam prior to China's initiation of hostilities, which it began reinforcing during the conflict (Chen 1987, pp. 26, 92). China's leaders sought to contain the escalation of the conflict by keeping its incursion land-based and not involving naval or air forces (Chen 1987, pp. 93, 94). The limited scale of China's military incursion contributed to the Soviet Union's decision not to directly intervene militarily (Chen 1987, p. 110). Presumably, the Soviet Union's satellite imagery helped it to ensure that China's military incursion had not escalated too far and China's satellite imagery aided its leaders in determining that the Soviet Union was not preparing for a major intervention. So while the MIDs dataset codes this case as a salient conflict, direct, casualty-laden fighting between China and Soviet Union did not occur.

statistically significant.[33] This should not be taken to imply that satellite-enabled militaries do not intervene in other countries now and then. Obviously the United States and the Soviet Union engaged in several large wars during the sample period (e.g., Vietnam and Afghanistan). The finding, rather, is that states with satellites are relatively less likely to be involved in larger MIDs. If the United States and the Soviet Union fought several wars despite having satellites, perhaps they would have fought even more wars in a counterfactual world without them.

While the absolute likelihood of a dyad experiencing a salient MID in a given year is generally low, reconnaissance satellites substantially reduce the probability of such conflicts. Shifting from neither side having reconnaissance satellites to the aggressor having the capability decreases the relative risk of a salient conflict by 0.38. If the target obtains them alternatively, the relative risk declines by 0.33. Having both states possessing reconnaissance satellites reduces the estimated relative risk of a salient MID by 0.12. For comparison, shifting from both the aggressor and potential target being non-democracies to both being democracies only reduces their relative risk of a serious MID by 0.46. The power of the reconnaissance peace is thus on par with the better-known democratic peace![34]

The Reconnaissance Peace

President Carter was right: the proliferation of reconnaissance satellite technology appears to have a pacifying effect on the politics of nations. Reconnaissance satellites provide a unique and durable source of defensive advantage. Not only do they enable monitoring of compliance with arms control agreements, the role that Carter stressed; but satellites also provide a more direct contribution to the politics of war.

Eyes in the sky dramatically reduce the chances that hostile states can leverage the element of surprise in major military actions. They can also

---

[33] The post-2000 variable that controls for the availability of commercial satellite imagery has a negative and statistically significant effect in constrained models but its effects wash out when controls are included. We include a number of control variables to account for dyad members' economic and military power, relationships, and regime type. We also include variables to account for salient political relationships. Rivals are more apt to engage one another in significant conflicts. We control for whether the states in a directed dyad were experiencing a strategic rivalry in a given year. To account for the effects of regime type on satellite reconnaissance and on conflict behavior, we use data from the Polity IV Project coding the nature of states' formal political institutions.

[34] Oneal and Russett 1997; Dafoe, Oneal, and Russett 2013.

296 ELEMENTS OF DETERRENCE

provide potential aggressors with credible, durable intelligence that they can exploit in compellent bargaining situations, enabling aggressors to achieve their objectives without having to engage in the actual use of force. When two states possess reconnaissance satellites, their deployment of military forces are highly transparent to one another. Reducing private information about adversaries' capabilities substantially diminishes the potential advantages and risks of surprise attacks.

Uncertainty is a major, if not *the* major, cause of war in international politics. Satellites have resolved a major source of historical uncertainty in world politics by lifting the cloak of secrecy on invading armies, both by informing the potential target of the mobilization and, since satellites are robust to revelation, informing the potential aggressor of the target's knowledge. Satellite reconnaissance is stabilizing, therefore, because it improves mutual knowledge about the balance of power (and may even provide some clues about intentions).

In the period of 1950 to 2010, accordingly, we find that reconnaissance satellites reduce the likelihood of substantial military conflicts when either or both states in a dyad possess them. Our findings have substantive implications for international affairs. Reconnaissance satellites enhance the role of intelligence in promoting peace. Spying from space makes a state's informational advantages transparent to other nations, affecting not only potential outcomes of conflict, but also the bargaining that takes place before conflicts occur. By denying aggressors the ability to exploit surprise, satellites can reduce both the incentives to launch significant offensive actions and the ability to use threats of such attacks coercively. Greater transparency created when both states possess reconnaissance satellites allows leaders to bargain effectively and avoid the need to resort to war.

But so long as there are residual sources of uncertainty about the balance of interests and capabilities, there will still be risks of war. An important case outside of our sample illustrates this point. In mid-2021, Russia began mobilizing forces on the Ukrainian border. It was impossible to hide this activity from US intelligence and commercial imaging satellites. It was also possible for the United States to publicly share this intelligence without losing access to future collection. The space-based spotlight on the Russian military buildup gave Ukraine strategic warning to prepare its defenses and enabled Western nations to mobilize public opinion and respond more rapidly. The Russians were unable to achieve strategic surprise; nevertheless, Russia invaded in February 2022. How do we explain this?

While satellite reconnaissance revealed Russian preparations in exquisite detail, there were several other sources of uncertainty. First, there was uncertainty about Russian intentions. Observers debated whether the buildup was an invasion or a bluff. Second, Russia woefully misjudged the balance of power, both overestimating Russian capabilities and underestimating Ukrainian capabilities. Third, Russia misjudged Western willingness to provide material and intelligence support to Ukraine. Russia thus believed, incorrectly, that it still had the advantage despite its lack of strategic surprise. A poorly informed Russia gambled that it could take Kyiv easily, while a better-informed Ukraine defeated Moscow's intemperate lunge. Satellite reconnaissance not only denied Russian strategic surprise; it also provided battlefield advantages to Ukraine as the United States began sharing operational intelligence derived from overhead imagery. Russia appears to have misunderstood the ways in which satellites weakened its own position and strengthened Ukraine's. The Russian invasion in 2022 ranks among the greatest strategic blunders of all time. Technical reconnaissance should have improved mutual information and improved the prospects for peace in this case, but there is no patch for human stupidity.

The initial Russian incursion into Ukraine in 2014 offers another variation on the theme of uncertainty. Rather than massing armies, Russia infiltrated light forces in unmarked uniforms—the "little green men"—to take Crimea by fait accompli. Russian "gray-zone conflict" became an attractive work around to the reconnaissance-supported Western deterrence. Russia chose an ambiguous form of conflict because Western deterrence succeeded to some extent in 2014, but Western deterrence failed in 2022 because Ukraine improved in the gray zone. Chapter 14 will return to the complicated dynamics of gray-zone conflict in more detail.

Our approach could perhaps interpreted as a minor intervention to repair offense-defense theory.[35] The theory contains useful insights about state behavior, but relevant mechanisms triggering decisions to go to war remain poorly conceptualized. Notably, our findings are *not* consistent with the predictions of the classical theory. While our findings with respect to targets with satellites could support a traditional interpretation that reconnaissance satellites are defense-dominant as a technology, that view does not predict the negative effect of *aggressors* with satellites nor that salient conflicts

---

[35] Lynn-Jones 1995; Van Evera 1999. Chapter 6 offers other reasons to be generally suspicious of offense-defense theory.

298   ELEMENTS OF DETERRENCE

between satellite possessors *almost never* occur. By focusing instead on a capability that offers informational advantages rather than kinetic ones, we provide a perspective that is distinct from the classical tradition but more consistent with current thinking about the causes of war, which emphasizes the paramount importance of uncertainty.

Looking ahead, scholars should explore whether other technological capabilities can, or are likely to, operate in ways that complement or substitute for reconnaissance satellites. Our period of analysis tails off at roughly the time that high-resolution commercial satellite imagery has become widely available, a phenomenon with interesting implications for international affairs. On the one hand, it could be that many more states will behave as if they possess reconnaissance satellite capabilities, given wider access to intelligence through commercial satellites. Given our findings, this possibility implies an optimistic forecast. One the other hand, an abundance of reconnaissance makes it harder to demonstrate the impact of this capability in the future, as co-variance is required to demonstrate cause and effect.

Another implication of our findings appears more pessimistic and all too plausible. No one likes to be spied on, least of all sovereign powers. The advent of satellite surveillance and a widening awareness of their effects may drive states to seek new forms of secrecy and new forms of espionage that lack the transparency that characterizes satellite reconnaissance. Cyberspace is the obvious alternative, and, as we shall see in Chapter 13, the picture is not as genial. Eyes in the sky may also encourage threat actors to operate in cluttered urban environments that increase the vulnerability and targeting of civilians by terrorists and others, thus reinforcing the counterproductive effects of drones described in the previous chapter.

A final caveat is that this chapter has focused only on reconnaissance satellites. Satellites carry other mission packages for communications (SATCOM) and positioning, navigation, and timing (PNT) that enable maneuver warfare, which Chapter 9 suggests could be destabilizing. Space-faring nations can also employ a range of anti-satellite (ASAT) capabilities ranging from kinetic direct ascent and co-orbital weapons to non-kinetic jamming and dazzling, which probably introduce additional strategic dynamics, especially as rival military forces become more dependent on space for SATCOM, PNT, and tactical intelligence. ASAT capabilities are shrouded in secrecy (and so cannot be revealed because of the military commitment problem), and employment can result in rapid changes in relative operational capability on the battlefield (and so create potential for miscalculation and incentives preemption). Indeed, once the operational applications of space are included, there may be more similarities with cyberspace. Thus, while we find evidence that space-based intelligence is generally stabilizing, we make no equivalent claims for space-based operational support, nor do we speculate on the implications of entangling different space capabilities across, say, conventional and nuclear missions or military and commercial platforms. This area is ripe for future research. The fact that this caveat is necessary, finally, only underscores the overarching theme of this book that "means matter" because military force structure and posture are politically salient.

No advantage is permanent. In the cat-and-mouse game of international security, innovations that clarify will lead to efforts to obscure. The ambiguous implications of intelligence in explaining international conflict warrants increased analytical attention.

PART IV

STRATEGIC IMPLICATIONS OF COMPLEXITY

The availability of multiple means for multiple ends increases the complexity of strategy. On the battlefield, combined-arms warfare and joint military operations combine specialized capabilities to improve military performance. It is natural to assume that multidomain forces will produce integrated deterrence at the grand strategic level as well. Yet, as we have seen in the previous section, strategies that combine different types of military capabilities, for example using using offensive cyber operations in nuclear deterrence or introducing automated drones into conventional war, can create painful political trade-offs.

In this section we explore some additional implications of strategic complexity. Adding to the challenges of military complexity across domains, military rivals may also be trading partners. States that cooperate in some areas may also compete in others. Here we show how low levels of conflict can coexist, and may even be encouraged by, the deterrence of high levels of conflict. Classic liberal perspectives expect interdependence to have a pacifying effect, and there is some empirical evidence for this view. Chapter 12 offers more a more nuanced perspective by linking trade interdependence to the bargaining model of war described in Chapter 4. Chapter 13 returns to where we began with a more empirical view of cyberconflict. We show how the same economic trends that are making militarized conflict less attractive are making informational conflict more attractive. But a more economically globalized world does not mean the end of war. An obvious counterexample is Russia's war in Ukraine, which began in 2014 and escalated dramatically in 2022. Chapter 14 uses this motivating case to explain why "gray-zone conflict" may be symptomatic of successful deterrence, ironically enough. Deterrence in practice is often more about influencing *how* challenges will emerge rather than simply *whether*.

The Conclusion summarizes our findings and reflects on general implications for policy and future research. We focus in particular on US strategy toward China, where various priorities for strategic stability, military power, political influence, or economic prosperity imply different specialized ways and means to achieve these goals. But all good things do not go together, and with more complex means available, political choices about where to prioritize, and where to compromise, become that much more difficult.

12

Trade

Asymmetry and Multipolarity

with Oliver Westerwinter

Geopolitical competition in the twenty-first century is characterized by an extreme degree of economic interdependence. During the Cold War there was plenty of trade *within* politically aligned blocs of countries, but not so much *across* superpower rivals. The military balance between the United States and the Soviet Union, therefore, had an outsized influence on superpower strategy. Today, by contrast, the United States and China are simultaneously military rivals and major trading partners. Even as their economies have begun gradually decoupling (or "de-risking") in recent years, with rising trade barriers and efforts to repatriate supply chains, China and the United States are still more knit together than any geopolitical competitors in history. Contemporary militarized interaction plays out within a dense web of global economic networks in a complex multipolar environment. Intensive economic interaction, conversely, occurs in the shadow of war between nuclear powers.

In this chapter, therefore, we focus on non-military instruments of power. If variation in military means is as consequential for the success or failure of deterrence as we argue it is, then variation beyond the military realm might be consequential as well. Here we focus on variation in patterns of economic trade as an existence proof of the further complexity of deterrence. Complex economic networks may create incentives to limit conflict in some situations, while motivating it in others. Just as considerations of political cost can affect strategic risk, as we have seen throughout this book, the ways in which states pursue the goal of prosperity can be consequential for the goal of stability as well. A full discussion of deterrence across domains in the twenty-first century, therefore, should consider interaction across the military and economic domains.

Elements of Deterrence: Strategy, Technology, and Complexity in Global Politics. Erik Gartzke and Jon R. Lindsay, Oxford University Press. © Oxford University Press 2024. DOI: 10.1093/oso/9780197754443.003.0012

304 ELEMENTS OF DETERRENCE

Indeed, to the extent that the cyber domain (which connects all domains) has been a central preoccupation of "multidomain strategy" and "integrated deterrence," the economic "domain" has already been an implicit part of our discussion. "Cyberspace" is really just shorthand for the digital infrastructure of economic globalization. Most of the key information and communication technologies are owned and operated by commercial organizations, and digital interdependence has enhanced the prosperity of interconnected governments and corporations alike. The condition for the possibility of cyber "conflict," therefore, is extensive public and private cooperation in building, connecting, and maintaining a common information infrastructure. In cyberspace, as a fundamental condition for the possibility of competition, actors must cooperate to constitute the domain in the first place.[1] This makes cyberspace rather different from other military domains; indeed, it is not really a domain of war-fighting at all, but rather of intelligence competition.[2]

Later in Chapter 13, we are going to argue that the same historical economic trends that are making war less attractive are making informational contests more attractive. We will use internet connectivity as a proxy for these general trends to show that states with more connectivity tend to be engaged in fewer militarized disputes but more cyberconflict. But before delving into the data on cyberconflict, we want to first provide some additional nuance and empirical evidence for the general claim that economic interdependence tends to discourage militarized conflict. Just as deterrence is complex, displaying different dynamics in different circumstances, interdependece is complex and ambiguous too. Some aspects of trade could discourage warfare, while other aspects appear more likely to encourage various forms of conflict.

In its simplest form, our argument is that the complexity of trade networks may account for ambiguity in the observed effects of commerce on conflict. Trade ties produce several effects, each of which has different consequences for cooperation and conflict. We characterize these effects as interdependence, asymmetry, and multipolarity, discussing each below. There is an inevitable increase in analytical complexity when we address trade and conflict from an explicitly networked perspective.[3] Bringing economic networks into the analysis of trade and conflict is essential, nevertheless, for unraveling

---

[1] Lindsay 2017.   [2] Lindsay 2021; Chesney and Smeets 2023.
[3] For extensive technical discussion of data and findings see Gartzke and Westerwinter 2016.

TRADE 305

the multiple causal pathways through which commerce operates on war and peace. By doing so, we are better able to explain previous empirical riddles and to provide a larger, more comprehensive theoretical framework for assessing the commercial peace.[4]

The Push and Pull of Commerce

Research on the relationship between trade and conflict is both durable and dialectical. Liberal theory emphasizes the pacific effects of commerce on world politics.[5] A more diverse tradition argues that capitalist interactions exacerbate international tensions.[6] Despite sustained interest and effort, it has proven difficult to resolve this dialectic empirically. While the balance of evidence favors the commercial peace,[7] the results are often weak, attenuated, or measured inconsistently.[8]

Why has evidence for the commercial peace remained relatively weak? We argue that this ambiguity stems from the fact that trade ties generate not one relationship, but several. Distinguishing among disparate consequences of commerce on conflict is critical for improved theory and for proper assessment of these empirical relationships. There are at least two general ways in which trade might influence decisions about conflict.

First, trade may affect states' decisions to fight by shaping the opportunity costs that nations face in going to war.[9] The prospect of trade losses might discourage conflict in cases where the risk posed to commerce from fighting is large relative to the value of the stakes in a dispute. To deter conflict, trade partners must prefer the status quo to making, or resisting, demands for change. But for trade to act as a barrier to conflict, the commercial

---

[4] Our analysis also serves as an illustration of how network theory and measures can be applied to enrich existing theoretical arguments and empirical models in the study of international conflict. In doing so, we add to a growing literature on networks in international relations that has begun to show how the accumulation of ties among nations affect a broad range of international outcomes, inter alia, Dorussen and Ward 2008; Hafner-Burton and Montgomery 2008; Hegre, Oneal, and Russett 2010; Maoz 2011; Chyzh 2016; Lupu and Poast 2016.

[5] Montesquieu 1989 [1748]; Cobden 1903 [1867]; Angell 1909; Rosecrance 1985; Oneal and Russett 1997; Polachek 1997; Pevehouse 2004.

[6] Thucydides 1996; Lenin 1975 [1917]; Carr 1939; Krasner 1976; Waltz 1979; Gasiorowski 1986; Grieco 1988; Waltz 1999.

[7] Gartzke 2007.

[8] Barbieri and Schneider 1999; Mansfield and Pollins 2001; Mansfield and Pollins 2003; G. Schneider 2014; Gartzke and Zhang 2015.

[9] Polachek 1980; Russett and Oneal 2001; Polachek and Jun 2010.

306 ELEMENTS OF DETERRENCE

losses anticipated from fighting must be large relative to the overall cost of fighting. Relatively few bilateral trade relationships are substantial enough to accomplish this, though more will apply to minor (rather than major) disputes. Trading states also tend to be prosperous and are therefore capable of inflicting (and absorbing) high conflict costs. This does not rule out opportunity cost (i.e., deterrence) arguments,[10] but it does imply that the effects of trade will depend on the nature of conflict. Insofar as the cost of fighting varies with the intensity of a dispute, then the deterrent effect of commercial ties should do more to alter the *intensity* of contests than their *propensity*.

Second, trade relationships could also serve as a means to signal resolve to adversaries in disputes over contested issues.[11] While trade can deter, it can also inform. Trade ties provide a different mechanism allowing states to act out their differences through non-militarized conflict. Indeed, trade can substitute for force; trading relationships need only be valuable to both sides in a dyad to be used as politics by yet another means. To the degree that interdependence mimics key attributes of militarized contests, it can supplant more deadly or risky disputes. However, interdependence does not necessarily imply the end of disagreement among states. Tensions may persist, and while they are less likely to produce casualties, trading partners may actually *increase* incidents of low-intensity non-militarized conflict,[12] to include cyberconflict, "gray-zone conflict," and other diplomatic friction.

But not all trade relationships are equal. A country is more trade dependent when its imports and exports make up a larger proportion of its gross domestic product (GDP). Asymmetric trade relationships can undermine the pacific effects of commerce by decoupling the dual functions of conflict, namely imposing costs and signaling resolve.[13] The *less* dependent partner in an asymmetric trade relationship can coerce the *more* dependent partner by imposing costs (e.g., by imposing tariffs, boycotts, or blockades), but the former does not incur a significant cost for doing so, precisely because its economy is not as affected by the restriction of trade. Just as the use of drones conveys little information about resolve (Chapter 10), coercing cheaply is not informative. The dependent target of asymmetric trade coercion, therefore, must find some other way to test the resolve of the less dependent partner, perhaps by starting a militarized dispute. Meanwhile, the more dependent

---

[10] Polachek and Jun 2010.   [11] Morrow 1999; Gartzke 2001b; Gartzke 2007.
[12] Gartzke 2003.   [13] Hirschman 1945; Keohane and Nye 1977.

state in the asymmetric relationship can demonstrate resolve by suffering through the trade restrictions imposed by the less dependent state; however, it derives little benefit from doing so because the less dependent state suffers relatively little cost in the process. The more dependent actor can coerce but not inform, while the less dependent actor can inform but not coerce.

These tendencies reverse themselves to some degree with increasing multilateral trade ties. Multilateral asymmetric trade networks (i.e., situations in which states have asymmetric trade dependencies with more than one state) should be less conflict-prone than isolated asymmetric trade relationships. An increase in multilateral trade ties implies that both states in an asymmetric network are able to substitute away from any given dyadic dependency. For the dependent state, a network of dependent relationships tends to undermine the coercive leverage of the less dependent state and thus limits the need to escalate conflict within the dyad to resist coercion. Similarly, for the less dependent partner in an asymmetric trade dyad, increasing the number of asymmetric ties creates more opportunities for coercion, marginally lowering the utility of coercing any particular partner.

The complex, contrasting tendencies of trade networks continue for symmetric (interdependent) dyads. Increasing the number of a state's symmetric trade ties again leads to the opportunity for substitution, but this time the effect is to *decrease the decrease* in conflict associated with bilateral interdependence. Symmetric trade networks reduce the constraining effect of interdependence on conflict and can also limit the informational value of competition through commercial ties. In short, extra-dyadic trade ties are likely to shape the way that dyadic dependence and interdependence affect interstate conflict, something that scholars have only recently begun to assess systematically.[14]

Figure 12.1 summarizes key relationships leading to six empirical hypotheses, which we will describe below. Solid lines indicate bilateral trade relationships. Dashed lines indicate prospective increases (+) or decreases (−) in militarized conflict. Subfigures (a) and (b) indicate interdependent bilateral trade relationships, and subfigures (c) and (d) are asymmetric trade relationships. Relevant hypotheses are indicated in brackets.

---

[14] Crescenzi 2005; Martin, Mayer, and Thoenig 2008; Dorussen and Ward 2010; Kinne 2012; Kinne 2014b.

(a) Bilateral interdependence tends to *reduce* military conflict [H1] but *increase* non-military conflict [H2]

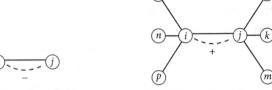

(b) Multilateral ties weaken the effects of interdependence [H6]

(c) Bilater asymmetry tends to *increase* military conflict [H3]

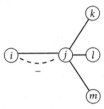

(d) Multilateral ties dampen the effects of asymmetry [H4 & H5]

Fig. 12.1 The effects of asymmetric and multilateral trade on conflict

Interdependence

Conflict consists of harming and being harmed. Actors harm in order to compel or to favorably alter the balance of power. Destruction weakens an opponent's productive capacity, prosperity, or material might, advantaging adversaries. The prospect of future harm can also induce compromise or acquiescence, obviating the need for actual force. Bargains that were previously unacceptable become appealing, even as deals that were once preferred become less attractive to the winning side.[15] By harming and being harmed, states eventually become better informed about the private information that initially led to bargaining failure and war.[16]

One way to avoid war is to find mechanisms that serve as proxies for fighting. Viable alternatives to violence must prove costly for both sides in a dispute. The ability to impose harm makes an action attractive to actors interested in influencing or weakening an adversary. The necessity of absorbing harm makes a given method informative. The difficulty in finding alternatives to military violence as a way of simultaneously imposing and incurring harm has led to its persistence in political affairs. Actors fight

---

[15] Wittman 1979.   [16] Powell 2004a.

TRADE 309

to win, to advantage themselves over others. However, it is the willingness to suffer that convinces adversaries to act with discretion. Interdependence allows actors to impose costs on one another, but to do so, actors must also incur harm, and further risk retaliation. Interdependence allows contests that are costly and risky, and therefore informative.[17]

Interdependence can serve as a vehicle for defusing violence by shifting conflict behavior to lower, non-militarized levels. Competing through economics rather than warfare makes the use of force unnecessary if the economic costs incurred and imposed are sufficiently informative. If interdependence informs, then trading states should tend to substitute non-militarized for militarized conflict, doing more to reduce the intensity of disputes than to lower frequency.[18]

All things being equal, symmetric trade ties should tend to discourage interstate conflict. The top left subfigure indicates a negative sign, meaning that bilateral interdependence is associated with a reduction in militarized conflict. While this prediction is the conventional expectation of the capitalist peace, controversy continues about how trade encourages peace. If trade deters conflict by creating opportunity costs, then it is the prospect of losses that is critical.[19] Big, militarized disputes should be less affected in most cases than contests of more modest scope, since the loss of trade is finite and bigger disputes are more expensive. Smaller, non-militarized conflicts should be most affected, since trade losses most alter the overall cost of small contests and since the risk of escalation should also deter.

But in addition to deterring, trade can also substitute for violence in acting out conflict. Economic conflict can replace militarized disputes if trade facilitates the dual functions of harming and informing. Yet, rather than deterring conflict that is most affected by the costly loss of trade, the informational logic implies that symmetric ties actually *increase* minor, non-militarized conflict. At the same time, because conflict that is informative at lower intensities supplants more intense violence, interdependence should disproportionately reduce militarized conflict.[20]

- *Hypothesis 1*: Interdependent dyads are less likely to experience militarized conflict.
- *Hypothesis 2*: Interdependent dyads are more likely to experience non-militarized conflict.

[17] Morrow 1999.   [18] Gartzke 2003.
[19] Polachek and Jun 2010.   [20] Gartzke 2003.

310 ELEMENTS OF DETERRENCE

Asymmetry

Interdependence can deter as well as inform. However, to do this, the value of trade must be sufficient to change the ordinal preferences of actors over the issues at stake in a dispute. This may often turn out to be even more difficult than the requirement that trade ties be valuable relative to the costs of militarized conflict. Given the zero-sum nature of contests, changes in the balance of power, cost, or risk that discourage one state from acting aggressively encourage increased aggression from the other side. Deterrence involves increasing the costs or risks of an attack and maintaining or reducing incentives to exploit newfound advantages with larger demands. As Theodore Roosevelt put it, deterrence requires that one "speak softly" *and* "carry a big stick." By itself, a big stick will not yield deterrence because the big stick can be used to compel, rather than just to deter. To the extent that the ability to harm, or equivalently the ability to take away benefits, is used to coerce concessions, the effect of trade as a deterrent to conflict is reduced.

Peace requires that both sides in a dispute prefer the status quo or a negotiated bargain to the costly lottery of war.[21] Trade can be a reason to prefer peace where both sides view the economic costs of a contest as more onerous than the likely fruits of victory. This is much less likely where the benefits of trade are asymmetric. If one economy is much more dependent on a given bilateral trade relationship than its partner, then the less dependent state can use the relationship to coerce. However, doing so is not particularly informative because the coercing state is not dependent on its partner. Similarly, the dependent state can demonstrate resolve through resisting coercion. But this state has little incentive to do so, given that it cannot reciprocally coerce its partner. Asymmetric trade relationships thus fail to mimic conflict because they do not link harm imposed with harm incurred. Because one side can coerce, but not inform, there is little reason for the less dependent state to refrain from seeking redistribution or punishment.

- *Hypothesis 3*: Asymmetrically dependent dyads are more likely to exhibit militarized conflict.

---

[21] Fearon 1995.

Multipolarity

Increasing the number of bilateral trade ties complicates an already complex picture in several ways. In particular, multipolarity (i.e., situations in which states have trade ties to more than one state) should tend to attenuate the tendencies just delineated above for interdependence and asymmetry. Consider again an asymmetric bilateral trade relationship. Dependent states in a two-state world have limited options; they can knuckle under to coercion from the less dependent partner, or resist by demonstrating resolve by incurring costs and possibly escalating a dispute.

Now imagine that the dependent trade partner possesses additional bilateral relationships. These additional ties could also be asymmetric. Even while dependent in each case, the dependent state now has options created by its trade network. Increasing the number of partners both decreases the leverage available to any given partner (partners can coerce but each bilateral tie is less important) and diversifies risk (the dependent state can shift some trade to another partner).[22]

A similar logic applies to the less dependent state in an asymmetric trade relationship. As the number of extra-dyadic relationships in which the less dependent state in the dyad is also the less dependent trade partner increases, the less dependent state has more relationships to choose from in deciding which state to coerce. This should lead to a decrease in the marginal utility for coercing any given partner because of the availability of a larger number of potential targets.

The effect of extra-dyadic trade dependencies in lessening dependence, coercion and conflict could easily be missed if one were to focus exclusively on bilateral trade ties. Two pairs of asymmetric trade ties with the same nominal characteristics should behave differently, depending on whether the more dependent state is uniquely dependent on one partner or whether dependence is distributed across multiple bilateral relationships. Asymmetrically dependent dyads where the more dependent state has no or only a few extra-dyadic trade partnerships should experience more conflict, while those where the dependent state has a large number of extra-dyadic trade

---

[22] Researchers have also measured the sensitivity of states to changes in the supply of particular traded goods; Gasiorowski 1986; Polachek, Robst, and Chang 1999; Crescenzi 2003.

312 ELEMENTS OF DETERRENCE

ties should experience less conflict. Likewise, two otherwise identical asymmetric trade relationships should differ in their conflict behavior depending on whether the less dependent state has other relationships in which it is also the less dependent state. Asymmetric dyads, where the less dependent state has no or only a few extra-dyadic trade partnerships, should be more conflict prone, while less dependent states with many extra-dyadic trade ties should experience less conflict.

- *Hypothesis 4*: The tendency for asymmetry to increase militarized conflict should decline in the number of asymmetric partners of the *more* dependent state in a dyad.
- *Hypothesis 5*: The tendency for asymmetry to increase militarized conflict should decline in the number of asymmetric partners of the less dependent state in a dyad.

Economic ties beyond the dyad should also impact symmetric trade ties, weakening cooperation rather than encouraging it. Imagine again a solitary, but symmetrically dependent, dyad. Increasing trade ties should make it possible for a dyadic counterpart to substitute away from a particular relationship in the event of conflict. In opportunity cost/deterrence terms, marginal reductions in a state's reliance on a given trade relationship will tend to make the state less reluctant to press its demands. Additional trade ties also tend to undermine the signaling value of interdependence, since adversaries have more options beyond the dyad. Even nominally symmetric benefits can turn into a vehicle for coercion when one party is better able to take the relationship to the brink.

Therefore, symmetric trade ties should be less pacifying when states have numerous trade partners. States signal resolve to the degree that they endure costs for damaging or suspending trade relationships. The ties themselves may also deter. To the degree that states possess a network of trade relationships, ties become a "substitute for the substitute," reducing in particular the informational value of a particular bilateral trade linkage. The cost of harming a given symmetric bilateral tie is reduced, and the inhibiting or informational effect of a given bilateral relationship declines. While some informational value is retained as long as existing trade linkages remain valuable, the effect of networks in weakening the pacific effects of trade should be greatest in the case of opportunity costs, where peace is a function of deterrence, rather than by revealing information.

- *Hypothesis 6*: The tendency for interdependence to reduce militarized conflict should decline in the number of interdependent trade partnerships used by states in a dyad.

Summary of Empirical Findings

Testing our hypotheses involves examining the effect of interdependence, asymmetry, and multipolarity of trade on both militarized and non-militarized conflict. We use three dependent variables that count all conflicts, militarized conflicts, and non-militarized conflicts in an undirected dyad-year. For our main independent variables, we interact measures of extra-dyadic asymmetric dependence and interdependence with dyadic variables for asymmetric dependence and interdependence, and we add a number of econometric controls that have been used in previous research.[23]

We find some support for hypothesis 1 that bilateral interdependence is associated with decreased militarized conflict.[24] This is broadly consistent with previous literature. Perhaps more interestingly, regarding hypothesis 2 about the positive effect of dyadic interdependence on non-militarized conflict, states are more (not less) likely to experience non-militarized conflict as the threshold of dependence in a dyad increases. Figure 12.2 shows that states that are more interdependent (measured in terms of the least dependent state in a dyad) are estimated to experience more non-militarized conflict events.

Asymmetry militates against the pacific effects of bilateral interdependence. Figure 12.3 shows, holding other variables constant, that as our measure of asymmetric dependencies increases, we observe an increase in the number of predicted militarized conflict events between states. While pairs of states with low levels of asymmetric dependence are predicted to experience close to zero militarized conflicts, those with higher levels of asymmetric dependence are predicted to be engaged in more militarized conflict events. These findings lend credence to hypothesis 3.

---

[23] For technical details on our research design see Gartzke and Westerwinter 2016 and its online appendix. Note that we refrain from using MIDs as in previous chapters because we are also interested in non-military conflicts. Here we use two different conflict events datasets to code the dependent variables, the Conflict and Peace Data Bank (COPDAB) 1948–78 and the World Event Interaction Survey (WEIS) 1966–92, to mitigate statistical anomalies or artifacts. We lead the dependent variables by one year to limit reverse causation.

[24] Results are significant for WEIS data but insignificant for COPDAB data.

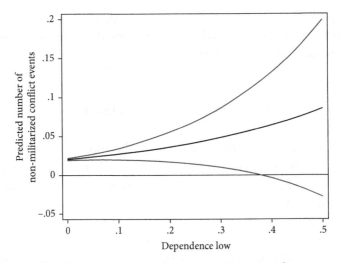

Fig. 12.2 Trade interdependence increases non-miltiary conflict

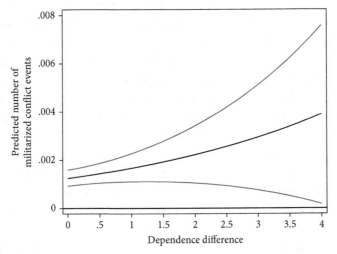

Fig. 12.3 Asymmetric dependency increases militarized conflict

However, the destabilizing effect of dyadic asymmetric trade dependency is mitigated by a network of extradyadic trade dependencies. The effect of dyadic asymmetry even becomes statistically insignificant for dyads where the more dependent state has many extradyadic asymmetric trade ties. Supporting hypothesis 4, Figure 12.4 illustrates how the extradyadic network dependencies of the more dependent state in a dyad decrease the conflict-enhancing effect of asymmetric dyadic trade dependence.

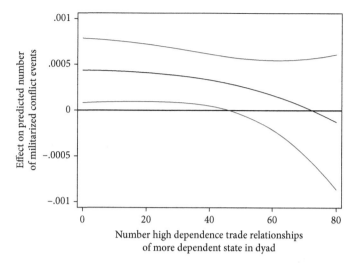

Fig. 12.4 Multilateral trade reduces conflict for more dependent states

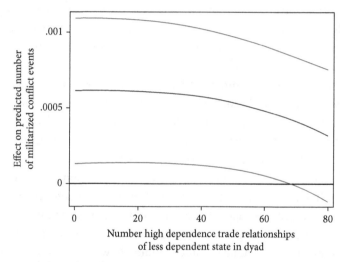

Fig. 12.5 Multilateral trade slightly reduces conflict for less dependent states

Supporting hypothesis 5, Figure 12.5 shows a similar effect of the extradyadic dependence of the less dependent state in the dyad on the conflict-enhancing effect of dyadic asymmetric dependence.

We do not find compelling support for hypothesis 6, which argued that the conflict-diminishing effect of dyadic interdependence on militarized conflict may itself diminish as the number of extra-dyadic interdependencies of the two states in a dyad increases. The dyadic interdependence

316   ELEMENTS OF DETERRENCE

is negatively associated with militarized conflict, and this negative effect increases (i.e., becomes less negative) in the number of extra-dyadic interdependent trade ties in the dyad. However, both the main effect of dyadic interdependence as well as the interaction term are statistically insignificant at conventional levels.

The Mixed Blessings of Interdependence

The classical liberal perspective is that economic interdependence tends to reduce the incidence of armed conflict. The reality is more complicated. Just as deterrence is not just one thing, interdependence is also not one thing. Different kinds of trade relationships can either encourage or discourage different kinds of conflict.

We find that multilateral trade ties tend to reduce the effects of bilateral trade relationships in tempering or inflaming conflict. Symmetric (dyadic) trade dependencies tend to reduce the likelihood of militarized conflict, in accordance with classical liberal expectations of interdependence. However, the same symmetric dependencies tend to increase non-militarized disputes. Asymmetric (dyadic) trade dependencies, meanwhile, will generally increase the likelihood of conflict. But asymmetric multilateral (extra-dyadic) trade relationships of both the more and less dependent state in the dyad mitigate the negative effects of dyadic asymmetric dependence on militarized conflict. In short, our analysis shows that networked trade dependencies lessen the impact of dyadic trade relationships. Combined with a better understanding of the countervailing tendencies of bilateral trade ties, recognition that extra-dyadic trade ties temper bilateral effects helps to reconcile existing controversies concerning trade and conflict.

Much remains to be done in understanding how trade interacts with war and peace. The traditional liberal perspective has always been incomplete, lacking a convincing mechanism for the stipulated reduction in conflict. Here we have tried to link it to the same theory of war that informs our view of deterrence. Commerce and conflict are each complex processes that separately deserve, and receive, considerable attention. Together, they exhibit compound complexity, something that is further magnified when looking at economic ties more holistically, as networks of relationships rather than as isolated dyads. We have provided hopefully convincing evidence that incorporating network effects beyond the dyad may be necessary in unraveling the relationship between commerce and conflict, even within dyads.

The relationship between trade and conflict does not disappear at the boundaries of the dyad. We find that states that share symmetric economic ties experience fewer militarized conflicts, but that interdependence is associated with increases in non-militarized conflict. By contrast, states that are asymmetrically dependent are likely to become entangled in more militarized contests. We find consistent support across datasets that the positive effect of asymmetric dependence on militarized conflict decreases in the number of extra-dyadic asymmetric trade ties of the less dependent state. This finding is in line with other network studies that find a conflict-mitigating relationship between various configurations of extra-dyadic ties in the trade network and the onset of international conflict.[25]

Processes do not occur in isolation in international affairs. They interact in ways that can confound simple, logical theoretical constructs that in their pure form may be largely correct. Trade does inhibit conflict, but inhibitions are also invitations to substitute away from one type of conflict to another, especially when the opportunity to exploit other forms of interaction are increased by economic interdependence. Trading states have less big militarized conflict, but they have more minor non-militarized scuffles. Depending on how researchers aggregate the effects of interdependence, they may find results supporting the trend of trade-diminishing conflict, the counter-trend, or they may conflate the two, finding no overall relationship. Similarly, asymmetry tends to work against the effects of symmetry, diminishing the conflict-diminishing effect of economic ties. Both of these relationships are further affected by trade networks. States with more trade ties are less dependent on any particular relationship, lessening coercion originally facilitated by dyadic asymmetry and thus reducing the conflict-inducing effects of asymmetric dependence.

Knowing a bit more about what these relationships look like and how these ties operate theoretically in influencing war and peace (and why) is perhaps more than a small step along the path to the kind of sophisticated parsimony

---

[25] Dorussen and Ward 2010; Kinne 2012; Kinne 2014a.

that is needed in the study of the interaction between trade and conflict. This interaction has always been relevant, but it is increasingly important in a world in which major military rivals are also trading partners. Any attempt to integrate deterrence strategy cannot be limited to military or intelligence domains, but must integrate economic and political domains as well.

13

Cyber

Complements and Substitutes

with Nadiya Kostyuk

If uncertainty makes deterrence failure more likely, then better information should improve strategic stability. Sure enough, Chapter 11 presented evidence on the stabilizing effect of intelligence. Reconnaissance satellites improve mutual information about the effective balance of power, which in turn improves strategic stability by making surprise attack less feasible. The "reconnaissance peace" further contributes to the "capitalist peace," whereby economic globalization makes militarized conflict less attractive, as discussed in Chapter 12.

Shared information infrastructure is a prominent feature of modern economic interdependence. Trading states rely on digital information systems to coordinate complex global supply chains and synchronize high volumes of financial transactions. The "capitalist peace" might even be described as a "digital peace." But few would describe cyberspace as peaceful. Lucas Kello describes a profound degree of "unpeace" in the digital era.[1] Many observers now consider cyberspace to be the "fifth domain" of warfare, alongside the traditional operational environments of land, sea, air, and space. Many governments have invested in cyber forces, and cyberconflict has become a normal aspect of geopolitical competition, for better or worse. If the information-improving domain of outer space appears to reduce conflict, why does the informational domain of cyberspace seem to increase it? How do we explain the apparent paradox that we now have *more conflict* due to *more information*?[2]

One answer is that "conflict" in cyberspace is more like an intelligence contest than military combat.[3] Insofar as intelligence and war are governed by different strategic logics, it is plausible that there could be more of the

[1] Kello 2017.　　[2] Lord 2007.　　[3] Rovner 2019a; Chesney and Smeets 2023.

Elements of Deterrence: Strategy, Technology, and Complexity in Global Politics. Erik Gartzke and Jon R. Lindsay, Oxford University Press. © Oxford University Press 2024. DOI: 10.1093/oso/9780197754443.003.0013

320 ELEMENTS OF DETERRENCE

former despite less of the latter. In Chapters 5 through 7, we discussed the strategic characteristics of cyberspace in detail, arguing that the domain is poorly suited for coercion marginally useful for defense in combination with conventional capabilities, and *extremely* useful for deception. As discussed in Chapter 6, the human-built domain of information-processing turns out, unsurprisingly enough, to be well suited for manipulating information. The specialization for deception in cyberspace also creates serious trade-offs. Most dramatically, as discussed in Chapter 7, offensive cyber operations might undermine nuclear deterrence. The "cyber commitment problem" becomes a source of relative uncertainty (asymmetric information), which in turn increases the risk of deterrence failure (war). But the problem of nuclear deterrence is an extreme edge case. Rarefied penetrations of specialized nuclear command and control systems via extremely sensitive technical capabilities may not offer the best guide to most cyberconflict in the wild. The vast majority of cyberthreat activity does not come anywhere near such sensitive systems, nor does it rely on such exquisite methods. On the contrary, the vast majority of cyber intrusions are possible only because states find it in their interest to establish connections to a common internet.

In this chapter, we argue that improvements in the general availability of information in and through cyberspace are correlated with other factors that make conventional war less likely. States that are getting rich through economic interdependence have less reason to go to war for economic resources. And economic interdependence depends increasingly on information technology. But the price of the modern informational peace is an increasing attractiveness of intelligence contests in and through cyberspace. The same developments that discourage conventional war, therefore, will also encourage information "conflict" or intelligence contests. Common information systems improve economic prosperity, and actors moderate the intensity of cybercrime and cyber espionage to preserve the benefits of digital globalization, which include opportunities for future exploitation.[4]

The rise of the internet not only enables more intensive forms of virtual competition, but it also heralds changes in the issues over which states and citizens compete. Economic and social changes associated with the information age reduce the utility of pursuing more traditional forms of conflict. Cyberspace offers an attractive domain in which to contest the balance of power, interests, and information in a technological era when

---

[4] Lindsay 2017.

territorial conquest becomes less attractive, if not anachronistic.[5] In short, the rising value of information invites intelligence contests.

The normalization of cyberconflict in international politics has at least one benefit: it is now possible to systematically investigate certain aspects of cyberconflict empirically. Here, we focus on the relationship between cyber operations and traditional tools of war. Much of the debate to date has focused on the question of whether cyberconflict can directly complement or substitute for traditional forms of conflict. As we have seen, there are reasons to be skeptical. But cyberspace could separately affect *both* virtual and kinetic dispute behavior. We argue that with an increase in a country's internet access, it is more likely to initiate or become a target of cyberconflict, but that it is also less likely to initiate or become a target of conventional conflict. We test our theory using an innovative estimation approach, applied to panel data on cyber versus conventional disputes.[6] We find no direct relationship between virtual or conventional conflict. Instead, increasing internet dependency simultaneously increases cyberconflict and discourages militarized disputes.

Our findings thus support the hypothesis that cyberconflict is an indirect substitute for conventional war. We describe it as indirect insofar as cyberconflict is a symptom of broader economic developments that are more directly responsible for changing patterns of violence. Advanced industrial states are not necessarily looking to cyberconflict as an alternative to war, but rather are engaging in cyberconflict for the same reasons that they are looking to war less often.

Linking Cyberconflict and War

There is a wealth of literature in the study of international security that examines military technologies as substitutes or complements. For example,

---

[5] The war in Ukraine, ongoing as of this writing, demonstrates that territorial conquest is not a thing of the past. Yet this war is remarkable precisely because Russia's blatant invasion stands out against the background trend, cf. Altman 2020. It also demonstrates the limits of substitution when a nation, rightly or wrongly, perceives its core interests to be imperiled. The indirect substitution of information conflict for kinetic conflict, as theorized below, is only a general trend, not an iron law. The war in Gaza, also ongoing as of this writing, seems to provide another rule-proving exception, but the irregular aspect of this largely internal war is notable.

[6] We apply our estimation approach to two datasets: the Dyadic Cyber Incident Dataset (DCID) (Valeriano, Jensen, and Maness 2018), and the Militarized Interstate Disputes (MIDs), (Maoz 2005). Details of estimation methods and regressions are reported in Kostyuk and Gartzke 2023 and its online appendix.

322   ELEMENTS OF DETERRENCE

conventionally weak states are likely to seek nuclear weapons as an "equalizer."[7] Nuclear, chemical, and biological weapons function as complements initially, but once a country has acquired nuclear weapons, it is less likely to pursue other types of weapons of mass destruction.[8] In a few cases countries are willing to give them up, or bargain them away.[9]

Recently, scholars have started paying attention to information technologies as substitutes or complements. For example, China uses the substitution of space, cyber, and conventional missile weapons as a source of strategic leverage in limited wars because it cannot respond to a worsening threat environment and credible threats with nuclear weapons or large conventional forces.[10] Most scholarship on cyber and conventional technologies focuses on the direct link between the two.[11] We start by summarizing arguments linking cyber operations as complements or substitutes of conventional operations. Then, we will introduce a missing link in existing explanations and show how a country's internet access helps account for increasing cyber operations, as opposed to conventional military operations.

A Complement to War

Cyber operations may be poor tools for coercive diplomacy, but states might use them to shape the balance of military power during combat operations. Cyber operations can exploit a target's unrecognized vulnerabilities, offering commanders the ability to quickly disrupt an opponent's command and control, hinder communication, and create other obstacles to sustaining military operations. In the Ukrainian conflict in Donbas, for example, hackers inundated the communications of combat units and commanders by flooding their phones with text messages and phone calls, collected operational intelligence via hacked closed-circuit television cameras, intercepted drones, and obtained control of Wi-Fi access points.[12] Once a conventional dispute is ongoing, therefore, cyber operations may be utilized to complement physical denial strategies on the ground.

---

[7] Paul 2012; Monteiro and Debs 2014.   [8] Horowitz and Narang 2014, p. 509.
[9] Mehta 2020.   [10] Cunningham 2022.
[11] Liff 2012; Rid 2012; Gartzke 2013; Valeriano and Maness 2015; Borghard and Lonergan 2017; Kostyuk and Zhukov 2019b; Maschmeyer 2021; Lonergan and Lonergan 2022b.
[12] Kostyuk and Zhukov 2019.

While some cyber operations are important during combat, others are most valuable prior to conflict onset.[13] Cyber espionage, which can prove fruitful on an ongoing basis, is especially useful in the lead-up to an active contest. For example, many of the cyber espionage campaigns associated with the Ukrainian conflict (e.g., Snake) were initiated years prior to the onset of hostilities. While some espionage operations continued during the conflict (e.g., Armageddon), many stopped—some due to their diminishing informational value, while others had become compromised.[14]

The above discussion highlights two distinct temporal dimensions of complementarity: co-occurrence and sequentiality. Co-occurrence involves operations in different domains happening more or less simultaneously. For instance, the fighting factions in the Ukrainian conflict used disruption operations during conventional combat. Sequentiality occurs when operations in one domain shape conflict in another domain, at a later time. For example, the intelligence obtained by cyber espionage preceding military operations in Ukraine was used in later combat. When formulating our hypotheses, we consider both forms of complementarity. Specifically, hypotheses 1a and 1b summarize existing scholarly perspectives on complementarity of cyber and military operations.

- *Hypothesis 1a.* Co-occurrent Complementarity: There is positive correlation between cyber operations in period t and military operations in period t.
- *Hypothesis 1b.* Sequential Complementarity: There is positive correlation between cyber operations in period $t - 1$ and military operations in period t.

A Substitute for War

Rather than attempting to initiate costly conventional conflicts, states can use cyber operations to degrade or destroy enemy capabilities in peacetime. These operations allow leaders to deny responsibility for damaging, invasive, or compromising operations and, as a result, they lower the chance of retaliation from the target, as well as limiting blowback at home, compared with traditional tools. Consequently, states that lack the motivation to act

---

[13] Buchanan and Cunningham 2020.   [14] Kostyuk and Zhukov 2019.

324 ELEMENTS OF DETERRENCE

in another, costlier domain may deem cyber aggression to be an attractive alternative.

States can potentially use cyber operations meant to sabotage a target's networks, operations, or systems instead of conventional military operations, both through "rare cyber-attacks that generate an effect felt in the physical world, and the more common destruction of digital information, which can be almost as dire as physical attack for many pieces of infrastructure."[15] The Stuxnet worm, allegedly designed by the United States and Israel and intended to slow the development of the Iranian nuclear enrichment program, is an example of the former. Stuxnet was a part of Operation Olympic Games—a covert, unacknowledged sabotage campaign by the United States and Israel that targeted Iranian nuclear facilities using cyber means. The George W. Bush administration initiated Olympic Games in 2006, believing that the operation would prevent Israel from launching air strikes on Iranian nuclear facilities, an act that might have involved the United States in yet another major conflict in the Middle East.[16] Retaliatory cyberattacks have escalated in recent years as Iranian hackers improve their operational skills and Iranian officials become more confident in cyber operations.[17]

Reputed Russian cyberattacks against infrastructure and other targets in Ukraine both reflect the substitution dynamic and pose an interesting analytical dilemma.[18] Attacks against the Ukrainian power grid that could have been conducted conventionally by Russian military units or Russian-backed separatists operating in Ukraine have instead been prosecuted virtually. The choice to mount cyberattacks against the power grid, instead of using kinetic forms of military violence, is of course subject to many factors. At the same time, the presence of both cyber and conventional operations could tend to exaggerate the extent of complementarity.

As explained earlier, we consider both co-occurent and sequential manifestations of substitution when formulating our hypotheses. Hypotheses 2a and 2b summarize existing scholarly perspectives on substitution of cyber and military operations.

[15] Borghard and Lonergan 2017, p. 16.   [16] Lindsay 2013.
[17] Perlroth and Clifford 2018.   [18] Cerulus 2019.

- *Hypothesis 2a.* Co-occurent Substitution: There is negative correlation between cyber operations in period t and military operations in period t.
- *Hypothesis 2b.* Sequential Substitution: There is negative correlation between cyber operations in period $t - 1$ and military operations in period t.

The Indirect Link

Most studies of cyberconflict tend to directly link it to conventional operations, as either complements or substitutes for one another. An alternative possibility is indirect substitution between the digital and kinetic fronts. We start by providing reasons that these two types of domains are likely to operate independently of each other, at least initially. We then introduce the missing link—internet access—that connects the two modes of dispute, indirectly triggering substitution between them. Thus a country's increasing internet access is likely to be associated with more cyberconflict and less conventional conflict.

Independence

While it is certainly plausible that cyber operations interact with conventional conflict, it is also possible for conflict in one domain to function independently of conflict in other domains. At minimum, this prospect should be considered for logical completeness; nothing appears to obviously preclude cyber and terrestrial conflict from being occasionally, often, or even generally uncoordinated. Independence might diminish over time or vary cross-sectionally (nationally or dyadically), but complements or substitutes may be limited in an initial phase of the emergence of cyberconflict, as governments deploy capabilities that are as yet poorly integrated with other defense capabilities.

It is actually quite difficult to coordinate complex activities in different domains. Amphibious warfare has famously been considered the most difficult kind of warfare in the twentieth century, precisely because it *requires* the

326 ELEMENTS OF DETERRENCE

careful orchestration of operations on land, sea, and air. Given the nature of social activities, and the all-too-human tendency to "keep things simple," unless there is a compelling reason to make such a coordinated effort— or conversely, a strong case has been made to commanders *not* to operate independently in one or several domains—the tendency would presumably be for actions taken in different domains to tend to occur independently of one another.

There is some evidence already of a lack of coordination between cyber and terrestrial domains. Evidence from daily accounts of disruptive cyberattacks and military operations from the Syrian and Ukrainian conflicts suggests that while there is a tit-for-tat response for military operations, cyber operations seem to operate in their own "bubble."[19] The authors explain this result in terms of force synchronization: "the lead time required to plan and implement a successful attack—studying the target system, collecting intelligence on its vulnerabilities, and writing code that exploits them—can make these efforts difficult to synchronize with conventional operations."[20]

Similarly, cyber and conventional conflict are often carried out by wholly different agencies of a given government. Compartmentalization and other issues get in the way of the free-flow of information. One operational unit may literally not know what others are doing. Even if they do coordinate superficially, turf battles and other concerns may make it difficult for different security agencies to successfully achieve the intensive integration of activities needed to synchronize operations in different domains.

More fundamentally, if cyberspace and physical space do different things, it is perhaps not that surprising that they are engaged differently, at different times, and in different ways. As an informational domain, cyberspace is primarily useful for conveying and containing information. Indeed, a key problem in cyberspace is limiting the diffusion of data, which can be replicated endlessly at near-zero cost. Organizations, including governments, seek to limit who knows what, when, and where. This implies that critical objectives in cyberconflict involve the control of information, as opposed to territory, tangible goods (such as airports or equipment), or institutions (like government offices or a leader). Putting aside disruptive events such as denial of service attacks and attempts to undermine or obstruct control systems (e.g., Stuxnet), a large portion of cyber activities are related to the control of information, rather than places or things.

---

[19] Kostyuk and Zhukov 2019, p. 319.   [20] Kostyuk and Zhukov 2019, p. 322.

Based on these perspectives, we argue that states are likely to use conventional military operations and cyber operations largely independently, at least for now. Thus, we are unlikely to find significant complementarity or substitution across cyber and military operations.

- *Hypothesis 3a*. Co-occurent Independence: Cyber operations in period t and military operations in period t operate independently of each other.
- *Hypothesis 3b*. Sequential Independence: Cyber operations in period $t - 1$ and military operations in period t operate independently of each other.

The Growing Usefulness of Informational Contests

If cyberconflict does not interact with conventional conflict directly, is there a mechanism that could potentially connect the two indirectly? That is, is there a common explanation for the coincidental rise in cyberconflicts and a corresponding decrease in conventional conflicts?

In the section above on substitution, we explained the benefits of using cyber operations over conventional operations, leading to a potential rise of the former. But there are no studies that explicitly consider a mechanism that could link the two phenomena, simultaneously explaining changes in both cyber and conventional fronts. The spread of the internet is one such mechanism, as the advent of cyberspace affects both virtual and terrestrial modes of fighting, indirectly causing substitution between them. Rather than simply being a scope condition, the spread of the internet actively creates an indirect relationship by increasing the likelihood that a country experiences cyberconflict and decreases the likelihood that the country experiences terrestrial conflict.

Two conditions must be met for this indirect relationship to hold. First, cyberspace as a domain must facilitate "useful" forms of international conflict. Second, traditional domains for conflict must no longer be adequate or functional to achieve competitors' aims. We discuss each necessary condition in turn.

The first condition is that cyberspace facilitates "useful" forms of international conflict. The internet or cyberspace more generally is an artificial domain, created entirely by human beings. The processes that led to cyberspace are at least trivially responsible for cyber operations, as clearly

328 ELEMENTS OF DETERRENCE

there can be no cyberconflict without cyberspace. But, the mere presence of a venue for conflict does not mean that (much) conflict will occur if actors have no reason to disagree in a specific manner, or if the domain does not lend itself to both prosecuting and practical resolution of differences.

Space, for example, was initially thought to be an important emerging domain for political violence. Yet, it quickly became clear that this ultimate "high ground" was much more useful as an observation post than as a firing platform. Space was hard to get to and difficult to operate or maintain equipment and weapons in (as opposed to transiting through, which was very useful indeed). Occupation was problematic and "control" offered only limited types of advantages to a competitor. Like space, cyberspace can be considered more an observation post than a weapons platform, but this distinction quickly becomes blurred due to ambiguities about the nature of cyber "weapons." In space, observation is free and open, provided one can get there. Surveillance satellites peer down on Earth with only limited natural or artificial obstruction. Because spying from space cannot be prevented, there is no need for nations to keep their espionage efforts secret. Since everyone knows about "eyes in the sky," the effect of space surveillance is disproportionately beneficial for deterrence. Thus, as discussed in Chapter 11, nations are discouraged from actions that would be degraded by revelation because they cannot conceal them.

Cyber espionage, by contrast, is preventable (at least potentially). Because of this, spying must be pursued in secret, even as penetrating other actors' networks involves actions and measures that look much more like warfare than does deploying cameras in the sky. Revelation of cyber-espionage activities typically degrades future access to sources of information. The secrecy that must be maintained to operate clandestinely in cyberspace means that cyber operations are more like traditional espionage than space surveillance. Indeed, the penetration of enemy systems required for cyber spying may be indistinguishable to targets from efforts designed to degrade or destroy these same systems. Access is essential and contested, whether one is preparing an attack or just listening.

Information has been a valuable currency and a concern in warfare for centuries, but information has become an even more attractive commodity in the information age. Knowledge has been an ascendant component of wealth and power for millennia, but it has arguably never been more important than it is today. While there are multiple ways to access insights about the world (e.g., human and signals intelligence sources), cyberspace is an attractive environment in which to manage, distribute, and obtain information.

The world's governments are increasingly turning to the internet or cellular technology to obtain secrets or access compromising information about foreign governments or important individuals. China, notably, has made extensive use of cyber operations to acquire military and civilian industrial technology from the West. Western nations have also increasingly relied on cyberspace as a domain of espionage. For example, the US National Security Agency (NSA) partnered with Danish intelligence officials to monitor the internet traffic of European leaders.[21] While German leaders like Angela Merkel expressed outrage, Germany has its own tradition of spying on friends and neighbors.[22] There are of course many other examples, only some of which are known to the general public, given the covert nature of a high proportion of cyber operations.

As these examples suggest, cyberspace is an extremely attractive domain for both aggressors and targets, given their respective objectives. Chinese spies could, and have, sought to obtain sensitive technologies through physical means, but these operations are costly, risky, and difficult to conceal. The theft of intellectual property through cyberspace can be conducted by operators that are physically remote from a given target. At the same time, targets continue to house sensitive data in the virtual domain, due to the benefits of managing and disseminating information in cyberspace.

The examples above suggest the contexts where cyber operations are more attractive as a mode of conflict. Governments appear to prefer acting in cyberspace when their costs are low and their objectives are readily obtainable. The increasing value and availability of knowledge and information make cyber operations more useful tools for states that also have economies that are, or seek to be, structured around informational technologies. A high level of internet access both reflects and affects the value of information in a nation's economy, even as using conventional tools of conflict to obtain information is much less effective.

[21] Henley 2021.   [22] Dobson 2020.

The Declining Usefulness of War

The second condition for an indirect relationship is that the same historical forces that have produced the internet have also altered the ability or usefulness of traditional warfare to achieve competitors' aims. Previous research suggests a number of mechanisms capable of explaining a decline in interstate conflicts since 1945, including norms development, changing power distributions, and the spread of knowledge of how to avoid the use of armed force.[23] These same mechanisms have been conducive for building out the digital infrastructure of economic globalization.

For much of history, the foundations of civilization rested on control and exploitation of physical territory. More land meant more wealth. Today, prosperity is no longer derived primarily from agriculture, or from extracting minerals from the soil. Much more of the productive (and destructive) capacity of states rests with human and financial capital. Unlike empires of the past, modern nations seldom seek conquest and plunder to sustain and enrich themselves.[24] Instead, they use or threaten force to extract political concessions—to tell others how they must behave, not what property they can possess—rather than taking territory or other tangible goods.

This transition in the motives of states has begun to transform international conflict. Long the focus of military aggression, territorial conquest holds less appeal than it once did.[25] More precisely, there has been a decline of outright wars of territorial conquest, even as states still engage in marginal territorial revision through faits accomplis.[26] With the decline in the value of territory as a means of achieving wealth and power, the utility of conventional conflict has also declined, at least in its most traditional forms. Military violence remains, but it is much more focused on the projection of influence or the acquisition of strategic territory, than on physical conquest or economic plunder. Force is used to punish, coerce, or deny, not to take.[27]

---

[23] Gartzke 2007; Pinker 2011; Gleditsch et al. 2013; Holsti 2016. Cf. Braumoeller 2019.

[24] As an exception to this pattern, it appears that the objectives of Russian authorities in conducting a physical invasion of Ukraine in early 2022 have less to do with obtaining information and more to do with more traditional goals, such as political influence and strategic depth. Indeed, the invasion seems to hinge on a worldview that is backward looking and out of step with the new realities of an informational world. Despite that, the flow of information and sustaining government and citizen communication via internet-connected technologies remain top priorities in this conflict; Kostyuk and Gartzke 2022. We return to Russia's war in Ukraine in Chapter 14.

[25] Gartzke and Rohner 2011.

[26] Altman 2020. Territorial control still plays an important role in internal wars, such as the ongoing conflict in Gaza, where state institutions are not consolidated.

[27] It is not surprising that countries continue investing in their armed forces because they serve various functions, and war is only one of them. Unlike these other functions, such as maintaining

The global spread of the internet increased the need to acquire and control information. Cyberspace is a great medium for ideas, those that owners wish to share as well as those they do not. If information is power, then increasingly contestation is over the control of information, raising the value of the stakes over information as a commodity. While cyber operations are not limited to espionage, the need to gain access, regardless of one's motives for doing so, and the range of actions that are possible, once access has been achieved, mean that a high proportion of cyber operations will look like espionage. Indeed, most cyber operations contain elements of spying, regardless of what other objectives may be planned or contemplated. Put more simply, spying is where conflict is at in cyberspace.

By the same token, it is not always clear that conventional military force is likely to advantage actors seeking to acquire or control information. Airstrikes, fishing disputes, or border clashes will seldom penetrate or compromise a target's command and control apparatus, the industrial secrets of leading firms, or a party headquarters. Similarly, while airstrikes can damage an opponent's capabilities such as, for example, nuclear enrichment facilities, they are not subtle. Kinetic attacks often cause collateral or environmental damage and leave an attacker open to international condemnation and possible retribution. In contrast, cyber operations can allow an attacker to rebalance power anonymously, or at least quietly, further demonstrating why using cyber operations is apparently cheaper than conventional tools.

Cyber operations, as discussed in chapter 5, possess several drawbacks in pursuing the traditional goals of military force, i.e., as direct substitutes or even complements. These drawbacks include problems like limited destructiveness, a minimum of psychological shock, the temporal boundedness of damage, and a lack of credibility. At the same time, their strengths play to exactly the needs of a growing list of nations in the twenty-first century, while also offering a contrasting set of advantages from conventional modes of conflict. Cyber operations allow actors to benefit at a target's expense (slightly shifting or shaping the balance of power) at relatively low cost and

---

domestic stability, peacekeeping, or coercion of rivals, wars are less fruitful now because (1) they are quite costly; and (2) there are other cheaper ways of obtaining a country's strategic objectives. Given that interstate conflict is the most useful tool for capturing territory, physical conquest generally holds less appeal in the twenty-first century. Modern armies largely refrain from the venerable tactics of raid and pillage, not due to superior morals, but because there is little profit in using extremely expensive organizations to steal relatively cheap stuff.

332 ELEMENTS OF DETERRENCE

risk of escalation. They are particularly practical when the stakes in a contest involve intangibles (information, control, and actors' beliefs).

Thus, if a country can use cyber operations to obtain sensitive information to shift the balance of power, it has few incentives to also execute a more costly military action. In other words, the advent of cyberspace effects an indirect substitution between different conflict domains. The claim is not that the internet is causing a decline in war, but rather that it is correlated with broader economic trends that are.[28] Information advantages become more salient in a world where controlling arable acres and manual labor are not as important as competing effectively in a globally integrated economy. Given the growing value of information, nations are mostly interested in using cyberspace to achieve new objectives. But not all nations can.

We are not trying to make and test any claims about why states increase their internet access per se. For various reasons, some do. We do claim that increasing a country's internet access is likely to be associated with an increase in that country's propensity to engage in cyberconflict, and to reduce the nation's likelihood of engaging in conventional conflict. Since we are interested in studying an effect of an exogenous variable, a country's internet access, this relationship is co-occurent in some sense. Thus, we do not distinguish between co-occurence and sequentiality in these hypotheses.

- *Hypothesis 4a.* With an increase in a country's internet access, it is likely to initiate *more cyberconflicts* (i.e., attack) and *fewer conventional* conflicts.
- *Hypothesis 4b.* With an increase in a country's internet access, it is likely to become a target of *more cyberconflicts* and of *fewer conventional* conflicts.

Furthermore, we can formulate a stronger version of hypothesis 4 by focusing on the most informational aspects of cyberconflict. If the critical objectives in cyberconflict involve the control of information, then the "main event" in cyberconflict is espionage, as well as derivative activities designed to facilitate or interrupt spying. Other things happen in cyberconflict, such as denial of service attacks and attempts to undermine or obstruct control systems (e.g., Stuxnet), but a large portion of cyber activities are related to

---

[28] Gartzke 2007.

the control of information, rather than places or things.[29] This point aligns with the recent scholarship which views actors' behavior in cyberspace primarily as an "intelligence contest."[30] Therefore, we are more likely to observe the indirect substitution of cyber espionage operations with conventional operations than such substitution of disruption and degradation operations with conventional operations. We hypothesize that increasing a country's internet access is likely to lead to an increase in that country's propensity to engage in, and defend against, cyber espionage, and to reduce (somewhat) a nation's utility for engaging in conventional operations.

- *Hypothesis 5a.* With an increase in a country's internet access, it is likely to initiate more cyber *espionage* operations.
- *Hypothesis 5b.* With an increase in a country's internet access, it is likely to become a target of more cyber *espionage* operations.

Summary of Findings

This study seeks to determine why nations choose particular domains in which to fight. Rivalries are ideal for this purpose, since they involve pairs of nations with demonstrated hostility, but that may or may not fight in a given time period. Samples of rivalries generally capture around 80 percent of interstate conflict over the past 200 years. Since we are interested in explaining when states use cyber, conventional, or both types of operations, we combine the dyads identified as conventional rivalries[31] with the dyads identified as cyber rivals[32] to create the population of rivalries that we use in our analysis.

A focus on rivalries also allows us to favorably assess the complement/substitution arguments (hypotheses and 1 and 2), while likely biasing against our theory (hypotheses 3 through 5). Nations that experience few conventional disputes do not qualify as rivals. As such, the predictions of our indirect argument, if fulfilled, will lead more states with a high internet access and dyads to be under-counted as conventional rivals, compared to

---

[29] Perhaps this reality may change as the "internet of things" becomes more widespread, or perhaps there will be even more return on investment in informational conflict. Even with the internet increasingly integrating with the physical world, however, the ability to control or obstruct physical space through cyberspace will remain limited.

[30] Chesney and Smeets 2023.   [31] Thompson and Dreyer 2011.

[32] Valeriano and Maness 2014.

states that have a low internet access; nevertheless, states with a high internet access may continue to exhibit a significant number of cyberconflicts than states with a low internet access. More generally, it is difficult to assess how countries might behave differently in terms of their conflict behavior if they exhibit little or no conflict.

We follow existing political science scholarship that uses DCID data to examine the dynamics of non-cyber international trends in interstate rivalries.[33] As in the previous studies in this book, we use MIDs to measure conventional military conflict. We also consider a number of variables that might affect a nation's willingness to fight, in addition to our key independent variable of *internet access*, measured by internet users per capita based on World Bank data.

To determine whether digital and conventional conflict domains shape each other sequentially or concurrently (or not), we introduce a new approach that estimates both versions of complementarity and substitutability. A logistic regression with lagged dependent variables approximates sequential effects of cyber and conventional conflict. We allow for concurrent substitution or complementarity by jointly estimating factors associated with cyber and conventional operations. Because the methods are quite technical, we will simply summarize our findings here.[34]

Our main findings are that a rival's internet access explains its propensity towards cyber versus conventional conflict. This is especially the case for cyber-espionage operations. We find support for our primary hypotheses of indirect substitution (hypotheses 4a and 4b). Specifically, with an increase in its internet access, a state is more likely to use cyber means, and less likely to use conventional means, to engage in conflict (hypothesis 4b). Moreover, with an increase in its internet access, a state is more likely to become a target of cyberconflict and less likely to become a target of conventional conflict (hypothesis 4a).

We further confirm this indirect substitution effect of a rival's internet access on its propensity towards different modes of conflict by showing that

[33] I.e., interstate trade in Akoto 2021. We ran robustness checks that consider the possibility that cyber operations remain under/over-reported in DCID. Our results generally hold. DCID is compiled from public reporting of cyber campaigns, which means it is potentially affected by reporting bias and almost certainly by missingness, given the clandestine nature of most intrusions. Yet, the omission of data would tend to work against our hypotheses, so if we detect an increase in internet-based conflict in a truncated dataset of internet conflict, the real trend may be even more pronounced than we report here.

[34] Readers interested in the details of estimation methods and regressions are encouraged to consult Kostyuk and Gartzke 2023 and its online appendix.

rivals do not use cyber and conventional military operations as concurrent complements or substitutes. While rivals are likely to sequentially use cyber and conventional operations against the same targets, they use these two types of operations independently from each other. This evidence provides support for hypothesis 3 and refutes hypothesis 1 and 2.

We also test our theoretical expectations for different types of cyber-operations. We expect cyber espionage as well as combined disruption-degradation operations to operate independently from conventional operations (hypothesis 3). But we expect to find a more likely indirect substitution effect for cyber espionage operations (hypotheses 5a and 5b) than for combined disruption-degradation operations. Indeed, we find that rivals do not use different types of cyber operations and conventional military operations as concurrent complements or substitutions. But they are likely to sequentially use these operations against the same targets yet independently from each other. This evidence again supports hypothesis 3 and refutes hypothesis 1 and 2. Importantly, we find evidence for the indirect substitution effect of cyber espionage operations, supporting hypotheses 5a and 5b.

In addition to our main results explained above, we also investigate how additional factors help explain how different features of a given dyad affect whether countries engage in cyber and/or conventional conflict, and why. Specifically, we show that there is a positive, statistically significant association between an attacker's overall capabilities (CINC) score and its likelihood of cyberconflict.[35] We find no association between distance and conflict, perhaps because the internet allows countries to dispute with others far from home. But there is a positive, statistically significant relationship between a target possessing (sharing) nuclear weapons and the probability of any dispute. This result can be explained by a widespread perception that cyber operations are non-escalatory,[36] and the fact that most MIDs involve disputes short of wars.

To visualize the influence of the country's internet access on its likelihood of engaging in either form of conflict, Figures 13.1 and 13.2 presents interaction plots that visualize the results of our best-fit model. The x-axis

[35] The association between attacker's CINC score and its likelihood of conventional conflict is not statistically significant, but this is not unusual; see De Mesquita and Lalman 1988. It is likely that strategic interaction plays a critical role. Because all actors know that power matters in winning wars, the effects of power on conflict onset are largely absorbed in expectations about relative military performance, and thus manifest through bargaining and diplomacy, rather than through more easily observable warfare; see Powell 1999b.

[36] Lonergan and Lonergan 2023.

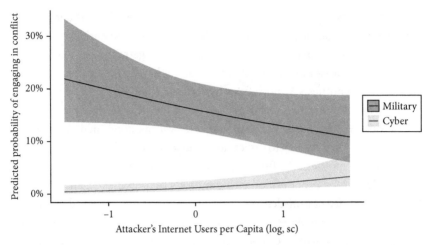

Fig. 13.1 Attacker's internet access and its likelihood of experiencing conflict

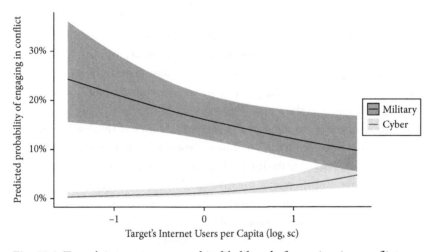

Fig. 13.2 Target's internet access and its likelihood of experiencing conflict

displays a measure of a country's internet users per capita: zero is the mean of a country's internet users per capita, and the other numbers are standard deviations from the mean. The y-axis displays its probability of engaging in either military disputes (dark line) or cyberconflict (light line).

We find that as actor's internet users per capita increases, its likelihood of engaging in conventional disputes *decreases* while its likelihood of engaging in cyberconflict *increases*. This trend is consistent for both the initiators and targets of conflict, as shown respectively in Figure 13.1 and Figure 13.2.

These findings provide evidence that cyberconflict is substituting indirectly for military conflict.

Discussion and Implications

Much remains to be done in assessing the impact of new forms of conflict on war and peace. We began with a pair of contrasting conventional wisdoms about how cyber and conventional conflict interact. We have provided tentative evidence that largely contradicts both of these dialectical accounts: cyber neither triggers or substitutes for conventional conflict behavior. Instead, cyberconflict exists at present largely independently from conventional military operations. Further, the decline in militarized conflict identified in recent decades cannot be explained simply by the rise of "cyberwar." To the contrary, we provide evidence for a common root in terms of technology.

Specifically, we introduced a missing link—internet access as a proxy for informational interdependence—to explain both the decline in conventional conflict and the increase in cyberconflict. The global internet is both a symptom and an enabler of economic interdependence. As broad historical economic trends make military conflict less attractive, for reasons discussed in Chapter 12, the same trends are making cyberconflict more attractive. Countries have thus been utilizing cyberspace to pursue and control information, an increasingly attractive commodity in political and economic competition. Given that cyberspace allows actors to compete over information, we can expect increased friction in this new medium as technologically sophisticated states use espionage and subversion to pursue their strategic goals.

Our findings contribute to policy debates regarding both within- and cross-domain conflict by suggesting that observers may have overestimated the role that cyber operations play in conventional conflict. These findings provide preliminary support for recent scholarship that views actors' behavior in cyberspace primarily as an "intelligence contest" primarily.

Our findings also reveal the effect of additional variables on a country's decision to engage in cyber or conventional conflict. Specifically, the fact that a target possesses (or shares) nuclear weapons increases the likelihood of a state using *less escalatory* means to resolve a dispute via cyber operations or militarized disputes. States possessing nuclear weapons are more likely to engage in any conflict, implying stability-instability, as nuclear status deters high-intensity war but allows more risk-taking at lower levels of dispute intensity.[37] Geographical distance between states appears irrelevant for both types of conflict. Given the rapid spread of the internet in recent decades, it is not surprising that the distance between two states does not significantly affect the ability of rivals to engage in digital or physical exchanges.[38] Lastly, we show that overall national capabilities differentially shape the propensity to engage in cyber and conventional conflict.

Our study is not without limitations. Even though our results suggest that digital and conventional fronts are generally independent, this may certainly change as more nations deploy information campaigns alongside war "on the ground." Cyber and conventional operations could also complement (e.g., Russia's use of conventional and cyber operations against Ukraine, US use of conventional and cyber operations against the Islamic State) or substitute over longer intervals (e.g., a delayed US response to the 2014 Sony hack). Moreover, nations have begun a shift in cyberstrategies predicated on a greater presence in adversarial networks. Such "defend forward" doctrines might produce more rapid responses in the future, similar to the 2019 US cyberattack against Iranian Republican Guard systems in response to the bombing of oil tankers in the Gulf of Oman. Countries might also resort to conventional force in response to cyber operations, as for example when the Israeli Defense Force conducted an air strike against a building said to house a Hamas hacking group accused of mounting cyberattacks against Israel, but this runs against historical trends of cyber operations not provoking escalation and, on the contrary, sometimes associated with deliberate de-escalation.[39]

While historical trends continue to propel more internet-dependent nations away from traditional forms of warfare and toward cyberconflict, we do expect to see a few exceptions from this general trend. Conflict is inherently uncertain, and countries will get creative with how they achieve their strategic objectives. Ongoing wars in Ukraine and Gaza and intermittent US drone strikes around the world show that in certain cases some advanced industrial states will still find conventional military options useful in the digital era. To limit access to sensitive control systems

[37] George, Smoke, et al. 1974.
[38] Evidence from previous research suggests that proximity affects selection into rivalry, e.g., Buhaug and Gleditsch 2006.
[39] Lonergan and Lonergan 2022.

vulnerable to catastrophic cyber-physical attack, countries will continue to "air-gap" their computer systems to make them less accessible, even at the cost of foregoing economic exchange. And, some countries may continue prioritizing territorial conquest.[40] But a few outliers in these categories do not necessarily suggest new trends. Deviant cases with consistent qualifications (i.e., exceptions that prove the rule) are unlikely to change our main theoretical prediction that technologically sophisticated states will continue to compete over information more than territory as they pursue their strategic goals.

---

[40] Altman 2020.

14

Gray Zone

Ambiguity and Escalation

with J. Andrés Gannon and Peter Schram

There is increasing concern that conventional conceptions of deterrence are inadequate to address burgeoning threats in the gray zone.[1] Deterrence is typically believed to have failed if a challenger disrupts the status quo or resorts to military violence. From this perspective, traditionally capable defenders appear ill-equipped to respond to revisionism in the gray zone.[2] As a recent Chairman of the US Joint Chiefs of Staff commented, "Our traditional approach is either we're at peace or at conflict. And I think that's insufficient to deal with the actors that actually seek to advance their interests while avoiding our strengths."[3]

Russia's 2014 intervention in Crimea with "little green men" (soldiers whose uniforms lacked insignia or other identifying information) together with "active measures" to manipulate information emerged as a paradigmatic example of "hybrid warfare" designed to challenge the status quo without triggering broader conflict.[4] Similar tactics and imagery have emerged elsewhere, with Chinese "little blue men" eroding "red lines" in maritime East Asia.[5] According to former British Defense Secretary Michael Fallon, "That is not a Cold War. It is a grey war. Permanently teetering on the edge of outright hostility. Persistently hovering around the threshold of what we would normally consider acts of war."[6] The emergence of new domains of conflict is often portrayed as a disaster for deterrence. The escalation of limited war in Ukraine into large-scale land warfare in 2022 adds to the pessimism.

---

[1] Holmes and Yoshihara 2017; Matisek 2017; Hicks and Friend 2019; Pettyjohn and Wasser 2019.
[2] Van Jackson 2017.   [3] Dunford 2016.   [4] Marten 2015; Lanoszka 2016.
[5] M. Green et al. 2017.   [6] Fallon 2017.

Elements of Deterrence: Strategy, Technology, and Complexity in Global Politics. Erik Gartzke and Jon R. Lindsay,
Oxford University Press. © Oxford University Press 2024. DOI: 10.1093/oso/9780197754443.003.0014

We suggest, however, that gray-zone conflict (GZC) is neither novel nor inherently a deterrence failure. Rather than repudiating deterrence, gray-zone challenges could actually reflect a certain respect for existing frameworks, both to avoid major war and preserve interests in common with status quo powers. Deterrence not only determines *whether* a challenge emerges but also *how*. Restricting other nations' behaviors could certainly prove valuable, even in the absence of peace and a full retention of the status quo. An enemy that engages "with one hand tied behind its back" to avoid triggering a larger contest is not fighting as effectively as it could. Even if the challenger resorts to force and the defender does not escalate immediately, fear of subsequent intervention by the defender could cause the challenger to adopt a more furtive military strategy. As horrendous as the combat has been in Ukraine, as of this writing, it has remained largely contained within the (2013-era) borders of Ukraine, and restricted to the conventional level, with several classes of weapons withheld, or only introduced gradually. Even this can be interpreted as partial success for deterrence.

The argument in this chapter is based on a formal game theoretical model in which a challenger and defender can select from variable intensities of limited conflict, or they can resolve the crisis with a decisive war.[7] We find that actors will behave differently depending on if the actor is constrained by their internal cost-benefit balancing (i.e. driven by costs, efficacy, innovation, etc.), or if the actor is constrained by an external deterrent threat. We then derive a series of observations that connect empirically observable behavior to the challenger's constraints and motivations for GZC (i.e. whether a challenger is constrained internally or externally). We find evidence that the external deterrent threat of NATO intervention seemed to shape recent Russian moves into the gray zone.

An additional result from our formal model is that a defender that becomes better at GZC may incentivize a challenger to risk war. This result arises because as the defender gets better at fighting within GZC, GZC becomes less beneficial to the challenger. For a challenger who would otherwise conduct GZC, this change in the defender's gray-zone capabilities can result in the challenger giving up on GZC altogether and accepting the status quo, or (more surprisingly) can result in the challenger acting more aggressively and risking war. This result offers some insight into why Russia

---

[7] For detailed description and analysis of this model, along with empirical tests, see Gannon et al. 2023.

342   ELEMENTS OF DETERRENCE

escalated in February 2022 in its invasion of Ukraine, after its disappointing performance in eight years of GZC.

Between Peace and War

Despite the analytical convenience afforded by conceptualizing war and peace as discrete outcomes, there is nothing new about conflict that falls between these two extremes. The literature on conflict is replete with both examples and frameworks, including limited war,[8] salami slicing,[9] low-intensity conflict,[10] hybrid wars,[11] frozen conflict,[12] covert operations,[13] cyberwar,[14] and hassling.[15]

Early Cold War writings on "weakening the enemy with pricks instead of blows" emphasized that states may choose to pursue limited political objectives in the shadow of nuclear escalation.[16] The Korean War seemed a then-underappreciated type of war fought to achieve political ends short of total victory with military means short of a total commitment.[17] Contemporary treatments understood limited war as a conflict between actors that had the capacity to increase battlefield commitments but did not want to do so, creating a third option between major war and acquiescence.[18] Strategists introduced the "stability-instability paradox" to describe how disincentives for nuclear war, or even major conventional war, encourage conflict at lower levels of intensity, or in peripheral theaters.[19] Similarly, Powell notes that "how much power the challenger brings to bear limits how much risk the defender can generate."[20] As George and Smoke explain, adversaries can "design around" deterrence by discovering new options that offer "an opportunity for gain while minimizing the risk of an unwanted response."[21]

The renewal of interest in low-intensity conflict between more capable competitors represents a return to these themes. A common thread in definitions of GZC is that it involves "a carefully planned campaign operating in the space between traditional diplomacy and overt military aggression" employed by challengers with grand geopolitical ambitions and

---

[8] Kissinger 1955; Osgood 1969   [9] Schelling 1966.   [10] Turbiville 2002.
[11] Lanoszka 2016.   [12] Driscoll and Maliniak 2016.
[13] Carson 2018a; O'Rourke 2018b.   [14] Lindsay and Gartzke 2018.
[15] Schram 2021, 2022.   [16] Hart 1967, p. 186.
[17] Osgood 1969.   [18] Brodie 1957; Kissinger 1957b.   [19] Snyder 1965; Jervis 1984.
[20] Powell 2015, p. 598.   [21] George and Smoke 1989, p. 173.

potent capabilities.[22] A number of practitioners and journalists highlight the worrying expansion of technologies by which low-intensity conflict can be practiced.[23] Scholars similarly note the technological novelty of this phenomenon as a form of aggression against which the US is unprepared.[24] This pessimism concerning adversaries' ability to overthrow the existing military balance with "innovative doctrines or cunning strategies"[25] has even led some to advocate revamping deterrence to focus on gray-zone threats.[26] The policy prescription emerging from this conventional wisdom is that the United States—and other targets of gray-zone aggression—must use more of the tools available at its disposable to re-assert deterrence and counter innovations in this unconventional battlespace.[27]

We wish to push back on this growing consensus that an expanded repertoire of potent tools for conflict short of war means GZC represents the new modal form of conflict. Indeed, militaries have been innovating novel technologies in *all* domains of warfare, at *all* levels of intensity.[28] Yet in most conflicts, many of the sharpest arrows remain in the quiver. Therefore, the choice to use select innovations but not others represents a restriction, rather than an expansion, of the total means available. This shift in perspective, which views GZC as a relative reduction rather than an absolute expansion of options, calls into question claims about its effectiveness, and even its novelty.

In the last decade of the Cold War, US Secretary of State George Shultz offered a note of cautious optimism in this regard:[29]

> The ironic fact is, these new and elusive challenges have proliferated, in part, because of our success in deterring nuclear and conventional war. Our adversaries know they cannot prevail against us in either type of war. So they have done the logical thing: they have turned to other methods. Low-intensity warfare is their answer to our conventional and nuclear strength— a flanking maneuver, in military terms.

---

[22] Mazarr 2015. On ambiguity concerning how practitioners define and interpret GZC see Bragg 2017 and Janičatová and Mlejnková 2021.
[23] Olson 2015.
[24] F. Hoffman 2007; Thornton 2015; Brands 2016; C. Jackson 2016b; Wirtz 2017; Hughes 2020.
[25] L. Goldstein 2017, p. 906.   [26] Tor 2015; Matisek 2017.
[27] Hicks and Friend 2019; McCarthy, Moyer, and Venable 2019.
[28] Gannon 2022.   [29] Shultz 1986, p. 204.

344 ELEMENTS OF DETERRENCE

Below we develop Shultz's insight, leveraging the conceptual framework of this book that recognizes a diversity of both means and ends in deterrence strategy, to explore whether modern GZC should be viewed as similarly reassuring or newly alarming.

Modeling Gray-Zone Conflict

We define GZC as occurring when a militarily capable challenger intentionally limits the intensity and capacity with which they conduct military operations, and the defender engages but chooses not to escalate to a decisive war. Our definition means that GZC must be preferred by both sides in a contest. Both actors have the capacity to escalate to a larger war but both also prefer not to, meaning that GZC is an equilibrium.

Motivating Case

The conflict in Ukraine was often held up, prior to 2022, as the paradigmatic example of GZC. Thus we use it as a motivating illustration of our formal model of GZC. The conventional wisdom prior to 2022 presents a puzzle in retrospect: if Russian subversion in the gray zone had been as effective as many assumed before 2022, then Russia would not have needed to escalate to a more costly war in 2022. We offer a more nuanced account of this case. We developed a formal model prior to the Russian escalation in 2022, to explain decisions made in 2014, yet the model contains within it a suggestive explanation for Russia's decisions in 2022.

The Euromaidan Revolution (2013–14) presented Russia with a new political reality: Kyiv was abruptly realigning with the West. In response, Russia quickly set about attempting to revise this realignment. From 2014 to late 2021, Russia's actions were finite and often indirect, far below the threshold of Russian military capabilities. We refer to behaviors like these as limited "challenges," implicitly to the status quo. The notion of "status quo" is inherently contextual, of course. Russia, of course, has justified its intervention as an attempt to restore the status quo prior to Western influence over Kyiv. As a modeling convenience, we treat the status quo simply as whatever political conditions prevail at a given point in time when the analysis begins, since we are most interested in how and whether actors attempt to alter it.

In response to Russian challenges, NATO quickly increased its presence in the Black Sea, reinforced its support for capacity-building in Ukraine, and stepped up its presence and cooperation in other countries in Eastern Europe. This helped Ukraine counter the Russian-sponsored separatist movement in eastern Ukraine, while Russian cyber campaigns failed to influence the political alignment of Kyiv. In this way, Ukraine became engaged in GZC characterized by limited proxy warfare, disinformation operations, and sporadic cyberattacks.

This low-level conflict lasted for eight years, until the February 2022 Russia invasion of Ukraine. The question, of course, is why did Russia change its strategy? We offer the counter-intuitive explanation that Ukraine's defensive succcesses in the gray zone prompted Russia to *escalate* to war, even though Russia's original decision to mount a gray-zone challenge was motivated by its desire to *avoid* war. The later decision to escalate only makes sense in the context of the earlier decision to avoid escalation. Put simply, escalation is path-dependent. Western-enabled improvements in Ukrainian GZC created incentives for a resolved Russian challenger to escalate to open war.

Modeling Assumptions

We model these general dynamics in terms of a challenger (C) and a defender (D) in a crisis.[30] Crisis bargaining proceeds through several stages. In the initial stages, the challenger selects some level of GZC, and the defender responds, either by initiating war or responding in the gray zone at some level. Later stages describe future crisis bargaining in the context of these

---

[30] Many gray-zone challenges involve either state or non-state proxies; see Lanoszka 2016a. For parsimony, we will consider a target's allies as part of the target's capabilities. For simplicity, this means that the NATO-Ukraine coalition is considered as a unified coalition. This is obviously not the case, and Russian strategy self-consciously attempts to exploit fissures in the defending coalition. Since we are focusing here on the onset and escalation behavior of the challenger, however, we will not explicitly model alliance dynamics. Yet, even in our model, these alliances politics and frictions can be encapsulated in the deterrence threshold of the defender, which is imperfectly known by the challenger, and the defender's costs of GZC. Intra-alliance frictions can be expected to increase the deterrence threshold (by undermining collective resolve and credibility) and increase gray-zone costs (by undermining coordination and resupply).

346 ELEMENTS OF DETERRENCE

choices, with the defender offering an ultimatum and the challenger either accepting or going to war.[31]

Whereas most formal models of crisis bargaining offer a binary option of war or peace, our model offers an intermediate range of conflict in the gray zone. There are costs associated with both kinds of conflict. While general war can accomplish an aggressor's goals, war may be unnecessary and inefficient if partial victories or faits accomplis can be achieved at lower cost.[32] Our approach thus offers insight into three central questions. First, why do capable states engage in GZC, thereby withholding some of their military capability? Second, once they do, what explains variation in the intensity with which they engage in it? Third, under what conditions do defensive actions in the gray zone encourage counterproductive escalation?

Throughout this book we have emphasized trade-offs across key strategic objectives: actors want to influence a political dispute, minimize the costs of doing so, avoid a major war in the process, but also prevail in war if necessary. These desperate goals also motivate and constrain challengers to initiate limited conflict or, potentially, escalate to general war. Here we focus on the challengers twin goals of minimizing costs and avoiding war while attempting to gain a favorable settlement of the dispute.

GZC may range from harassing protests to intensive proxy warfare. Challengers that attempt to alter the status quo must choose a level of aggression. A more intensive challenge can yield greater political gains, but could introduce costs: (1) the costs of protracted GZC, and (2) the risks of a costly general war. The selected degree of challenge thus faces two possible constraints: an *internal efficiency constraint*, and an *external deterrent constraint*.

1. *Internal efficiency constraint*: The challenger freely chooses the scope and intensity of conflict that it believes is most efficient for accomplishing its objectives *without concerns of provoking an escalation*. The challenger restricts their level of force based only on its own internal cost-benefit calculations (e.g., relative to other policy priorities it might have). Here the challenger is most sensitive to its own valuation of the stakes and the costs of its challenge.

---

[31] To offer yet another empirical example, Chinese behavior in the South China Sea (circa 2022) is a limited challenge, and neighboring countries responding to these challenges (whether through indirect measures like patrols or through direct confrontation) is the gray-zone response. This mutual gray-zone activity will influence whatever eventual political settlement, stalemate, or later war that emerges between China and its neighbors.

[32] Tarar 2016; Altman 2018.

2. *External deterrent constraint*: The challenger must scale back from its optimal low-level challenge in order to avoid triggering a larger contest. If the challenger is resolved enough to reject the status quo, yet still averse to the costs of open war, the challenger will engage at a lower level of force to avoid a greater risk of war. Here the challenger is most reactive to the defender's willingness to go to war, even as this cannot be perfectly known.

In practice these considerations interact, but to different degrees. This theoretical distinction is empirically consequential. Those who claim that Russia (or any other state engaging in GZC) conducts whatever kind of GZC it wants and operates outside the realm of standard deterrence dynamics are describing a challenger behaving based on their internal efficiency constraint. However, it could also be that Russia is limiting its challenges in order to avoid a greater escalation—which is more consistent with the external deterrent threat binding. Our model establishes that, depending on which constraint binds (i.e., shapes the challenger's strategic choice), we may observe distinct comparative statics. Our model and results allow us to connect observable relationships in the data to what constrains and motivates a challenger's GZC decision.

This distinction calls into question the conventional wisdom that a defender should always try to improve its performance in GZC. When a defender is effective at fighting GZC, then GZC becomes less efficient for the challenger. This can encourage the challenger to pursue options outside of GZC. On one hand, becoming effective at GZC could be productive for the defender if, upon the challenger's low-level activity becoming ineffective, the challenger abandons the use of force altogether and accepts the status quo ex ante. On the other hand, it could be counterproductive for the defender to become better at GZC if, upon the challenger's low-level activity becoming ineffective, the challenger instead escalates to war.

The wisdom of defending more effectively in the gray zone depends on a careful assessment of the costs and values of each side of the interaction. We attempt to capture some of this problem by incorporating incomplete information regarding the defender's private costs from war. This means that the challenger does not know ex ante how great a challenge it can make in the gray zone before the defender opts for war. This assumption captures the intuition that GZC may be used as a "salami slicing" strategy to probe defender resolve, yet with the risk of tiggering inadvertent escalation.

348 ELEMENTS OF DETERRENCE

The Challenger's Payoff in Gray-Zone Conflict

Any formal model to capture all these trade-offs will naturally be complicated, as each actor can make multiple choices depending on multiple parameters, some of which are imperfectly known. In the next few sections we will attempt to convey an informal understanding of our assumptions and findings through a series of figures that illustrate key relationships in the model.[33]

Figures 14.1 and 14.2 depict the payoff to the challenger (increasing along the vertical y-axis) as a function of GZC at a given level (increasing along the horizontal x-axis). The curves reflect the challenger's expected value for war (i.e., the payoff from war, should the defender initiate it, less the challenger's costs of fighting it). The challenger's optimal level of GZC (i.e., the highest point on the utility curve) is marked by asterisks. The kink in the left side of the curve reflects the defender's ability to effectively counter challenges in the gray zone up to a given point (GZ-DEF).[34]

Each sub-figure is divided into three regions. The boundaries of these regions reflect sharp discontinuities in the challenger's utility curve, reflecting disparate assessments of how the defender will respond to a selected level of GZC. Put another way, the defender's external deterrent threat (EDT) is more or less credible in these three regions:[35]

- On the left side of the boundary labeled GZ-EDT, the defender always engages in GZC because its EDT is not credible at that level.
- On the right side of the boundary labeled W-EDT, the defender always goes to war, because its EDT is always credible at that level.
- In between GZ-EDT and W-EDT, defenders will respond differently for reasons that the challenger does not perfectly understand, so the challenger is taking a risk here.

---

[33] The full technical specification and analysis of the model is presented in Gannon et al. 2023 and its online appendix.

[34] This means that the challenger's efforts in the gray zone, independently of deterrence considerations, tend be relatively more effective above GZ-DEF.

[35] The defender's costs of war can range from $\underline{\kappa}_D$ (defenders of this type will always go to war within the center region, since war is relatively costly and they are more resolved) to $\bar{\kappa}_D$ (defenders of this type will always engage in GZC within the center region, since war is more costly and they are less resolved). The challenger knows these bounds ($0 \leq \underline{\kappa}_D < \bar{\kappa}_D$) but not the actual costs for the defender (κ_D).

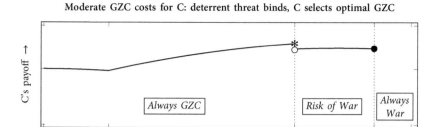

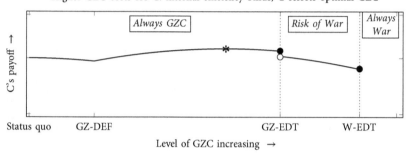

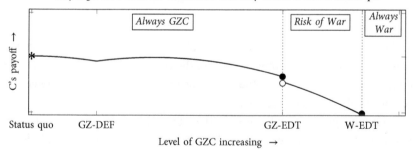

Fig. 14.1 Challengers select gray-zone conflict without risking war

In the center region, the most resolved defenders will go to war for any challenge larger than GZ-EDT, while the least resolved defenders will not go to war until the challenge exceeds W-EDT. The challenger knows these bounds, but not the true threshold of deterrence. Cautious challengers that are worried about the *most dangerous* outcome will assume that any defender could be the high-resolve type, and thus avoid the center area altogether,

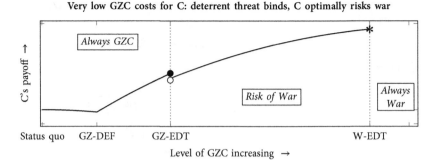

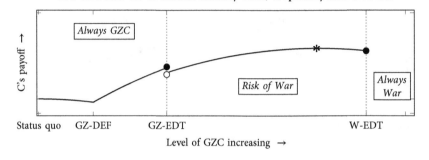

Fig. 14.2 Challengers risk war in gray-zone conflict

as illustrated by Figure 14.1. Aggressive challengers that are only concerned with the *most likely* outcome can assess the probability that they are facing a low-resolve defender, and thus risk war by escalating GZC in the center region, as illustrated by Figure 14.2.

Each sub-figure within Figure 14.1 depicts the effects of external and internal constraints as described above. All sub-figures have the same underlying parameters, except the costs of GZC for the challenger, which varies across sub-figures, increasing from top to bottom.

- In the top sub-figure, GZC is cheap for the challenger, so the *external deterrent constraint binds*. Under this set of parameters, the challenger maximizes its GZC activity right up to the point where different types of defender might be willing to choose war (i.e., the boundary GZ-EDT).
- In the middle sub-figure, GZC is a little more costly for the challenger, so the *internal cost constraint binds*. The challenger chooses an optimal

challenge short of the defender's threshold of deterrence. It doesn't matter what kind of defender the challenger faces, as it's decision is driven by internal cost considerations.

- In the bottom sub-figure, the *internal cost constraint binds* as well, but now GZC is prohibitively costly for the challenger. The challenger decides that it is better off with the status quo and does not challenge at all.

Figure 14.2 considers a different set of parameters and illustrates other possible equilibria to the game. Here the challenger makes a probabilistic assessment about the defender's resolve. The deterrent constraint binds more weakly in Figure 14.2 than Figure 14.1. In the top figure of Figure 14.2, a very aggressive challenger escalates its GZC challenge all the way to W-EDT. Therefore, it will have to fight a war if the defender is the most resolved type, which is bad for the challenger, but it can mount a more aggressive challenge against a less resolved type, which is good for the challenger. Together, the expected payoff from taking a more aggressive challenge and risking war is greater than the expected payoff from never risking war at GZ-EDT. Finally, in the bottom panel of Figure 14.2, the challenger faces slightly greater costs to challenging. This results in the challenger scaling back their selected challenge due to the internal efficiency constraint.

In sum, there are two underlying, rational mechanisms for how challengers conduct GZC. First, when the *external deterrent* threat binds, the challenger may select their challenges based on the external deterrent threat, essentially pulling their punches in GZC to avoid a risk of war. Second, when the external deterrent threat does not bind, the challenger selects their challenge based on their own *internal efficiency*, essentially choosing their optimal challenge unconstrained by the risk of further escalation.

Explaining Variation in Gray-Zone Activity

Next we establish how observable patterns can be used to interpret whether the challenger's behavior is shaped by their internal efficiency or their external deterrent threat. This will allow us to use the relationships uncovered by empirical analysis below to infer whether a challenger is behaving based on the logic of deterrence or efficiency.

352 ELEMENTS OF DETERRENCE

Figure 14.3 provides a different visualization of relationships in the model. The vertical y-axis in all three sub-figures plots the optimal level of GZC for the challenger (equivalent to the asterisk in Figures 14.1 and 14.2). This optimum is a function of several different factors that push and pull in different directions. The sub-figures plot the optimum as a function of different factors, holding everything else constant.

- The top sub-figure plots the challenger's optimal GZC as a function of the defender's deterrent threat. As the defender's war costs decrease, all things being equal, its threat becomes more credible.
- The middle sub-figure plots the optimum as a function of the challenger's resolve. More resolved challengers are willing to accept more risk and thus increase their challenge.
- The bottom sub-figure plots the optimum as a function of the challenger's costs for engaging in GZC. All things being equal, increasing GZC costs lead a challenger to reduce its level of effort.

One reason why GZC dynamics are so complex, therefore, is that there are multiple factors that determine escalation dynamics. These factors are often changing at the same time as the actors interact over time. All things are usually not equal. Still, it is helpful to understand how variation in any given factor may lead a challenger to modulate the level of its GZC (or not).

The dashed lines in each figure depict points at which different constraints bind or fall away, as discussed above.[36] We will use these to make several observations about the empirical dynamics of GZC. These should not be understood as tests of the model, per se, but rather heuristic guides for developing empirical explanations. Shifts in the level of challenge, along with other observable indicators of each explanatory factor, may be used to infer which zone the challenger is in and thus which constraint binds. If we observe specific empirical patterns in the data, therefore, then we can back out whether external deterrence or the challenger's internal optimization is driving the challenger's behavior.

---

[36] The relative position of these points is what is important. The absolute positions are based on mathematical expressions without an intuitive interpretation and parameters chosen for illustration.

GRAY ZONE 353

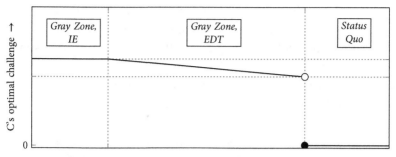

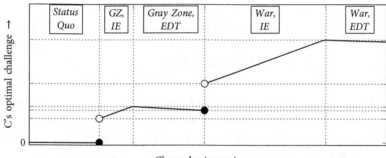

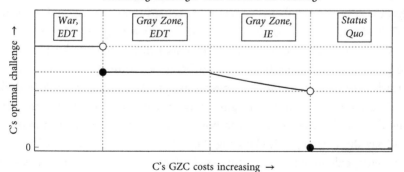

Fig. 14.3 Determining the optimal level of gray-zone conflict

354 ELEMENTS OF DETERRENCE

On the Defender's Deterrent Threat

In the top sub-figure of Figure 14.3, moving from left to right, the defender's costs for war steadily decrease and thus its deterrent threat improves. When the defender's costs of war are greatest, the challenger is unconstrained by the external deterrent threat. This means that the challenger can freely select their challenge based on their own internal efficiency. Thus, the defender's costs of war do not play a role in the challenger's decision making here.

Moving to the right (to the second region), the defender gets better at war, and the challenger cannot conduct the same level of challenge without provoking the defender. Here, the external deterrent threat starts to bind, and, to remain in GZC, the challenger must scale back their challenge.

Moving to the right further (to the third region), the defender is very willing to fight. Here the challenger is so constrained in what challenges they can conduct that will still result in GZC that the challenger no longer finds GZC to be productive. Under these very low costs of war for the defender, the challenger will select into the status quo and avoid GZC altogether.

Furthermore, there is an important interaction between the defender's threat and the challenger's resolve (i.e., the top and middle sub-figures of Figure 14.3). A more resolved challenger may not be willing to accept the status quo at all. If the deterrence threshold decreases enough, the challenger may feel constrained within GZC, yet still switch to risking war. As the defender becomes better at war, the challenger will either opt into the status quo and end the gray-zone challenge or select an even greater challenge and risk war. What distinguishes these cases is the challenger's willingness to fight.

When the challenger responds to increases in the defender's willingness to go to war by scaling back their challenge to nothing, the challenger is clearly deterred. When the challenger responds to increases in the defender's willingness to go to war by engaging in more aggressive and riskier behavior, the defender's deterrent threat is not constraining the challenger, and we will say the challenger is choosing their challenge based on their internal efficiency calculations (e.g., guns vs. butter or the discretionary costs of consuming military resources).

A similar dynamic can play out when the challenger begins by sometimes risking war. If the external deterrent threat constraint binds and the threshold decreases, the challenger will either decrease their challenge, or revert to selecting into the peaceful status quo. Alternatively, if the challenger sometimes risks war, the challenger's internal efficiency

GRAY ZONE 355

constraint binds, and the threshold decreases, then the challenger will be non-responsive until the threshold decreases enough so that the external deterrent threat constraint binds.

How the challenger's responds to changes in the defender's deterrence posture can be summarized in observations 1 and 2:

- *Observation 1*: If increasing the defender's willingness to go to war results in the challenger decreasing their selected challenge, then the *external deterrent* threat shapes the challenger's selected challenge.
- *Observation 2*: If increasing the defender's willingness to go to war results in the challenger not changing their selected challenge, increasing their selected challenge, or risking war more, then the challenger's *internal efficiency* shapes the challenger's selected challenge.

On the Challenger's Resolve

In the middle sub-figure of Figure 14.3, moving from left to right, the challenger places increasing value on the stakes of the dispute. Unresolved challengers will not bother to challenge at all. They will simply accept the status quo. Moving to the right, as the challenger values the asset more, the challenger eventually begins engaging in GZC. Within the next equilibrium space (GZ, IE), the challenger's challenges are not aggressive enough to reach the defender's threshold for declaring war; this means that the internal efficiency constraint binds, and the challenge is increasing in the challenger's resolve.

As challenger resolve increases further, and its level of GZC increases, the challenger eventually becomes constrained by the defender's willingness to go to war. This is when the external deterrent threat binds. Within this region (Gray Zone, EDT), as discussed above, the challenger's optimal challenge is decreasing. If we observe less aggressive challenges over issues that challengers care more about, then we know the challenger's decisions are influenced by deterrence (and vice versa).[37]

---

[37] This (counter-intuitive) relationship stems from the bargaining component of the game. As the challenger's resolve increases, the defender must offer the challenger a greater policy concession in the fourth stage to avoid the challenger declaring war in the fifth stage. Specifically, whenever the deterrent threat binds, the challenger scales back its challenge, knowing it will be compensated later for doing so. For this reason, whenever the challenger is responding to the external deterrent threat, as the challenger's resolve decreases, the challenger will pursue more aggressive challenges.

356   ELEMENTS OF DETERRENCE

As the challenger's resolve increases, it is more willing to risk war with less-effective defenders in order to conduct a greater challenge against more-effective defenders. As discussed above, the challenger can only make a probabilistic judgment about what type of defender it faces. This is where war sometimes occurs. There is a similar relationship between the challenger's internal efficiency (War, IE) and defender's deterrent threat (War, EDT) as challenger resolve increases even further.

How the challenger's responds to changes in its level of resolve is summarized in observations 3 and 4:

- *Observation 3*: If increasing the challenger's resolve results in the challenger increasing their selected challenge, then the challenger's *internal efficiency* shapes the challenger's selected challenge.
- *Observation 4*: If increasing the challenger's resolve results in the challenger decreasing their selected challenge, then the *external deterrent threat* shapes the challenger's selected challenge.

On the Challenger's Gray-Zone Costs

In the bottom sub-figure of Figure 14.3, moving from left to right, the costs of engaging in GZC increase for the challenger. When the external deterrent threat constraint binds, the challenger bases their challenges on the defender's willingness to go to war, which is independent of the internal costs of challenging. If we observe no change in the selected challenges as the challenger's costs are increasing, therefore, then we might infer that the challenger's decisions are based on the external deterrent threat.

In contrast, when the internal efficiency constraint binds, the challenger bases their challenges on how much they care about the asset and how costly it is to engage in more aggressive challenges. If the costs of GZC are very high, all things being equal, then the game is not worth the candle and the challenger begrudgingly accepts the status quo. If we observe less aggressive challenges as the challenger's costs increases, then we might infer that the challenger's decisions are based on its internal efficiency.

Across all equilibria, as the challenger's challenge costs decrease, the challenger will select weakly more aggressive challenges. We do not discuss these results at length because these findings are relatively straightforward. How the challenger's responds to changes in its challenge costs can be summarized in observations 5 and 6.

- *Observation 5*: If decreasing the challenger's challenge costs results in the challenger increasing their selected challenge, then the challenger's *internal efficiency* shapes the challenger's selected challenge.
- *Observation 6*: If decreasing the challenger's challenge costs results in the challenger not changing their selected challenge, then the *external deterrent* threat shapes the challenger's selected challenge.

There is a very important seventh observation that we will discuss later. Here we will simply note that the results on the challenger's costs are quite different from the results on the defender's costs. This distinction is directly relevant to the problem of escalation, exemplified by the 2022 Russian invasion of Ukraine. Thus we will return to it after our empirical discussion of Russian GZC.

Russian Gray-Zone Conflict

In this section we use ideas derived from our formal model to assess whether Russian gray-zone behavior in Europe is shaped by NATO's deterrent threat or not. We focus on Russia because its interventions are referenced as paradigmatic examples of GZC.[38] From 1994 to 2018, Russia has been involved in election interference in the United Kingdom and Moldova, cyber attacks in Estonia and Georgia, and special operations in Ukraine and Yugoslavia. The diversity of Russian targets and means provides an opportunity to conduct an analysis of Russian choices under different deterrent circumstances.

We will summarize the findings of a statistical analysis and provide a brief comparative analysis of three cases: Estonia, Ukraine, and Georgia.[39] We find that the possibility of a NATO intervention is associated with more limited Russian gray-zone operations. By no means is this analysis causal, as our key independent variables—NATO membership, for example—are not exogenous treatments. Our results should be viewed as suggestive and taken with the necessary caveats.

---

[38] Marten 2015; Driscoll and Maliniak 2016; Jasper 2020.
[39] See Gannon et al. 2023 and online appendices for a detailed technical discussion of data, findings, and robustness checks.

358   ELEMENTS OF DETERRENCE

Observation 1 suggests that if we observe a negative relationship between NATO's willingness to fight and the intensity of Russian aggression, then deterrence is shaping Russian behavior. Below, our statistical analysis suggests that Russia does appear to scale back its challenges when the risk of escalation is high, which is consistent with the external deterrent threat binding at times (though this is subject to standard endogeneity concerns that exist in the multivariate regression setting).

Additionally, we also find that Russian activity is inversely associated with decreased resolve and increased costs of its challenges, as approximated by a geographical "loss of strength gradient."[40] Based on observations 3 and 5, this suggests that Russian behavior is also driven by its internal efficiency constraint binding at times.

Statistical Findings

To explain observed patterns of Russian GZC, we analyze independent variables such as NATO membership and geographical proximity, and control variables such as democracy, GDP per capita, population, nuclear status, military expenditure, etc. We find that both NATO membership and distance from Russia decrease the intensity of Russian intervention against European states. These results provide evidence that Russian behavior is shaped by NATO's deterrent threat.

Figure 14.4 plots the count and average intensity of Russian gray-zone operations since 1994. The line represents annual average intensity. Bars denote the number of interventions annually. Contrary to descriptions of GZC as the product of an expansive technological portfolio, there does not appear to be a clear temporal pattern in the intensity or frequency of activity. Instead, 2004 represents the most intense overall Russian interventions and 2014 experienced the highest number of interventions (most of which were associated with Ukraine).

Figure 14.5 depicts a pattern of the geographical coverage of Russian conflict events in Europe. Shading represents the highest intensity of Russian intervention in each European state. Russia appears to be willing to use

---

[40] Boulding 1962; Posen 2003.

GRAY ZONE 359

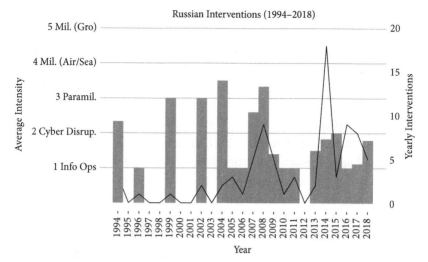

Fig. 14.4 Intensity of Russian intervention across time

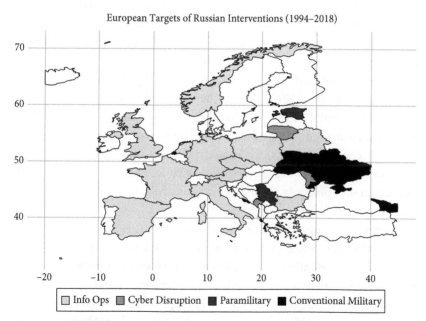

Fig. 14.5 Geographic representation of Russian intervention

360 ELEMENTS OF DETERRENCE

more force in countries in its "near abroad," relative to countries further away. Interpreting this geographic pattern on its own is difficult, as distance from Russia is plausibly related to Russian interest or resolve, ease of conducting operations, or the impact, or even the determinants of NATO membership. This pattern thus highlights the need for more sophisticated analysis.

Consistent with the discussion on the external deterrent threat (observation 1), we propose that NATO's willingness (or unwillingness) to fight critically shapes Russian gray-zone behavior. NATO members plausibly possess lower costs for fighting since they can rely on collective security, meaning they may possess a reduced willingness to tolerate aggressive low-level behavior from Russia. If Russia is responding to NATO's deterrent threat, we expect NATO states to experience less intense Russian activity.

Consistent with observation 1, when facing NATO members, Russia undertook lower-intensity challenges. For relevant NATO states, the odds of a non-cyber, non-information attack (categories 3, 4, or 5) are 46% lower than the odds of experiencing a cyberattack, an information attack, or no attack. Consistent with the discussion of the internal-efficiency constraint in observations 3 and 5, insofar as military power is affected by a loss of strength gradient, Russian gray-zone operations will decrease as Russia has less resolve over the issue or faces greater costs for conducting operations when the internal efficiency constraint binds.

Naturally these findings can co-exist, suggesting that Russian motives for the scope of their GZC vary case-by-case. Plausibly, Russian valuation for the stakes and ease of operation arguably increases in regions deeper within its "Near Abroad" than for areas well beyond it; when Russia's internal efficiency constraint binds, we should (and do) observe less revisionist behavior as distance grows. Nevertheless, what we observe is still consistent with deterrence plausibly playing a restraining role in Russia's level of gray-zone challenge.

Together, this suggests that Russian behavior is shaped by the external deterrent threat in some cases and its own internal efficiency constraint in other cases. Importantly, it is not just that NATO membership deters Russian aggression, but that NATO membership alters the intensity of Russian aggression. NATO members are not increasingly the victims of GZC because Russia is using a novel form of effective conflict they could not before. Rather, our results suggest that Russia is using gray-zone forms of conflict because Western deterrence has taken its best options off the table.

Selected Case Studies

The quantitative analysis can be thought of as a coarse technique for considering empirical trends. Our quantitative analyses proxy NATO membership and geographical distance for the deterrence gradient. A qualitative analysis allows us to add more nuance by considering relative Russian and Western interests.

Here we briefly consider three major cyber campaigns attributed to Russia that feature prominently in cybersecurity literature on cyberconflict: Estonia, Georgia, and Ukraine. These cases are typically highlighted as examples of the increasing potential of GZC, making them a most likely case for the conventional efficiency logic. We follow a most similar case study design in selecting cases that feature cyberattacks by the same contiguous challenger (Russia) but differ in other military instruments employed.[41] A summary of the extent of Russian intervention in each case is provided in Table 14.1.

Russia has an interest in all of its border states and could intervene with relative ease. If Russian intervention were motivated only by internal values in every case, we should not expect to see a systematic pattern correlated with indicators of deterrence. But that is not what we find. Instead, we see a gradient of Western deterrence conditioning Russian choices.

There are many potential explanations for Russian aspirations in each instance. Here we set aside Russia's foreign policy formulation and focus instead on geopolitical context and military effectiveness. As the deterrent threat from NATO becomes more salient moving eastward from Estonia (where NATO intervention is most plausible) to Georgia (where NATO intervention is least plausible), Russia pursues its international objectives with greater intensity. As a Western deterrent response becomes less likely,

Table 14.1 Deterrence gradient in major Russian gray-zone conflicts

Russian Operations	Estonia (2007)	Ukraine (2014–21)	Georgia (2008)	Ukraine (2022–)
Nuclear Threats				X
Conventional Warfare			X	X
Special Operations		X	X	X
Cyber Operations	X	X	X	X

[41] Bennett and Elman 2007.

362   ELEMENTS OF DETERRENCE

and as Russia is more invested in the stakes of the conflict, for various reasons, Russia is more willing to bring more force to bear.

Ukraine is the exception that proves the rule. Ukraine in 2014 (where NATO intervention was less plausible than Estonia but perhaps more plausible than Georgia) sees a middle level of intensity, with cyberattacks and obfuscated ground forces but no open conventional warfare. Whereas Russia had a relatively free hand in Georgia, it was more constrained in Ukraine, even though it arguably cared more about the stakes in Ukraine. While it is plausible that Russia was more constrained by internal efficiency in Georgia, external deterrence seems more relevant in Ukraine.

For Ukraine in 2022, this case exhibits the highest intensity of all, replete with nuclear threats missing from the previous cases. This is an obvious exception to the geographical deterrence gradient. However, we argue that the complicating dynamics of Ukraine in 2022 can only be understood path-dependently in the context of Ukraine in 2014–21. Deterrence failed in 2022, ironically enough, because it succeeded in 2014. Moreover, intrawar deterrence has kept the fighting largely confined to the conventional level and within the borders of Ukraine (as of this writing).

Estonia (2007)

Estonia is the case with the most restrained Russian aggression. The Baltic states formally joined NATO in 2004 receiving only muted protests from Moscow. Later in 2007, as Putin's foreign policy took on a more combative tenor, the relocation of a Soviet statue in Tallinn triggered a wave of DDoS attacks targeting Estonian banks and government sites.[42] A symbolic affront to Russian pride was met with symbolic protest. The attacks were carried out by "patriotic hackers" with tacit encouragement from Moscow and constituted one of the most disruptive cyber campaigns witnessed up to this time.

Yet no one issued any clear demands or claimed responsibility, the attacks were effectively mitigated, and Estonia did not reinstall the statue.[43] Estonia's defense minister considered but ultimately rejected invoking Article V, the

---

[42] Schmidt 2013.

[43] In the context of our model, the relocated statue represented a new "status quo," where Estonia could engage in independent, nationalist, possibly anti-Russian policy choices. The Russian cyberattack was a (largely futile) attempt to undermine the Estonian government's ability to behave in this manner.

GRAY ZONE 363

collective defense clause of the NATO treaty, instead treating the episode as a domestic law enforcement matter.[44]

Had Estonia not been a NATO member, this consideration would not even have been a possibility, and Russia might well have chosen to act more aggressively.[45] Although counterfactuals for the Estonian case are by definition not observable, the fact that Russia engaged in high-intensity aggression against Moldova and Georgia during the 2005 to 2009 period while limiting its attacks against Lithuania, Poland, and the United States to cyberattacks and information operations provides suggestive evidence that Russia was clearly using much less force in cases where the defender was more capable or better protected than in cases where a target was weak and isolated politically. The unsettled legal status of a cyberattack in 2007 both enabled and constrained Russia in this respect.[46]

Russia and Estonia each understood that NATO was highly unlikely to retaliate for an ambiguous and plausibly deniable outburst, so long as Russia did not inflict serious harm and the level of aggression remained well below the perceived threshold for an Article V response. Overall, in the Estonian case Russian moves are consistent with a desire to avoid escalation. In the aftermath, Estonia overhauled its cyber defenses and established a NATO cybersecurity center, inhibiting future Russian provocations in the gray zone.

Georgia (2008)

Georgia is the case with the most Russian aggression (prior to 2022). The NATO Bucharest Summit Declaration in April 2008 announced the potential for a Georgian and Ukrainian pathway to NATO membership. This, alongside Kosovo's declaration of independence, triggered a secession crisis in South Ossetia and Abkhazia. Russia announced that it would unilaterally increase peacekeepers in Abkhazia, and hostilities broke out later that year. Georgia was wracked by DDoS service attacks that were encouraged by Moscow, much like Estonia.[47]

Unlike the Estonia case, Russia also deployed columns of conventional armor, naval bombardments, and special operations forces. This case is often cited as an example of how cyberspace can enhance military cross-domain operations, but even more important was Russia's relatively free hand. Russia

[44] Traynor 2007.
[45] Estonians also may not have felt emboldened to provoke Russia in the first place without NATO protection.
[46] Joubert 2012.   [47] Deibert, Rohozinski, and Crete-Nishihata 2012.

364   ELEMENTS OF DETERRENCE

chose whatever tools it needed to accomplish its objectives and did not pull its punches. NATO counteraction in the Caucuses was unlikely because Georgia was deep in Russia's traditional sphere of influence and NATO members were publicly worried about Russia's reaction to Georgia joining NATO's Membership Action Plan (MAP).

While Russia's tactical performance left much to be desired, the mission was a strategic success that ended the conversation about Georgia joining NATO. Georgia's location—with Tbilisi a mere 80 miles from the Russian border—makes it a security liability in the eyes of many Western leaders.[48] Indeed, the Russian intervention served to clarify the stakes of Western interference in Russia's near abroad.

Ukraine (2014–21)

The first phase of the war in Ukraine falls in between Estonia and Georgia in terms of conflict intensity. Consistent with the logic of NATO's deterrent threat binding, as discussed above, Russian actions in Ukraine were more extensive than those in Estonia, but (prior to 2022) much less than what occurred in Georgia.

In eight years of protracted low-level conflict, there occurred neither large-scale combined arms warfare, as in Georgia, nor unrestrained ethnic cleansing.[49] Russia could have exerted greater military effort, but instead it emphasized cyberattacks,[50] disinformation campaigns, special operations, and military aid to proxy forces. Even though NATO had no formal commitment to Ukraine, conflict in a country that borders four NATO allies (Poland, Slovakia, Hungary, Romania) was implicitly shaped by the possibility of Western intervention, risking nuclear escalation in the process.

As a result, we conjecture that Russia acted circumspectly and relatively ineffectively. Endemic Russian cyberattacks and information operations had little impact on battlefield events during the proxy war phase of the conflict.[51] Even as social media manipulation is supposedly a Russian specialty, pro-Kremlin narratives did not take hold in western ukraine.[52] By and large, Russian subversion failed to influence Kyiv (other than pushing it further westward).[53]

---

[48] Driscoll and Maliniak 2016, p. 590.   [49] Driscoll and Steinert-Threlkeld 2020.
[50] This includes a pair of disruptions of the electrical power grid more severe than anything witnessed in the other cases, yet still temporary and reversible.
[51] Kostyuk and Zhukov 2019.   [52] Driscoll and Steinert-Threlkeld 2020.
[53] Maschmeyer 2021.

The alternative hypothesis is that efficiency rather than deterrence drives variation in Russian intervention in all cases. One might argue that Russia simply tends to use more force in the conflicts it cares more about. For example, one might argue that Russia places a very different value on the outcome in Ukraine than Estonia. Russia's historical ties with Estonia are weaker, so Russia let Estonia join NATO without a fight in 2004. By contrast, Russia had supported Georgian separatists since the early 1990s and was highly resolved to prevent Western encroachment. Russia had more expansive goals in Georgia, and so it used more force. In Georgia, Russia used as much force as needed. The internal efficiency constraint was binding.

The same cannot be said about Ukraine, however, especially in comparison with Georgia. While Georgia may be the birthplace of Stalin, it is also a peripheral outpost in the Caucuses far from Moscow. By contrast, the Black Sea port of Sevastopol makes Crimea strategically important, and NATO forces in Ukraine would be perceived as a dagger pointing at Moscow. The seat of the medieval Kievan Rus empire is also more salient in Russian nationalist mythology than Georgia ever was. If Russian moves in Ukraine were motivated by only internal value calculations and not constrained by external deterrence, then we would expect far more robust, and more overt, Russian military efforts in Ukraine.

Yet, despite Russia's undoubted higher valuation for the stakes in Ukraine, Russia showed more restraint there for eight years. The pattern of Russian intervention is consistent with the deterrence gradient despite variation in Russian valuation of the stakes.

Of course, Russian restraint ended spectacularly in the February 2022 invasion. Clearly, geography is not destiny. Deterrence held in Ukraine, until it didn't. What changed?

Ukraine (2022–)

Russia employed far more force in Ukraine than Georgia, and for a much longer time, from 2022 onward. Russia began a major mobilization in late 2021 and a full scale invasion in February 2022. Russia initially lunged for the Kyiv but its offensive was defeated. The war shifted to the east in a grinding war of attrition and occasional breakthroughs, and Russia stepped up a campaign of punishment bombings against civilian targets. More ominously, both Moscow and Washington have made not-so-veiled threats to use nuclear weapons if the conflict spills over onto Russian or NATO soil, respectively.

366 ELEMENTS OF DETERRENCE

At first blush, this seems like an exception to the geographical deterrence gradient. Russia's initial decision to enter the gray zone followed the geographical deterrence gradient, as argued above. We believe that the external deterrent constraint was binding in the first phase of the war in Ukraine, leading Russia to pull its punches. The prospect—and reality—of Western support for Ukraine continued to increase throughout the gray-zone period of the war, exemplified by Ukraine becoming a NATO Enhanced Opportunities Program Partner in 2020.

Yet, the 2022 escalation must be understood in terms of Russian declining performance in the gray zone prior to 2022. It is clear that Russia has long placed great value on the political future of Ukraine. It placed a high value on the stakes of the conflict, but it initially pulled its punches because of deterrence. As the future prospects of its gray-zone strategy in Ukraine soured, however, Russia became willing to run more risk by mobilizing conventional forces on Ukraine's border and preparing a swift regime change operation.

Such a move may not have been attractive in 2014, but it may have become Russia's least bad option in 2022. Russia thus made the decision to escalate from a losing GZC to a more intensive conventional war. Russia became willing to risk a war in 2022 that it was not in 2014. How can we explain this?

Escalation Dynamics

In this section we explore one further implication of our model and use it to offer a tentative explanation for Russian escalation in 2022.

Consider a scenario where, in equilibrium, the challenger chooses a conservative challenge that always results in GZC and avoids the risk of war. The challenger eschews more aggressive moves that might constitute a more productive form of GZC but would sometimes result in war. As the defender becomes more capable at GZC, however, this constrains how productive GZC can be for the challenger. The challenger's payoff to GZC declines, while the challenger's war payoffs remain the same. This means that the "downside" of a more aggressive challenge—the game ending in war—now does not look as bad to the challenger given that it is doing worse playing it safe.

It may seem intuitive that improvements in a defender's capacity to counter gray-zone aggression should reinforce the strength of deterrence, but this is not necessarily the case. Sometimes the defender getting better at GZC will effectively deter the challenger—convince the challenger not to challenge and accept the "status quo"—but other times this change will encourage the challenger to behave more aggressively and risk a war.

On the Defender's Gray-Zone Costs

Figure 14.6 illustrates this argument. This figure has the same dimensions as Figures 14.1 and 14.2 above. The difference is that, whereas the previous sub-figures varied the GZC costs for the *challenger*, here we vary the GZC costs for the *defender*. This makes all the difference.

The intuition here is that there is a difference between costs and power, as we have argued throughout the book. Power is about creating effects on the battlefield by countering and overcoming enemy action. Costs are more about generating power and absorbing the impact of enemy power. The costs

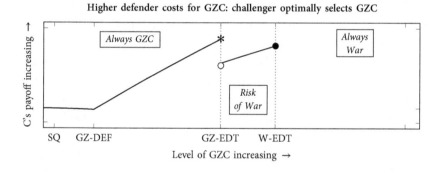

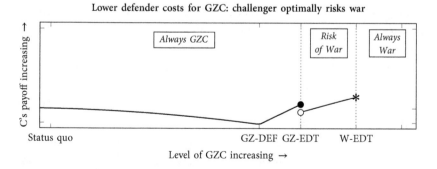

Fig. 14.6 Escalation dynamics in gray-zone conflict

368 ELEMENTS OF DETERRENCE

of GZC are simply a measure of efficiency. Power in GZC depends on the interaction of two forces. Increases in power for one side of a contest must translate into a relative decrease in power for the other. Insofar as one side can increase its battlefield performance at lower cost (e.g., through more precise weapons, better intelligence, better training, more proxy forces, etc.), a decline in costs for one side might also translate into a decline in power for the other.

We capture this relationship in the model as the point at which the defender can effectively counter the challenger in GZC. In the figures this is the point labeled GZ-DEF, or the kink in the GZC curve. A challenger will generally perform better above GZ-DEF, otherwise all of its efforts will be countered by the defender. In Figures 14.1 and 14.2 above, GZ-DEF was fixed. We allowed the challenger's costs to change, but the GZC effectiveness of the defender did not. In Figure 14.6, however, we allow the defender's GZC costs to vary. As the defender's costs decline—as the defender gets better at GZC—the point GZ-DEF shifts to the right.

In the top panel of Figure 14.6, defender GZC costs are high, and GZ-DEF is low. Here the challenger attains the greatest payoff by going all the way to GZ-EDT, yet never risking war. It is worthwhile noting what the challenger is *not* doing. It could risk war by going to W-EDT, which would result in a greater payoff if the game ends in GZC against an unresolved defender, but would also result in a much lower payoff if the game ends in war against a resolved defender. Here, the downside of going to W-EDT and risking war is so much worse than the payoff of playing it safe and stopping at GZ-EDT that it will not take the risk.

In the bottom panel, defender GZC costs are low, and GZ-DEF is high. Here the challenger is better off going all the way to W-EDT and sometimes risking war. Why? As the defender gets better at GZC, the challenger's payoff for all GZC outcomes is much worse, certainly compared to the top panel (i.e., the utility curve is much lower). Given this general decline in its fortunes, the challenger now thinks about its least bad options. Going only to GZ-EDT as before is now so much worse for the challenger, in fact, that the downside of risking war is only slightly less than the payoff at GZ-EDT. The challenger now does so poorly in GZC that war now does not look nearly as bad. The risk of war at W-EDT now becomes relatively more attractive.

The tragedy is readily apparent. In the upper panel, the challenger maximizes GZC without risking war. This is a classic manifestation of the stability-instability paradox. Deterrence is credible at a high level but not at a low lever. The challenger goes right up to the red line. Given the failure of deterrence at this lower level, it is natural for the defender to start investing in defensive strategies. By doing so however, the defender begins to change the challenger's calculus. Restrained GZC is no longer attractive as a way of designing around deterrence. In the bottom panel, the challenger is more willing to risk the very war that it hoped to avoid in the top panel. Thus the challenger is willing to tolerate the downside risk of war in order to attain a greater upside of a more aggressive challenge.

We do not claim that decreases in the defender's gray-zone costs always leads to war. As the defender gets better at GZC, the challenger could instead be pressured out of challenging altogether and instead accept the status quo. A key factor that determines whether decreases in defender gray-zone costs result in the challenger switching from GZC to war or peace is the challenger's *resolve*.

When the challenger possess a high resolve, a decrease in defender costs are more likely to result in war. These finding can be summarized in observation 7.

Observation 7: Decreases in the defender's gray-zone costs can lead to war, especially when the challenger's resolve is high.

Explaining Russian Escalation in Ukraine

Until this point, we have discussed the defender's gray-zone capabilities stemming from technological capabilities. There is an alternate interpretation as well; defender costs could be influenced by the defender's prior, unmodeled moves in the game that set up current gray-zone operations. For example, if the defender aggressively pursued counterinsurgency operations against foreign-backed rebels before this game began, the defender could be in a better position to pursue aggressive GZC within the game. This interpretation illustrates how it is not just latent, exogenous costs that influence the challenger's activity. Rather, war can result from the defender behaving too aggressively in prior gray actions against a highly resolved challenger.

This final interpretation has important policy consequences for interpreting events in Ukraine since February 2022. After roughly eight years of GZC in Ukraine, Russia dramatically changed course by invading Ukraine, thus initiating a highly aggressive war. This escalation raises an important question about GZC: why, if subversion is such an efficient way of revising

370 ELEMENTS OF DETERRENCE

the status quo without triggering open war, would Russia choose to accept the costs and risks of threatening just such a war?

Our research poses one answer to this question. Over the previous eight years, through internal improvements and external support, Ukraine improved at fighting in the gray zone. This made the gray-zone strategy increasingly untenable for Russia. Indeed, the war was just pushing Kyiv further West over time and encouraging more Western support in terms of training, intelligence, and some material capabilities. Our model suggests there could be a connection between Western-enabled improvements in Ukrainian gray-zone capabilities (2014–21) and the Russian escalation that followed (2022 onward).

Of course, we cannot say for certain that this element drove Russia escalation; it is exceptionally difficult to identify what drives international decision making. For example, it could be that Russia came to view itself as more of a declining power in the lead up to the 2022 invasion, perhaps due to arms transfers to Ukraine or the warming relations between NATO and Ukraine.[54] It could have been something peculiar in the transition between the Trump and Biden administrations. Thus, its decision to invade would have been independent from battlefield events in Ukraine. Yet this decision remains puzzling if we assume that GZC was delivering more benefits than costs for Russia.

The initial phase of the invasion is also suggestive. Russia appears to have wildly overestimated its capabilities and underestimated Ukraine (to include Western willingness to provide weapons and intelligence). Moscow's initial lunge on Kyiv attempted to achieve regime change on the cheap, but it failed. In other words, Russia was willing to move into the center region of Figure 14.6, but it misjudged the willingness and ability of the defender to go to war.

In the later phases of the war, as well, it is notable that the war has remained restricted (as of this writing) to the borders of Ukraine. Several classes of weapons have not yet been employed within them. At this higher level, then, the deterrent constraint is still binding. Intrawar deterrence continues to shape the conduct of the war, even as interwar deterrence failed to prevent it.

Our model suggests an important implication for future policy: challengers with high resolve, when faced with worse options within the GZC policy space, may seek more aggressive means of conducting international

---

[54] Benson and Smith 2022.

politics. In effect, because of the defender's improvements in GZC, it ceases to become an attractive intermediate option for the challenger. The gray zone becomes more black and white. The counter-intuitive implication is that for defenders that wish to avoid a war, it may be worthwhile to make some concessions in the gray zone. If GZC is a pressure release valve short of war, defensive improvements in GZC can shut off the valve.

Every Silver Lining's Got a Touch of Gray

Gray-zone conflict occurs when capable actors intentionally limit the intensity or capacity of aggression and refrain from escalation. Deterrence shapes the way that conflict emerges, but it may not suppress conflict altogether. The good news is that GZC may be symptomatic of deterrence success. Adversaries could be "designing around" deterrence in an effort to avoid the anticipated retaliation of the defender.[55] The bad news is that GZC probes the threshold of deterrence effectiveness. We expect conflict severity to be greater wherever there are questions about the willingness or ability of defenders to respond forcefully.

An adversary is seldom passive. There will always be attempts at end-runs or push-back, even when deterrence is credible. It is thus important to think carefully before overextending commitments where credibility is in doubt.

Just as there is a gray zone between war and peace, the distinction between effective and ineffective deterrence is also fuzzy. Doubling down on deterrence in the gray zone can mitigate conflict in some cases but provoke escalation in the others. Wherever deterrence is credible, or the challenger's resolve is low, challengers can be expected to exercise restraint as they probe to see what they can get away with. Wherever deterrence is not credible or challengers are highly resolved, however, a challenger will be more emboldened to use whatever means they have at their disposal to meet their objectives, limited only by internal efficiency constraints.

We have used the same cases that have raised alarm about the dangers of GZC to suggest the validity of an alternative explanation. The evidence suggests that Russia may systematically reduce the intensity of its interventions due to deterrence, employing a greater variety of means with more

---

[55] Stein 1982; Lieberman 2012.

lethal intensity where deterrence is weakest but conducting only ambiguous information operations where deterrence is most robust.

The conventional wisdom is right that Russian interventions are paradigmatic exemplars of GZC, but it is wrong about Russian motivations and the effectiveness of these operations. Revisionist powers have not discovered a secret formula or novel tools destined to destabilize Western democracies or undermine NATO's deterrence posture. Rather it acts opportunistically as circumstances enable it to hassle adversaries and their clients without risking a costly military confrontation.

The flip side of this logic, however, is that Russia is willing to call NATO's bluffs in cases where it can reasonably expect that NATO is unwilling to intervene. In Georgia, and even more so in Chechnya, Russian willingness to prioritize effectiveness at the price of efficiency is clear. Ukraine after 2021 provides a more nuanced, and more dangerous, illustration of this general logic.

The very fact that an adversary opts to engage in limited conflict suggests both vulnerabilities and opportunities. Instead of worrying about Western paralysis in response to Russian cunning, we can acknowledge that NATO has already blocked Russia from wielding even greater influence. NATO's implicit general deterrence posture has arguably succeeded in keeping more extreme forms of Russian aggression in check. The unfortunate fact remains, however, that a simple remedy for GZC does not exist, if only because there is always some ability to "design around" deterrence.

We may be able to choose *how* our adversary confronts us, but not *whether*. Deterrence is not an on/off switch, but a rheostat, providing a range of causes and variable effects. Gray-zone conflict is, then, not simply deterrence failure but also a modest kind of success.

15

Conclusion

Summary and Implications

The past thirty years have borne witness to a highly unusual historical period. In the aftermath of the implosion of the Soviet Union, the United States became the indisputable "hegemon," or the most powerful state in the international system. For a transitory "unipolar moment," America's role as dominant power went largely uncontested, not only because the United States was so powerful, but also because it appeared to be uninterested in blatant territorial conquest or physical plunder. The bulk of US objectives seemed at least minimally acceptable to other capable states.

But America's unipolar moment began to fade almost as soon as it began. The United States dissipated its strength and global goodwill through a series of unpopular, protracted military interventions in the Balkans, Afghanistan, Iraq, and elsewhere. Numerous governments and domestic populations grew dissatisfied or resentful about US leadership. The American liberal order enabled China to grow rich, in turn financing China's military build up. Russia invaded Ukraine and initiated the largest land war in Europe since World War II, right on NATO's doorstep. And war is raging between Israelis and Arabs once again. The new century thus presents a set of complex, dangerous, and tragic tensions, conditions that seem more reminiscent of the Cold War than the "End of History."

The world is reorienting to a more typical historical environment in which political and military advantages are contextual rather than absolute. Where and how nations choose to compete, fight, deter, or deceive affects their prospects for success. Choices about whether and how to respond to any given action by an adversary—subject to a range of available options— become more consequential. American hegemony is no longer assured, but neither is Chinese ascendancy. War between these two nations cannot be ruled out, motivated perhaps by opportunity or prevention. Nor can the course of great power war be readily predicted, with outcomes ranging from interminable gray-zone conflict or protracted stalemate to thermonuclear

Elements of Deterrence: Strategy, Technology, and Complexity in Global Politics. Erik Gartzke and Jon R. Lindsay, Oxford University Press. © Oxford University Press 2024. DOI: 10.1093/oso/9780197754443.003.0015

annihilation. In other words, strategy matters again, as it typically has throughout history.

As the world reverts to normal in strategic terms, "winning" in any given competitive arena has also become more complex, contingent, and incomplete. The calculus of power is complicated by the availability of a growing range of technologies that can be used to exchange, reassure, impose, subvert, or subdue. Developments in networking, data processing, artificial intelligence, embedded computing, robotics, commercial space, and quantum computing may improve both economic and military performance, cooperation as well as competition. The implications are profoundly uncertain for the future of world affairs; this should be troubling given the role of uncertainty in precipitating warfare emphasized throughout this book. Even if the costs of great power war remain restrictive, the same cannot be said about other forms of conflict.

Power has often enabled strong nations to achieve their most cherished goals, or even (occasionally) to get most of what they want, but no nation can typically expect to get everything. Establishing priorities, and following through on them, thus becomes the most important step in re-centering the national security policy of the United States; this must be reflected in force planning, posture, diplomacy, and crisis response. Yet the very complexity of these activities in the modern context makes implementing national security policy ever more demanding and incomplete.

This concluding chapter proceeds in three sections. First, we summarize our core argument about the multiple elements of deterrence. We highlight some of the trade-offs imposed by four different aspects of deterrence strategy, and we review the empirical evidence for the effects of specialized military technologies on strategic stability. Second, we apply these concepts to the contemporary debate over US grand strategy toward the People's Republic of China (PRC). As we demonstrate, the various schools of thought in this debate stand as effective proxies for the four types of preferences over outcomes and policy trade-offs that we describe in our effort to disaggregate deterrence theory. Factions differ to a much greater extent in terms of what they want to achieve than in how they imagine the United States can get there. Indeed, each perspective espouses the same nominal approach: "deterrence." Differences between perspectives in the grand strategy debate are largely characterized by which of the elements of deterrence a given faction chooses to highlight or alternately discount. Finally, we conclude that the problem of political preferences trumps the issue of technological

CONCLUSION   375

complexity. There is no meaningfully "right" way to combine the means of competition and conflict without a clear sense of preferred political ends.

The Complexity of Deterrence

Whenever there is competition in multiple domains and uneven rates of innovation across them, political and military strategy takes on a "rock, paper, scissors" quality. Competitors tend to seek out and exploit each other's weaknesses, rather than confronting their strengths directly, regardless of how much nations or actors prepare. Actors may try to encourage an adversary to focus on apparent opportunities and then exploit their initiative, rather than expecting an attacker to engage with the target's strengths. Military defense-in-depth, for example, works by deliberately presenting a vulnerable avenue of approach to lure enemy forces deep into a kill zone. After German U-boats sank the RMS Lusitania in 1915, to take another example, the Royal Navy began deploying decoy cargo vessels known as "Q Ships" to entice U-boats into conducting an attack, revealing their position, and thereby enabling the British to attack German submarines with hidden guns or friendly submarines.[1] Strategy consists of careful planning, assessment, and implementation of ways to lure an adversary toward preferred, apparent vulnerabilities, and away from other, more harmful weakness or inadequacies.

But in a complex, multidomain environment, there are invariably more ways to do this, and an increasing number of ways to fail. An underappreciated aspect of this process of growing strategic complexity is that conflict involves not only combinations of multiple types of forces or policy instruments but also multiple political objectives. Discussions about the technological complexity of "cross-domain," "comprehensive," or "integrated" deterrence have become a fixture in national security discourse. At the same time, they often paper over difficult political trade-offs embodied in technological capabilities. Deterrence in practice mobilizes a variety of moving parts, even as the classical theory of deterrence tends to conflate these differences.

In this book we have sought to unravel and analyze these different elements of deterrence. We have argued that deterrence strategy is actually a

[1] Couillard 2023, pp. 19–22.

376   ELEMENTS OF DETERRENCE

bundle of different means *and ends*. We have also argued, and presented systematic evidence to show, that differentiated instruments of war tend to be specialized for the pursuit of different objectives. Different tools of national power will alternately favor, or discount, various aspects of the deterrence rubric. The core tension and challenge in conducting strategy is then prioritizing among the multiple objectives subsumed within the idea of "integrated" deterrence. No technology or combination of technologies can realize all desirable objectives at the same time, to the same degree. Indeed, it is in the nature of specialization that, with each innovation in our ability to harm, more tensions emerge among the various competing goals housed within the deterrence rubric.

Deterrence strategy cannot be a "silver bullet" for achieving every national objective in all situations. To the contrary, the effort to dissuade is an invitation to struggle among different, competing national security goals. This means that deterrence cannot be fully "integrated" for all ends, ways, and means. Governments must figure out what they are willing to fight for, how they are willing to fight, and where they are willing to compromise. Policy makers often show an aversion to reckoning with value trade-offs, at least in public. Domestic rivals are sure to seize on any disagreement, so it is tempting to put off answering them, or promise constituents that a strategy or a candidate will deliver all things. Adversaries who suspect that an ambiguous deterrence policy covers over a lack of consensus or resolve may be more willing to call a bluff. Waiting for a crisis to figure out what matters is a recipe for miscalculation, and deterrence failure. Deferring is not deterring. At least in the context of deterrence, a national strategy that does not involve an explicit delineation of preferences is tantamount to no strategy at all.

Multiple Objectives

The rationality of deterrence theory has been extensively criticized.[2] These critiques are important, in part because psychology, organizations, and cultures may affect the determination of preferences. Yet, rationality may not be the most significant obstacle to implementing a successful deterrence policy. Even if we assume that actors make perfectly rational choices, they still have to choose what to prioritize from a bundle of different objectives.

---

[2] Jervis, Lebow, and Stein 1985; Lebow and Stein 1989; Stein 1992; Stein 2017.

CONCLUSION   377

At the same time, what has often been characterized as *ir*rationality may in fact be better characterized as completely comprehensible, if unfortunate, rational pathologies (i.e., bureaucratic politics and other unit-level collective action problems associated with competing domestic political interests and objectives). Indeed, the rational bargaining model itself implies unappreciated tensions across multiple preferences that complicate decision making even for perfectly rational decision makers.

Actors may want to improve strategic stability by reducing the risk of war, or increase prosperity through peaceful commerce. They might also want to improve their confidence in their ability to retain the status quo in any given dispute, or maximize their ability to win a war should significant fighting become necessary. Many would be interested in reducing the political or economic costs of any policy they adopt to achieve these objectives. Each of these is individually desirable. But they are collectively incompatible. Augmenting influence by making more imposing threats generally requires assuming some increased risk of war. Preparing to fight more effectively by enhancing maneuver and stealth is at odds with visibly committing to fight in a particular place. Policies that are cheap, or simple to implement, are easily confused with cheap talk.

Actors thus have to figure out what they care about most in any given situation: political influence, military effectiveness, policy efficiency, or strategic stability. These goals can be pursued through different strategies that we describe in terms of *accommodation, coercion, defense,* and *deception,* respectively. Actors also have to choose what specific tools, plans, postures, and declaratory statements they will employ out of a menu of different options, each of which have different implications for competitors, and for the world around them.

The maintenance of strategic stability, or the absence of escalation, is an important objective—some would claim *the* objective—of any deterrence policy. But peace or stability is not, in fact, the only objective of deterrence. Peace at any price is often considered to be too costly. Appeasement and/or compromise also accomplish the objective of war avoidance, possibly more reliably, at least in the short term. Another objective of deterrence beyond peace and stability, therefore, is the maintenance of the status quo, or even its enhancement. Deterrence, therefore, is also a form of political influence over the distribution of contested assets (i.e., the stakes).

One country's interpretation of the status quo, of course, may look like revisionism to others. The "One China" policy regarding Taiwan is only the most obvious example, with Washington hoping to preserve an independent Taiwan and China looking to reintegrate a wayward province. In

378 ELEMENTS OF DETERRENCE

Eastern Europe, similarly, NATO countries interpret Russian aggression as revisionism, while Russia claims to be re-asserting its historical dominance over a subordinate polity, while also countering an expansionist NATO threat. Either sincerely or for strategic reasons, policy makers will be tempted to identify and focus on a flattering baseline. Countries can, and do, also interpret the status quo more restrictively. Governments will point to elements or aspects of existing conditions as "the status quo" that they want to retain, ignoring features that do not favor their position, or that are relatively unimportant or unattractive from their perspective. Competitors are very likely to refer to competing conceptions of what was, is, and should be the status quo, a reality that is problematic from the perspective of classical deterrence.

Actors will often be tempted to extend promises a bit further than is entirely genuine or necessary in order to increase the scope of their influence. There are many places the United States might like to protect. However, expanding the scope and scale of one's commitments also heightens the risk that an adversary will perceive that any particular commitment is an aggression or a bluff, correctly or incorrectly. The mere ecological presence of bluffing—getting something for next to nothing—also encourages rivals to doubt the credibility of deterrent threats unless they are backed up with costly signals of resolve. A great power seeking to deter must thus balance peace with the extent of its commitments to protect, making an assessment of how much in relative terms it values stability or influence. For a given level of defense effort, increasing the portion of actors, borders, or prerogatives that are subject to promises of protection or retaliation are only achieved at a heightened risk of challenges and, probabilistically, deterrence failure.

Failure to consider this dilemma should tend to make deterrence look fantastic in both senses of the word: very appealing, and totally unrealistic. A more realistic and practical way to think about deterrence is in terms of the trade-off between the objectives of risk and reward. How much of the status quo is one willing to secure, at what price or risk? What costs or risks is the defender willing to absorb in return for an additional increment of influence? One might expect a defender to only extend deterrence to cover portions of its political system and external relationships that it deems sufficiently valuable. However, the notion of "sufficient" is malleable, both relative to circumstances (what is the balance of power, say, between potential adversaries) and to national values (some countries, leaders, or populations care more about some things than others). How will actors decide what issues, territory, or prerogatives matter to them? Classic nuclear deterrence

CONCLUSION 379

theory assumes that survival matters most, and this is certainly plausible, but what goals are worth more moderate risks? What indeed beyond survival might a nation risk a great deal to pursue? The answers are not to be found in deterrence theory.

Policy makers have still other issues to resolve in terms of the means chosen in making deterrence work. These factors are vital in practice but are not well integrated into deterrence theory. At a minimum, the means of deterrence must be cheap relative to the cost of warfare for actors to prefer deterrence to a fight. Leaders who are sensitive to the costs of conflict, or who prefer to expend resources on butter rather than guns, will find deterrence appealing. Deterrence strategy operates through threats of costs or risks, rather than through the actual imposition of such costs (i.e., talk versus action), offering hope of avoiding the financial and humanitarian burden of war. Fighting despoils at least some of the value of the issues or territory in dispute, reducing whatever stakes are being fought over. War also dissipates resources that could be invested in other priorities at home. Preparations for war sink scarce resources into expensive weapons and readiness postures. Deterrence might be attractive, therefore, as a way to avoid the costs of fighting.

However, if the desire for influence is more than a casual bluff, then more effective capabilities will be needed as an insurance policy to hedge against the increased risk of deterrence failure. The more expansive the aims of deterrence, the more that an actor will have to prioritize more expensive forms of power to favorably influence political outcomes. The US decision to develop and sustain a nuclear deterrence strategy to secure Western European allies during the Cold War was at least as much a cost-saving measure as it was an effort to retain the status quo. This might have been achieved through a much larger investment in, and deployment of, conventional military force in Europe, or alternately through commensurate mobilization of NATO's European member states. Yet, the United States eventually invested in additional battlefield options to shore up the lower end of the so-called stability-instability paradox. The Kennedy administration's doctrine of Flexible Response aimed to field additional capability to counter Soviet aggression below the threshold of credible nuclear retaliation. The US military eventually implemented its AirLand Battle doctrine and expensive combined-arms forces to boost American military power in Europe. It was not cheap, and it courted additional risk.[3]

[3] Posen 1991.

380 ELEMENTS OF DETERRENCE

If implementing a credible deterrence policy is costly, then practicing deterrence may become even less appealing, particularly for cost-sensitive actors. If the present value of a heightened military readiness posture for decades on end is more costly than a short, sharp conflict, then possibly the latter will be preferred. If an adversary can capitalize on one's own military advantages relatively quickly and cheaply, perhaps it is better to use one's military power, rather than brandish it.[4]

Innovations that reduce the costs of fighting can make a limited war (or subverting cooperative endeavors) more attractive than trying to credibly defend all possible targets. This may be part of the justification for using drones for counterterrorism.[5] Similarly, cyber exploitation and disinformation operations are attractive precisely because they are so much cheaper than trying to credibly coerce a target into handing over intellectual property or changing opinions. Yet, insofar as many new technologies (cyber operations in particular) rely on secrecy, they are unlikely to persist in the face of disclosure and countermeasures, but non-transparency undermines credible coercion. Military advantages that are difficult to counter and that are likely to persist lend themselves to coercion, while those that are permeable or perishable do not.

Multiple Strategies

In Chapter 3, we went back to first principles to make these implicit trade-offs in deterrence more apparent. Bargaining models of war are increasingly utilized in international relations to account for conflict.[6] Classical deterrence theory assumes that actors make rational choices but does not explicitly incorporate bargaining, which has the effect of artificially restricting deterrence outcomes. Applying modern conceptions of war puts deterrence on a more stable foundation, but also makes the effects of deterrence on war and the stakes more complex and contingent.

Uncertainty is a core cause of war, perhaps *the* cause of war, in bargaining models.[7] Any source of uncertainty can potentially lead to deterrence failure.

---

[4] Other versions of this logic appear as commitment problems, power transitions, or the mis-named Thucydides Trap. Winning today is better than losing tomorrow, whatever the actual time horizon.

[5] Zegart 2018.   [6] Fearon 1995; Wagner 2000; Powell 2002.

[7] Gartzke 1999; W. Reed 2003; Meirowitz and Sartori 2008; Debs and Monteiro 2014; Lindsey 2015; Ramsay 2017; Kaplow and Gartzke 2021. Imperfect information about power or resolve is

CONCLUSION 381

Conversely, improvements in relevant information should enhance stability. We showed in Chapter 11 how information-improving space reconnaissance is associated with (negative) peace and in Chapter 9 that uncertainty-increasing naval forces are associated with more militarized disputes. In Chapter 10, similarly, we showed that reliance on drones creates uncertainty about resolve, which can expand or prolong conflicts.

Stripped to the basics, bargaining models contain four key parameters: demands, power, costs, and uncertainty.[8] Yet the bargaining model is agnostic about whether or why actors should be concerned about any of these in particular situations. Preferences about parameters are exogenous to the model, meaning that we have to look beyond purely strategic interaction to unit-level factors like psychology, ideology, and domestic or organizational politics. Our focus in this book is not the sources of preference, per se, but the systematic patterns of trade-offs that they imply for strategic bargaining processes. We will return to the problem of preferences below.

Actors can manipulate the basic parameters to alter bargaining outcomes like payoffs or stability. An actor can attempt, for instance, to shift the bargaining range or increase its expected value by pressing its *demands*, augmenting its *power*, economizing on *costs*, or reducing *uncertainty*. This, in turn, suggests that there are at least four different objectives that any deterrence policy must balance, namely increasing political *influence*, ensuring military *effectiveness*, improving policy *efficiency*, and bolstering strategic *stability* or reducing the risk of war. To pursue these various objectives, we can identify four "pure" or ideal types of strategy that might be mixed in practice. We described these in Chapter 4, respectively, as *accommodation* (not discussed extensively in this book except in the context of mutually-beneficial economic trade in Chapter 12), *coercion* through costly and thus credible signaling, *defense* through reliable military performance, and *deception* through the exploitation of the efforts or systems of other actors.

Table 15.1 summarizes the relationship between the four basic parameters of the bargaining model, (exogenous) preferences over each, and the general strategies for pursuing them. Table 15.1 also provides an example of specialized means to be used for each strategy. This does not mean that

distinguished from commitment problems—the inability to keep to a deal due to anticipated changes in the balance of power. The latter can also be understood as imperfect information about future behavior. Perfect information about the outcome of future wars that emerge through commitment problems should allow actors to avoid fighting in the first place.

[8] More complex models are possible, but these are the variables used in Fearon 1995. This model already contains multiple trade-offs and is sufficient to reveal how preferences matter.

382 ELEMENTS OF DETERRENCE

Table 15.1 The multiple elements of deterrence

Bargaining Model Parameter	Political Preference	General Strategy	Specialized Means (example)
Demand	Political Influence	Coercion	Nuclear Weapons
Power	Military Effectiveness	Defense	Maneuver Forces
Cost	Policy Efficiency	Deception	Cyber Operations
Uncertainty	Strategic Stability	Accommodation	Economic Trade

instruments cannot be used for multiple strategies, or that there are no other means available, simply that these exemplify the most obvious relationships. We further summarize the differential implications of various means for strategic stability in Table 15.2 and the discussion below.

All of these strategies may be combined together. Deception may be used in war, as in a feinting maneuver or concealment of an ambush. Limited war, similarly, can be used in support of influence or deterrence. And a spy may be coerced into giving up secrets. Yet they each work by a different logic, which gives rise to trade-offs. One important trade-off that came up again and again in this book is between credibility and efficiency. Secrecy, obfuscation, and misdirection are what make it possible for strategies of deception to provide an efficiency advantage. If clandestine sources and methods are revealed, however, the enemy can adopt countermeasures that compromise efficiency and may undermine effectiveness altogether. Similar things can be said about stealthy or maneuverable platforms that spread influence around the battlefield by being difficult to track and target. Capabilities that rely on secrecy and deception are generally ill suited for clear and credible communication.[9]

Multiple Trade-Offs

Figure 15.1 provides a graphical summary of some of the most salient trade-offs confronting decision makers in balancing deterrence objectives. For the axes of Figure 15.1 we have chosen the parameters that are most controllable by policy makers. Policy makers can decide how much of any

---

[9] Some clandestine capabilities or covert activities may be revealed for strategic communication under certain restrictive conditions, as discussed by Carson and Yarhi-Milo 2017; Poznansky and Perkoski 2018; B. Green and Long 2020.

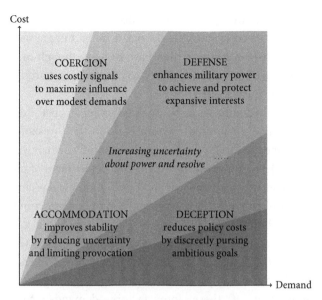

Fig. 15.1 Stability of strategies with different preferences over cost and demand

given contested issue they want to demand, and they can decide how much they want to spend on military capabilities for whatever purpose. The other two parameters are harder to manipulate directly since they depend on the effects of interacting with other, competing actors. Relative military power depends not only on the proportion of military personnel and weapons a state purchases, but also on spending patterns and responses by other states. Power is of course also affected by "soft" factors like doctrine, organization, and morale, the effects of which are again conditional on relational efforts between one's own nation and other states.[10] Uncertainty has many origins, ranging from deliberate bluffing and secrecy to the fog and friction of intelligence and politics.[11] As with power, the presence of ecological uncertainty is social; one state cannot eliminate its own uncertainty about others without their active cooperation.

Although policy makers cannot directly manipulate power and uncertainty, they can affect them indirectly by manipulating costs and demands, which are the factors that sovereign states can control more directly. As costs increase, the bargaining range opens up, which is represented by the

---

[10] S. Biddle 2004; Castillo 2014; Talmadge 2015; Grauer 2016; Lindsay 2020.
[11] Beyerchen 1992; Slantchev and Tarar 2011; Yarhi-Milo 2014; Kaplow and Gartzke 2021.

384 ELEMENTS OF DETERRENCE

expanding gray zone in Figure 15.1.[12] Indeed, one way to conceptualize nuclear war is that its costs subsume the entire bargaining range. Each side would rather concede everything than have to fight, though of course this creates instability within nuclear stability, as competitors search for ways to compete below the nuclear threshold.

These additional resources can be invested either in costly signaling for coercion (deterrence) or limited revision beneath the threshold of armed conflict (gray-zone conflict). Another implication of increasing costs, given the nature of modern military power, is that the deployment of more expensive military forces with exquisite capabilities in multiple domains will tend to create more uncertainty about how they will operate in combat (uncertainty about capabilities). As demands increase, there will also tend to be more uncertainty about how much actors are willing to pay to achieve these higher demands. This increasing uncertainty is represented in Figure 15.1 by growing error bars around the central bargaining range or gray zone.[13]

The combination of these four factors—demands, costs, power, uncertainty—affects the initiation and escalation of crises and conflict (strategic stability), which is one of the most important dynamics in the theory and practice of international politics. Figure 15.1 thus depicts this variation with shades of gray ranging from the highest probability of peace in light gray to the greatest risk of war in dark gray.[14] The expanding gray zone between peace and war in Figure 15.1 captures some of the stability-instability dynamic discussed elsewhere.[15] Even as deterrence may be stable at high cost levels (costly signaling, expensive punishment, large deployments, etc.), actors who really care about an issue have many options

---

[12] This relationship can be understood intuitively by comparing Figure 15.1 with Figures 3.1 and 3.2 in Chapter 3. These are slightly different graphs. The vertical axis of Figures 3.1 and 3.2 represent relative power with *fixed* costs *of war* in Figure 3.1 (and variable costs *of war* in Figure 3.2), but the vertical axis in Figure 15.1 represents the *variable* costs *of all security policies*. The actual balance of power is not perfectly knowable or controllable in Figure 15.1. The different notions of cost in each model are related; some of the assets consumed in war are also reflected in the investments in the forces that can be used in war, peace, or gray-zone conflict. There is a correlation between the costs of preparing for a given war and the costs suffered in that war. The size of the bargaining range in Figure 3.1 is defined by the sum of costs for both actors, which implies that the bargaining range grows with increasing costs. This is reflected in the expanding gray zone in both Figure 3.2 and Figure 15.1. This growing gray zone creates a space for diverse negotiating tactics, short of war.

[13] See Chapter 3 for further discussion about the effects of uncertainty about reservation points.

[14] Note that the bargaining model does not make point predictions. War may or may not emerge due to numerous other "necessary" factors (Gartzke 1999). As uncertainty and options increase with expanding investment in capabilities to influence more expansive demands, the probability of a variety of different manifestations of conflict will increase.

[15] Powell 2015.

CONCLUSION 385

for negotiating "by other means." A general consensus of classical deterrence theory is that threats of mutual assured destruction in the context of state survival offer the greatest strategic stability, but as Glenn Snyder observed, stable deterrence for core interests encourages instability in more peripheral areas, where nations continue to vie for influence through limited, proxy, secret, or guerrilla war.[16]

As modeled in Chapter 14, the emergence of "gray-zone conflict" can be seen as a symptom of successful deterrence. Russia's war in Ukraine, for example, combines high-intensity ground combat bounded by both explicit and implicit nuclear threats in a context of ongoing trade and extensive information operations. A modern twist is that these limited forms of conflict provide a "pressure release valve" for power politics, reducing the likelihood of escalation to major war.[17] In Chapters 13 and 12 we provided an argument and evidence that cyber and non-military conflict, respectively, can be understood in this way. Inverting Snyder's concept thus implies a "instability-stability paradox" as well. If disincentives for wider or more severe conflicts produce incentives for smaller or more limited conflicts, then more opportunities to "go small" may also help competitors not to "go big."

We can thus map the four strategies in Table 15.1 onto Figure 15.1. The "pure" strategy of coercion embodied in classical deterrence finds itself in the top left quadrant. We might describe this as the Theodore Roosevelt theory of deterrence: "speak softly and carry a big stick." States that have modest demands and invest in costly signals to clarify how and where they are willing to act are best able enact coercion—influence without war. However, states are often tempted to use these same capabilities to not only protect the status quo, but improve it. Greater demands—speaking loudly and carrying a big stick—entail greater risk of deterrence failure, which in turn means that a state must be willing and able to fight. The strategy of defense thus maps onto the top right quadrant, where the practice of deterrence can become quite complicated by both posturing and limited conflict in an expanded bargaining range. Taken to the logical extreme, the goal of "pure" defense, of course, is to win the war at any price, not (necessarily) to avoid it.

But countries competing over expansive goals naturally search for ways to limit their risks or costs in blood and treasure. Maneuver, precision targeting, and subversion are attractive ways to increase the coverage of military power at a reduced cost. The strategy of deception thus maps onto the bottom right

---

[16] G. Snyder 1965.   [17] Carson 2018b; Poznansky 2020; Lonergan and Lonergan 2023.

386 ELEMENTS OF DETERRENCE

quadrant of Figure 15.1—demanding more (but perhaps not speaking at all) with a smaller stick. This is the least stable quadrant (deception), located diagonally opposite the most stable quadrant (coercion). Low-cost options and secret maneuvers are antithetical to credibility, and war avoidance. We discussed the tension between technologies that provide efficient military advantages at the price of reduced credibility in Chapter 7 on offensive cyber operations, Chapter 9 on naval forces, and Chapter 10 on automated drones.

The strategy of accommodation, finally, maps onto the bottom left quadrant. Like coercion, accommodation focuses on more limited aims, but unlike coercion, accommodation forgoes provocative military means. Instead, accommodation aims to solve the commitment problem discussed above, whereby capable states with limited aims may be tempted to demand a little bit more. This temptation reflects the classic logic of the security dilemma, in which one state's efforts to improve its security makes other states insecure.[18] This is a dilemma because reducing military costs to reassure other actors also opens a state up to exploitation from revisionists. Increasing military costs will improve strategic stability, but other actors will worry that capabilities will be leveraged for greater influence, prompting arms races to offset capability. Accommodation is a gamble that compromise in demands and defenses will lessen the security dilemma and reduce incentives for arms racing and preventative or preemptive war. In this more stable environment, if the gamble pays off, actors can produce more butter and fewer guns.

The strategy of accommodation is increasingly salient given the growing non-military dimensions of international politics. Economic interdependence matters more in security terms for at least two reasons. First, states that participate in more commercial relationships and other joint endeavors enjoy more (negative) peace. Strategies of accommodation work by fostering bargains, entering into common institutions, or engaging in economic exchange to realize benefits without fighting. As we argued in Chapter 12, economic interdependence encourages states to work within the bargaining range of mutually beneficial deals, rather than going to war. As we showed in Chapter 13, increasing internet penetration, which is a reflection of growing economic globalization, predicts a decrease in war. Yet Chapter 13 also demonstrated an increase in cyberconflict with the rise in interconnectivity.

---

[18] Jervis 1978.

CONCLUSION   387

Second, the same social institutions and mutually beneficial exchange relationships that encourage strategies of accommodation also enable strategies of deception. The difference is that the former involves open cooperation while the latter extracts a secret advantage. Chapter 6 thus argued that intelligence, covert action, and counterintelligence all work by exploiting trust in common organizations and shared systems. Deception actively shapes the balance of power, not unlike strategies of defense as described above. But whereas defense works by forcibly overcoming the target's resistance, deception seeks to trick the target into acting against its own best interests. With more economic interdependence, there is perhaps less military conflict, but more cyber and limited conflict. Accommodation thus tends to lead to a paradoxical sort of stability, with less warfare but more intelligence contests.

Multiple Domains

The trade-offs illustrated in Figure 15.1 tend to manifest as different specialized force structures and postures. In Chapter 4 we explored the subtle strategic differences associated with diverse forms of military and non-military power. Military capabilities are often differentiated according to "domains" such as land, sea, air, space, and cyberspace. Domains may be salient enough to merit a dedicated military service (e.g., the US Army, Navy, Air Force, and Space Force, plus the service-like US Cyber Command which combines like capabilities from the other services). However we label them, there exist different sets of platforms and interactions that have specialized material or operational properties. We have argued that these operational features lend themselves to different strategies, which in turn engage the trade-offs between aspects of deterrence (warning, winning, watching, working) in different ways.

We have presented evidence that different military domains or types of technologies are more or less suited for different political strategies. Forward deployed land forces enhance warning by providing allies and adversaries alike with a costly signal of commitment. Globally mobile naval forces make it possible to project power in more places (more winning), adding to influence, but they are also less effective as commitments to fight in any given location (less warning). Unmanned aerial vehicles or drones can improve battlefield performance while reducing the risk to military personnel (less, cost), but they undermine the informativeness of military force for the same

388 ELEMENTS OF DETERRENCE

reasons (more uncertainty). Satellite reconnaissance, meanwhile, improves mutual information about the balance of power, which lowers the risk of war (more stability). Yet as traditional war becomes less attractive as a means of political competition (more working together), other forms of conflict may become more alluring, exemplified by the growth in cyberconflict (more watching for opportunity).

This implies that integrating all domains for a grand strategy of deterrence, scaling up the benefits of combined arms operations at the tactical or operational level of war, may be a quixotic aspiration. The reason is that combined arms warfare is optimized for winning, but grand strategy is also interested in warning, working, and watching. While combinations of domains can "dial in" overall *military* performance, they are unlikely to overcome *political* trade-offs themselves. A stealthy military capability that can help win a contest with surprise is not likely to be effective at signaling intent. Similarly, troop deployments will not overcome the winning-warning trade-off, at least in terms of platforms. An adversary may remain uncertain about the true level of resolve or balance of power, given any combination of capabilities.

Strategic stability is only one goal among many for deterrence, but it is an important one. In the empirical studies reported in this book, we have used the outbreak of military disputes to operationalize and measure deterrence failure. Deterrence is hard to assess in any given case without extensive evidence of the thinking of decision makers, since success means that nothing happens. But tendencies can be measured with more confidence. When wars are systematically less likely under conditions that theory anticipates, we gain confidence in the theory. We thus use the weakening of negative peace as an indication of the instability of deterrence. In Table 15.2 we summarize evidence for how specific choices of means affect the risk of conflict. Each of them can have a stabilizing or destabilizing effect for different reasons, which are detailed in the middle column. Note that a recurrent theme is the importance of information (uncertainty) for strategic stability. There are many nuances here, of course, as these mechanisms may have implications for different types of conflict (indicated in parentheses in the right column as needed).

In sum, actors that are concerned about controlling the chances of escalation and other adverse outcomes will prioritize the stabilization and minimization of risks. Political accommodation and economic trade both have the potential to reduce the risks of war, perhaps at some sacrifice in terms of power or influence. However, actors that seek to influence others to accede

CONCLUSION   389

Table 15.2 Implications of different means for strategic stability

Means	Mechanism	Risk of Conflict
Nuclear Weapons (Ch. 2)	Extreme Lethality	↓ (major war)
Cyber Operations (Chs. 5 & 6)	Secret & Reversible	↓ (war), ↑ (deception)
Cyber vs. Nuclear C3 (Ch. 7)	Secret Advantage	↑ (nuclear instability)
Ground Deployments (Ch. 8)	Costliness	↓
Naval Forces (Ch. 9)	Flexibility	↑
Remotely Piloted Vehicles (Ch. 10)	Force Protection	↑ (protraction)
Space Reconnaissance (Ch. 11)	Visible Collection	↓
Interdependence (Ch. 12)	Substitution	↓ (mil.), ↑ (non-mil.)
Asymmetric Trade (Ch. 12)	Nonsubstitution	↑ (bilateral)
Internet Penetration (Ch. 13)	Information Value	↓ (mil.), ↑ (cyber)
Alliance (Ch. 14)	Cautious Challenger	↓ (war), ↑ (gray zone)
Gray-Zone Defenses (Ch. 14)	Resolved Challenger	↑ (escalation)

to their demands to revise or maintain the status quo, will attempt to bolster the credibility of threats and assurances. Nuclear weapons and forward deployments of land forces have attractive features for deterrence strategies that prioritize influence. If actors care most about gaining and maintaining a favorable balance of power, they should try to maximize war-fighting effectiveness. Highly mobile and lethal multidomain forces, particularly in the air and sea domains, are well suited for defense strategies, but with some liabilities in terms of credibility. Actors that need to economize, finally, either because of resource constraints or in order to realize other domestic policy objectives, will adopt ways and means that improve efficiency. Means that rely on information and deception, in particular in space and cyberspace, are especially useful for controlling costs, but may pose more harmful effects in terms of strategic stability if clandestine advantages cannot be revealed.

What does this process of disaggregating deterrence theory provide, in terms of value to practitioners? Our reformulation of deterrence theory reveals that there is considerable complexity lurking at the heart of even a relatively simple, logically coherent, rationalist model of conflict. Any increase in the complexity of an explanation must be justified in terms of an at least commensurate increase in explanatory power. Our answer is that doing so helps to account for a number of theoretical and empirical anomalies that were previously disruptive of deterrence theory or were ignored. In particular, it addresses the increasing sense among observers and practitioners that something is missing from classical conceptions of deterrence. There are many ways in theory and in practice to connect multiple means to multiple ends. Deterrence "success" or "failure" depends as much on one's perspective (i.e., on what the deterring state sought to

390 ELEMENTS OF DETERRENCE

achieve) as on objective factors such as whether a threat was explicit and whether a challenger attacked. This makes deterrence theory more complex, to be sure, but it also allows deterrence to be more relevant to contemporary conditions, and thus practically useful.

Deterrence Trade-Offs in US-China Strategy

An application of these concepts involving the elements of deterrence will prove helpful, to allow us to apply, and readers to "see," the efficacy and utility of the theoretical framework we have outlined here. Contemporary debates about US deterrence strategy in East Asia offer a particularly important and salient example.

In a rare public speech on April 14, 2022, CIA Director William Burns described "an increasingly adversarial China" as "the single most important geopolitical challenge as far out as I can see into the 21st century."[19] Burns chose to give his speech at the Georgia Institute of Technology to highlight "the main arena for competition with China—the revolution in technology." He emphasized the complex, multidomain nature of the strategic threat to the United States: "The People's Republic of China is a formidable competitor, lacking in neither ambition nor capability. It seeks to overtake us in literally every domain, from economic strength to military power, and from space to cyber space. . . . China is intent upon building the capabilities to bully its neighbors, replace the United States as the preeminent power in the Indo-Pacific, and chip away with other authoritarians at the rules-based international order that we and our allies have worked so hard to sustain."

This CIA-sponsored assessment is broadly consistent with the 2021 Department of Defense annual report to Congress on *Military and Security Developments Involving the People's Republic of China*, which describes China as the "pacing challenge" for the US military. The report declares that "Beijing seeks to reshape the international order to better align with its authoritarian system and national interests, as a vital component of its . . . national strategy to achieve 'the great rejuvenation of the Chinese nation' by 2049 [which] is deeply integrated with its ambitions to strengthen the PLA [People's Liberation Army]." In the first decades of the twenty-first

---

[19] Burns 2022.

century, the PLA has made remarkable strides in its ambition "to modernize its capabilities and improve its proficiencies across all warfare domains so that as a joint force it can conduct the range of land, air, and maritime operations as well as space, counterspace, electronic warfare (EW), and cyber operations."

If the rise of China presents a complex challenge across multiple domains, it has also provoked numerous proposals designed to reform US strategy. Most of these proposals involve bolstering deterrence, but there are important differences in how each advocate or perspective envisions doing so. Perspectives differ in their emphasis on the credibility of threats and assurances, limiting the costs of US China policy, improving strategic stability between nuclear rivals, and enabling the US military to defeat the People's Liberation Army (PLA) in a possible war. Indeed, the only thing all proposals have in common is the use of the words "China" and "deterrence."

Contemporary strategists have propounded contrasting visions of how to revise current US strategy and doctrine, ranging from "primacy" and "deep engagement" to "restraint" or "offshore balancing." On the surface, such controversies are peculiar and confusing, given that each perspective interacts with, and is applied to, a similar world reality, and all perspectives claim to be advocating a common strategy: deterrence. How can it be that all of these alternative grand strategies are equally aimed at enhancing deterrence, when each differs from the others in important respects? Surely some are better at deterring than others? Which one is the "best"?

The discourse on China strategy is often framed in terms of military and/or political truths, as if the overriding goal, achievable through dialectical debate, is to discern, and eventually agree upon, an objectively "best" approach to US grand strategy, one that presumably would also apply to other countries with similar conditions and capabilities.

Instead, we suggest that the variety of claims about how the United States ought to conduct its national security policy reflect different priorities concerning the heterogeneous elements and outcomes of deterrence. The geopolitical rivalry between the United States and China is distinct from previous historical epochs, both in terms of the high levels of economic interdependence and given the tremendous (and growing) level of military complexity. Thus it is plausible that all four of the strategies above could be relevant in this case. Military and non-military means can be used alternatively to lower costs, enhance prosperity, limit risk, gain influence, signal credibly, or increase the prospects for military victory.

In our view, the origin of these debates lies in important but underappreciated differences between what each perspective seeks to achieve—how each differs in how it defines deterrence, or alternately how it prioritizes among the deterrence trade-offs described above—and how these discrepancies in objectives biases the practice and likely outcomes of deterrence. These differences in emphasis on goals are obscured by the opaque aggregation of objectives in traditional deterrence theory. Bundling together disparate objectives ensures that observers and practitioners fail to note the sources of difference in the forms of deterrence advocated by different perspectives in crafting national policy. It also creates a false debate over their relative merits, in which rhetorical positions assume that one perspective is inherently more effective at achieving a common goal ("deterrence") rather than differentially effective at achieving competing goals. Disaggregating the ends of deterrence, in debates about China strategy and in general, helps to explain why different strategic perspectives arrive at disparate ways and means to practice what each claims is deterrence.

Figure 15.2 plots five different China strategies (and one supporting cyberstrategy) using the same trade-off space described in Figure 15.1. "Military Primacy" and "Deep Engagement" reflect more expansive demands for US influence in East Asia, with the latter perhaps more willing

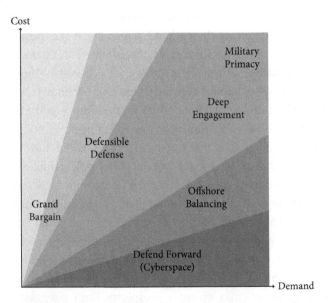

Fig. 15.2 Proposed strategies to deter China reflect different preferences

CONCLUSION 393

to make accommodations in the name of preserving mutually beneficial commercial ties. Both envision a costly, capable US force structure. The other three perspectives highlight differences that are often lumped together as "Restraint" but differ in their valuations for different parameters. The "Grand Bargain" school envisions making significant concessions to China about the future of Taiwan and significantly drawing down US forces in Asia. The "Defensible Defense" strategy, by contrast, imagines equipping allies and partners with the capability to defend themselves and thereby deter Chinese aggression while limiting the role of the US military (somewhat akin to the Ukraine model where NATO is supporting but not directly participating in combat against Russia). The "Offshore Balancing" school, meanwhile, foresees using US air and naval forces to cover a wide variety of US interests, while drawing down forward deployed forces and land defenses. While often pitched as a deterrence strategy, it is closer to deception in our framework. We also plot, but do not discuss in detail, US Cyber Command's "Defend Forward" cyberstrategy. This is not a China strategy, per se, but it illustrates an ambition of widely contesting digital resources at low cost via chronic "Persistent Engagement," which is usually deemed to be an explicit alternative to deterrence in cyberspace.[20] Each strategy, moreover, advocates a different mix of means. However, proponents often do not recognize or acknowledge the diversity of implications for strategic stability reflected in Table 15.2.

Below we review and reconcile the deterrence perspectives advanced by different factions in the debate over US grand strategy vis-à-vis China, demonstrating how each emphasizes different elements of deterrence, while discounting others. US pundits and policy makers may want Beijing to do what Washington wants, at low cost, without fighting, while retaining the ability to prosecute a successful war if deterrence fails. But these are different goals and each competes with the others, at least in part. The ways and means of doing deterrence will vary as strategists emphasize disparate ends such as influence, efficiency, stability, or effectiveness.[21]

---

[20] Schneider, Goldman, and Warner 2020.
[21] There is yet another layer of differences, over politics. Pundits may advocate different states of the world. For example, many differ in their support for Taiwan. Should Taiwan be allowed to chart its own independent course or is defense of Taiwan limited to protection from invasion? We will not attempt to weigh in on debates about what America should value, and how much. However, we can model such differences in terms of more or less expansive demands, insofar as the United States and China have opposing preferences about the political future of Taiwan.

394 ELEMENTS OF DETERRENCE

Primacy: Winning at War

A prominent view in the US defense establishment is that deterrence is best achieved by improving the ability of the US military to fight and win a war. This perspective is championed in a 2020 article by Michele Flournoy, US Undersecretary of Defense for Policy in the Obama administration.[22] Deterrence will best be bolstered by war-fighting prowess: "To reestablish credible deterrence of China, the United States must be able to prevent the success of any act of military aggression by Beijing, either by denying the PLA's ability to achieve its aims or by imposing costs so great that Chinese leaders ultimately decide that the act is not in their interest. And Xi and his advisers must believe that the United States has not just the capability but also the resolve to carry through on any deterrent threat it makes."

Flournoy highlights two prongs of this grand strategy. The first is "shoring up the capabilities of allies and partners." She calls for the United States to "work closely with its allies and partners to make a clear-eyed assessment of what each country can contribute to stabilizing the region and deterring increasingly aggressive behavior. This will also require reassuring them in words and deeds that they can count on the United States to have their backs in disputes with Beijing and ultimately to help defend them against gray-zone coercion or outright attacks."

Second, she urges investments in "new capabilities that will ultimately determine military success—such as resilient battlefield networks, artificial intelligence to support faster decision-making, fleets of unmanned systems, and hypersonic and long-range precision missiles." While not discussed as such in Flournoy's article, this is broadly consistent with US operational concepts such as "Joint Concept for Access and Maneuver in the Global Commons" (JAMGC) and "Joint All-Domain Command and Control" (JADC2). These war-fighting concepts champion the use of advanced automation technologies and coordinated doctrine for networking intelligence, maneuver, and strike platforms across all domains. It is assumed that these technologies and doctrines will enable the US military to fight more efficiently (projecting power across a larger area) and effectively (defeating Chinese revisionism).

---

[22] Flournoy 2020.

In this view, allies mainly provide the geographic platform that will enable the United States to carry the primary burden of deterrence, and if deterrence fails, of war-fighting. As Flournoy writes, "China will try to disrupt the US ability to re-enforce forward forces from the outset of a conflict, in all domains—air, sea, undersea, space, cyberspace. Accordingly, US forces, bases, logistics networks, and C4ISR networks must be made more survivable and resilient. This will require investments in stronger cyber and missile defenses; more geographically dispersed bases and forces; more unmanned systems to augment manned platforms; and resilient networks that can continue to function under attack." These systems are supposed to enable the United States to intervene successfully in any Western Pacific scenario.

The question is whether the same measures adopted to improve war-fighting effectiveness also (equally) improve deterrence credibility. Throughout this book, we have argued and presented evidence that calls this into question. The advanced space, cyber, and networked forces that Flournoy highlights depend on stealth and maneuver for their efficacy. They also provide important efficiency advantages, which can allow the US military to spread its forces over a substantial area. Yet, as we have seen, these same measures raise questions about resolve. When and where will the United States commit its exquisite forces to risky fights over variable stakes? The ability to engage in an ever greater number of places does not equate to the willingness to do so. Indeed, a mobile and stealthy force has inherent difficulty generating, and demonstrating, a commitment to intervene, if necessary. The war-avoidance manifestation of deterrence has long been tied closely to predictability. Uncertainty about the (true) localized balance of power is a recipe for miscalculation and instability. One cannot simultaneously rely on stealth and mobility—effectively surprise—to achieve victory and at the same time minimize the prospects for a war.

Concerns about instability and a heightened risk of war are potentially compounded by the need to rely on and protect third parties. The issue of chain-ganging, discussed in Chapter 8, emerges as the United States contends with Asian allies that have different goals vis-à-vis China. Some will prove excessively cautious, forcing the US military to shoulder not only the burden of collective defense, but also the risk that the mobility and strike potential of American forces will be hampered in times of crisis or war. Other

396 ELEMENTS OF DETERRENCE

allies may become emboldened by a primacist American grand strategy, forcing US officials to carefully constrain allied efforts to convert protection into influence, in the form of more assertive demands on China, demands that eat away at the conflict-inhibiting effects of US security largesse.

Engagement: Maximizing American Influence

A complement to primacy is "deep engagement."[23] Originally proposed in the mid-1990s by Joseph Nye, then serving as an Assistant Secretary of Defense, the notion was, and is, that America is the essential pillar of a globally valued and valuable global order, providing the public security goods that make widespread prosperity and stability possible. Also described as "liberal internationalism" (or by its critics as "liberal hegemony"), this mutually beneficial system would suffer and decline without active US leadership or, alternately, would be forced to fall back on secondary, more parochial, less effective, and more self-motivated protectors, such as China.

The notion of America as the indispensable nation has been taken up by a range of advocates, reflecting shades on a common theme.[24] Good things have happened because the United States is "out there," actively managing the liberal order, and these good things will cease, or at least decline, when and if the United States, and in particular the US military, decides to retrench. The world needs America, even if sometimes they, and we, don't know it.

Everyone does not benefit equally from US engagement, of course, least of all US adversaries. But even here the argument is that countries such as China (in particular) and Russia and Iran (as oil-exporting nations) on the whole prefer the US provision of public goods to likely alternatives. While often left unsaid, there are also private US benefits for wielding influence. A seat at every negotiating table is maintained for US diplomats, while Washington is consulted by a multitude of allies and partners, to say nothing of the economic payoff for hegemony. Where the United States expresses a preference, it is listened to and often accommodated.

Where engagement advocates differ from primacists is in the former's focus on military power. For internationalists, US military capabilities are largely a means to an end. Primacy is not a goal and might even

---

[23] Nye 1995.
[24] Wohlforth 1999; Brooks and Wohlforth 2000; Brooks, Ikenberry, and Wohlforth 2013.

be counter-productive. Indeed, the emphasis on war-fighting potential is unattractive to internationalists, who prefer to avoid contests, rather than plan for them. At the same time, internationalists accept warfare as a risk of projecting power, at least implicitly. Internationalists downplay the costs of engagement, but they appear to accept the potential need for larger outlays for defense. At the same time, embracing the necessity for engaging assertively in a large number of contested spaces abroad implies an acceptance of more frequent overt conflict. Liberal internationalists seem to diverge to some degree on whether they are more eager to maintain US fingers in more pies, with a commensurate increase in defense spending, or prefer to leverage US capabilities with some heightened risk of opposition, and possibly conflict, internationally.

Retrenchment: Minimizing the Risk of War

A contrasting proposal by Eugene Gholz, Benjamin Friedman, and Enea Gjoza labeled "Defensive Defense" prioritizes strategic stability over US military power.[25] Whereas the strategy of primacy (advocated by Flournoy) is designed to penetrate and defeat China's anti-access and area-denial (A2/AD) strategy, this perspective seeks to turn A2/AD against China by improving the capabilities of US allies to defend against Chinese aggression. Mutual denial would make conflict unattractive for all: "The goal should be to create a fortified A2/AD zone on both sides of the seas inside Asia's first island chain—what would be a 'no man's sea' in wartime."

Gholz et al. worry that the primacist approach, which they describe as "Offensive Defense" will have the effect of exacerbating the security dilemma with China, since US operations will have to depend on preemptive attacks on Chinese command and control networks. Primacy is also very expensive, since the US military has to fight far from home with exposed communication and logistics networks. They argue that the "current offensive operational concept results from Washington's tendency to confuse its security needs with total military dominance of adversaries." They advocate an alternative approach that "would contain US costs while improving security in East Asia and reducing the risk of unwanted escalatory spirals."

---

[25] Gholz, Friedman, and Gjoza 2019.

398 ELEMENTS OF DETERRENCE

Gholz et al. urge the United States to "push its wealthy allies in Asia to more energetically improve their own A2/AD capabilities, rather than trying to emulate the US military's strike capability." They argue that this "would allow the United States to purchase fewer of the expensive, vulnerable assets that underpin its current offensive defense approach (for example, carrier strike groups and hypersonic land-attack missiles)." Security partners, including treaty allies such as Japan and South Korea, and tacit allies like Taiwan, would become more responsible for their own defense, as they "prepare to fight with weapons that impede an adversary's advance rather than pre-emptively striking the adversary's forces in the adversary's home territory." While this strategy does rely on forces in all domains, it focuses on extending the defensive engagement envelopes of allies' land-based fortifications.

Gholz et al. emphasize that this strategy is based on a more limited conception of US national security interests in Asia: "to preserve allies' territorial integrity by maintaining a stable balance of power among regional states." This means accepting a reduction in US power to dictate its preferred policy outcomes and settling instead for a more limited policy aim that equates to "live and let live": "Accommodating China's ability to defend its territory—which is necessary for it to believe it is secure and thus act less aggressively—does not meaningfully damage US ability to deter potential attacks on US allies, let alone attacks on US territory."

An even more restrained proposal is advanced by Charles Glaser, who calls for a "grand bargain" with China that would cede US interests in Taiwan's political future in exchange for China resolving its other maritime disputes in the South and East China Seas.[26] Glaser argues that changes in the balance of power make it too risky for the US military to enforce the status quo going forward. In other words, Glaser explicitly prioritizes stability (the absence of war with China) over influence (the pursuit of US interests in Taiwan's political future).

Both of these retrenchment strategies—empowering Taiwan and others to defend themselves or ceding Taiwan to China's sphere of influence—are articulations of military "restraint."[27] However, they do not necessarily imply economic retrenchment. On the contrary, a lessening of tensions through accommodating China's core interests is supposed to make it easier for both China and the United States to re-commit to their joint gains from trade

[26] Glaser 2015. [27] Posen 2014.

(and non-military coordination on issues of common concern like climate change). This would retain the economic aspect of liberal internationalism while ditching the military assertiveness of primacy.

Offshore Balancing: Reducing Costs

There are other alternatives that seek to combine or balance restraint with the primacist position. Gholz et al. highlight the benefits from their perspective of fortifying allied geography and enabling the United States to "come home." By contrast, the "offshore balancing" position espouses the use of US naval and air forces as a mobile counter to possible aggression. This perspective seeks to keep the United States involved in the region, but not with the same robust footprint as that of primacy. Offshore Balancing thus reflects variation in conceptions of "restraint," depending on the degree to which proponents prioritize stability or residual influence.

The chief appeal of an "offshore balancing" strategy for its supporters is that it ends costly military adventures overseas. As John Mearsheimer and Stephen Walt write, "The United States would maintain substantial naval and air assets and modest but capable ground forces, and it would stand ready to expand its capabilities should circumstances require. But for the foreseeable future, the US government could spend more money on domestic needs or leave it in taxpayers' pockets."[28]

Mearsheimer and Walt argue that the United States can afford to embrace a more restrained grand strategy: "Offshore balancing is a grand strategy born of confidence in the United States' core traditions and a recognition of its enduring advantages. It exploits the country's providential geographic position and recognizes the powerful incentives other states have to balance against overly powerful or ambitious neighbors." This puts Mearsheimer and Walt starkly at odds with liberal internationalists who espouse robust US military engagement in Europe and the Middle East. Yet there is less daylight between these perspectives on China because "if China continues its impressive rise, it is likely to seek hegemony in Asia. The United States should undertake a major effort to prevent it from succeeding."

Mearsheimer in particular argues that "great powers are doomed to compete" and thus with regard to US China policy in recent decades, liberal

---

[28] Mearsheimer and Walt 2016.

400 ELEMENTS OF DETERRENCE

"engagement was a colossal strategic mistake."[29] In Mearsheimer's view, it will not be possible to rectify this error without accepting some cost and risk. Effective management of the China rivalry "would require Washington to maintain formidable conventional forces in East Asia to persuade Beijing that a clash of arms would at best yield a Pyrrhic victory. Convincing adversaries that they cannot achieve quick and decisive wins deters wars. Furthermore, US policy makers must constantly remind themselves—and Chinese leaders—about the ever-present possibility of nuclear escalation in wartime."

Offshore balancing seems attractive, particularly as framed by its advocates. One achieves much of what could be achieved by more comprehensive means, but at a lower cost. Yet the caution in all sales pitches remains; let the "buyer" beware, don't believe you can get something for nothing. An important downside of offshore balancing stems from its reliance on mobility and a reactive, networked military capability to intervene, if and when one chooses to do so. On the one hand, offshore balancing does not really limit interventionism, a core concern for advocates. With mobile forces, the United States (or any other country) can still intervene wherever and whenever it chooses to do so. It just cannot sustain a large, permanent occupation, which is a different, though important (and vexing) issue. On the other hand, the reliance on a mobile, reactive force for defense undermines deterrence credibility in much the same way as reliance on new and emerging technologies. The United States *may* intervene in a crisis in Asia (or elsewhere) but it is not compelled to do so. This lack of pre-commitment keeps allies and potential adversaries guessing, which is not what one wants if the stability portion of deterrence is a priority.

Multiple Preferences in US-China Strategy

The dramatic rise of China, and its military modernization in all domains, is the preeminent geopolitical challenge for US grand strategy in the twenty-first century. But this simple fact does not translate automatically into an obvious policy response. Different commentators, looking at the same problem with access to the same information, have come to starkly different conclusions as to how the United States should posture towards China.

---

[29] Mearsheimer 2021.

CONCLUSION   401

These differences seem to us to have as much to do with different values and priorities as with different approximations of one, coherent analytical truth. Indeed, they reflect the diversity of the impact of military means on different, competing notions of deterrence. Whether one prioritizes stability, influence, power, or efficiency will determine the sort of grand strategic posture toward China that is best suited to one's (diverse) objectives.

American attempts to "pivot" to Asia—primarily a reallocation of naval forces despite aspirations to lead with diplomacy—have proven controversial, not least among European allies who fear abandonment. Sea power increases influence at the price of heightened diplomatic friction, tempting competitors to challenge naval powers on issues where the challenger is relatively more resolved. Forward presence at sea, therefore, does not translate into increased determination or willingness. The findings reported in Chapter 8 on the land domain, by contrast, suggest that forward basing of troops on allied soil, and in general greater proportionate spending specific to that ally, provide more credible signals of commitment to defend that ally.

The findings reported in Chapter 9 on the maritime domain suggest that sea power poses an inherent trade-off between being effective in the event of war and increasing the risk that war will occur. This finding is at odds with the conventional view that a strong defense is the best deterrent. While defense certainly contributes to deterrence, the details of force structure and posture also matter. Maintaining a strong navy encourages a national force posture that ensures contests occur farther from home when they happen. At the same time, reliance on sea power as a primary instrument of influence and power projection—a key feature of proposed US grand strategies that advocate drawing down overseas troop deployments and relying on offshore balancing—means contests are likely to occur more often. Navies can be in more places, but always only in a decidedly finite number of places at any one time. Navies can defend a nation's distant interests, but those interests are usually less vital than interests close to home. Of course, these realities are in tension.

Shortly before his departure in early November 2020, Secretary of Defense Mark Esper unveiled "Battle Force 2045," an ambitious plan for "500 manned and unmanned ships by 2045, and a fleet of 355 traditional battle force ships by 2035."[30] Even in the wake of Esper's departure, however, discussion of the plan among naval strategists continued, implying that some

---

[30] Eckstein 2020.

402 ELEMENTS OF DETERRENCE

version of Battle Force 2045 may persist.[31] The plan represents a significant increase from the current US naval force of roughly 300 (manned) vessels, as well as significant changes to naval force structure (adding new light aircraft carriers, reducing large carriers, and nearly doubling the inventory of attack submarines, amphibious warfare ships, small surface combatants, and logistics ships, with unprecedented automation). The addition of light carriers and amphibious vessels, which could marginally improve the US Navy's ability to "show the flag" and enhance political influence in more places, is more than offset by a major investment (nearly 200 vessels) in attack submarines and surface combatants, which can be expected to complicate deterrence and increase instability due to their emphasis on speed and stealth.

Most problematic for the goal of stability in the Pacific is the emerging US emphasis on automated weapons and artificial intelligence. Heavy dependence on unmanned vessels and aircraft will tend to exacerbate the naval commitment problem. An adversary faced with unmanned systems—which reduce the cost of war for their user—will have difficulty determining a combatant's true resolve, precisely because these systems make fighting cheaper and less risky. How does the target of deterrence figure out whether robot warships and warplanes are being used because they are more effective in combat or because an adversary is reluctant to risk human casualties? As discussed in Chapter 10, unmanned systems acquired in the hopes of reducing the costs of war could thus increase the risk, and possibly the duration, of contests by introducing uncertainty about the resolve of nations that rely on them.

While militarily effective automated systems make it hard for the target to measure resolve (since resolved and unresolved types pool together), military secrets make it hard for a target to evaluate an adversary's capabilities. This is especially concerning in the realm of cyber warfare and in nuclear counterforce operations that depend on surprise and first-mover advantages. Improvements in US battlefield reconnaissance and precision targeting have tended to make the second-strike forces of other nuclear states less secure.[32] This is part of the reason why China has embarked on a serious effort to expand and modernize the survivability of its nuclear forces, which in turn makes "left of launch" counterforce measures more desirable for US damage limitation efforts where deterrence appears likely to fail. The tragedy is that

[31] Filipoff 2020.   [32] Lieber and Press 2006; B. Green 2020.

efforts to "win" the war after a deterrence failure make deterrence failures more likely in the first place, as we emphasized in Chapter 7. It is at least important to make this trade-off consciously and deliberately.

The "multidomain" military challenge of China has thus reinvigorated debates about deterrence. Chinese military modernization, with its focus on war-fighting capabilities in space and cyberspace, has raised doubts about the long-term stability of US extended deterrence in Asia. The modernization and expansion of the Chinese navy, in particular the development of so-called A2/AD capabilities in the East and South China Seas, is significantly changing the naval balance of power in the Western Pacific.[33] The US military responded with the operational concept of "AirSea Battle"—later renamed the ponderous and imponderable "Joint Access and Maneuver in the Global Commons"—which aims to proactively defeat A2/AD in the event of war with China.[34] Such a forward posture probably does enhance US influence in the Pacific. However, it appears likely to achieve this objective only by also increasing the risk of eventual conflict or inadvertent escalation.

It is not our intention to adjudicate among alternative strategies for deterring China. Instead, we hope to move forward this critical debate by clarifying which deterrence attributes a given nation should emphasize, given national preferences over outcomes. The strategies that have been proposed for competing with China are not simply different conceptions about the most effective way to confront China, but involve different preferences regarding US national security interests (i.e., political influence over the status quo in East Asia, military effectiveness in multidomain battle, the policy cost of deterring and perhaps fighting China, and strategic stability with China). The last of these different objectives can be further disaggregated into a reduced propensity for arms racing, crisis onset, or escalation to conventional or nuclear war, which are not necessarily governed by the same preferences and dynamics. Americans—indeed the citizens of any country— should evaluate their collective national priorities and decide which of the elements of different deterrence strategies are likely to produce the greatest collective benefit for their society. This of course requires recognition that deterrence itself is not a unitary objective, but a set of contrasting actions, goals, and priorities, as we point out.

In doing so, we hope also to highlight the persistent conceptual problems lurking beneath most discussions of deterrence. As contemporary reality

---

[33] Montgomery 2014.   [34] Greenert and Schwartz 2012; Hutchens et al. 2017.

404 ELEMENTS OF DETERRENCE

moves beyond the confines of the Cold War and nuclear weapons, it becomes increasingly important that we recognize that the classical model was artificially constrained by assumptions that, while adequate for an earlier era and dynamic, are no longer sufficient today. By advancing a framework that allows practitioners, experts, and the public to consider the different elements and trade-offs in any deterrence strategy more clearly and explicitly, we hope to ensure that policy discussions and the ensuing implementation of deterrence strategies more often achieve their intended results.

The Inevitable Choices in Deterrence Strategy

There are at least four key variables tied to deterrence, as we have noted several times in this book. Each of these variables clearly matter to states and other political actors, but all cannot be pursued with equal vigor simultaneously. Avoiding war is clearly important and a major private and social benefit of successful deterrence. Yet so is avoiding capitulation and having some influence over retaining or improving the status quo. Lowering the costs of deterrence and military operations in general is also desirable, because greater efficiency enables governments to pursue other policy goals or husband scarce resources. A fourth important objective is enhancing military power in the event that deterrence fails, which may or may not contribute to deterrence success depending on the composition of military forces.

These four factors are further influenced and constrained by military force structures and postures; what nations buy, build, deploy, and maintain determines, at least in part, what it is possible for deterrence to look like, for states and for their national counterparts. Countries opting for deterrence are making a "middle of the spectrum" claim about goals. They are not intrinsically revisionist or pacifist, but somewhere in between. Beyond this, they have to balance trade-offs between the four variables discussed here in concocting their national deterrence "recipe."

There is no inherent, prima facie reason for dispassionate decision makers to prefer any of the four objectives subsumed within the deterrence rubric over the others. Preferences are exogenous. The ways in which actors prioritize the objectives of deterrence—minimizing risk, maximizing influence, minimizing costs, and maximizing power—ultimately depends on what they want politically and how much they are willing to pay to get it, now

CONCLUSION 405

and in the future. There are unavoidable tensions across these aims, and some tensions are especially fraught (notably between deception-efficiency and deterrence-influence, or between accommodation-stability and defense-power). Deterrence theory per se does not tell us which of these goals is most important. Indeed, in our formulation prioritizing across them is not a function of objective truth. Their proper relationship depends on value-laden factors, contextual circumstances, and the preferences of populations and their leaders.

Actors who are not attached to a disputed good and are not very resolved to retain what they have should most wish to minimize the risk of war. They should be more willing to compromise or appease potential aggressors in order to avoid the costs and risks of credible deterrence or effective defense. Actors who have minimal aims yet, by contrast, are more resolved to retain key portions of the status quo should be more interested in maximizing deterrence credibility. They should be less willing to compromise on their core interests and more willing to pay a high price to convince potential aggressors that they should avoid harming those interests. Classical nuclear deterrence theory tends to focus on this quadrant, running the risk of a horrifically costly war in order to secure fundamental national interests.

In practice, however, actors often have more expansive aims: they desire to achieve political or economic benefits above and beyond mere survival. Such actors will entertain liberal interpretations of the status quo, and thus their efforts at deterrence are more likely to look like compellence to others. Nevertheless, they can vary in their willingness to pay for the opportunity to achieve their more expansive aims. Less resolved actors who prefer to invest resources for purposes other than defending, stabilizing, or expanding the status quo should be most interested in minimizing the costs of deterrence. They should be more attracted to military stratagems that offer the prospect of marginal benefits without the costs and risks associated with a major confrontation. More highly resolved actors, by contrast, should attempt to maximize their military power to prevail in war. They are willing to pay for more effective military capabilities and they employ them more assertively, in the event that deterrence fails. Indeed, maximizing military power can even make deterrence failure more likely, thus further increasing the potential cost and risk associated with a given policy.

Deterrence is not a single coherent strategy but rather a bundle of factors. Indeed, deterrence might be better described as the process of managing tensions across conflicting goals and complex instruments of national power.

Deterrence encompasses the promotion of peace, advocacy for a particular set of interests, minimization of costs, and enhancement of war-fighting potential. To the degree that these outcomes are different and distinct, realizing them requires contrasting actions. To the degree that these objectives are in tension, or simply compete for the same finite set of resources (equipment, personnel, time, a leader's attention), they cannot all be pursued with equal vigor. Recognizing the trade-offs involved in any act of deterrence is critical to ensuring success by the standards of the actor implementing the strategy.

In the final analysis, there is no such thing as value-free deterrence. Attempts to formulate a value-neutral theory of deterrence or indeed other aspects of national security or international relations theory have led to contortions that diminish the utility of the analytical framework. One of the main reasons that deterrence theory has appeared increasingly out of touch is that it has been called on to provide judgments about processes that were assumed away in the original, nuclear formulation. As we move from an era of superpower nuclear brinkmanship, where survival was uncontested in the hierarchy of human needs, to a period where subtle competition is ongoing across many domains and regions, the need for a theoretical framework that explicitly considers the trade-offs across alternative objectives of national security has been brought to the fore. The United States in the Cold War perceived an existential threat, and it risked all to contain it. Today the problems of non-state actors and the rise of near-peer competitors re-asserts the need to consider the consequences of specific military potential. Yet not all provocations are worthy of a concerted national effort, or even a military response. Indeed, many can be set aside without fundamental risk to the nation. Under these conditions, one of the greatest challenges in US foreign policy may be to rediscover inaction or restraint, choosing wisely how to balance the inherent trade-offs in any initiative designed to deter.

A defender cannot guarantee that an adversary will refrain from attacking, or that an attack will fail if it occurs. Deterrence can only shape how and where aggression is expressed. It may be that the defender's biggest concern is to limit penetration of the border. This implies a different defensive posture than the goal of preventing an attacker from taking key terrain or capturing other objectives, such as communication or transportation hubs. It may be that the defender is more concerned about force protection and sustainability than about an enemy's temporary acquisition of territory. In each instance, the best defense depends on a defender's objectives and on inherent trade-offs between alternative objectives intrinsic to defense.

What we prefer shapes how we deter. Because deterrence has a number of different, often incompatible objectives, the means selected to deter matter immensely. Different means of deterrence or defense have different advantages or disadvantages for different deterrence ends. Because these ends are often in tension, or the same means cannot serve different ends equally well, values matter. Actors must decide what is most important, and where they are willing to compromise. Because decision makers will inevitably compromise on some objectives, uncertainty emerges as a critical concern. Deterrence will fail in some places precisely because it is working in others. Indeed, deterrence tends to fail in time in part because of the conditions that ensured its initial success. An immovable object is eventually bypassed. An irresistible force is eventually deflected or slowed. Stymieing an adversary ensures that it will seek other avenues to advance its objectives.

Actors will try to shore up their own deterrence failures and challenge the deterrence posture of their opponents. Because of this, process matters. Deterrence is an ongoing balancing act between evolving technologies, interdependencies, and political situations. The things that worked yesterday will eventually prove ineffective or irrelevant, as an adversary evolves its operations, strategy, equipment, and force structure to adapt and overcome. Finally, because there are both a growing number of means and ends in the practice of modern deterrence, complexity takes a toll on efficacy, even as it taxes the minds of force planners and operational commanders. The combinatory possibilities of ends, ways, and means in national security strategy are growing exponentially. This makes planning and decision making intrinsically more challenging. By the same token, it is more imperative than ever to understand the trade-offs intrinsic to deterrence. Even a marginal improvement in the ability to understand and manage complexity can provide a critical advantage. After all, contests are won on the margin, not by perfect strategies, plans, and execution, but just by being a little bit better, and luckier.

The temptation is always to reach for some new concept like "integrated deterrence" to cut through technological and political complexity. But deterrence cannot be integrated, not across all domains, all interests, and the entire spectrum of conflict. In deterrence strategy, all good things do not go together. Technological complexity is a hard problem, to be sure, but it is not the hardest one. The hardest problem is figuring out what matters.

Bibliography

Max Abrahms and Philip B. K. Potter. "Explaining Terrorism: Leadership Deficits and Military Group Tactics." In: *International Organization* 69.2 (2015), pp. 311–49.

Christopher Achen and Duncan Snidal. "Rational Deterrence Theory and Comparative Case Studies." In: *World Politics* 41.2 (1989), pp. 143–69.

Elliot Ackerman and James Stavridis. *2034: A Novel of the Next World War.* New York: Penguin, 2021.

James M. Acton "Escalation through Entanglement: How the Vulnerability of Command-and-Control Systems Raises the Risks of an Inadvertent Nuclear War." In: *International Security* 43.1 (2018), pp. 56–99.

Karen Ruth Adams. "Attack and Conquer? International Anarchy and the Offense-Defense-Deterrence Balance." In: *International Security* 28.3 (2003), pp. 45–83.

Dima Adamsky. "From Israel with Deterrence: Strategic Culture, Intra-war Coercion and Brute Force." In: *Security Studies* 26.1 (2017), pp. 157–84.

Dima Adamsky. "From Moscow with Coercion: Russian Deterrence Theory and Strategic Culture." In: *Journal of Strategic Studies* 41.1–2 (2018), pp. 33–60.

Dima Adamsky. "Russian Orthodox Church and Nuclear Command and Control: A Hypothesis." In: *Security Studies* 28.5 (2019), pp. 1010–39.

Emanuel Adler. "Complex Deterrence in the Asymmetric-Warfare Era." In: *Complex Deterrence: Strategy in the Global Age.* Ed. T. V. Paul, Patrick M. Morgan, and James J. Wirtz. Chicago: University of Chicago Press, 2009, pp. 85–107.

George A. Akerlof. "The Market for 'Lemons': Quality Uncertainty and the Market Mechanism." In: *Quarterly Journal of Economics* 84.3 (1970), pp. 488–500.

William Akoto. "International Trade and Cyber Conflict: Decomposing the Effect of Trade on State-Sponsored Cyber Attacks." In: *Journal of Peace Research* (2021), pp. 1083–97. https://doi.org/10.1177/0022343320964549.

Keith Alexander. "Cyber Warfare in Ukraine Poses Threat to Global System." In: *Australian Financial Review* (2022). https://www.ft.com/content/8e1e8176-2279-4596-9c0f-98629b4db5a6.

C. Kenneth Allard. *Command, Control, and the Common Defense.* Revised. Washington, DC: National Defense University Press, 1996.

Michael A. Allen, Michael E. Flynn, and Carla Martinez Machain. "US Global Military Deployments, 1950–2020." In: *Conflict Management and Peace Science* 39.3 (2022), pp. 351–70.

Michael A. Allen, Michael E. Flynn, Carla Martinez Machain, and Andrew Stravers. "Outside the Wire: US Military Deployments and Public Opinion in Host States." In: *American Political Science Review* 2.114 (2020), pp. 326–41.

Joshua Alley and Matthew Fuhrmann. "Budget Breaker? The Financial Cost of US Military Alliances." In: *Security Studies* 30.5 (2021), pp. 661–90.

Michael F. Altfeld. "The Decision to Ally: A Theory and Test." In: *Western Political Quarterly* 37.4 (1984), pp. 523–44.

410 BIBLIOGRAPHY

Dan Altman. "By Fait Accompli, Not Coercion: How States Wrest Territory from Their Adversaries." In: *International Studies Quarterly* 61.4 (2017), pp. 881–91.

Dan Altman. "Advancing without Attacking: The Strategic Game around the Use of Force." In: *Security Studies* 27.1 (2018), pp. 58–88.

Dan Altman. "The Evolution of Territorial Conquest after 1945 and the Limits of the Territorial Integrity Norm." In: *International Organization* 74.3 (2020), pp. 490–522.

Marc Ambinder. "Failure Shuts Down Squadron of Nuclear Missiles." In: *The Atlantic* (Oct. 26, 2010).

Christopher Andrew. "Intelligence, International Relations and 'Under-theorisation.' " In: *Intelligence and National Security* 19.2 (2004), pp. 170–84.

Norman Angell. *Europe's Optical Illusion*. London: Norman Angell, 1909.

Hannah Arendt. *On Violence*. New York: Harcourt, Brace & Co., 1970.

Ivan Arreguin-Toft. How the Weak Win Wars: A Theory of Asymmetric Conflict. New York: Cambridge University Press, 2005.

Robert J. Art. "Geopolitics Updated: The Strategy of Selective Engagement." In: *International Security* 23.3 (1998), pp. 79–113.

Robert J. Art and Kelly M. Greenhill. "Coercion: An Analytical Overview." In: *Coercion: The Power to Hurt in International Politics*. Ed. Kelly M. Greenhill and Peter J. P. Krause. New York: Oxford University Press, 2018, pp. 3–32.

Lloyd J. Austin. *Secretary of Defense Remarks for the US INDOPACOM Change of Command*. Speech. Camp H. M. Smith, HI, 30 Apr 2021 Source: https://www.defense. gov/news/Speeches/Speech/Article/2592093/secretary-of-defense-remarks-for-the- us-indopacom-change-of-command/.

Paul C. Avey, Jonathan N. Markowitz, and Robert J. Reardon. "Disentangling Grand Strategy: International Relations Theory and US Grand Strategy." In: *Texas National Security Review* 2.1 (2018). pp. 28–51. http://dx.doi.org/10.26153/tsw/869.

Francis Bacon. *Essays, Civil and Moral: and The New Atlantis*. New York: P. F. Collier & Son, 1909.

Benjamin Bahney and Jonathan Pearl. "Why Creating a Space Force Changes Nothing." In: *Foreign Affairs* (2019).

Benjamin Bahney, Jonathan Pearl, and Michael Markey. "Anti-Satellite Weapons and the Instability of Deterrence." In: *Cross-Domain Deterrence: Strategy in an Era of Complexity*. Ed. Jon R. Lindsay and Erik Gartzke. New York: Oxford University Press, 2019, pp. 121–43.

Uri Bar-Joseph. *The Watchman Fell Asleep: The Surprise of Yom Kippur and Its Sources*. SUNY series in Israeli studies. Albany: State University of New York Press, 2005.

Paul Baran. *On Distributed Communications Networks*. Tech. rep. Santa Monica: RAND Corporation, 1962.

Katherine Barbieri and Gerald Schneider. "Globalization and Peace: Assessing New Directions in the Study of Trade and Conflict." In: *Journal of Peace Research* 36.4 (1999), pp. 387–404.

Jo Becker and Scott Shane. "Secret 'Kill List' Tests Obama's Principles." In: *New York Times* (May 29, 2012).

Michael Beckley. "The Emerging Military Balance in East Asia: How China's Neighbors Can Check Chinese Naval Expansion." In: *International Security* 42.2 (2017), pp. 78–119.

Michael Beckley. *Unrivaled: Why America Will Remain the World's Sole Superpower*. Ithaca: Cornell University Press, 2018.

BIBLIOGRAPHY   411

Richard Bejtlich. *The Practice of Network Security Monitoring: Understanding Incident Detection and Monitoring*. San Francisco: No Starch Press, 2013.

J. Bowyer Bell. "Toward a Theory of Deception." In: *International Journal of Intelligence and Counterintelligence* 16.2 (2003), pp. 244–79.

Mark S. Bell. "Examining Explanations for Nuclear Proliferation." In: *International Studies Quarterly* 60.3 (2016), pp. 520–29.

Tim Benbow. *The Magic Bullet? Understanding the Revolution in Military Affairs*. London: Brassey's, 2004.

James R. Beniger. *The Control Revolution: Technological and Economic Origins of the Information Society*. Cambridge, MA: Harvard University Press, 1986.

Andrew Bennett and Colin Elman. "Case Study Methods in the International Relations Subfield." In: *Comparative Political Studies* 40.2 (2007), pp. 170–95.

Brett V. Benson and Bradley C. Smith. "Commitment Problems in Alliance Formation." In: *American Journal of Political Science* n/a.n/a (2022). https://doi.org/10.1111/ajps.12693.

Richard K. Betts. *Surprise Attack: Lessons for Defense Planning*. Washington, DC: Brookings Institution, 1982.

Richard K. Betts. "Is Strategy an Illusion?" In: *International Security* 25.2 (2000), pp. 5–50.

Richard K. Betts. "Fixing Intelligence." In: *Foreign Affairs* 81.1 (2002), p. 43.

Alan Beyerchen. "Clausewitz, Nonlinearity, and the Unpredictability of War." In: *International Security* 17.3 (1992), pp. 59–90.

Stephen Biddle. "The Past as Prologue: Assessing Theories of Future Warfare." In: *Security Studies* 8.1 (1998), pp. 1–74.

Stephen Biddle. "Rebuilding the Foundations of Offense-Defense Theory." In: *Journal of Politics* 63.3 (2001), pp. 741–74.

Stephen Biddle. *Military Power: Explaining Victory and Defeat in Modern Battle*. Princeton: Princeton University Press, 2004.

Stephen Biddle. "Speed Kills? Reassessing the Role of Speed, Precision, and Situation Awareness in the Fall of Saddam." In: *Journal of Strategic Studies* 30.1 (2007), pp. 3–46.

Stephen Biddle and Ivan Oelrich. "Future Warfare in the Western Pacific: Chinese Antiaccess/Area Denial, US AirSea Battle, and Command of the Commons in East Asia." In: *International Security* 41.1 (2016), pp. 7–48.

Tami Davis Biddle. *Rhetoric and Reality in Air Warfare: The Evolution of British and American Ideas about Strategic Bombing, 1914–1945*. Princeton: Princeton University Press, 2002.

Tami Davis Biddle. "Coercion Theory: A Basic Introduction for Practitioners." In: *Texas National Security Review* 3.2 (2020), pp. 94–109. http://dx.doi.org/10.26153/tsw/8864.

Wiebe E. Bijker et al., ed. *The Social Construction of Technological Systems: New Directions in the Sociology and History of Technology*. Cambridge, MA: MIT Press, 1987.

Joseph L. Billingsley, ed. *Integrated Deterrence and Cyberspace: Selected Essays Exploring the Role of Cyber Operations in the Pursuit of National Interest*. Washington, DC: National Defense University, College of Information and Cyberspace, 2023.

Geoffrey Blainey. *The Causes of War*. New York: Free Press, 1973.

Geoffrey Blainey. *The Causes of War*, 3rd ed. New York: Simon and Schuster, 1988.

Bruce Blair. *Strategic Command and Control*. Washington, DC: Brookings Institution May 1985.

Bruce Blair. "Could Terrorists Launch America's Nuclear Missiles?" In: *Time* (Nov. 11, 2010). https://content.time.com/time/nation/ article/0,8599,2030685,00.html.

412 BIBLIOGRAPHY

Brian Blankenship and Erik Lin-Greenberg. "Trivial Tripwires? Military Capabilities and Alliance Reassurance." In: *Security Studies* 31.1 (2022), pp. 92–117.

Sean Bodmer et al. *Reverse Deception: Organized Cyber Threat CounterExploitation.* New York: McGraw-Hill, 2012.

Charles Boehmer, Erik Gartzke, and Timonthy Nordstrom. "Do Intergovernmental Organizations Promote Peace?" In: *World Politics* 57 (2004), pp. 1–38.

Sergei Boeke and Dennis Broeders. "The Demilitarisation of Cyber Conflict." In: *Survival* 60.6 (2018), pp. 73–90.

Tobias Bohmelt, Ulrich Pilster, and Atsushi Tago. "Naval Forces and Civil-Military Relations." In: *Journal of Global Security Studies* 2.4 (2017), pp. 346–63.

Erica D. Borghard and Shawn W. Lonergan. "The Logic of Coercion in Cyberspace." In: *Security Studies* 26.3 (2017), pp. 452–81.

Kenneth Boulding. *Stable Peace.* Austin: University of Texas Press, 1978.

Kenneth Boulding. *Conflict and Defense: A General Theory.* New York: Harper and Row, 1962.

Bleddyn E. Bowen. *War in Space: Strategy, Spacepower, Geopolitics.* Edinburgh: Edinburgh University Press, 2020.

Paul J. Bracken. *Command and Control of Nuclear Forces.* New Haven: Yale University Press, 1985.

Belinda Bragg. *Integration Report: Gray Zone Conflicts, Challenges, and Opportunities.* Tech. rep. Arlington, VA, July 13, 2017. Source: https://nsiteam.com/social/ wp-content/uploads/ 2017/07/Integration-Report-Final-07-13-2017-R.pdf.

Jordan Branch. "What's in a Name? Metaphors and Cybersecurity." en. *International Organization* 75.1 (2021), pp. 39–70.

Hal Brands. *Paradoxes of the Gray Zone.* SSRN Scholarly Paper ID 2737593. Rochester, NY: Social Science Research Network, 2016.

Sergey Bratus et al. "Exploit Programming: From Buffer Overflows to 'Weird Machines' and Theory of Computation." In: *USENIX; login:* 36.6 (2011). https://www.usenix. org/publications/login/ december-2011-volume-36-number-6/exploit-programming-buffer-overflows-weird.

Bear F. Braumoeller. *Only the Dead: The Persistence of War in the Modern Age.* New York: Oxford University Press, 2019.

Shawn Brimley. "Promoting Security in Common Domains." In: *Washington Quarterly* 33.3 (2010), pp. 119–32.

Bernard Brodie. *A Guide to Naval Strategy.* Princeton: Princeton University Press, 1944.

Bernard Brodie. "More about Limited War." In: *World Politics* 10.1 (1957). Ed. RN Rear Admiral Sir Anthony W. Buzzard, Robert E. Osgood, and P. M. S. Blackett, pp. 112–22.

Bernard Brodie et al. *The Absolute Weapon: Atomic Power and World Order.* New York: Harcourt, Brace and Co., 1946.

Stephen Brooks, G. John Ikenberry, and William C. Wohlforth. "Don't Come Home, America: The Case against Retrenchment." In: *International Security* 37.3 (2013), pp. 7–51.

Stephen G. Brooks and William C. Wohlforth. "Power, Globalization, and the End of the Cold War: Reevaluating a Landmark Case for Ideas." In: *International Security* 25.3 (2000), pp. 5–53.

Stephen G. Brooks and William C. Wohlforth. *America Abroad: The United States' Global Role in the 21st Century.* New York: Oxford University Press, 2016.

Stephen G. Brooks and William C. Wohlforth. "The Rise and Fall of the Great Powers in the Twenty-First Century: China's Rise and the Fate of America's Global Position." In: *International Security* 40.3 (2016), pp. 7–53.

Jason M. Brown. "To Bomb or Not to Bomb? Counterinsurgency, Airpower, and Dynamic Targeting." In: *Air and Space Power Journal* (2007), pp. 1–13.

Dino A. Brugioni. "The Art and Science of Photoreconnaissance." In: *Scientific American* 274.3 (1996), pp. 78–85.

Bruce Bueno De Mesquita. "The War Trap Revisited: A Revised Expected Utility Model." In: *The American Political Science Review* 79.1 (1985), pp. 156–77.

Bruce Bueno De Mesquita and David Lalman. "Empirical Support for Systemic and Dyadic Explanations of International Conflict." In: *World Politics: A Quarterly Journal of International Relations* (1988), vol 41 issue 1 pp. 1–20.

Erik Brynjolfsson and Adam Saunders. *Wired for Innovation: How Information Technology Is Reshaping the Economy.* Cambridge, MA: MIT Press, 2010.

Ben Buchanan. *The Cybersecurity Dilemma: Hacking, Trust and Fear between Nations.* New York: Oxford University Press, 2017.

Ben Buchanan. *The Hacker and the State: Cyber Attacks and the New Normal of Geopolitics.* Cambridge, MA: Harvard University Press, 2020.

Ben Buchanan and Fiona S. Cunningham. "Preparing the Cyber Battlefield: Assessing a Novel Escalation Risk in a Sino-American Crisis (Fall 2020)." In: *Texas National Security Review* 3.4 (2020), pp. 54–81.

Ethan Bueno de Mesquita et al. "Measuring Political Violence in Pakistan: Insights from the BFRS Dataset." In: *International Interactions* 32.5 (2015), pp. 536–58.

Halvard Buhaug and Nils Petter Gleditsch. "The Death of Distance? The Globalization of Armed Conflict." In: *Territoriality and Conflict in an Era of Globalization.* Ed. Miles Kahler and Barbara F. Walter. New York: Cambridge University Press, 2006, pp. 187–216.

Carl H. Builder. *The Masks of War: American Military Styles in Strategy and Analysis.* Baltimore: Johns Hopkins University Press, 1989.

M. Elaine Bunn. *Can Deterrence Be Tailored?* Strategic Forum 225. Washington, DC: Institute for National Strategic Studies, National Defense University, 2007.

Bureau of Investigative Journalism. Drone Wars: The Full Data. https://www.thebureauinvestigates.com/stories/2017-01-01/drone-wars-the-full-data 1 January 2017.

William Burns. *The Role of Intelligence at a Transformational Moment.* Atlanta: Georgia Institute of Technology. Speech. Apr 14, 2022. https://www.cia.gov/static/21993f0aa96849f2dbdfafcc2d6598e6/Director-Burns-Speech-and-QA-Georgia-Tech.pdf.

William Burr. "Sino-American Relations, 1969: The Sino-Soviet Border War and Steps towards Rapprochement." In: *Cold War History* 1.3 (2001), pp. 73–112.

Antonio Calcara et al. "Why Drones Have Not Revolutionized War: The Enduring Hider-Finder Competition in Air Warfare." In: *International Security* 46.4 (2022), pp. 130–71.

Andrew Callam. "Drone Wars: Armed Unmanned Aerial Vehicles." In: *International Affairs Review* 18.3 (2010).

Shannon Carcelli and Erik Gartzke. "The Diversification of Deterrence: New Data and Novel Realities." In: *Oxford Research Encyclopedia of Politics.* Oxford: Oxford University Press, 2017. https://doi.org/10.1093/acrefore/9780190228637.013.745.

Allison Carnegie. "Secrecy in International Relations and Foreign Policy." In: *Annual Review of Political Science* 24.1 (2021), pp. 213–33.

414 BIBLIOGRAPHY

Edward H. Carr. *The Twenty Years' Crisis: 1919–1939*. London: Macmillan, 1939.

Austin Carson. "Facing Off and Saving Face: Covert Intervention and Escalation Management in the Korean War." In: *International Organization* 70.1 (2016), pp. 103–31.

Austin Carson. *Secret Wars: Covert Conflict in International Politics*. Princeton Studies in International History and Politics. Princeton: Princeton University Press, 2018.

Austin Carson and Keren Yarhi-Milo. "Covert Communication: The Intelligibility and Credibility of Signaling in Secret." In: *Security Studies* 26.1 (2017), pp. 124–56.

Ashton B. Carter. "Satellites and Anti-Satellites: The Limits of the Possible." In: *International Security* 10.4 (1986), pp. 46–98.

Ashton B. Carter, John B. Steinbruner, and Charles A. Zracket. *Managing Nuclear Operations*. Washington, DC: Brookings Institution 1987.

Jasen J. Castillo. *Endurance and War: The National Sources of Military Cohesion*. Stanford: Stanford University Press, 2014.

James Cavallaro, Stephan Sonnenberg, and Sarah Knuckey. *Living under Drones: Death, Injury and Trauma to Civilians from US Drone Practices in Pakistan*. Tech. rep. Stanford and New York: International Human Rights, Conflict Resolution Clinic, Stanford Law School, and NYU School of Law, Global Justice Clinic, 2012.

Jonathan D. Caverley. *Democratic Militarism: Voting, Wealth, and War*. Cambridge: Cambridge University Press, 2014.

Central Intelligence Agency. *Soviet Acquisition of Militarily Significant Western Technology: An Update*. Tech. rep. Sept. 1985. https://apps.dtic.mil/sti/pdfs/ADA160564.pdf.

Laurens Cerulus. "How Ukraine Became a Test Bed for Cyberweaponry." In: *Politico* (Feb. 14, 2019).

Sambuddho Chakravarty et al. "Detecting Traffic Snooping in Tor Using Decoys." In: *Recent Advances in Intrusion Detection*. Ed. Robin Sommer, Davide Balzarotti, and Gregor Maier. Berlin; Heidelberg Springer, 2011, pp. 222–41.

Michael S. Chase and Arthur Chan. *China's Evolving Approach to "Integrated Strategic Deterrence."* Tech. rep. Santa Monica: RAND Corporation, Apr. 2016. https://doi.org/10.7249/RR1366.

Michael S. Chase, Jeffrey Engstrom, et al. *China's Incomplete Military Transformation*. Santa Monica: RAND Corporation, 2015.

King C. Chen. *China's War with Vietnam, 1979: Issues, Decisions, and Implications*. Stanford: Hoover Institution, 1987.

Robert Chesney and Max Smeets, ed. *Deter, Disrupt, Or Deceive: Assessing Cyber Conflict as an Intelligence Contest*. Washington, DC: Georgetown University Press, 2023.

Chia Yuan Cho et al. "Insights from the Inside: A View of Botnet Management from Infiltration." In: *Proceedings of the 3rd USENIX Conference on Large-Scale Exploits and Emergent Threats: Botnets, Spyware, Worms, and More*. LEET'10. Berkeley: USENIX Association, 2010.

Nazli Choucri and David D. Clark. *International Relations in the Cyber Age: The Co-Evolution Dilemma*. Cambridge, MA: MIT Press, 2018.

Thomas J. Christensen and Jack Snyder. "Chain Gangs and Passed Bucks: Predicting Alliance Patterns in Multipolarity." In: *International Organization* 44.2 (1990), pp. 137–68.

Olga Chyzh. "Dangerous Liaisons: An Endogenous Model of International Trade and Human Rights." In: *Journal of Peace Research* 53.3 (2016), pp. 409–23.

Stephen J. Cimbala. "Nuclear Crisis Management and 'Cyberwar': Phishing for Trouble?" In: *Strategic Studies Quarterly* (2011), Vol 5, Issue 1 pp. 117–31. https://www.airuniversity.af.edu/Portals/10/SSQ/documents/Volume-05_Issue-1/Cimbala.pdf.

Stephen J. Cimbala. *Nuclear Weapons in the Information Age*. London: Continuum International Publishing, 2012.

Stephen J. Cimbala. "Nuclear Deterrence and Cyber: The Quest for Concept." In: *Air & Space Power Journal* (2014), Vol 28 Issue 2 pp. 87–107. https://www.airuniversity.af.edu/Portals/10/ASPJ/journals/Volume-28_Issue-2/V-Cimbala.pdf.

David D. Clark. "A Cloudy Crystal Ball: Visions of the Future." Plenary presentation presented at the 24th meeting of the Internet Engineering Task Force, Cambridge, MA, July 17, 1992. https://groups.csail.mit.edu/ana/People/ DDC/future_ietf_92.pdf.

Richard A. Clarke and Robert K. Knake. *Cyber War: The Next Threat to National Security and What to Do about It*. New York: Ecco, 2010.

Carl von Clausewitz. *On War*. Trans. Michael Howard and Peter Paret. Princeton: Princeton University Press, 1976.

Richard Cobden. *Political Writings of Richard Cobden*. Vol. I. London: T. Fisher Unwin, 1903 [1867].

Elbridge Colby. "Cyberwar and the Nuclear Option." In: *The National Interest* June 24, 2013. https://nationalinterest.org/commentary/cyberwar-the- nuclear-option-8638.

Luke N. Condra and Jake N. Shapiro. "Who Takes the Blame? The Strategic Effects of Collateral Damage." In: *American Journal of Political Science* (2010).

Julian Corbett. *Some Principles of Maritime Strategy*. London: Longmans, Green and Co., 1911.

Herley Cormac. "Why Do Nigerian Scammers Say They Are from Nigeria?" Workshop on the Economics of Information Security (WEIS 12), Berlin, June 25, 2012. https://www.microsoft.com/en-us/research/wp-content/uploads/2016/02/WhyFromNigeria.pdf.

James W. Cortada. *The Digital Hand*. Volume III, Oxford; New York: Oxford University Press, 2008.

Mathieu Couillard. "The Role of Deceptive Defense in Cyber Strategy." MA thesis. Monterey, CA: Naval Postgraduate School, June 2023.

Conrad C. Crane. *Bombs, Cities, and Civilians: American Airpower Strategy in World War II*. Lawrence: University Press of Kansas, 1993.

Timothy Crawford. *Pivotal Deterrence: Third-Party Statecraft and the Pursuit of Peace*. Ithaca: Cornell University Press, 2003.

Madelyn R. Creedon. "Space and Cyber: Shared Challenges, Shared Opportunities." In: *Strategic Studies Quarterly* (2012), Vol 6, issue 1 pp. 3–8. https://www.airuniversity.af.edu/Portals/10/SSQ/documents/Volume-06_Issue-1/creedon.pdf.

Mark Crescenzi. "Economic Exit, Interdependence, and Conflict: An Empirical Analysis." In: *Journal of Politics* 65.3 (2003), pp. 809–32.

Mark J. C. Crescenzi. *Economic Interdependence and Conflict in World Politics*. Lanham, MD: Lexington Books, 2005.

Mark J. C. Crescenzi et al. "Reliability, Reputation, and Alliance Formation." In: *International Studies Quarterly* 56.2 (2012), pp. 259–74.

Brian B. Crisher. "Naval Power, Endogeneity, and Long-Distance Disputes." In: *Research & Politics* 4.1 (2017). https://doi.org/10.1177/2053168017691700.

Rebecca Crootof. "The Killer Robots Are Here: Legal and Policy Implications." In: *Cardozo Law Review* 36 (2014), p. 1837.

Fiona S. Cunningham. "Strategic Substitution: China's Search for Coercive Leverage in the Information Age." In: *International Security* 47.1 (2022), pp. 46–92.

Allan Dafoe. "On Technological Determinism: A Typology, Scope Conditions, and a Mechanism." In: *Science, Technology, & Human Values* 40.6 (2015), pp. 1047–76.

416 BIBLIOGRAPHY

Allan Dafoe, John R. Oneal, and Bruce Russett. "The Democratic Peace: Weighing the Evidence and Cautious Inference." In: *International Studies Quarterly* 57.1 (2013), pp. 201–14.

James W. Davis et al. "Taking Offense at Offense-Defense Theory." In: *International Security* 23.3 (1998), pp. 179–206.

Alexandre Debs and Nuno P. Monteiro. "Known Unknowns: Power Shifts, Uncertainty, and War." In: *International Organization* 68.1 (2014), pp. 1–31.

Defense Science Board. "Resilient Military Systems and the Advanced Cyber Threat." Washington, DC: Office of the Under Secretary of Defense for Acquisition, Technology, and Logistics, January 2013.

Ronald J. Deibert, Rafal Rohozinski, and Masashi Crete-Nishihata. "Cyclones in Cyberspace: Information Shaping and Denial in the 2008 Russia–Georgia War." In: *Security Dialogue* 43.1 (2012), pp. 3–24.

Ronald J. Deibert. "Toward a Human-Centric Approach to Cybersecurity." In: *Ethics & International Affairs* 32.4 (2018), pp. 411–24.

Ronald J. Deibert. "Subversion Inc: The Age of Private Espionage." In: *Journal of Democracy* 33.2 (2022), pp. 28–44.

Laura DeNardis. *The Global War for Internet Governance.* New Haven: Yale University Press, 2014.

Abraham M. Denmark and James Mulvenon, ed. *Contested Commons: The Future of American Power in a Multipolar World.* Washington, DC: Center for a New American Security, 2010.

Dorothy E. Denning. "Barriers to Entry: Are They Lower for Cyber Warfare?" In: *IO Journal* April 2009, pp. 6–10. https://faculty.nps.edu/dedennin/publications/ Denning-BarriersToEntry.pdf.

Department of Defense. *2022 National Defense Strategy of the United States of America.* Washington, DC, Oct. 2022.

Daniel Deudney. *Whole Earth Security: A Geopolitics of Peace.* Worldwatch Paper 55. Washington, DC: Worldwatch Institute, July 1983.

Karen DeYoung. "Pakistani Ambassador to US Calls CIA Drone Strikes a 'Clear Violation.'" In: *Washington Post* (Feb. 5, 2013). Section: National Security. https:// www.washingtonpost.com/world/national-security/pakistani-ambassador-to-us-calls-cia-drone-strikes-a-clear-violation/2013/02/05/1a620fc2-6fa9-11e2-ac36-3d8d9dcaa2e2_story.html

Janina Dill. *Legitimate Targets?: Social Construction, International Law and US Bombing.* New York: Cambridge University Press, 2014.

Michael Dobbs. *One Minute to Midnight: Kennedy, Khrushchev, and Castro on the Brink of Nuclear War.* 1st ed. New York: Alfred A. Knopf, 2008.

Melina J. Dobson. "Operation Rubicon: Germany as an Intelligence 'Great Power'?" In: *Intelligence and National Security* 35.5 (2020), pp. 608–22.

Everett C. Dolman. *Astropolitik: Classical Geopolitics in the Space Age.* London: Routledge, 2001.

Han Dorussen and Hugh Ward. "International Organizations and the Kantian Peace: A Network Perspective." In: *Journal of Conflict Resolution* 52.2 (2008), pp. 189–212.

Han Dorussen and Hugh Ward. "Trade Networks and the Kantian Peace." In: *Journal of Peace Research* 47.1 (2010), pp. 29–42.

Alexander B. Downes and Mary Lauren Lilley. "Overt Peace, Covert War? Covert Intervention and the Democratic Peace." In: *Security Studies* 19.2 (2010), pp. 266–306.

Daniel W. Drezner. "Economic Sanctions in Theory and Practice: How Smart Are They?" In: *Coercion: The Power to Hurt in International Politics*. Ed. Kelly M. Greenhill and Peter Krause. New York: Oxford University Press, 2018, pp. 251–70.

Jesse Driscoll and Daniel Maliniak. "With Friends Like These: Brinkmanship and Chain-Ganging in Russia's Near Abroad." In: *Security Studies* 25.4 (2016), pp. 585–607.

Jesse Driscoll and Zachary Steinert-Threlkeld. "Social Media and Russian Territorial Irredentism: Some Facts and a Conjecture." In: *Post-Soviet Affairs* 36.2 (2020), pp. 101–21.

Thomas Dullien. "Weird Machines, Exploitability, and Provable Unexploitability." In: *IEEE Transactions on Emerging Topics in Computing* 8.2 (2020), pp. 391–403.

Joseph Dunford. *Gen. Dunford's Remarks and Q&A*. Center for Strategic and International Studies, December 14, 2015. Washington, DC. https://www.cnas.org/publications/transcript/gen-dunfords-remarks-and-q-a-at-the-cnas-inaugural-national-security-forum.

Myriam Dunn Cavelty. *Cyber-Security and Threat Politics: US Efforts to Secure the Information Age*. New York: Routledge, 2008.

Myriam Dunn Cavelty. "From Cyber-Bombs to Political Fallout: Threat Representations with an Impact in the Cyber-Security Discourse." In: *International Studies Review* 15.1 (2013), pp. 105–22.

Bryan R. Early. "Exploring the Final Frontier: An Empirical Analysis of Global Civil Space Proliferation." In: *International Studies Quarterly* 58.1 (2014), pp. 55–67.

Bryan R. Early and Fahrenkopf, Nolan, Shooting for the Stars: Introducing the National Space and Ballistic Missile (NSBM) Dataset (July 13, 2017). Available at SSRN: http://dx.doi.org/10.2139/ssrn.3001913.

Bryan R. Early and Erik Gartzke. "Spying from Space: Reconnaissance Satellites and Interstate Disputes." In: *Journal of Conflict Resolution* 65.9 (2021), pp. 1551–75.

Megan Eckstein. *SECDEF Esper Calls for 500-Ship Fleet by 2045, With 3 SSNs a Year and Light Carriers Supplementing CVNs*. USNI News. Oct. 6, 2020. https://news.usni.org/2020/10/06/secdef-esper-calls-for-500-ship-fleet-by-2045-with-3-ssns-a-year-and-light-carriers-supplementing-cvns.

Benjamin Edelman. "Adverse Selection in Online 'Trust' Certifications and Search Results." In: *Electronic Commerce Research and Applications* 10.1 (2011), pp. 17–25.

Florian J. Egloff. *Semi-State Actors in Cybersecurity*. New York: Oxford University Press, 2021.

Florian J. Egloff and James Shires. "The Better Angels of Our Digital Nature? Offensive Cyber Capabilities and State Violence." In: *European Journal of International Security* (2021), vol 8 is 1 pp. 130–149.

David Elliott. "Deterring Strategic Cyberattack." In: *IEEE Security & Privacy* 9.5 (2011), pp. 36–40.

Stephen Engelberg and Michael Wines. "US Says Soldier Crippled Spy Post Set Up in Berlin." In: *New York Times* (May 7, 1989). Section: World.

Andrew S. Erickson. "Rising Tide, Dispersing Waves: Opportunities and Challenges for Chinese Seapower Development." In: *Journal of Strategic Studies* 37.3 (2014), pp. 372–402.

Andrew S. Erickson et al. "Correspondence: How Good Are China's Antiaccess/Area- Denial Capabilities?" In: *International Security* 41.4 (2017), pp. 202–13.

David Ettinger and Philippe Jehiel. "A Theory of Deception." In: *American Economic Journal: Microeconomics* 2.1 (2010), pp. 1–20.

418 BIBLIOGRAPHY

Michael Fallon. *Speech Delivered by Secretary of State for Defence Sir Michael Fallon at the RUSI Landwarfare Conference*. Speech. June 29, 2017. https://www.gov.uk/government/speeches/secretary-of-states-speech-to-the-rusi-land-warfare-conference.

James D. Fearon. "Rationalist Explanations for War." In: *International Organization* 49.3 (1995), pp. 379–414.

James D. Fearon. "Signaling Foreign Policy Interests: Tying Hands versus Sinking Costs." In: *Journal of Conflict Resolution* 41.1 (1997), pp. 68–90.

James D. Fearon. "Cooperation, Conflict, and the Costs of Anarchy." In: *International Organization* 72.3 (2018), pp. 523–59.

Larrie D. Ferreiro. "Horatio Nelson Never Wrote 'A Ship's a Fool to Fight a Fort'; It Was Jackie Fisher Who Invented the Attribution." In: *Journal of Military History* 80.3 (2016), pp. 855–56.

John Ferris. "The Intelligence-Deception Complex: An Anatomy." In: *Intelligence and National Security* 4.4 (1989), pp. 719–34.

Dmitry Filipoff. *Fleet Force Structure Perspectives Series*. Center for International Maritime Security. Oct. 26, 2020. Center for International Maritime Security (CIMSEC) Web forum. https://cimsec.org/fleet-force-structure-series/.

Benjamin B. Fischer. "CANOPY WING: The US War Plan That Gave the East Germans Goose Bumps." In: *International Journal of Intelligence and CounterIntelligence* 27.3 (2014), pp. 431–64.

Michael P. Fischerkeller, Emily O. Goldman, and Richard J. Harknett. *Cyber Persistence Theory: Redefining National Security in Cyberspace*. New York: Oxford University Press, 2022.

Michèle A. Flournoy. "How to Prevent a War in Asia." Foreign Affairs June 18. 2020. https://www.foreignaffairs.com/articles/united-states/2020-06-18/how-prevent-war-asia.

Christopher Ford and David Rosenberg. *The Admirals' Advantage: US Navy Operational Intelligence in World War II and the Cold War*. Annapolis: Naval Institute Press, 2005.

Ulrike Esther Franke. "Drones, Drone Strikes, and US Policy: The Politics of Unmanned Aerial Vehicles." In: *Parameters* 44.1 (2014), pp. 121–30.

M. Taylor Fravel. "Shifts in Warfare and Party Unity: Explaining China's Changes in Military Strategy." In: *International Security* 42.3 (2018), pp. 37–83.

Bryan Frederick et al. *Understanding the Deterrent Impact of US Overseas Forces*. Santa Monica: RAND Corporation, 2020.

Lawrence Freedman. "The First Two Generations of Nuclear Strategists." In: *Makers of Modern Strategy: From Machiavelli to the Nuclear Age*. Ed. Peter Paret. New York: Oxford, 1986, pp. 735–78.

Lawrence Freedman. *Deterrence*. New York: Polity Press, 2004.

Lawrence Freedman. *Strategy: A History*. New York: Oxford University Press, 2013.

Norman Friedman. *Seapower and Space: From the Dawn of the Missile Age to Net-centric Warfare*. Annapolis: Naval Institute Press, 2000.

Norman Friedman. *Seapower as Strategy: Navies and National Interests*. Annapolis: Naval Institute Press, 2001.

Norman Friedman. *Network-centric Warfare: How Navies Learned to Fight Smarter through Three World Wars*. Annapolis: Naval Institute Press, 2009.

Jason Fritz. *Hacking Nuclear Command and Control*. Research Paper. Canberra, Australia: International Commission on Nuclear Non-proliferation and Disarmament, July 2009.

Mitsuo Fuchida. *Midway: The Battle That Doomed Japan*. New York: Ballan-tine, 1986.

BIBLIOGRAPHY 419

Matthew Fuhrmann and Michael C. Horowitz. "Droning On: Explaining the Proliferation of Unmanned Aerial Vehicles." In: *International Organization* 71.2 (2017), pp. 397–418.

Francis Fukuyama. "The End of History?" In: *The National Interest* 16 (1989), pp. 3–18.

David A. Fulghum. *Why Syria's Air Defenses Failed to Detect Israelis.* Aviation Week, Ares Blog. Oct. 5, 2007.

Jonathan Fuller et al. "C3PO: Large-Scale Study of Covert Monitoring of C&C Servers via Over-Permissioned Protocol Infiltration." In: *Proceedings of the 2021 ACM SIGSAC Conference on Computer and Communications Security.* CCS '21. New York: Association for Computing Machinery, 2021, pp. 3352–65.

Andrew Futter, "Hacking the Bomb: Nuclear Weapons in the Cyber Age" (paper presented at the ISA Annual. Conference, New Orleans, LA, February 2015).

Andrew Futter. "The Double-Edged Sword: US Nuclear Command and Control Modernization." In: *Bulletin of the Atomic Scientists* June 29, 2016. Blog post https://thebulletin.org/2016/06/the-double- edged-sword-us-nuclear-command-and-control-modernization/.

Johan Galtung. *Peace by Peaceful Means: Peace and Conflict, Development and Civilization.* London: SAGE, 1996.

J. Andrés Gannon. "One if by Land, and Two if by Sea: Cross-Domain Contests and the Escalation of International Crises." In: *International Studies Quarterly* 66.4 (2022). https://doi.org/10.1093/isq/sqac065.

J. Andrés Gannon et al. "The Shadow of Deterrence: Why Capable Actors Engage in Contests Short of War." In: *Journal of Conflict Resolution* (2023). https://doi.org/10.1177/00220027231166345.

Ben Garfinkel and Allan Dafoe. "How Does the Offense-Defense Balance Scale?" In: *Journal of Strategic Studies* 42.6 (2019), pp. 736–63.

Erik Gartzke. "War Is in the Error Term." In: *International Organization* 53.3 (1999), pp. 567–87.

Erik Gartzke. "Democracy and the Preparation for War: Does Regime Type Affect States' Anticipation of Casualties?" In: *International Studies Quarterly* 45.3 (2001), pp. 467–84.

Erik Gartzke. "War, Bargaining, and the Military Commitment Problem." New Haven: Yale University Press, 2001.

Erik Gartzke. "The Classical Liberals Were Just Lucky: A Few Thoughts about Interdependence and Peace." In: *Economic Interdependence and International Conflict. New Perspectives on an Enduring Debate.* Ed. Edward D. Mansfield and Brian M. Pollins. Ann Arbor: University of Michigan Press, 2003, pp. 96–110.

Erik Gartzke. "Globalization, Economic Development, and Territorial Conflict." In: *Territoriality and Conflict in an Era of Globalization.* Ed. Miles Kahler and Barbara Walter. Cambridge: Cambridge University Press, 2006, pp. 156–86.

Erik Gartzke. "The Capitalist Peace." In: *American Journal of Political Science* 51.1 (2007), pp. 166–91.

Erik Gartzke. "The Myth of Cyberwar: Bringing War in Cyberspace Back Down to Earth." In: *International Security* 38.2 (2013), pp. 41–73.

Erik Gartzke. "Blood and Robots: How Remotely Piloted Vehicles and Related Technologies Affect the Politics of Violence." In: *Journal of Strategic Studies* 44.7 (2021), pp. 983–1013.

Erik Gartzke and Koji Kagotani. "Trust in Tripwires: Deployments, Costly Signaling and Extended General Deterrence." Typescript. University of California, San Diego and Osaka University of Economics, 2016.

420 BIBLIOGRAPHY

Erik Gartzke and Koji Kagotani. "Being There: US Troop Deployments, Force Posture and Alliance Reliability." Working Paper, 2017.

Erik Gartzke, Jeffrey M. Kaplow, and Rupal N. Mehta. "The Determinants of Nuclear Force Structure." In: *Journal of Conflict Resolution* 58.3 (2014), pp. 481–508.

Erik Gartzke and Matthew Kroenig. "Nukes with Numbers: Empirical Research on the Consequences of Nuclear Weapons for International Conflict." In: *Annual Review of Political Science* 19.1 (2016), pp. 397–412.

Erik Gartzke and Jon R. Lindsay. "Weaving Tangled Webs: Offense, Defense, and Deception in Cyberspace." In: *Security Studies* 24.2 (2015), pp. 316–48.

Erik Gartzke and Jon R. Lindsay. "The Influence of Sea Power on Politics: Domain- and Platform-Specific Attributes of Material Capabilities." In: *Security Studies* 29.4 (2020), pp. 601–36.

Erik Gartzke and Jonathan Markowitz. "Leveraging in US Alliance Policy: Tactics and Tipping-Points." Typescript. UC San Diego and USC, 2015.

Erik Gartzke and Dominic Rohner. "The Political Economy of Imperialism, Decolonization and Development." In: *British Journal of Political Science* 41.3 (2011), pp. 525–56.

Erik Gartzke and James Igoe Walsh. "The Drawbacks of Drones: The Effects of UAVs on Militant Violence in Pakistan." In: *Journal of Peace Research* 59.4 (2022), pp. 463–77.

Erik Gartzke and Jiakun Jack Zhang. "Trade and War." In: *The Oxford Handbook of the Political Economy of International Trade.* Ed. Lisa L. Martin. New York: Oxford University Press, 2015.

Erik Gartzke, Shannon Carcelli, et al. "Signaling in Foreign Policy." In: *Oxford Research Encyclopedia of Politics* (2017). https://doi.org/10.1093/acrefore/9780190228637.013.481.

Erik Gartzke and Oliver Westerwinter. "The Complex Structure of Commercial Peace Contrasting Trade Interdependence, Asymmetry, and Multipolarity." In: *Journal of Peace Research* 53.3 (2016), pp. 325–43.

Mark J. Gasiorowski. "Economic Interdependence and International Conflict: Some Cross-National Evidence." In: *International Studies Quarterly* 30.1 (1986), pp. 23–38.

Hans Gatzke, trans. *Carl von Clausewitz's Principles of War.* New York: Dover, 1999.

Francis J. Gavin. *Nuclear Statecraft: History and Strategy in America's Atomic Age.* Ithaca: Cornell University Press, 2012.

Francis J. Gavin. "Rethinking the Bomb: Nuclear Weapons and American Grand Strategy." In: *Texas National Security Review* 2.1 (2019), pp. 74–100.

Alexander George and Richard Smoke. "Deterrence and Foreign Policy." In: *World Politics* 41.2 (1989), pp. 170–82.

Alexander George, Richard Smoke, et al. *Deterrence in American Foreign policy: Theory and Practice.* New York: Columbia University Press, 1974.

George Lee Butler. *Uncommon Cause: A Life at Odds with Convention,* Volume II: *The Transformative Years.* Denver: Outskirts Press, 2016.

Josh Gerstein. Ex-DNI rips Obama White House. POLITICO. July 29, 2011.

Eugene Gholz, Benjamin Friedman, and Enea Gjoza. "Defensive Defense: A Better Way to Protect US Allies in Asia." In: *Washington Quarterly* 42.4 (2019), pp. 171–89.

Eugene Gholz, Daryl G. Press, and Harvey M. Sapolsky. "Come Home, America: The Strategy of Restraint in the Face of Temptation." In: *International Security* 21.4 (1997), pp. 5–48.

Douglas Gibler. "The Costs of Reneging: Reputation and Alliance Formation." In: *Journal of Conflict Resolution* 52.3 (2008), pp. 426–54.

Lilach Gilady. *The Price of Prestige: Conspicuous Consumption in International Relations.* Chicago: University of Chicago Press, 2018.

David V. Gioe, Michael S. Goodman, and Tim Stevens. "Intelligence in the Cyber Era: Evolution or Revolution?" In: *Political Science Quarterly* 135.2 (2020), pp. 191–224.

Charles L. Glaser and Chaim Kaufmann. "What Is the Offense-Defense Balance and How Can We Measure It?" In: *International Security* 22.4 (1998), pp. 44–82.

Charles L. Glaser. *Analyzing Strategic Nuclear Policy.* Princeton: Princeton University Press, 1990.

Charles L. Glaser. *Rational Theory of International Politics: The Logic of Competition and Cooperation.* Princeton: Princeton University Press, 2010.

Charles L. Glaser and Steve Fetter. "Should the United States Reject MAD? Damage Limitation and US Nuclear Strategy toward China." In: *International Security* 41.1 (2016), pp. 49–98.

Nils Petter Gleditsch et al. "The Forum: The Decline of War." In: *International Studies Review* 15.3 (2013), pp. 396–419.

Roy Godson and James J. Wirtz. "Strategic Denial and Deception." In: *International Journal of Intelligence and Counterintelligence* 13.4 (2000), pp. 424–37.

James M. Goldgeier and Joshua R. Itzkowitz Shifrinson, ed. *Evaluating NATO Enlargement: From Cold War Victory to the Russia-Ukraine War.* London: Palgrave MacMillan, 2023.

James M. Goldgeier and Philip E. Tetlock. "Psychology and International Relations Theory." In: *Annual Review of Political Science* 4.1 (2001), pp. 67–92.

Jack Goldsmith. *Cybersecurity Treaties: A Skeptical View.* Tech. rep. Stanford: Hoover Institution, 2011.

Jack Goldsmith and Tim Wu. *Who Controls the Internet? Illusions of a Borderless World.* Oxford: Oxford University Press, 2006.

Avery Goldstein. "First Things First: The Pressing Danger of Crisis Instability in US-China Relations." In: *International Security* 37.4 (2013), pp. 49–89.

Lyle Goldstein. "The US-China Naval Balance in the Asia-Pacific: An Overview." In: *China Quarterly* 232 (2017), pp. 904–31.

Miguel Alberto Gomez and Christopher Whyte. "Breaking the Myth of Cyber Doom: Securitization and Normalization of Novel Threats." In: *International Studies Quarterly* 65.4 (2021), pp. 1137–50.

David C. Gompert and Martin Libicki. "Cyber Warfare and Sino-American Crisis Instability." In: *Survival* 56.4 (2014), pp. 7–22.

David C. Gompert and Phillip C. Saunders. *The Paradox of Power: Sino- American Strategic Restraint in an Age of Vulnerability.* Washington, DC: National Defense University Press, 2011.

Jeff Goodwin. *No Other Way Out: States and Revolutionary Movements, 1945–1991.* New York: Cambridge University Press, 2001.

Yoav Gortzak, Yoram Z. Haftel, and Kevin Sweeney. "Offence-Defence Theory: An Empirical Assessment." In: *Journal of Conflict Resolution* 49.1 (2005), pp. 67–89.

Robert Gorwa and Max Smeets. "Cyber Conflict in Political Science: A Review of Methods and Literature." International Studies Association Annual Convention, Toronto, 2019. https://doi.org/10.31235/osf.io/fc6sg.

Government Accountability Organization. *Nuclear Command, Control, and Communications: Update on DOD's Modernization.* Tech. rep. GAO-15-584R. Washington, DC, June 2015.

422   BIBLIOGRAPHY

Ryan Grauer. *Commanding Military Power: Organizing for Victory and Defeat on the Battlefield*. New York: Cambridge University Press, 2016.

Colin S. Gray. *Modern Strategy*. New York: Oxford University Press, 1999.

Stefano Grazioli and Sirkka L. Jarvenpaa. "Consumer and Business Deception on the Internet: Content Analysis of Documentary Evidence." In: *International Journal of Electronic Commerce* 7.4 (2003), pp. 93–118.

Brendan Rittenhouse Green. *The Revolution That Failed: Nuclear Competition, Arms Control, and the Cold War*. New York: Cambridge University Press, 2020.

Brendan Rittenhouse Green and Austin Long. "Conceal or Reveal? Managing Clandestine Military Capabilities in Peacetime Competition." In: *International Security* 44.3 (2020), pp. 48–83.

Brendan Rittenhouse Green and Austin G. Long. "Signaling with Secrets—Evidence on Soviet Perceptions and Counterforce Developments in the Late Cold War." In: *Cross-Domain Deterrence: Strategy in an Era of Complexity*. Ed. Jon R. Lindsay and Erik Gartzke. New York: Oxford University Press, 2019.

Michael Green et al. *Countering Coercion in Maritime Asia: The Theory and Practice of Gray Zone Deterrence*. Tech. rep. Washington, DC: Center for Strategic and International Studies, May 2017.

Andy Greenberg. *Sandworm: A New Era of Cyberwar and the Hunt for the Kremlin's Most Dangerous Hackers*. New York: Doubleday, 2019.

Andy Greenberg. "Russia's New Cyberwarfare in Ukraine Is Fast, Dirty, and Relentless." In: *Wired* (Nov. 10, 2022).

Jonathan W. Greenert and Norton A. Schwartz. "Air-Sea Battle." In: *The American Interest* (Feb. 10, 2012). https://www.the-american-interest.com/2012/02/20/air-sea-battle/.

Kelly M. Greenhill. "Asymmetric Advantage: Weaponizing People as Nonmilitary Instruments of Cross-Domain Coercion." In: *Cross-Domain Deterrence: Strategy in an Era of Complexity*. Ed. Jon R. Lindsay and Erik Gartzke. New York: Oxford University Press, 2019, pp. 259–89.

Kelly M. Greenhill and Peter Krause, ed. *Coercion: The Power to Hurt in International Politics*. New York: Oxford University Press, 2018.

Ted Greenwood. "Reconnaissance, Surveillance and Arms Control: Introduction." In: *Adelphi Papers* 12.88 (1972), pp. 1–4.

Shaun Gregory. *The Hidden Cost of Deterrence: Nuclear Weapons Accidents*. London: Brassey's, 1990.

Joseph M. Grieco. "Anarchy and the Limits of Cooperation: A Realist Critique of the Newest Liberal Institutionalism." In: *International Organization* 42.3 (1988), pp. 485–507.

Emilie M. Hafner-Burton and Alexander H. Montgomery. "Power or Plenty. How Do International Trade Institutions Affect Economic Sanctions?" In: *Journal of Conflict Resolution* 52 (2008), pp. 213–42.

Paul Halpern. *A Naval History of World War I*. Annapolis: Naval Institute Press, 2012.

Michael I. Handel. "The Yom Kippur War and the Inevitability of Surprise." In: *International Studies Quarterly* 21.3 (1977), pp. 461–502.

Michael I. Handel. *Masters of War: Classical Strategic Thought*. 3rd rev. and expanded ed.; repr. London: Cass, 2005.

Cecil D. Haney. *Testimony*. Washington DC: 2015. Mar 19, 2015 Senate Armed Services Committee Washington DC. https://www.stratcom.mil/speeches/2015/130/Senate_Armed_Services_Committee_Testimony/.

Lene Hansen and Helen Nissenbaum. "Digital Disaster, Cyber Security, and the Copenhagen School." In: *International Studies Quarterly* 53.4 (2009), pp. 1155–75.

Richard J. Harknett. "The Risks of a Networked Military." In: *Orbis* 44.1 (2000), pp. 127–43.

Richard J. Harknett and Michael P. Fischerkeller. "Deterrence is Not a Credible Strategy for Cyberspace." In: *Orbis* 61.3 (2017), pp. 381–93.

Richard J. Harknett and Max Smeets. "Cyber Campaigns and Strategic Outcomes." In: *Journal of Strategic Studies* 45.4 (2022), pp. 534–67.

Basil Henry Liddell Hart. *Strategy: The Indirect Approach*. London: Faber & Faber, 1967.

Brian Harvey, Henk Smid, and Théo Pirard. *Emerging Space Powers: The New Space Programs of Asia, the Middle East and South-America*. Berlin: Springer, 2010.

Phil M. Haun and Colin F. Jackson. "Breaker of Armies: Air Power in the Easter Offensive and the Myth of Linebacker I and II in the Vietnam War." In: *International Security* 40.3 (2016), pp. 139–78.

Phil M. Haun. *Coercion, Survival, and War: Why Weak States Resist the United States*. Stanford: Stanford University Press, 2015.

Phil M. Haun. "Air Power versus Ground Forces—Deterrence at the Operational Level of War." In: *Cross-Domain Deterrence: Strategy in an Era of Complexity*. Ed. Jon R. Lindsay and Erik Gartzke. New York: Oxford University Press, 2019, pp. 144–62.

Daniel R. Headrick. *The Invisible Weapon: Telecommunications and International Politics, 1851–1945*. New York: Oxford University Press, 1991.

Jason Healey and Robert Jervis. "The Escalation Inversion and Other Oddities of Situational Cyber Stability." In: *Texas National Security Review* 3.4 (2020), pp. 30–53.

Kristin E. Heckman and Frank J. Stech. "Cyber-Counterdeception: How to Detect Denial & Deception (D&D)." In: *Cyber Wargames*. Ed. Sushil Jajodia. New York: Springer, 2015.

Eric Heginbotham. "The Fall and Rise of Navies in East Asia: Military Organizations, Domestic Politics, and Grand Strategy." In: *International Security* 27.2 (2002), pp. 86–125.

Havard Hegre, John R. Oneal, and Bruce Russett. "Trade Does Promote Peace: New Simultaneous Estimates of the Reciprocal Effects of Trade and Conflict." In: *Journal of Peace Research* 47.6 (2010), pp. 763–74.

Jon Henley. "Denmark Helped US Spy on Angela Merkel and European Allies—Report." In: *The Guardian* (May 31, 2021).

Iain D. Henry. "What Allies Want: Reconsidering Loyalty, Reliability and Alliance Interdependence." In: *International Security* 44.4 (2020), pp. 45–83.

Paul R. Hensel. "Territory: Theory and Evidence on Geography and Conflict." In: *What Do We Know about War?* Ed. John A. Vasquez. New York: Rowman & Littlefield, 2000, pp. 57–84.

Cormac Herley. "When Does Targeting Make Sense for an Attacker?" In: *IEEE Security & Privacy* 11.2 (2013), pp. 89–92.

Cormac Herley and D. Florêncio. (2008). Protecting Financial Institutions from Brute-Force Attacks. In: Jajodia, S., Samarati, P., Cimato, S. (eds) *Proceedings of The IFIP TC 11 23rd International Information Security Conference, IFIP SEC'08, September 7–10, 2008, Milano, Italy*. The International Federation for Information Processing, vol 278. New York: Springer, 2008.

Michael Herman. *Intelligence Power in Peace and War*. New York: Cambridge University Press, 1996.

424   BIBLIOGRAPHY

Geoffrey L. Herrera. *Technology and International Transformation: The Railroad, the Atom Bomb, and the Politics of Technological Change.* Albany: State University of New York Press, 2006.

Drew Herrick and Trey Herr. Combating Complexity: Offensive Cyber Capabilities and Integrated Warfighting (February 2016). Available at SSRN: https://ssrn.com/abstract=2845709 or http://dx.doi.org/10.2139/ssrn.2845709.

Richards J. Heuer, Jr. "Strategic Deception and Counterdeception: A Cognitive Process Approach." In: *International Studies Quarterly* 25.2 (1981): 294–327.

Beatrice Heuser. *The Evolution of Strategy: Thinking War from Antiquity to the Present.* New York: Cambridge University Press, 2010.

Beatrice Heuser. "Regina Maris and the Command of the Sea: The Sixteenth Century Origins of Modern Maritime Strategy." In: *Journal of Strategic Studies* 40.1–2 (2017), pp. 225–62.

Kathleen H. Hicks and Alice Hunt Friend. *By Other Means*, Part I: *Campaigning in the Gray Zone.* Tech. rep. Lanham: Center for Strategic & International Studies, 2019.

Albert O. Hirschman. *National Power and the Structure of Foreign Trade.* Berkeley: University of California Press, 1945.

David Hoffman. *The Dead Hand: The Untold Story of the Cold War Arms Race and Its Dangerous Legacy.* New York: Random House, 2009.

Frank G. Hoffman. *Conflict in the 21st Century: The Rise of Hybrid Wars.* Tech. rep. Arlington, VA: Potomac Institute for Policy Studies, 2007, p. 72.

James R. Holmes and Toshi Yoshihara. "An Ocean Too Far: Offshore Balancing in the Indian Ocean." In: *Asian Security* 8.1 (2012), pp. 1–26.

James R. Holmes and Toshi Yoshihara. "Deterring China in the 'Gray Zone': Lessons of the South China Sea for US Alliances." In: *Orbis* 61.3 (2017), pp. 322–39.

Kalevi Holsti. "The Decline of Interstate War: Pondering Systemic Explanations." In: *Kalevi Holsti: Major Texts on War, the State, Peace, and International Order.* New York: Springer, 2016, pp. 43–64.

Michael C. Horowitz and Neil Narang. "Poor Man's Atomic Bomb? Exploring the Relationship between 'Weapons of Mass Destruction'." In: *Journal of Conflict Resolution* 58.3 (2014), pp. 509–35.

Michael Howard. *Strategic Deception in the Second World War.* London: Pimlico, 1994.

Geraint Hughes. "War in the Grey Zone: Historical Reflections and Contemporary Implications." In: *Survival* 62.3 (2020), pp. 131–58.

Peter J. Hugill. *Global Communications since 1844: Geopolitics and Technology.* Baltimore: Johns Hopkins University Press, 1999.

Michael Allen Hunzeker and Alexander Lanoszka. "Landpower and American Credibility." In: *Parameters* 45.4 (2015), pp. 17–26.

Michael E. Hutchens et al. "Joint Concept for Access and Maneuver in the Global Commons: A New Joint Operational Concept." In: *Joint Force Quarterly* 84 (2017), pp. 134–39.

Paul K. Huth and Bruce Russett. "Deterrence Failure and Crisis Escalation." In: *International Studies Quarterly* 32.1 (1988), pp. 29–45.

Paul K. Huth. "Extended Deterrence and the Outbreak of War." In: *American Political Science Review* 82.2 (1988), pp. 423–43.

Paul K. Huth. *Extended Deterrence and the Prevention of War.* New Haven: Yale University Press, 1988.

Paul K. Huth. "Deterrence and International Conflict: Empirical Findings and Theoretical Debates." In: *Annual Review of Political Science* 2.1 (1999), pp. 25–48.

BIBLIOGRAPHY   425

Paul K. Huth and Bruce Russett. "What Makes Deterrence Work? Cases from 1900 to 1980." In: *World Politics* 36.4 (1984), pp. 496–526.

Paul K. Huth and Bruce Russett. "Testing Deterrence Theory: Rigor Makes a Difference." In: *World Politics* 42.2 (1990), pp. 466–501.

G. John Ikenberry. *After Victory: Institutions, Strategic Restraint, and the Rebuilding of Order after Major Wars*. Princeton: Princeton University Press, 2001.

Viktor Levonovich Israelyan. *Inside the Kremlin during the Yom Kippur War*. University Park: Pennsylvania State University Press, 1997.

Colin F. Jackson. "Information Is Not a Weapons System." In: *Journal of Strategic Studies* 39.5–6 (2016), pp. 820–46.

Galen Jackson. "The Offsore Balancing Thesis Reconsidered: Realism, the Balance of Power in Europe, and America's Decision for War in 1917." In: *Security Studies* 21.3 (2012), pp. 455–89.

Van Jackson. "Tactics of Strategic Competition: Gray Zones, Redlines, and Conflict before War." In: *Naval War College Review* 70.3 (2017), pp. 39–61.

Silvie Janièatová and Petra Mlejnková. "The Ambiguity of Hybrid Warfare: A Qualitative Content Analysis of the United Kingdom's Political-Military Discourse on Russia's Hostile Activities." In: *Contemporary Security Policy* 42.3 (2021), pp. 312–44. https://doi.org/10.1080/13523260.2021.1885921.

Scott Jasper. *Russian Cyber Operations: Coding the Boundaries of Conflict*. Washington, DC: Georgetown University Press, 2020.

Robert Jervis. *The Logic of Images in International Relations*. Princeton: Princeton University Press, 1970.

Robert Jervis. *Perception and Misperception in International Politics*. Vol. 49. Princeton: Princeton University Press, 1976.

Robert Jervis. "Cooperation under the Security Dilemma." In: *World Politics* 30.2 (1978), pp. 167–214.

Robert Jervis. *The Illogic Of American Nuclear Strategy*. Ithaca: Cornell University Press, 1984.

Robert Jervis. *The Meaning of the Nuclear Revolution: Statecraft and the Prospect of Armageddon*. Ithaca: Cornell University Press, 1989.

Robert Jervis. *System Effects: Complexity in Political and Social Life*. Princeton: Princeton University Press, 1998.

Robert Jervis. "Reports, Politics, and Intelligence Failures: The Case of Iraq." In: *Journal of Strategic Studies* 29.1 (2006), pp. 3–52.

Robert Jervis, Richard Ned Lebow, and Janice Gross Stein, ed. *Psychology and Deterrence*. Baltimore: Johns Hopkins University Press, 1985.

Chalmers Johnson. *Blowback: The Costs and Consequences of American Empire*. New York: Owl Books, 2001.

Nicholas L. Johnson. "Orbital Debris: The Growing Threat to Space Operations." 33rd Annual Guidance and Control Conference, Breckenridge, CO, Feb. 6, 2010. https://ntrs.nasa.gov/search.jsp?R=20100004498.

Paul E. Johnson et al. "Detecting Deception: Adversarial Problem Solving in a Low Base-Rate World." In: *Cognitive Science* 25.3 (2001), pp. 355–92.

Joan Johnson-Freese. *Space as a Strategic Asset*. New York: Columbia University Press, 2007.

Alastair Iain Johnston. "Is Chinese Nationalism Rising? Evidence from Beijing." In: *International Security* 41.3 (2017), pp. 7–43.

426 BIBLIOGRAPHY

Patrick B. Johnston. "Does Decapitation Work? Assessing the Effectiveness of Leadership Targeting in Counterinsurgency Campaigns." In: *International Security* 36.4 (2012), pp. 47–79.

Patrick B. Johnston and Anoop K. Sarbahi. "The Impact of US Drone Strikes on Terrorism in Pakistan." In: *International Studies Quarterly* 60.2 (2016), pp. 203–19.

Joint Chiefs of Staff. A Historical Study of Strategic Connectivity, 1950–1981. Special Historical Study Washington, DC: Joint Chiefs of Staff, Joint Secretariat, Historical Division, July 1982.

Joint Chiefs of Staff. *Cyberspace Operations.* Joint Publication 3–12. Washington, DC: Joint Chiefs of Staff, June 2018.

Jenna Jordan. "When Heads Roll: Assessing the Effectiveness of Leadership Decapitation." In: *Security Studies* 18.4 (2009), pp. 719–55.

Jenna Jordan. "Attacking the Leader, Missing the Mark." In: *International Security* 38.4 (2014), pp. 7–38.

Vincent Joubert. *Five Years after Estonia's Cyber Attacks: Lessons Learned for NATO?* Tech. rep. 76. Rome: NATO Defense College, 2012, p. 8.

Jenny Jun. *The Political Economy of Ransomware.* War on the Rocks. June 2021. Volume 42, 2021 - Issue 3, pp 312–344. https://www.tandfonline.com/doi/full/10.1080/13523260.2021.1885921.

Timothy J. Junio. "How Probable is Cyber War? Bringing IR Theory Back In to the Cyber Conflict Debate." In: *Journal of Strategic Studies* 36.1 (2013), pp. 125–33.

David Kahn. "An Historical Theory of Intelligence." In: *Intelligence and National Security* 16.3 (2001), pp. 79–92.

Herman Kahn. *On Thermonuclear War.* Princeton: Princeton University Press, 1960.

Stathis N. Kalyvas. *The Logic of Violence in Civil War.* New York: Cambridge University Press, 2006.

Monica Kaminska. "Restraint under Conditions of Uncertainty: Why the United States Tolerates Cyberattacks." In: *Journal of Cybersecurity* 7.tyab008 7:1 pp. 1–15. https://academic.oup.com/cybersecurity/article/7/1/tyab008/6162971.

Tim J. Kane. Global US Troop Deployment, 1950–2005 (May 24, 2006). Available at SSRN: https://ssrn.com/abstract=1146649 or http://dx.doi.org/10.2139/ssrn.1146649.

Fred Kaplan. *The Wizards of Armageddon.* New York: Simon and Schuster, 1986.

Fred Kaplan. " 'WarGames' and Cybersecurity's Debt to a Hollywood Hack." In: *New York Times* (Feb. 19, 2016).

Jeffrey M. Kaplow and Erik Gartzke. "The Determinants of Uncertainty in International Relations." In: *International Studies Quarterly* 65.2 (2021), pp. 306–19.

Lucas Kello. "The Meaning of the Cyber Revolution: Perils to Theory and Statecraft." In: *International Security* 38.2 (2013), pp. 7–40.

Lucas Kello. *The Virtual Weapon and International Order.* New Haven: Yale University Press, 2017.

Paul Kennedy. *The War Plans of the Great Powers (RLE The First World War): 1880–1914.* London: Routledge, 2014.

Paul Kennedy. *The Rise And Fall of British Naval Mastery.* Revised. London: Penguin Random House, 2017.

Robert O. Keohane and Joseph S. Nye. *Power and Interdependence. World Politics in Transition.* Boston and Toronto: Little, Brown and Company, 1977.

David Kilcullen and Andrew McDonald Exum. "Opinion: Death from Above, Outrage Down Below." In: *New York Times* (May 16, 2009). Section: Opinion.

Marc D. Kilgour and Frank Zagare. "Credibility, Uncertainty, and Deterrence." In: *American Journal of Political Science* 35.2 (1991), pp. 305–34.

Tongfi Kim. *The Supply Side of Security: A Market Theory of Alliances.* Stanford: Stanford University Press, 2016.

Tongfi Kim and Luis Simon. "A Reputation versus Prioritization Trade-Off: Unpacking Allied Perceptions of US Extended Deterrence in Distant Regions." In: *Security Studies* 30.5 (2021), pp. 1–36.

Tongfi Kim and Luis Simon. "Greater Security Cooperation: US Allies in Europe and East Asia." In: *Parameters* 51.2 (2021), pp. 61–71.

Gary King, Jennifer Pan, and Margaret E. Roberts. "How Censorship in China Allows Government Criticism but Silences Collective Expression." In: *American Political Science Review* 107.2 (2013), pp. 326–43.

Brandon J. Kinne. "Dependent Diplomacy: Signaling, Strategy, and Prestige in the Diplomatic Network." In: *International Studies Quarterly* 58.2 (2014), pp. 247–59.

Brandon J. Kinne. "Multilateral Trade and Militarized Conflict: Centrality, Openness, and Asymmetry in the Global Trade Network." In: *Journal of Politics* 74.1 (2012), pp. 308–22.

Brandon J. Kinne. "Does Third-Party Trade Reduce Conflict? Credible Signaling versus Opportunity Costs." In: *Conflict Management and Peace Science* 31.1 (2014), pp. 28–48.

Henry Kissinger. "Military Policy and Defense of the 'Grey Areas'. " In: *Foreign Affairs* 33.3 (1955), pp. 416–28.

Henry Kissinger. *Nuclear Weapons and Foreign Policy.* New York: Harper & Row, 1957.

Henry Kissinger. "Strategy and Organization." In: *Foreign Affairs* 35.3 (1957), pp. 379–94.

Jeffrey W. Knopf. "The Fourth Wave in Deterrence Research." In: *Contemporary Security Policy* 31.1 (2010), pp. 1–33.

Matthew Adam Kocher, Thomas B. Pepinsky, Stathis N. Kalyvas. "Aerial Bombing and Counterinsurgency in the Vietnam War." In: *American Journal of Political Science* 55.2 (2011), pp. 201–18.

Stephen W. Korns and Joshua E. Kastenberg. "Georgia's Cyber Left Hook." In: *Parameters* 38.4 (2008), pp. 60–76.

Nadiya Kostyuk and Erik Gartzke. "Why Cyber Dogs Have Yet to Bark Loudly in Russia's Invasion of Ukraine (Summer 2022)." In: *Texas National Security Review* 5.3 (2022), pp. 113–26.

Nadiya Kostyuk and Erik Gartzke. "Fighting in Cyberspace: Internet Access and the Substitutability of Cyber and Military Operations." In: *Journal of Conflict Resolution* (2023). Forthcoming. https://doi.org/10.1177/00220027231160993.

Nadiya Kostyuk and Yuri Zhukov. "Invisible Digital Front: Can Cyber Attacks Shape Battlefield Events?" In: *Journal of Conflict Resolution* 63.2 (2019), pp. 317–47.

Stephen D. Krasner. "State Power and the Structure of International Trade." In: *World Politics* 28 (1976), pp. 317–43.

Sarah Kreps and Jacquelyn Schneider. "Escalation Firebreaks in the Cyber, Conventional, and Nuclear Domains: Moving beyond Effects-Based Logics." In: *Journal of Cybersecurity* 5.1 (2019), pp. 1–11. https://academic.oup.com/cybersecurity/article/5/1/tyz007/5575971.

Kristensen, Hans M., and Robert S. Norris. "United States Nuclear Forces, 2016." Bulletin of the Atomic Scientists 72, no. 2 (March 3, 2016): 63–73. https://doi.org/10.1080/00963402.2016.1145901.

428 BIBLIOGRAPHY

Matthew Kroenig. *The Logic of American Nuclear Strategy: Why Strategic Superiority Matters*. New York: Oxford University Press, 2018.

Yang Kuisong. "The Sino-Soviet Border Clash of 1969: From Zhenbao Island to Sino-American Rapprochement." In: *Cold War History* 1.1 (2000), pp. 21–52.

Andrew H. Kydd and Barbara F. Walter. "The Strategies of Terrorism." In: *International Security* 31.1 (2006), pp. 49–80.

Andrew Lambert. *Seapower States: Maritime Culture, Continental Empires and the Conflict That Made the Modern World*. New Haven: Yale University Press, 2018.

Alexander Lanoszka. "Russian Hybrid Warfare and Extended Deterrence in Eastern Europe." In: *International Affairs* 92.1 (2016), pp. 175–95.

Alexander Lanoszka. *Atomic Assurance: The Alliance Politics of Nuclear Proliferation*. Ithaca: Cornell University Press, 2018.

Alexander Lanoszka. *Military Alliances in the Twenty-First Century*. Medford, MA: Polity, 2022.

Alexander Lanoszka and Michael A Hunzeker. "Evaluating the Enhanced Forward Presence After Five Years." The RUSI Journal 168, no. 1–2 (February 23, 2023): 88–97. https://doi.org/10.1080/03071847.2023.2190352.

Jeffrey Larsen and Kerry Kartchner. *On Limited Nuclear War in the 21st Century*. Stanford: Stanford University Press, 2014.

Harold D. Lasswell. *Politics: Who Gets What, When, How*. New York: Whittlesey House, McGraw-Hill, 1936.

Sean Lawson. "Beyond Cyber-Doom: Assessing the Limits of Hypothetical Scenarios in the Framing of Cyber-Threats." In: *Journal of Information Technology & Politics* 10.1 (2013), pp. 86–103.

Sean Lawson and Michael K. Middleton. "Cyber Pearl Harbor: Analogy, Fear, and the Framing of Cyber Security Threats in the United States, 1991–2016." In: *First Monday* 24.3–4 (2019).

Christopher Layne. "From Preponderance to Offshore Balancing." In: *International Security* 22.1 (1997), pp. 86–124.

Christopher Layne. "Offshore Balancing Revisited." In: *Washingtion Quarterly* 25.2 (2002), pp. 233–48.

Christopher Layne. "The (Almost) Triumph of Offshore Balancing." In: *National Interest* 27 (2012). https://nationalinterest.org/commentary/almost-triumph-offshore-balancing-6405.

Richard Ned Lebow and Janice Stein. "Rational Deterrence Theory: I Think, Therefore I Deter." In: *World Politics* 41.2 (1989), pp. 208–24.

Brett Ashley Leeds. "Alliance Reliability in Times of War: Explaining State Decisions to Violate Treaties." In: *International Organization* 57.4 (2003), pp. 801–27.

Brett Ashley Leeds and David Davis. "Domestic Political Vulnerability and International Disputes." In: *Journal of Conflict Resolution* 41.6 (1997), pp. 814–34.

Brett Ashley Leeds, Michaela Mattes, and Jeremy S. Vogel. "Interests, Institutions, and the Reliability of International Commitments." In: *American Journal of Political Science* 53.2 (2009), pp. 461–76.

Vladimir Lenin. *Imperialism, the Highest Stage of Capitalism*. Beijing: Foreign Languages Press, 1975 [1917].

Kirill Levchenko et al. "Click Trajectories: End-to-End Analysis of the Spam Value Chain." In: *Proceedings of the 2011 IEEE Symposium on Security and Privacy*. SP '11. Washington, DC: IEEE Computer Society, 2011, pp. 431–46.

BIBLIOGRAPHY 429

Bahar Leventoglu and Branislav L. Slantchev. "The Armed Peace: A Punctuated Equilibrium Theory of War." In: *American Journal of Political Science* 51 (2007), pp. 755–71.

Carl Levin, C. Robert Kehler, and Keith B. Alexander. *Hearing to Receive Testimony on US Strategic Command and US Cyber Command in Review of the Defense Authorization Request for Fiscal Year 2014 and the Future Years Defense Program*. Washington, DC. U.S. Senate, 113th Congress, 1st Session, Committee on Armed Services Mar. 12, 2013.

Ariel Levite. *Intelligence and Strategic Surprises*. New York: Columbia University Press, 1987.

Saul Levmore and Martha C. Nussbaum, ed. *The Offensive Internet: Speech, Privacy, and Reputation*. Cambridge, MA: Harvard University Press, 2011.

Jack S. Levy and William R. Thompson. "Balancing on Land and at Sea: Do States Ally against the Leading Global Power?" In: *International Security* 35.1 (2010), pp. 7–43.

James A. Lewis. *Cross-Domain Deterrence and Credible Threats*. Tech. rep. Washington, DC: Center for Strategic and International Studies, July 1, 2010.

James A. Lewis. "Five Myths about Chinese Hackers." In: *Washington Post* (Mar. 22, 2013).

Martin C. Libicki. *Conquest in Cyberspace: National Security and Information Warfare*. New York: Cambridge University Press, 2007.

Martin C. Libicki. *Cyberdeterrence and Cyberwar*. Santa Monica: RAND, 2009.

Mark Lichbach. *The Rebel's Dilemma*. Ann Arbor: University of Michigan Press, 1995.

Keir Lieber. "The Offense-Defense Balance and Cyber Warfare." In: *Cyber Analogies*. Ed. Emily O. Goldman and John Arquilla. Monterey, CA: Naval Postgraduate School, 2014, pp. 96–107.

Keir A. Lieber. *War and the Engineers: the Primacy of Politics over Technology*. Ithaca: Cornell University Press, 2005.

Keir A. Lieber. "Grasping the Technological Peace: The Offense-Defense Balance and International Security." In: *International Security* 25.1 (2000), pp. 71–104.

Keir A. Lieber and Daryl G. Press. "The End of MAD? The Nuclear Dimension of US Primacy." In: *International Security* 30.4 (2006), pp. 7–44.

Keir A. Lieber and Daryl G. Press. "Why States Won't Give Nuclear Weapons to Terrorists." In: *International Security* 38.1 (2013), pp. 80–104.

Keir A. Lieber and Daryl G. Press. "The New Era of Counterforce: Technological Change and the Future of Nuclear Deterrence." In: *International Security* 41.4 (2017), pp. 9–49.

Keir A. Lieber and Daryl G. Press. "The Return of Nuclear Escalation." In Foreign Affairs 102.6 (2023), pp. 45–55.

Elli Lieberman. *Reconceptualizing Deterrence: Nudging toward Rationality in Middle Eastern Rivalries*. London: Routledge, 2012.

Adam P. Liff. "Cyberwar: A New 'absolute weapon'? The Proliferation of Cyberwarfare Capabilities and Interstate War." In: *Journal of Strategic Studies* 35.3 (2012), pp. 401–28.

Jon R. Lindsay. "Stuxnet and the Limits of Cyber Warfare." In: *Security Studies* 22.3 (2013), pp. 365–404.

Jon R. Lindsay. "The Impact of China on Cybersecurity: Fiction and Friction." In: *International Security* 39.3 (2014), pp. 7–47.

Jon R. Lindsay. "Tipping the Scales: The Attribution Problem and the Feasibility of Deterrence against Cyberattack." In: *Journal of Cybersecurity* 1.1 (2015), pp. 53–67.

Jon R. Lindsay. "Restrained by Design: The Political Economy of Cybersecurity." In: *Digital Policy, Regulation and Governance* 19.6 (2017), pp. 493–514.

Jon R. Lindsay. "Cyber Conflict vs. Cyber Command: Hidden Dangers in the American Military Solution to a Large-Scale Intelligence Problem." Intelligence and National Security 36, no. 2 (2021): 260–78.

Jon R. Lindsay. *Information Technology and Military Power*. Ithaca: Cornell University Press, 2020.

Jon R. Lindsay. "Cyber Operations and Nuclear Escalation: A Dangerous Gamble." In: *Nuclear Command, Control, and Communications: A Primer on US Systems and Future Challenges*. Ed. James J. Wirtz and Jeffrey A. Larsen. Washington, DC: Georgetown University Press, 2022, pp. 121–44.

Jon R. Lindsay and Erik Gartzke. "Politics by Many Other Means: The Comparative Strategic Advantages of Operational Domains." In: *Journal of Strategic Studies* 45.5 (2022), pp. 743–76.

Jon R. Lindsay and Erik Gartzke. "Coercion through Cyberspace: The Stability-Instability Paradox Revisited." In: *Coercion: The Power to Hurt in International Politics*. Ed. Kelly M. Greenhill and Peter Krause. New York: Oxford University Press, 2018, pp. 179–203.

Jon R. Lindsay and Erik Gartzke, ed. *Cross-Domain Deterrence: Strategy in an Era of Complexity*. 1st ed. New York: Oxford University Press, 2019.

David Lindsey. "Military Strategy, Private Information, and War." In: *International Studies Quarterly* 59.4 (2015), pp. 629–40.

Erica D. Lonergan and Shawn W. Lonergan. "Cyber Operations, Accommodative Signaling, and the De-Escalation of International Crises." Security Studies 31, no. 1 (January 1, 2022): 32–64. https://doi.org/10.1080/09636412.2022.2040584.

Erica D. Lonergan and Shawn W. Lonergan. *Escalation Dynamics in Cyberspace*. New York: Oxford University Press, 2023.

Austin Long. *Deterrence—From Cold War to Long War: Lessons from Six Decades of RAND Research*. Santa Monica: RAND Corporation, 2008.

Austin Long. *The Soul of Armies: Counterinsurgency Doctrine and Military Culture in the US and UK*. Ithaca Cornell University Press, 2016.

Austin Long and Brendan Rittenhouse Green. "Stalking the Secure Second Strike: Intelligence, Counterforce, and Nuclear Strategy." In: *Journal of Strategic Studies* 38.1–2 (2014), pp. 38–73.

Kristin M. Lord. *The Perils and Promise of Global Transparency: Why the Information Revolution May Not Lead to Security, Democracy, or Peace*. Albany: State University of New York Press, 2007.

Amir Lupovici. "The Emerging Fourth Wave of Deterrence Theory—Toward a New Research Agenda." In: *International Studies Quarterly* 54.3 (2010), pp. 705–32.

Amir Lupovici. "The 'Attribution Problem' and the Social Construction of 'Violence': Taking Cyber Deterrence Literature a Step Forward." In: *International Studies Perspectives* 17.3 (2014), pp. 322–342.

Yonatan Lupu and Paul Poast. "Team of Former Rivals: A Multilateral Theory of Non-aggression Pacts." In: *Journal of Peace Research* 53.3 (2016), pp. 344–58.

Jason, Lyall. Bombing to Lose? Airpower, Civilian Casualties, and the Dynamics of Violence in Counterinsurgency Wars (September 3, 2017). Available at SSRN: https://ssrn.com/abstract=2422170 or http://dx.doi.org/10.2139/ssrn.2422170.

Jason Lyall. *Bombing to Lose? Airpower and the Dynamics of Violence in Counterinsurgency Wars*. Working Paper. Social Science Research Network, 2017.

Jason Lyall, Graeme Blair, and Kosuke Imai. "Explaining Support for Combatants during Wartime: A Survey Experiment in Afghanistan." In: *American Political Science Review* 107.4 (2013), pp. 679–705.

William J. Lynn, III. "Defending a New Domain: The Pentagon's Cyberstrategy." In: *Foreign Affairs* 89.5 (2010), pp. 97–108.

Sean M. Lynn-Jones. "Offense-Defense Theory and Its Critics." In: *Security Studies* 4.4 (1995), pp. 660–91.

Halford J. Mackinder. "The Geographical Pivot of History." In: *Geographical Journal* 23.4 (1904), pp. 421–37.

Alfred Thayer Mahan. *The Influence of Sea Power upon History, 1660–1783*. Boston: Little, Brown, and Co., 1890.

Thomas G. Mahnken. *Uncovering Ways of War: US Intelligence and Foreign Military Innovation, 1918–1941*. Ithaca: Cornell University Press, 2002.

Edward D. Mansfield and Brian Pollins. "The Study of Interdependence and Conflict: Recent Advances, Open Questions, and Directions for Future Research." In: *Journal of Conflict Resolution* 45.6 (2001), pp. 834–59.

Edward D. Mansfield and Brian M. Pollins. "Interdependence and Conflict: An Introduction." In: *Economic Interdependence and International Conflict: New Perspectives on an Enduring Debate*. Ed. Edward D. Mansfield and Brian M. Pollins. Ann Arbor: University of Michigan Press, 2003, pp. 1–28.

Mark E. Manyin et al. *Pivot to the Pacific? The Obama Administration's Rebalancing toward Asia*. Tech. rep. R42448. Congressional Research Service, 2012.

Vincent Manzo. *Deterrence and Escalation in Cross-Domain Operations: Where Do Space and Cyberspace Fit?* Strategic Forum 272. Washington, DC: Institute for National Strategic Studies, National Defense University, Dec. 2011. https://inss.ndu.edu/Portals/68/Documents/ stratforum/SF-272.pdf.

Zedong Mao. *On Guerrilla Warfare*. New York: Praeger, 1961.

Zeev Maoz, 2008, "Dyadic Militarized Interstate Disputes Dataset Version 2.0 (DYDMID2.0)", https://doi.org/10.7910/DVN/EN67CI, Harvard Dataverse.

Zeev Maoz. *Networks of Nations. The Evolution, Structure, and Impact of International Networks, 1816–2001*. New York: Cambridge University Press, 2011.

Zeev Maoz et al. "The Dyadic Militarized Interstate Disputes (MIDs) Dataset Version 3.0: Logic, Characteristics, and Comparisons to Alternative Datasets." In: *Journal of Conflict Resolution* Forthcoming (2019). Volume 63, Issue 3, March 2019, pp. 811–35.

Kimberly Marten. "Putin's Choices: Explaining Russian Foreign Policy and Intervention in Ukraine." In: *Washington Quarterly* 38.2 (2015), pp. 189–204.

Philippe Martin, Thierry Mayer, and Mathias Thoenig. "Make Trade Not War?" In: *Review of Economic Studies* 75.3 (2008), pp. 865–900.

Lennart Maschmeyer. "The Subversive Trilemma: Why Cyber Operations Fall Short of Expectations." In: *International Security* 46.2 (2021), pp. 51–90.

Robert K. Massie. *Castles of Steel: Britain, Germany and the Winning of the Great War at Sea*. New York: Random House, 2007.

Jahara W. Matisek. "Shades of Gray Deterrence: Issues of Fighting in the Gray Zone." In: *Journal of Strategic Security* 10.3 (2017), pp. 1–26.

Aleksandar Matovski. "Strategic Intelligence and International Crisis Behavior." In: *Security Studies* 29.5 (2020), pp. 964–90.

Michaela Mattes. "Reputation, Symmetry, and Alliance Design." In: *International Organization* 66.4 (2012), pp. 679–707.

Michael Mayer. "The New Killer Drones: Understanding the Strategic Implications of Next-Generation Unmanned Combat Aerial Vehicles." In: *International Affairs* 91.4 (2015), pp. 765–80.

Michael Mazarr. *Struggle in the Gray Zone and World Order*. Dec. 22, 2015. https://warontherocks.com/2015/12/struggle-in-the-gray-zone-and-world-order/.

432 BIBLIOGRAPHY

Robert McCabe, Deborah Sanders, and Ian Speller, ed. *Europe, Small Navies and Maritime Security: Balancing Traditional Roles and Emergent Threats in the 21st Century*. New York: Routledge, 2021.

Michael C. McCarthy, Matthew A. Moyer, and Brett H. Venable. *Deterring Russia in the Gray Zone*. Tech. rep. Carlisle Barracks, PA: Strategic Studies Institute, Mar. 20, 2019.

H. R. McMaster. *Crack in the Foundation: Defense Transformation and the Underlying Assumption of Dominant Knowledge in Future War*. Tech. rep. S03–03. Carlisle Barracks, PA: US Army War College Center for Strategic Leadership, 2003.

H. R. McMaster, "Continuity and Change: The Army Operating Concept and Clear Thinking About Future War," Military Review, March-April 2015, pp. 6–21. https://www.armyupress.army.mil/Portals/7/military-review/Archives/English/MilitaryReview_20150430_art005.pdf

Gregory S. McNeal. "Targeted Killing and Accountability." In: *Georgetown Law Journal* 102 (2014), pp. 681–794.

William H. McNeill. *The Pursuit of Power: Technology, Armed Force, and Society since A.D. 1000*. Chicago: University of Chicago Press, 1982.

James F. McNulty. "Naval Presence: The Misunderstood Mission." In: *Naval War College Review* 27.2 (1974), pp. 21–31.

William H. McRaven. *Spec Ops: Case Studies in Special Operations Warfare: Theory and Practice*. New York: Presidio Press, 1995.

John J. Mearsheimer. *The Tragedy of Great Power Politics*. New York: Norton, 2001.

John J. Mearsheimer. "Manuever, Mobile Defense, and the NATO Central Front." In: *International Security* 6.3 (1981), pp. 104–22.

John J. Mearsheimer. *Conventional Deterrence*. Ithaca: Cornell University Press, 1985.

John J. Mearsheimer and Stephen M. Walt. "The Case for Offshore Balancing: A Superior US Grand Strategy." In: *Foreign Affairs* 95.4 (2016), pp. 70–83.

Rupal N. Mehta. *Delaying Doomsday: The Politics of Nuclear Reversal*. New York: Oxford University Press, 2020.

Rupal N. Mehta. "Extended Deterrence and Assurance in Multiple Domains." In: *Cross-Domain Deterrence: Strategy in an Era of Complexity*. Ed. Jon R. Lindsay and Erik Gartzke. New York: Oxford University Press, 2019, pp. 234–56.

Adam Meirowitz and Anne E. Sartori. "Strategic Uncertainty as a Cause of War." In: *Quarterly Journal of Political Science* 3.4 (2008), pp. 327–52.

Microsoft Threat Intelligence. "Volt Typhoon Targets US Critical Infrastructure with Living-off-the-Land Techniques." Microsoft Security (blog), May 24, 2023. https://www.microsoft.com/en-us/security/blog/2023/05/24/volt-typhoon-targets-us-critical-infrastructurewith-living-off-the-land-techniques/.

Asfandyar Mir. "What Explains Counterterrorism Effectiveness? Evidence from the US Drone War in Pakistan." In: *International Security* 43.2 (2018), pp. 45–83.

Asfandyar Mir and Dylan Moore. "Drones, Surveillance, and Violence: Theory and Evidence from a US Drone Program." In: *International Studies Quarterly* (2019), sqz040. Volume 63, Issue 4, December 2019, pp. 846–62.

Pilla Vaishno Mohan et al. "Leveraging Computational Intelligence Techniques for Defensive Deception: A Review, Recent Advances, Open Problems and Future Directions." In: *Sensors* 22.6 (2022), p. 2194.

James Clay Moltz. *The Politics of Space Security: Strategic Restraint and the Pursuit of National Interests*. Stanford: Stanford University Press, 2008.

James Clay Moltz. *Crowded Orbits: Conflict and Cooperation in Space*. New York: Columbia University Press, 2014.

BIBLIOGRAPHY   433

Nuno P. Monteiro and Alexandre Debs. "The Strategic Logic of Nuclear Proliferation." In: *International Security* 39.2 (2014), pp. 7–51.

Baron de Montesquieu. *Spirit of the Laws.* Cambridge: Cambridge University Press, 1989 [1748].

Evan Braden Montgomery. "Contested Primacy in the Western Pacific: China's Rise and the Future of US Power Projection." In: *International Security* 38.4 (2014), pp. 115–49.

Forrest E. Morgan. *Deterrence and First-Strike Stability in Space.* Tech. rep. Santa Monica: RAND, 2010.

Patrick M. Morgan. *Deterrence Now.* Cambridge: Cambridge University Press, 2003.

Patrick M. Morgan. *Deterrence: A Conceptual Analysis.* Los Angeles: Sage, 1977.

James D. Morrow. "Alliances and Asymmetry: An Alternative to the Capability Aggregation Model of Alliances." In: *American Journal of Political Science* 35.4 (1991), pp. 904–33.

James D. Morrow. "How Could Trade Affect Conflict?" In: *Journal of Peace Research* 36.4 (1999), pp. 481–89.

James D. Morrow. "Alliances: Why Write Them Down?" In: *Annual Review of Political Science* 3.1 (2000), pp. 63–83.

James D. Morrow. "International Law and the Common Knowledge Requirements of Cross-Domain Deterrence." In: *Cross-Domain Deterrence: Strategy in an Era of Complexity.* Ed. Jon R. Lindsay and Erik Gartzke. New York: Oxford University Press, 2019.

Louis Morton. "Japan's Decision for War." In: *Command Decisions.* Ed. Kent Roberts Greenfield. Center of Military History, Department of the Army. Washington, DC: US GPO, 2000, pp. 99–124.

Lewis Mumford. *Technics and Civilization.* Chicago: University of Chicago Press, 2010.

Michael Nacht, Patricia Schuster, and Eva Uribe. "Cross-Domain Deterrence in American Foreign Policy." In: *Cross-Domain Deterrence: Strategy in an Era of Complexity.* Ed. Jon R. Lindsay and Erik Gartzke. New York: Oxford University Press, 2019.

Ellen Nakashima. "US Accelerating Cyberweapon Research." In: *Washington Post* (Mar. 18, 2012).

Vipin Narang. *Nuclear Strategy in the Modern Era: Regional Powers and International Conflict.* Princeton: Princeton University Press, 2014.

Vipin Narang. "Strategies of Nuclear Proliferation: How States Pursue the Bomb." In: *International Security* 41.3 (2017), pp. 110–50.

National Research Council. *Proceedings of a Workshop on Deterring Cyberattacks: Informing Strategies and Developing Options for US Policy.* Washington, DC: National Academies Press, 2010.

Sean Naylor. *Not a Good Day to Die: The Untold Story of Operation Anaconda.* New York: Penguin, 2005.

David Paull Nickles. *Under the Wire: How the Telegraph Changed Diplomacy.* Cambridge, MA: Harvard University Press, 2003.

Mark David Nieman et al. "An International Game of Risk: Troop Placement and Major Power Competition." In: *Journal of Politics* 83.4 (2021), pp. 1307–21.

Cathal Nolan. *The Allure of Battle: A History of How Wars Have Been Won and Lost.* New York: Oxford University Press, 2017.

North Atlantic Treaty Organization. *NATO Cyber Defence Factsheet.* Feb. 2018. https://www.nato.int/nato_static_fl2014/assets/pdf/pdf_2018_02/20180213_1802-factsheet-cyber-defence-en.pdf.

Joseph S. Nye. "Deterrence and Dissuasion in Cyberspace." In: *International Security* 41.3 (2017), pp. 44–71.

434 BIBLIOGRAPHY

Joseph S. Nye. "The Case for Deep Engagement." In: *Foreign Affairs* 74.4 (1995), pp. 90–102.

Lindsey O'Rourke. *Covert Regime Change: America's Secret Cold War.* Cornell Studies in Security Affairs. Ithaca: Cornell University Press, 2018.

Office of Public Affairs. "Seven Iranians Working for Islamic Revolutionary Guard Corps-Affiliated Entities Charged for Conducting Coordinated Campaign of Cyber Attacks Against US Financial Sector." Department of Justice, March 24, 2016. https://www.justice.gov/opa/pr/seven-iranians-working-islamic-revolutionary-guard-corps-affiliated-entities-charged.

Office of the Deputy Assistant Secretary of Defense for Nuclear Matters. "Nuclear Command and Control System." In: *Nuclear Matters Handbook 2015.* Washington, DC: Government Printing Office, 2015, pp. 73–81.

Office of the Federal Register. "Weekly Compilation of Presidential Documents." National Archives and Records Administration, October 9, 1978.

Office of the Secretary of Defense. *Nuclear Posture Review.* Tech. rep. Washington, DC: US Department of Defense, Feb. 2018.

Office of the Secretary of Defense. *Nuclear Posture Review.* Tech. rep. Washington, DC: US Department of Defense, Oct. 2022.

Erik Olson. *America's Not Ready for Today's Gray Wars.* https://www.defenseone.com/ideas/2015/12/americas-not-ready-todays-gray-wars/124381/. 2015.

John R. Oneal and Bruce Russett. "The Classical Liberals Were Right: Democracy, Interdependence, and Conflict, 1950–1985." In: *International Studies Quarterly* 41.2 (1997), pp. 267–93.

Stefano Ortolani and Bruno Crispo. "NoisyKey: Tolerating Keyloggers via Keystrokes Hiding." In Proceedings of the 7th USENIX Conference on Hot Topics in Security, 2. HotSec'12. USA: USENIX Association, 2012.

Robert Osgood. "The Reappraisal of Limited War." In: *Adelphi Papers* 9.54 (1969), pp. 41–54.

William A. Owens, Kenneth W. Dam, and Herbert S. Lin, ed. *Technology, Policy, Law, and Ethics Regarding US Acquisition and Use of Cyberattack Capabilities.* Washington, DC: National Academies Press, 2009.

Leon E. Panetta. "Remarks by Secretary Panetta on Cybersecurity." Presented at the Business Executives for National Security, New York, October 11, 2012. https://www.hsdl.org/?view&did=724128.

Robert A. Pape. *Bombing to Win: Air Power and Coercion in War.* Ithaca, NY: Cornell University Press, 1996.

Robert A. Pape and James K. Feldman. *Cutting the Fuse: The Explosion of Global Suicide Terrorism and How to Stop It.* Chicago: University of Chicago Press, 2010.

Robert A. Pape. *Bombing to Win: Air Power and Coercion in War.* Ithaca: Cornell University Press, 1996.

Jonathan Parshall and Anthony Tully. *Shattered Sword: The Untold Story of the Battle of Midway.* Herndon, VA: Potomac, 2007.

T. V. Paul, Patrick M. Morgan, and James J. Wirtz, ed. *Complex Deterrence: Strategy in the Global Age.* Chicago: University of Chicago Press, 2009.

Thazha V. Paul. "Disarmament Revisited: Is Nuclear Abolition Possible?" In: *Journal of Strategic Studies* 35.1 (2012), pp. 149–69.

Nicole Perlroth and Krauss Clifford. "A Cyberattack in Saudi Arabia Had a Deadly Goal. Experts Fear Another Try." In: *New York Times* (Mar. 15, 2018).

Charles Perrow. *Normal Accidents: Living with High Risk Technologies*. 2nd ed. Princeton: Princeton University Press, 1999.

Dale Peterson. "Offensive Cyber Weapons: Construction, Development, and Employment." In: *Journal of Strategic Studies* 36.1 (2013), pp. 120–24.

Scott Peterson. "Old Weapons, New Terror Worries." In: *Christian Science Monitor* (Apr. 15, 2004).

Stacie L. Pettyjohn and Becca Wasser. *Competing in the Gray Zone: Russian Tactics and Western Responses*. Tech. rep. Santa Monica: RAND Corporation, 2019.

Jon C. Pevehouse. "Interdependence Theory and the Measurement of International Conflict." In: *Journal of Politics* 66.1 (2004), pp. 247–66.

Steven Pinker. "Decline of Violence: Taming the Devil within Us." In: *Nature* 478.7369 (2011), pp. 309–11.

Avery Plaw and Matthew S. Fricker. "Tracking the Predators: Evaluating the US Drone Campaign in Pakistan." In: *International Studies Perspectives* (2012), pp. 1–22.

Avery Plaw, Matthew S. Fricker, and B. G. Williams. "Practice Makes Perfect? The Changing Civilian Toll of CIA Drone Strikes in Pakistan." In: *Perspectives on Terrorism* 5.5–6. (2011), pp. 51–69.

Solomon W. Polachek. "Conflict and Trade." In: *Journal of Conflict Resolution* 24.1 (1980), pp. 55–78.

Solomon W. Polachek. "Why Democracies Cooperate More and Fight Less: The Relationship between International Trade and Cooperation." In: *Review of International Economics* 5.3 (1997), pp. 295–309.

Solomon W. Polachek and Xiang Jun. "How Opportuntiy Costs Decrease the Probability of War in an Incomplete Information Game." In: *International Organization* 64.1 (2010), pp. 133–44.

Barry R. Posen. "Command of the Commons: The Military Foundation of US Hegemony." In: *International Security* 28.1 (2003), pp. 5–46.

Barry R. Posen. *The Sources of Military Doctrine: France, Britain, and Germany between the World Wars*. Ithaca: Cornell University Press, 1984.

Barry R. Posen. *Inadvertent Escalation: Conventional War and Nuclear Risks*. Ithaca: Cornell University Press, 1991.

Barry R. Posen. *Restraint: A New Foundation for US Grand Strategy*. Ithaca: Cornell University Press, 2014.

Abigail Post. "Flying to Fail: Costly Signals and Air Power in Crisis Bargaining." In: *Journal of Conflict Resolution* 63.4 (2019), pp. 869–95.

Robert Powell. "The Theoretical Foundations of Strategic Nuclear Deterrence." In: *Political Science Quarterly* 100.1 (1985), pp. 75–96.

Robert Powell. "Nuclear Brinkmanship with Two-Sided Incomplete Information." In: *American Political Science Review* 82.1 (1988), pp. 155–78.

Robert Powell. *Nuclear Deterrence Theory: The Search for Credibility*. Cambridge: Cambridge University Press, 1990.

Robert Powell. *In the Shadow of Power: States and Strategies in International Politics*. Princeton: Princeton University Press, 1999.

Robert Powell. "Bargaining Theory and International Conflict." In: *Annual Review of Political Science* 5 (2002), pp. 1–30.

Robert Powell. "Bargaining and Learning While Fighting." In: *American Journal of Political Science* 48.2 (2004), pp. 344–61.

436 BIBLIOGRAPHY

Robert Powell. "The Inefficient Use of Power: Costly Conflict with Complete Information." In: *American Political Science Review* 98 (2004), pp. 231–41.

Robert Powell. "War as a Commitment Problem." In: *International Organization* 60.1 (2006), pp. 169–203.

Robert Powell. "Defending against Terrorist Attacks with Limited Resources." In: *American Political Science Review* 101.3 (2007), pp. 527–541.

Robert Powell. "Nuclear Brinkmanship, Limited War, and Military Power." In: *International Organization* 69.3 (2015), pp. 589–626.

David A. Powner. *Information Technology: Federal Agencies Need to Address Aging Legacy Systems.* Tech. rep. GAO-16-468. Washington, DC: US Government Accountability Office, May 25, 2016.

Michael Poznansky. *In the Shadow of International Law: Covert Intervention in the Postwar World.* New York: Oxford University Press, 2020.

Michael Poznansky and Evan Perkoski. "Rethinking Secrecy in Cyberspace: The Politics of Voluntary Attribution." Journal of Global Security Studies 3, no. 4 (October 1, 2018): 402–16.

Gordon W. Prange. *At Dawn We Slept: The Untold Story of Pearl Harbor.* New York: McGraw-Hill, 1981.

Gordon W. Prange. *Miracle at Midway.* New York: Penguin, 1983.

Daryl G. Press, Scott D. Sagan, and Benjamin A. Valentino. "Atomic Aversion: Experimental Evidence on Taboos, Traditions, and the Non-Use of Nuclear Weapons." In: *American Political Science Review* 107.1 (2013), pp. 188–206.

Bryan C. Price. "Targeting Top Terrorists: How Leadership Decapitation Contributes to Counterterrorism." In: *International Security* 36.4 (2012), pp. 9–46.

Stephen L. Quackenbush and Frank C. Zagare. "Modern Deterrence Theory: Research Trends, Policy Debates, and Methodological Controversies." In Oxford Handbook Topics in Politics, edited by Oxford Handbooks Editorial Board. Oxford University Press. Accessed October 5, 2023. https://doi.org/10.1093/oxfordhb/9780199935307.013.39.

George H. Quester. *Offense and Defense in the International System.* New York: John Wiley & Sons, 1977.

Abraham Rabinovich. *The Little-Known US-Soviet Confrontation during Yom Kippur War.* The World from PRX. Oct 26, 2012.

Kristopher W. Ramsay. "Information, Uncertainty, and War." In: *Annual Review: of Political Science* 20.1 (2017), pp. 505–27.

Thomas C. Reed. *At the Abyss: An Insider's History of the Cold War.* New York: Random House, 2004.

William Reed. "Information, Power, and War." In: *American Political Science Review* 97.4 (2003), pp. 633–41.

Dan Reiter. "Exploring the Bargaining Model of War." In: *Perspectives on Politics 1* (2003), pp. 27–43.

Dan Reiter and Paul Poast. "The Truth about Tripwires: Why Small Force Deployments Do Not Deter Agression." In: *Texas National Security Review* 4.3 (2021), pp. 33–53.

Charles A. Richard. *Statement of Charles A. Richard Commander United States Strategic Command before the Senate Armed Services Committee.* Washington, DC. 117th Congress, 2nd Session 8 March 2022.

Jeffrey Richelson. *America's Secret Eyes in Space: The US Keyhole Spy Satellite Program.* New York: Harper & Row, 1990.

J. A. Richmond. "Spies in Ancient Greece." In: *Greece and Rome* 45.1 (1998), pp. 1–18.

Thomas Rid. "Cyber War Will Not Take Place." In: *Journal of Strategic Studies* 35.1 (2012), pp. 5–32.

Thomas Rid. *Cyber War Will Not Take Place.* London: Hurst, 2013.

Thomas Rid. *Active Measures: The Secret History of Disinformation and Political Warfare.* New York: Farrar, Straus and Giroux, 2020.

Thomas Rid and Peter McBurney. "Cyber-Weapons." In: *RUSI Journal* 157.1 (2012), pp. 6–13.

Robert C. Rubel. "Command of the Sea: An Old Concept Resurfaces in a New Form." In: *Naval War College Review* 65.4 (2012), pp. 21–34.

Alex Roland. "Technology, Ground Warfare, and Strategy: The Paradox of the American Experience." In: *Journal of Military History* 55.4 (1994), pp. 447–67.

Richard Rosecrance. *The Rise of the Trading State: Commerce and Conquest in the Modern World.* New York: Basic Books, 1985.

Michael Ross. "The Political Economy of the Resource Curse." In: *World Politics* 51.2 (1999), pp. 297–332.

Robert Ross. "The Problem with the Pivot." In: *Foreign Affairs* 91.6 (2012), pp. 70–82.

Robert Ross. "The Geography of the Peace: East Asia in the Twenty-First Century." In: *International Security* 23.4 (1999), pp. 81–118.

Joshua Rovner. *Fixing the Facts: National Security and the Politics of Intelligence.* Ithaca: Cornell University Press, 2011.

Joshua Rovner. "Cyber War as an Intelligence Contest." War on the Rocks (blog), September 16, 2019. https://warontherocks.com/2019/09/cyber-war-as-an-intelligence-contest/.

Joshua Rovner. "Sea Power versus Land Power—Cross-Domain Deterrence in the Peloponnesian War." In: *Cross-Domain Deterrence: Strategy in an Era of Complexity.* Ed. Jon R. Lindsay and Erik Gartzke. New York: Oxford University Press, 2019, pp. 163–85.

Joshua Rovner and Caitlin Talmadge. "Hegemony, Force Posture, and the Provision of Public Goods: The Once and Future Role of Outside Powers in Security Persian Gulf Oil." In: *Security Studies* 23 (2014), pp. 548–81.

Neil C. Rowe, E. John Custy, and Binh T. Duong. "Defending Cyberspace with Fake Honeypots." In: *Journal of Computers* 2.2 (2007), pp. 25–36.

RSA. *Social Engineering and Cyber Attacks: The Psychology of Deception.* White Paper. July 17, 2013.

Bruce Russett and John R. Oneal. *Triangulating Peace: Democracy, Interdependence, and International Organizations.* New York: Norton, 2001.

Scott D. Sagan. *The Limits of Safety: Organizations, Accidents, and Nuclear Weapons.* Princeton: Princeton University Press, 1995.

Scott D. Sagan and Kenneth N. Waltz. *The Spread of Nuclear Weapons: An Enduring Debate.* 3rd ed. New York: W. W. Norton & Company, 2012.

Ilai Saltzman. "Cyber Posturing and the Offense-Defense Balance." In: *Contemporary Security Policy* 34.1 (2013), pp. 40–63.

David E. Sanger and William J. Broad. "Downing North Korean Missiles Is Hard. So the US Is Experimenting." In: *New York Times* (Nov. 16, 2017).

Anne E. Sartori. *Deterrence by Diplomacy,* Princeton: Princeton University Press, 2013.

Raphael Satter. "Undercover Agents Target Cybersecurity Watchdog." In: *AP News* (Jan. 26, 2019).

Ralph Sawyer, trans. *Sun Tzu's the Art of War.* New York: Fall River Press, 1984.

Ronald Schaffer. *Wings of Judgement: American Bombing in World War II.* Oxford: Oxford University Press, 1988.

Thomas C. Schelling. *The Strategy of Conflict*. Cambridge, MA: Harvard University Press, 1960.

Thomas C. Schelling. *Arms and Influence*. New Haven: Yale University Press, 1966.

Thomas C. Schelling. *Arms and Influence: With a New Preface and Afterword*. New Haven: Yale University Press, 2008.

Thomas C. Schelling. "A World without Nuclear Weapons?" In: *Daedalus* 138.4 (2009), pp. 124–29.

Andreas Schmidt. "The Estonian Cyberattacks." In: *A Fierce Domain: Conflict in Cyberspace, 1986 to 2012*. Ed. Jason Healey. Cyber Conflict Studies Association, Washington, DC, 2013, pp. 174–93.

Eric Schlosser. *Command and Control: Nuclear Weapons, the Demascus Accident, and the Illusion of Safety*. New York: Penguin, 2014.

Michael N. Schmitt and Jeffrey S. Thurnher. "Out of the Loop: Autonomous Weapons Systems and the Law of Armed Conflict." In: *Harvard National Security Journal* 4 (2012), p. 231.

Gerald Schneider. "Peace through Globalization and Capitalism? Prospects of Two Liberal Propositions." In: *Journal of Peace Research* 51.2 (2014), pp. 173–83.

Jacquelyn Schneider. "Deterrence in and through Cyberspace." In: *CrossDomain Deterrence: Strategy in an Era of Complexity*. Ed. Jon R. Lindsay and Erik Gartzke. New York: Oxford University Press, 2019.

Jacquelyn Schneider. "The Capability/Vulnerability Paradox and Military Revolutions: Implications for Computing, Cyber, and the Onset of War." In: *Journal of Strategic Studies* 42.6 (2019), pp. 841–63.

Jacquelyn Schneider, Benjamin Schechter, and Rachael Shaffer. "Hacking Nuclear Stability: Wargaming Technology, Uncertainty, and Escalation." In: *International Organization* Volume 77, Issue 3, Summer 2023, pp. 633–67.

Jacquelyn Schneider, Emily O. Goldman, and Michael Warner, ed. *Ten Years In: Implementing Strategic Approaches to Cyberspace*. Newport Papers 45. Newport, RI: US Naval War College, 2020.

Peter Schram. "Hassling: How States Prevent a Preventive War." In: *American Journal of Political Science* 62.2 (2021), pp. 294–308.

Peter Schram. "When Capabilities Backfire: How Improved Hassling Capabilities Produce Worse Outcomes." In: *The Journal of Politics* 84.4 (2022), pp. 2246–60.

Schulte, Stephanie Ricker. " 'The WarGames Scenario': Regulating Teenagers and Teenaged Technology (1980–1984)." In: *Television & New Media* 9:6 (2008), pp. 487–513.

Norton Schwartz. "Airpower in Counterinsurgency and Stability Operations." In: *Prism* 2.2 (2003), pp. 127–34.

Randall L. Schweller. "Unanswered Threats: A Neoclassical Realist Theory of Underbalancing." In: *International Security* 29.2 (2004), pp. 159–201.

Len Scott and Huw Dylan. "Cover for Thor: Divine Deception Planning for Cold War Missiles." In: *Journal of Strategic Studies* 33.5 (2010), pp. 759–75.

Paul Seabright. *The Company of Strangers: A Natural History of Economic Life*, revised ed. Princeton: Princeton University Press, 2010.

Todd S. Sechser. "Goliath's Curse: Coercive Threats and Asymmetric Power." In: *International Organization* 64.4 (2010), pp. 627–60.

Todd S. Sechser and Matthew Fuhrmann. *Nuclear Weapons and Coercive Diplomacy*. New York: Cambridge University Press, 2017.

Todd S. Sechser, Neil Narang, and Caitlin Talmadge. "Emerging Technologies and Strategic Stability in Peacetime, Crisis, and War." In: *Journal of Strategic Studies* 42.6 (2019), pp. 727–35.

Paul Senese. "Territory, Contiguity, and International Conflict: Assessing a New Joint Explanation." In: *American Journal of Political Science* 49.4 (2005), pp. 769–79.

Aqil Shah. "Do US Drone Strikes Cause Blowback? Evidence from Pakistan and Beyond." In: *International Security* 42.04 (2018), pp. 47–84.

Ryan Shandler, Michael L. Gross, and Daphna Canetti. "Cyberattacks, Psychological Distress, and Military Escalation: An Internal Meta-Analysis." In: *Journal of Global Security Studies* 8.1 (2023), ogac042. pp. 1–19.

Jacob N. Shapiro. *The Terrorist's Dilemma: Managing Violent Covert Organizations.* Princeton: Princeton University Press, 2013.

Sharman, J. C. "Power and Profit at Sea: The Rise of the West in the Making of the International System." In: *International Security* 43.4 (2019), pp. 163–96.

Michael S. Sherry. *The Rise of American Air Power: The Creation of Armageddon.* New Haven: Yale University Press, 1987.

Keith L. Shimko. *The Iraq Wars and America's Military Revolution.* New York: Cambridge University Press, 2010.

Dany Shoham and Michael Liebig. "The Intelligence Dimension of Kautilyan Statecraft and Its Implications for the Present." In: *Journal of Intelligence History* 15.2 (2016), pp. 119–38.

George Shultz. *Low-Intensity Warfare: The Challenge of Ambiguity.* Conference Address. National Defense University, Washington, DC, Jan. 15 1986.

George Shultz, Sidney D. Drell, and James E. Goodby, ed. *Deterrence: Its Past and Future.* Stanford: Hoover Institution, 2011.

John Simpson, Philip Acton, and Simon Crowe. "The Israeli Satellite Launch." In: *Space Policy* 5.2 (1989), pp. 117–28.

Peter W. Singer. *Wired for War: The Robotics Revolution and Conflict in the Twenty-First Century.* New York: Penguin, 2009.

Branislav L. Slantchev. "Military Coercion in Interstate Crises." In: *American Political Science Review* 99.4 (2005), pp. 533–47.

Branislav L. Slantchev. "Feigning Weakness." In: *International Organization* 64.3 (2010), pp. 357–88.

Branislav L. Slantchev. *Military Threats: The Costs of Coercion and the Price of Peace.* Cambridge: Cambridge University Press, 2011.

Branislav L. Slantchev and Ahmer Tarar. "Mutual Optimism as a Rationalist Explanation of War." In: *American Journal of Political Science* 55.1 (2011), pp. 135–48.

Rebecca Slayton. "What Is the Cyber Offense-Defense Balance? Conceptions, Causes, and Assessment." In: *International Security* 41.3 (2017), pp. 72–109.

Julia Slupska and Leonie Maria Tanczer. "Threat Modeling Intimate Partner Violence: Tech Abuse as a Cybersecurity Challenge in the Internet of Things." In: *The Emerald International Handbook of Technology-Facilitated Violence and Abuse.* Ed. Jane Bailey, Asher Flynn, and Nicola Henry. Emerald Studies In Digital Crime, Technology and Social Harms. Emerald Publishing Limited, 2021, pp. 663–88.

Max Smeets. "A Matter of Time: On the Transitory Nature of Cyberweapons." In: *Journal of Strategic Studies* 41.1–2 (2017), pp. 6–32.

Max Smeets. "Cyber Arms Transfer: Meaning, Limits and Implications." In: *Security Studies* 31.1 (2022), pp. 65–91.

440   BIBLIOGRAPHY

Megan Smith and James Igoe Walsh. "Do Drone Strikes Degrade Al Qaeda? Evidence from Propaganda Output." In: *Terrorism and Political Violence* 25.2 (2013), pp. 311–27.

Merritt Roe Smith and Leo Marx, ed. *Does Technology Drive History? The Dilemma of Technological Determinism*. Cambridge, MA: MIT Press, 1994.

Glenn H. Snyder. "The Balance of Power and the Balance of Terror." In: *The Balance of Power*. Ed. Paul Seabury. San Francisco: Chandler, 1965, pp. 184–201.

Glenn H. Snyder. "The Security Dilemma in Alliance Politics." In: *World Politics* 36.4 (1984), pp. 461–95.

Glenn H. Snyder. *Deterrence and Defense*. Princeton: Princeton University Press, 1961.

Etel Solingen. "Pax Asiatica versus Bella Levantina: The Foundations of War and Peace in East Asia and the Middle East." In: *American Political Science Review* 101.4 (2007), pp. 757–80.

Jonathan Solomon. "Cyberdeterrence between Nation-States Plausible Strategy or a Pipe Dream?" In: *Strategic Studies Quarterly* 5.1 (2011), pp. 1–25.

Lance Spitzner. "Honeypots: Catching the Insider Threat." In: *Computer Security Applications Conference, 2003. Proceedings. 19th Annual*. 2003, pp. 170–79.

Nicholas J. Spykman. "Geography and Foreign Policy, II." In: *American Political Science Review* 32.2 (1938), pp. 213–36.

Paul B. Stares. *The Militarization of Space: US Policy, 1945–1984*. Ithaca: Cornell University Press, 1985.

Sean Starrs. "American Economic Power Hasn't Declined—It Globalized! Summoning the Data and Taking Globalization Seriously." In: *International Studies Quarterly* 57.4 (2013), pp. 817–30.

Janice Gross Stein. "Military Deception, Strategic Surprise, and Conventional Deterrence: A Political Analysis of Egypt and Israel, 1971–73." In: *Journal of Strategic Studies* 5.1 (1982), pp. 94–121.

Janice Gross Stein. "Extended Deterrence in the Middle East: American Strategy Reconsidered." In: *World Politics* 39.3 (1987), pp. 326–52.

Janice Gross Stein. "Deterrence and Compellence in the Gulf, 1990–91: A Failed or Impossible Task?" In: *International Security* 17.2 (1992), pp. 147–79.

Janice Gross Stein. "The Micro-Foundations of International Relations Theory: Psychology and Behavioral Economics." In: *International Organization* 71.S1 (2017), S249–S263.

Tim Stevens. "A Cyberwar of Ideas? Deterrence and Norms in Cyberspace." In: *Contemporary Security Policy* 33.1 (2012), pp. 148–70.

Tim Stevens. *Cyber Security and the Politics of Time*. Cambridge: Cambridge University Press, 2016.

Clifford Stoll. *The Cuckoo's Egg: Tracking a Spy through the Maze of Computer Espionage*. New York: Doubleday, 1989.

Jon Tetsuro Sumida. *Inventing Grand Strategy and Teaching Command: The Classic Works of Alfred Thayer Mahan Reconsidered*. Baltimore: Johns Hopkins University Press, 1997.

Sun-tzu. *The Art of War: The Essential Translation of the Classic Book of Life*. Trans. John Minford. New York: Penguin Books, 2002.

Craig L. Symonds. *The Battle of Midway*. New York: Oxford University Press, 2011.

Caitlin Talmadge. "Deterring a Nuclear 9/11." In: *Washington Quarterly* 30.2 (2007), pp. 21–34.

Caitlin Talmadge. *The Dictator's Army: Battlefield Effectiveness in Authoritarian Regimes.* Ithaca: Cornell University Press, 2015.

Caitlin Talmadge. "Would China Go Nuclear? Assessing the Risk of Chinese Nuclear Escalation in a Conventional War with the United States." In: *International Security* 41.4 (2017), pp. 50–92.

Ahmer Tarar. "A Strategic Logic of the Military Fait Accompli." In: *International Studies Quarterly* 60.4 (2016), pp. 742–52.

Terror Free Tomorrow. Public Opinion in Pakistan's Tribal Regions. New America Foundation, 2010. Washington, DC (September 2010).

Hugh Thompson et al. *Anomaly Detection at Multiple Scales (ADAMS), Final Report.* Tech. rep. Sponsored by the Defense Advanced Research Projects Agency, Issued by US Army Aviation and Missile Command under Contract No. W31PQ-11-C-0229, Nov. 9 2011. https://apps.dtic.mil/sti/citations/tr/ADA552461.

Ken Thompson. "Reflections on Trusting Trust." In: *Communications of the ACM* 27.8 (1984), pp. 761–63.

William Thompson and David Dreyer. *Handbook of International Rivalries.* Washington DC: CQ Press, 2011.

Rod Thornton. "The Changing Nature of Modern Warfare." In: *RUSI Journal* 160.4 (2015), pp. 40–8.

Thucydides. The Landmark Thucydides: A Comprehensive Guide to The Peloponnesian War. Edited by Robert B. Strassler. Translated by Richard Crawley. New York: Free Press, 1996.

Volkan Topalli, Richard Wright, and Robert Fornango. "Drug Dealers, Robbers and Retaliation: Vulnerability, Deterrence and the Contagion of Violence." In: *British Journal of Criminology* 42 (2002), pp. 337–51.

Uri Tor. ' "Cumulative Deterrence' as a New Paradigm for Cyber Deterrence." In: *Journal of Strategic Studies* 40.1–2 (2015), pp. 92–117.

Marc Trachtenberg. *History and Strategy.* Princeton: Princeton University Press, 1991.

Marc Trachtenberg. "The Past and Future of Arms Control." In: *Daedalus* 120.1 (1991), pp. 203–16.

Robert F. Trager and Dessislava P. Zagorcheva. "Deterring Terrorism: It Can Be Done." In: *International Security* 30.3 (2006), pp. 87–123.

Ian Traynor. "Russia Accused of Unleashing Cyberwar to Disable Estonia." In: *The Guardian* (May 16 2007).

Graham Turbiville. "Preface: Future Trends in Low Intensity Conflict." In: *Low Intensity Conflict & Law Enforcement* 11.2–3 (2002), pp. 155–63.

Stephen Twigge and Len Scott. "Strategic Defence by Deception." In: *Intelligence and National Security* 16.2 (2001), pp. 152–57.

Christopher P. Twomey. *The Military Lens: Doctrinal Difference and Deterrence Failure in Sino-American Relations.* Ithaca: Cornell University Press, 2011.

US Army. *The US Army in Multi-Domain Operations 2028.* TRADOC Pamphlet 525-3-1. Fort Eustis, VA: US Army Training and Doctrine Command, Dec 6, 2018.

David Ucko. *The New Counterinsurgency Era: Transforming the US Military for Modern Wars.* Washington, DC: Georgetown University Press, 2009.

United Nations. *Review of Maritime Transport 2017.* Tech. rep. New York: United Nations Conference on Trade and Development, 2017.

Brandon Valeriano, Benjamin M. Jensen, and Ryan C. Maness. *Cyber Strategy: The Evolving Character of Power and Coercion.* New York: Oxford University Press, 2018.

442 BIBLIOGRAPHY

Brandon Valeriano and Ryan C. Maness. "The Dynamics of Cyber Conflict between Rival Antagonists, 2001–2011." In: *Journal of Peace Research* 51.3 (2014), pp. 347–60.

Brandon Valeriano and Ryan C. Maness. *Cyber War versus Cyber Realities: Cyber Conflict in the International System.* Oxford: Oxford University Press, 2015.

Stephen Van Evera. "Offense, Defense, and the Causes of War." In: *International Security* 22.4 (1998), pp. 5–43.

Stephen Van Evera. *Causes of War: Power and the Roots of Conflict.* Ithaca: Cornell University Press, 1999.

Paul K. Van Riper, "Information Superiority." Testimony to US House of Representatives National Security Committee, Washington, DC, March 20, 1997.

John A. Vasquez. "The Realist Paradigm and Degenerative versus Progressive Research Programs: An Appraisal of Neotraditional Research on Waltz's Balancing Proposition." In: *The American Political Science Review* 91.4 (1997), pp. 899–912.

Kristin Ven Bruusgaard. "Russian Strategic Deterrence." In: *Survival* 58.4 (July 2016), pp. 7–26.

Tristan A. Volpe. "Atomic Leverage: Compellence with Nuclear Latency." In: *Security Studies* 26.3 (2017), pp. 517–44.

Solomon W. Polacheck, John Robst, and Yuan-Ching Chang. "Liberalism and Interdependence: Extending the Trade-Conflict Model." In: *Journal of Peace Research* 36.4 (1999), pp. 405–22.

R. Harrison Wagner. "Bargaining and War." In: *American Journal of Political Science* 44 (2000), pp. 469–84.

Thomas Waldman. *War, Clausewitz and the Trinity.* New York: Routledge, 2016.

James Igoe Walsh and Marcus Schulzke. *Drones and Support for the Use of Force.* Ann Arbor: University of Michigan Press, 2018.

James Igoe Walsh. *The Effectiveness of Drone Strikes in Counterinsurgency and Counterterrorism Campaigns.* Tech. rep. Carlisle Barracks, PA: Strategic Studies Institute, Sept. 1 2013.

James Igoe Walsh. "Precision Weapons, Civilian Casualties, and Support for the Use of Force." In: *Political Psychology* 36.5 (2015), pp. 507–23.

James Igoe Walsh and M. Schulzke. "The Ethics of Drone Strikes: Does Reducing the Cost of Conflict Encourage War?" Carlyle Barracks, PA: The Army War College, 2015.

Kenneth N. Waltz. *Theory of International Politics.* Reading, MA: Addison-Wesley Pub. Co., 1979.

Kenneth N. Waltz. "The Spread of Nuclear Weapons: More May Be Better." In: *Adelphi Papers* 21.171 (1981). https://doi.org/10.1080/05679328108457394.

Kenneth N. Waltz. "Globalization and Governance." In: *PS: Political Science and Politics* 32.4 (1999), pp. 693–700.

Michael Warner. "The Divine Skein: Sun Tzu on Intelligence." In: *Intelligence and National Security* 21.4 (2006), pp. 483–92.

Michael Warner. "Cybersecurity: A Pre-history." In: *Intelligence and National Security* 27.5 (2012), pp. 781–99.

Michael Warner. "A Matter of Trust: Covert Action Reconsidered." In: *Studies in Intelligence* 63.4 (2019), pp. 33–41.

Becca Wasser et al., ed. *Comprehensive Deterrence Forum: Proceedings and Commissioned Papers.* Santa Monica: RAND Corporation, 2018.

Nicholas Weaver. "A Close Look at the NSA's Most Powerful Internet Attack Tool." In: *Wired* Mar 13, 2014. https://www.wired.com/2014/03/quantum/.

Russell F. Weigley. *The American Way of War: A History of United States Military Strategy and Policy.* Bloomington, IN: Indiana University Press, 1973.

Gus W. Weiss. "The Farewell Dossier: Duping the Soviets." In: *Studies in Intelligence* 39.5 (1996), pp. 121–126.

Alexander Wendt. "Anarchy Is What States Make of It: The Social Construction of Power Politics." In: *International Organization* 46.2 (1992), pp. 391–425.

Barton Whaley. "Toward a General Theory of Deception." In: *Journal of Strategic Studies* 5.1 (1982), pp. 178–92.

Hugh White. *Losing the War in an Afternoon: Jutland 1916.* The Strategist. Autralian Strategic Policy Institute, May 13, 2016. https://www.aspistrategist.org.au/losing-the-war-in-an-afternoon-jutland-1916/.

Sarah P. White. "Subcultural Influence on Military Innovation: The Development of US Military Cyber Doctrine." PhD Dissertation. Harvard University, Aug. 2019.

Adam Wick. *Deceiving the Deceivers: Active Counterdeception for Software Protection.* 2012. US Small Business Innovation Research Award FA8650-12-M-1396. https://www.sbir.gov/sbirsearch/detail/393779.

Alex S. Wilner. *Deterring Rational Fanatics.* Philadelphia: University of Pennsylvania Press, 2015.

Langdon Winner. *Autonomous Technology: Technics-Out-of-Control as a Theme in Political Thought.* Cambridge, MA: MIT Press, 1977.

James J. Wirtz. "Life in the 'Gray Zone': Observations for Contemporary Strategists." In: *Defense & Security Analysis* 33.2 (2017), pp. 106–14.

James J. Wirtz and Jeffrey A. Larsen, ed. *Nuclear Command, Control, and Communications: A Primer on US Systems and Future Challenges.* Washington, DC: Georgetown University Press, 2022.

Donald Wittman. "How War Ends: A Rational Model Approach." In: *Journal of Conflict Resolution* 23.4 (1979), pp. 743–63.

William C. Wohlforth. "The Stability of a Unipolar World." In: *International Security* 21.1 (1999), pp. 5–41.

Albert Wohlstetter. "The Delicate Balance of Terror." In: *Foreign Affairs* 37.2 (1959), pp. 211–34.

Albert Wohlstetter et al. "Is There a Strategic Arms Race? (II): Rivals but No 'Race'. " In: *Foreign Policy* 16 (1974), pp. 48–92.

Markus Wolf and Anne McElvoy. *Man without a Face: The Autobiography of Communism's Greatest Spymaster.* New York: Public Affairs, 1997.

J. D. Work. "Evaluating Commercial Cyber Intelligence Activity." In: *International Journal of Intelligence and Counterintelligence* 33.2 (2020), pp. 278–308.

J. D. Work and Richard J. Harknett. *Troubled Vision: Understanding Recent Israeli-Iranian Offensive Cyber Exchanges.* Tech. rep. Washington, DC: Atlantic Council, Jul 22, 2020.

J. C. Wylie. *Military Strategy: A General Theory of Power Control.* Ed. John B. Hattendorf. Annapolis: Naval Institute Press, 1989.

Keren Yarhi-Milo. "Tying Hands behind Closed Doors: The Logic and Practice of Secret Reassurance." In: *Security Studies* 22.3 (2013), pp. 405–35.

Keren Yarhi-Milo. *Knowing the Adversary: Leaders, Intelligence, and Assessment of Intentions in International Relations.* Princeton: Princeton University Press, 2014.

444 BIBLIOGRAPHY

JoAnne Yates. *Control through Communication: The Rise of System in American Management*. Baltimore: Johns Hopkins University Press, 1989.

Toshi Yoshihara and James R. Holmes, ed. *Strategy in the Second Nuclear Age: Power, Ambition, and the Ultimate Weapon*. Washington, DC: Georgetown University Press, 2012.

Jim Yuill, Dorothy E. Denning, and Fred Feer. "Using Deception to Hide Things from Hackers: Processes, Principles, and Techniques." In: *Journal of Information Warfare* 5.3 (2006), pp. 26–40.

Frank C. Zagare. "Rationality and Deterrence." In: *World Politics* 42.2 (1990), pp. 238–60.

Frank C. Zagare. "Classical Deterrence Theory: A Critical Assessment." In: *International Interactions* 21.4 (1996). London: Routledge, pp. 365–87.

Frank C. Zagare and D. Marc Kilgour. "Asymmetric Deterrence." In: *International Studies Quarterly* 37.1 (1993), pp. 1–27.

Frank C. Zagare and D. Marc Kilgour. *Perfect Deterrence*. Cambridge: Cambridge University Press, 2000.

Steven J. Zaloga. *The Atlantic Wall (2): Belgium, The Netherlands, Denmark and Norway*. Oxford: Osprey, 2011.

Amy Zegart. "Cheap Fights, Credible Threats: The Future of Armed Drones and Coercion." In: *Journal of Strategic Studies* 43.1 (2018), pp. 6–46.

Amy Zegart. *Flawed by Design: The Evolution of the CIA, JCS, and NSC*. Stanford: Stanford University Press, 2000.

Jun Zhuang, Vicki M. Bier, and Oguzhan Alagoz. "Modeling Secrecy and Deception in a Multiple-Period Attacker–Defender Signaling Game." In: *European Journal of Operational Research* 203.2 (2010), pp. 409–18.

Jonathan L. Zittrain. "The Generative Internet." In: *Harvard Law Review* 119.7 (2006), pp. 1974–2040.

E. L. Zorn. "Israel's Quest for Satellite Intelligence." In: *Studies in Intelligence* 10 (2001), pp. 33–38.

Index

Note: Page references followed by a "*t*" indicate table; "*f*" indicate figure.

A2/AD strategy. *See* anti-access and
 area-denial strategy
Abrahms, Max 259–60
abstraction 25–26
accommodation
 deception and 78, 377, 383*f*
 disarmament and 151
 government and 83
 after negotiations 8
 stability and 381, 382*t*
 strategy of 386
Acheson, Dean 59
Aegis Ashore batteries 176
Aegis Ballistic Missile Defense
 System 176
Aenid (Virgil) 147
Afghanistan 253, 259, 273
aggression
 by challengers 366–67
 by China 60
 cyber 121
 defense against 65, 68–69
 military 163–64, 287–88
 with nuclear deterrence 60–61
 psychology of 163, 371–72
 purpose of 116–17
 response to 38
 by Russia 89
 as strategy 31
 subversion and 293
Aidid, Muhamed Farrah 262
aircraft carriers
 battleships and 245
 conflict dynamics and 245
 diplomacy and 225–28, 237, 241–43,
  243*f*
 influence of 245–46, 246*f*
 submarines and 247–48
 in war 59, 103, 125

air warfare
 air power 252–55, 274n37,
  278–81
 automation in 278–81
 drones in 255–60, 264–69, 269f,
  270–73, 282
 economics of 252–55, 260–63
 geopolitics of 273–78
 land warfare and 210
 policy in 94–95, 273–78
Alexander, Keith 109, 170
Allen, Michael E. 207
alliances
 alliance theory 200–202
 commitments to 211–12
 credibility of 221–23
 for defense 210, 214–15
 dynamics of 7–8, 209–10
 in Europe 401
 mobile forces and 218n61
 networks of 222–23
 politics of 198
 security with 204–5
 for stability 395–96
 ties to 203–4
 with US 214, 216–17
 in war 22–23
 in World War I 276–77
 after World War II 200
ambiguous attacks 156–57
ambiguous policy 58
anonymous hackers 139–40, 156,
  159n87
anti-access and area-denial (A2/AD)
 strategy 397–98, 403
anti-ballistic missile systems 178
anti-satellite weapons 31–32, 298–99
APRANET program 171–72
Arms and Influence (Schelling) 18

446 INDEX

arms-races 27n24
arsenals 24–25
ASAT technology 99–100, 99n81
Asia. See also *specific countries*
  East 392–93, 403
  Europe and 198
  geopolitics in 237, 399–404
  hegemony in 399
  scholarship on 196–97, 196n3
  US and 230, 249–50
assassinations 129
assorted measures and signatures 150n63
assumptions, in GZC 345–47
assurance 22
asymmetry
  interdependence and 313–18, 314f
  multipolarity and 303–5, 311
  scholarship on 308f, 310
  in trade 306–7, 311–12
attack submarines 246–47, 247f
attribution, for coercion 114
Austin, Lloyd, III 33–34
Australia 195
automation 253n5, 261–62, 263, 278–81
Azerbaijan 274, 274n37

Bacon, Francis 91
ballistic missile submarines 93
Baran, Paul 171–72
bargaining model
  canonical 78
  defense in 385
  denial and 11
  goals in 7t
  leadership in 52–53
  parameters in 53–54, 53f
  psychology of 7–8, 48f, 50–51
  research on 20n17
  scholarship from 384n14
  strategy of 56–57, 381–82, 382t
  of war 6–7, 9, 41–44, 48–49, 48f
battleships 245–46, 246f
beliefs 145n48
Berlin Crisis 178
Betts, Richard 288
bilateral trade 307–8, 307–9, 308f, 311
biological weapons 322
Blankenship, Brian 202, 205, 219

Botnet 160
Brennan, John O. 255
brinkmanship crises 178, 183–85, 191,
  249, 279
Brodie, Bernard 152, 228, 232n36
brute force. See coercion
bureaucratic politics 47–48
Bureau of Investigative
  Journalism 268–69
Burns, William 390

Caesar, Julius 284–85
Cambodia 28
Canada 118
canonical bargaining model 78
Canopy Wing program 172–76, 187
Carter, Jimmy 282–84, 295
Carver, Raymond 54
Central Intelligence Agency
  (CIA) 148–49
challengers
  aggression by 366–67
  defenders and 344–45, 354–56,
    367–69, 367f
  economics to 356–57
  psychology of 355–56
  scholarship on 345–47, 351–52, 353f
  status quo to 346–47
  strategy of 348–51, 349f
China. See also US-China strategy
  A2/AD strategy by 397–98, 403
  aggression by 60
  Central Military Commission 190
  in coercive diplomacy 22
  in Cold War 104, 303
  in cyberspace 31–32
  defense against 10
  espionage by 185–86
  force posture in 196n3
  France and 185
  geopolitics and 392–93, 392f
  India and 185
  international law to 58–59
  Israel and 30, 292
  Japan and 124
  military in 229, 373–75, 400–401
  nuclear deterrence in 175–76
  People's Liberation Army 33

INDEX   447

to political pundits 393n21
Russia and 31, 67, 98–99, 291, 294
scholarship on 390–91
strategy of 251
substitution by 322
Taiwan and 92, 377–78
in Taiwan Strait Crisis 60
US and 12, 33–34, 127, 166, 223n64,
224, 302, 396–99
to US National Defense Strategy 4
Vietnam War to 294
weapons tests by 98n74
Christensen, Thomas J. 211
Churchill, Winston 92
CIA. See Central Intelligence Agency
Cimbala, Stephen 182
Citizen Lab 160
civilians
defense for 277–78
drones and 95
government and 268
non-combatants and 262–63
in Pakistan 267
in Palestine 280
power of 71–72
technology for 142–43, 277
violence against 263n27, 269, 269f,
271–73
classical deterrence
allies in 22–23
arsenals in 24–25
coercion in 21–22
complexity in 28
counterforce in 24–25
expansion in 26–27
history of 20
international security in 69–70
in MAD 55–56
model 1
orthodox deterrence and 6–8, 7t
peace in 21
theory 17–20, 19–20, 43
of war 54–56
war-fighting in 23
Clausewitz, Carl von
on force 47
on military 76, 153
reputation of 105, 114

strategy to 77
on surprise 287
uncertainty to 44, 90
on war 41–42, 74–75
Clinton, Bill 262
coastline length 243–44, 244f
coercion
attribution for 114
benefits of 180
coercive diplomacy 22–23
coercive strategy 90
in cyberspace 111–12
deception 83
defense and 78, 85–86, 86t, 134, 151,
377, 381, 382t, 383f
as deterrence 21–22, 79
with drones 306–7
effectiveness of 66, 254
with information 310
military 102–3, 133–34
by Nazis 147–48
with nuclear deterrence 86
power in 232–33
Schelling on 23n21, 66, 79–80, 123
in Vietnam War 28
war-fighting and 17–18
coercive diplomacy 80
cognitive domain 85
cognitive psychology 78
coherent intelligence 287–88
Cold War
brinkmanship crises in 279
China in 104, 303
CIA in 148–49
conflict dynamics in 185, 290
counterforce in 172–73
defense in 82–83
end of 373
Europe after 206
Germany in 158, 207–8
history 187
MAD in 19–20
NATO in 59, 90n43
nuclear deterrence in 2, 291, 403–4
politics 179–80, 340
power in 118
reconnaissance in 286–87
Russia in 226

448 INDEX

Cold War (*Continued*)
  scholarship on 342
  security in 1
  society during 178–79
  stability-instability paradox in 101–2
  strategy 29–31, 178
  technology in 29, 99
  US in 19–20, 88–89, 99, 176, 406
colonialism 279
commerce 304–13, 305–13, 308*f*, 316–18
commercial space industry 98n76
comparative advantages 85–88, 86*t*
compellence
  coercion and 57
  by denial 24
  deterrence contrasted with 11, 21–22,
    80, 88, 107, 121, 123, 199, 239, 250,
    286, 405
  stealth technology and 122
  terrorism as 129
complexity
  in classical deterrence 28
  complex deterrence 32–33
  cultural 88
  of deterrence 375–80, 387–90, 389*t*
  of networks 316–18
  scholarship on 85n34
  sociotechnical 162
  strategy and 102–5, 301–2, 380–82,
    382*t*
  of trade-offs 382–87, 383*f*
comprehensive deterrence 32–33
computer programming 145–46
computer viruses 109–10, 137, 143, 146,
  155–57
concession, in war 276n40
conflict dynamics
  aircraft carriers and 245
  of asymmetric trade 311–12
  in Cold War 185, 290
  costless conflict 254
  in cyberspace 118–19, 135–36
  cyber vigilantism as 157–58
  empirical patterns in 288–95, 294*f*
  geography in 338
  in GZC 59, 344–52, 349*f*, 353*f*, 354–57
  instability in 46–47
  interdependence in 308–9

  with military 44–45
  mobile forces in 62
  with multipolarity 314–15, 315*f*
  multipolarity in 307–8, 308*f*
  non-combatants in 277–78
  outcomes and 335–37, 336*f*
  peace and 313n23
  risk in 305–6, 310
  scholarship on 117–21, 305n4, 333–39,
    388–89, 389*t*
  technology for 12
  trade-offs in 8
  traditional conflict 327–28
  with transparency 296
convergent evolution 159–60
cooperation 144
Corbett, Julian 75–76, 91, 227–28
costless conflict 254
cost reduction 399–400
counterforce 24–25, 97, 172–73, 180, 187
counterintelligence 387
counterterrorism 254–55, 259–60, 268
The Count of Monte Cristo
  (Dumas) 149n61
COVID-19 pandemic 230
credibility
  of alliances 221–23
  commitment to 204, 214, 216–17, 217*t*
  credible communication 177–80
  in cyberspace 35
  after deception 87
  of defense 61
  of deterrence 371
  deterrence and 221–23
  dynamics of 217, 217*t*
  economics of 48*f*, 49
  generating 216
  of intelligence 296
  in land wars 195–200, 218–21, 219*t*
  lowering 193
  militarized interstate disputes and 194,
    293n30
  nuclear 96–97, 103–4
  power and 215, 236n42, 237
  presence and 216
  scholarship on 35
  signaling 210, 239
  with status quo 57–61

in substitution 331–32
subversion and 8
of threats 122–23
Crimea 340
crises 23, 38–39
cross-domain deterrence 4, 15, 28,
32–33, 104
Cuban Missile Crisis 178, 185, 287,
290–91, 290–92
cultural complexity 88
cyber aggression 121
cyberconflict 321–25, 386
cyber deception
NC3 and 167–76, 187–89
nuclear deterrence and 165–67, 166n4,
177–86
policy implications with 186–91
cyber espionage 320, 323, 328, 332–33,
335
cybersecurity 166
cyberspace. See also *specific topics*
ambiguous attacks in 156–57
China in 31–32
coercion in 111–12
commitment to 180–81
conflict dynamics in 118–19, 135–36
credibility in 35
DCID 321n6, 334, 334n33
DDoS attacks 109–10, 145–46, 362–63
deception in 155–58, 161–64
deterrence in 10, 151–55
economics of 11–12, 100, 304
electronic warfare 391
empirical anomaly in 138–39
in Estonia 363–64
exploitation in 104
geography of 84n29
to government 139–42, 158–60
history of 73n1
independence in 325–29
influence in 184–85
information and 319–21, 333–39, 336f
Internet and 130–32
Internet hackers 136–37, 139–40, 156,
159n87, 162–63
malware 143, 143n40, 146
military commitment to 180–81
military in 165

network-attacks in 110–11
neutron bombs and 119n35
nuclear deterrence and 73–74
nuisances 161–62, 161n93
ontology of 3n1
politics of 100–102, 142–50
power in 127–30, 229
risk in 5
satellites and 298
secret statecraft and 139–42, 140n25
space and 102–3
technology in 114–17
trade-offs in 3
traditional war and 330–33
US Cyber Command 76
violence in 32
war in 2–3, 100–102, 107, 111–14,
117–27, 133–36
war strategy in 109–11
weapons in 31
webpage defacement 27
cyberspies 155–56
cyberstrategy 393
cyberterrorism 129–30
cyber vigilantism 157–58

damage limitation 24–25, 29, 61, 172
DCID. *See* Dyadic Cyber Incident Dataset
DDoS attacks. *See* distributed denial of
service attacks
deception. *See also* cyber deception
accommodation and 78, 377, 383f
balance of 161–64
coercion 83
credibility after 87
in cyberspace 155–58, 161–64
denial and 151
engineering 158–60
by Great Britain 154
historiography of 154n74
influence and 134n6
with information 144n44, 149n61
as intelligence 8
measures 173
mutually assured 161, 290
offensive 138–39, 153–55, 161
in practice 147–49
psychology of 101, 150–51

450 INDEX

deception (*Continued*)
  risk in 152n65
  scholarship on 143–47, 381, 382*t*
  strategy of 103, 133–36, 151–53, 193
  technology of 142–50
  in war 85–86, 86*t*
defense
  against aggression 65, 68–69
  with air power 274n37
  alliances for 210, 214–15
  in bargaining model 385
  against China 10
  for civilians 277–78
  coercion and 78, 85–86, 86*t*, 134, 151,
    377, 381, 382*t*, 383*f*
  in Cold War 82–83
  credibility of 61
  defenders 202–4, 210–11, 210–13,
    220–21, 344–45, 348n35, 354–56,
    367–69, 367*f*, 406
  Defense Advanced Research Projects
    Agency 158–59
  Defense Science Board 154–55, 188
  defensible defense strategy 392–93,
    392*f*
  defensive 251
  as deterrence 155–58, 354–55
  deterrence compared to 23, 107
  direct 197
  economics of 201–2
  force posture and 198
  Ground-based Midcourse Defense
    System 176
  against hackers 162–63
  of Japan 250
  military 8, 11, 152n65
  mobile forces for 75–76
  to NATO 207–8
  network defenders 155
  offshore balancing and 210–11
  in Pakistan 185
  peace and 310
  planning for 153
  policy for 65
  with reconnaissance satellites 297–98
  scholarship on 138–39
  stability in 71
  of status quo 64

strategy for 80
with technology 262
against terrorism 30n32
THAAD 176
trade-offs for 101
US 32
US Department of Defense 10, 390–91
US National Defense Strategy 4, 32,
  35–37
US Secretary of Defense 190
denial 11, 24, 36–37, 81–82, 151
Denmark 329
Department of Defense, US 10, 34–35,
  34–37, 390–91
deployments
  automation and 261–62
  extended deterrence and 200–202
  force posture and 207–13
  foreign 196–97
  in land wars 204–7
  military 211
  offshore balancing and 200–201,
    200n14
  peace and 203–4, 208
deterrence. *See specific topics*
digital networks 2–3, 142–43
diplomacy
  aircraft carriers and 225–28, 237,
    241–43, 243*f*
  automation and 263
  coastline length and 243–44, 244*f*
  coercive 22–23, 80
  efficiency in 253
  government and 42
  influence in 235–37, 236n43
  with Japan 122
  military 37, 62
  naval tonnage and 242–43, 242*f*
  power in 225
  risk in 63
  subversion and 52
direct defense 197
direct deterrence 22–23
disarmament 136n7, 151
disinformation 158–59
dispute propensity 245*f*
distributed denial of service (DDoS)
  attacks 109–10, 145–46, 362–63

Dr. Strangelove (film) 2, 175, 178–79
domains. *See specific topics*
domestic policy 9
drones
  in air warfare 255–60, 264–69, 269f, 270–73, 282
  in Azerbaijan 274n37
  coercion with 306–7
  drone warfare 245, 402
  economics and 278–81
  in maritime environments 12
  in Pakistan 128–29
  satellites and 282–83
  tactical 275–76
  technology for 95, 267n32
  trade-offs with 252–53
  UAVs and 253–60, 262–64, 266–68, 273–74, 402
  in Ukraine 338–39
  to US 338–39
Dumas, Alexandre 149n61
Dyadic Cyber Incident Dataset (DCID) 321n6, 334, 334n33
dyadic variation 185–186

East Africa 273–74
East Asia 392–93, 403
Ebay 115
economics. *See also* trade
  of air warfare 252–55, 260–63
  to challengers 356–57
  of cost reduction 399–400
  of credibility 48f, 49
  of cyberspace 11–12, 100, 304
  of defenders 348n35, 367–69, 367f
  of defense 201–2
  of destruction 9
  drones and 278–81
  economic exchanges 8
  economic interdependence 230
  economic ties 312
  of geopolitics 230–31, 305–8, 308f
  goals and 56
  government and 213–14
  gross domestic product 306, 358
  of military 218n60
  of mobile forces 330n27
  of non-military tools 391

of policy efficiency 6
power and 44–45, 404–5
punishment with 24n23
risk and 137, 329
society and 320–21
sunk costs 217t
of technology 255–60
of war 48f, 49–50, 61–62, 138–39
effectiveness
  of coercion 66, 254
  of deterrence 61–66
  efficacy and 184
  influence and 57
  military 47, 52
  of power 381
  of strategy 152–53
  of technology 329
efficiency
  in diplomacy 253
  internal efficiency constraints 346–47, 350–51, 350f, 355, 357
  scholarship on 6, 47–48, 52, 56–57
Egypt 154
Eisenhower, Dwight D. 286
electromagnetic domains 85
electronic warfare 172–73, 391
emerging technology 10
empirical anomaly 138–39
empirical anomaly, in cyberspace 138–39
endogeneity effect 244–45
engineering deception 158–60
escalation
  dynamics 12
  in gray zones 340–42
  in GZC 340–42, 366–71, 367f
  of NC3, 182–83
  nuclear deterrence and 337–38
  risk of 331–32, 388–89, 389t
  scholarship on 26–27, 344–45
  status quo and 348–51, 349f
  in Ukraine 357
  virtual 28
  of war 25–26
Esper, Mark 401–2
espionage
  by China 185–86
  cyber 320, 323, 328, 332–33, 335
  cyberspies 155–56

452   INDEX

espionage (*Continued*)
  Group spyware 160
  Hall on 174
  to leadership 329
  low-risk 162–63
  with photographic imagery 291,
    291n20
  by Russia 148–49, 148n55, 286–87
  from space 284–87
  subversion and 100–101, 107, 112,
    166, 337
  technological 150, 284
  traditional 114, 285
  undercover agents 159
Estonia 357, 361–63, 361–65, 361t,
    362–63, 362n43
Europe
  alliances in 401
  Asia and 198
  after Cold War 206
  colonialism by 279
  Euromaidan Revolution 344–45
  force posture in 210
  Germany and 329
  Great Britain and 125, 148
  history of 88–89
  Maginot Line in 65
  Middle East and 399
  NATO and 64, 195–96, 379
  Radio Free Europe 173–74
  Russia and 358, 359f, 360
  after Warsaw Pact 59
Van Evera, Stephen 140n25
exploitation 104, 144n41, 185,
    285–86
extended deterrence 22–23, 200–204,
    208–9, 222
external deterrent constraints 347,
    350–51, 350f, 355, 355n37, 357
extortion 79

Fearon, James D. 44, 44n11, 201–2,
    381n8
Federally Administered Tribal Areas, of
    Pakistan 257–58
flexible responses 97n71
Flournoy, Michèle A. 394–95, 397
fog of war 82, 153

force posture 196n3, 198, 207–13, 223,
    235–36
force structure 74–75
foreign deployments 196–97
Fort Ticonderoga 64n38
France 65, 90–91, 137, 185, 226, 232n36
Freedman, Lawrence 20
Fricker, Matthew S. 258
Friedman, Benjamin 397–99
Friedman, Norman 228

general deterrence 23
geography
  in conflict dynamics 338
  of cyberspace 84n29
  geographic endowments 55
  mobility and 232
  naval tonnage and 240–41, 241f
  of Pakistan 274
  political 234–35
  power and 234–35
  Russia and 359f
  strategy and 216
  technology and 83–84, 139
geopolitics
  of air warfare 273–78
  in Asia 237, 399–404
  China and 392–93, 392f
  economics of 230–31, 305–8, 308f
  global thermonuclear war 32–33
  government in 329
  hegemony in 396
  influence in 237–38
  Internet and 117, 131–32, 331–33,
    331–34, 331–39, 336f
  NATO in 357–58
  nuclear deterrence and 19–20, 29–30,
    179
  policy for 61–66
  risk aversion in 57–58
  Russia in 296–97, 321n5, 324, 371–72,
    385
  in Russian gray-zones 357–58, 359f,
    360–66, 361t
  scholarship on 195–200
  sea power in 225
  stability in 288–95, 294f
  Taiwan in 398–99

INDEX 453

trade in 303–5, 313, 314*f*, 315–16
Ukraine in 97n73
uncertainty in 319
US in 373–75
after World War II 29–31
George, Alexander 342
Georgia 132, 357, 361, 361*t*, 363–65, 372
Germany
Berlin Crisis 178
Canopy Wing program to 174
in Cold War 158, 207–8
Europe and 329
Great Britain and 120–21, 375
history of 59, 92
intelligence in 172–73
to NATO 89
in naval warfare 278–79
US and 213
in World War I 241–42
in World War II 147–48
Gholz, Eugene 397–99
Gjoza, Enea 397–99
Glaser, Charles 398
global domains 84n29
Global Positioning System (GPS) 100
global survival 15
global thermonuclear war 32–33
Goldgeier, James 206
Göring, Herman 120–21
GPS. *See* Global Positioning System
Gray, Colin 287–88
gray zone conflict (GZC)
ambiguity in 342–44
assumptions in 345–47
conflict dynamics in 59, 344–52, 349*f*,
353*f*, 354–57
deterrence and 371–72, 385
escalation in 340–42, 366–71, 367*f*
risk in 349–50, 350*f*
Russia and 357–58, 359*f*, 360–66, 361*t*
scholarship on 383–84, 383*f*
stalemates in 373–74
subversion in 73–74, 344, 364, 369–70
variation in 351–52, 353*f*
war in 132
Great Britain
deception by 154
Europe and 125, 148

France and 226
Germany and 120–21, 375
history of 91–92, 227–28, 232
Israel and 185–86
Rome and 284–85
US and 147–48, 195, 276–77
in World War I 278–79
Greece 147, 226–27, 230–31
gross domestic product 306, 358
Ground-based Midcourse Defense
System 176
Group spyware 160
Gulf War 95, 275
gullibility 143, 161n93
GZC. *See* gray zone conflict

hackers 136–37, 139–40, 156, 159n87,
162–63
Hall, James 174
Hamas 131, 280
Haney, Cecil 170–71
Heartbleed bug 146
hegemony 396, 399
Heuer, Richards J., Jr. 144–45, 145n48
Hitler, Adolf 147–48
human intelligence 150n63, 286, 290–91
Hunzeker, Michael A. 205–6
Hussein, Saddam 275

ICBMs. *See* intercontinental missiles
immediate deterrence 23
implicit strategic objectives 47–54,
48*f*, 53*f*
incentives, in war 199–200
independence, in cyberspace 325–29
India 185–86
indirect substitution 334–35
influence
of aircraft carriers 245–46, 246*f*
in cyberspace 184–85
deception and 134n6
in diplomacy 235–37, 236n43
effectiveness and 57
in geopolitics 237–38
of leadership 221
political 47, 52, 117–18, 377, 381, 382*t*
in politics 15
power and 251

454 INDEX

influence (*Continued*)
  Schelling and 134n6
  stability and 56–57, 60
  US 396–97
information
  coercion with 310
  control of 326
  cyberspace and 319–21, 333–39, 336f
  deception with 144n44, 149n61
  disinformation 158–59
  informational contests 327–29
  informational logic 309
  knowledge and 284–85, 328–29
  leaks 157n80
  peace and 312–13
  revolution 135
  subversion and 31
  technology 136–37
  in war 325–29, 380n7
instability 27–28, 46–47, 101–2, 185–86,
  199, 395–96
institutional politics 9, 44
insurgent forces 263
integrated deterrence 4, 15, 30–37, 107,
  141n36, 407
intelligence
  agents 149–50
  coherent 287–88
  collection 148
  contests 333
  counterintelligence 387
  credibility of 296
  deception as 8
  evolution of 164
  in Germany 172–73
  human 150n63, 286, 290–91
  intelligence gain-loss dilemma 69
  to KGB 158
  leaks 181, 329
  scholarship on 282–84
  space and 288–95, 294f
  stability and 295–99
  subversion and 187
  traditional 285
  vulnerability and 122–23
  war and 319–20
intelligence, surveillance, reconnaissance
  (ISR) 82, 103–4

intensity 306
intercontinental missiles (ICBMs 167–69,
  177, 187–88
interdependence 303–5, 308–9, 313–18,
  314f, 316–18
internal efficiency constraints 346–47,
  350–51, 350f, 355, 357
international relations. *See specific topics*
Internet
  communication on 330n24
  computer programming and 145–46
  cyberspace and 130–32
  deterrence with 171–72
  exploitation on 144n41
  faith in 147
  geopolitics and 117, 131–32, 331–33,
  331–34, 331–39, 336f
  hackers 136–37, 139–40, 156, 159n87,
  162–63
  military and 114–15
  networks 304–5
  spammers 161n93
  of things 333n29
  vandals 113–14
  war on 130–32
Iran 110, 176, 324, 338, 396
Iraq 67–68, 95, 259, 275
Islamic State 338
ISR. *See* intelligence, surveillance,
  reconnaissance
Israel
  China and 30, 292
  Egypt and 154
  Great Britain and 185–86
  Hamas and 280
  Iran and 338
  US and 109–10

JADC2. *See* Joint All-Domain Command
  and Control
JAMGC. *See* Joint Concept for Access and
  Maneuver in the Global Commons
Japan
  China and 124
  defense of 250
  diplomacy with 122
  Pearl Harbor and 154
  Al Qaeda and 280

INDEX 455

US and 68, 125–26, 181, 209, 250, 283
in World War II 125n45
Jellicoe, John 92
Johnston, Patrick B. 257, 267n32
Joint All-Domain Command and Control
(JADC2) 394
Joint Concept for Access and Maneuver in
the Global Commons (JAMGC) 394

Kautilya 147
Kehler, Robert 169–71
Kello, Lucas 137
Kennan, George 58
Kennedy Space Center 282
KGB 158
kinetic warfare 120
knowledge, information and 284–85,
328–29
Kosovo 253
Kuwait 95, 275

labor 276, 278–81
land wars
alliance theory in 200–202
credibility in 195–200, 218–21, 219t
deployments in 204–7
extended deterrence in 203–4
mobile forces in 250–51
offshore balancing in 207–13
scholarship on 210, 213–17, 217t,
221–23, 233–34, 401
strategy in 76, 88–93
Lanoszka, Alexander 205–6
Laos 28
Lawrence Berkeley Laboratory 158
leadership
in bargaining model 52–53
espionage to 329
influence of 221
military 71–72
of mobile forces 63–64, 249–50
psychology of 45–46
punishment of 54
in Russia 185, 196
in society 2
surprise attacks to 288
trade-offs to 65–66
in war 121–22

leverage 103, 238
Levy, Jack 229
liberal hegemony 396
Lin-Greenberg, Erik 202, 205, 219
Lithuania 363
long peace 29
low-risk espionage 162–63
Lusitania (ship) 375
Lynn, William, III 113

machine learning 159
MAD. *See* mutual assured destruction
Maginot Line 65
Mahan, Alfred Thayer 225n4, 227–28,
229
malware 143, 143n40, 146
maneuver strategies 89–90, 224–25,
240–48, 241f
maritime domain 12, 231–40, 249–50,
401
Mary II (queen) 232n36
maximal deterrence 25
McNamara, Robert 277
Mearsheimer, John 89, 208n45, 229–30,
399–400
Merkel, Angela 329
Middle East 324, 338, 399
militant organizations 263–69, 269f,
270–73
militarized interstate disputes 194, 218,
240, 244, 292–94, 293n30, 334
military
aggression 163–64, 287–88
automation 278–81
in China 229, 373–75, 400–401
choices 74
Clausewitz on 76, 153
coercion 102–3, 133–34
commitment 180–81
conflict dynamics with 44–45
cultures 84
in cyberspace 165
defense 8, 11, 152n65
deployments 211
digital networks for 2–3
diplomacy 37, 62
disputes 237–40
domains 85–86, 86t

456 INDEX

military (*Continued*)
  economics of 218n60
  effectiveness 47, 52
  engagement 396–97
  espionage 114
  experts 196–97
  information revolution for 135
  intent 66
  Internet and 114–15
  labor 276
  leadership 71–72
  mobile forces and 387–88
  mobilization 46
  modern 67
  negotiations with 7
  networks 157n80
  non-military tools 10, 34–35,
    50–51, 391
  offshore balancing with 216
  options 25, 94–95
  personnel 200n14, 204, 216–17
  policy 178
  politics of 10, 388
  power 50, 182, 196, 231–32, 250
  presence 236
  psychology 2
  sea power and 244
  specialization 15, 18, 30–31, 75–85,
    103–4, 193
  strategy 4–5, 66–69
  support 181
  technology 63, 380
  trade-offs 69
  US 34, 124, 127–28, 207
  US National Defense Strategy for 36
  violence 256, 330–31
  war-fighting 24
*Military and Security Developments
  Involving the People's Republic of
  China* (US Department of
  Defense) 390–91
minimal deterrence 25
missile domains 84, 94
mobile forces
  alliances and 218n61
  for defense 75–76
  economics of 330n27
  force posture 196n3, 198, 207–13

insurgent forces and 263
in land wars 250–51
leadership of 63–64, 249–50
military and 387–88
in modernity 89–90
in offshore balancing 210n52
policy for 195–200, 198–99
power of 62, 67
Schelling on 89
trade-offs with 91–92
uniforms for 151–52
Moldova 363
Morrow, James D. 201
multipolarity 303–5, 307–8, 308f,
    311–15, 315f
mutual assured destruction
    (MAD) 19–20, 55–56, 96–97,
    178, 186

Nagorno-Karabakh 255, 274
Napoleon Bonaparte 90–92
National Aeronautics and Space
    Administration 115
National Defense Strategy, US 4, 32,
    35–37
National Security Agency, US 143,
    157n80, 165–66, 181, 329
National Security Strategy, US 24n22, 31
NATO. *See* North Atlantic Treaty
    Organization
naval warfare
  Germany in 278–79
  history of 225n4
  in maritime domain 231–40
  naval punishment 248
  naval tonnage 240–41, 241f, 242–43,
    242f, 248
  power of 195
  scholarship on 75–76, 91–93, 152,
    240–48, 241f, 401–2
  sea power and 224–31, 235, 248–51
Nazis 147–48
NC3. *See* nuclear command, control, and
    communications
negative peace 21
Nelson, Horatio 92, 230
network attacks 110–11
network defenders 155

network operations 163–64
networks 157n80, 158, 222–23, 304–5, 316–18
network technology 153
neutron bombs 119n35
New Zealand 195
Nieman, Mark David 207
non-combatants 262–63, 277–78
non-lethal weapons 120n36
non-military tools 10, 34–35, 50–51, 391
North Atlantic Treaty Organization (NATO)
   in Cold War 59, 90n43
   defense to 207–8
   deterrence postures by 372
   as deterrent 341
   doctrine 208n45
   in Estonia 362–63
   Europe and 64, 195–96, 379
   in geopolitics 357–58
   in Georgia 363–65
   Germany to 89
   history of 46
   in Kosovo 253
   membership 357–58, 360
   Russia and 206, 357–58
   scholarship on 358, 359f, 360–62, 361t
   strategy 208n46
   in Ukraine 345n30, 364–66
   US and 46, 377–78
   war to 174
North Korea 29–30, 59, 167, 176–77
North Vietnamese Army 28
nuclear command, control, and communications (NC3)
   cyber deception and 167–76, 187–89
   escalation of 182–83
   exploitation 185
   policy 181, 184, 186, 190–91
   scholarship on 189
   technology for 170–71
   vulnerability 172, 188–89
nuclear deterrence
   aggression with 60–61
   biological weapons and 322
   in China 175–76
   coercion with 86

   in Cold War 2, 291, 403–4
   cyber deception and 165–67, 166n4, 177–86
   cyberspace and 73–74
   deterrence with 29–31
   escalation and 337–38
   force structure of 73n2
   geopolitics and 19–20, 29–30, 179
   in Iran 324
   Nuclear Command and Control System (NCCS) 189
   nuclear credibility 96–97, 103–4
   in nuclear deterrence theory 38–39
   Nuclear Posture Review 32, 32n46, 168, 171, 190–91
   nuclear security and 35–36, 54–55
   nuclear terrorism 155n77
   policy implications with 186–91
   politics of 95–97
   psychology of 373–74
   punishment with 95–96
   Schelling on 21n20
   scholarship on 405
   strategy with 17–18
   trade-offs with 87
   in US 190–91
   war after 152–53
   Warsaw Pact and 208n46
   after World War II 29
Nye, Joseph 396

Obama, Barack 113, 196n3, 255
offensive deception 138–39, 153–55, 161
offshore balancing
   defense and 210–11
   deployments and 200–201, 200n14
   in land wars 207–13
   with military 216
   mobile forces in 210n52
   peace and 214
   presence and 218–20, 219t, 220t
   strategy in 198–99
   theories for 213–17, 217t
   in US-China strategy 399–400
   US in 221–22
Operation Olympic Games 176, 324
operational deterrence 25–26, 94–95
operational domains 11

458   INDEX

operational features 82–85
Operation Mincemeat 147–48
orthodox deterrence 5–8, 7t
outer space. *See* space

Pakistan
    Afghanistan and 259
    civilians in 267
    counterterrorism in 259–60, 268
    defense in 185
    drones in 128–29
    Federally Administered Tribal Areas
        of 257–58
    geography of 274
    India and 186
    North Korea and 29–30
    scholarship on 268n33
    urban terrorism in 268–69, 269f,
        271–73
    US and 255–56
Palestine 280
Panetta, Leon 109–10, 124
paradoxical trinity 41, 105
paranoia 157
partial automation 253n5
Patton, George S. 147–48
peace
    in classical deterrence 21
    commerce and 304–5
    conflict dynamics and 313n23
    defense and 310
    deployments and 203–4, 208
    deterrence and 199
    information and 312–13
    long 29
    offshore balancing and 214
    peacetime 249
    politics and 260–61
    positive 21
    presence in 243
    reconnaissance 295–99
    to Russia 295
    unpeace 319
    war and 163–64, 317–18, 342–44
Pearl Harbor 68, 109, 124–27, 154, 163,
        283, 286
People's Liberation Army, of China. *See*
    China; US-China strategy

perception 202
Pericles 226–27
personality strikes 272
Philippines 195
photographic imagery 150n63, 291,
        291n20, 295n33
photoreconnaissance satellites 282
physical deployment of forces.
        See presence
physical violence 118
pilotless vehicles 261
Pistone, Joseph 159
Plaw, Avery 258
Poast, Paul 205
Poland 363
policy
    in air warfare 94–95, 273–78
    alliance dynamics in 7–8
    ambiguous 58
    debates 337
    for defense 65
    deterrence 40–41, 71
    domestic 9
    efficiency and 6, 47–48, 52
    for geopolitics 61–66
    implications 186–91
    military 178
    for mobile forces 195–200, 198–99
    NC3, 181, 184, 186, 190–91
    with non-military tools 34–35
    NSA 165–66
    options 193–94
    policy makers 40, 96n67, 250, 381t,
        382–83, 382–84
    scholarship and 3–4, 11–12
    security 48f, 383f, 384n12
    for stability-instability paradox 27–28
    sufficiency and 378–79
    trade-offs in 70–71
    US 19, 29–30, 196n3
political actors 112
political geography 234–35
political influence 47, 52, 117–18, 377,
        381, 382t
political liabilities 232–33
political probability 111, 114–17
political pundits 393n21
political science 229

INDEX 459

political trade-offs 231–40
political violence 328
politicians 58, 71
politics
  of air warfare 94–95
  of alliances 198
  in brinkmanship crises 249
  bureaucratic 47–48
  Cold War 179–80, 340
  comparative advantages in 85–88, 86t
  concerns of 42
  of cyberspace 100–102, 142–50
  of deterrence 26, 73–75
  government 6
  influence in 15
  institutional 9, 44
  of land wars 88–93
  of MAD 19–20
  of military 10, 388
  of nuclear deterrence 95–97
  of operational features 82–85
  peace and 260–61
  of sea power 229n26
  of security 3–4, 69–72
  for space domains 97–99
  status quo 69
  strategic complexity and 102–5
  of subversion 79–83
  of technology 9–10, 43, 72
  of UAVs 262
  of uncertainty 296
  in US 195–200
  of war 75–81
Posen, Barry R. 229
positioning, navigation, and
    timing 298–99
positive peace 21
potential agreement 50–51
Potter, Philip B. K. 259–60
Powell, Robert 38–39
power. *See also* sea power
  air 252–55, 274n37, 278–81
  balance of 380n7
  of civilians 71–72
  in coercion 232–33
  in Cold War 118
  credibility and 215, 236n42, 237
  in cyberspace 127–30, 229

  in diplomacy 225
  economics and 44–45, 404–5
  effectiveness of 381
  geography and 234–35
  to hurt 79–80
  influence and 251
  in IR 69–70
  military 50, 182, 196, 231–32, 250
  of mobile forces 62, 67
  of naval warfare 195
  sea 224–31, 235, 244, 248–51, 249
  of secret capabilities 121–24
  soft 383
  of stealth 239
  strategy for 34
  of submarines 279
  substitution and 331–32
  of subversion 385–86
  of technology 67–68
  of US 121–22
preemptive war 182
prescience 45
presence (physical deployment of forces)
  credibility and 216
  extended deterrence with 222
  force posture as 235–36
  offshore balancing and 218–20,
      219t, 220t
  in peace 243
  scholarship on 196–97, 207–13
  strategic stability from 219t
prestige 236n42
preventative war 45
propaganda 258–59
propensity 306
protective strategies 138–39
protégés. *See specific topics*
psychology
  of aggression 163, 371–72
  in arms-races 27n24
  of bargaining model 7–8, 48f, 50–51
  of behavior 42–43
  of beliefs 145n48
  of challengers 355–56
  cognitive 78
  of deception 101, 150–51
  of demands 53n24
  of deterrence 203

460 INDEX

psychology (*Continued*)
  of government 51
  gullibility 143, 161n93
  of institutional politics 44
  of integrated deterrence 31–37, 407
  of leadership 45–46
  military 2
  of nuclear deterrence 373–74
  of objectives 4–5
  paranoia 157
  perception 202
  of preferences 70
  of risk 1
  sociology and 43
  of strategy 55–56
  of trade-offs 40
  of uncertainty 380–81
  of violence 21, 116
  of war 11–12
punishment 24, 24n23, 54, 95–96,
    123–24, 248, 252
Putin, Vladimir 45–46, 185, 196, 362

Al Qaeda 154, 258–59, 280, 283

Radio Free Europe 173–74
Raleigh, Walter 227
ransomware 101
rationality 42–43
Reagan, Ronald 165–66
reconnaissance 286–87, 295–99. *See also*
    satellites
Reiter, Dan 205
restraint 224
retrenchment 397–99
Richard, Charles 171, 188–89
Rid, Thomas 114
risk
  for anonymous hackers 156
  aversion 57–58
  with battleships 246
  in brinkmanship crises 183–84
  in conflict dynamics 305–6, 310
  in cyberspace 5
  in deception 152n65
  in diplomacy 63
  economics and 137, 329
  of escalation 331–32, 388–89, 389t

  in escalation dynamics 12
  in GZC 349–50, 350f
  of instability 395–96
  low-risk espionage 162–63
  in naval warfare 92–93
  with pilotless vehicles 261
  psychology of 1
  retrenchment and 397–99
  scholarship on 144–45
  with UAVs 273–74
  war and 2, 350–51, 354–55,
    367–69, 367f
Rome 284–85
Roosevelt, Franklin Delano 208
Roosevelt, Theodor 310
Rovner, Joshua 204, 226
Rumsfeld, Donald 183
Russia
  aggression by 89
  in Canopy Wing program 173–74
  China and 31, 67, 98–99, 291, 294
  in Cold War 226
  espionage by 148–49, 148n55, 286–87
  in Euromaidan Revolution 344–45
  Europe and 358, 359f, 360
  geography and 359f
  in geopolitics 296–97, 321n5, 324,
    371–72, 385
  government of 378
  GZC and 357–58, 359f, 360–66, 361t
  Iran and 110, 396
  Iron Curtain in 179
  KGB in 158
  leadership in 185, 196
  NATO and 206, 357–58
  peace to 295
  threats from 97n73
  Ukraine and 45–46, 92, 98n76, 131,
    275–76, 301, 330n24, 341–42,
    369–71
  US and 172–75, 179–80, 185–86,
    290–92, 303
  in Warsaw Pact 172–73
  after World War II 58

safety, trade-offs for 77, 81–82
salami tactics 208
Sarbahi, Anoop K. 257, 267n32

satellites
anti-satellite weapons 31–32, 298–99
communication with 282n2, 298
in Cuban Missile Crisis 292
cyberspace and 298
drones and 282–83
photographic imagery from 295n33
reconnaissance 98–99, 282–84,
289–90, 292–93, 292–95, 294f,
297–98
Space-Based Infrared System 98
surprise and 295–96
surveillance 328
warnings and 288–89
Schelling, Thomas
on brinkmanship crises 191
on coercion 23n21, 66, 79–80, 123
on deterrence 18
influence and 134n6
on mobile forces 89
on nuclear deterrence 21n20
Schwartau, Winn 124
scrambling devices 174
sea power
in geopolitics 225
military and 244
naval warfare and 224–31, 235, 248–51
politics of 229n26
scholarship on 224–31, 225n4, 248–51
to US 249
secret agents 148
secret capabilities 121–24
secret statecraft 139–42, 140n25
security
with alliances 204–5
in Cold War 1
cybersecurity 166
to government 2
in IR 69–70
leaks 144–45
nuclear 35–36
policy 48f, 383f, 384n12
politics of 3–4, 69–72
US National Security Agency 143,
157n80, 165–66, 181, 329
selective violence 257
Shamoon virus 109–10
Shifrinson, Joshua 206

Shultz, George 343–44
signaling credibility 210, 239
sinking costs signal 51n23
Smoke, Richard 342
Snowden, Edward 157n80, 181, 186
Snyder, Jack 211
social constructions 84–85
social engineering 146–47
society 2, 10, 12–13, 178–79, 236n42,
320–21
sociology 43
sociotechnical complexity 162
soft power 383
software 145–46, 161n93
Somalia 262
South Korea 59, 195
Soviet Union. See Russia
space
commercial space industry 98n76
cyberspace and 102–3
domains 97–99
espionage from 284–87
intelligence and 288–95, 294f
Kennedy Space Center 282
National Aeronautics and Space
Administration 115
political violence in 328
reconnaissance peace in 295–99
space-based ISR 104
stability in 282–84, 287–88
Space-Based Infrared System satellites
98
Space X 98n76
specialization
military 15, 18, 30–31, 75–85,
103–4, 193
scholarship on 85–86
special forces 90
strategic 165
of technology 11
in war 74
spies. See espionage
Spitzner, Lance 158
stability
accommodation and 381, 382t
alliances for 395–96
in defense 71
in geopolitics 288–95, 294f

462 INDEX

stability (*Continued*)
  to government 79
  influence and 56–57, 60
  instability 27–28, 46–47, 101–2,
    185–86, 199, 395–96
  intelligence and 295–99
  with MAD 186
  protection and 64, 64n38
  in space 282–84, 287–88
  stability-instability paradox 101–2
  strategic 27, 48–49, 52–53, 219*t*, 220*t*,
    290, 377, 383*f*, 388
  technology for 284–87
status quo
  to challengers 346–47
  credibility with 57–61
  defense of 64
  in East Asia 403
  escalation and 348–51, 349*f*
  influence over 57
  politics 69
  uncertainty in 51, 51n22
stealth 233, 239
Stoll, Clifford 158
Strategic Automated Command and
    Control System 171
strategic complexity 102–5
strategic deterrence 25–26
strategic interaction 104–5
strategic specialization 165
strategic surprise 287–88
strategy. *See also* US-China strategy
  A2/AD strategy 397–98, 403
  of accommodation 386
  advertising 25
  aggression as 31
  of bargaining model 56–57, 381–82,
    382*t*
  of challengers 348–51, 349*f*
  of China 251
  to Clausewitz 77
  coercive 90
  Cold War 29–31, 178
  complexity and 102–5, 301–2, 380–82,
    382*t*
  counterforce 180
  cyberstrategy 393
  of deception 103, 133–36, 151–53, 193

for defense 80
defensible defense 392–93, 392*f*
for Department of Defense 36–37
deterrence 37–38, 41, 375–76, 379,
    404–7
effectiveness of 152–53
geography and 216
goals 5
implicit strategic objectives 47–54, 48*f*,
    53*f*
for integrated deterrence 30
in land wars 76, 88–93
maneuver strategies 89–90, 224–25,
    240–48, 241*f*
in maritime domain 249–50
military 4–5, 66–69
of military specialization 75–85
with mobility 62
NATO 208n46
with non-military tools 10
with nuclear deterrence 17–18
objectives 12–13
in offshore balancing 198–99
in operational domains 11
positioning, navigation, and
    timing 298–99
for power 34
protective strategies 138–39
psychology of 55–56
of punishment 252
scholarship on 226–31
Strategic Air Command 168
strategic complexity 102–5
strategic stability 27, 48–49, 52–53,
    219*t*, 220*t*, 290, 377, 383*f*, 388
with submarines 225, 239
with technology 9
of trade-offs 12
trickery and 80–81
of Ukraine 296–97, 341
of US 15, 343
US National Defense Strategy 4, 32,
    35–37
US National Security
    Strategy 24n22, 31
US Strategic Command 169, 171
in Vietnam War 277
in war 95–97, 109–11

INDEX 463

structural realism 70
Stuxnet worm 109–10, 143, 163, 176, 181, 186, 324
submarines
    aircraft carriers and 247–48
    attack 246–47, 247f
    ballistic missile 93
    battleships and 246f
    history of 152, 225, 239
    power of 279
    submarine-launched ballistic missiles 167–68, 177, 187–88, 239–40, 247–48, 247f
    in war 241–42
    in World War I 375
substitution 322–25, 322–27, 331–32, 334–39. *See also specific topics*
subterfuge 309
subversion
    aggression and 293
    credibility and 8
    diplomacy and 52
    espionage and 100–101, 107, 112, 166, 337
    in GZC 73–74, 344, 364, 369–70
    information and 31
    intelligence and 187
    politics of 79–83
    power of 385–86
Suez Canal 230
sufficiency 378–79
Sun Tzu 147, 148n56, 153, 287
surprise 284, 287–88, 295–96
surveillance satellites 328
Syria 326

tactical drones 275–76
tactics, in war 151–52
Taiwan 59–60, 92, 377–78, 393n21, 398–99
Talmadge, Caitlin 204
technology
    ASAT 99–100, 99n81
    for civilians 142–43, 277
    in Cold War 29, 99
    for conflict dynamics 12
    convergent evolution and 159–60

for cross-domain deterrence 4
in cyberspace 114–17
of deception 142–50
defense with 262
for deterrence 33–34
domains 30–31
for drones 95, 267n32
economics of 255–60
effectiveness of 329
emerging 10
evolution of 145
geography and 83–84, 139
history of 86t, 87–88
human intelligence and 150n63
information 136–37
labor and 278–81
military 63, 380
for NC3 170–71
network 153
politics of 9–10, 43, 72
power of 67–68
sociotechnical complexity 162
software 145–46
specialization of 11
for stability 284–87
strategy with 9
technical possibility 111, 114–17
technical vulnerabilities 101
technological espionage 150, 284
for UAVs 253
in US 122
in World War II 276–77
Terminal High Altitude Air Defense (THAAD) 176
terrorism
    counterterrorism 254–55, 259–60, 268
    cyberterrorism 129–30
    defense against 30n32
    Hamas 131, 280
    by Islamic State 338
    in Nagorno-Karabakh 274
    nuclear 155n77
    at Olympic Games 176
    Al Qaeda 154, 258–59, 280, 283
    UAVs against 254–55, 266–68
    urban 268–69, 269f, 271–73
    war on 264–69, 269f, 270–73
Tet Offensive 154

464 INDEX

THAAD. *See* Terminal High Altitude Air
 Defense
Thompson, William 229
Tora! Tora! Tora! (film) 124
trade
 asymmetry in 306–7, 311–12
 bilateral 307–8, 307–9, 308*f*, 311
 commerce and 305–13, 308*f*
 deterrence and 382*t*
 in geopolitics 303–5, 313, 314*f*, 315–16
 interdependence in 308–9, 316–18
trade-offs
 complexity of 382–87, 383*f*
 in conflict dynamics 8
 in cyberspace 3
 in damage limitation 61
 for defense 101
 with drones 252–53
 with force structure 74–75
 with goals 55
 to leadership 65–66
 military 69
 with mobile forces 91–92
 with nuclear deterrence 87
 in orthodox deterrence 5
 in policy 70–71
 political 231–40
 psychology of 40
 for safety 77, 81–82
 strategy of 12
 in US-China strategy 390–93, 392*f*
traditional conflict 327–28
traditional espionage 114, 285
traditional intelligence 285
traditional war 119–20, 330–33
transparency 180, 239–40, 296
tripwires 204–5
tying hands signal 51n23

UAVs. *See* unmanned aerial vehicles
Ukraine
 brinkmanship crises in 185
 cyberattacks against 110, 113
 drones in 338–39
 escalation in 357
 in geopolitics 97n73
 Georgia and 132, 372
 history of 344–45, 361*t*

Nagorno-Karabakh and 255
NATO in 345n30, 364–66
operational advantages of 276n39
Russia and 45–46, 92, 98n76, 131,
 275–76, 301, 330n24, 341–42,
 369–71
strategy of 296–97, 341
Syria and 326
US and 338, 365–66
war in 321n5, 323, 344–45, 385
uncertainty
 to Clausewitz 44, 90
 of efficacy 184
 in geopolitics 319
 maneuver strategies and 224–25,
 240–48, 241*f*
 in military disputes 237–40
 politics of 296
 psychology of 380–81
 scholarship on 48*f*
 in status quo 51, 51n22
 war and 44–47, 44n11, 282–83
undercover agents 159
underwater acoustics 150n63
uniforms, for mobile forces 151–52
United States (US). *See also* US-China
 strategy
 Afghanistan and 273
 Air Force 169, 174
 alliances with 214, 216–17
 Asia and 230, 249–50
 Canopy Wing program in 172–76, 187
 China and 12, 33–34, 127, 166,
 223n64, 224, 302, 396–99
 CIA in 148–49
 in Cold War 19–20, 88–89, 99, 176,
 406
 counterterrorism by 254–55
 in Cuban Missile Crisis 287
 Cyber Command 76, 113, 136–37, 141
 as defenders 220–21
 defense 32
 Department of Defense 10, 390–91
 drones to 338–39
 Fort Ticonderoga in 64n38
 in geopolitics 373–75
 Germany and 213
 Great Britain and 147–48, 195, 276–77

in Gulf War 95
history 226
Indo-Pacific Command 33
influence 396–97
integrated deterrence in 4
Iraq and 67–68
Israel and 109–10
JADC2 in 394
JAGMC in 394
Japan and 68, 125–26, 181, 209, 250, 283
in Middle East 324
in militarized interstate disputes 218, 292–94
military 34, 124, 127–28, 207
National Defense Strategy 4, 32, 35–37
National Security Agency 143, 157n80, 165–66, 181, 329
National Security Strategy 24n22, 31
NATO and 46, 377–78
North Korea and 167, 177
nuclear deterrence in 190–91
Nuclear Posture Review and 32n46
in offshore balancing 221–22
Pakistan and 255–56
Pearl Harbor to 286
personality strikes by 272
policy 19, 29–30, 196n3
political pundits in 393n21
politics in 195–200
power of 121–22
Russia and 172–75, 179–80, 185–86, 290–92, 303
sea power to 249
Secretary of Defense 190
Somalia and 262
South Korea and 59
Space-Based Infrared System satellites in 98
Strategic Command 169, 171
strategy of 15, 343
Taiwan to 59–60
technology in 122
UAVs from 255–60, 402
Ukraine and 338, 365–66
in Vietnam War 28
in war on terrorism 264–69, 269f, 270–73

to Yamamoto 125n45
in Yom Kippur War 291
unmanned aerial vehicles
(UAVs) 253–60, 262–64, 266–68, 273–74, 402. *See also* drones
unpeace 319
urban terrorism 268–69, 269f, 271–73
urban violence 267, 267n31
US. *See* United States
US-China strategy
engagement in 396–97
offshore balancing in 399–400
scholarship on 400–404
trade-offs in 390–93, 392f
war in 394–96, 397–99

variation, in GZC 351–52, 353f
Vietnam War 28, 154, 259, 277, 294
vigilantism 157–58
violence
capacities for 143
against civilians 263n27, 269, 269f, 271–73
in cyberspace 32
by militant organizations 266–69, 269f, 270–73
military 256, 330–31
physical 118
political 328
propaganda for 258–59
psychology of 21, 116
selective 257
threats of 77
urban 267, 267n31
in war-fighting 22
Virgil 147
virtual escalation 28
vulnerability 54, 115, 122–23, 172, 188–89

Walt, Stephen 399
Waltz, Kenneth 70
war. *See also specific topics*
aircraft carriers in 59, 103, 125
alliances in 22–23
bargaining model of 6–7, 9, 41–44, 48–49, 48f
classical deterrence of 54–56

466 INDEX

war (*Continued*)
Clausewitz on 41–42, 74–75
commerce and 316–18
comparative advantages in 85–88, 86*t*
concession in 276n40
cyberconflict and 321–25
in cyberspace 2–3, 100–102, 107,
111–14, 117–27, 133–36
deception in 85–86, 86*t*
domains of 102–5
drone warfare 402
economics of 48*f*, 49–50, 61–62,
138–39
electronic warfare 172–73
escalation of 25–26
fog of 82, 153
government and 164
GZC and 132
implicit strategic objectives in 47–54,
48*f*, 53*f*
incentives in 199–200
information in 325–29, 380n7
intelligence and 319–20
on Internet 130–32
kinetic warfare 120
leadership in 121–22
to NATO 174
after nuclear deterrence 152–53
operational features of 82–85,
99n79
partial automation in 253n5
peace and 163–64, 317–18, 342–44
politics of 75–77, 75–81
preemptive 182
preventative 45
psychology of 11–12
risk and 2, 350–51, 354–55, 367–69,
367*f*
salami tactics in 208
scholarship and 78n16, 206, 348–51,
349*f*

in space domains 97–99
specialization in 74
strategy in 95–97, 109–11
submarines in 241–42
tactics in 151–52
on terrorism 264–69, 269*f*, 270–73
traditional 119–20, 330–33
in Ukraine 321n5, 323, 344–45, 385
uncertainty and 44–47, 44n11, 282–83
in US-China strategy 394–96, 397–99
war-fighting 17–18, 22–24, 23, 26, 29,
66–67
warships 248
after World War II 18
WarGames (film) 165–66
warnings 285–86, 288–89
Warsaw Pact 59, 172–73, 208, 208n46
weapons of mass destruction 186–87.
See also nuclear deterrence
webpage defacement 27
Wolf, Markus 172–73
World War I 241–42, 276–79,
278–79, 375
World War II
alliances after 200
France in 65, 137
geopolitics after 29–31
Germany in 147–48
history of 124–27
Japan in 125n45
nuclear deterrence after 29
Pearl Harbor in 68, 124
Russia after 58
technology in 276–77
traditional war after 330
war after 18
World Wide Web. *See* Internet

Yamamoto, Isoroku 125, 125n45
Yemen 273–74
Yom Kippur War 154, 291

Printed in the USA/Agawam, MA
May 17, 2024

866226.005